MW01286037

MARSHAL OF
VICTORY

The Stackpole Military History Series

THE AMERICAN CIVIL WAR
Cavalry Raids of the Civil War
Ghost, Thunderbolt, and Wizard
In the Lion's Mouth
Witness to Gettysburg

WORLD WAR I
Doughboy War

WORLD WAR II
After D-Day
Airborne Combat
Armor Battles of the Waffen-SS, 1943–45
Armoured Guardsmen
Army of the West
Arnhem 1944
The B-24 in China
Backwater War
The Battalion
Battle of Paoli
The Battle of France
The Battle of Sicily
Battle of the Bulge, Vol. 1
Battle of the Bulge, Vol. 2
Battle of the Bulge, Vol. 3
Beyond the Beachhead
Beyond Stalingrad
The Black Bull
Blitzkrieg Unleashed
Blossoming Silk Against the Rising Sun
Bodenplatte
The Breaking Point
The Brigade
The Canadian Army and the Normandy
    Campaign
Coast Watching in World War II
Colossal Cracks
Condor
A Dangerous Assignment
D-Day Bombers
D-Day Deception
D-Day to Berlin
Decision in the Ukraine
The Defense of Moscow 1941
Destination Normandy
Dive Bomber!
A Drop Too Many
Eager Eagles
Eagles of the Third Reich
The Early Battles of Eighth Army
Eastern Front Combat
Europe in Flames
Exit Rommel
The Face of Courage
Fatal Decisions
Fist from the Sky
Flying American Combat Aircraft of World
    War II, Vol. 1
Flying American Combat Aircraft of World
    War II, Vol. 2
For Europe
Forging the Thunderbolt
For the Homeland
Fortress France

The German Defeat in the East, 1944–45
German Order of Battle, Vol. 1
German Order of Battle, Vol. 2
German Order of Battle, Vol. 3
The Germans in Normandy
Germany's Panzer Arm in World War II
GI Ingenuity
Goodbye, Transylvania
Goodwood
The Great Ships
Grenadiers
Guns Against the Reich
Hitler's Final Fortress
Hitler's Nemesis
Hitler's Spanish Legion
Hold the Westwall
Infantry Aces
In the Fire of the Eastern Front
Iron Arm
Iron Knights
Japanese Army Fighter Aces
Japanese Naval Fighter Aces
JG 26 Luftwaffe Fighter Wing War Diary,
    Vol. 1
JG 26 Luftwaffe Fighter Wing War Diary,
    Vol. 2
Kampfgruppe Peiper at the Battle of
    the Bulge
The Key to the Bulge
Kursk
Luftwaffe Aces
Luftwaffe Fighter Ace
Luftwaffe Fighter-Bombers over Britain
Luftwaffe Fighters and Bombers
Massacre at Tobruk
Mechanized Juggernaut or Military
    Anachronism?
Messerschmitts over Sicily
Michael Wittmann, Vol. 1
Michael Wittmann, Vol. 2
Mission 85
Mission 376
Mountain Warriors
The Nazi Rocketeers
Night Flyer / Mosquito Pathfinder
No Holding Back
On the Canal
Operation Mercury
Panzer Aces
Panzer Aces II
Panzer Aces III
Panzer Commanders of the Western Front
Panzergrenadier Aces
Panzer Gunner
The Panzer Legions
Panzers in Normandy
Panzers in Winter
Panzer Wedge, Vol. 1
Panzer Wedge, Vol. 2
The Path to Blitzkrieg
Penalty Strike
Poland Betrayed
Prince of Aces
Red Road from Stalingrad

Red Star Under the Baltic
Retreat to the Reich
Rommel Reconsidered
Rommel's Desert Commanders
Rommel's Desert War
Rommel's Lieutenants
The Savage Sky
The Seeds of Disaster
Ship-Busters
The Siege of Brest, 1941
The Siege of Küstrin
The Siegfried Line
A Soldier in the Cockpit
Soviet Blitzkrieg
Spitfires and Yellow Tail Mustangs
Stalin's Keys to Victory
Surviving Bataan and Beyond
T-34 in Action
Tank Tactics
Tigers in the Mud
Triumphant Fox
The 12th SS, Vol. 1
The 12th SS, Vol. 2
Twilight of the Gods
Typhoon Attack
The War Against Rommel's Supply Lines
War in the Aegean
War of the White Death
Warsaw 1944
Winter Storm
The Winter War
Wolfpack Warriors
Zhukov at the Oder

THE COLD WAR / VIETNAM
Cyclops in the Jungle
Expendable Warriors
Fighting in Vietnam
Flying American Combat Aircraft:
    The Cold War
Here There Are Tigers
Land with No Sun
Phantom Reflections
Street without Joy
Through the Valley
Tours of Duty
Two One Pony

**WARS OF AFRICA AND THE
MIDDLE EAST**
The Rhodesian War

GENERAL MILITARY HISTORY
Carriers in Combat
Cavalry from Hoof to Track
Desert Battles
Guerrilla Warfare
The Philadelphia Campaign, Vol. 1
Ranger Dawn
Sieges
The Spartan Army

MARSHAL OF VICTORY

Vol. 2: The WWII Memoirs of
General Georgy Zhukov, 1941–1945

Georgy Zhukov
Edited by Geoffrey Roberts

STACKPOLE
BOOKS

TO THE SOVIET SOLDIER

Published in Paperback in the U.S. in 2015 by
STACKPOLE BOOKS
5067 Ritter Road
Mechanicsburg, PA 17055
www.stackpolebooks.com

First published in Russian in 1974.
Published in the United Kingdom in 2013 by Pen & Sword Military, an imprint of Pen
& Sword Books Limited. This edition published by arrangement with Pen & Sword.

Printed in the United States of America

10 9 8 7 6 5 4 3 2 1

Cover design by Wendy A. Reynolds

ISBN 978-0-8117-1554-6 (v. 2)

The Library of Congress has cataloged the first volume as follows:

Zhukov, Georgii Konstantinovich, 1896–1974.
  [Vospominaniia i razmyshleniia. English]
  Marshal of victory : the WWII memoirs of General Georgy Zhukov / Georgy
Zhukov ; edited by Geoffrey Roberts.
    2 volumes ; cm. — (Stackpole military history series)
  Originally published: Barnsley, South Yorkshire : Pen & Sword Military, 2013.
  Original edition has subtitle: The autobiography of General Georgy Zhukov.
  Includes bibliographical references and index.
  Contents: v.1. Through 1941 — v. 2. 1941–1945.
  Translated from the Russian.
  ISBN 978-0-8117-1553-9 (v. 1)
1. Zhukov, Georgii Konstantinovich, 1896–1974. 2. Marshals—Soviet Union—
Biography. 3. World War, 1939–1945—Campaigns—Eastern Front. 4. World War,
1939–1945—Personal narratives, Soviet. I. Roberts, Geoffrey, 1952– editor. II. Title.
III. Title: WWII memoirs of General Georgy Zhukov.
  DK268.Z52A313 2015
  940.54'147092–dc23
  [B]   2015005918

Contents

Acknowledgements

The second English edition of Zhukov's memoirs is reproduced with the permission of his daughter Maria.

Geoffrey Roberts would like to acknowledge the collaboration of his co-translator Svetlana Frolova and the editorial input of his partner Celia Weston. He would also like to thank Rupert Harding and his team at Pen & Sword for taking on this project and making Zhukov's memoirs available again to a new generation of readers.

The preparation of this volume was aided greatly by the financial support of the College of Arts, Celtic Studies and Social Sciences, University College Cork, Ireland.

Chronology of the Life and Career of Georgy Zhukov

1896   *1 December*: Birth of Georgy Konstantinovich Zhukov in Strelkovka, Kaluga Province, Russia.

1915   *August*: Conscripted into the Tsar's Army and assigned to the cavalry.

1918   *1 October*: Joins the Red Army.

1919   *March*: Becomes a candidate member of the Soviet communist party.

1920   Marries Alexandra Dievna Zuikova.

1923   *July*: Appointed commander of the 39th Buzuluk Cavalry Regiment.

1924   *October*: Attends Higher Cavalry School in Leningrad.

1928   Birth of daughter Era.

1929   Birth of daughter Margarita.
      Attends Frunze Military Academy in Moscow.

1930   *May*: Promoted to command of 2nd Cavalry Brigade of the 7th Samara Division.

1931   *February*: Appointed Assistant Inspector of the Cavalry.

1933   *March*: Appointed commander of the 4th (Voroshilov) Cavalry Division.

1937   Birth of daughter Ella.
      July: Appointed commander of the 3rd Cavalry Corps in Belorussia.

1938   *June*: Appointed Deputy Commander of the Belorussian Military District.

1939   *May*: Posted to the Mongolian–Manchurian border.
      June: Appointed commander of the 57th Special Corps at Khalkhin-Gol.
      20 August: Launch of attack on Japanese forces at Khalkhin-Gol.

1940   *May*: Appointed commander of the Kiev Special Military
       District.
       2 June: First meeting with Stalin.
       5 June: Promoted to General of the Army.
       25 December: Delivers report on 'The Character of
       Contemporary Offensive Operations' to Higher Command
       conference in Moscow.

1941   *January*: Takes part in General Staff war games.
       14 January: Appointed Chief of the General Staff.
       February: Elected to the central committee at the 18th party
       conference.
       22 June: German invasion of the Soviet Union.
       29 July: Transferred from Chief of the General Staff to
       command of the Reserve Front.
       August: Leads counter-offensive at Yel'nya.
       11 September: Appointed commander of the Leningrad Front.
       11 October: Appointed commander of the Western Front.
       5 December: Beginning of Moscow counter-offensive.

1942   *17 July*: Beginning of the battle for Stalingrad.
       26 August: Appointed Stalin's Deputy Supreme Commander.
       19 November: Operation Uranus – Red Army counter-
       offensive at Stalingrad.

1943   *January*: Supervises operation to end the German blockade of
       Leningrad.
       18 January: Promoted to Marshal of the Soviet Union.
       July: Kursk battle.

1944   Death of Zhukov's mother.
       June: Operation Bagration.
       12 November: Appointed commander of 1st Belorussian Front.

1945   *January*: Launch of Vistula-Oder Operation.
       16 April: Launch of attack on Berlin.
       May: Red Army captures Berlin and Zhukov accepts German
       surrender.
       30 May: Appointed commander of Soviet occupation forces in
       Germany.
       24 June: Leads Victory Parade in Red Square.

1946   *February*: Elected to the Supreme Soviet.
       22 March: Appointed Commander-in-Chief of Soviet ground
       forces.

June: Dismissed as Commander-in-Chief of Soviet ground forces and posted to Odessa.

1947　*February*: Expelled from membership of the party central committee.

1948　*January*: Censured for extracting war booty from Germany.

February: Transferred to the command of the Urals Military District.

1952　*October*: Attends 19th party congress and is re-elected to central committee.

1953　*March*: Returns to Moscow and is appointed Deputy Defence Minister.

June: Arrests Beria.

1954　Death of Zhukov's sister Maria.

1955　*February*: Appointed Minister of Defence.

July: Attends Geneva Summit and meets President Eisenhower.

1956　*February*: Elected to the Presidium at the 20th party congress.

November: Oversees Soviet military intervention in Hungary.

1957　*June*: Leads defence of Khrushchev against attempted coup by Molotov's 'anti-party group'.

June: Birth of daughter Maria.

October: Central Committee dismisses Zhukov for distancing army from the party.

1958　*February*: Retires from the armed forces.

1965　Divorces Alexandra Dievna.

1966　Marries Galina Semonovna.

1967　*December*: Death of Alexandra Dievna.

1968　*January*: Suffers stroke.

1969　*April*: Publication of 1st edition of Zhukov's memoirs.

1973　*November*: Death of Galina Semonovna.

1974　*18 June*: Dies in the Kremlin hospital.

Publication of the 2nd edition of Zhukov's memoirs.

Introduction: The Memoirs of Georgy Zhukov

By Geoffrey Roberts

Georgy Zhukov's life and career as soldier, politician and memoirist was long, complex and dramatic. It was the story of a peasant lad who rose from poverty to become the greatest Soviet general of the Second World War. After the war Zhukov seemed set for an equally glorious postwar career as the Soviet Union's top soldier. But he soon fell out with dictator Joseph Stalin and was banished to the provinces. Zhukov survived this fall from grace and after Stalin's death in 1953 he became Soviet Defence Minister. He allied himself with Stalin's successor as party leader, Nikita Khrushchev, but fell out with him, too, and in October 1957 he was dismissed from office. In 1958 Zhukov was forced to retire from the armed forces. He retreated to his country dacha and wrote his famous memoirs – a fascinating and seminal insider account of the Soviet High Command at war. The memoirs were not published until several years after Khrushchev's fall from power in 1964 but by the time Zhukov died in 1974 he had been rehabilitated politically and restored to the Soviet military pantheon. Thousands queued to pay their respects as his body lay in state in the Central House of the Soviet Army in Moscow. Zhukov's state funeral was the biggest since the death of Stalin and it marked the beginning of the rise of a Zhukov cult, internationally as well as in the USSR.[1]

Russia's Hero

In Russia, Zhukov is a national hero, seen as the man who defeated Hitler to save Europe and the world from the Nazis. Zhukov's exploits are said to surpass even those of such national icons as Alexander Suvorov, the eighteenth-century Tsarist general who never lost a battle, and Field Marshal Mikhail Kutuzov, who defeated Napoleon's Grand Armée when it invaded Russia in 1812. Indeed, the books, articles, monuments, exhibitions and celebrations devoted to Zhukov in post-communist Russia are far more numerous than are those dedicated to Kutuzov and Suvorov.

Zhukov's reputation in the rest of the world is no less exulted, not least because of his memoirs' influence. The American historian and journalist Harrison Salisbury memorably described Zhukov as 'the master of the art of mass warfare in the twentieth century', while to John Erickson, the foremost British authority on the Soviet army, he was the century's greatest soldier, who, like Suvorov, never lost a battle.[2]

David Glantz, the premier western historian of the Soviet–German war of 1941–1945, compared Zhukov to the American general Ulysses S. Grant as 'a superb strategist and practitioner of operational art who, nevertheless, displayed frequent tactical errors. Just as bloody military defeats at Cold Harbour and Spotsylvania in 1864 during the American Civil War did little to diminish Grant's fame, so also Zhukov's failures should not diminish the fact that he was one of the pre-eminent architects of the Soviet victory over Hitler's vaunted Wehrmacht.'[3]

The comparison between Zhukov and Grant may be taken further. Both were from poor backgrounds and became excellent cavalrymen. Both commanded armies in wars of national survival and were relentlessly forceful in pursuit of victory. Like Grant, Zhukov has been accused of being a 'butcher' with callous disregard for the lives of his troops – a charge he vehemently denied, pointing out that armchair generals could always tell you – after the event – how to win battles more cheaply and easily. Both men worked for charismatic leaders (Lincoln and Stalin) who kept faith with them even when defeat threatened. Then, after their respective wars, Grant and Zhukov were naïve in pursuit of postwar political careers that ultimately ended in failure but achieved further fame by writing best-selling memoirs.[4]

Like Grant, and most great generals, Zhukov is not everyone's hero. Even in Russia he has his critics. Among the most vociferous have been Viktor Suvorov and his supporters. Suvorov (whose real name is Rezun) is a former Soviet intelligence officer who defected to the west in 1978. He is most famous for his contention that in the summer of 1941 Stalin was preparing a pre-emptive strike on Germany. This was the same argument used by Hitler and Nazi propagandists to justify the German invasion of the Soviet Union on 22 June 1941.[5]

Suvorov is also committed to debunking the Zhukov cult.[6] According to Suvorov, all Soviet leaders were scoundrels, including Zhukov, whom he describes as a 'war criminal' because of the harsh disciplinary regime he imposed on his troops.

Suvorov's writings attacked Zhukov on three broad fronts. First, he assembled every negative statement about Zhukov's personality made by members of the Soviet High Command: 'All the top military leaders of the country were against Zhukov,' concludes Suvorov. 'The Generals knew, the Marshals knew, that Zhukov was vainglorious. They knew he was both a dreadful and a dull person. They knew he was rude and a usurper. They knew he was in a class of his own as a careerist. They knew he trampled over everyone in his path. They knew of his lust for power and the belief in his own infallibility.'[7] His second line of attack was to ascribe all Zhukov's successes and achievements to the work of other people and to accuse him of failing to acknowledge their contribution. Thirdly, Suvorov subjected Zhukov's memoirs to a forensic examination, pointing to their many omissions, evasions and contradictions.

Yet Zhukov's memoirs are no more self-serving and error-ridden than most autobiographical works by military and political leaders. Like generals the world over, Zhukov glossed over his own mistakes and defeats, while blaming others for the failures. Zhukov was certainly a flawed character, albeit one of epic achievements, but Suvorov accentuated only the negatives.

More measured criticism has come from Robert Forczyk, who highlighted Zhukov's successes as well as his setbacks but pointed out that his operational methods were often crude and brutal. However, his portrayal of an aloof, bullying and self-centred general will be unrecognisable to the reader of Zhukov's memoirs, too easily dismissed by Forczyk in favour of the negative commentaries that suit his critique.[8]

Often depicted as a cruel general, Zhukov was a commander fighting a savage war for the very highest stakes. The Soviet victory over Hitler's Germany saved Russia and Europe from a Nazi racist empire and from genocide on a continental scale. The single most important individual on the Soviet side of the war was Stalin. It was Stalin's violent, authoritarian communist system that defeated Hitler's Nazi regime and the Soviet system depended for its survival on Stalin performing exceptionally well as a war leader.[9] As Zhukov himself said, 'Stalin was a splendid Supreme Commander'. But if Stalin was the indispensable Supreme Commander, Zhukov and the Soviet High Command were the equally indispensable military architects of victory. The price of that victory was paid with the blood and suffering of tens of millions of

Soviet people, including the eight million fatalities incurred by the Red Army. The death toll could be said to have made this a pyrrhic victory but the alternative of Nazi enslavement would have been far worse.

A Soldier's Life

Zhukov made his name as a general at the battle of Khalkhin-Gol on the Mongolian–Manchurian border in August 1939, on the eve of the Second World War. In a border war with Japan's Kwantung Army, Zhukov inflicted a bloody defeat on the enemy, one that helped persuade the Japanese to expand towards the United States rather than in the Soviet direction, leading to their fateful decision to attack Pearl Harbor in December 1941.

Zhukov missed the disastrous Soviet–Finnish war of 1939–1940 but he was recalled from the Far East in May 1940 and given command of the Kiev Special Military District – the Red Army's largest and on the front line of the coming war with Nazi Germany. This was the platform for Zhukov's appointment as Chief of the General Staff in February 1941. Zhukov was not renowned as a staff officer – he much preferred front-line operational command – but Stalin wanted someone he could rely on to counterattack when the German invasion came.

When the Germans invaded the Soviet Union with massive force in June 1941 Zhukov did order a series of counter-offensives. But these actions exposed Soviet troops to encirclement by the Germans and compounded the disaster of an invasion that inflicted on the Red Army one of the greatest defeats of any army in history.[10] By the end of 1941 the Red Army had lost four million soldiers and had been pushed back to the gates of Leningrad and Moscow. The Soviet Union teetered on the brink not only of defeat but of complete collapse.

In the meantime Zhukov had stepped aside as Chief of the General Staff (he claimed in his memoirs to have been sacked by Stalin) and was given command of a reserve army of about fifty divisions. At Yel'nya in the Smolensk region in August 1941 Zhukov launched the Red Army's first successful large-scale counter-offensive against the Germans, re-capturing a big tract of territory and blocking Hitler's path to Moscow – at least for a while.

Zhukov's next assignment was to save Leningrad from imminent capture by the Germans in September 1941. With that city's defences bolstered, Zhukov was recalled to defend Moscow from a German attack that succeeded in advancing to within a few miles of the Soviet capital. In December Zhukov launched a counter-offensive in front of

Moscow, driving the Germans back 100 miles and ending Hitler's dream of conquering the Soviet Union in a single blitzkrieg campaign.

In the summer of 1942 Hitler tried again to inflict a devastating defeat on the Soviet Union. No longer capable of waging a broad-front campaign, the Germans opted for a single strategic operation in the south. Their aim was to seize the Soviet oilfields at Baku on the other side of the Caucasus and it was this campaign that led to the siege at Stalingrad later that year.

The German southern campaign was quite successful initially as Hitler's armies advanced hundreds of miles, inflicting a series of defeats on the Red Army and capturing hundreds of thousands of prisoners. By the end of August the Germans had reached the outskirts of Stalingrad. If they could capture the city, its strategic location on the Volga would enable them to block vital oil supplies to northern Russia and protect their advance on Baku.

On the eve of the battle for Stalingrad, Stalin appointed Zhukov his Deputy Supreme Commander. Zhukov's task was to save Stalingrad and to prepare counter-actions to halt and then roll back the German southern campaign.

During three months of ferocious fighting in and around Stalingrad the Red Army barely retained a foothold in the city but in so doing drained German human and material resources. In November 1942 Zhukov unleashed a multi-pronged counter-offensive at Stalingrad. Operation Uranus destroyed the Hungarian, Italian and Romanian armies defending the Germans' flanks, encircled 300,000 German troops in Stalingrad and threatened to cut off Wehrmacht forces heading south to Baku. When the battle was over the Germans and their Axis allies had lost fifty divisions and suffered 1.5 million casualties. In Stalingrad alone 150,000 German soldiers perished. The Germans were able to withdraw their other troops from the south but by early 1943 were back where they started when they had launched their war for oil in June 1942.

Launched at the same time as Operation Uranus was Operation Mars – an attack on Army Group Centre in front of Moscow. David Glantz has claimed that Mars was Zhukov's preferred operation because he believed the Germans could only be beaten if Army Group Centre was destroyed. Mars was much less successful than Uranus but, according to Zhukov, it was a diversionary operation designed to draw German forces away from Stalingrad and the south.[11]

Zhukov also played a central role in the next great battle of the Soviet–German war – at Kursk in July 1943, when hundreds of German and Soviet tanks clashed in open warfare. The outcome was another German defeat and the loss of Hitler's panzer reserves. Kursk was to be the last significant German offensive of the war. Thereafter it was retreat all the way back to Berlin.

Zhukov was in the forefront of the Soviet strategic offensive of 1943–1945. In November 1943 he rode into Kiev with the Soviet forces that had recaptured the Ukrainian capital. A few months later he supervised Operation Bagration – the campaign to liberate Belorussia from Nazi occupation. Bagration took the Red Army into Poland and to the outskirts of Warsaw. In August 1944 Zhukov drafted plans to capture the Polish capital but, exhausted by its advance and with over-stretched supply lines, the Red Army was incapable of achieving this goal. However, Zhukov did capture Warsaw in January 1945 after the Soviets launched an operation that advanced the Red Army from the Vistula to the Oder – the two great rivers bisecting eastern Poland and eastern Germany respectively.

By this time Zhukov was in charge of the 1st Belorussian Front, tasked by Stalin to take Berlin. Zhukov hoped to seize the German capital in February 1945 but was forced to divert forces to deal with enemy threats on his northern flank. The advance on Berlin resumed in April and it was Zhukov's troops who led the triumphant capture of Hitler's last redoubt, albeit at the cost of 80,000 Soviet soldiers' lives. Fittingly, it was Zhukov who formally accepted Germany's unconditional surrender on 9 May 1945.

Zhukov's fame had been growing since the battle of Moscow and his renown was reinforced by newsreel footage of the victory parade in Red Square in June 1945 at which he took the salute astride a magnificent white horse. Zhukov delivered the victory speech and then stood alongside Stalin as 200 captured Nazi banners were piled against the Kremlin wall, just as Marshal Kutuzov's soldiers had thrown French standards at the feet of Tsar Alexander I after they defeated Napoleon in 1812.

Zhukov had no idea that only a year later he would be sacked as commander-in-chief of Soviet ground forces and dispatched to a provincial military command in Odessa. The charges against him were that he was arrogant, disrespectful of his colleagues – especially Stalin – and claimed too much credit for wartime victories. His situation went from bad to worse when he was expelled from the communist party Central Committee in 1947. Zhukov was then accused of looting while serving as commander of the Soviet occupation forces in Germany immediately after the war. In 1948 he was further demoted to the command of the Urals Military District in Sverdlovsk. Many of his associates were arrested and imprisoned and arrest seemed to loom for Zhukov, too. 'In 1947 I feared arrest every day', he later recalled, 'and I had a bag ready with my underwear in it.'[12]

Fortunately for Zhukov, Stalin's ire against him was limited and in the late 1940s and early 1950s he was gradually rehabilitated, being re-admitted to the Central Committee in 1952. After Stalin's death Zhukov was brought back to Moscow and appointed Deputy Minister of Defence. An early assignment in his new role was the arrest of Lavrenty Beria, the Soviet security chief, accused of plotting to seize supreme power. In 1955 Zhukov became Defence Minister and attended the Geneva Summit of July 1955, where he conversed with President Eisenhower, another general-turned-politician, with whom he had worked in Germany after the war.

Zhukov's new boss, Khrushchev, launched a vitriolic attack on Stalin's brutal record of mass repression in a secret speech to a closed session of the 20th Congress of the Soviet communist party in February 1956. Zhukov was uneasy about Khrushchev's critique of the dictator's war leadership but he later contributed to criticism of Stalin's deva-stating prewar purge of the Soviet military in which thousands of officers, including most of the top command, were arrested or executed.

In June 1957 Zhukov played a starring role in resisting an attempt to oust Khrushchev made by a hard-line faction headed by Vyacheslav Molotov, former foreign minister. Without Zhukov's support Khrush-chev would have fallen from power. But, ironically, Zhukov's bravura performance against Molotov transformed him, in Khrushchev's eyes, into a political threat. Zhukov remained a soldier who had no high political ambitions beyond service to the Soviet state but in October 1957 Khrushchev accused him of undermining the role of the com-munist party in the armed forces. On this pretext Zhukov was sacked as Minister of Defence and forced to retire, thus bringing to an end his military as well as his political career – an outcome for which he never forgave Khrushchev.

The Memoirist

In retirement Zhukov worked on his memoirs but with Khrushchev still in power there was no chance they would be published. Zhukov told his daughters that he was writing for posterity. This context for their construction was important to the content of the memoirs. During his period of disgrace under Stalin, Zhukov's name had all but disappeared from historical accounts of the Great Patriotic War, as the Soviets called it. The same process happened under Khrushchev but as well as being omitted or sidelined in official narratives Zhukov also came under sharp and public critical attack.

The first salvo was fired by his wartime rival Marshal Ivan S. Konev in an article in *Pravda* in November 1957, published after the Central Committee plenum that deposed Zhukov as Minister of Defence. Konev attacked various aspects of Zhukov's war record. More criticism followed in other publications. Zhukov was accused, as he had been in Stalin's time, of claiming too much credit for wartime victories. He was faulted for failing to prepare adequately for the German invasion in June 1941. The finger of blame was pointed in his direction for defeats such as the loss of Kiev in September 1941 and the disastrous battle of Kharkov in May 1942. He was accused of mishandling the battle of Berlin and of failing to capture the German capital when he had a chance to do so in February 1945. Military memoirists mocked his command style, portraying him as an ineffectual bully and martinet. Needless to say, the war service of Khrushchev and his allies among the Soviet generals received a much better press.[13]

Zhukov wrote his memoirs in response to these criticisms and to set the record straight as he saw it. Not surprisingly, he was inclined to gloss over mistakes, reluctant to admit fault and wary of providing his critics with any ammunition. In his armoury were documents from Soviet military archives which he deployed to show his centrality, importance and prescience during the great events of the war.

When Khrushchev was deposed in 1964 Zhukov returned to public life and was gradually rehabilitated as a significant military figure. Soviet books and journals began to publish his accounts of the war's great battles – Moscow, Stalingrad, Kursk and Berlin. These articles later became key chapters in his memoirs and were published in English in 1969 as *Marshal Zhukov's Greatest Battles*. Zhukov was annoyed by this unauthorised book, which pre-empted publication of his memoirs. In an article published in the main party journal *Kommunist* he attacked the editor – Harrison Salisbury – for propagating two myths. The first was the myth of a specific 'Zhukov strategy' or a 'Zhukov style' of leadership during the Great Patriotic War, as opposed to the collective efforts and strategies of the Soviet High Command. The second myth was that Soviet victories had been won at the cost of a lot more casualties than was strictly necessary. Zhukov insisted that only those forces required for any particular operation had been expended and commented sarcastically that 'the right thing to have done during the war would have been to entrust Mr Salisbury with the high command, and he would doubtless have shown how Hitler's armies could be smashed with "small forces" and, as he says, "refined" tactics.'[14]

In 1965 Anna Mirkina, an editor at the publishing arm of the Novosti Soviet press agency, APN, approached Zhukov about publication of his memoirs. In August 1965 a contract was signed and by autumn 1966 Zhukov had delivered a 1,430-page typed manuscript.[15]

One of Zhukov's authorial role models was Winston Churchill, who had published a multi-volume memoir-history of the Second World War in the late 1940s and early 1950s, which Zhukov read in a restricted-circulation Russian translation. As a former Prime Minister, Churchill was allowed privileged access to British archives. He and his team of researchers used this access to great effect, publishing many long extracts from the archives in the memoirs, adding greatly to their authority and authenticity as well as making them an indispensable source for historians in the absence of direct archival access. Unlike Churchill, Zhukov worked mostly on his own but he was given special access to the archives of the Soviet military. He used the documents he extracted to underpin his personal narrative of the strategic history of the Great Patriotic War, a story in which he played a central role. The archive sources Zhukov used did not become generally accessible until the 1990s. Hence the influence his memoirs had in shaping western as well as Soviet narratives of the Great Patriotic War.

Zhukov's other highly effective technique was to make extensive use of inverted commas to report verbatim conversations he supposedly had with various people, including Stalin. This technique in memoirs and autobiography was common and Zhukov's readers were aware that he could not possibly remember in such detail what had been said decades before. The point was to establish that Zhukov had a good and reliable memory of the conversations he recalled and of their essential meaning. It also served as a dramatic device to bring his memoirs to life and flesh out their characters.

Censorship

All Soviet war memoirs had to be passed by the censors and Zhukov's were no exception, despite his high status. The official vetting and editing proved to be a long-drawn-out process, much to Zhukov's frustration. He wanted them to be published as soon as possible so that the malicious stories about him dating from the Khrushchev era could be corrected. Eventually, in April 1968, a group headed by Marshal Grechko, Minister of Defence, reported to the party leadership on the memoirs. The group's appraisal was generally positive but critical of Zhukov's tendency to inflate his own role in the war and his lack of attention to the collective contribution of the party, especially its leadership. The report focused in particular on Zhukov's treatment of the immediate prewar period, arguing that he undervalued the significance of the party's preparations for war. One specific point was that Zhukov was deemed to attribute too much importance to the negative impact of the 1930s purges of the Red Army. The group reported, too, that the importance of Stalin's role was exaggerated to the detriment of the contributions of the State Defence Committee, the General Staff and Front commanders. Grechko concluded that the memoirs should be published but only after further editing and amendment.[16]

The memoirs were then handed over to a specialist editorial group headed by the historian G.A. Deborin. The Deborin group became, in effect, the censorship team, working on the required changes in consultation with Zhukov and with V.G. Komolov, a journalist employed by APN to mediate between author and editors. According to Komolov, the editing was a fraught process and Zhukov bridled at many of the proposed changes. Nevertheless, the work proceeded quite quickly, even though – and perhaps because – Zhukov was in poor health. By the summer of 1968 an approved text for publication had been agreed by the Central Committee. The hundreds of photographs published in the book also had to be approved by the censor.[17]

The memoirs, dedicated by Zhukov 'to the Soviet soldier' (*Sovetskomu Soldatu Posvyashchau*), were published in April 1969 to great acclaim and huge sales. Over the years millions of copies have been sold, not only in Russia and the Soviet Union but also in numerous translations. The first English edition was published in 1971.[18]

After publication Zhukov received a huge amount of correspondence from the Soviet public – about 10,000 letters in all – praising the book but also pointing out mistakes and suggestions for improvement. It was decided to prepare a revised edition incorporating these corrections and adding new chapters on topics that interested readers: the siege of Leningrad, the Yel'nya battle and the workings of Stavka – the headquarters of the Soviet High Command. To help Zhukov with the Stavka chapter, the publishers drafted in the historian Evgeny Tsvetaev, who had worked with General Shtemenko on his memoirs, the first volume of which had been published in 1968. Shtemenko was Chief of Operations during the war and his memoirs provided a detailed account of the workings of Stavka.[19] Tsvetaev wanted Zhukov to produce something similar but Zhukov insisted he was writing a memoir, not a scientific tract. The resultant compromise was a chapter combining elements of memoir with a general description of Stavka procedures. Even so, it was a chapter that was destined to become a key text for historians seeking to understand how the Soviet High Command operated during the war.[20]

Preparation of the revised edition began in 1973 but was complicated by the aftermath of the severe stroke Zhukov had suffered in 1968 that left him paralysed on his left side. He had recovered somewhat but his speech remained slurred and he could only walk with assistance. He also needed frequent treatments. On doctors' orders he was allowed to work only one hour a day. Then, after the death of his second wife in November 1973, Zhukov's health deteriorated further. But he did manage to complete the revised edition, including writing a new preface. Zhukov died in June 1974, only a few weeks before his revised memoirs were published.

The memoirs had expanded into two volumes and the revised edition was published in English in 1985.[21] A facsimile of that edition is reproduced in this present publication.

The revised edition of Zhukov's memoirs was republished in Russian several times in the 1970s and 1980s, latterly in a three-volume version. In 1990 a 10th, expanded Russian edition of the memoirs was published that incorporated a significant amount of new material from Zhukov's original, uncensored, typescript. This material was supplied by Zhukov's youngest daughter Maria, who had inherited part of his personal archive (other papers were taken away by the Soviet authorities). In 1992 an 11th edition of the memoirs included yet more material from Maria.[22] The 10th edition had added 125 pages to previous editions, while the 11th contained a further 35 pages.[23] Conveniently, these two editions italicised the material previously excluded. These expanded memoirs have been reprinted several times since but the reprints do not contain any new material.

Before analysing in detail the differences between the Soviet and post-Soviet editions of the memoirs it is worth asking the question: which is the most authentic version? The natural answer is the 'uncensored' or 'unexpurgated' post-Soviet version, the one that Zhukov wrote originally. The difficulty is that Zhukov did not authorise the post-Soviet versions, whereas he did authorise the Soviet versions, albeit under protest. Moreover, the post-Soviet version of the memoirs contains a lot of material that was cut for editorial rather than political reasons, probably with Zhukov's approval. There is a further complication, too. In the absence of the complete original typescript (in his daughter's personal possession) it is impossible to know which additions to the Soviet-era edition of the memoirs were made by the censors and which by Zhukov himself, or what else was excluded from the post-Soviet version. Nevertheless, it is clear that the post-Soviet version does contain material Zhukov would have wished to publish had he been allowed to do so by the censors.

The account of Zhukov's memoirs is further complicated by the existence of additional material. The two most important additional memoirs to have emerged are those translated and published in this volume. The first piece, 'Briefly about Stalin', comes from Zhukov's private papers held by his daughter Maria and published in *Pravda* in 1989, when it was the official newspaper of the Soviet communist party. According to Maria, this was one of several pieces that Zhukov wrote for 'the writing table' (in English we would say 'for the desk drawer'). They were written in longhand by Zhukov and typed up by his mother-in-law Klavdiya (Maria's grandmother), who did all his transcribing. They were kept in a safe so were saved from confiscation by the state after his death.[24]

In this memoir Zhukov was critical of Stalin but the piece confirmed Zhukov's mixed feelings when he blamed others for the dictator's misdeeds and recognised Stalin's abilities as a military leader. The villains of the piece were Konev, who had betrayed Zhukov in 1957, and Nikolai Bulganin, who had served under Zhukov as a political commissar during the war. Zhukov clashed with Bulganin when he became Stalin's right-hand man in the defence ministry after the war. It is clear, too, that Zhukov did not particularly blame Stalin for his postwar troubles; indeed, he expressed gratitude to the dictator for saving him from the deadly clutches of the Soviet security apparatus.

All editions of Zhukov's published memoirs begin with his early life and conclude in 1946, on the eve of his demotion and exile by Stalin. They are war memoirs, not a full life-story. This is a great pity because his postwar political career was almost as colourful as his military life. Hence the importance of the second, much longer, additional memoir published in this volume, which covers the initial period after Stalin's death. Immediately after Zhukov died the Soviet authorities took away his private papers (apart from those hidden by Maria). Thirty years later those papers were released into the Russian State Military Archive (Russian acronym RGVA). The collection consists of about 190 files containing manuscripts and materials relating to his memoirs, speeches, articles, correspondence, personal memorabilia and photographs.[25] In one of these files may be found the typescript of Zhukov's memoir about the post-Stalin period, which appears to date from 1963–1964, and is a text based on his conversations, not something that he wrote.[26]

This 'memoir' covers the period from Stalin's death in March 1953 until Zhukov's dismissal by Khrushchev in October 1957. It deals with the post-Stalin succession struggle among the Soviet leaders and provides a fascinating first-hand account of some of the important events of this period: the arrest of Beria, the attempt to overthrow Khrushchev in June 1957 and the central committee plenum that ended Zhukov's career. But its coverage is highly selective. There is very little on the 20th party congress, nothing on the crushing of the Hungarian uprising in November 1956 (a military operation supervised by Zhukov and executed by Konev) or on Zhukov's meeting with Eisenhower at the Geneva summit. It is notable for its hostility to Khrushchev and for its unflattering portrait of the other Soviet leaders. It has the air of an account related by Zhukov at the height of his exile and alienation from the party.

There are many other Zhukov files in the RGVA that contain memoir material, most importantly handwritten and typed variants of sections of the published memoirs. These unpublished materials reveal a Zhukov who is more willing to be self-critical and to admit mistakes. He is frank about his unpreparedness for the position of Chief of the General Staff when he was appointed. The disaster of 22 June 1941 is depicted as a fundamental failure of the overly offensive orientation of Soviet military doctrine and preparation for war. He is also much freer in his criticism of his peers, especially those generals who had sided with Khrushchev at the October 1957 plenum. For example, he describes Marshal Semyon Timoshenko, who was People's Commissar for Defence in 1941, as a 'dilettante' when it came to grand strategy and preparing the country for war.[27]

A particular detail worth noting here is Zhukov's variant account of his departure from the post of Chief of the General Staff in July 1941. In the published memoirs Zhukov wrote that he was sacked by Stalin because he urged a withdrawal of Soviet troops from Kiev. The fall of the Ukrainian capital to the Germans in September 1941 was an unmitigated disaster for the Red Army and the failure to withdraw in time resulted in the encirclement and capture of several hundred thousand Soviet troops. Zhukov's memoir account was designed to distance him from that disaster and to fend off Khrushchev-era criticism of his role as Chief of the General Staff. An alternative account by Zhukov of what happened is preserved in the archive – that he asked to be relieved as Chief of Staff and given a front-line command, i.e. of the reserve armies that mounted the successful Yel'nya counter-offensive.[28] We may never know which story is true but it does pose the question: which is the more authentic memoir – the one he constructed for public consumption or the one contained in his unpublished writings?

The Memoirs Compared

The post-Soviet edition of Zhukov's memoirs is approximately 40,000 words longer than the Soviet-era edition (the English-language version of which is the one published in these pages). The additional 40,000 words were cut from Zhukov's original manuscript during the process of vetting and censorship prior to the publication of the first and second Russian editions of the memoirs.[29]

Of these cuts about a quarter were editorial – the deletion of excessive detail and repetitions. It is difficult to imagine Zhukov objecting to such cuts and their omission from the censored Soviet-era editions was no great loss. But most of the deletions were politically motivated. The censors' aim was twofold: first, to make sure the memoirs did not contain too much material that was embarrassing to the Soviet regime and, second, to ensure Zhukov's memoirs were not overly colourful or idiosyncratic but conformed to the norms applied to all Soviet war memoirs. This meant an emphasis on collective rather than personal exploits; lauding the role of the communist party and the Soviet state; no signs of outright political dissent; and a narrative focus on the public not the private life of the memoirist.

In analyses of the difference between memoirs and autobiography a distinction is often made between the person-centred life narrative of autobiography and the situation-centred narrative of memoirs in which the writer is an observer as well as a participant in events. Autobiographies tell what happened to the subject, whereas memoirs show what happened more generally. It is a distinction that disintegrates in practice as life stories often consist of a hybrid of memoir and autobiography. Such is the case with Zhukov's 'reminiscences and reflections' (*Vospominaniya i Ramyshleniya*), which contain much third-person narration of the war and of the related history of the Soviet army, party and state. But the central subject of the story, and the focus of attention throughout, remains Zhukov and his personal views, experiences and relationships. To restrain this personal thrust in the memoirs, the team working with Zhukov secured a number of different types of cut prior to publication.

First, they reduced the number of Zhukov's criticisms of his fellow Soviet generals. Throughout the memoirs Zhukov explicitly or implicitly criticises those Soviet generals who had attacked him during the Khrushchev era. Zhukov also expresses disagreement with the claims of other Soviet military memoirists. Quite a lot of this kind of material survived into the published Soviet edition of the memoirs but there was much that did not. For example, in his original memoir Zhukov recalled a visit to his regiment in the 1920s by Chief of the Cavalry Semyon Budenny and Zhukov's divisional commander Semyon Timoshenko. He recalled the two visitors exchanging some smart remarks suggesting they had been treated with disrespect. When Zhukov asked a colleague what he had done wrong, he was told that he had not greeted Budenny and Timoshenko with enough fuss, such as getting the troops to cheer them.[30] This vignette was immediately followed by a description of a visit by A.I. Yegorov, who was the commander of the military district. Yegorov, later arrested and executed by Stalin, comes across as much more straightforward and less egotistical than either Budenny and Timoshenko. But the Soviet censors cut Zhukov's critical remarks about Budenny and Timoshenko so the story of their visit to his regiment becomes blandly anodyne, leaving readers to wonder why it featured at all.

The most frequent target of Zhukov's criticism was Konev. Zhukov and Konev, both strong personalities, rubbed each other up the wrong way. During the war a rivalry developed between them that was manipulated by Stalin, most famously when he urged both men to be the first to drive their armies to Berlin. When Stalin demoted Zhukov in 1946 Konev gave his fellow marshal some lukewarm support (which was about as much as could be expected in the circumstances) but he was in the vanguard of the Khrushchevite attack on Zhukov in 1957. In his memoirs Zhukov took the moral high ground – criticising Konev but praising him too. For example, Zhukov tarred Konev with the brush of career progress at the expense of a purge victim: 'after the arrest of divisional commander B.I. Bobrov at the end of 1937 I.S. Konev was named divisional commander'. But Zhukov goes on to say that he met Konev often during this period and that 'he was always active and made a good impression on me'.[31] While many of Zhukov's criticisms of Konev made it into print, this one was cut by the censors.

In another deleted passage Zhukov complained about Konev going behind his back to Stalin in connection with the liquidation of an enemy grouping in the Korsun–Shevchenkovskii area in the Ukraine in 1944. According to Zhukov, Konev, the commander of an adjacent front, telephoned Stalin to say the operation against the Korsun–Shevchenkovskii grouping might fail if it wasn't given to him to finish off. Zhukov's memory of this incident may well have been coloured by the fact that at the time he had received a stinging rebuke from Stalin for the failure of his liquidation operation. The operation was taken over by Konev and, much to Zhukov's chagrin, his rival received all the credit for its success.

Zhukov's attitude to Marshal Kliment Voroshilov, the People's Commissar for Defence in the 1930s, verged on the contemptuous in another passage deleted by the censors: 'It is well-known that in military affairs he was weak. Apart from participation in the civil war he had no practical or theoretical basis in the sphere of military science and military art and depended on his closest aides to lead the defence commissariat and build the armed forces.'[32] Zhukov was even more critical of Voroshilov's fecklessness in his unpublished memoir of the post-Stalin period, where he points out that one of his daughters was married to Voroshilov's grandson (they later divorced).

Zhukov had a great deal of respect for Marshal Boris Shaposhnikov, the prewar Chief of the General Staff who took on the position again when Zhukov vacated the post in July 1941. But Zhukov was critical of Shaposhnikov's tendency to remain silent during arguments with Stalin (he made the same complaint about other Soviet generals, Rokossovsky, for example). In one instance – deleted by the censors – Zhukov argued with Stalin that they should remain on the strategic defensive in the spring and summer of 1942, launching just one or two major offensive operations. Shaposhnikov agreed with Zhukov but did not support him in front of Stalin.[33]

Zhukov was keen to correct the mistakes of other military memoirists, sometimes sharply so. In his account of the Kursk battle Zhukov noted a new method of artillery preparation, devised by General P.S. Semyonov, for tanks and infantry to attack during the artillery barrage without waiting for its completion so as to catch the enemy by surprise.

In a deleted passage Zhukov expressed his amazement that Marshal Nikolai Voronov, the Soviet artillery chief, instead claimed credit for the new technique in front of Stalin – a claim repeated in Voronov's memoirs.[34]

Zhukov had a particular dislike of Marshal A.I. Yeremenko, who together with Khrushchev claimed the credit for the spectacular Stalingrad counter-offensive of November 1942. People did not like him, noted Zhukov in a censored sentence, because he was arrogant and an idolater.[35] Zhukov was also keen to record that Yeremenko was wrong when he claimed in his memoirs that Stalin had attended the high command conference in December 1940. But the censors cut this passage, too.[36]

Nor was Zhukov impressed by General P.A. Rotmistrov's claim that at Kursk his 5th Tank Army played the decisive role in the defeat of the Germans' Army Group South's armoured forces. Zhukov pointed to all the fighting done by other units before Rotmistrov arrived to face a weakened German army.[37] Similarly, Zhukov was critical of Marshal Vasily Chuikov's memoir of the battle of Stalingrad. Chuikov was in charge of the Red Army's successful defence of the city but Zhukov said he did not give enough credit to the support of the Soviet armies fighting on his flanks.[38] Neither comment was included in the published memoirs.

Before the publication of Zhukov's memoirs the most detailed and informed account of high-level Soviet military decision-making during the war was Shtemenko's *The General Staff at War*. Zhukov contested Shtemenko's memoirs on several points but relatively gently since he and Shtemenko were allies in the struggle for the historical memory of the war against Khrushchev's supporters. Even so, most of the points he made were deleted by the censors. For example, Zhukov stated that Shtemenko was wrong to claim Stalin had consulted Front commanders about strategic questions. According to Zhukov these matters were reserved for discussions between himself, Stalin and the General Staff. Front commanders (i.e. Konev and Yeremenko) were consulted only about implementation.[39]

Another theme of Zhukov's writing that caught the censors' wary eyes concerned his efforts to humanise his memoirs with personal touches and colourful descriptions. When Yegorov visited Zhukov's regiment he asked Zhukov what he had donated to the country's gold fund to help build new factories and plants. Zhukov told him four cigarette cases and his wife's ring and earrings, adding that he had no more to give. This last phrase was censored, as was Yegorov's reply: 'Never mind, comrade, some day we will all be rich.'[40]

In his account of the Kursk battle Zhukov described the calmness of a staff officer, General Boikov, in the face of a multitude of tasks but added the censored passage: 'Looking at Boikov it was possible to think for a while of fishing in some picturesque reservoir near Moscow, not of the great battle that was about to begin.'[41]

Nor were the humourless censors amused by Zhukov's story about the Soviet occupation of Bessarabia and Northern Bukovina in June 1940. Zhukov's task was to occupy the then Romanian territories following the delivery of a Soviet ultimatum demanding the return of these lost lands (Bessarabia was occupied by Romania in 1918 and Bukovina was ethnically Ukrainian). Zhukov despatched two airborne brigades and two tank brigades to seize control of bridges over the Prut river. The next day Stalin telephoned him and said the Romanian ambassador had complained about Soviet tanks landing on the river. Stalin wanted to know how that was possible and laughed when Zhukov explained that only the airborne troops had flown to the bridges; the tanks made their way there by road.[42]

Neither were the censors enamoured of Zhukov's description of a dinner with Stalin attended by A.A. Zhdanov, the Leningrad party boss. When Stalin proposed a toast to the gallant people of Leningrad, Zhdanov burst into his favourite song – about the Volga – and everyone joined in enthusiastically.[43] One final example of deletions in this vein – and there are many – was Zhukov's description of the meal after signature of the German unconditional surrender agreement: 'The dinner was glorious! Headed by Chief of Supplies General N.A. Antipenko and chef V.M. Petrov, our people prepared a fantastic spread which went down well with our guests.'[44] Presumably this was felt to be too frivolous a detail for such a solemn occasion. But the censors did allow Zhukov to publish that he celebrated by doing a Russian dance!

Most of the censorship of Zhukov's original manuscript was straightforwardly political, beginning with the deletion of the names of Soviet political figures still in disgrace in the 1960s – for example, Georgy Malenkov and Lazar Kaganovich, leaders of the so-called 'anti-party group' who had tried to overthrow Khrushchev in 1957 and who remained unrehabilitated even after Khrushchev's fall. Molotov was the third and main leader of the group but, as Stalin's right-hand man, he was too central and pervasive a figure in Zhukov's memoirs to be omitted too frequently from the text.

The censorship that must have rankled most was the excision of his extensive writing on the prewar purge of the Red Army. Like most memoirists, Zhukov used the opportunity to go on the record about people he admired and respected, many of whom were military officers who had been purged in the 1930s. Zhukov made a point of naming these purged officers, noting they had been unjustly arrested and repressed.

Zhukov also wrote a long general account of the purges and of his own brushes with the process which, he claimed, had almost led him to become a victim, too. Zhukov began the censored section by noting that the year 1937 was a severe test for the Soviet people and armed forces:

> Arrested were a majority of the commanders of military districts and fleets, members of military councils, corps commanders, and commanders and commissars of formations and units. There were more arrests among honest workers of the organs of state security. In the country there was a terrible atmosphere. No one trusted anyone, people feared each other, avoided conversations and were afraid of talking in front of third persons. There was an unprecedented epidemic of slander. Honest people were slandered, sometimes by their closest friends. This happened because people feared being suspected of disloyalty. And this terrible situation continued to worsen. The Soviet people did not understand why the arrests were so widespread and went to sleep worried that they, too, would be taken away during the night.[45]

Zhukov then went on to recount in detail the cases of some of the military purge victims he knew and how, to no avail, he had tried to defend them from false accusations.[46] He came under suspicion himself, later recalling: 'The most difficult emotional experience in my life was connected with the years 1937–1938. The necessary fatal documents were prepared on me; apparently they were already sufficient, someone somewhere was running with a briefcase in which they lay. In general the matter went like this: I would end up the same way as had many others.'[47] According to Zhukov, what saved him was being sent to Khalkhin-Gol, but it is difficult to credit that he would have been given such an important mission if his arrest were imminent.

In the Soviet edition of Zhukov's memoirs the many pages on the purges were reduced to the statement that in 1937 there were 'unfounded arrests in the armed forces . . . in contravention of socialist legality' and 'prominent military leaders were arrested, which, naturally, affected the development of our armed forces and their combat readiness'.[48]

Zhukov's original manuscript was peppered with critical remarks about the performance and shortcomings of the Red Army. Many survived the censorship process, but not all. For example, a passage criticising the Red Army's strategy during the Russian civil war as being based on manoeuvres that it did not have the reserves to conduct was cut.[49] Deleted, too, was Zhukov's comment that until 1940 the Soviet High Command did not have a very good understanding of how to make use of large-scale tank and mechanised formations.[50] Similarly Zhukov remarked in several places how in the early part of the war the Red Army had performed badly but became better with experience. In one instance, the censors allowed Zhukov to say in his description of his tank commanders during the battle of Berlin that he 'could only marvel at our commander tank-men, how they had raised their operational and tactical skills during the war'. Unpublished were Zhukov's immediately subsequent sentences: 'I could not help recalling that during the first months of the war, when our commanders were insufficiently prepared, they frequently found themselves in difficult situations from which they were unable to extract themselves. But now these experienced cadres could fulfil any mission.'[51] A slightly different example is the deletion of Zhukov's comment that the receipt of high-performance Studebaker trucks from the United States' Lend-Lease programme was important for the motorisation of Soviet artillery prior to the Kursk battle. The point was to avoid giving too much credit to the Cold War enemy, although during the war itself the Soviets had been fulsome in their thanks for American material aid, a view to which Zhukov fully subscribed.[52] In the same vein was the censors' cut of a favourable remark by Zhukov about Eisenhower: 'I liked his simplicity, informality and sense of humour.' Zhukov was also known to have called Eisenhower 'Ike' on occasion.[53]

The biggest challenge facing the censors was what to do about Zhukov's treatment of Stalin, especially in view of the Grechko group's comment that the dictator had been given too much coverage. After Khrushchev's fall in 1964 Stalin was partially rehabilitated by the new leadership headed by Leonid Brezhnev. He remained condemned for his crimes against the party and the Soviet people but his role in building socialism was recognised, as was his significant contribution to the war effort. But the official preference was to say as little as possible about Stalin, thereby avoiding either too much condemnation or too much praise. If Stalin's name could be avoided by referring to the 'General Secretary' or the 'Supreme Commander', then so much the better. But it was inevitable that Stalin as a person as well as the boss would loom large in Zhukov's memoirs. Indeed, Zhukov's appraisal of Stalin as Supreme Commander was instrumental in the restoration of Stalin's reputation as a great, if unpalatable, war leader. The censors responded by trimming Zhukov's extensive descriptions of his relations with Stalin.

One early cut was Zhukov's critical dissection of a laudatory account by Voroshilov about Stalin's role in the Russian civil war, specifically that he had come up with a plan to defeat General Denikin's counter-revolutionary White Army in the south of the country. Zhukov pointed out that all Stalin had proposed were a few ideas about the direction of the campaign against Denikin, which Lenin had promptly ignored.[54] In another censored passage Zhukov wrote that, unlike Voroshilov, Deputy Defence Commissar Marshal Mikhail Tukhachevsky – executed in 1937 – did not toady before Stalin, who had never forgiven him for the failed Soviet march on Warsaw in 1920.[55]

Zhukov's first meeting with Stalin was in June 1940 and his story of the encounter was retained in his Soviet-era memoirs. Zhukov was suitably impressed and remarked that 'if he was like this with everyone, then why was there all this talk about him being such a terrible person? At that time one didn't want to believe anything bad' – comments that were censored.[56]

In relation to 22 June 1941, Zhukov recalled a number of occasions on which he tried to persuade Stalin to step up the preparations for war with Germany and to take measures that would ensure the Red Army would be ready when the Germans attacked. Some of this material made it past the censors but not all. In one deleted passage Zhukov complained that Stalin was not interested in the work of the General Staff and that he, Zhukov, had not been given the opportunity to properly brief the dictator on the country's defence.[57] Equally problematic were the effects of the Stalin cult that led to the belief that the dictator knew more about the conduct of war than the General Staff. But Zhukov was adamant it was possible to raise difficult issues with Stalin and to have sharp discussions with him if necessary. According to Zhukov, Stalin was suspicious of Great Britain but was sure that while the British fought on, Hitler would not attack the USSR and undertake a risky two-front war: 'Hitler is not such a fool that he doesn't understand that the Soviet Union is not like Poland, or France or even England.'[58]

During the war there were many disagreements between Zhukov and Stalin about operational matters. Again, some of these disputes made it into the published memoirs while others were censored. There appears to be no particular pattern to these deletions. Maybe the censorship team, who were themselves historians, thought some of Zhukov's claims for prescience were rather retrospective. For example, Zhukov went to considerable trouble to establish how in the summer of 1944 he had favoured an advance into East Prussia rather than an attack on German-occupied Warsaw. Zhukov's point is that had his advice been taken then the later Soviet advance on Berlin would not have been complicated by having to contain strong German forces in East Prussia and the adjacent province of Pomerania. The allusion here is to a dispute Zhukov had in the 1960s with Chuikov about whether or not Berlin could have been captured by the Red Army as early as February 1945, thus ending the war sooner and saving hundreds of thousands of lives. Zhukov's side of the argument was that this was not possible because of the threat posed to the northern flank of his 1st Belorussian Front by German forces in Pomerania. Zhukov's preference for an East Prussian operation made it into the published memoirs, although some of the detail was omitted.[59]

A related issue was the question of when to abandon Soviet efforts to capture Warsaw. According to Zhukov, in October 1944 he argued strongly that the advance on Warsaw should be called off because it was getting nowhere. Rokossovsky, who commanded the 1st Belorussian Front which was conducting this operation, agreed with Zhukov but backed away from the argument when it became apparent that Stalin was not happy with the idea of calling off the offensive. Zhukov was unhappy with Rokossovsky's attitude but stuck to his guns and, with the support of some other members of the Politburo, was able to persuade Stalin to halt offensive operations in the Warsaw area. Stalin was still displeased, however, and Zhukov links this episode to Stalin's decision to take direct command of all the Fronts, whereas previously he had controlled operations via Stavka representatives and coordinators such as Zhukov. The knock-on from this decision was that Zhukov was placed in charge of the 1st Belorussian Front – the one that was head-ing directly for Berlin – while Rokossovsky was transferred to the 2nd Belorussian Front, which would protect the northern flank of Zhukov's advance on the German capital. Rokossovsky was disgruntled and his relationship with Zhukov never recovered. Stalin's decision to take direct command of the Fronts was recorded in the published memoirs but not the background and consequences of that decision, as recalled by Zhukov.[60]

When Zhukov's advance on Berlin in April 1945 encountered some initial difficulties, there were some tensions with Stalin, only some of which are recorded in the published memoirs. In his original manuscript Zhukov said neither he nor Stalin phoned each other for three days (17–19 April 1945). But Zhukov was not too worried because he knew that 'when even the smallest things were not going well, [Stalin] got very irritable'.[61]

In this section of his memoirs Zhukov was also keen to contest the idea, propagated by Shtemenko, that depending on how the operation progressed, Stalin contemplated allowing his rival Konev's 1st Ukrainian Front, advancing on Berlin from the south, to take the German capital. But the censors did not think the differences between Zhukov's and Shtemenko's accounts merited an explicit public airing.[62]

More personal material also fell foul of the censors. For example, Zhukov described meeting Stalin at the dictator's dacha in March 1945 and going for a walk with him. The published memoirs stated that 'Stalin unexpectedly began telling me about his childhood'. But omitted was what Stalin reportedly told Zhukov: 'He said that he was a very sickly child. His mother loved him very much and had not left his side until he was almost six. In accordance with his mother's wishes he went to study in a seminary to become a priest. But he had always been a bit of a rebel, didn't get on with the administration, and was expelled from the seminary.'[63]

One now well-known story about Stalin omitted from the censored memoirs concerned Zhukov's meeting with the dictator's son Vasily just before the June 1945 victory parade. Vasily told Zhukov that Stalin had wanted to take the salute at the victory parade himself but had fallen off the horse during practice.[64] It has to be said, however, that Vasily was not the most reliable of sources and there is no evidence that Stalin ever learned to ride.

The Costs of Censorship

The overall effect of all these deletions was to strip Zhukov's original memoir of much of its negative and critical content in relation to the Soviet system. The result is a memoir very positive in tone that reflects well not only on Zhukov but on Soviet communism. From the censors' point of view it was a job well done. As a lifelong communist and a loyal Soviet citizen, Zhukov could not have been too displeased. From the readers' point of view the loss was injurious but not fatal. Zhukov's sharp tongue in relation to some of his colleagues had been toned down and the memoirs had lost much of their judgemental, political edge, especially in relation to Stalin's military purges, but what remained was still an interesting, colourful and revealing account of Zhukov's life and military career.

Zhukov's memoirs were and remain an indispensable first-hand account of the Great Patriotic War by a participant in all the war's great battles and campaigns, who served throughout the conflict at the very highest levels of Soviet high command, and in close partnership with Stalin. The memoirs are not great literature but they are clear, vigorous and highly informative. Readers are also fortunate to have available such a good English translation.

The diminution of Zhukov's personal voice in the narrative was a definite loss. Zhukov's carping about his colleagues and his efforts to inject a little colour and humour into the memoirs were revealing of his character. This absence was made all the more important because there had been so little of a personal nature in the memoirs to begin with. In conformity with Soviet conventions, Zhukov's memoirs were predominantly a narrative of his public life as a soldier. They revealed little about his inner world or his private life. This suited Zhukov because even in private he tended to be reticent. His temperament changed after the war, as he grew older and as a result of his political travails, during which he acquired a little humility. But for accounts of the later, more emotionally mature, open, self-reflective and vulnerable Zhukov, we are overly-reliant on the memoirs of others.[65]

Zhukov did admit to being a bit of a disciplinarian but argued this was because he was a perfectionist who strove to elicit the best from those under his command and to help save their lives in battle. That anodyne self-description masked the reality of Zhukov as a tough, brutal and unrelenting commander, who cursed, threatened and occasionally hit people to impose his will. Such bullying was not uncommon in the Red Army and was commensurate with Zhukov's own experience of being disciplined as a child, as an apprentice and as a conscript in the Tsarist army during the First World War. During the Great Patriotic War the Soviets executed some 158,000 of their own troops, a good many of them on Zhukov's orders. While he never expressed regret for his harsh actions during the war, there is no evidence that Zhukov was personally cruel or callous with regard to the lives of his soldiers. His stern approach to military leadership, which is not to everyone's taste, was his command style, his way of getting things done at the time and in the circumstances that confronted him.

Away from military command Zhukov was a more gentle and, indeed, cultured soul. He was not a self-consciously intellectual general but he was widely read in literature, history and military theory and, by the time he died, had amassed a library of some 20,000 books (about the same number as Stalin).[66] Zhukov liked ballet, opera and films, as well as the more traditional manly pursuits of hunting, fishing and shooting.

Zhukov is sometimes portrayed as self-centred and egotistical. He was certainly full of himself, particularly when younger and at the peak of his glory days at the end of the war. But, as these memoirs show, he could also be unstinting in his praise of other people's contributions and qualities. His memoirs became a testament to others as well as to himself. And while Zhukov nursed grudges against those he felt betrayed by, he remained loyal to his friends and was prepared to recognise the talents of even his worst rivals, such as Konev.

Zhukov had an unusually complicated family life: two wives, two long-term mistresses, serial adultery and four daughters by three different women.[67] All these women remained loyal to Zhukov. Although this could be attributed as devotion to a Great Man, their loyalty also reflected the care, attention and affection Zhukov gave them when he could. But his military career always came first. It was Zhukov's public persona and commitments that dominated his life and defined his identity. He was, indeed, who he presented himself to be – a tough, energetic and dedicated soldier and a loyal servant of the Soviet state.

Zhukov relished the discipline, order and predictability of military life and never mastered the vagaries of Soviet political intrigue. At the same time he loved the energy and activism of military affairs. 'Routinism is a dangerous thing', he told the Soviet writer Konstantin Fedin in an unpublished interview dating from 1945. 'Military affairs are changing all the time. I love military affairs because you are always busy. It is easy to become decrepit. This we know.'[68] As his memoirs testify, Zhukov fought to retain this zest into old age.

In common with many military and political leaders, Zhukov's inner life was shaped by his public identity. Admittedly, this identity was more frayed and contradictory than the seamless version presented in his memoirs. But knowledge of his record as a military man of action is the starting point for any understanding of Zhukov the person. In this respect there is no better introduction to Zhukov than through his own memoirs.

Notes

1. For a full biography of Zhukov see: G. Roberts, *Stalin's General: The Life of Georgy Zhukov*, Random House: New York, 2012.

2. E. Salisbury (ed,), *Marshal Zhukov's Greatest Battles*, Sphere Books: London, 1971, p. 4. John Erickson's comment appears in a review of the Salisbury book in the *Sunday Times* in July 1969.

3. D. Glantz, introduction to *Marshal Zhukov's Greatest Battles*, Cooper Square Press: New York, 2002, pp. xxv–xxvi.

4. I am indebted to Tim Morris's blog for this comparison between Grant and Zhukov: http://www.uta.edu/english/tim/lection/130313.html.

5. V. Suvorov, *Icebreaker: Who Started the Second World War?*, Hamish Hamilton: London, 1990. An updated version of Suvorov's argument was published as *The Chief Culprit: Stalin's Grand Design to Start World War II*, Naval Institute Press: Annapolis MD, 2008. For a critical assessment of Suvorov's work and the debate it has provoked, see T.J. Uldricks, 'The Icebreaker Controversy: Did Stalin Plan to Attack Hitler?', *Slavic Review*, vol. 58, no. 3, Fall 1999.

6. V. Suvorov, *Ten' Pobedy* and *Beru Svoi Slova Obratno*, Harvest: Donetsk, 2003 and 2005. Other critics of Zhukov include B.V. Sokolov, *Georgii Zhukov: Triumfi i Pandeniya*, Ast: Moscow, 2003, and A.N. Mertsalov & L.A. Mertsalova, *Inoi Zhukov*, Moscow, 1996.

7. *Ten' Pobedy*, pp. 17, 26.

8. R. Forczyk, *Georgy Zhukov*, Osprey Publishing: Oxford, 2012. A more radical critique of Zhukov is Arsen Martirosyan's, who argues that he was involved in a military conspiracy to overthrow Stalin through engineering a German defeat of the USSR. Martirosyan links this conspiracy to a plot by Marshal Tukhachevsky, executed for treason in 1937. According to Martirosyan, Zhukov and a second generation of military conspirators deliberately changed Soviet strategy from one of active defence in the event of a German invasion to a series of disastrous counter-offensives. Like all conspiracy theorists Martirosyan confuses mistakes and cover-up with evidence of a plot. The Red Army's counter-offensives of June 1941 were badly conceived and led to disastrous defeats but this offensivist policy was not Zhukov's invention – it was deeply ingrained in Soviet military doctrine. Zhukov as Chief of the General Staff shared responsibility for the ensuing disaster but what happened was the result of strategic errors, not a conspiracy. See A. Martirosyan, *22 Iunya*, two vols, Veche: Moscow 2012. An interview with the author may be found here: http://www.youtube.com/watch?v=vFmJU6wAwt4e.

9. See G. Roberts, *Stalin's Wars: From World War to Cold War, 1939–1953*, Yale University Press: London, 2006.

10. On the Red Army's failure in the face of German encirclement operations, see R.R. Reese, *Why Stalin's Soldiers Fought*, University Press of Kansas, 2011, ch. 3.

11. See D. Glantz, *Zhukov's Greatest Defeat: The Red Army's Epic Disaster in Operation Mars, 1942*, Ian Allan Publishing: Shepperton, 2000.

12. A. Mirkina, *Vtoraya Pobeda Marshala Zhukova*, Vniigmi-Mtsd: Moscow, 2000, p. 24.

13. For some examples see S. Bialer (ed.), *Stalin and His Generals: Soviet Military Memoirs of World War II*, Souvenir Press: London, 1969.

14. G. Zhukov, 'Velichie Pobedy SSSR i Bessilie Fal'sifikatorov Istorii', *Kommunist*, January 1970 (published in English as *The Soviet High Command and the War*, Soviet Weekly Booklet: London, 1970). In his memoirs Zhukov further attacked Salisbury for his anti-Soviet treatment of the blockade of Leningrad in the latter's book, *900 Days: The Siege of Leningrad*, Harper & Row: New York, 1969. This was quite unfair since Salisbury's classic book actually provided quite a balanced account of the siege that gave the Soviets their due for maintaining such a stout and heroic, albeit also tragic, defence of the city.

15. Mirkina, *Vtoraya Pobeda Marshala Zhukova*, passim.

16. *Georgy Zhukov: Stenogramma Oktyabr'skogo (1957g) Plenuma TsK KPSS i Drugie Dokumenty*, Mezhdunarodnyi Fond 'Demokratiya': Moscow, 2001, part 6, doc. 14.

17. Ibid, docs 16–17; Mirkina, *Vtoraya Pobeda Marshala Zhukova*, pp. 53–5.

18. *The Memoirs of Marshal Zhukov*, Jonathan Cape: London, 1971.

19. Shtemenko's memoirs were published in English as: S.M. Shtemenko, *The Soviet General Staff at War, 1941–1945*, 2 vols, Progress Publishers: Moscow, 1970, 1986.

20. E. Tsvetaev, 'Poslednii Podvig G.K. Zhukova', in S.S. Smirnov et al, *Marshal Zhukov: Kakim My Ego*, Pomnim, Politizdat: Moscow, 1988.

21. G.K. Zhukov, *Reminiscences and Reflections*, 2 vols, Progress Publishers: Moscow, 1985.

22. G.K. Zhukov, *Vospominaniya i Razmyshleniya*, 3 vols, 10th and 11th editions, APN: Moscow, 1990 and 1992.

23. O. Preston Chaney, *Zhukov*, revised edition, University of Oklahoma Press, 1996, p. 527.

24. 'Korotke o Staline', *Pravda*, 20 January 1989.

25. Rossiiskii Gosudarstvennyi Voennyi Arkhiv (RGVA), F.41107, Op.1, D.1-189 and Op.1, D.1-4.

26. RGVA, Op.2, D.1. The typescript was published in *Zhukov: Stenogramma Oktyabr'skogo (1957g) Plenuma TsK KPSS i Drugie Dokumenty*, pp. 620–39.

27. RGVA, F.41107, Op.1, D.17, ll. 38–41.

28. RGVA, D.54, l. 57.

29. The post-Soviet edition of the memoirs also incorporates a small amount of material from other manuscripts by Zhukov, i.e. from sources other than the original typescript of his memoirs as first submitted to the publishers in 1966.

30. Zhukov, *Vospominaniya i Razmyshleniya*, vol. 1, pp. 153–4 (vol. 1, p. 116). All references are to the 11th Russian edition of Zhukov's memoirs published in 1992. The number in brackets refers to the page in the second English edition of the memoirs (the one published in this volume), where the censored material would have appeared had it been allowed to remain in.

31. *Vospominaniya i Razmyshleniya*, vol. 1, p. 237 (vol. 1, p. 172).

32. *Vospominaniya i Razmyshleniya*, vol. 1, p. 186 (vol. 1, p. 137).

33. *Vospominaniya i Razmyshleniya*, vol. 2, p. 288 (vol. 2, p. 74).

34. *Vospominaniya i Razmyshleniya*, vol. 3, p. 52 (vol. 2, p. 187).

35. *Vospominaniya i Razmyshleniya*, vol. 1, p. 248 (vol. 1, p. 176).

36. *Vospominaniya i Razmyshleniya*, vol. 1, p. 311 (vol. 1, p. 224).

37. *Vospominaniya i Razmyshleniya*, vol. 3, p. 58 (vol. 2, p. 193).

38. *Vospominaniya i Razmyshleniya*, vol. 2, p. 317 (vol. 2, p. 98).

39. *Vospominaniya i Razmyshleniya*, vol. 3, p. 183 (vol. 2, p. 310).
40. *Vospominaniya i Razmyshleniya*, vol. 1, p. 156 (vol. 1, p. 118).
41. *Vospominaniya i Razmyshleniya*, vol. 3, p. 45 (vol. 2, p. 181).
42. *Vospominaniya i Razmyshleniya*, vol. 1, pp. 290–1 (vol. 1, p. 208).
43. *Vospominaniya i Razmyshleniya*, vol. 3, p. 97 (vol. 2, p. 232).
44. *Vospominaniya i Razmyshleniya*, vol. 3, p. 284 (vol. 2, p. 401).
45. *Vospominaniya i Razmyshleniya*, vol. 1, p. 229 (vol. 1, p. 171).
46. A detailed summary of this section of the uncensored memoirs may be found in Chaney, *Zhukov*, pp. 46–54.
47. Chaney, *Zhukov*, p. 55.
48. Zhukov, *Reminiscences and Reflections*, vol. 1, p. 171.
49. *Vospominaniya i Razmyshleniya*, vol. 1, pp. 118–19 (vol. 1, p. 88).
50. *Vospominaniya i Razmyshleniya*, vol. 1, p. 304 (vol. 1, p. 220).
51. *Vospominaniya i Razmyshleniya*, vol. 3, p. 242 (vol. 2, p. 363).
52. *Vospominaniya i Razmyshleniya*, vol. 3, p. 27 (vol. 2, p. 164).
53. *Vospominaniya i Razmyshleniya*, vol. 3, p. 317 (vol. 2, p. 433). When Eisenhower, accompanied by Zhukov, visited Moscow in August 1945 one of those who greeted him was Kathleen Harriman, the daughter of the American ambassador, who wrote in a letter to her sister: 'I took a great shine to Marshal Zhukov that evening. He's very genial & fun & apparently easy to work with. Once during the evening he called Eisenhower "Ike", a great departure for a Soviet!'
54. *Vospominaniya i Razmyshleniya*, vol. 1, pp. 103–4 (vol. 1, p. 76).
55. *Vospominaniya i Razmyshleniya*, vol. 1, p. 188 (vol. 1, p. 138).
56. *Vospominaniya i Razmyshleniya*, vol. 1, p. 287 (vol. 1, p. 206).
57. *Vospominaniya i Razmyshleniya*, vol. 1, p. 345 (vol. 1, p. 249).
58. *Vospominaniya i Razmyshleniya*, vol. 1, p. 384 (Vol. 1, p. 275).
59. *Vospominaniya i Razmyshleniya*, vol. 3, pp. 151–2 (vol. 2, p. 283).
60. *Vospominaniya i Razmyshleniya*, vol. 3, pp. 174–5 (vol. 2, p. 303).
61. *Vospominaniya i Razmyshleniya*, vol. 3, p. 247 (vol. 2, p. 367).
62. *Vospominaniya i Razmyshleniya*, vol. 3, pp. 225–6 (vol. 2, p. 348).
63. *Vospominaniya i Razmyshleniya*, vol. 3, p. 215 (vol. 2, p. 339).
64. *Vospominaniya i Razmyshleniya*, vol. 3, p. 308 (vol. 2, p. 424).
65. The two important texts are Konstantin Simonov's 'Notes Towards a Biography of G.K. Zhukov' – based on the writer's meetings and conversations with Zhukov from the 1930s through to the 1960s – published in his *Glazami Cheloveka Moego Pokoleniya*, Novosti: Moscow, 1989; the memoirs collected in I.G. Aleksandrov (ed.), *Marshal Zhukov: Polkovodets i Chelovek*, 2 vols, Novosti: Moscow, 1988; and the memoir of Zhukov's youngest daughter Maria: *Marshal Zhukov – Moi Otets*, Sretenskogo Monastyriya: Moscow, 2005.
66. V.S. Astrakhansky, 'Biblioteka G.K. Zhukova', *Arkhivno-Informatsionnyi Bulleten'*, no. 13, 1996.
67. Zhukov's personal life is covered extensively in Roberts, *Stalin's General*. Some more details may be found in Sheila Fitzpatrick's review of the book: "Who gets the dacha?", *London Review of Books*, 24 January 2013. But the discerning reader should be aware that while there are many claims about Zhukov's private life, not all of them are to be taken at face value.
68. RGVA, F.41107, Op.1, D.86, l.9.

The 'Drang nach Osten'.

Panzers under fire.

This is how the Germans marched through Moscow!

Air defences in Moscow.

The battle for Stalingrad.

Street fighting in Berlin.

Marshal G.K. Zhukov, General N.E. Berzarin and Arthur Pieck beside the Reichstag, 3 May 1945.

The Commanders-in-Chief of the Allied troops. (Left to right): Field Marshal Bernard Montgomery, General Dwight D. Eisenhower, Marshal G.K. Zhukov and General Delattre de Tassigny.

Georgy Zhukov with his daughters (right to left), Ella, Era and Masha.

Georgy Zhukov and his wife Galina on holiday near Moscow.

CHAPTER 1

The Battle of Moscow

On October 5, 1941, I received a message from General Headquarters: "Stalin wants to speak with Front Commander over direct line."

From the communications room of Leningrad Front HQ I telegraphed to General Headquarters over the Baudot: "Zhukov here." General Headquarters replied: "Stand by." In less than two minutes the other end of the line telegraphed: "Stalin here."

Stalin: "How do you do."

Zhukov: "How do you do."

Stalin: "Comrade Zhukov, can you get on a plane and immediately come to Moscow? The Stavka would like to discuss with you the necessary measures to rectify the situation on the left wing of the Reserve Front in the vicinity of Yukhnov. Leave someone in your place — Khozin, perhaps."

Zhukov: "May I fly out early in the morning of October 6?"

Stalin: "Excellent. We'll expect you in Moscow tomorrow."

However, certain important events in the sector of the 54th Army made it impossible for me to leave on the morning of the 6th, and, with permission of the Supreme Commander, the flight was postponed.

In the evening on October 6 Stalin again phoned me in Leningrad.

"How are things with you? What's new in enemy actions?"

"German pressure has slackened. According to what prisoners say, German troops sustained heavy losses in September and are taking up defensive positions near Leningrad. Artillery is shelling the city, and it is being bombed from the air. Our aerial reconnaissance has detected large columns of motorized infantry and tanks moving southward from the Leningrad area — evidently, in the direction of Moscow."

Having reported the situation, I asked the Supreme Commander if his order for me to fly to Moscow still stood.

"Leave General Khozin or Fedyuninsky in your place," Stalin repeated, "and fly to Moscow."

I bade farewell to the members of the Leningrad Front Military Council and left for Moscow. Since General Khozin had to be rushed to the 54th Army, I delegated temporary command of the Leningrad Front to General Fedyuninsky.

In Moscow I was met by the chief of Stalin's bodyguard. From him I learned that the Supreme Commander was ill and was working at home. We went there at once.

Stalin had a cold; he didn't look very well, and received me curtly. He acknowledged my greeting with a nod and called my attention to a map, where he pointed out the Vyazma area.

"Look at this," he said. "A very grave situation has developed. I can't get a detailed report from the Western and Reserve Fronts on the true situation there. And we cannot make any decisions without knowing where and with what strength the enemy is mounting the offensive, or what the fighting value of our troops is. You are to go at once to Western Front Headquarters to investigate the situation thoroughly. Phone me from there at any hour, day or night. I'll be waiting for your call."

After a moment Stalin asked:

"What's your opinion? Do you think the Germans can soon mount an offensive against Leningrad?"

"I don't think so. They suffered heavy losses and moved out tanks and motorized divisions all along the way from outside Leningrad to the central direction. They are not in a position, given the strength they have now, to mount a new offensive operation."

"And where do you think they are going to send those tank and motorized forces that Hitler moved out of the Leningrad area?"

"Obviously in the direction of Moscow. But only after they are brought up to full strength again and repairs made to the equipment."

Throughout our discussion Stalin stood at the table, on which there was a topographical map of the Western, Reserve and Bryansk Fronts. Pointing to the Western Front, he said: "Apparently they've already been moving in that direction."

I immediately went to see B. M. Shaposhnikov, Chief of General Staff, and gave him a detailed picture of the situation as of October 6 in the Leningrad area.

"The Supreme Commander has just phoned," he said. "Ordered us to prepare a map of the Western sector for you. It will soon be ready. Western Front Command is where Reserve Front HQ was in August when you conducted operations to crush the enemy near Yelnya."

Shaposhnikov filled me in on the details of the situation on the Moscow sector. He gave me the Supreme Command order which stated:

"To the Commander of the Reserve Front.

"To the Commander of the Western Front.

"By order of the Supreme Command General of the Army Zhukov is assigned to command the Reserve Front and represent the Stavka.

"The Stavka requests that Comrade Zhukov be informed of the situation. All decisions taken by Comrade Zhukov in the future, regarding the utilization of the troops and on questions of conducting operations are to be heeded absolutely.

"For the Supreme Command
"Chief of General Staff Shaposhnikov
"October 6, 1941, 19:30 hrs."

While we were waiting for the map, Shaposhnikov poured me a cup of strong tea. He said he was very tired, and he looked it. I left Shaposhnikov and went straight to Western Front Headquarters.

On the way I studied the situation on the map using a pocket flash-light. I was very sleepy, so every now and then I had the driver stop the car and took short runs to shake off sleep.

It was night when I reached Western Front HQ. The duty officer reported that the commanding officers were in conference with the Front Commander. The Commander's office was dimly lit with stearin candles. Sitting at a table were Konev, Sokolovsky, Bulganin and Malandin. Everyone looked exhausted. I told them I was there on the Supreme Commander's order to investigate the situation and phone in a report at once.

What Lt.-Gen. Malandin, Chief of the Front HQ Operations

Division, was able to tell me in reply to my questions about the latest developments, supplemented and specified the information we already had.

What had happened on the Western sector?

At the time the German troops started advancing on Moscow, three Fronts were defending the far approaches to the capital. They were: the Western (Commander Col.-Gen. Konev), the Reserve (Commander Marshal Budenny) and the Bryansk (Commander Lt.-Gen. Yeremenko). In late September the three Fronts had a combined strength of about 1,250,000 men, 990 tanks, and 7,600 mortars and guns, 677 planes. Most of the troops, means and equipment were on the Western front.[1]

After regrouping his troops on the Moscow sector, the enemy had a force superior to the combined strength of our three Fronts. He had 40 per cent more men, 70 per cent more tanks, 80 per cent more mortars and guns, and twice as many planes.[2]

The German offensive, code-named Typhoon, began on September 30 with attacks by Guderian's tank group and the 2nd Army on the Bryansk Front forces in the sector between Zhukovka and Shostka. On October 2 the enemy dealt powerful blows at the troops of the Western and Reserve Fronts. Hitting especially hard from areas north of Dukhovshchina and east of Roslavl, he succeeded in piercing our defences. The enemy shock units lunged forward from the south and the north, enveloping the Vyazma grouping of the Western and Reserve Fronts.

An extremely grave situation developed to the south of Bryansk where the 3rd and 13th armies of the Bryansk Front found themselves faced with the threat of encirclement. Encountering no real opposition, Guderian's troops headed for Orel, where we did not have the forces to repulse the offensive.

On orders of the Supreme Command, a reinforced 1st Guards Rifle Corps was formed under Major-General Lelyushenko on October 2. Its mission was to hold up the enemy advance and enable the Bryansk Front to withdraw its troops.

On October 3, developing their offensive, the Guderian forces captured practically undefended Orel, with the Nazi

---

[1] *A History of the Second World War, 1939-1945*, in twelve volumes, Vol. 4, Moscow, Voenizdat, 1975, p. 93 (in Russian).

[2] Ibid.

24th Motorized Corps emerging in the rear of the Bryansk
Front. The lst Guards Rifle Corps, deployed in the Mtsensk
area, engaged the enemy's motorized group and panzers. It
held them at bay for several days, inflicting considerable
casualties and destroying much of their weaponry. For the
first time, the tankmen of our 4th and llth brigades hit enemy
vehicles from ambush. And the troops of the Bryansk Front
took advantage of the good show. put up by the lst Guards
Rifle Corps to withdraw to the appointed line.

Here are the recollections of the episode by General Guderian,
commander of the Nazi 2nd Panzer Army: "2nd October...
Simultaneously in the operational zone of the 24th Panzer
Corps near Mtsensk, north-east of Orel, bitter fighting broke
out, involving the 4th Panzer Division... A large number of
Russian T-34s was engaged in the battle, causing considerable
losses to our panzers. The superiority that our panzers had so
far was now lost and seized by the adversary. This wiped out
the chances of a rapid and unintermittent success."

He added: "The planned swift offensive on Tula had had
to be put off."

True enough. Not only had Guderian put off the offensive
on Tula, he also never captured the city. But the Bryansk
Front was cut. Suffering losses, its troops were rolling back
east, fighting all the way. A menacing situation took shape on
the Tula sector.

Col.-Gen. Konev, Commander of the Western Front, ordered
a counter-offensive from the north of Vyazma against the
enemy's northern grouping that was trying to outflank his
troops. Unfortunately, that counter-offensive was not successful. Late on October 6 a considerable part of the troops of the
Western and Reserve Fronts was encircled west of Vyazma.

From my talks with the officers at Western Front Headquarters and an analysis of the situation I got the impression
that the disaster in the area of Vyazma could have been
averted. Despite the enemy's superiority in manpower and
materiel, our troops could have avoided encirclement. To do so
it had been necessary to determine more exactly and in time
the directions of the enemy's main effort and concentrate on
those directions the bulk of the troops and weapons at the
expense of the inactive defence sectors. However, this was not

done, and our defences were not able to sustain the enemy's concentrated blows. Large gaps were made in our defence line, which we had nothing to close with — there were no reserves at the Command's disposal.

At 2:30 a.m. on October 8 I phoned Stalin. He was still up and working. After outlining the situation on the Western Front I said:

"The main danger now lies in the weak Mozhaisk defence line. Because of this, enemy armoured troops may suddenly appear near Moscow. We must bring up forces quickly from every place possible to the Mozhaisk line."

"Where are the 19th and 20th armies, and Boldin's group of the Western Front?" Stalin asked. "Where are the 24th and 32nd armies of the Reserve Front?"

"They've been encircled to the west and north-west of Vyazma," I replied.

"What do you propose to do?"

"I'm leaving at once for the Reserve Front to see Budenny."

"Do you know where the Reserve Front's headquarters is?"

"I'll look for it in the neighbourhood of Maloyaroslavets."

"All right. Go to Budenny and call me from there."

A steady drizzle was falling, and the thick fog clinging to the ground restricted visibility. When on the morning of October 8 we drove up to the Obolenskoye railway station we saw two signalmen laying a cable from the bridge across the River Protva to Maloyaroslavets.

"Where are you pushing these wires to, comrades?" I called out to them.

"Right where we've been ordered to push them," one of them, a huge man, replied without even looking up.

I had to tell them who I was, and that we were looking for Reserve Front HQ.

The huge signalman stood at attention and said:

"Excuse me, Comrade General, did not know you by sight. That's why I answered the way I did. You've already passed headquarters. It was moved here two hours ago, and housed in the cottages over there in the forest on the hill. The sentries there will show you the way."

The car turned around. Soon I was in the room of Army

Commissar 1st Class L. Z. Mekhlis, a GHQ representative, who was with Major-Gen. A. F. Anisov, Chief of Staff of the Front. Mekhlis was on the phone, giving someone hell.

I asked them where the Commander was, and the Chief of Staff answered:

"Nobody knows. He was with the 43rd Army during the day. I'm afraid that something unpleasant may have happened to Budenny."

"Have you taken steps to find him?"

"Yes, I've sent liaison officers but they haven't come back yet."

Mekhlis addressed a question to me then:

"And what assignment brings you here?" he asked.

"I've come as a Stavka member on the Supreme Commander's instructions to investigate the situation here."

"You can see that the situation is none too good. Right now I'm rounding up the stragglers. At assembly points we'll arm them and form new units out of them."

My talks with Mekhlis and Anisov gave me very little concrete about the situation of the Reserve Front troops or about the enemy. So I got in the car and rode on to Yukhnov, hoping to quickly find out more on the spot.

As we drove across the Protva River I involuntarily recalled my childhood. I knew the area very well, as I had walked through it many times in my youth. My native village of Strelkovka was ten kilometres away from Obninskoye where Reserve Front HQ was located. My mother, my sister and her four children were living in Strelkovka. "How are they? Suppose I call on them?" But that was impossible, there wasn't time. I asked myself what would happen to them if the fascists came to the village. What would they do to a Red Army general's relatives? Shoot them, surely. "First chance I get," I thought, "I'll have them brought to Moscow."

Two weeks later the Germans occupied Strelkovka as well as all of the Ugodsky-Zavod District. Luckily, I was able beforehand to send my mother, sister and her children to Moscow.

My fellow villagers did not sit around doing nothing. A guerilla detachment was formed in the region with Victor Karasev, a YCL member and former frontier guard, at the head. He was an exceptionally brave man and a clever organizer. His commissar was Alexander Kurbatov, secretary of the Ugodsky-Zavod District Party Committee. The chairman of the Ugodsky-Zavod District Executive Committee, M. A. Guryanov, whom I would describe as a dauntless people's avenger, was also in that detachment.

The Ugodsky-Zavod partisans made bold raids on enemy headquarters, logistical establishments and small units.

Unfortunately, in November 1941 the Germans took Communist Guryanov prisoner. They beat him up brutally and hanged him. To this day my fellow villagers tend this hero's grave with loving care.

When the enemy retreated he burnt down Strelkovka along with several other villages. My mother's house went up in flames too.

Among the other strong partisan units operating in the region was that commanded by V. V. Zhabo. This unit played a crucial role in all the operations against the 12th German Army Corps, which was preparing to move in the direction of Moscow. On November 29, 1941, Sovinform reported one of these operations:

"We have received information on the great success of the partisan units in the ... region. On November 24, partisan units raided an important locality (meaning Ugodsky Zavod.— G. Zh.). They destroyed the enemy headquarters, and seized important documents."

Zhabo was born in Donetsk in 1909. As a border-guard officer, he displayed great courage and gallantry. He was recommended to me as a conscientious and resolute commander. I received him personally, and was impressed by his careful preparation of everything he did. As a native of the region where these units were operating, I knew well the terrain where the enemy forces were moving, and was able to give advice as to how things could best be accomplished. The operation was successfully carried out. Vladimir Zhabo died a hero's death on August 8, 1943, in fighting near the village of Dubrovo, Khotynets District in the Orel Region, where he was in command of the 49th Mechanized Brigade of the 6th Guards Mechanized Corps.

The Ugodsky-Zavod District was liberated by the 17th Rifle Division under General D. M. Seleznev.

A town, Obninsk, was built after the war on the site of the village of Pyatkino (burnt down by retreating German troops) where in 1941 the headquarters of the Reserve Front, and later, of the Western Front, had been. The town of Obninsk is now known far and wide as the place where the world's first atomic power station was built. Today Obninsk is a major scientific centre.

But back to the events of that time.

Once in Maloyaroslavets, we drove to the centre of the town without meeting a soul. The town looked abandoned. In front of the building of the District Executive Committee, I saw two cars. I shook the driver of one of them awake.

"Whose cars are these?" I asked.

"Marshal Budenny's, Comrade General."

"Where is he?"

"Inside."

"How long have you been here?"

"About three hours."

I entered the District Executive Committee building, and saw Budenny pouring over a map.

We shook hands warmly. One could tell that he had gone through a lot in those difficult days.

"Where are you from?" Budenny asked.

"From Konev."

"How are things with him? We've been out of touch for two days. While I was at the 43rd Army's headquarters yesterday, Front HQ moved. I don't know whereto."

"I've found it in a forest beyond the railway bridge across the Protva. They are waiting to hear from you. The bulk of our forces on the Western Front have been encircled."

"We're no better off here," Budenny said. "The 24th and 32nd armies have been cut off. Yesterday I myself was nearly captured between Yukhnov and Vyazma. I saw large tank and motorized infantry columns moving in the direction of Vyazma. Evidently the enemy wants to encircle the town by a turning movement from the east."

"Who controls Yukhnov?"

"I don't know now. There were up to two infantry regiments, but without any artillery, on the Ugra. I think Yukhnov is in the hands of the enemy."

"And who's covering the road from Yukhnov up to Maloya-roslavets?"

"As I was riding here, all I met were three militiamen in Medyn, no one else. The local government has left Medyn."

"Go to Front headquarters now," I told Budenny, "see what's what there, and inform General Headquarters of the situation. I'll go to the Yukhnov area. Report our meeting to the Supreme Commander, tell him I went to Kaluga. We've got to find out what's happening there."

When I got to Medyn I found no one there. I saw only an old woman rummaging through the ruins of a house which had been turned into a pile of rubble by an aerial bomb.

"What are you looking for, granny?" I asked. She raised her head. Wide wandering eyes stared at me vacantly.

"What's the matter with you, granny?"

Without a word in reply she went back to digging at the rubble. Another woman carrying a sack that was half full emerged from among the ruins.

"Don't ask her. She's gone mad with grief. There was an air raid the day before yesterday. The Germans bombed and machine-gunned us. This woman lived in this house with her grandchildren. She was at the well getting a pail of water when a bomb hit the house right in front of her very eyes. The children were killed. Our house was also destroyed. I'd be off in a hurry but I thought I'd look for some clothes and shoes under the wreckage."

Tears streamed down her cheeks as she talked.

With a heavy heart I started again in the direction of Yukhnov. Ever so often I had to stop and look around careful-ly so as not to drive into enemy-occupied territory.

I had gone 10 or 12 kilometres when my car was suddenly stopped on a forest road by armed soldiers wearing overalls and tankmen's helmets. One of them came up to the car and said:

"You can't go any farther. Who are you?" I told him, and asked in turn where their unit was located.

"Here in this forest," he replied. "Headquarters of our tank brigade is only a hundred metres away."

"Very well. Take me to headquarters."

I was glad that a tank brigade was here. A short man in neat blue overalls and tankman's goggles over his service cap rose to greet me. I thought I had seen him somewhere.

"FHQ Reserve Tank Brigade Commander Colonel Troitsky reporting," he began.

"Troitsky! What a surprise! I didn't expect to meet you here."

I remembered Troitsky from the action on the Khalka River (Khalkhin-Gol), where he was Chief of Staff of the 11th Tank Brigade, the brigade commanded by Hero of the Soviet Union M. P. Yakovlev. That brigade was the dread of the Japanese.

"I didn't expect to meet you here either, Comrade General," said Troitsky. "I knew you were in command of the Leningrad Front, but I didn't know you had left it."

"Well, what's happening here? Let's hear it. First of all, where is the enemy?"

"The enemy is about to capture Yukhnov," Col. Troitsky told me. "His advance units have crossed the bridge over the Ugra. I've sent out reconnaissance to Kaluga. Enemy troops have not yet entered the town, but bitter fighting is going on at the approaches. The 5th Rifle Division and several withdrawn units of the 43rd Army are in action there. The brigade under my command is part of the Supreme Command Reserve. This is the second day I've been here, and I have had no instructions."

"Send a liaison officer to Reserve Front Headquarters. It's located in the area of the Obninskoye railway station beyond the bridge across the Protva in the village of Pyatkino. Report the situation to Marshal Budenny. Deploy part of the brigade to protect the entire Medyn direction. Through Reserve Front Headquarters report the orders I've given you to the General Staff, and tell them that I have gone on to Kaluga to the 5th Rifle Division."

Later I learned that the bridge across the Ugra had been blown up by the detachment of Major I. G. Starchak, chief of the para-drop service of the Western Front. This 400-strong detachment had been formed on October 4 on his own initiative, and was made up of frontier guards trained for operation in the enemy rear.

Having blown up the bridge, the detachment under Starchak took up a defensive position along the bank of the Ugra. Soon it was reinforced by a detachment of military school students from Podolsk under the command of Sr.-Lt. L. A. Mamchik and Capt. Y. S. Rossikov. The epic stand of these two detachments prevented the enemy from forcing the Ugra and breaking through to Medyn.

There were few men left alive after five days of bitter fighting, but that heroic self-sacrifice frustrated the enemy plans of an early seizure of Maloyaroslavets, and enabled our troops to gain time and organize defences at the approaches to Moscow. At the same time, students from the artillery and the machine-gunners schools in Podolsk arrived in the Maloyaroslavets area, where they took up positions to strengthen the sector.

A liaison officer caught up with me in the neighbourhood of Kaluga and handed over a message received by phone from the Chief of General Staff which said that the Supreme Commander ordered me to report at Western Front Headquarters on October 10.

As October 8 drew to a close I again left for Reserve Front Headquarters.

I was met by the Chief of Staff of the Front, who handed me the Supreme Command order removing Budenny and appointing me Commander of the Reserve Front. Immediately after that, I received orders requesting me to arrive at Western Front Headquarters on October 10.

I phoned Shaposhnikov, and in reply to my question as to which Front to proceed to, he said:

"The thing is that the State Defence Committee is examining the question of dissolving the Reserve Front and combining its forces with those of the Western Front. It is suggested that you assume command of the Western Front. Up to October 10, you look after the situation on the Reserve Front, and do what you can to ensure that the enemy does not advance along the Mozhaisk-Maloyaroslavets line, nor from the Aleksin area on the Serpukhov sector."

On October 10, almost immediately after I arrived at Western Front Headquarters located in Krasnovidovo, I was called to the phone. Stalin was on the line.

"The Supreme Command has decided to appoint you Commander of the Western Front. Konev will be your deputy. Any objections?"

"No, what objections can there be? I think Konev should be put in command of the forces on the Kalinin sector. That sector is far too isolated, and we've got to make it a secondary division of the Front."

"Very well," Stalin agreed. "The remaining units of the Reserve Front, the troops of the Mozhaisk defence line, are to come under your command. Assume control of the Western Front and act quickly. I've already signed the order, and it has been sent to the Fronts."

"I'll act on your instructions right away, but I'm asking for larger reserves to be sent as soon as possible, since we may expect an intensification of the enemy thrust towards Moscow any time now."

I soon received the order from General Headquarters:

"Directly to the Military Council of the Western Front, the Military Council of the Reserve Front, to Commander of the Reserve Front Comrade Zhukov, and to Comrades Molotov and Voroshilov.

"October 10, 1941, 17:00. In relation to the uniting of the commands of forces operating on the Western sector, the Supreme Command orders:

"1) To unite the Western and Reserve Fronts in the Western Front.

"2) To appoint Comrade Zhukov Commander of the Western Front.

"3) To appoint Comrade Konev Deputy Commander of the Western Front.

"4) To appoint Comrades Bulganin, Khokhlov and Kruglov members of the Military Council of the Western Front.

"5) Comrade Zhukov is to assume command of the Western Front as of 18:00, on October 11, 1941.

"6) The Reserve Front is to be dissolved and used to complement the Western and Moscow Reserve Fronts.

"Please acknowledge receipt.

"Stavka of the Supreme Command
"J. Stalin
"B. Shaposhnikov"

I discussed the situation with Konev and we decided that Front Headquarters should be moved to Alabino. Konev and a group of officers and the necessary control means were to go to the Kalinin sector to coordinate the actions of the body of troops there. The Military Council of the Front was to go to Mozhaisk to look into the situation on that sector and discuss it with Colonel S. I. Bogdanov, Commandant of the Mozhaisk fortified area.

So the Front's staff began moving to Alabino, while Bulganin, member of the Military Council, and I arrived in Mozhaisk a couple of hours later. From his office we could hear the sound of artillery fire and bomb explosions. Bogdanov told us that the 32nd Rifle Division, supported by artillery and tanks, was in action against the enemy's advance mechanized and armoured units at the approaches to Borodino. The Division Commander was Colonel V. I. Polosukhin, a highly experienced man. The 32nd Rifle Division could be relied on.

Giving Bogdanov the necessary instructions, we left for Front Headquarters.

It was temporarily housed in camp cabins in Alabino. The staff immediately got down to organizational and operational matters — there was a great deal to be done.

We had to quickly organize a solid defence system along the Volokolamsk-Mozhaisk-Maloyaroslavets-Kaluga line. We had to develop it in depth, and also to constitute second echelons and Front reserves so we could move them to threatened areas; organize ground and air reconnaissance and effective control of the troops; and provide logistic support. The most important task was to step up party-political work, to raise the morale of the troops and their confidence in their strength and inevitable victory over the enemy on the approaches to Moscow.

Work in these directions was proceeding day and night. People were literally falling off their feet with fatigue, but motivated by a sense of responsibility for the destiny of Moscow and of their Motherland, and following the directives of the Communist Party they continued to extend the defences on the approaches to Moscow.

In the summer and autumn of 1941 the Central Committee of the Party, the State Committee for Defence and the Supreme Command undertook several major measures to rein-

force the Moscow defences, raise considerable manpower reserves, and replenish the army in the field with personnel and
equipment. Extra measures were undertaken to stop the enemy.

In the early hours of October 7 the troops of the Supreme
Command Reserve and the Fronts adjacent to the Mozhaisk
area were transferred to the Mozhaisk defence line; 14 rifle
divisions, 16 armoured brigades, over 40 artillery regiments
and other units arrived; the 16th, the 5th, the 43rd and the 49th
armies were being formed anew. By mid-October they were
90,000 strong. Obviously, for an enduring and reliable defence
these forces were clearly insufficient. But the Supreme Command could not expend more troops at the time; troop dispatch-
ment from the Far East and other remote areas was delayed for
a number of reasons. Therefore we first and foremost decided
to organize the Volokolamsk, Mozhaisk, Maloyaroslavets and
Kaluga sectors, where we concentrated the main artillery and
anti-tank forces.

The 16th Army, whose staff and command personnel was
headed by Rokossovsky, Lobachev and Malinin, was assigned
to the Volokolamsk sector. The Army comprised new elements,
since its divisions previously assigned to the 20th Army had
been encircled west of Vyazma. The 5th Army under Maj.-
Gen. Lelyushenko (after he was wounded, he was replaced by
General Govorov) concentrated on the Mozhaisk sector. The
33rd Army, which Lt.-Gen. Yefremov had been quickly
assigned to command, was concentrated in the Naro-
Fominsk area; the 43rd Army under Maj.-Gen. Golubev —
on the Maloyaroslavets sector; and the 49th Army under
Lt.-Gen. Zakharkin, on the Kaluga sector.

They were all experienced military leaders, and had
our full confidence. We were sure that they, at the head
of their troops, would do everything possible to stop the
enemy advance on Moscow.

Here I must mention the really excellent work of the Staff
of the Front with Lt.-Gen. Sokolovsky as Chief and Lt.-Gen.
Malandin as Chief of Operations, as well as the energetic efforts
by Maj.-Gen. Psurtsev, signal troops commander, in providing
adequate communications with the troops of the Front.

Extensive engineering and sapper work was being done in
the rear of the first echelon units to develop the defence

system in depth. Anti-tank defences had been built in all tank-threatened directions. Front reserves were being drawn to the likely directions of the main attack.

Front HQ was soon moved from Alabino to Perkhushkovo. Telephone and telegraph lines connected it with headquarters of the ground and air forces of the Front, and with the Supreme Command's General Headquarters.

In this way, an actually new Western Front was organized. It was confronted with a truly historic task — the defence of Moscow.

Led by its Central Committee, the Party began extensive work to make the people aware of the grave situation that had developed, of the imminent danger looming over Moscow. The Central Committee called on the people to do their duty to the country with honour, and to halt the enemy advance on Moscow.

West and north-west of Vyazma, our troops continued to fight heroically behind enemy lines, trying to break out of encirclement and link up with the Red Army forces. But all their attempts were futile. The Command of the Front and the Supreme Command helped the surrounded troops by bombing the enemy battle formations and by air-dropping provisions and ammunition. But this was all they could do, since they lacked both manpower and equipment.

Having found themselves surrounded by the enemy, the troops did not lay down their arms but continued to fight courageously. In this way they pinned down the main forces of the enemy, and did not allow the offensive towards Moscow to gather momentum.

Twice, on October 10 and 12, we radioed messages to the army commanders of the surrounded forces. These messages contained brief information on the enemy and the assignment of breakthrough missions under the overall control of General M. F. Lukin, Commander of the 19th Army. The army commanders were to immediately present their breakthrough plans, report the disposition of their forces, and make requests for air support, indicating the sector where they wanted it. However there was no reply to either of our messages. They must have reached the surrounded troops too late — when control of them was lost. Only isolated groups managed to break out of encirclement.

The former commander of the 45th Cavalry Division, Stuchenko, later told me the following: "What was left of our division broke out of encirclement in order to link up with the Front; we engaged the Germans whenever we could afford to, killing several thousands of them. Around the middle of October there was hardly a day without, a fight, each new one more fierce than the last. Many outstanding commanders, commissars, and soldiers were killed."

With deep feeling Stuchenko told me about the heroic death of the divisional commissar A. G. Polekhin who, despite the obvious mortal danger, took personal charge of a reconnaissance party.

"Although most of the division had been destroyed, the surviving officers and men fought with a single purpose — to link up with the forces of the Front as quickly as possible, and together to defend Moscow. It was the happiest day for all of us, when we broke out of encirclement and joined the forces of the Front in order to repulse the hateful enemy..."

Thanks to the persistence and staunchness of our troops who fought in encirclement near Vyazma, we had gained invaluable time which enabled us to strengthen the Mozhaisk defence line. And so the surrounded troops did not lay down their lives nor shed their blood, in vain. Their heroic deeds and their enormous contribution to the defence of Moscow still wait writing of.

On October 13 heavy fighting began on all the important sectors leading to Moscow.

Those were grim days. The Party's Central Committee and the State Committee for Defence decided to immediately move some of the central agencies and all of the diplomatic corps from Moscow to Kuibyshev, as well as to evacuate the more important objects of national value from the capital.

Air raids on Moscow were intensifying daily. The alarm was sounded nearly every night. By that time the Party had done a great deal of work to fortify local air defences. Millions of Moscow residents were actively being trained for air defence duties. Muscovites soon learned not to be afraid of incendiary bombs.

The Supreme Command concentrated large groups of fighters, strafers and bombers in the Moscow area.

On October 20 the State Committee for Defence announced a state of siege in Moscow and the areas immediately around it. Rigid order was established in all the fighting forces defending Moscow. Stern measures were introduced to prevent any possible breach of discipline. Moscow residents quickly cut short any actions by panic-mongering accomplices of the enemy.

The Soviet capital faced the imminent danger with fortitude. The appeals of the Central Committee and of the Moscow Committee of the Party to defend the capital went straight to the heart of every Muscovite, every soldier, and of all the Soviet people. The people of Moscow did everything they could to turn Moscow and its approaches into an impregnable fortress.

When we speak of the heroism displayed in the Battle of Moscow, we refer not only to the actions of our army, to our heroic Soviet soldiers, commanders, and political officers. What was achieved on the Western Front in October, and also in the battles that followed, was made possible by the unity and the common efforts of the troops and the populace of Moscow and Moscow Region, and by the effective aid given the army and the defenders of the capital by the rest of the country, the entire Soviet people.

As many as 12 people's volunteer divisions had been formed by the Party's organizations in the city in early July. Among the volunteers were people of many different civilian trades — workers, engineers, technicians, scientists, art workers, and so on. None of them were skilled soldiers, and what they learned of warcraft was picked up directly in the battlefield. But there was one thing all of them had in common — a fervent patriotism, unshakeable tenacity, and confidence in victory. And it was no accident that once they had picked up the requisite experience of combat, these volunteer units became an excellent fighting force.

Volunteers made up the nucleus of many special scout and ski squads, and were active in partisan detachments. The Western Front received highly valuable assistance from the Moscow populace.

Hundreds of thousands of Muscovites worked day and night building fortified lines round the city. Something like

250,000, with women and teenagers comprising three-quarters of that number, erected the interior defensive perimeter in October and November alone. They built as much as 72,000 metres of anti-tank ditches, some 80,000 metres of escarpments and counter-escarpments, and 52,500 metres of anti-tank and other obstacles, and dug nearly 128,000 metres of communication and other trenches. All in all, they moved more than 3,000,000 cubic metres of earth by hand!

The showing of the workers and engineers at plants that had not been evacuated from Moscow was truly selfless and dedicated. They worked with obsolete equipment, for all the good machinery had been evacuated. There was a shortage of manpower, but military production was started in an amazingly short time. The Moscow Motor Works began making sub-machine-guns, with the First Ball-Bearings Plant and the Sergo Ordzhonikidze Works supplying the breechblocks for them.

In December, Moscow's plants were ordered to produce 35 times as much as they had produced in November. And they coped with the assignment! The Second Watch and Clock Factory started production of mine detonators. The trolleybus depot in Moscow's Leningradsky District started making hand-grenades, while the Serp i Molot Works and Krasny Proletary Plant repaired tanks and produced ammunition.

All garages and car depots were busy repairing tanks and other army vehicles. The Rot Front Confectionary was making concentrated foods. And the smaller enterprises that in peacetime had supplied the populace with fancy goods were now making anti-tank grenades and detonators.

The men in the front lines knew the whole country was pitching in to defend the capital, and this countrywide backing was an inspiring and dependable spur for the Soviet victories in the Battle of Moscow.

In answer to the appeal issued by the Party Central Committee many thousands of Communists and YCL members from Moscow and other cities and towns joined the acting army as political instructors and inspired the soldiers by their example.

In the critical days of October the Military Council of the Western Front issued an appeal which said:

"Comrades! In this grim hour of mortal danger to our

State, the life of every soldier belongs to the Motherland. She demands of each of us the utmost effort, courage, fortitude and heroism. The Motherland calls on us to rise like an unbreakable wall in the way of the fascist hordes and to defend our beloved Moscow. Vigilance, iron discipline, organization, resolute action, an unbending will to win, and readiness for self-sacrifice are required today more than ever before."

Decisive events were imminent.

Since the defence line running through Volokolamsk, Mozhaisk, Maloyaroslavets and Serpukhov was still being held with insufficient strength and the enemy had been able to penetrate it at several points, the Military Council made the Novozavidovsky-Klin-Istra Reservoir-Istra-Krasnaya Pakhra-Serpukhov-Aleksin line its main line of defence.

Because of the enormously wide frontage and the difficulty of controlling the troops of the Kalinin group, the Military Council of the Western Front asked the Supreme Command to shorten the front and put these troops under another command. So the Supreme Command ordered the Western Front on October 17 to detach its 22nd, 29th, and 30th armies, which were assigned to the Kalinin Front which was to be formed anew. Col.-Gen. Konev was put in command of the Kalinin Front; Corps Commissar Leonov was appointed member of the Military Council, and Maj.-Gen. Ivanov — Chief of Staff. The newly-formed Kalinin Front reduced the Western Front defence zone and improved troop control.

The situation on the Bryansk Front, which was in the charge of Lt.-Gen. Yeremenko, was also bad. Most of the troops found themselves encircled, and were fighting their way to the east. Thanks to heroic efforts they managed to break out of encirclement on October 23. Pursuing the scattered forces of the Bryansk Front the advance units of Guderian's army captured Orel, and approached Tula on October 29.

In October, apart from logistical establishments of the 50th Army there were no troops capable of defending Tula. Three badly damaged infantry divisions had withdrawn to the Tula area in the latter part of the month. These units numbered between 500 and 1,500 combatants, while an artillery regiment had only four guns left. The troops were battle-fatigued.

The people of Tula helped our troops tremendously tailoring uniforms, and repairing arms and combat equipment. Led by the city Party organization they worked day and night to get the troops back in fighting shape.

The Defence Committee of Tula headed by V. G. Zhavoronkov, Secretary of the Regional Party Committee, quickly managed to raise and arm workers' detachments, which fought courageously alongside the units of the Bryansk Front 50th Army at the near approaches to the city, and did not let the enemy enter the city.

Particular staunchness and valour were displayed by the Tula workers' regiment headed by Captain A. P. Gorshkov and Commissar G. A. Ageyev. This regiment took up a defensive position along with the withdrawn units in the vicinity of Kosaya Gora. General V. S. Popov, commander of the Tula defence area, deployed an anti-aircraft artillery regiment for use in anti-tank defence. All the forces defending Tula displayed exceptional courage.

Guderian counted on taking Tula on the march and then moving on to Moscow from the south. But he failed to do so.

The offensive mounted on October 30 was repulsed by defenders of Tula, with the enemy sustaining heavy losses.

On November 10, by decision of the Supreme Command, the Bryansk Front was disbanded, and the defence of Tula passed to the control of the Western Front.

In November 1941 the enemy made repeated attempts to seize Tula and thus clear the way to Moscow, but failed again. The city was like an impregnable fortress. The right flank enemy grouping was completely tied up from head to foot. The enemy then decided to encircle Tula by a turning movement, for which he had to spread out his forces. As a result, Guderian's army lost its operational and tactical troop density.

The city of Tula and its people played an important role in defeating the Germans at the approaches to Moscow.

I do not think there is any need to recount here the entire chain of events, since they have already been described in detail in many works. The result of the defensive battles at the approaches to Moscow is also well known. In a month of heavy fighting, the enemy succeeded in advancing about

230 to 250 kilometres. However, the German Command's plan of capturing Moscow by mid-October was frustrated, enemy strength was sapped considerably, and his striking forces had been greatly dissipated.

The German offensive began to peter out as the days went by. At the end of October it was finally halted at a front line running through Turginovo, Volokolamsk, Dorokhovo, Naro-Fominsk, a point west of Serpukhov and Aleksin. The Kalinin Front's defence area near Kalinin had been stabilized as well.

It is impossible to list all the heroes who distinguished themselves during the heroic defence of Moscow in October 1941. Whole military units who displayed mass heroism — not only individual soldiers — won fame in the battles for the Motherland. Such hero units were at every sector of the front.

The Volokolamsk sector, towards which the 5th Army Corps of the enemy — later joined by two motorized corps — was advancing, was staunchly defended by the units of the Fortified Areas. The units of the newly-formed 16th Army also stood fast. The 316th Rifle Division under Maj.-Gen. I. V. Panfilov fought with particular valour.

A composite rifle regiment of Moscow Infantry Commanders School trainees was deployed in the most crucial sector of the 16th Army. It was supported by three artillery anti-tank regiments.

Sending the trainees off to their stations, the regimental commander and chief of the school, S. I. Mladentsev, said to them:

"The bestial enemy is thrusting towards Moscow, the heart of our country. We must stop him, we must defend our capital. And it is our duty to fight as well as our elder brothers, the Kremlin trainees who covered themselves with glory, had once fought. This is no time to pass exams. You will pass them at the front, grappling with the enemy. And I am sure that each one of you will pass these exams with honours..."

The regiment covered the 85 kilometres from Solnechnogorsk in double quick time and arrived in the Volokolamsk area by nightfall on October 7. The school commanders had made no mistake — the trainees spurned danger and death, and

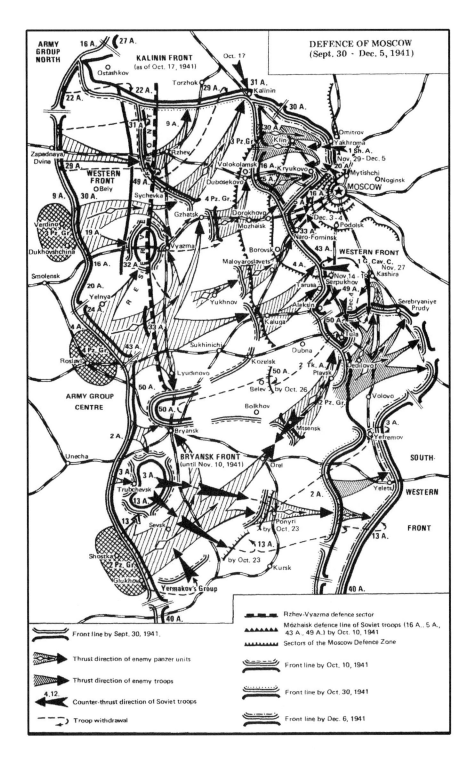

DEFENCE OF MOSCOW
(Sept. 30 - Dec. 5, 1941)

clung firmly to their defence line. Their closest neighbour was the 316th Rifle Division under General Panfilov, which covered itself with glory in the fighting for Moscow and was in due course renamed the 8th Guards Division.

Owing to the general shortage of manpower and materiel battalions were extended to hold a frontage of 7 to 10 km as much as three kilometres in depth. There was no unbroken line of defence at Volokolamsk at the time. Only support points were manned, while the terrain between them was covered with artillery fire, and at some places by long-range machine-guns.

On the Mozhaisk sector, the 32nd Rifle Division under Col. V. I. Polosukhin took on the enemy's 40th Motorized Corps supported by a strong group of planes. Almost 130 years after the Great Patriotic War of 1812 on Borodino Field, that same Borodino field, which was an eternal monument to Russian military glory, again became the scene of a patriotic battle.

On the Maloyaroslavets sector, units of the enemy's 12th Army and 57th Motorized Corps were advancing. Troops of the 312th Rifle Division under Col. Naumov and cadets of the Podolsk infantry and artillery schools fought valiantly at the approaches to Maloyaroslavets. The tankmen of Col. Troitsky, the man whom I have already mentioned, fought in the area of Medyn, where they stood to the last. The troops of the 110th Rifle Division and the 151st Motorized Infantry Brigade distinguished themselves near the ancient Russian town of Borovsk.   Shoulder to shoulder with them, the tankmen of the 127th Tank Battalion were staunchly repulsing enemy attacks. At the cost of heavy losses, the enemy managed to press our troops to the River Protva and then to the River Nara; but he could penetrate no farther.

The 33rd Army was deployed between the 5th and 43rd armies in the area of Naro-Fominsk. The 43rd Army was deployed to the south of Naro-Fominsk along the eastern bank of the Nara, while the 49th Army took up positions along the line running through a point west of Serpukhov, east of Tarusa, and Aleksin.

Having fortified their positions all along the line, the troops were ready to stand up to the enemy attacks.

The soldiers of the Western Front had learned a lot in the three weeks of fighting in October. Extensive party-political work was conducted among the troops, the programme concentrated primarily on popularizing destruction-of-the-enemy methods, individual and mass heroism, and combat prowess, and valour.

I would like to particularly emphasize the great role played in the organization of political work in the Army by Division Commissar D. A. Lestev, Chief of the Western Front Political Department, a fine Communist and a fearless soldier.

On November 1, 1941, I was summoned to General Headquarters. Stalin said to me:

"Besides a ceremonial meeting, we'd like to hold a military review in Moscow on the anniversary of the October Revolution. What do you think — will the situation on the front allow us to hold this ceremony?"

I replied: "The enemy is not going to begin any major offensive in the next few days. He has suffered considerable casualties, and has been forced to replace losses and regroup troops. To neutralize his aviation, which is likely to remain active, I suggest that Moscow's air defence be strengthened with fighter planes from the neighbouring fronts."

On the eve of the holiday, a ceremonial meeting on the occasion of the 24th anniversary of the Great October Revolution was held in the Mayakovskaya station of the Moscow underground, and on November 7 there was the traditional military march-past in Red Square. The soldiers went to the front right from Red Square.

This event played a tremendous role in further strengthening the morale of the army and of the Soviet people, and was also of great international importance. Stalin's speeches showed once again that the Party and Government were confident that the invaders would be defeated.

Meanwhile, anti-tank defences were being organized in depth, and tank-proof facilities built in threatened areas. Losses were being replaced, arms and ammunition were being supplied, as well as engineering, communication and other technical facilities and equipment. From November 1 to 15 the Western Front was reinforced with 100 thousand officers and men, 300 tanks, and 2,000 guns.

From these reserves, raised deep in the rear of the country, the Supreme Command reinforced the Front with infantry and tank units which were concentrated on the more threatened sectors. Large forces were amassed on the Volokolamsk-Klin and Istra sectors, where we expected the main attack by the enemy's armour. Reserves were being brought up to the Tula-Serpukhov area — the German 2nd Panzer and 4th Field armies were ready to strike again.

At the beginning of November I had a none too pleasant conversation with Stalin over the phone.

"What's the enemy doing?" he asked.

"Completing the concentration of his striking forces. It's obvious that he's soon going to take the offensive," I replied.

"Where do you expect his main attack?"

"From the Volokolamsk area. Guderian's tank forces will evidently bypass Tula and move towards Kashira."

"Shaposhnikov and I believe that we have to forestall the enemy through counterblows. One counterblow should be delivered in the area of Volokolamsk, the other from the area of Serpukhov against the flank of the German 4th Army. Large forces are obviously gathering there to strike at Moscow."

"With what forces, Comrade Stalin, will we be able to deliver these counterblows?" I asked. "The Western Front cannot spare any forces. We have only troops for defence."

"In the Volokolamsk area you can use the right wing units of Rokossovsky's army, the tank division, and Dovator's cavalry corps. In the Serpukhov area you can use Belov's cavalry corps, Getman's tank division and some of the 49th Army units."

"I don't believe we can do that now, we cannot commit the Front's last reserves to counterblows whose success is doubtful. We'll have nothing to strengthen our defences with when the enemy brings his main attack forces into action."

"Your Front has six armies. Do you think that's nothing?"

"The Western Front is holding defences over a greatly extended frontage, and if stretched out in a straight line, it would total 600 kilometres. We have very small reserves in depth, especially in the central sector."

"Consider the question of counterblows settled. Report your plan of operations tonight," Stalin snapped out with displeasure.

About fifteen minutes later Bulganin looked in and said from the door:

"Did I ever get hell!"

"What for?"

"Stalin said: 'You and Zhukov have an overly high opinion of yourselves. But we'll get to you yet!' He told me to see you at once and work out counterblows."

"All right, sit down and let's call up Sokolovsky and inform army commanders Rokossovsky and Zakharkin."

Two hours later, Front HQ issued orders to the commanders of the 16th and 49th armies and their units concerning counterblows, and we reported to General Headquarters accordingly. However, these counterblows, in which cavalry was the main force, did not yield the results that the Supreme Commander expected. The enemy was still very strong, and his pugnacity had not yet been dampened. It was only in the Aleksin area that things went well; the German 4th Army suffered heavy losses, and was unable to take part in the overall advance on Moscow.

To continue the thrust towards Moscow the German Command brought up more forces; by November 15 it had in the Western Front zone 51 divisions, including 31 infantry, 13 tank and 7 motorized divisions, which were fully manned, and well equipped with tanks, artillery and combat materiel.

On the Volokolamsk-Klin and Istra sectors the enemy had, against Rokossovsky's army, concentrated the 3rd and 4th Panzer groups, consisting of seven tank, three motorized, and four infantry divisions, supported by about 2,000 artillery pieces and a powerful air group.

The enemy striking force against the 50th Army on the Tula-Kashira sector comprised the 24th and 47th Motorized corps, 53rd and 43rd Army corps totalling twelve divisions, including four tank and three motorized divisions, and also having powerful air support.

The German 4th Field Army comprising six army corps had been deployed on the Zvenigorod, Kubinka, Naro-Fominsk, Podolsk and Serpukhov sectors. Through frontal attacks, this Army was to pin down the troops of the Western Front, sap them of their strength, and then strike a blow in the central sector towards Moscow.

The second stage of the Moscow offensive began on November 15 with an attack against the 30th Army of the Kalinin Front, which had weak defences south of the Volga Reservoir. Simultaneously, the enemy struck against the troops of the Western Front, specifically against the right flank of the 16th Army south of the River Shosha. A secondary attack was also launched in the zone of that Army in the area of Teryaeva Sloboda.

The defences of the 30th Army were soon pierced by the enemy's 300 tanks, while our troops had only 56 light tanks with little firepower. The defence was not able to hold out, and was soon broken.

On the morning of November 16, the enemy began stepping up his attack from the Volokolamsk area towards Klin. We did not have sufficient reserves in that sector, since they had been moved, on orders from GHQ, to the Volokolamsk area to mount a counterblow, and were subsequently pinned down by the enemy.

That day the enemy struck a powerful blow in the area of Volokolamsk. Two enemy tank and two enemy infantry divisions advanced in the direction of Istra. On the Istra sector the enemy had concentrated 400 medium tanks against our 150 light tanks. Fierce fighting ensued. The 316th Rifle Division under General Panfilov, the 78th Rifle Division under Colonel Beloborodov, the 18th Rifle Division under General Chernyshev, Mladentsev's detached cadet regiment, the lst Guards, the 23rd, 27th and 28th Detached Tank brigades, and Maj.-Gen. Dovator's cavalry group put up especially stiff resistance.

At 23:00 hrs. on November 17, the 30th Army of the Kalinin Front passed, by the Supreme Command order, to the control of the Western Front; this further extended the Front's positions to the north (up to the Volga Reservoir). Maj.-Gen. Lelyushenko was put in command of the 30th Army.

On November 16 through 18 our troops had some very gruelling engagements. Paying no attention to his losses, the enemy repeatedly attacked our positions, trying at all costs to break through to Moscow with his tank spearheads.

However, the depth of our artillery and anti-tank defences, as well as excellent cooperation between all fighting forces, prevented the enemy from penetrating the defence lines of the

16th Army. It would deliberately and gradually withdraw from action and retire to positions held by our artillery, where it would offer resistance again, repulsing the fierce attacks of the Nazi troops.

Exceptional gallantry was displayed by the lst Guards Tank Brigade of the 16th Army. In October this unit — then the 4th Tank Brigade — had fought heroically near Orel and Mtsensk, for which it was honoured with the title of lst Guards Tank Brigade. Now, in November, its men enhanced their unit's brilliant combat reputation by courageously defending the approaches to Moscow.

The State Committee for Defence, and part of the leadership of the Party Central Committee and of the Council of People's Commissars were working in Moscow as usual. Moscow workers toiled from 12 to 18 hours a day providing the fronts that covered the approaches to Moscow, with arms, ammunition and equipment.

The capital was still in danger. The enemy, albeit slowly, was advancing towards Moscow.

I don't remember exactly what day it was — but it was certainly soon after the German tactical breakthrough in the 30th Army sector of the Kalinin Front — Stalin phoned me and asked:

"Are you sure we'll be able to hold Moscow? It hurts me to ask you this. Answer me truthfully, as a Communist."

"We'll definitely hold Moscow. But we'll need at least two more armies and another two hundred tanks."

"It's good that you are so confident. Call the General Staff and make arrangements for the assignment of the two reserve armies you are asking for. They will be ready by late November. Right now we can't get you any tanks yet."

Half an hour later Vasilevsky and I agreed that the lst Shock Army and the 10th Army would be sent to the Western Front, where they would join the 20th Army. The lst Shock Army would be assigned to the Yakhroma area, and the 10th Army — to the Ryazan area.

The enemy initiated the offensive in the Moscow-Tula zone of operations on November 18. His 3rd, 4th and 17th Panzer divisions began thrusting forward in the Venev area where the defence was being conducted by the 413th and 299th Rifle divisions of the 50th Army. That group penetrated our defences and captured the area of Bolokhovo and Dedilovo. The 239th Rifle and the 41st Cavalry divisions were hastily deployed to counter the enemy in the area of Uzlovaya. Our troops displayed mass heroism in the fierce fighting that lasted day and night. The units of the 413th Rifle Division fought with particular gallantry. On November 21 the main force of Guderian's Panzer Army captured Uzlovaya and Stalinogorsk. The enemy's 47th Motorized Corps was advancing in the direction of Mikhailov. The consequence was that a rather complicated situation developed in the area of Tula.

In these circumstances the Military Council of the Front decided to bolster the Kashira defence area with the 112th Armoured Division under Colonel (now General of the Army) Getman; the Ryazan defence area was to be strengthened with a tank brigade and other units; the Zaraisk sector, with the 9th Tank Brigade and the 35th and 127th Detached Tank battalions; and the Laptevo sector, with the 510th Rifle Regiment and a tank company.

On November 26 the enemy's 3rd Panzer Division pressed our units back and straddled the railway line and the Tula-Moscow highway at a point north of Tula. However the 1st Guards Cavalry Corps under General P. A. Belov, the 112th Tank Division and several other units repulsed the enemy's attacks in the area of Kashira and halted the enemy. The 173rd Rifle Division and the 15th Guards Mortar Regiment were sent to the Kashira area as reinforcements for the units fighting there.

On November 27, Belov's Cavalry Corps, coordinating operations with the 112th Tank Division, the 173rd Rifle Division and other units, struck a counterblow at Guderian's troops and drove them 10-15 kilometres back south towards Venev.

Up to November 30, gruelling battles were fought in the areas of Kashira and Mordves. But the enemy was not successful. Guderian began feeling certain that it was impossible to break down the stubborn resistance of our troops in the area of Kashira and Tula and to smash through to Moscow. The Nazi troops were forced to assume the defensive in that sector.

The Soviet troops fighting in this sector repulsed all attacks by the enemy, inflicted heavy losses and did not let him break through to Moscow.

Things were not so bright, however, on the right flank of the Front in the area of Istra, Klin and Solnechnogorsk, where the 16th Army was putting up stubborn resistance.

On November 23, enemy tanks burst into Klin. To avoid encirclement the 16th Army had to withdraw in the early hours of the 24th to the next rear line. Following heavy engagements, the 16th Army retreated from Klin. The loss of Klin created a gap between the 16th and 30th armies, which was protected by a small body of troops that had been hastily mustered together for the purpose.

On November 25, the 16th Army retreated from Solnechnogorsk. An alarming situation evolved there. The Military Council sent everything it could from the other sectors of the Front, including armoured units, anti-tank personnel, artillery batteries, and anti-aircraft artillery battalions taken from General M. S. Gromadin, Commander of the Moscow Air Defence, etc. The enemy absolutely had to be halted in that important sector until the 7th Guards Rifle Division was brought up from the Serpukhov sector, along with two tank brigades and two anti-tank artillery regiments from the Supreme Command Reserve.

Our frontage curved dangerously, forming weak spots here and there. The irreparable seemed likely to happen any moment. But no! The soldiers had not lost heart; they organized an impenetrable defence as soon as reinforcements arrived.

On the evening of November 29, an armoured enemy unit took advantage of our weak defences at a bridge across the Moscow Canal near Yakhroma, seized the bridge and began pushing forward. There it was stopped by the advance units of the lst Shock Army under Lt.-Gen. V. I. Kuznetsov and, after a fierce engagement, driven back beyond the canal.

The situation in that zone of action was exceedingly complicated. This sometimes produced events which could have occurred only as a result of the great tenseness of the situation. Here is an example.

The Supreme Commander somehow received information that our troops had given up the town of Dedovsk northwest of Nakhabino. This would have been very near Moscow.

Naturally, Stalin was extremely worried by that report, especially since on November 28 and 29, the 9th Guards Rifle Division under Maj.-Gen. Beloborodov was successfully beating back the enemy's repeated and fierce attacks in the area of Istra. And now, twenty-four hours later, it was reported that the Germans had taken Dedovsk.

Stalin got me on the phone:

"Do you know that Dedovsk has been captured?"

"No, Comrade Stalin, I don't."

The Supreme Commander was quick to give me a piece of his mind. "A commanding general should know what's happening on his front. Go to the spot at once, and organize a counterattack personally to recapture Dedovsk."

I tried to argue:

"Leaving Front Headquarters in a situation as tense as this would be rather ill-advised."

"We'll manage, don't worry. Let Sokolovsky stand in for you for the time."

I hung up and immediately contacted Rokossovsky to ask why we at Front HQ knew nothing about the fact that Dedovsk had been given up. And I learned that the town of Dedovsk had not been captured by the enemy; that it could only have been the village of Dedovo. I also learned that in the Khovanskoye, Dedovo, Snigiri area and to the south of it the 9th Guards Rifle Division was waging a furious battle, preventing an enemy breakthrough along the Volokolamsk highway towards Dedovsk and Nakhabino.

I decided to call General Headquarters and explain that clearly there had been a mistake. But I was butting my head against a brick wall. Stalin became so angry that he ordered me to go to Rokossovsky at once and arrange for the ill-starred village to be recaptured by all means. I was also to take with me Govorov, Commander of the 5th Army. "He is an artilleryman," Stalin had said, "let him help Rokossovsky organize artillery fire to assist the 16th Army."

Under the circumstances there was no sense in arguing. When I summoned General Govorov and explained his mission, he quite reasonably pointed out that such a trip was not necessary. The 16th Army had its own artillery officer, Maj.-Gen. V. I. Kazakov, and besides, the Commanding General knew best

what to do and how to do it. So why should he — Govorov —
leave his army at a frenzied time like this?

To avoid further discussion I had to tell the General that those
were Stalin's orders.

On the way to Beloborodov's division we called for Rokossovsky. The division commander was not especially overjoyed
to see us in his perimeter. He was up to his neck in detail as it
was, and here he had to make explanations concerning a few
houses across the gully in the village of Dedovo that had been
seized by the enemy.

Reporting the situation, General Beloborodov showed us
convincingly that recapturing those houses was tactically inex-
pedient. Unfortunately, I could not tell him that in that particular case I was not guided by tactical considerations. And so I
ordered him to send a rifle company with two tanks to dislodge
the German squad holding the houses. But let us turn back to
serious things.

On December 1, the German forces unexpectedly effected a
breakthrough in the central sector at the junction between the
5th and 33rd armies and began advancing along the highway
towards Kubinka. However, they were halted near the village
of Akulovo by the 32nd Rifle Division, whose artillery destroyed
some of their tanks. Many more enemy tanks were blown up on
mine fields.

Reeling back with heavy losses, the German armoured units
turned to Golitsino, where they were utterly routed by the
Front reserve forces and units of the 5th and 33rd armies. The
breakthrough was ultimately halted on December 4, the enemy
leaving on the battlefield over 10,000 dead and 50 tanks, and
a great deal of other combat materiel destroyed.

From the nature of operations and the strength of attacks of
all the enemy groupings it became obvious by the end of November that the Germans were losing strength and had neither the
manpower nor the weapons to continue the offensive.

Having deployed his striking forces over an extended frontage and made a wide swing with his armoured fist, the enemy
had, in the course of the battles near Moscow, spread out his
troops so thin that they lost their ramming ability in the final
engagements at the near approaches to Moscow. The Nazi
Command had not expected their losses to be as great as those

sustained by its troops in the Battle of Moscow. Moreover, it was unable to replace those losses and reinforce its Moscow grouping.

Interrogation of prisoners revealed that some companies had only 20-30 men left, that the morale of the German troops had greatly deteriorated, and that they no longer believed that it was possible to capture Moscow.

The troops of the Western Front had also suffered heavily, and were totally battle-fatigued, but held on to their defences, and reinforced by reserves, they fought the enemy with renewed strength.

In the 20 days of the second stage of their Moscow campaign German casualties were over 155,000 killed and wounded; they lost about 800 tanks, hundreds of artillery pieces and a great number of planes. The heavy losses, the unfulfilled strategic tasks, sowed the seeds of doubt in the German soldiers' minds that they would win the war. In the eyes of people around the world, the Nazi military and political leadership lost its reputation of invincibility.

Former Nazi generals and field marshals have tried to blame Hitler for the failure of the plan to capture Moscow and of the entire Eastern Campaign. Hitler, they say, did not heed their advice and slowed down the advance of the Army Group Centre on Moscow in August by diverting part of the forces to the Ukraine.

General Mellenthin, for instance, writes: "The drive on Moscow, which was favoured by Guderian, and temporarily abandoned in August in favour of the conquest of the Ukraine, might have yielded decisive results if it had been ruthlessly pursued as the dominating *Schwerpunkt* of the invasion. Russia might have been paralyzed by a thrust at the heart of Stalin's power..."[1]

Generals Guderian, Hoth and others consider the severe Russian climate, coupled with Hitler's miscalculations, to be the main reason for their defeat near Moscow.

Of course, weather and climate play a definite role in any combat action, and equally affect the combatants on both

---

[1] F. W. von Mellenthin, *Panzer Battles 1939-1945*, Cassell and Co. Ltd., London, 1956, p. 149.

sides. It is true that Nazi soldiers wrapped themselves up in clothes seized from the population and walked about shod in unsightly home-made straw "galoshes". Warm clothes and uniforms are also a weapon. Our country fed and clothed her soldiers. But the Nazi army was not prepared for the winter. The German leaders believed the Russian campaign would be little short of a walk-over, taking just months or weeks. Obviously the Nazi ringleaders grossly miscalculated politically and strategically, and not simply with the climate.

Other generals and bourgeois historians put all the blame on mud and lack of roads. There is nothing new about this version either. Napoleon, who lost his army of 800,000, also blamed the Russian winter. But I was there to see thousands upon thousands of Moscow women, not particularly suited for the arduous job of sapping, who had left their comfortable homes to dig anti-tank ditches and trenches, put up barricades, construct "asparagus" and other obstacles and carry sandbags. Mud stuck to their feet and to the wheels of the barrows in which they carried earth. Mud stuck to the blades of the spades, making them unwieldy in the feminine hands.

For the benefit of those who are inclined to hide behind the mud as the real reason for the Germans' defeat near Moscow, I would like to add that the period of slush in October 1941 was comparatively short. Cold weather set in and snow fell in early November, making the terrain and roads passable everywhere. At the time of the all-out German offensive in November, the temperature in the Moscow area was from 7° to 10° below zero, which, as one can well imagine, means there was no slush.

No! It was neither rain nor snow that stopped the fascist troops near Moscow. The grouping of picked Nazi troops, over one million strong, was routed by the courage, iron staunchness and valour of the Soviet troops which had the people, Moscow and their country behind them.

As for the temporary suspension of the Moscow offensive and the diversion of part of the forces to the Ukraine, we may assume that without that operation, the situation of the German central grouping might have been even worse than it turned out to be. For the Supreme Command reserves, which were used to fill the gaps in the South-Western sector in September, could have been used to strike at the flank and the rear of the

Army Group Centre which was advancing on Moscow.

Enraged by the failure of the second stage of the advance on Moscow and of the *blitzkrieg* plan, and looking for scapegoats, Hitler relieved of command Field Marshal General Brauchitsch, Commander-in-Chief of the Land Forces; Field Marshal General von Bock, Commander of the Army Group Centre; General Guderian, Commander of the 2nd Panzer Army, and many other generals on whom he had lavishly bestowed Knight's Crosses and other high awards just one and a half to two months before. Hitler appointed himself Commander-in-Chief of the Land Forces, apparently believing that this would have a magic effect on the troops.

On December 11, 1941, the Hitler Government declared war against the United States. By this act Hitler evidently wanred to accomplish two things. First, he wanted to show that Germany, ignoring her losses, was becoming even stronger, and was capable of carrying on the war not only against the Soviet Union and Britain, but against the United States as well. Second, he wanted to quickly push Japan into action against the USA in order to ensure that the United States would not be involved in the war against Germany in Europe. When Stalin heard the news, he smiled ironically:

"Interesting... What forces and what resources can Germany use in fighting against the United States? For this kind of war she has neither long-distance air strength, nor appropriate naval strength."

I was often asked how it was that the Soviet troops managed to defeat the powerful German groupings near Moscow and in conditions of severe winter drive what remained of them back west.

The Germans' defeat near Moscow has been described by many authors and, on the whole, correctly. However, I as former Commander of the Western Front, would like to give my own view of that battle.

As is known, when it began Operation Typhoon on the Moscow sector the German Command planned to rout the Soviet forces in the Vyazma-Moscow and the Bryansk-Moscow sectors, and outflank Moscow to the north and south so they could seize the city as soon as possible. The enemy had intended to achieve that strategic aim in two consecutive stages by double envelopment: during the first, he planned to envelop and rout our troops in the area of Bryansk and Vyazma; while during the second he intended to envelop and capture Moscow by skirting it with the armoured units from the north-west via Klin and Kalinin, and from the south, via Tula and Kashira, completing the strategic pincer movement in the area of Noginsk.

However, when they were preparing this very complex operation the German Command woefully miscalculated in estimating the necessary manpower and materiel. It had seriously underrated the capabilities of the Red Army, and overrated those of its own troops.

The forces concentrated by the German Command carried only enough punch to break through our defence line at Vyazma and Bryansk, and to press back the forces of the Western and Kalinin Fronts to a line running through Kalinin, Yakhroma, Krasnaya Polyana, Kryukovo, the rivers Nara and Oka, Tula and Kashira.

As a result, although he attained his immediate objective in early October, the enemy was not able to carry out the second stage of Operation Typhoon.

There were also considerable defects in the build-up of the striking forces for carrying out the second stage. The enemy flank forces were not strong enough, particularly those operating near Tula, and included few all-arms units. Given the conditions counting on armour alone was not justified. The German armoured troops were worn out and greatly depleted — they had lost their fighting value. The German Command failed to strike a simultaneous blow in the centre of our Front, although its forces were sufficient for that. This circumstance enabled us to move all our reserves freely, including divisional reserves, to the Front's flanks, where the fighting was the fiercest, and send them into action against the enemy's striking forces.

Some works on military history claim that the series of operations during the Battle of Moscow should not include the October action of the Western, Reserve and Bryansk Fronts; that the enemy had been finally halted at the Mozhaisk defence line, and that after this the German Command had to work out a "new general offensive operation".

All that was said above about the failure of Operation Typhoon disproves this claim. Alluding to the fact that in November the Germans had to considerably reinforce their troops and materiel and somewhat regroup the armoured units on their left flank proves nothing, since such measures are to be expected in any large-scale offensive operation, and so cannot be considered factors determining the beginning or the end of a strategic operation.

The important thing is that at the beginning of November, the concentrations of the enemy striking forces on our Front's flanks had been detected in good time, which allowed us to correctly anticipate the directions of the enemy's main effort. The enemy punches encountered defences widely dispersed in depth and sufficiently equipped with anti-tank and engineering resources. Our main armour forces were also concentrated on the most threatened sectors.

Enemy communications spanned more than a thousand kilometres, and were constantly harassed by guerilla detachments whose acts of heroism disrupted the work of the enemy supply and logistical agencies.

Heavy German losses, the length of Operation Typhoon, and the stubborn resistance of the Soviet troops had a great impact on the enemy's fighting efficiency, caused confusion in his ranks, and dissipated his belief in the success of the offensive operation.

The Soviet forces also sustained heavy losses in the Battle of Moscow but the country was providing them with the necessary support, and they maintained their fighting efficiency right to the very end of the defensive actions, and were always confident of victory. The most difficult time had passed.

The Red Army had foiled Hitler's plan of seizing Leningrad and linking up with Finland's Armed Forces. Now on the counter-offensive, the Red Army routed the enemy in the area of Tikhvin, and took the city. The forces of the Southern Front also launched a counter-offensive, and captured Rostov-on-Don.

This was the setting in which we prepared the counter-offensive at Moscow. The idea for it was conceived back in November. The plan took final shape during the defensive battles, and became an important and constant element of all the operational planning of the Supreme Command Stavka.

The counter-offensive had been prepared all through the

defence actions and the methods for its realization definitely took shape when to all appearances the Nazi troops could no longer sustain our counterblows. The Soviet troops, fired with successes scored in the defence battles, launched the counter-offensive at Moscow without a let-up.

On November 29, I called up the Supreme Commander and, having reported the situation, asked him for orders so that we could begin our counterattack.

Stalin listened to me attentively, then asked:

"Are you sure that the enemy has reached a critical point and is in no position to bring some new large force into action?"

"The enemy has been bled white. But if we don't eliminate the dangerous enemy penetrations now, the enemy can later reinforce his troops in the area of Moscow with large reserves at the expense of his north and south groupings, and then the situation may become adverse."

Stalin said he would discuss this with the General Staff.

I asked Sokolovsky, Chief of Staff of the Front, who also thought it was time to send our reserve armies into action, to call up the General Staff and back our suggestion urging a counter-offensive without further delay.

Late at night on November 29, we were informed that the Supreme Command had decided to launch the counter-offensive and wanted us to show it our plan of the operation. In the morning of November 30, we submitted our ideas, which were graphically put down on a map, for no details were required since we had agreed all the basics in advance with Stalin, Shaposhnikov and Vasilevsky. I merely attached a short note to Vasilevsky: "Please urgently let People's Commissar of Defence Comrade Stalin have the Western Front's plan of the counter-offensive and issue a directive that we may launch the operation, for otherwise we might miss the bus."

A note attached to the map showed that owing to the situation, the armies of the Front could not simultaneously go on the counter-offensive. We set the following schedule:

"1. Considering the detrainment and concentration of troops and their rearming, the time the attack is to begin shall be between the morning of the 3rd and the 4th of December for the lst Shock, the 20th, the 16th and Golikov's armies, and between the 5th and 6th of December for the 30th Army."

In the next clause of the note we explained that the armies we were committing in the offensive were listed in the Stavka's directive, and described the objectives of the Western Front:

"The immediate objective is to strike at Klin and Solnechnogorsk and thrust in the direction of the Istra, crushing the main enemy group on the right flank, and to strike at Uzlovaya and Bogoroditsk, hitting the flank and rear of the Guderian group, thus smashing the enemy on the left flank of the Western Front armies.

"To pin down enemy forces along the rest of the front and deny the enemy any chance of rushing in troops, the Western Front's 5th, 33rd, 43rd, 49th and 50th armies shall assume the offensive with limited objectives on the 4th-5th of December.

"The main air group (three quarters of all aircraft) shall cooperate with the shock group on the right, while the rest shall cooperate with Lieutenant-General Golikov's army on the left."

Stalin wrote "I agree" on the plan, and signed it.

The objectives set for the individual armies of the Western Front were:

The 1st Shock Army under the command of Lt.-Gen. Kuznetsov was to deploy for attack in the area of Dmitrov and Yakhroma, and, in cooperation with the 30th and 20th armies, strike towards Klin, and then advance in the general direction of Teryaeva Sloboda.

The 20th Army in cooperation with the 1st Shock and the 16th armies was to launch an attack from the Krasnaya Polyana and Bely Rast area in the general direction of Solnechnogorsk, enveloping it from south, and then advance on Volokolamsk. Besides, the right wing of the 16th Army was to thrust towards Kryukovo, and then develop the attack depending on the situation.

The 10th Army in cooperation with the units of the 50th Army was to launch an attack in the direction of Stalinogorsk-Bogoroditsk and further on to the south of the River Upa.

Under the counter-offensive plan the initial task for the troops on the flanks of the Western Front was to smash up the striking forces of Army Group Centre, thus removing the immediate threat to Moscow. We would need more forces to assign farther-going and more categorical missions. As it was,

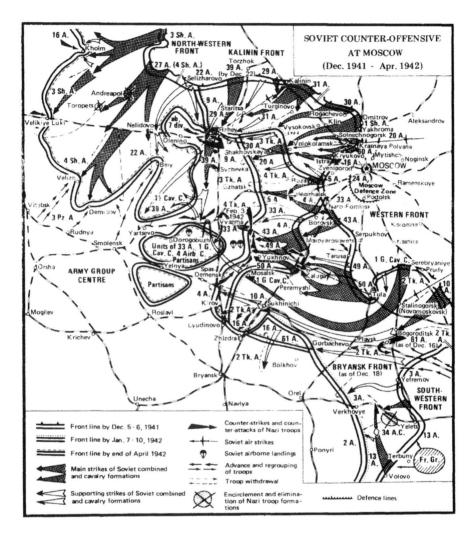

our purpose was to throw the enemy as far away from Moscow as we could, causing him maximum casualties.

Although the Western Front had been given three more armies, this had given us no numerical superiority over the enemy (except in aircraft). He still had more tanks and artillery. This circumstance determined the plan of the counter-offensive.

In the early morning of December 1, 1941, having made a thorough study of the battles fought by the Kalinin Front and of their results, the Supreme Command came to the conclusion that its method of separate attacks in different directions, as witnessed on November 27 through 29, was ineffective in the given circumstances.

The Stavka ordered the Kalinin Front to concentrate a shock force of not less than five or six divisions within the next two or three days, and strike out at Turginovo in order to emerge in the rear of the enemy's group in Klin and thus assist the troops of the Western Front in wiping it out.

General Konev, who was in command of the Kalinin Front, reported to the Stavka that he could not carry out its order because he lacked strength and had no tanks. Instead of the powerful blow in depth planned by the Supreme Command, he suggested a separate bid to capture Kalinin.

The Stavka objected, noting that the proposal of the Kalinin Front commander ran counter to the common aim of launching a resolute counter-offensive at Moscow.

Stalin instructed the Deputy Chief of General Staff, General Vasilevsky, who had also attached his signature to the directive that required the Kalinin Front to form a shock force, to have a talk with General Konev, to explain his mistake and the substance of the case. Vasilevsky coped with his mission splendidly. He had a thorough knowledge of the situation of the Front, he knew its strength and potential, and telegraphed the following to Konev on December 1:

"Nothing but active operations with a decisive objective can botch the German offensive on Moscow and thereby not only save Moscow but also lay the foundation for seriously defeating the enemy. If we do not accomplish this within the next few days, it will be too late. The Kalinin Front holds an exceedingly advantageous operational position for this purpose, and must not look on idly. It is your duty to gather literally everything in order to hit the enemy, who is weak in your sector. Believe me, success is certain."

Thereupon, Vasilevsky made a detailed study of the Front, named the divisions he thought should be used, and said how to reinforce them with guns from the Front's own artillery.

"Literally every hour counts," he concluded, "and you must therefore do everything you can to launch the operation not later than the morning of the fourth."

The Front commander could only admit that the Stavka had been right, and assure the Supreme Command that he would gather all needed strength for the strike.

"I'm taking a risk," Konev remarked, however, in conclusion.

Late on December 4, the Supreme Commander called me up and asked:

"Aside from what has already been done, how else can we help the Front?"

I replied that air support was necessary from the Supreme Command Reserve and the National Air Defence Forces. Besides, we needed at least two hundred manned tanks. The Front had an insignificant number of tanks, and without armour we could not rapidly step up the counter-offensive.

"We can give you no tanks," Stalin said, "but you will have aircraft. Talk it over with the General Staff. I'll phone there now. Don't forget that the Kalinin Front assumes the offensive on December 5, and the task force on the right wing of the South-Western Front does the same on December 6, in the area of Yelets."

The General Staff clarified the following:

Troops of the Kalinin Front were being engaged to assist the counter-offensive of the Western Front. Their objective was to strike in a south-westerly direction and emerge in the rear of the enemy group at Klin and Solnechnogorsk, thus contributing to its final defeat by troops of the Western Front.

The South-Western Front's thrust against the enemy in Yelets was to assist the Western Front in crushing the enemy troops south-west of Moscow.

Deep snow greatly hampered concentration and regrouping of troops, and their movement to assault positions. However, the troops overcame these difficulties, and by the morning of December 6 were ready to launch the counter-offensive.

On December 6, 1941, the troops of the Western Front began their counter-offensive to the north and south of Moscow. The neighbouring fronts moved forward in the area of Kalinin and Yelets. A large-scale battle developed.

On the first day of the offensive the forces of the Kalinin Front penetrated the forward line of defence but could not topple the enemy. It was only after ten days of bitter fighting and changing of tactics of the offensive that our troops began pushing forward. They were facilitated in that by the right wing of the Western Front which had smashed up the enemy grouping in the Rogachevo-Solnechnogorsk area and turned Klin.

On December 13, the 30th Army commanded by Lelyushenko and some of the units of the lst Shock Army of the Western Front approached Klin. Having enveloped the city on all sides, the Soviet troops burst into Klin and, after fierce battles, liberated it in the small hours of December 15.

The 20th and 16th armies' offensive was also gathering momentum. Towards the end of the day on December 9 the 20th Army, having broken down the enemy's stubborn resistance, approached Solnechnogorsk. The enemy was dislodged from that city on December 12. Meanwhile, the 16th Army liberated Kryukovo on December 8, and began stepping up the offensive towards the Istra Reservoir.

The right wing units of the 5th Army under General Govorov were advancing as well. The 5th Army's advance largely contributed to the success of the 16th Army.

After Klin was liberated, British Foreign Minister Anthony Eden came there on a visit.

At the end of December we saw in the *Pravda* Eden's statement made on his return to London. Speaking of the impressions of his visit to the Soviet Union, he said: "I was happy to see some of the feats of the Russian armies, feats that were truly magnificent."

The deaths of Maj.-Gen. Dovator, 2nd Guards Cavalry Corps Commander, and Lt.-Col. Tavliev, Commander of the 20th Cavalry Division, on December 19 near the village of Palash-kino — 12 km north-west of Ruza — were a terrible shock to all of us. On the recommendation of the Military Council of the Front the Presidium of the USSR Supreme Soviet posthumously awarded Maj.-Gen. Dovator the title of Hero of the Soviet Union.

The counter-offensive operations of the Western Front's right wing continued and were invariably supported by the air force of the Front, the National Air Defence and the long-range aviation. Under the command of General Golovanov, the long-range aviation hit powerful blows on artillery positions, tank formations and command posts. When the enemy began rolling back, the long-range aviation bombed and strafed his infantry formations, tank and truck columns. As the German troops withdrew westward, they left the roads behind them jammed with motor vehicles and combat equipment.

The Command of the Front sent ski units, cavalry and airborne troops to batter the retreating enemy, along withdrawal routes and in the rear. In coordination with the military councils of the Fronts, guerilla detachments intensified action in the enemy rear. Their operations seriously complicated the situation for the German Command.

On the left wing of the Front the 50th Army and General Belov's Cavalry Corps began on December 3 smashing up Guderian's 2nd Panzer Army in the area of Tula. Having lost about 70 tanks on the battlefield, the 3rd and 17th Panzer divisions and the 29th Motorized Division of Guderian's army beat a hasty retreat towards Venev.

The 10th Army entered combat in December in the area of Mikhailov where the enemy clung to his positions with the aim of protecting the flank of the retreating 2nd Panzer Army. Other units of the 50th Army launched the offensive on December 8 from the area of Tula, threatening to cut off the enemy's withdrawal routes from Venev and Mikhailov.

The Front and Supreme Command Reserve Air Forces rendered continuous support to General Belov's Cavalry Corps in attack, as well as to the 50th and 10th armies.

Deeply enveloped on both flanks, Guderian's army did not have the strength to parry counter-offensive thrusts of the Western Front and of the South-Western Front's task force, and began hastily to roll back in the general direction of Uzlovaya, Bogoroditsk and further on to Sukhinichi, abandoning heavy weapons, trucks, tractors and tanks.

In the course of ten days' fighting the left wing forces of the Western Front inflicted a heavy defeat on Guderian's 2nd Panzer Army and advanced 130 km.

To the left of the Western Front zone the units of the newly-formed Bryansk Front were also gaining ground rapidly. Our approach to the Oreshki-Staritsa-rivers Lama and Ruza-Maloyaroslavets-Tikhonova Pustyn-Kaluga-Mosalsk-Sukhinichi-Belev-Mtsensk-Novosil line marked the end of the first phase of the Moscow counter-offensive.

The threat overhanging Tula was removed at last. The Tank Division under Getman and the Cavalry Corps under

Belov played the decisive role in the counter-offensive. The task force of the 50th Army under Lt.-Gen. Popov struck a decisive blow at the enemy when freeing Kaluga.

Badly battered and battle-fatigued the Nazi armies were rapidly losing manpower and materiel, and under the pressure of the Soviet forces, rolling back west. The next phase of the counter-offensive, as we saw it, should have been for the western zone of action (Western, Kalinin and Bryansk Fronts) upon replenishing them with manpower and materiel, to press the counter-offensive to completion — that is until recapture of the positions held before the Germans started their Operation Typhoon.

Had we received from the Supreme Command at least four reinforcement armies (one for the Kalinin Front, one for the Bryansk Front and two for the Western Front), we would have had a real possibility of inflicting new defeats on the enemy and throwing him farther away from Moscow, and reaching the Vitebsk-Smolensk-Bryansk line.

Of course, the success of the December counter-offensive in the central strategic direction was considerable. Having suffered a major defeat the German striking forces of the Army Group Centre were retreating.

But on the whole the enemy was still strong. In the central part of the Front the enemy had offered stubborn resistance, and the offensive operations near Rostov and Tikhvin, though successfully begun, were not properly completed and lost momentum.

The Supreme Commander, however, impressed by the rout of the Nazi forces at the approaches to Moscow, and by the successes in the course of the counter-offensive, was highly optimistic. He believed that in the other theatres of operations, the Germans would not be able to sustain the Soviet Army's blows either, and could do nothing other than move to the defensive. This gave him the idea of an earliest possible offensive all along the line from Lake Ladoga to the Black Sea.

Late on January 5, 1942, I was summoned to the Stavka as its member to discuss the draft overall offensive plan.

After Shaposhnikov had made a brief report on the situation at the front and outlined the draft plan, Stalin said:

"The Germans are taken aback after their defeat near

Moscow. They have prepared for the winter badly. Now is just the time to take the general offensive. The enemy expects to hold it up until spring in order to gather his forces and again launch active operations. He wants to win time and some breathing space."

None of those present, as I recall, had any objections to what was said, and Stalin elaborated on his thought.

"Our objective," he said, pacing up and down his study as was his wont, "is to deny the Germans any breathing space, to drive them westward without let-up, to make them use up their reserves before spring comes..."

He laid special stress on the words "before spring", paused, and finally explained:

"By that time we'll have fresh reserves, while the Germans will have none..."

Having set forth what he thought was the probable course of the war, the Supreme Commander examined the practical actions of various fronts.

The Supreme Command had the following concept of operations: in view of the successful counter-offensive in the western theatre of operations, the enemy's defeat on all fronts was to be made the objective of the general offensive.

The main blow was to be delivered against the Army Group Centre. It was planned that the left wing forces of the North-Western Front together with the Kalinin and Western Fronts were to rout the group by double envelopment with subsequent encirclement and destruction of the enemy's main forces in the area of Rzhev, Vyazma and Smolensk.

The Leningrad Front, the Volkhov Front, and the right wing forces of the North-Western Front were to rout the Army Group North.

The task for the South-Western and Southern Fronts was to inflict a defeat on the Army Group South and liberate the Donbas. The Caucasian Front and the Black Sea Fleet were to liberate the Crimea.

The general offensive was to be assumed in the shortest time possible.

Stalin then asked for our opinion of the outlined draft.

"We must go on with the offensive in the western theatre of operations where the situation is more favourable for us and where the enemy hasn't had time to restore his fighting efficiency," I said. "However, to ensure success of the operation the western theatre forces must be replenished with manpower and weapons, reserves must be built up — tank units above all. Otherwise the offensive will be a failure."

"As for the Leningrad and south-western offensive operations, I must say that our troops are up against strong enemy defences. Without powerful artillery means they will not be able to pierce the defence line but will only unjustifiably sustain great casualties and wear themselves out. I'm for strengthening the western theatre and stepping up the offensive there."

"We don't have the means to ensure simultaneous offensive operations on all the fronts now," Voznesensky observed.

"I have spoken to Timoshenko," Stalin said. "He is for the offensive in the south-western direction. We have to pound the Germans to pieces as soon as possible so that they won't be able to mount an offensive in spring. Who else would like to speak?"

There was no reply. The discussion of Stalin's suggestions was thus left up in the air.

As we left the conference room, Shaposhnikov said to me:

"You shouldn't have argued, the Supreme Commander had that question settled."

"Why was our opinion asked then?"

"That, my dear fellow, I do not know," Shaposhnikov said, sighing heavily.

Front Headquarters received the letter of instructions for the offensive on January 7, 1942. In compliance with these instructions the Military Council assigned the Front's forces additional tasks to continue the counter-offensive:

— the right flank of the Front (the lst Shock, 20th and 16th armies) were to continue advancing in the general direction of Sychevka, and, in cooperation with the Kalinin Front, to rout the Sychevka-Rzhev enemy grouping;

— the centre forces of the Front (the 5th and 33rd armies) were to advance in the general direction of Mozhaisk-Gzhatsk; the job of the 43rd, 49th and 50th armies was to strike towards Yukhnov, rout the Yukhnov-Kondrov enemy grouping and exploit the success towards Vyazma;

— the reinforced Cavalry Corps under General Belov was to move out to the Vyazma area and link up with the Kalinin Front's 11th Cavalry Corps under Maj.-Gen. Sokolov for a combined blow against the rear of the Vyazma enemy grouping (at that time large partisan detachments were active in the Vyazma area);

— the 10th Army's mission was to advance on Kirov protecting the Front's left flank.

Our neighbour on the right, the Kalinin Front, as we already pointed out, was to advance in the general direction of Sychevka-Vyazma, circumventing Rzhev, with its 22nd Army stepping up the offensive towards Bely.

The North-Western Front had to mount an offensive in two diverging directions. Its 3rd Shock Army under Lt.-Gen. Purkayev was to advance in the general direction of Velikiye Luki, while its 4th Shock Army under Col.-Gen. Yeremenko was to press towards Toropets and Velizh.

The right flank armies of the South-Western and Bryansk Fronts were to contain the enemy, preventing him from transferring forces to his central zone of action and the Donbas area.

The forces in the south-western zone of advance were to capture Kharkov, and seize bridgeheads near Dnepropetrovsk and Zaporozhye.

It was an imposing plan. But in several directions, especially the main direction — west — it was not backed up with sufficient manpower or weapons. This the Supreme Commander knew perfectly well. But he believed that even the available strength was enough to crush the Nazi defences if we followed the principle of amassing shock forces and conducting our artillery offensives skilfully.

On January 10, commanders of Fronts and armies received a Supreme Command Directive, which contained an assessment of the war situation in the spirit of Stalin's utterances at the afore-mentioned meeting of January 5, 1942, and instructed the Fronts to operate with shock forces and to organize artillery offensives.

Let me cite the more important passages of the said Directive:

"To secure successes in 1942, our troops must learn to break through the enemy's defence line, to organize the breaches to its entire depth, and thus open the way for our infantry, our tanks, our cavalry. The Germans have more than one defence line — they are building and will soon have a second and a third. If our troops do not learn to breach and crash through the enemy's defence line swiftly and substantially, our advance will become impossible..."

Then the Directive set forth two conditions which Stalin thought had to be carried out if we wanted to succeed.

The first was actions by shock forces. "Our troops usually advance as separate divisions or brigades deployed along the front in a chain. This organization of an offensive cannot be effective, of course, because it gives us no edge in strength at some particular place. Such an offensive is doomed to failure. An offensive can be effective only if we concentrate a considerably superior force vis-à-vis the enemy in one of the sectors of the front. It is essential for this that each army setting out to breach the enemy's defence should have a shock force of three or four divisions massed for a strike at some specific point along the front. That, indeed, is the prime task of the army command, because that is the only way to gain a decisive edge in strength and secure success in breaching the enemy's defence at some definite sector of the front."

This was followed by the second instruction concerning "artillery offensives".

"Often," the Directive said, "we send the infantry into an attack against the enemy's defence line without artillery, without any artillery support whatsoever, and after that we complain that the infantry won't rise against an enemy who has dug in and is defending himself. It is clear, however, that such an 'offensive' cannot yield the desired effect. It is not an offensive but a crime — a crime against the Motherland, and against the troops which are forced to suffer senseless losses...

"This means, first, that the artillery must not confine itself to separate actions for an hour or two before an offensive, and that it must advance together with the infantry and must sustain the shelling all through the offensive with just short breaks until the enemy's defence line is broken up to its entire depth.

"This means, second, that the infantry must not wait until after the shelling to attack, as this occurs following the so-called 'artillery preparation', and that it must attack together with the artillery, to the thunder of gunfire, to the tune of the artillery.

"This means, third, that the artillery should not fire at random, but massively, and not massively at any point of the front but in the zone of the shock force of the Army or Front, and exclusively in that zone because otherwise the artillery offensive is inconceivable."

The instructions contained in the Stavka Directive were adopted for unconditional fulfilment. I take the liberty of saying once more, however, that in the winter of 1942 we did not have the requisite strength and weaponry to put these ideas of a broad offensive, which were in general correct, into effect. And lacking such strength, the troops could not form the desired shock forces and carry out artillery offensive effectively enough to crush so powerful and proficient an enemy as the Nazi Wehrmacht.

And the events bore this out. The advance of the North-Western Front was the only one that developed well, because here the enemy had no unbroken line of defence.

In early February 1942, the 3rd and 4th Shock armies of this Front having covered about 250 km, moved up to Velikiye Luki, Demidov and Velizh. The Kalinin Front's 22nd Army was then fighting for the town of Bely, while the 11th Cavalry Corps was moving out to an area northwest of Vyazma. The Kalinin Front's 39th and 29th armies were pushing forward slowly west of Rzhev. Faced by a well-organized defence system, the left flank troops of the Kalinin Front were unable to obtain any success.

The enemy's actions at that time were determined by Hitler's order of January 3, 1942, which said in part: "We must cling to every town and village, retreating not a step, fighting to the last cartridge, to the last grenade — that is what the present situation demands."

"Herren Commanders," went an order from the commander of the 23rd Infantry Division. "The general combat situation urgently demands that the rapid withdrawal of our troops be stopped on the River Lama line, and that the division organize firm resistance. Positions along the Lama must be held to the last man. It is a question of life and death..."

What prompted the German Command to call on its troops peremptorily to stop and take a stand on the Lama line?

It proceeded from the fact that there were defensive positions that our troops had organized back in October and November where the enemy could temporarily consolidate his hold. These positions ran north to south along both banks of the Lama linking with positions on the rivers Ruza and Nara.

Besides, by bringing from the deep rear all sorts of composite and reserve divisions, as well as units freshly drawn off from occupied territory, the enemy managed by mid-December further to develop the positions for defence. Organization of the ground was completed by the time the retreating German troops reached the line along the said rivers.

Permit me to briefly recall to the reader the Soviet offensive near Moscow at the beginning of 1942.

On January 10, 1942, following a 90-minute artillery preparation, our Western Front's forces (the 20th Army, part of the lst Shock Army, the 2nd Cavalry Corps under Maj.-Gen. I. A. Pliev, the 22nd Tank Brigade and five ski battalions) launched an attack to penetrate the front line in the area of Volokolamsk. After two days of fighting tooth and nail, the enemy defences were broken through. Major-General Pliev's Cavalry Corps, with the five ski battalions and the 22nd Tank Brigade, were sent into the gap.

On January 16 and 17, the Front's right flank forces, in cooperation with partisan detachments, captured Lotoshino and Shakhovskaya cutting the Moscow-Rzhev railway. It would seem that it was right at that point that we should have built up strength to exploit the success. But it did not turn out that way.

On January 19 the order came from the Supreme Command to withdraw the lst Shock Army from action and assign it to the Supreme Command Reserve. Both Sokolovsky and I phoned the General Staff asking for permission to keep the lst Shock Army. We got the same reply — that was the Supreme Commander's order.

I called up Stalin. I insisted that pulling the army out would weaken our attack forces.

The answer I got was: "Enough of this stupid talk. You have a lot of troops. Count your armies."

I tried to continue: "Comrade Stalin, we are fighting on a

very wide front, fierce battles are being fought all along the line, and that rules out regrouping. I ask you not to withdraw the lst Shock Army from the Western Front's right flank so as not to lessen pressure on the enemy."

Stalin hung up without a reply. My talks with Shaposhnikov on the matter were to no avail either.

"My dear fellow, there is nothing I can do," Shaposhnikov said. "It is the Supreme Commander's own decision."

We had to stretch the 20th Army over a wide frontage. When they reached Gzhatsk, the weakened right flank forces were' stopped by organized enemy defence. Their further advance was checked.

By January 20, the 5th and 33rd armies advancing in the centre of the Front liberated Ruza, Dorokhovo, Mozhaisk and Vereya. The 43rd and 49th armies reached the area of Domanovo, and engaged the enemy's Yukhnov grouping.

Here I would like to give a more detailed examination of the operations of the Soviet troops in the area of Vyazma. Between January 18 and 22, two battalions of the 201st Airborne Brigade and the 250th Airborne Regiment were dropped in the area of Zhelanye (40 km south of Vyazma) to cut off enemy communications with the rear. The 33rd Army under Lt.-Gen. Yefremov was given the job of exploiting the breakthrough in the direction of Vyazma, and in cooperation with General Belov's lst Cavalry Corps, the airborne force, partisan detachments and the 11th Cavalry Corps of the Kalinin Front, to seize Vyazma.

On January 27, General Belov's corps broke through beyond the Warsaw Highway, 35 km south-west of Yukhnov, and three days later linked up with the airborne force and partisan detachments south of Vyazma. On February 1 three infantry divisions of the 33rd Army (113th, 338th and 160th) under the personal command of Lt.-Gen. Yefremov moved out to that area and engaged the enemy at the approaches to Vyazma. To reinforce the lst Cavalry Corps under General Belov and ensure coordination with the 11th Cavalry Corps of the Kalinin Front, the Supreme Command ordered the 4th Airborne Corps to be dropped in the area of Ozerechnya. However, because of insufficient transport planes, it was possible to drop only the 2,000-strong 8th Airborne Brigade.

Pressing the offensive from the Naro-Fominsk area towards Vyazma, on January 31 the 33rd Army emerged into the area of Shansky Zavod and Domanovo, where it found a wide and utterly unprotected gap in the enemy defences. The fact that there was no unbroken line gave us reason to believe that the Germans did not have sufficient forces on that sector for the well-organized defence of Vyazma. Therefore we decided to take Vyazma on the march before the enemy brought up his reserves. The fall of the city would put the enemy's entire Vyazma grouping in an exceptionally difficult position.

Lt.-Gen. Yefremov decided to personally lead the striking force of his army, and began to rapidly advance towards Vyazma.

When on February 3 and 4 the main forces of that grouping, comprising two divisions, were at the approaches to Vyazma, the enemy struck against the base of the breakthrough wedge and re-established his defence line along the Ugra, cutting off the striking force. The second echelon of the army had managed to fall behind near Shansky Zavod, while the advance of its neighbour on the left, the 43rd Army, had been slowed down in the area of Medyn. The 43rd Army did not carry out in time the mission assigned to it by the Front Staff — to help out General Yefremov's force.

Belov's Cavalry Corps, committed on the Vyazma sector, had moved out to the nieghbourhood of Vyazma and linked up with Yefremov's troops, with the result that they themselves became cut off from the rear.

By that time the German Command had brought large reserves to the Vyazma area from France and from other fronts, and had managed to stabilize the situation. Hard as we tried, we were unable to pierce the enemy's defences.

The result was that we had to leave that entire grouping in the enemy rear in a wooded area south-west of Vyazma, where many partisan detachments had their bases.

Finding itself in the enemy's rear, for two months Belov's corps, Yefremov's group and the airborne units joined with the partisans to harass the enemy, destroying his manpower and materiel.

On February 10, the 8th Airborne Brigade and partisan detachments raided the headquarters of the German 5th Panzer

Division, capturing a considerable amount of equipment, and occupied the area of Morshanovo-Dyagilevo. That same day, General Belov and Yefremov were informed of it and ordered to coordinate their actions with the commander of the 8th Airborne Brigade, whose headquarters was in Dyagilevo.

Having established radio contact with Belov and Yefremov, the Front Command organized, as far as it was possible, the air supply of ammunition, medicines and provisions. Many of the wounded were air-lifted to the rear. Maj.-Gen. V. S. Golushkevich, Chief of the Front Headquarters Operations Division, and liaison officers, made several flights to the grouping.

At the beginning of April, the grouping's position became seriously worse. Having built up considerable strength, the enemy increased pressure on the grouping, aiming to eliminate this dangerous "splinter" by spring. A thaw at the end of April almost totally robbed the grouping of its possibility to manoeuvre, as well as of its communication with the partisan-controlled area from which it received provisions and fodder.

At the request of Generals Belov and Yefremov, the Front Command gave them permission to begin leading out their troops so they could link up with the main forces. The grouping was given strict orders to leave the Vyazma area through partisan-held forests, moving in the general direction of Kirov where the 10th Army was preparing to break through the enemy's defence which was weaker in that sector.

General Belov's Cavalry Corps and the airborne units followed these instructions to the letter, and after passing along a long U-shaped route, reached the area of the 10th Army on July 18, 1942. Skilfully skirting around large enemy groupings and destroying small ones in its way, most of the party emerged through a breach created by the 10th Army into the front line. It had lost many of its heavy weapons and combat materiel during the operation in the enemy rear and on the way out. Yet the majority of the men did reach our troops. How joyous was the meeting between the men who had broken out of the enemy rear, and those who had backed up their manoeuvre. Neither the officers nor the men were ashamed

of their tears, as they were tears of happiness, of comradeship-
in-arms.

However, the route was difficult, and unfortunately not
everyone managed it. Lt.-Gen. Yefremov considered the route
too long for his worn-out troops, and directly radioed the
General Staff, asking for permission to effect a breakthrough
along the shortest route — across the Ugra.

Immediately after, Stalin called me and asked whether
I approved Yefremov's suggestion. I replied that I emphatically did not. However, the Supreme Commander said that
General Yefremov was an experienced army commander, and
that we should accede to his request. The Supreme Command
ordered a counterattack by the forces of the Front. This
attack was prepared and carried out by the 43rd Army.
However, no counterattack came from General Yefremov's
troops.

We later learned that the Germans had spotted General
Yefremov's force en route to the Ugra and destroyed it.
Fighting a losing battle Army Commander General Yefremov,
who fought with great gallantry, was seriously wounded. To
escape being taken prisoner, Yefremov shot himself. This
was the tragic death of that valiant military leader. Most of his
heroic men fell alongside him.

Lt.-Gen. Yefremov assumed command of the 33rd Army on
October 25, 1941, when the Germans were thrusting towards
Moscow. In the Battle of Moscow his troops fought valiantly,
and did not let the enemy break through their lines. For valour displayed in the Battle of Moscow, General Yefremov was
awarded the Order of the Red Banner.

Army artillery commander Maj.-Gen. P. N. Afrosimov, a
remarkable man and an extremely capable artillery officer,
and some other commanders and political workers who had
distinguished themselves in the Battle of Moscow, fell in the
same fighting in which General Yefremov died.

Viewing the events of 1942 critically, I can say now
that we misjudged the situation in the Vyazma area. We had
overrated the potential of our troops and underrated the enemy.
He proved to be a harder nut to crack than we believed...

In February and March, the Supreme Command demanded
that the offensive in the western zone of operations be

stepped up, but the Fronts had neither the manpower nor the equipment for this to be done.

The country's entire resources were strained to the utmost at the time. It was not able to satisfy the requirements of the armed forces which the situation and current tasks demanded. Things came to such a point that every time we were summoned to General Headquarters, we took the opportunity to coax out of the Supreme Commander at least 10-15 anti-tank rifles, or anti-tank guns, or submachine-guns, or what was to us the bare minimum of mortar and artillery shells. Whatever we could obtain in this way was immediately loaded onto trucks and sent to the armies that most needed it.

Ammunition was especially in short supply. Of the total ammunition supplies planned for the first ten days of January, the Front in fact received one per cent of the 82-mm mortar shells and 20-30 per cent of the artillery rounds. For January as a whole, the percentages were: 50-mm mortar shells, 2.7 per cent; 82-mm mortar shells, 55 per cent; 120-mm mortar shells, 36 per cent; artillery rounds, 44 per cent.

Things were even worse in February: of the 316 carloads of ammunition scheduled for the first ten days of the month, none arrived. Because of the shortage of ammunition some of the rocket artillery had to be sent to the rear.

Believe it or not, the normal rate of ammunition expenditure we had to establish was one to two rounds per artillery piece per day. And that during an offensive campaign! The Front Command's report to the Supreme Commander on February 14, 1942, stated:

"Combat experience has shown that the shortage of ammunition is preventing us from launching artillery attacks. As a result, enemy fire systems are not being disrupted, while our units, attacking insufficiently neutralized enemy defences, are suffering heavily without scoring the expected successes."

In late February and early March of 1942, the Supreme Command decided to bolster the Fronts on the Western sector with manpower and materiel. However, the decision was taken too late. Worried by the turn of events, the enemy had greatly strengthened his Vyazma grouping and, using his well-organized positions as support, began active operations against the Western and Kalinin Fronts.

It was becoming more and more difficult for our worn out and depleted troops to overcome the enemy's resistance. Our repeated pleas to halt the advance so that we could consolidate the captured ground were turned down by the Supreme Command. Moreover, in his letter of instructions of March 20, 1942, the Supreme Commander insisted that we conduct our mission even more energetically.

Following those instructions, the Fronts of the western theatre of operations attempted in late March and early April to crush the Rzhev-Vyazma grouping, but with no success.

At last the Supreme Command was compelled to accept our proposal to pass over to the defensive along the line running through Velikiye Luki-Velizh-Demidov-Bely-Dukhov-shchina-the Dnieper-Nelidovo-Rzhev-Pogoreloye Gorodishche-Gzhatsk-the Ugra-Spas-Demensk-Kirov-Lyudinovo-Kholmi-shchi-the Oka.

During the winter offensive, the forces of the Western Front had advanced from 70 to 100 km, which somewhat improved the overall operational and strategic situation on the Western sector.

What were the overall results of the great Battle of Moscow?

In his account of Operation Typhoon, Nazi General Westphal had to admit that "the German army — previously considered invincible — was on the brink of collapse". Many of Hitler's other former generals agreed, such as Tippelskirch, Blumentritt, Bayerlein and Manteuffel.

In the Battle of Moscow, the Germans lost more than half a million officers and men; 1,300 tanks; 2,500 artillery pieces; over 15,000 motor vehicles, and a great deal more combat equipment. The enemy troops were rolled back west between 150 and 300 km from Moscow.

The 1941-1942 Soviet winter counter-offensive was conducted in difficult conditions, but even more important, as I already pointed out, without numerical superiority over the enemy. Besides, our Fronts did not have full armoured and mechanized units, without which, as combat experience had shown, no large-scale, extensive offensive operations were possible. Only powerful armoured and mechanized forces can forestall enemy manoeuvres, swiftly outflank him, cut off his supply routes from the rear, and envelop and cut up his groupings.

In the Battle of Moscow the Red Army inflicted the first major defeat in the six months of the war on the Wehrmacht's main grouping. Before this, the Soviet Armed Forces had carried out several important operations that slowed the enemy's advance on all three directions of his main blow. But none of the operations was the equal, either in scope or outcome of the great battle at the approaches to the Soviet capital.

The skilful conduct of defensive operations, the well-timed execution of counterblows and the prompt assumption of the counter-offensive were a substantial contribution to Soviet military science. They also testified to the Soviet military leaders' maturity in operational and strategic questions, and demonstrated the greater combat skill of men in all the fighting services.

The result of the Battle of Moscow and the winter offensive by the Red Army showed that the German forces could be defeated provided things were made difficult for them.

The rout of the German troops on the approaches to Moscow was of great significance for the world. People in all the countries of the anti-Hitler coalition greatly rejoiced at the news of the marvellous victory by the Soviet forces. This victory inspired hope among progressives everywhere of deliverance from fascist slavery.

The German setbacks near Leningrad, Rostov and Tikhvin and in the Battle of Moscow had a sobering effect on reactionary circles in Japan and Turkey, and made them exercise more caution in their policies towards the Soviet Union.

The German troops were now on the defensive. To restore their fighting efficiency, the Nazi military and political leadership had to take several extreme measures, as well as redeploy considerable forces from occupied countries of Europe and fling them into the Soviet-German theatre. Germany had put pressure on the governments of the satellite countries so that they would send more troops and equipment to the East, and this aggravated the political situation in those countries.

After the Nazi defeat near Moscow, many German officers and generals, to say nothing of the rank and file, became convinced that the Soviet Union was a mighty power, and that the Soviet Armed Forces were an insurmountable obstacle in the way of the goals set by the Nazi military leaders.

I am often asked about Stalin's role in the Battle of Moscow.

Throughout the whole time, Stalin was in Moscow, organizing the troops and weapons for the enemy's defeat. As head of the State Committee for Defence, and with the help of the executive staff of the People's Commissariats he must be given credit for the enormous work in organizing necessary strategic, material and technical resources. By his strict exactingness Stalin achieved, one can say, the near-impossible.

When I am asked what event in the last war rests most strongly in my memory, I always say: the Battle of Moscow.

In gruelling and often unbelievably difficult conditions, our troops matured, accumulating battle wisdom and experience. As soon as they received the minimum necessary technical resources, they turned from a retreating defensive into a powerful offensive force. Grateful generations to come will always remember the tremendous organizational work of the Party, the heroic labour of the Soviet people, and the glorious feats of their Armed Forces.

I would like to pay tribute to all who took part in the Battle of Moscow and who survived and to bow my head in deep respect to the memory of those who laid down their lives but did not let the enemy through to the heart of our country, the Hero City of Moscow. All of us owe them a debt of gratitude too great to be repaid.

The Communist Party and the Government lavished rewards on those who won the historic victory in grim 1941 against a formidable enemy. Thirty-six thousand officers and men were decorated during the period of the counter-offensive at Moscow and the Red Army's winter offensive. The title of Hero of the Soviet Union was awarded to 110 soldiers for special merit in combat. More than a million people earned the medal "For the Defence of Moscow".

By a decree of the Presidium of the USSR Supreme Soviet of May 8, 1965, Moscow was named a Hero City and was decorated with the Order of Lenin and the Gold Star medal. The remains of the Unknown Soldier who laid down his life in defending the capital have now been laid to rest beside the Kremlin wall. These words are inscribed on his tombstone:

> Your name is unknown,
> Your deed is immortal.

The eternal flame of glory lit for the heroes who fell defending the capital will never be extinguished. It will serve forever as a reminder of the courage and heroism of the Soviet people who had selflessly defended their socialist Motherland.

CHAPTER 2

The Ordeal Continues (1942)

For a number of reasons our country was once again subjected to severe trials in 1942. But as in 1941, in the Battle of Moscow, the Soviet people and their armed forces, led by the Party of Lenin, overcame every setback with great courage. They routed the strategic concentration of German forces in the area between the Don and the Volga and thus set the stage for the complete expulsion of the Nazi armies from our country.

To understand the events that took place in the south one must acquire at least a cursory knowledge of the military and political situation that developed at the beginning of the summer of 1942.

The end of spring had seen some improvement in the Soviet Union's international and domestic situation. The anti-fascist front continued to expand and consolidate. In January, 26 countries signed a declaration in which they agreed to use all the means at their disposal to combat the aggressor states and not conclude any separate cease-fire or separate peace with them. An understanding was reached with the United States and Britain that a second front would be opened in Europe in 1942. All these and other factors, especially the defeat of the German forces at Moscow and the disruption of the plans for a *blitzkrieg*, gave a powerful boost to the anti-fascist forces in all countries.

A lull had set in on the Soviet-German front. Both sides were on the defensive. The troops were digging trenches, building dug-outs, mining the approaches to forward positions, erecting barbed wire entanglements and carrying out other defence measures. Commanders and headquarters staffs were busy tightening up fire systems, coordinating the various services, and tackling other problems.

The Stavka, the General Staff and individual military units were summing up the results of the fighting, analyzing and critically assessing successes and failures, and trying to get a deeper insight into the enemy's methods of warfare, his strengths and weaknesses.

The Soviet people, inspired by the Red Army's great victory at Moscow, which had laid the foundation for a fundamental turning-point in the war, were making good headway with the task of putting the economy on a war footing. Increasing quantities of new tanks, aircraft, artillery, rockets and ammunition were reaching the armed forces.

After the completion of the winter offensive, however, the Soviet Armed Forces were still markedly inferior to the enemy in numbers and in equipment. At that time we had no properly prepared reserves or substantial material resources. New strategic reserves for all the services had therefore to be built up in the rear. The successes of our tank and artillery industry enabled the Supreme Command to start forming tank corps and tank armies, equipped with the most up-to-date weapons of those days.

Modernized 45-mm anti-tank guns and new 76-mm guns were coming into service. New artillery units and formations were being mustered. Anti-aircraft defences for the troops and the country as a whole were being organized on a grand scale. Our air force was able to start forming air armies. By June we had eight such armies. The long-range bomber formations were substantially reinforced. The total strength of the army in the field rose to 5.6 million men, 3,882 tanks, 44,900 guns and mortars (not counting 50-mm mortars, of which we had 21,400), and 2,221 aircraft. Combat training was vastly expanded, the lessons of the recent fighting were mastered and skill was acquired in handling the new weapons.[1]

The Nazi Command was also preparing for its summer campaign and still regarded the Eastern Front as the main theatre. The Nazi leaders sent more and more fresh forces eastward. On the fronts stretching from the Barents to the

---

[1] *A History of the Second World War, 1939-1945,* Vol. 5, pp. 92 and 121.

Black Sea Nazi Germany and her allies had 217 divisions and 20 brigades, including 178 divisions, 8 brigades and 4 air fleets manned by Germans. Owing to the absence of a second front, Germany was able to keep not more than 20 per cent of its armed forces on the other fronts and in the occupied countries.

By May 1942 the enemy had deployed on the Soviet-German front an army of more than six million men (including 810,000 satellite troops), 3,229 tanks and self-propelled guns, nearly 57,000 artillery pieces and mortars, and 3,395 combat aircraft. The enemy remained superior in manpower. We had a small numerical superiority in tanks, but in quality most of them fell short of the German panzers.

On the whole the Nazi High Command's political and military strategy for the coming months of 1942 could be summed up as the destruction of our forces in the south, the occupation of the Caucasus, a breakthrough to the Volga, and the capture of Stalingrad and Astrakhan, thus paving the way for the destruction of the USSR as a state.

In planning offensive operations for the summer of 1942 the Nazi Command had to take into account the fact that despite its numerical advantage over the Soviet forces, it no longer possessed the resources to launch simultaneous offensives in all strategic directions, as it had done in 1941, under the Barbarossa Plan.

By the spring of 1942 the German forces were strung out from the Barents to the Black Sea, with a consequent sharp decline in their operational density.

By great efforts the Nazi Command was able to build up Army Group South to full strength and concentrate forces that substantially outnumbered our armies on the South-Western sector.

Hitler's Directive No. 41, of April 5, 1942, envisaged the seizure of the Soviet Union's richest industrial and agricultural regions, acquisition of additional economic resources (above all Caucasian oil) and the capture of a dominant strategic position from which to pursue his military and political goals.

Hitler and his associates hoped that as soon as success was achieved in the south they would be able to thrust forward in the other strategic directions and renew their attacks on Leningrad and Moscow.

The plan for the Moscow strategic sector in 1942 was restricted to separate offensive operations for the destruction of the Soviet forces deeply wedged into the German defences, with a dual aim in view. First, to improve the German forces' operational position and, second, to divert the Soviet Command's attention from the Southern sector, where the enemy's main blow was to fall.

A specific aim of the capture of the Caucasus and the Volga was to cut the Soviet Union's means of communication with its allies in the anti-Hitler coalition.

In the spring of 1942 I spent a good deal of time at General Headquarters and took part in discussions with the Supreme Commander concerning various fundamental strategic questions, so I had a good idea of how he assessed the situation and the prospects for 1942.

It was obvious that he did not fully believe the assurances by Churchill and Roosevelt that a second front would be opened in Europe, but he had not lost hope that they would undertake some kind of operation elsewhere. Stalin trusted Roosevelt more than he did Churchill.

The Supreme Commander assumed that in the summer of 1942 the Germans would be capable of waging major offensive operations simultaneously in two strategic directions, most likely the Moscow and the southern. In the north and north-west, he maintained, the enemy's activity would be of little significance. At most he might try to cut off salients in our defence line and improve the deployment of his troops.

Of the two sectors in which Stalin expected strategic offensive operations, he was most concerned about the Moscow sector, where the Germans had assembled more than 70 divisions.

With regard to our plans for the spring and early summer of 1942 Stalin assumed that we were not yet strong enough to develop major offensive operations. He believed we should confine ourselves for the immediate future to an active strategic defence. At the same time, however, he thought it necessary to mount a number of offensive operations in the

Crimea, in the Kharkov area, on the Lgov-Kursk and Smolensk sectors, and also in the Leningrad and Demyansk areas.

I knew that Marshal Shaposhnikov wanted to have only an active strategic defence, which would wear down and bleed the enemy in early summer, after which, when we had built up our reserves, we would be able to launch a broad summer counter-offensive. While generally supporting Shaposhnikov, I believed that on the Western sector we should in early summer try to wipe out the enemy's Rzhev-Vyazma grouping, where the Germans held a large bridgehead and had concentrated powerful forces.

After additional study of the situation, the Stavka and the General Staff reached the conclusion that the Orel-Tula and Kursk-Voronezh sectors were the most dangerous, since they harboured the threat of an enemy thrust at Moscow and encirclement of the capital from the south-west. Hence the decision: by the end of spring a considerable portion of the Supreme Command's reserve should be concentrated on the Bryansk Front for the defence of Moscow, and massive reinforcements were sent to this area. By the middle of May the Bryansk Front comprised four tank corps, seven infantry divisions, eleven separate infantry brigades, four separate tank brigades and a large amount of artillery. In addition the Front was supported by the 5th Tank Army of the Supreme Command Reserve, which would be used for a powerful counterblow in the event of any enemy offensive in this area.

I was basically in agreement with the Supreme Commander's operational and strategic predictions, but I did not see eye to eye with him over the number of offensive operations to be launched by our Fronts, because I believed they would swallow up our reserves without achieving much and thus make it more difficult to prepare for a subsequent Soviet general offensive.

When I reported my ideas on the subject, I proposed to Stalin and the General Staff, as I have said, that powerful blows should be struck in the Western strategic direction with the aim of destroying the enemy's Vyazma-Rzhev concentration. These blows would be delivered by the forces of the Western and Kalinin Fronts, and those adjoining them, and also by the air forces of the Supreme Command and the Moscow Air Defence Force. The enemy's defeat in the western direction would seriously undermine his strength, forcing him to abandon large-scale offensive operations, at least for the near future.

Today, of course, when I look back, this argument does not seem so indisputable as it did then, but at the time in the absence of complete information about the enemy I was sure I was right.

In view of the complexity of the problem Stalin ordered that the general situation and the possible options for action by our forces during the summer campaign should be discussed once again.

Special attention was to be devoted to the proposals submitted by the command of the South-Western sector concerning a massive offensive operation with the forces of the Bryansk, South-Western and Southern Fronts. The aim of this operation would be to rout the enemy on the southern flank and reach a line running through Gomel, Kiev, Cherkassy, Pervomaisk, and Nikolayev.

The meeting of the State Defence Committee at the end of March was attended by Voroshilov, Timoshenko, Shaposhnikov, Vasilevsky and myself.

Shaposhnikov made a very detailed report, which generally reflected Stalin's predictions. But in view of the enemy's numerical superiority and the lack of a second front in Europe, he proposed that we should confine ourselves in the near future to active defence. The basic strategic reserves should not be committed to action but concentrated on the Central sector and partly in the Voronezh area, where the General Staff expected the main events of summer 1942 to unfold.

In considering the plan for an offensive operation presented by the command of the South-Western sector, Shaposhnikov expressed disagreement with this plan of the General Staff and drew attention to the organizational difficulties of the operation, and the absence of the necessary reserves.

But the Supreme Commander interrupted him.

"We can't stay on the defensive and do nothing until the Germans strike the first blow! We must launch several preemp-

tive strikes on a broad front and test the enemy's intentions.
Zhukov proposes launching an offensive on the Western sector
and remaining on the defensive everywhere else. I think that is
a half measure."

The next to speak was Timoshenko. Having reported on the
situation of the South-Western sector, he said: "The troops
on this sector are ready and should unquestionably strike
a preemptive blow to disrupt the Germans' offensive plans
against the Southern and South-Western Fronts; otherwise we
shall have a repetition of what happened at the beginning of
the war. As for launching an offensive on the Western sector,
I support Zhukov. That will hold down the enemy's forces."

Voroshilov supported Timoshenko's view.

I spoke up again in opposition to the launching of several
offensive operations at once. But this view was not taken into
consideration and an ambivalent decision was reached. On the
one hand, the Supreme Commander agreed with the General
Staff, which was firmly opposed to a major offensive operation
by the Soviet Fronts grouped around Kharkov. On the other,
he gave Timoshenko permission to carry out a separate offensive operation with the forces of the South-Western sector. The
enemy's Kharkov concentration was to be routed by attacks
from the Volchansk area and the Barvenkovo bridgehead and
Kharkov was to be recaptured, thus paving the way for
liberation of the Donbas.

This is how Vasilevsky, a direct participant in the events,
recalls the situation:

"Realizing the risks attached to an offensive from such
an operational trap as the Barvenkovo salient presented for
the forces of the South-Western Front that were to carry out
this operation, Shaposhnikov proposed that it should not be
undertaken. But the command of the sector insisted on its
proposal and assured Stalin that it would be entirely successful. Stalin gave his permission and ordered the General Staff
to consider the operation the internal affair of the sector and
not interfere in any matters concerned with it."

The events of May and June showed that an extremely grave
miscalculation had been made. At the end of April our offensive in the Crimea collapsed. The forces of the Crimean Front,
led by General D. T. Kozlov, suffered considerable losses

without achieving their objective. The Supreme Command ordered the Front Command to take up firm defensive positions.

On May 8, the enemy concentrated a shock force and massive air support against the Crimean Front and broke through its defences. Our troops found themselves in a dangerous situation and were compelled to abandon Kerch.

The defeat at Kerch seriously complicated the situation at Sebastopol, where the city's defenders had been fighting fiercely since October 1941. Now that it had captured Kerch, the German Command was able to concentrate all its forces against Sebastopol.

On July 4, after nine months of siege and continuous fierce fighting in which Soviet sailors and soldiers won immortal glory, Sebastopol was abandoned by our forces. This meant the complete loss of the Crimea, which greatly complicated the overall situation for us and naturally made things easier for the enemy, who was able to free one of its active armies and considerable reinforcements for operations elsewhere.

On May 3, the North-Western Front launched its offensive against the 16th German Army in the Demyansk area. The battle lasted a month without bringing success. Admittedly, the enemy suffered heavy losses.

During a telephone conversation concerning the Crimean Front and the South-Western sector the Supreme Commander said to me: "Now you see what comes of defence... We must punish Kozlov, Mekhlis and Kulik severely for their carelessness, and as a warning to others not to be so passive. Timoshenko will start his offensive soon."

On May 12 the South-Western Front launched its offensive on Kharkov with the planned double thrust, from Volchansk and from the Barvenkovo salient.

At first the operation went well. Our forces broke through the enemy's defences and advanced 25-50 km in three days. Stalin was pleased and, as Vasilevsky recalls, used this advance to have a dig at the General Staff, whose objections had almost led him to cancel such a successful operation.

Soon, however, the situation changed. The Southern Front (commanded by Colonel-General Malinovsky) had been assigned to cover the operation on the Lozovaya-Barvenkovo-Slavyansk sector but it had not fully appreciated the threat from Kramatorsk, where a massive offensive force of German armoured and motorized troops was in the final stages of concentration for attack.

On the morning of May 17, eleven German divisions in Kleist's Army Group struck from the Slavyansk-Kramatorsk area against the 9th and 57th armies of the Southern Front. The defences crumbled and in two days the enemy broke out on the flank of the left wing of the South-Western Front in the Petrovsky area.

That evening, Vasilevsky, who was temporarily in charge of the General Staff owing to Shaposhnikov's illness, contacted the 57th Army's chief of staff General Anisov, who reported that the situation was critical.

Vasilevsky immediately passed this information to the Supreme Commander and proposed halting the South-Western Front's offensive and diverting part of its shock force to eliminate the threat from Kramatorsk. This was the only way of saving the situation because the Supreme Command had no reserves in the area.

Stalin did not like changing his decisions. After a talk with Timoshenko he told the Chief of General Staff: "...the measures taken by the sector command are quite sufficient to repel the enemy's thrust at the Southern Front. The South-Western Front will therefore continue its offensive..."

On May 18 the situation on the South-Western Front suddenly deteriorated. The General Staff once again suggested halting the offensive operation around Kharkov and turning the main forces of the Barvenkovo strike force to liquidate the enemy breakthrough and restore the position of the Southern Front's 9th Army.

That day I was present at General Headquarters during a conversation Stalin had with the Commander of the South-Western Front. I clearly remember that the Supreme Commander made it quite plain to Timoshenko that he was deeply disturbed by the enemy's successes in the Kramatorsk area.

Towards evening on May 18 he discussed the problem with Khrushchev, the South-Western Front's Military Council member, who expressed the same ideas as the Front Command: the threat from the enemy's Kramatorsk group had been greatly exaggerated and there was no reason to halt the operation. On the basis of these reports from the Military Council of the South-Western Front on the need to continue the offensive, the Supreme Commander rejected the arguments of the General Staff. The existing version that the Military Councils of the Southern and South-Western Fronts sent warnings to General Headquarters does not correspond to the facts. I can testify to this because I was present during the Supreme Commander's conversations.

On May 19 the situation on the South-Western sector became catastrophic. The enemy's strike force broke through into the rear of the Soviet troops. And only at this juncture was the order given to halt our offensive on Kharkov and turn the main forces of the Barvenkovo strike force against Kleist's armies. But it was too late.

On May 23, the 6th and 57th armies, part of the 9th Army and General Bobkin's operations group were encircled. Many units succeeded in breaking out, but for some it was impossible and, refusing to surrender, they fought to the last drop of blood. General Kostenko, a hero of the Civil and Patriotic wars, the Front's Deputy Commander and former Commander of the 19th Manych Regiment of the 4th Don Cossack Division, was killed in these engagements. General Podlas, Commander of the 57th Army, and General Bobkin, Commander of the operations group, also lost their lives. I had studied with them on refresher courses for senior commanders. They were splendid officers and true sons of our Party and the Motherland.

If one analyzes the course of the Kharkov operation, it is not difficult to see that the main reason for our defeat lay in the underestimation of the serious threat posed by the South-Western strategic direction, where the necessary Supreme Command reserves had not been concentrated.

If a few reserve armies had been marshalled in readiness on the operational rear lines of the South-Western sector, the disaster would never have occurred.

In June fierce battles continued along the whole South-Western sector. Our outnumbered forces were compelled to pull back beyond the River Oskol and attempt to consolidate on the rear lines.

On June 28 the enemy launched offensive operations on a broader scale. From the Kursk area he struck in the direction of Voronezh, at the 13th and 40th armies of the Bryansk Front. On June 30 the German 6th Army pounced on Ostrogozhsk and pierced the defences of the 21st and 28th armies. The position of our troops on the Voronezh sector substantially deteriorated and some of them were encircled.

This is how Marshal Vasilevsky assesses the situation in his memoirs.

"The situation on the Voronezh sector deteriorated rapidly at the end of July 2. The defences at the junction of the Bryansk and South-Western Fronts had been torn open to a depth of 80 km. The Front's reserves on this sector were thrown into the fighting. There was a clear danger of the enemy's strike force breaking through to the Don and capturing Voronezh. To prevent this the Supreme Command gave Lieutenant-General Golikov, the Commander of the Bryansk Front, two field armies from its reserve (the 6th and the 60th.— *G. Zh.*), ordering him to deploy them along the right bank of the Don between Zadonsk and Pavlovsk and to take charge of combat operations in the Voronezh area.

"At the same time the 5th Tank Army was placed at the disposal of this Front. Together with the Front's tank formations it was to launch a counterattack at the flank and rear of the Nazi forces attacking Voronezh. In the early hours of July 3 the corps of the 5th Tank Army completed their concentration on the south of the River Yelets. An immediate and decisive thrust at the enemy driving towards Voronezh could have changed the situation sharply in our favour, particularly as his main forces had suffered considerable losses, were extended over a broad front and engaged in heavy fighting with our troops.

"But the tank army received no instructions from the Front Command. On orders from the Supreme Command I had to go at once to the Yelets area to speed up the commitment of the tank army to action. Before leaving, I telegraphed orders to the army commander and the Commander of the Bryansk Front to prepare at once to launch a counterattack."

Despite the massive support given by the Supreme Command and the General Staff, the situation on the Bryansk

Front grew worse day by day. This process was aggravated considerably by the defects in troop control at front and army level. In view of this, the Supreme Command took organizational measures to divide the Bryansk Front into two. Vatutin was put in command of the new, Voronezh Front, and Rokossovsky was sent to replace Golikov as Commander of the Bryansk Front.

The 6th and 60th field armies and the 5th Tank Army took part in the fighting in the Voronezh area and this somewhat stabilized the defence, but it did not eliminate the grave danger of a breakthrough across the Don and a thrust along the Don in the direction of Stalingrad.

As a result of the loss of the Crimea, the defeat in the Barvenkovo area, in the Donbas and at Voronezh, the enemy again seized the strategic initiative, brought up fresh reserves and advanced rapidly towards the Volga and the Caucasus. By mid-July the enemy had driven back our troops across the Don between Voronezh and Kletskaya and from Surovikino to Rostov and were fighting in the great bend of the Don in an attempt to break through to Stalingrad.

The forced withdrawal of our troops gave the enemy control of the richest regions of the Don and the Donbas and created a direct threat to the Volga and the North Caucasus. We were in danger of losing the Kuban area and all communications with the Caucasus, the crucial economic region that kept the army and industry supplied with oil.

On July 28, 1942, People's Commissar for Defence Stalin published Order No. 227. This order introduced severe measures to deal with panic-mongers and violators of discipline and resolutely condemned "defeatist" tendencies. It stated that the iron rule for the troops must be "not one step back!" The order was reinforced by intensive party-political work.

In June 1942, the Party's Central Committee reviewed the state of political work in the Red Army and drew up measures for its further improvement. The Central Committee demanded that the political agencies should step up political education among the troops. All commanders and political workers, including the senior ranks, were instructed to conduct agitation and propaganda personally among the men. Analysis of the results of political work among the troops was improved.

Better organizers were put in charge of this important and difficult work. Mekhlis was replaced as head of the Main Political Administration of the Red Army by A. S. Shcherbakov, an alternate member of the Political Bureau, and a secretary of the Party's Central Committee and its Moscow Committee. Capable political workers who had given a good account of themselves in the active Army were brought into the Main Political Administration. Conferences of members of Military Councils and the chiefs of the political agencies of the Army and Navy were addressed by Central Committee secretaries M. I. Kalinin, E. M. Yaroslavsky, D. Z. Manuilsky and many other prominent statesmen and party people.

The Central Committee required the Military Councils of the Fronts and armies to improve their work among the soldiers and officers in order to tighten up discipline, and strengthen the troops' steadiness and fighting ability. Communists and Komsomol members were specially mobilized. The influx of Communists into the active Army stiffened the morale of our armed forces. Prominent propagandists regularly visited the units that were engaged in the fiercest fighting.

Above all, the Germans had to be denied access to the Volga. The Supreme Command set up a new, Stalingrad Front, comprising the 62nd Army under the command of Major-General V. Y. Kolpakchi, the 63rd Army commanded by Lieutenant-General V. I. Kuznetsov, the 64th Army commanded by Lieutenant-General V. I. Chuikov, and also the 21st Army under Major-General A. I. Danilov, which was made up of units from the disbanded South-Western Front.

The Military Council of the former South-Western Front was transferred intact to the newly-formed Stalingrad Front. The Front was strengthened with the recently-formed 1st and 4th Tank armies and the surviving units of the 28th, 38th and 57th armies. The Volga Naval Flotilla was also made subordinate to the Front Command as a task force.

Defence lines and fortified areas were energetically prepared on the approaches to Stalingrad. As at Moscow, thousands of citizens came out to build fortifications and laboured devotedly to prepare the city for defence.

The Stalingrad Regional and City Party Committees did a lot to recruit and train people's volunteers and workers' self-defence detachments, to reorganize production for the needs of the Front, and to evacuate children and old people, as well as state valuables.

By July 17 the Stalingrad Front was positioned on the following defence line: Pavlovsk-on-Don, and further along the bank of the Don to Serafimovich, then Kletskaya through Surovikino and as far as Verkhne-Kurmoyarskaya.

During the retreat the Southern Front had suffered heavy losses. Its four armies numbered only a little more than one hundred thousand men. To strengthen troop control on the North-Caucasian sector, the Supreme Command abolished the Southern Front and transferred what remained of its forces to the North-Caucasian Front, which was placed under the command of Marshal S. M. Budenny.

The 37th and 12th armies of the North-Caucasian Front were given the task of covering the Stavropol sector, and the 18th, 56th and 47th armies, that of covering the Krasnodar sector.

At the end of July and the beginning of August the development of events on the North-Caucasian sector was clearly not in our favour. The enemy's superior forces were pushing stubbornly forward and German troops soon reached the River Kuban.

In August fierce battles also developed on the Maikop sector. Enemy forces captured Maikop on August 10 and Krasnodar on the 11th.

In mid-August the enemy occupied Mozdok and broke through to the River Terek. By September 9 the Soviet 46th Army had been dislodged and enemy forces were in possession of nearly all the mountain passes. The city of Sukhumi was seriously threatened.

In these testing days the peoples of the Caucasus did not waver or lose faith in the strength and viability of the Soviet multinational state.

The Party organizations of Georgia, Armenia and Azerbaijan undertook to supply and service the armies in the field; armed detachments were formed and volunteers poured into the ranks of the Red Army. These measures made it possible to consolidate the Fronts. The Nazis' calculation that when their troops arrived the peoples of the Caucasus would break away from the Soviet Union proved unfounded.

The army in the field was greatly helped by the partisan detachments of Caucasian mountaineers, who knew the country well, every pass and trail across the mountains. Their daring raids sowed fear among the enemy and caused them substantial losses.

By July 22 the Stalingrad Front comprised 38 divisions. Of these only 16 divisions (the 63rd and 62nd armies, two divisions of the 64th Army, and one division each from the 4th and 1st Tank armies) were able to occupy the defensive positions in the main zone. They were confronted by the German 6th Army, which at that time possessed 18 fully manned and equipped divisions. The balance of forces was in the enemy's favour with advantages of 20% in manpower, 100% in tanks, and 260% in aircraft. Only in artillery and mortars were the forces more or less equal.[1]

Subsequently, thanks to the stubborn resistance of our troops on the approaches to Stalingrad the enemy was forced to bring up the 4th Panzer Army from the Caucasian sector for their attack from Kotelnikovo, and to deploy additional forces from the satellite armies.

According to the Wehrmacht High Command's Directive No. 45, of July 23, 1942, Army Group B, shielded in the north along the middle reaches of the Don (where Hungarian, Italian and Romanian troops were being deployed), was to sweep forward and capture Stalingrad and Astrakhan, then consolidate on the Volga, thus cutting off the Caucasus from the centre of the Soviet Union. Support for this operation was to be provided by the main forces of the 4th Air Fleet (1,200 combat aircraft).

On July 26, armoured and motorized German forces broke through the defences of the 62nd Army and reached the Kamensky area. To counter this breakthrough, the Supreme Command immediately ordered into battle the 1st and 4th Tank armies, which were still being formed and had only 240 tanks and two

---

[1] *A History of the Second World War, 1939-1945*, Vol. 5, p. 161.

infantry divisions. These armies were unable to halt the enemy's advance but did to some extent delay it.

Of course, the engaging of units that were still in the process of formation can not be considered correct but at that time the Supreme Command had no alternative, because the routes to Stalingrad were poorly protected.

Heavy fighting also ensued along the front line of the 64th Army, but the enemy could not take Stalingrad on the march in this sector either.

Savage fighting continued through the first half of August on the approaches to Stalingrad. Our forces clung to their defence lines and fought valiantly for every inch of ground, launching counterattacks and wearing down and depleting the enemy troops which were driving towards Stalingrad.

In view of the fact that the forces of the Stalingrad Front were spread out over a distance of 700 kilometres and were experiencing difficulty in troop control, the Supreme Command decided to divide the Front into two: the Stalingrad and the South-Eastern Fronts. This was done on August 5.

The Stalingrad Front remained under the command of Lieutenant-General V. N. Gordov, who had replaced Marshal Timoshenko. His chief of staff was Major-General Nikishev. The Front comprised the 63rd, 21st and 62nd armies, and the 4th Tank Army, and also the 16th Air Army, which was being formed under the command of Major-General S. I. Rudenko.

The South-Eastern Front was made up of the 57th, 51st, 64th and the 1st Guards armies, and the 8th Air Army. Colonel-General A. I. Yeremenko was appointed Front Commander.

On August 12, the State Committee for Defence commissioned Colonel-General Vasilevsky, Chief of General Staff, to coordinate troop actions at Stalingrad. Operationally, the Stalingrad Front was subordinated to the Commander of the South-Eastern Front.

On August 23, after many days of bitter fighting the enemy's 14th Panzer Corps broke through near Vertyachi and, having split the Stalingrad defence in two, reached the Volga in the Latoshinka-Rynok area. The 62nd Army was cut off from the main forces of the Stalingrad Front and had to be transferred to the South-Eastern Front.

German bombers made savage raids on Stalingrad, reducing the city to rubble, killing the civilian population and destroying industrial enterprises, art treasures and other objects of cultural value.

On the morning of August 24, part of the forces of the enemy's 14th Panzer Corps struck in the direction of the Tractor Works, but failed to achieve its objective. Armed workers from the Stalingrad factories took part in the bitter fighting in this sector.

At the same time the forces of the Stalingrad Front, which had withdrawn to the north-west, attacked southwards and forced the enemy to divert considerable forces that had been assigned to capture Stalingrad. This manoeuvre took much of the punch out of the enemy's attack on the city. His 14th Panzer Corps was cut off from its support services and for several days had to rely on supplies flown in by air.

Having ferried his main forces across the Don, the enemy developed a vigorous offensive backed up by massive air attacks.

By August 30 the troops of the South-Eastern Front had been forced by the enemy's superior numbers to withdraw to the outer and then the inner defence line. The 62nd and 64th armies manned the defences along a line running from Rynok through Orlovka, Gumrak and Peschanka to Ivanovka. At that time the 62nd Army was commanded by Lieutenant-General A. I. Lopatin. He did all that his duty as a soldier demanded of him, and more, since he was well aware that his army was outnumbered by the enemy. From September 10, 1942, the 62nd Army was commanded by Lieutenant-General Chuikov.

During this critical period the Supreme Command launched various separate offensive operations to tie down the enemy's reserves and prevent them from being brought up to the Stalingrad area.

On the Western Front, of which I was then in command, events took the following course. At the beginning of July, on the Front's left wing, the 10th, 16th and 61st armies attacked from the Kirov-Bolkhov area towards Bryansk. In August, on the right wing, in the Pogoreloye Gorodishche area, the reinforced 20th Army in cooperation with the left wing of the Kalinin Front launched a successful offensive with the objective

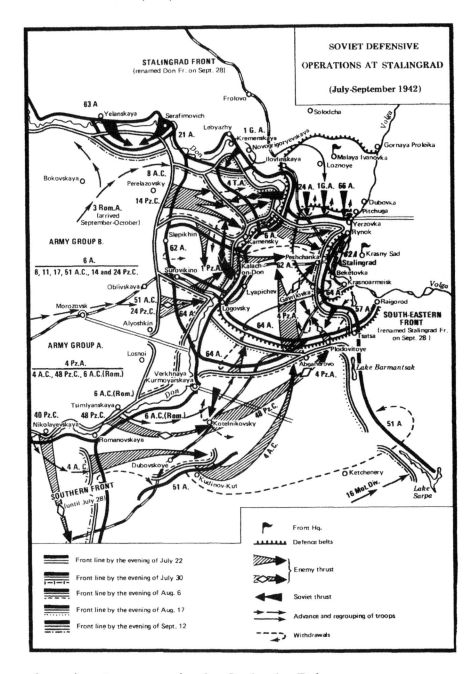

SOVIET DEFENSIVE

OPERATIONS AT STALINGRAD

(July-September 1942)

Front line by the evening of July 22
Front line by the evening of July 30
Front line by the evening of Aug. 6
Front line by the evening of Aug. 17
Front line by the evening of Sept. 12

Front Hq.
Defence belts
Enemy thrust
Soviet thrust
Advance and regrouping of troops
Withdrawals

of routing the enemy in the Sychevka-Rzhev area.

After piercing the German defences and reaching the Rzhev-Vyazma railway the Western Front's offensive was checked. The Kalinin Front failed to reach its objective and the city of Rzhev remained in enemy hands.

In the Pogoreloye Gorodishche-Sychevka area the enemy suffered heavy losses. To parry the Western Front's successful thrust, the Nazi Command had to rush in several divisions intended for the Stalingrad and Caucasus offensives.

The German General Kurt Tippelskirch writes on this point: "A breakthrough was prevented only when three panzer and several infantry divisions that had been about to move to the Southern Front were detained and thrown into the battle, first to localize the breakthrough and then to counterattack."[1]

With one or perhaps two more armies at our disposal we could have combined with the Kalinin Front under General I. S. Konev and defeated the enemy not only in the Rzhev area but the entire Rzhev-Vyazma German force and substantially improved the operational situation in the whole Western strategic direction. Unfortunately, this real opportunity was missed by the Supreme Command.

On the whole, I must say that the Supreme Commander realized that the unfavourable situation that developed in the summer of 1942 was due in part to his own personal mistake in endorsing the plan of action by Soviet forces in that year's summer campaign. And he did not seek any other guilty party among the leaders in General Headquarters or the General Staff.

On August 27, 1942, when I was in the Pogoreloye Gorodishche area, where we were in the midst of our offensive, I received a phone call from A. N. Poskrebyshev. He told me that the day before, August 26, the State Defence Committee had reviewed the situation in the south of the country and decided to appoint me Deputy Supreme Commander.

Poskrebyshev warned me to be at my command post at 14:00, in readiness to receive a phone call from Stalin. Poskrebyshev was a man of very few words, and the only thing he would say in answer to all my questions on this occasion was: "I don't know. I suppose he will tell you himself." But even from these words I realized that the State Defence Committee was deeply concerned about the outcome of the struggle at Stalingrad.

Soon Stalin came through on the HF line. After asking about the situation on the Western Front, he said: "You must come to

---

[1] K. Tippelskirch, *A History of the Second World War*, Moscow, 1956, p. 241 (retranslated from the Russian).

General Headquarters as soon as possible. Leave your chief of staff in charge of things. And think who we can appoint in your place."

The conversation ended there. Stalin said nothing about making me Deputy Supreme Commander. Apparently he wanted to tell me that in person. In general, the Supreme Commander spoke on the telephone only of matters that had to be dealt with at that particular moment. He also expected us to be extremely careful about what we said on the telephone, particularly in combat areas, where there was no stationary coding equipment.

I set off for Moscow without calling at Front headquarters.

It was late evening when I arrived in the Kremlin. Stalin was working in his office. Several members of the State Defence Committee were there with him.

The Supreme Commander said that things were going badly in the south and the Germans might take Stalingrad. The situation in the North Caucasus was no better. He then told me that the State Defence Committee had decided to appoint me Deputy Supreme Commander and send me to the Stalingrad area. Vasilevsky, Malenkov and Malyshev were there already.

"Malenkov will remain with you, but Vasilevsky must return to Moscow. When can you take off?" he asked me.

I replied that I should need twenty-four hours to study the situation and should be able to fly to Stalingrad on the 29th.

"Well, that's good. But aren't you hungry?" Stalin asked suddenly. "A little refreshment wouldn't do us any harm."

Tea and a dozen or so sandwiches were brought in. Over tea Stalin gave us a brief report on the situation as of 20:00 hrs on August 27. After summing up what had happened at Stalingrad, he said that the Supreme Command had decided to reinforce the Stalingrad Front with the 24th and 1st Guards armies and the 66th Army.

"In view of the grave situation at Stalingrad," he told us, "we have ordered the immediate transfer of the 1st Guards Army, under Moskalenko, to the Loznoye area, and on the morning of September 2 to use it and other units of the Stalingrad Front to counterattack the enemy forces that have broken through to the Volga, and join up with the 62nd Army. At the same time General Malinovsky's 66th Army and General

Kozlov's 24th Army are being transferred to the Stalingrad Front.

"You must see to it that the 1st Guards Army under General Moskalenko counterattacks on September 2 and use this as a cover for bringing up the 24th and 66th armies to their starting positions," he said to me. "Those two armies must be brought into action without delay. Otherwise we shall lose Stalingrad."

It was clear that the forthcoming battle was of the utmost military and political importance. With the fall of Stalingrad, the enemy command would be able to cut off the south of the country from the centre. We might also lose the Volga, the country's most important waterway, which carried a constant flow of goods from the Volga area and the Caucasus.

The Supreme Command was sending to Stalingrad everything it could possibly spare at the time. Only the newly-formed strategic reserves, intended for the further operations, had not yet been committed to action. Urgent measures were being taken to boost the production of aircraft, tanks, guns, ammunition and other equipment, so that they would be available in time to defeat the enemy forces concentrated in this area.

We took off from Moscow's Central Airport on August 29 and landed four hours later on an airstrip in the Kamyshin area on the Volga. I was met by Vasilevsky, who at once briefed me on the latest events. After a short discussion we drove to the headquarters of the Stalingrad Front, at Maloye Ivanovo.

It was about noon when we reached our destination.

Lieutenant-General Gordov was out on the forward positions. Chief of Staff Nikishev and Operations Chief Rukhle reported on the situation. From what they said I had the impression they were not quite sure that the enemy could be stopped in the Stalingrad area.

I called up the headquarters of the 1st Guards Army, where General Gordov was at the time, and told him to wait for us at the HQ of Army Commander Moskalenko where Vasilevsky and I intended to go.

Gordov and Moskalenko were at the command post when we arrived. We were much encouraged by their reports and by the generals themselves. We felt that both of them were well aware of the enemy's strength and the potential of their own troops.

After discussing the situation and the condition of our units, we concluded that the armies that were being concentrated for the counterattack could not be ready before September 6. I reported this at once to the Supreme Commander on the HF line. He listened to what I had to say and replied that he had no objections.

Vasilevsky had been ordered to return immediately to Moscow, and, if I remember rightly, he took off from Stalingrad on September 1.

The Supreme Command had set the date for the attack by the 1st Guards Army as September 2. But it could not be carried out on that day. Owing to lack of fuel and the long distances involved, its troops did not reach their starting positions by the morning of September 2. At General Moskalenko's request I postponed the attack till the 3rd. In my report to General Headquarters I stated:

"The 1st Guards Army could not launch its offensive on September 2 because the units had not yet reached their starting positions, brought up their ammunition and fuel and organized for battle. To avoid a disorganized start to the attack and consequent unnecessary losses, I decided after a personal on-the-spot investigation to postpone the attack until 05:00 hrs on September 3.

"I have set the offensive of the 24th and 66th armies for September 5 or 6. At the moment the whole command is engaged in drawing up detailed objectives. We are also taking steps to ensure material support for the operation..."

On the morning of September 3, after an artillery preparation, troops of the 1st Guards Army passed over to the offensive but were unable to advance more than a few kilometres in the direction of Stalingrad, and did the enemy little damage. Their further advance was halted by constant air attacks and counterattacks by enemy infantry and armour, supported by artillery from the Stalingrad area.

On September 3, I received a telegram signed by Stalin. "Situation at Stalingrad worsened. Enemy about three versts from the city. Stalingrad may fall today or tomorrow, unless northern group renders immediate assistance. Demand of commanders of armies north and north-west of Stalingrad to attack enemy immediately and help Stalingraders. There must be no delay. At this moment delay is criminal. Send all air forces to Stalingrad's aid. There are hardly any aircraft left in Stalingrad."

I called up the Supreme Commander at once and reported that I could order the attack to begin the next morning but the troops of all three armies would be forced to start fighting with almost no ammunition, because supplies could be brought up to the artillery positions only on September 4. Moreover, coordination of artillery, tanks and aircraft could not be organized before the date, and without such coordination nothing would be achieved.

"You think the enemy will wait for you to get organized?... Yeremenko says the enemy can take Stalingrad in one push unless you strike at once from the north."

I replied that I did not share this view and requested permission to begin the general offensive on the 5th, as planned. As for air support, I would give orders at once for a total bombing effort against the enemy.

"Very well," the Supreme Commander agreed. "If the enemy starts a general offensive against the city, you must attack at once, even if you are not fully prepared. Your main task now is to divert the German forces from Stalingrad and, if possible, wipe out the corridor separating the Stalingrad and South-Eastern Fronts."

As we had expected, nothing special occurred around Stalingrad before the morning of September 5. At 3 a.m. the Supreme Commander called Malenkov and asked whether the troops of the Stalingrad Front were ready for the offensive. Having assured himself that his order was being carried out, he did not call me to the telephone.

At dawn on September 5, the preparatory artillery and air bombardment began all along the front of the 24th, 1st Guards and 66th armies. But even on the main lines of advance the density of the artillery fire was not great and did not yield the necessary results.

The attack began after Katyusha volleys. I watched it from the observation post of the 1st Guards Army headquarters.

From the intensity of the fire that met our attacking troops it was clear that the artillery preparation had failed to yield the required results, and that no deep penetration of the enemy's lines could be expected.

An hour or two later the reports coming in from the army commanders showed that in several sectors the enemy's fire had halted our advance and his infantry and tanks were counterattacking. Air reconnaissance had detected a northward movement of large enemy groups of tanks, artillery and motorized infantry from the Gumrak-Orlovka-Bolshaya Ros-soshka area. Enemy aircraft appeared and started bombing our formations. In the afternoon fresh enemy forces entered the battle and in some sectors our troops were pushed back to their starting lines.

The intense firing lasted all day and died down only towards evening. We summed up the results. After a day's battle our units had advanced not more than between two and four kilometres and the 24th Army was still not far from its initial positions.

In the evening the troops received additional supplies of shells, mines and other ammunition. In view of the information about the enemy gained during the day, we decided to prepare during the night for a fresh attack, regrouping our forces as far as was possible.

Late in the evening I had a call from the Supreme Commander.

"How are things going?"

I reported that the day's fighting had been very heavy. North of Stalingrad the enemy had been forced to throw in fresh forces brought up from the Gumrak area.

"That's good. It will divert the enemy's forces from Stalingrad."

I went on: "Our units have made insignificant advances, and in a number of cases are still on their starting lines."

"Why's that?"

"Our troops did not have time to prepare the offensive, carry out artillery reconnaissance and uncover the enemy's fire system. So naturally we could not neutralize the enemy fire. When we launched our attack, the enemy stopped it with fire and counterattacks. What's more, the enemy has had command of the air all day and has bombed our troops continuously."

"Keep up your attacks," Stalin ordered. "The main objective is to divert as many enemy forces as possible from Stalingrad."

The next day the fighting was resumed with even greater ferocity. All through the night of September 5 our air force bombed the enemy. In addition to the Front's aircraft, the long-range air force under Lieutenant-General A. E. Golovanov was thrown into the battle.

During the day we repeated our attack but once again it was repelled. During September 6 the enemy brought up new units from the Stalingrad area. On a number of commanding heights they had dug in their tanks and self-propelled guns and set up well-organized strong points, which could be smashed only by powerful artillery fire. But this we were still lacking.

On September 7, I was approached in the afternoon by Colonel Rukhle, Operations Chief of the Stalingrad Front.

"The Supreme Commander wants to know if you have enough forces to defeat the enemy?"

In the hope that a transfer of some forces from General Vatutin's Voronezh Front might put things right we sent the following reply:

"The forces available here are clearly insufficient for the defeat of the enemy at Stalingrad. Additional forces must be concentrated, so that a more powerful blow can be struck at the enemy as soon as possible..."

But the Supreme Command did not come up with any decision to transfer additional divisions. The third and fourth days of battle consisted mainly of artillery and air battles.

On September 10, after a fresh tour of the units and formations I became even more convinced that we could not pierce the enemy's lines or eliminate the corridor with the forces available and without regrouping. Generals Gordov, Moskalenko, Malinovsky and Kozlov were of the same opinion.

The same day I reported to the Supreme Commander:

"With the forces at the disposal of the Stalingrad Front we shall not be able to penetrate the corridor and join up with the troops of the South-Eastern Front in the city. The

Germans' defence front has been considerably strengthened by reinforcements brought up from around Stalingrad. Further attacks with the same forces in the same order will be pointless, and our troops will inevitably suffer heavy losses. Additional forces and time to regroup are needed for a more concentrated thrust by the Stalingrad Front. The armies' attacks lack the capability to overturn the enemy."

Stalin replied that it would not be a bad idea if I came to Moscow to report in person on these matters.

I took off for Moscow during the day on September 12 and four hours later was in the Kremlin. Stalin had also summoned the Chief of General Staff Vasilevsky. Vasilevsky reported on the movement of new enemy forces towards Stalingrad from the Kotelnikovo area, on the fighting that was going at Novorossiisk, and also on the fighting on the Grozny sector.

The Supreme Commander listened attentively and then summed up:

"They want to grab the oil at Grozny at any price. Now let's see what Zhukov has to say."

I repeated what I had said two days before on the telephone. I said that the 24th, 1st Guards and 66th armies that had taken part in the offensive from September 5 to 11 had shown themselves to be efficient fighting formations. Their basic weakness was the shortage of reinforcements. They were short of howitzers and tanks necessary for a direct support of the infantry.

The terrain was very unfavourable for offensive action by our troops. It was bare and cut by deep ravines, where the enemy could easily protect himself against our fire. With the commanding heights that he had captured he could maintain long-range artillery observation and manoeuvre his fire in all directions. He was also able to conduct long-range artillery fire from the Kuzmichi-Akatovka-Opytnoye Pole state farm area. Under these conditions the 24th, 1st Guards and 66th armies could not break through the enemy's defence.

"What does the Stalingrad Front need to be able to eliminate the enemy's corridor and link up with the South-Eastern Front?" Stalin asked.

"At least one more full-strength field army, a tank corps, three tank brigades, and not less than 400 howitzers. Added to that, not less than one air army must be concentrated in the area for the whole operation."

Vasilevsky gave my estimate his full support.

The Supreme Commander brought out his map showing the Supreme Command reserves and subjected it to a long and careful scrutiny. Vasilevsky and I moved away from the table and spoke very quietly to each other about the need to seek some other solution.

"What 'other' solution?" Stalin asked, raising his head suddenly.

I had never imagined Stalin had such a keen ear. We came back to the table.

"Now look here," Stalin said, "you had better go to the General Staff and think out what has to be done in the Stalingrad area. What troops should be moved in to strengthen the Stalingrad concentration and where from, and also give some thought to the Caucasian Front. Tomorrow we shall meet here again at nine in the evening."

Vasilevsky and I spent all the next day working at the General Staff. We concentrated on the possibility of a large-scale operation that would enable us to avoid squandering our prepared and half-prepared reserves on isolated operations. In October we should be completing the formation of the strategic reserves. By that time our industry would have substantially increased its output of the latest types of aircraft and of ammunition for the artillery.

After discussing all the possible options, we decided to offer Stalin the following plan of action: first, continue to wear down the enemy by an active defence; second, prepare for a counter-offensive that would hit the enemy in the Stalingrad area hard enough to radically change the strategic situation in the south of the country in our favour.

As for the specific plan of the counter-offensive, we could not, of course, work out all the details in one day, but we clearly saw that the main blows must be struck at the flanks of the Stalingrad concentration, which was covered by Romanian troops.

A preliminary calculation indicated that the necessary forces and weapons for the counter-offensive could not be assembled before the middle of November. In our assessment of the enemy we worked on the assumption that Nazi Germany was no longer capable of executing its strategic plan for 1942. The resources it had at its disposal in the autumn of 1942 were not sufficient to achieve its objectives in the North Caucasus or the Don and Volga areas.

The forces the Nazi Command could use in the Caucasus and in the Stalingrad area had been substantially weakened and depleted. The Germans had nothing more of any weight to throw into this theatre and they would undoubtedly be compelled, as after the defeat at Moscow, to take up defensive positions on all sectors.

We knew that von Paulus' 6th Army and Hoth's 4th Panzer Army, the most efficient fighting units in the Wehrmacht, had been drawn into prolonged and exhausting battles at Stalingrad and could not complete the operation for the capture of the city; they were stuck on the approaches.

In the mortal struggle on the outskirts of Stalingrad and later, in the city itself, the Soviet forces suffered terrible losses and lacked the manpower to defeat the enemy. But we were completing the preparation of massive strategic reserves, armed with the newest weapons and combat equipment. By November the Supreme Command would have mechanized and armoured formations equipped with the highly effective and manoeuvrable T-34 tanks, which would allow us to set our troops more exacting targets.

In addition to this, during the first period of the war our senior command personnel had learned much and revised their views about many things. In the rigorous school of struggle with a powerful enemy they had mastered the art of operational and tactical warfare. In the course of many ferocious engagements the command and political staff and the men of the Red Army had hardened themselves and assimilated the means and methods of combat in any situation.

On the basis of information from the Fronts the General Staff had studied strong and weak points of the German, Hungarian, Italian and Romanian forces. Compared with the Germans, the troops of the satellites were not so well armed, less experienced and less efficient, even in defence. Above all, their soldiers, and many of their officers, had no desire to die for interests alien to them in far-away Russia, to which they had been sent by Hitler, Mussolini, Antonescu, Horthy and other fascist leaders.

The enemy's position was further complicated by the fact that they had very few operational reserves in the Volga and the Don area — not more than six divisions, and these were scattered over a broad front. They could not be assembled as a strike force at short notice. We were also favoured by the operational configuration of the whole enemy front. Our troops were in an enveloping position and could with comparative ease strike out from their bridgeheads at Serafimovich and Kletskaya.

After making this analysis, we were ready to report to the Supreme Commander.

In the evening Vasilevsky called Stalin and told him we were ready to appear, as instructed, at 21:00. Stalin said he was still busy and would receive us at 22:00. At 22:00 we were in his office.

Shaking hands, he said indignantly: "Tens, hundreds of thousands of Soviet people are giving their lives in the struggle against fascism, and Churchill is haggling over twenty Hurricanes. And their Hurricanes are no good, our pilots don't like that plane..." Then without more ado, in a completely calm voice he said: "Well, what have you thought up? Who's going to report?"

"Whoever you say," Vasilevsky replied. "We're both of the same opinion."

Stalin came up to look at our map.

"What have you got there?"

"This is a preliminary outline of a plan for a counter-offensive in the Stalingrad area," Vasilevsky explained.

"What are those concentrations around Serafimovich?"

"That's a new front. It will have to be created to strike a powerful blow at the operational rear of the enemy in the Stalingrad area."

"Have you enough forces now for such a big operation?"

I reported that according to our calculations the operation could be provided with the necessary support and thoroughly prepared within forty-five days.

"Wouldn't it be better to confine ourselves to a thrust from north to south and another from south to north, along the Don?" Stalin asked.

"No, that would allow the Germans to swing round their armoured divisions from Stalingrad and parry our blows. A blow west of the Don will prevent the enemy from making any rapid manoeuvre or bringing up reserves to meet our groupings because of the water obstacle."

"Aren't you taking your strike forces too far?"

Vasilevsky and I explained that the operation would be divided into two main stages: (1) penetration of the defence and encirclement of the Stalingrad concentration of German forces and the creation of a reliable outer front to isolate the encircled enemy from external forces and (2) destruction of the encircled enemy and blocking of all attempts to relieve him.

"We shall have to give the plan further consideration and count up our resources," said the Supreme Commander. "At present the main task is to hold Stalingrad and prevent the enemy from advancing on Kamyshin."

Poskrebyshev came in and reported that Yeremenko was on the phone.

After his telephone conversation the Supreme Commander said: "Yeremenko reports that the enemy is bringing tank units up to the city. Tomorrow we must expect a fresh attack. Give orders to have Rodimtsev's 13th Guards Division sent across the Volga immediately and see what else you can send across tomorrow," he told Vasilevsky.

Turning to me, he went on: "Call up Gordov and Golovanov and tell them to launch air attacks at once. Gordov must attack first thing in the morning to tie down the enemy. You yourself must fly back to the troops of the Stalingrad Front and study the situation in the Kletskaya and Serafimovich areas. In a few days Vasilevsky will have to fly out to see Yeremenko on the South-Eastern Front and study the situation on his left wing. We shall continue our discussion of the plan later. For the time being no one else is to know what we have discussed here."

An hour later I took off for the headquarters of the Stalingrad Front.

September 13, 14, and 15 were difficult, far too difficult days for the people of Stalingrad. Regardless of everything, the enemy pressed forward step by step through the ruins of the city towards the Volga. At any moment, it seemed, our troops would crack under the strain. But as soon as the enemy made a rush, our valiant men of the 62nd and 64th armies met them with point-blank fire. The ruins of the city were turned into a fortress. But every day, every hour our forces grew less.

The turning-point in these grave and what seemed at times final hours was brought about by Rodimtsev's 13th Guards Division. It counterattacked as soon as it got across the Volga. Its blow came as a complete surprise to the enemy. On September 16, Rodimtsev's division won back the Mamayev Kurgan. The Stalingraders were helped by air strikes commanded by Golovanov and Rudenko, and also the attacks and artillery bombardments from the north by the troops of the Stalingrad Front against units of the German 8th Army Corps.

Full credit must be given to the men of the 24th, 1st Guards and 66th armies of the Stalingrad Front, the airmen of the 16th Air Army and the long-range air force, who rendered invaluable assistance without counting the cost to the 62nd and 64th armies of the South-Eastern Front in defending Stalingrad.

I can state with full responsibility that but for the persistent counterattacks of the Stalingrad Front and the systematic air strikes, Stalingrad might have endured something far worse.

It is of some interest to note what one of the German officers in von Paulus' army has to say on this point. "At the same time the units of our corps suffered enormous losses in September while repulsing the furious attacks of the enemy who was trying to break through our cut-off positions from the north. Our divisions in this sector were bled white; most of the companies were reduced to between 30 and 40 men."[1]

During a lull, Yeremenko and Khrushchev visited the headquarters of the 1st Guards Army on the orders of the Supreme Commander. Golovanov and I were also present. Yeremenko said he would like to be informed about the situation and discuss the position in Stalingrad. Gordov and Moskalenko gave him all the details and told him about their views.

---

[1] J. Wieder, *Die Tragödie von Stalingrad*, Verlag Buchdruckerei Jos Nothhaft, Deggendorf, 1955, S. 30.

Since the Supreme Commander had warned me to keep the draft plan for a big counter-offensive a strict secret, the conversation centred mainly on the reinforcement of the South-Eastern and Stalingrad Fronts. In reply to Yeremenko's question about a plan for a more powerful counterblow, I promptly answered that the Supreme Command would in the future arrange for a much stronger counter-offensive but that for the time being there were neither the forces nor weapons for such a plan.

At the end of September I was again summoned to Moscow by Stalin for a more detailed discussion of the plan for a counter-offensive. By this time Vasilevsky was back in Moscow after studying the conditions for a counter-offensive by the armies of the left wing of the South-Eastern Front.

Before going to General Headquarters, we got together to exchange impressions.

During the discussion of the situation on the Stalingrad Front's sector the Supreme Commander asked me what I thought of General Gordov. I reported that from the operational point of view Gordov was a skilled general but seemed unable to get along with his staff and commanders.

Stalin said that in that case another commander should be put in charge of the Front. Lieutenant-General Rokossovsky was proposed as a candidate for the post. Vasilevsky supported me. And it was decided straight away that the Stalingrad Front should be renamed the Don Front, and the South-Eastern Front the Stalingrad Front. Rokossovsky was appointed to command the Don Front and his chief of staff was to be Malinin.

Lieutenant-General Vatutin was named as a candidate for the post of Commander of the newly set up South-Western Front. The nucleus for the staff of the South-Western Front was to be the staff of the 1st Guards Army. Moskalenko, the commander of this army, was put in command of the 40th Army.

After a detailed discussion of matters concerned with the plan for a counter-offensive operation, the Supreme Commander turned to me and said:

"You must fly back to the front. Do everything you can to wear down and exhaust the enemy. Have another look at the areas detailed in the plan for the concentration of reserves and

the starting lines for the South-Western Front and the right
wing of the Stalingrad Front, particularly around Serafimovich
and Kletskaya. Comrade Vasilevsky must pay another visit to
the left wing of the South-Eastern Front for the same purpose,
and study all the problems connected with the plan."

After a thorough on-the-spot examination of all the conditions for the counter-offensive Vasilevsky and I returned to
General Headquarters, where the plan was once again discussed and finally approved.

Vasilevsky and I signed the map of the counter-offensive,
and the words "I approve" were added and signed by the Supreme Commander.

Stalin said to Vasilevsky:

"Without disclosing the essence of our plan the Front commanders must be asked for the views on future operations."

I was ordered to instruct the Military Council of the Don
Front personally on the character of the operations to render
all-out assistance to Stalingrad. I clearly remember the conversation I had on September 29 in a dug-out, in a ravine north of
Stalingrad, where Army Commander Moskalenko had his command post.

In response to my instructions to keep up active operations
to prevent the enemy taking troops and weapons from the
Don Front's sector for an assault on Stalingrad, Rokossovsky
said that the Front was very short of men and weapons and
would not be able to achieve any serious results in its sector.
He was right, of course. I shared the same opinion, but without
active assistance the South-Eastern Front (now the Stalingrad
Front) would not be able to hold the city.

On October 1, I returned to Moscow for further work on the
plan of the counter-offensive. The plane that took me from
Stalingrad to Moscow was piloted by Lieutenant-General
Golovanov in person. I gladly joined this experienced pilot
in his cockpit.

Before we reached Moscow I noticed that the plane was
making an unexpected turn and losing height. I decided that
we must have gone off course. After a few minutes, however,
Golovanov steered the plane to land in an unfamiliar locality.
We made a safe landing.

"What made you land here?" I asked Golovanov.

"Thank your lucky stars there was an airfield nearby or we might have crashed."

"What went wrong?"

"Icing."

While we were talking, my own plane taxied up. It had been tailing us and now it took me to the Moscow's Central Airport. Naturally these flights in difficult conditions with hurried take-offs could not always go smoothly.

I clearly recall yet another "air" incident that nearly cost us our lives. It also happened during a flight from Stalingrad to Moscow. The weather was bad and it was raining. Moscow told us that there was mist over the city and visibility was poor. But we had to fly because we had been summoned by the Supreme Commander.

We reached Moscow without mishap but around the city visibility was down to a hundred metres. Flight control radioed the pilot to proceed to a reserve airfield. But that would have meant being late at the Kremlin, where the Supreme Commander was waiting for us.

Taking full responsibility, I ordered pilot E. Smirnov to land at the Central Airport and sat with him in his cockpit. As we flew over Moscow we suddenly saw the top of a factory chimney only 10 or 15 metres from our left wing. I looked at Smirnov. Without batting an eyelid, as they say, he increased his altitude a little and in two or three minutes went in to land.

"It looks as if we were lucky to get out of a situation known as being 'up the chimney'!" I said when we had landed.

"Anything can happen in the air, if the crew ignores the weather conditions," the pilot replied with a grin.

"Yes, it was my fault!" I confessed, and shook his hand.

Smirnov was a fine man and a very experienced pilot. We did more than 130 flying hours together.

In October, by decision of the Supreme Command, more than six full-strength divisions were sent in across the Volga to Stalingrad because there was virtually nothing left of the former 62nd Army except for its staffs and support services. The Don Front was also given reinforcements. The Supreme Command and the General Staff showed special concern for the newly created South-Western Front.

The bitter fighting in the city and the adjoining areas continued. Hitler was urging Army Group B and the Commander of the 6th Army von Paulus to take Stalingrad without further delay.

As I have said, back in September, before the final storming of the city the Nazi Command had replaced the German troops on the flanks with Romanian troops, thus sharply reducing the efficiency of their defences in the Serafimovich area and south of Stalingrad.

In mid-October the enemy launched his new offensive in the hope of putting a final end to Stalingrad. But as before, they encountered a stubborn defence by Soviet troops. The 13th Guards Division under Rodimtsev, the 95th Division under Gorishny, the 37th Guards Division under Zholudev, the 112th Division under Yermolkin, Gorokhov's task force, the 138th Division under Lyudnikov, and Bely's 84th Tank Brigade fought with particular skill and determination.

The street fighting went on day and night, in houses, in the factories, on the bank of the Volga, in fact, everywhere. Our units suffered heavy losses and survived only on small "islands" in the city.

To help the defenders, the troops of the Don Front launched an offensive on October 19. The Germans were forced once again to divert a considerable part of their air force, artillery and tanks from the assault on the city and turn them against the attacking Don Front.

During the same period the 64th Army struck a counterblow from the south in the Kuporosnoye-Zelenaya Polyana area at the flank of the enemy's assault units. The Don Front's offensive and the 64th Army's counterblow made things easier for the hard-pressed 62nd Army and thwarted the enemy's efforts to gain possession of the city. But for the assistance of the Don Front and the 64th Army, the 62nd Army could not have held out and Stalingrad might have fallen to the enemy.

At the beginning of November, the enemy made several attempts to wipe out the remaining centres of defence in the city, and on November 11, when our troops were completing the grandiose preparations for the counter-offensive, they once again attempted to advance, but without success.

By this time the enemy had been reduced to almost total exhaustion. From the interrogation of prisoners it was established that their units and formations were a long way below strength, the moral and political mood of officers as well as men had slumped and few of them believed they would survive these hellish months of fighting.

In the period from July to November, in the battles along the Don and the Volga, and in Stalingrad itself, the enemy had lost 700,000 men, more than a thousand tanks, over two thousand guns and mortars, and nearly 1,400 aircraft. The general operational situation of the German troops in the Volga area had also deteriorated. We have already mentioned that they had no reserves at corps or divisional level, the flanks of Army Group B were covered by troops of inadequate fighting efficiency, who had begun to realize what a hopeless and dangerous situation they were in.

The Soviet forces on the Don were well placed to launch the counter-offensive of the South-Western and Don Fronts. Counterattacking on its own, the 51st Army had knocked the enemy out of the lake defile south of Stalingrad and taken a firm grip on the useful Sarpa-Tsatsa-Barmantsak line. On Vasilevsky's recommendation this area was chosen as the jumping-off ground for the November counter-offensive of the left wing of the Stalingrad Front.

The bitter battles for Stalingrad had lasted for more than three months.

The nations of the world held their breath as they watched this grandiose engagement on the Don, the Volga and in Stalingrad. The successes of the Soviet troops, their courageous struggle with the enemy were putting new heart into all progressive people and inspiring them with confidence in victory over fascism.

The Battle of Stalingrad was a great and testing school of victory for our troops. The commanders and staffs gained invaluable practical experience in organizing cooperation between the infantry, tanks, artillery and aircraft. The armies learned to combine stubborn defence of the city with manoeuvres on the flanks. The morale of our forces had risen substantially and all this, taken together, provided favourable conditions for our counter-offensive.

In mid-November 1942, the defensive battles in the Stalingrad area and the North Caucasus ended the first period of the Great Patriotic War, which stands apart in the life of the Soviet people. This period was extremely difficult for them and their armed forces, especially when Hitler's armies reached the approaches to Moscow and Leningrad, and occupied the Ukraine, leaving behind them a trail of death and destruction.

By November 1942 the enemy forces had occupied a huge slice of Soviet territory, about 1,800,000 square kilometres in area, inhabited by nearly 80 million people before the war. Many millions of Soviet people were caught up in the war, forced to leave their homes and flee eastwards to escape the enemy occupation. The military situation compelled the Soviet forces to retreat far into the interior, suffering considerable losses in men and equipment.

But even in these difficult days our people and armed forces did not lose faith in the possibility of defeating the enemy hordes. The mortal danger rallied them even more closely round the Communist Party and, despite the difficulties, the enemy was finally halted on all sectors.

In those sixteen months the enemy troops on the Soviet-German front encountered stubborn resistance from troops and from civilians in the occupied areas. Their casualties were enormous. By November 1942 these losses amounted to more than two and a half million killed, wounded and missing. And these were the Wehrmacht's crack troops for whom the Nazi Command at the end of the first period in the war had no replacements.

Thanks to the tremendous efforts of the Party and the people, the Soviet forces were kept supplied with modern tanks, aircraft and other equipment. In 1942 more than 21,000 combat aircraft and more than 24,000 tanks came off the production lines, and by the end of the year by decision of the State Defence Committee self-propelled guns went into mass production. The enthusiasm of the troops was backed up by reliable weapons and they were able to fight more efficiently and with substantial results.

The first period of the war, which ended with the Battle of Stalingrad, was a great school of armed struggle with a powerful enemy. The Soviet Supreme Command, the General Staff, the commands and staffs of the troops in the field acquired invaluable experience in organizing and executing active defensive battles and counter-offensive operations.

In the course of the bitter fighting of those days the mass heroism of the Soviet soldiers and the courage of their military leaders, nurtured by the Party of Lenin, showed themselves to the full. An especially positive role was played by the personal example set by Communists and Komsomol members, who, when necessary, sacrificed themselves for the sake of victory. Glorious pages in the chronicle of this period were contributed by the defenders of the Brest Fortress, of Leningrad, Moscow, Odessa, Sebastopol, Stalingrad, Kiev, Novorossiisk, Kerch and the Caucasus.

The first period of the war gave birth to the Soviet Guards. For mass heroism and success in the battles of 1941-1942 the Guards title was awarded to 798 groups, formations, separate units, and fighting ships of the Soviet Armed Forces.

The intense armed struggle entailed a huge expenditure of arms and equipment. Despite the loss of a substantial part of the crucial economic areas, of their factories and mills, our people laboured selflessly to provide the Soviet armies with the necessary means of waging war. By the end of 1942 the country had been turned into a huge military camp. Soviet people saw it as their duty to do everything possible for victory.

The logistic services of the Red Army performed heroic work. In one and a half years of war the railways transported 6,350,000 wagonloads of military supplies. More than 113,000 wagonloads of ammunition, about 60,000 wagonloads of arms and equipment and over 210,000 wagonloads of fuel and lubricants were delivered to armies. The motor units shipped 2,700,000 men, 12,300,000 tons of freight, 1,923 tanks and 3,674 guns in 1942 alone. Military transport aviation moved over 532,000 people, including 158,000 wounded.

The reorganization of the Red Army's logistic services that had been carried out at the beginning of the war proved effective. The correct selection of commanders, political workers and Party organizers in the logistic services ensured close business-like contact with the national economy and efficient utilization of the tremendous resources which were being delivered to the armed forces.

Our young generation must know what an arduous struggle the Soviet people endured in defence of the Motherland. Reading memoirs and works of fiction, one cannot always get the right idea of how experienced and powerful an enemy the Soviet soldiers had to grapple with.

First, then, about the main mass of the German troops — officers and men.

Intoxicated by easy victories over the armies of the countries of Western Europe, their minds poisoned by Goebbels' propaganda, convinced of the possibility of an easy victory over the Red Army and their own superiority over all other peoples, the German troops expected a walk-over when they invaded our country. Particularly militant were younger officers and men who belonged to Nazi organizations and were serving in the tank and air force units. In the first months of the war I had occasion to interrogate prisoners and, I must say, they really believed in all Hitler's adventurist promises.

As for the fighting efficiency of the German officers and men in the first period of the war, their special skills and combat training, it must be acknowledged that they indisputably attained a high standard in all the arms and services, especially in Panzer troops and aviation.

The German soldier knew his job both in battle and on the march; he was persistent, self-assured and disciplined.

After the defeat at Stalingrad, of course, both officers and men lost faith in the promised victory, their morale noticeably declined, and they could no longer compete with the Soviet troops in valour. But on the whole the Soviet soldier was faced with an experienced and powerful enemy, from whom victory would not easily be won.

At all levels the German staff officers were properly trained in modern methods of organizing combat actions, a battle, or an operation. Troop control during operations was effected mainly by radio, with which the Wehrmacht was amply supplied. In battle they showed great persistence in getting the troops to attain their objectives. And they were skilled in organizing air support, whose bombing and strafing often cleared the way for the ground forces.

During the initial period of the war I was quite impressed by the operational staffs of the German armed forces. It was clear that their attacks in all the strategic directions were scrupulously planned and organized. Experienced officers had been chosen to command formations and armies. In a number of cases they correctly estimated the direction, strength and composition of forces for their thrusts, aiming them at weaker sections in our defences. But despite all this, the military and political strategy of Nazi Germany proved adventuristic, profoundly erroneous and near-sighted. There were glaring faults in the enemy's political and strategic calculations. Even in 1941 the forces at Germany's disposal (even counting the reserves of the satellite countries) were insufficient to achieve the main objectives on the key sectors.

After the enormous losses he had suffered in the Battle of Smolensk, the enemy was compelled to halt the offensive against Moscow and resort to a temporary defence. He also had to redirect a considerable part of Army Group Centre to assist the forces of Army Group South, which were locked in combat with the troops of our Central and South-Western Fronts.

Having failed to take Leningrad, the German High Command was compelled to withdraw the air force and Panzer troops and regroup them on the Moscow sector to strengthen Army Group Centre. In October and November the Germans' main effort was concentrated on the Central sector, but even here the mounting Soviet resistance on the approaches to Moscow left them with insufficient forces to complete Operation Typhoon.

At the root of all these miscalculations lay the gross underestimation of the strength and vitality of our socialist country and the Soviet people, and overestimation of their own strength and potential.

In planning the invasion of the Soviet Union, Hitler and his associates counted on hurling all their forces and weapons against the USSR. This was a pure gamble. Despite the treachery of the Pétain Government, the working people of France did not bow to the Nazi occupying forces. Nor did the freedom-loving peoples of Yugoslavia, Poland, Czechoslovakia and several other countries. The Nazis had to deal with a mass movement of Resistance. Britain, too, did not give up the struggle, although she did not use her potential to the full.

The Nazis never anticipated that the Soviet people, rallying around the Communist Party, would find the strength to reorganize the country's economy and at such short notice launch the mass production of tanks, aircraft, artillery and ammunition, everything that the Soviet Armed Forces needed to gain the upper hand over the enemy, to bring about a fundamental turn in the war, to begin the expulsion of the Nazi forces from our territory and prepare the ground for the final and complete defeat of Nazi Germany.

The hardships they had to endure toughened and matured our troops, taught them invaluable lessons and, when they were supplied with the necessary weapons, were able to turn a defensive, retreating army into an invincible, offensive force.

The tremendous organizational and educational activities of our Leninist Party brought about excellent results both in the field of military build-up and in mobilizing the Soviet people for establishing a material and technical basis to back up the armed struggle of the Red Army against Nazi troops.

To sum up, the first period of the Great Patriotic War ended in the failure of all strategic plans of the Hitler Command and a considerable thinning out of German forces. This main result of the fight against the Nazi army largely predetermined the further course of the entire World War II.

CHAPTER 3

Strategic Nazi Defeat at Stalingrad

In October 1942 it was clear that the Nazi Command would be compelled to switch to a strategic defence along the entire Eastern front. The Nazis had sustained enormous losses and by that time were no longer capable of large-scale offensives; their war plans against the Soviet Union were failing.

Meanwhile, Nazi propaganda launched a campaign for "more thorough and timely preparation for a second winter in Russia". The Nazi Command insisted that its troops build up an impregnable line of active defence to pave the way for victory in 1943.

Why did the Nazi High Command find itself in such a complicated position? On the one hand, the Nazis had not achieved their strategic objectives, as was the case in 1941; were faced with an overextended front from the Black Sea through the Northern Caucasus, Stalingrad, the Don area and up to the Barents Sea; had no free strategic reserves on the front and in the rear; and faced low morale of both population and troops. On the other hand, the Soviet state was steadily increasing its strength and overcoming economic and military difficulties.

By early November 1942 the Nazis had on the Soviet-German front 266 divisions with a total strength of about 6.2 milion officers and men, around 51,700 guns and mortars, 5,080 tanks and assault weapons, 3,500 combat aircraft and 194 warships.[1]

By this same time the Soviet Union had in the field around 6.6 million officers and men, 77,800 guns and mortars, 7,350 tanks, and 4,544 combat aircraft.[2] The Soviet Supreme Com-

---

[1] *A History of the Second World War, 1939-1945*, in twelve volumes, Vol. 6, Voenizdat, Moscow, 1976, pp. 19, 20 (in Russian).

[2] Ibid.

mand had a strategic reserve of 27 rifle divisions, 5 independent tank and mechanized corps, and 6 independent rifle brigades.

Therefore, by the end of the first period of the war the balance of forces began to tilt in favour of the Soviet Union.

Another advantage of ours was that the Soviet Armed Forces had learned to conceal their plans, misinform and confuse the enemy on a large scale. Because of well-camouflaged regroupings and troop concentrations we were able to make surprise attacks.

After fierce fighting in the south, at Stalingrad and in the Northern Caucasus, the Nazi military leadership believed Soviet forces would not be able to launch a major offensive on these fronts. An operational order of the German Ground Forces High Command dated October 14, 1942, maintained:

"The Russians have been badly exhausted in recent combat actions. In the winter of 1942/43 they will not be able to raise forces as strong as they had last winter."

This, however, was far from true.

According to the Supreme Command's plan, the westward thrust our forces undertook in the summer and autumn of 1942 against the Nazi Army Group Centre was to disorient the enemy, to make the German Command think it was precisely at this point, and nowhere else, that we were preparing for a major winter operation. This is why in October the Nazi Command began building up large forces against our western fronts. Three divisions — armoured, motorized and infantry — were moved from the Leningrad area to the vicinity of Velikiye Luki. Another seven divisions were rushed from France and Germany to the area of Vitebsk and Smolensk. Two panzer divisions were brought up from Voronezh and Zhizdra to the vicinity of Yartsevo and Roslavl. Hence, by early November the Nazi Army Group Centre had gained 12 divisions, plus other reinforcements.

German operational blunders were aggravated by poor intelligence; they failed to spot preparations for the major counter-offensive near Stalingrad where there were 10 field, 1 tank and 4 air armies, a number of independent tank, mechanized and cavalry corps, brigades and independent units, 15,500 guns and mortars, 1,463 tanks and armoured self-propelled guns and 1,350 combat aircraft.

After the war, Jodl, former Chief of Staff Operations Division of the German Armed Forces, admitted they had failed to detect the Soviet build-up against the left flank of the army under Paulus: "We did not have the slightest idea of the Russian strength in that area. Previously, there had been nothing there and suddenly a powerful blow was struck, proving decisive."

At the beginning of the Soviet counter-offensive, in the south the enemy occupied the following operational and strategical positions.

The main forces of Army Group B were in the Middle Don area, at Stalingrad, and also southwards in the vicinity of Sarpinskiye Lakes. They comprised the 8th Italian Army, the 3rd and 4th Romanian armies and the German 6th and 4th Panzer armies. Each division held from 15 to 20 kilometres.

The effective strength of this group totalled over one million officers and men, 675 tanks and assault weapons, over 10,000 guns and mortars. Numerically the confronting forces were nearly equal, with the exception of a slight superiority in tanks on the Soviet side.

Army Group B was supported by the 4th Air Fleet and 8th Air Corps.

Planning to smash Army Group B, the Soviet Supreme Command believed an enemy rout in the Stalingrad area would disorganize the Nazis' North Caucasian Front compelling them to either beat a hasty retreat or fight from a pocket.

After Stalin's death it became unclear who was the actual architect of the wide-scale and effective counter-offensive. Although this question is perhaps not particularly important, and the plan's inception was described in the preceding chapter, I would still like to add some details.

Some people think the initial rough outline of the future offensive was drafted by the Supreme Command as early as August 1942 and was rather limited.

In reality, it was not an outline for the future counter-offensive, but merely a plan for a counterblow to check the enemy advance on the approaches to Stalingrad. At that time no one in the Supreme Command could plan on more, as we had neither sufficient resources nor means.

Another conjecture is that on October 6, 1942 the Military

Council of the Stalingrad Front, on its own initiative, put before the Supreme Command proposals for a counter-offensive. Here are comments on that by Vasilevsky:

"As soon as day broke on October 6, N. N. Voronov, V. D. Ivanov and myself ... set off to the observation post of the 51st Army where we heard Commander N. I. Trufanov's report. In the evening of the same day, at the Front command post, we met the Commander of the Front and the Member of the Military Council to discuss once again the Supreme Command's plan for the pending counter-offensive. Since the Front Command had no fundamental objections to the plan, that same night we wrote a report accordingly and sent it to the Supreme Commander-in-Chief.

"On October 7, on behalf of the Supreme Command I instructed the Commander of the Don Front to present similar considerations with respect to his own forces."

I believe no more need be said. The information presented by Vasilevsky is convincing evidence that the Supreme Command and the General Staff played the main role in planning the counter-offensive.

Some historians also say that somewhat later Vatutin, Commander of the South-Western Front, submitted his own plan. However, this raises some questions. How much later? What kind of a plan? A plan for his own Front or a general plan for the counter-offensive?

After all, the South-Western Front was formed only in late October, at a time when its forces had already finished concentrating in conformity with the plan for the counter-offensive, and the Supreme Command's overall plan had already been completed and approved.

Here I would like to note that each Front commander, in conformity with the prevailing practice and procedure for drafting plans for front-line operations, would necessarily submit such a plan for the approval of either the Supreme Command in Moscow or its representatives on the spot. The commander, of course, would also state his thinking about coordinating operations with his neighbours and what he needed from the Supreme Command.

To draft such a major counter-offensive plan, a plan for three Fronts at Stalingrad, it was absolutely imperative to proceed not only from operational considerations, but also from concrete calculations of equipment and materiel.

Who could do this for an operation of such scope? Of course, only the authority controlling such large resources, namely, the Supreme Command and the General Staff.

It's quite natural that the Supreme Command and the General Staff, in the process of hostilities, thoroughly analyzed all intelligence bearing on the enemy that the Fronts and forces were able to accumulate, and drew the appropriate conclusions from both Nazi and Soviet actions. They also studied the proposals of front-line staffs, commanders of all Fronts and arms of the service. After analyzing all this information they made one or another decision.

Consequently, plans for an operation of strategic scope could be fully conceived only as the upshot of protracted efforts by all the fighting arms, staffs and commanders.

I would like to reiterate that the Supreme Command and the General Staff unquestionably played the decisive role in planning and effecting the counter-offensive at Stalingrad.

There is also no doubt that credit for directly smashing the enemy goes to those who by their brave assault, accurate fire, courage, valour, and skill blasted the enemy to smithereens. They were the valiant troops, commanders and generals who had passed the grim trials of the initial part of the war with flying colours and on the eve of the counter-offensive were fully prepared to take the initiative and deal the enemy a deadly blow.

The Supreme Command and the General Staff deserve credit for their ability to analyze with scientific accuracy all the factors involved in this enormous operation and predict its progress and final result. Therefore, it is out of the question to attribute this counter-offensive to any particular individual.

I do not think it necessary to describe in detail the entire plan for the counter-offensive and the progress of the operation, since our historians have written much on the subject and most of it is accurate. There are some points, however, that I feel worthwhile discussing.

The dominant role in the initial phase of the counter-offensive was played by the South-Western Front commanded by Lieutenant-General N. F. Vatutin.

Delivering crippling, deep-thrusting blows, this Front struck out from bridgeheads in the vicinity of Serafimovich and Kletskaya on the right bank of the Don. Meanwhile, the Stalingrad Front was advancing from the Sarpinskiye Lakes area. The shock groupings of the two Fronts were to link up in the area between Kalach (Kalach-on-the-Don) and the small village of Sovetsky and thus complete the encirclement of the main enemy grouping at Stalingrad.

Deploying its central grouping, incorporating among other troops, the 21st Army, the 5th Tank Army and part of the lst Guards Army, and other strong forces from bridgeheads southwest of Serafimovich and in the vicinity of Kletskaya, the South-Western Front was to pierce the defence line of the 3rd Romanian Army and with its mobile formations race southeast to reach the Don in the area of Bolshenabatovskaya and Kalach. As a result of this thrust, the forces of this Front were to emerge in the rear of the Nazi grouping at Stalingrad and block all westward lines of retreat.

The mission of supporting the Front's shock group and of establishing the outer perimeter of encirclement in the southwest and west was assigned to the army operating on the right flank of the South-Western Front, to the lst Guards Army under Lieutenant-General D. D. Lelyushenko and subsequently to the 5th Tank Army under Lieutenant-General P. L. Romanenko. Thrusting forward in a western, south-western and southern direction, on the third day of the operation, these forces were supposed to reach the line stretching from Veshenskaya to Bokovskaya and farther out along the River Chir to Oblivskaya.

Ground operations along the South-Western Front were to be supported by the 2nd and 17th Air armies under Major-Generals K. N. Smirnov and S. A. Krasovsky.

Meanwhile, the Don Front was to deliver two secondary attacks. One was to be combined with the South-Western Front and, thrusting south-east from east of Kletskaya, smash enemy defences on the Don's right bank (this was to be effected by the 65th Army). The other was to thrust out from the area of Kachalinskaya along the left bank of the Don and southwards in the general direction of Vertyachy so as to cut off enemy forces operating in the Don's smaller loop from the Stalingrad grouping (this was to be effected by the 24th Army).

The 66th Army was to go into vigorous action north of Stalingrad to tie up the enemy and completely prevent him from manoeuvring with reserve forces. The ground forces of the Don Front were to be supported by the 16th Air Army under Major-General S. I. Rudenko.

The shock grouping of the Stalingrad Front (comprised of the 51st, 57th and 64th armies) was to launch an offensive on the line extending from Ivanovka to the northern tip of Lake Barmantsak. Its mission was to pierce enemy defences and, advancing in a north-westerly direction, reach the vicinity of Kalach and the small village of Sovetsky, where it was to link up with the forces of the South-Western Front and thus seal the encirclement of the enemy grouping at Stalingrad.

The 51st Army under Major-General Trufanov was to break enemy defences on the isthmuses between lakes Sarpa, Tsatsa and Barmantsak, concentrating forces to carry the offensive farther north-west in the general direction of Abganerovo.

Meanwhile, the 57th Army under General F. I. Tolbukhin and the 64th Army under General M. S. Shumilov were to attack westwards and north-west from the vicinity of Ivanovka to envelop the enemy grouping from the south.

The 62nd Army under General V. I. Chuikov was to pin down enemy forces by action inside the city and be prepared to launch an offensive.

The mission of supporting the offensive of the Stalingrad Front's shock force and building up an exterior perimeter of encirclement from the south-west was allotted to the 51st Army (including General T. T. Shapkin's 4th Cavalry Corps), which was to attack south-west in the general direction of Abganerovo and Kotelnikovo. The troops of the Stalingrad Front were to be supported by the 8th Air Army under the command of Major-General T. T. Khryukin.

To prepare the counter-offensive enormous movements of troops and materiel were effected for all the Fronts, especially the newly organised South-Western Front. One must give credit to the General Staff and the Staff of the Red Army Logistics Division for the brilliant way in which they coped with massing the forces for this operation.

A total of 27,000 lorries were employed to transport troops

and freight. The railways carried 1,300 freight cars daily. Troops and supplies for the Stalingrad Front were carried in the exceptionally difficult conditions of the autumn ice drifting on the Volga. Between the lst and 20th of November, 111,000 officers and men, 427 tanks, 556 artillery pieces, 14,000 lorries and nearly 7,000 tons of ammunition were ferried across the Volga.

Between late October and early November, Vasilevsky, other representatives of the Supreme Command, and myself, worked hard to help the command personnel, staffs and troops fully understand the counter-offensive plan and the methods to effect it. The meetings of staffs of Fronts, armies and troops showed that this complex, labour-consuming task was performed by the commanding and political officers with a great sense of responsibility and creative initiative.

Between November 1 and 4 the plans of the South-Western Front were discussed and corrected, and later plans of the 21st Army and the 5th Tank Army were ironed out in full detail and dovetailed.

The discussion of operation plans at the headquarters of the South-Western Front was attended by myself and other representatives of the Supreme Command. General N. N. Voronov represented artillery, generals A. A. Novikov and A. E. Golovanov, the air force, and General Ya. N. Fedorenko, armoured troops. All of them helped more comprehensively to plan the use and coordination of the major fighting arms.

On November 4 the headquarters of the 21st Army debated preparations for offensive operations of the 21st and the 65th armies. The commanders of the Don Front and the 65th Army were invited to this meeting. At that time Vasilevsky was inspecting preparations under way by the 51st, 57th and 64th Armies of the Stalingrad Front. We agreed that I would join him later.

When working with the troops we focussed on intelligence bearing on enemy dispositions, the character of its defence efforts, the overall fire system, deployment of anti-tank weapons and anti-tank strong points.

We determined the methods and plans for artillery preparation, its density, the probability of demolishing and suppressing the enemy's defences and also the system of artillery support for the advancing forces. We dovetailed plans for coordinating artillery and air force operations and assigned them their respective missions. We planned coordination with the armour during the breakthrough and after it had been sent into the gap. We determined flank contact with neighbouring forces, especially when sending mobile forces into the breakthrough and directing their action in the operational depth of enemy defences. At the same time we issued practical instructions on how much more intelligence bearing upon enemy positions and movements was required, what additional details might be needed, and what concretely should be done in the field.

The commanding and political officers concentrated chiefly on the objective of rapidly breaking the enemy's tactical defences. Enemy forces had to be dealt a telling blow and before they could recover it would be necessary to rush into action the second wave to develop a tactical breakthrough into an operational breakthrough.

In assigning missions to corps, divisions and units we pressed the commanding officers to carefully study these missions and ways of cooperating with reinforcements and adjacent units, especially when operating in the depth of the enemy defences.

All this represented a difficult task for all echelons of commanding and political officers, and required particular strain of all strength and capabilities; however, the dividends made it worthwhile.

Political bodies, Party and YCL organizations launched a party-political campaign among the troops. Their activities were skilfully directed by the Front Military Council and Political Administration under General M. V. Rudakov.

To finalize plans for offensive operations by the forces of the Stalingrad Front, as previously arranged with Vasilevsky, I arrived on the morning of November 10 at Tatyanovka, the command post of the 57th Army. Already waiting there with the Military Council were M. M. Popov, M. S. Shumilov, F. I. Tolbukhin, N. I. Trufanov, corps commanders V. T. Volsky, T. T. Shapkin and other generals. Before the conference, however, Vasilevsky, the commanders of the 51st and 57th armies, Trufanov and Tolbukhin, as well as Popov, other generals and myself visited the sectors on which these armies were operating. We wanted to reinspect the terrain across which we were to develop the offensive of the main forces of the Stalingrad Front.

After reconnoitering the ground we spoke at the conference about coordinating operations between the Stalingrad and South-Western Fronts, detailed the link-up between the advance units of the two Fronts in the vicinity of Kalach, and discussed further coordination following the sealing of encirclement and other pertinent problems.

We then heard army and corps commanders report on individual army plans.

The evening of November 11, I used the Baudot printer to wire the Supreme Commander the following report:

"Spent two days working with Yeremenko. Personally inspected enemy positions confronting 51st and 57th armies. Ironed out details of pending Uran objectives with divisional, corps, and army commanders. Inspection showed Tolbukhin ahead in preparations...

"Have ordered battle reconnaissance and finalization of combat plan and Army Commander's decision on the basis of intelligence thus acquired.

"Popov working well, knows what he's doing.

"Supreme Command's two infantry divisions — 87th and 315th — for Yeremenko still not entrained because transport and horses not yet arrived.

"Only one of mechanized brigades here.

"Supplies and delivery of munitions poor. Troops short of shells for Uran operation.

"Operation won't be ready on schedule. Have ordered readiness by November 15, 1942.

"Yeremenko must immediately have 100 tons of antifreeze without which advance of mechanised units impossible; early transfer of 87th and 315th Rifle Divisions essential; 51st and 57th armies require winter wear and ammunition urgently, no later than November 14, 1942.

"Konstantinov.[1]

"November 11, 1942"

The Supreme Commander-in-Chief usually paid due attention to air support for ground operations. As soon as he received

---

[1] Zhukov's code name.— *Ed.*

my wire on the unsatisfactory preparations for air support for the pending counter-offensive he cabled the following:

"To Comrade Konstantinov.

"If air support preparation unsatisfactory in the armies of Yeremenko and Vatutin, operation will fail. Experience in fighting the Germans shows that operations against them can be won only provided we have superiority in air. Therefore, our air force must carry out three following assignments:

"F i r s t, concentrate on our shock force offensive area. Suppress German aircraft and provide our troops with reliable cover.

"S e c o n d, open up field for our advancing units with systematic bombing of confronting German forces.

"T h i r d, pursue retreating enemy forces with systematic bombing and assault action to achieve complete disorganisation and prevent digging in on nearest defence lines.

"If Novikov believes our air force currently unable to carry out above-mentioned missions, advise temporary suspensions of operation and build-up of air force.

"Talk to Novikov and Vorozheikin, drive point home, and notify me of your general opinion.

"Vasilyev.[1]

"04:00, November 12, 1942"

Having finalised by November 12 the details of the Stalingrad Front operational plans, Vásilevsky and myself telephoned Stalin to say that we needed to report personally several considerations related to the pending operation.

The morning of November 13 we saw Stalin. He was in a cheerful mood; he asked us to detail the state of affairs at Stalingrad and the progress being made in preparing for the counter-offensive.

Our report covered the following main points.

In discussing the qualitative and quantitative balance of forces we pointed out that on the sectors where the South-Western and Stalingrad Fronts were to strike the main blows, units of the Romanian armies were still fighting a defensive operation. We had learned from pows interrogations that the overall combat standard of the Romanian forces was not

---

[1] Stalin's code name.— *Ed.*

high. In these sectors we would enjoy considerable numerical superiority provided the Nazi Command did not regroup reserves by our offensive zero hour. Thus far our intelligence had not discovered any signs of regrouping. Paulus's 6th Army and part of the 4th Panzer Army were tied up at Stalingrad by the troops of the Stalingrad and Don Fronts.

Our forces were massing in the designated areas according to plan. As far as we could judge, the enemy was ignorant of our regrouping. We had taken steps to envelop all movements of troops and materiel with the utmost secrecy.

The missions assigned to the various Fronts, armies, and formations had been finalized. On-the-spot coordination of operations between all arms of the services had been dovetailed. The details of the planned link-up between the shock forces of the South-Western and Stalingrad Fronts had been ironed out with the respective commanders and their staffs, including the commanding personnel of the forces which were to emerge in the area between Sovetsky and Kalach. The air armies would apparently complete preparations not earlier than November 15.

The variants had been developed for building up an interior perimeter of encirclement of the enemy grouping at Stalingrad and of an exterior perimeter for destroying the trapped enemy.

Delivery of ammunition, fuel and winter clothing was somewhat tardy, but there was every reason to believe that by the evening of either November 16 or 17 the troops would have these supplies.

The counter-offensive could be started by the South-Western and Don Fronts on November 19. The Stalingrad Front was to start operations 24 hours later.

The South-Western Front was to begin earlier because its tasks were more complicated; it was stationed far from the Kalach-Sovetsky area and had to force-cross the Don.

The Supreme Commander listened attentively. By the way he unhurriedly puffed his pipe, smoothed his moustache, and never interrupted once, we could see that he was pleased. Stalingrad counter-offensive operation implied that Soviet forces would henceforth control the initiative. We were confident the pending counter-offensive would be successful and do much for the ultimate liberation of our homeland from the Nazi invaders.

While we were presenting our report, members of the State Defence Committee and some members of the Politbureau came in and so we had to repeat some of the major points we had already covered.

After a brief discussion, the plan for the counter-offensive was given full approval.

Vasilevsky and I pointed out to the Supreme Commander that as soon as German troops at Stalingrad and in the Northern Caucasus found themselves in a desperate spot the Nazi High Command would be compelled to transfer some of its forces from other sectors, particularly from Vyazma, to assist the southern grouping.

To prevent this, it was essential to urgently prepare and conduct an offensive north of Vyazma and, first, smash the Germans in the Rzhev Salient. We suggested using troops in the Kalinin and Western Fronts for this operation.

"That would be fine," Stalin said, "but which of you two will take charge?"

As Vasilevsky and I had already agreed on that score, I explained, "The Stalingrad operation is completely ready. Vasilevsky can coordinate operations at Stalingrad while I take charge of the preparations for an offensive by the Kalinin and Western Fronts."

The Supreme Commander consented and instructed: "Fly out tomorrow morning to Stalingrad and once again check troop and command readiness for the start of the operation."

On November 14 I made another tour of Vatutin's forces. Vasilevsky meanwhile went to see Yeremenko. The next day I received a cable from Stalin saying:

"To Comrade Konstantinov (personal)

"Set day for resettlement of Fyodorov and Ivanov[1] at your discretion and subsequently report back to me upon arrival in Moscow. Should you believe it necessary for either of the two to start resettlement one or two days earlier or later, I authorize you to decide this matter, too, at your own discretion.

Vasilyev.

---

[1] The day Vatutin's and Yeremenko's armies were to begin offensive.— *Author*.

"13:10, November 15, 1942"

Vasilevsky and I discussed the matter and set November 19 as zero day for the South-Western Front and the 65th Army of the Don Front, and November 20 as zero day for the Stalingrad Front. The Supreme Commander endorsed our decision.

On November 17 I was summoned to the Supreme Command GHQ to work out in detail the operation for the Kalinin and Western Fronts.

At 07:30 on November 19 the troops of the South-Western Front struck a telling blow, breaking the defences of the 3rd Romanian Army on two sectors simultaneously. This was effected from a bridgehead south-west of Serafimovich by the 5th Tank Army under Lieutenant-General Romanenko and from the Kletskaya bridgehead by the 21st Army under Major-General I. M. Chistyakov.

The enemy buckled and, panic-stricken, fled or surrendered. German units holding positions behind the Romanian forces, mounted a powerful counterattack in an attempt to check our advance, but were crushed by the lst and 26th Tank corps. The tactical breakthrough on the South-Western Front was now an accomplished fact.

Army Commander Romanenko was in his element. A brave man and extremely capable general, he was perfectly suited to guide such rapid movements.

To oppose General Chistyakov's 21st Army, the enemy swung its reserves into action, including its 14th Panzer Division. The 22nd German Panzer Division, the lst Romanian Tank Division, and 7th Romanian Cavalry Division were deployed against the 5th Tank Army and primarily against Major-General V. V. Butkov's lst Tank Corps.

Major-General A. G. Rodin's 26th Tank Corps inflicted a telling defeat on the lst Tank Division and crushed the headquarters of the 5th Romanian Army Corps. Some of the men fled panic-stricken, but a large number surrendered.

As soon as our forces moved ahead in operational width and depth, the main forces of the 3rd Romanian Army, hitherto holding out against the South-Western Front, along with the German reserves rushed in to help out, were completely destroyed and, for all practical purposes, ceased to exist.

Rodin's 26th Tank Corps and Kravchenko's 4th Tank Corps

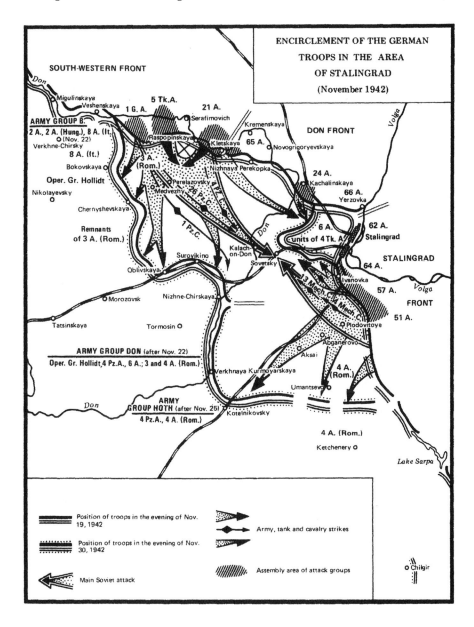

ENCIRCLEMENT OF THE GERMAN
TROOPS IN THE AREA
OF STALINGRAD
(November 1942)

raced through to the neighbourhood of Kalach to link up
with the 4th Mechanised Corps of the Stalingrad Front. The
65th Army of the Don Front under Lieutenant-General
P. I. Batov was advancing left of the 21st Army.

The night of November 22, Lieutenant-Colonel G. N. Filippov's advance guard of the 26th Tank Corps captured a bridge
across the Don in a daring raid.

Apparently the German sentries guarding the bridge had been expecting a relief detail and were taken by surprise when the advance detachment of Filippov's forces swooped down on them. The Nazis thought the group was on exercises using captured Russian tanks. When they realized the truth it was too late. After a brief engagement the bridge was taken. Though the Germans made several attempts to dislodge Filippov's group they got nowhere.

While holding the bridge, Filippov decided to send Lieutenant-Colonel N. M. Filippenko's armoured unit to capture Kalach which was just two kilometres away. Despite his small force, Lieutenant-Colonel Filippenko decided to attack from a march-column. The battle for Kalach raged all through the night. The Germans put up stiff resistance. However, soon the advance units of the Soviet corps' main forces reached the site and the town was liberated.

Regretfully, such heroes as Grigory Guryev, a Muscovite and Communist Party member, Alexander Ivanov and Grigory Davidyan, two exceptionally brave scouts, and other good comrades were killed in this battle. Lieutenant-Colonel Filippov and Lieutenant-Colonel Filippenko were awarded titles of Hero of the Soviet Union for bravery, and their men received decorations.

On November 24, having crushed the trapped Romanian force, the 21st and 5th armies of the South-Western Front captured more than 30,000 officers and men, including generals, and large amounts of enemy equipment.

The following are entries in a diary kept by the Romanian weather officer of an artillery brigade in the 6th Division:

"November 19

"Russians are fiercely shelling the left flank of the 5th Division. I've never been under such fire... Gun-fire so heavy the ground shudders and windows shatter... Enemy tanks appear on Height 163 and head for Raspopinskaya. Heard soon that tanks raced through our positions and broke into village, our guns having no effect... These heavy 52-ton tanks, which go at full speed, have very thick armour which our shells cannot pierce...

"November 20

"In morning enemy opened heavy artillery fire at sector held by the 13th Prut Division... Division wiped out. Tanks reached Gromki and Yevstratovskaya heading toward Perelazovsky in our rear. 5th Corps HQ at Perelazovsky was warned. No communication with higher command. 6th Division received by some miracle orders to hold out to last man. Currently we are encircled by enemy troops. In pocket are the 5th, 6th and 15th divisions and remnants of the 13th Division.

"November 21

"In desperate plight since early morning. We are surrounded... Great confusion in Golovsky... Now 10:05 hours. Don't know what to do. Officers are here from the 13th and 15th divisions after losing their units.

"A sorry situation! But fact.

"Friends staring at snapshots of their loved ones, wives and children. It hurts to think of my mother, brother, sisters and relatives. We're putting on our best clothing, even two sets of underclothes. We figure very tragic end in store... Everyone's talking and arguing about our situation... But we haven't lost hope... We think German troops will come to our aid...

"13:00 hours. General Mazarini, 5th Division commander, has assumed command of all divisions. Enemy ring tighter. Today is a big religious holiday. What sins have we or our forebears committed? Why must we suffer so? Two other officers and I discuss the situation and conclude we have no chance of escaping disaster. Unpleasant news from Osinovka confirms our fears. Several officers from the 5th Heavy Artillery Regiment arrive. They barely escaped.

"Divisional and regimental commanders again confer late at night to take final decision.

"Two alternatives discussed:

"1) Try to break out.

"2) Surrender.

"After long discussion the decision is surrender.

"We hear Russians have sent a truce envoy with surrender proposals."

The diary ends at this point, but we know what happened next: the entire group of Romanians surrendered.

The Supreme Commander, seriously concerned about the operations of the Don Front's right flank, dispatched the following directive the evening of November 23 to K. K. Rokossovsky, Commander of the Don Front:

"To Comrade Dontsov.[1]

"Copy to Comrade Mikhailov.[2]

"According to Mikhailov's report, the enemy's 3rd Motorized Division and the 16th Panzer Division are either wholly or partially transferred from your front and are now fighting against the 21st Army. This circumstance makes the situation favourable for all armies of your front to step up actions. Galanin is slack, instruct him to take Vertyachy on November 24 at the latest.

"Also instruct Zhadov to step up action and tie up the enemy.

"Give Batov a good push. He could be more energetic in the present situation.

"Stalin

"19:40, November 23, 1942"

As a result of the successful advance by Major-General Chistyakov's 21st Army, and the measures taken by the Don Front Command, the 65th Army was able to catch up and start advancing more vigorously.

The 24th Army of the Don Front launched its assault three days later, striking out along the Don's left bank. But because of its general weakness, the army failed to gain any particular success.

The 51st, 57th and 64th armies of the Stalingrad Front went into action on November 20, twenty-four hours after the South-Western and Don Fronts.

The 51st Army under Major-General Trufanov advanced in the general direction of Plodovitoye and even farther to Abganerovo.

The 57th Army under Major-General Tolbukhin attacked in the general direction of Kalach.

With its left flank the 64th Army under Lieutenant-General

---

[1] Code name for Rokossovky.— *Author.*

[2] Code name for Vasilevsky.— *Author.*

Shumilov struck out from the Ivanovka area in the general direction of Gavrilovka and Varvarovka, supporting the right flank of the 57th Army.

When the defences were pierced and the lst, 2nd, 18th and 20th Romanian Divisions and also the 29th German Motorized Division were crushed, the 51st Army rushed the 4th Mechanized Corps under General V. T. Volsky into the gap forced at Plodovitoye; meanwhile, in the sector controlled by the 57th Army, Major-General T. I. Tanaschishin's 13th Tank Corps went into action. Also rushed into the breach was General Shapkin's 4th Cavalry Corps, which captured the station of Abganerovo on the same day.

The enemy rushed the 16th and 24th Panzer Divisions from Stalingrad to this sector in an attempt to block the 57th Army's advance on Kalach. This movement, however, was belated, and did not have the strength to resist the powerful blows being dealt by the troops of the South-Western and Stalingrad Fronts, whose armoured units had by 16:00 hours on November 23 reached the vicinity of the small village of Sovetsky. There the 45th Tank Brigade of the 4th Tank Corps under Lieutenant-Colonel P. K. Zhidkov was the first to link up with the 36th Mechanized Brigade under Lieutenant-Colonel M. I. Rodionov of the 4th Mechanized Corps.

Crossing the Don, General A. G. Kravchenko's 4th Tank Corps of the South-Western Front and Volsky's 4th Mechanized Corps of the Stalingrad Front linked up in the vicinity of Sovetsky, thus sealing the encirclement of the Stalingrad enemy grouping deployed between the Don and the Volga.

This enabled the 64th, 57th, 21st, 65th, 24th and 66th armies to press ahead in the general direction of Stalingrad, compressing in a pincer movement the interior perimeter of encirclement of the enemy.

In their pursuit of the retreating enemy, the lst Guards Army, the 5th Tank Army of the South-Western Front and the 51st Army of the Stalingrad Front, which had been reinforced with armoured formations, were to hurl the smashed enemy units further back from the encircled Stalingrad grouping and build up a firm exterior perimeter so necessary for annihilation of the trapped enemy.

This concluded the first phase of the counter-offensive.

By early December the enemy had been hemmed in firmly. At that point our forces embarked upon the next phase, namely, of destroying the trapped grouping.

Vasilevsky and the General Staff kept me well posted on the progress of the counter-offensive. After the encirclement of the 6th German Army and units of the 4th Panzer Army it was crucial to prevent an enemy break-out.

On November 28 I discussed the pending offensive with the commanding officers of the Kalinin Front at their headquarters.

Late that night I received a call from the Supreme Commander who asked me whether I knew about the latest developments at Stalingrad. When I said I did, the Supreme Commander asked me what action I thought should be taken to destroy the Nazi forces encircled there.

The morning of November 29 I cabled the Supreme Commander:

"At the present juncture, unless there's a secondary enemy attack from Nizhne-Chirskaya and Kotelnikovo, the trapped German forces will not attempt a break-out.

"The Nazi Command will apparently try to hold on in the area of Stalingrad, Vertyachy, Marinovka, Karpovka and the Gornaya Polyana State Farm. They will also immediately try to mass a shock force at Nizhne-Chirskaya and Kotelnikovo to pierce our Front in the general direction of Karpovka, thus opening a corridor to supply the trapped grouping and subsequently enable it to escape.

"Under favourable circumstances the enemy may prove able to open up such a corridor in the sector of Marinovka, Lyapichev and Verkhne-Chirskaya, with its front facing north.

"The other side of this corridor with its front facing southeast may run along a line extending from Tsybenko through Zety and Gnilovskaya to Shebalin.

"To prevent a link-up of the Nizhne-Chirskaya and Kotelnikovo enemy groupings with the Stalingrad grouping, and the formation of such a corridor, I suggest the following:

"Hurl back as soon as possible the Nizhne-Chirskaya and Kotelnikovo groupings and deploy close battle formations along the Oblivskaya-Tormosin-Kotelnikovo line. We must have in reserve two armoured groups, each having at least one hundred tanks, at Nizhne-Chirskaya and Kotelnikovo.

"The encircled enemy grouping at Stalingrad must be cleft into two. This can be accomplished by striking a cutting blow in the direction of Bolshaya Rossoshka, and another from the opposite side in the direction of Dubininsky, Height 135. On all other sectors we must adopt defensive tactics, sending only individual units into action to bleed the enemy white.

"After the encircled enemy grouping is cleft, we should first destroy the weaker grouping and, subsequently, strike with all our force at the Stalingrad grouping.

"Zhukov

"November 29, 1942"

After submitting my report to the Supreme Commander, I telephoned Vasilevsky who supported my arguments. We also exchanged views on the pending operations of the South-Western Front. Vasilevsky agreed temporarily to suspend the Big Saturn Operation and direct the attack mounted by the South-Western Front at the flank of the enemy's Tormosin grouping. The General Staff held the same view.

The South-Western Front was assigned a mission coded Small Saturn. Under this plan the lst and 3rd Guards armies and the 5th Tank Army were to strike out in the general direction of Morozovsk and destroy the enemy grouping in that sector. This was to be supported by the 6th Army of the Voronezh Front, which was to advance in the general direction of Kantemirovka.

The Nazi Command badly needed reserves to remedy the catastrophic situation on the Stalingrad and Caucasian sectors. To prevent forces from being rushed from Army Group Centre, the Soviet Supreme Command decided to supplement the counter-offensive at Stalingrad with an offensive operation by the Western and Kalinin Fronts against the German troops holding the Rzhev salient. Between November 20 and December 8 the planning and preparation of this operation were finalized.

On December 8, 1942, the Fronts were issued the following directive:

"In combined operations the Kalinin and Western Fronts

are by January 1, 1943, to crush the Rzhev-Sychovka-Olenino-Bely enemy grouping and firmly dig in on the line running through Yarygino, Sychovka, Andreyevskoye, Lenino, Novoye Azhevo, Dentyalevo and Svity.

"The Western Front must:

"(a) pierce enemy defences in the Bolshoye Kropotovo and Yarygino sector on the 10th and 11th of December, take Sychovka no later than the 15th of December, and move into the Andreyevskoye Sector on the 20th of December no less than two rifle divisions to work with the 41st Army of the Kalinin Front to seal encirclement of the enemy;

"(b) after penetration of the enemy defences and the emergence of the main force on the railway line, turn the Front's mobile group and at least four rifle divisions north to attack the enemy's Rzhev-Chertolino grouping in the rear;

"(c) use the 30th Army to pierce defences in the sector stretching from Koshkino to the road junction north-east of Burgovo, and reach the railway line in the vicinity of Chertolino no later than December 15; upon reaching the railway line, enter into combined operations with the Front's mobile force and, striking out along the railway line, advance on Rzhev to take the city on December 23.

"The Kalinin Front must:

"(a) press ahead with its 39th and 22nd armies in the general direction of Olenino, crush the enemy grouping there by December 16 and emerge in the vicinity of Olenino;

"use the 22nd Army to mount a secondary attack in the direction of Yegorye to assist the 41st Army in smashing the enemy's Bely grouping;

"(b) use the 41st Army to crush by December 10 the enemy grouping breaking out in the Tsytsyno Sector and regain lost positions on the Okolitsa sector. Part of the force is to reach the Molnya-Vladimirskoye-Lenino area no later than December 20 in order to seal from the south, in conjunction with units of the Western Front, the encircled enemy grouping.

"Bely is to be taken no later than December 20.

"For the Supreme Command

"J. Stalin

"G. Zhukov"

This combined operation of the two Fronts was of major significance in destroying the enemy in the area of the Rzhev salient and should be described briefly.

The command of the Kalinin Front, led by Lieutenant-General M. A. Purkayev, had coped with its mission. Its troops were advancing south of Bely and, having successfully broken the enemy front, were pressing forward to Sychovka. Meanwhile, the Western Front group was, in turn, to pierce enemy defences and continue its movement to link up with troops in the Kalinin Front so as to seal encirclement of the Nazi grouping at Rzhev. However, the Western Front failed to penetrate enemy defences.

The Supreme Commander insisted I see Konev at once.

At the Western Front command post I realized it would be useless to repeat the operation because the enemy had seen through our plan and had moved up large forces from other sectors.

Meanwhile, a difficult situation also arose in the break-through sector in the Kalinin Front where the enemy struck at our flank and trapped Major-General M. D. Solomatin's Mechanized Corps.

We had to urgently assign another rifle corps from the Supreme Command reserve to help our troops break out of the encirclement. More than three days Solomatin's men fought fiercely in desperate conditions.

On the fourth night the Siberian troops, arriving in time, broke through the enemy defence; we managed to extricate Solomatin's exhausted troops and sent them at once to the rear to recuperate.

Though our troops failed to cope with the task assigned by the Supreme Command — destroy the Rzhev salient — their vigorous actions prevented the German Command from rushing large reinforcements from this sector to Stalingrad.

Moreover, to retain the Rzhev-Vyazma bridgehead, the Nazi Command was obliged to move up four panzer divisions and one motorized division to this sector.

Analyzing the reasons for the failure of the offensive taken by the Western Front, we concluded the main factor was underestimation of the rugged terrain in the theatre selected by the Front Command for the main attack.

Battle experience teaches us that whenever enemy defences are deployed on well-observable terrain lacking natural cover from artillery bombardment, such defences can easily be crushed by artillery and mortar fire, which will thus pave the way for a successful offensive.

If enemy defences, however, are located on poorly observable terrain with good cover behind reverse slopes and in ravines running parallel to the front, it is hard to suppress defences with artillery fire and penetrate them, especially when the use of armour is restricted.

In the given case, the rugged terrain occupied by German defences, which were well sheltered behind reverse slopes, was not taken into account.

Another reason for the failure sustained in this sector was the shortage of supporting armour, artillery, mortars and aircraft to pierce the enemy defences.

The Front Command endeavoured to correct the situation while the offensive was under way, but did not succeed. What aggravated the problem still more was that, contrary to our expectations, the Nazi Command had brought up considerable reinforcements to this sector from other Fronts.

Consequently, a group in the Kalinin Front, after penetrating enemy defences south of Bely, found itself all alone.

However, back to our operations at Stalingrad.

In the first half of December the destruction of the trapped enemy grouping by the Don and Stalingrad Fronts proceeded at a snail's pace.

Meanwhile, enemy forces, expecting Hitler's promised support, stubbornly contested every position. Since a large portion of our forces had been diverted to destroy the German grouping attacking from around Kotelnikovo, our offensive would not yield the desired results.

For the Germans a defeat at Stalingrad could very well develop into a disaster of major strategic importance.

The Nazi Command felt the best way to solve their problems was to stabilize defences on the Stalingrad sector and, under cover of these defences, withdraw Army Group A from the Caucasus. Therefore, it formed the new Army Group Don. General Field-Marshal Manstein was appointed the commander of this group.

The Nazi leadership considered Manstein the most suitable and capable of all their generals. Army Group Don was formed of the troops moved up from other sectors of the Soviet-German Front and in part from France and Germany.

We now know that Manstein's plan to rescue the encircled forces at Stalingrad was to organize two shock forces — at Kotelnikovo and Tormosin.

His plans, however, were not destined to succeed. The Wehrmacht felt an acute shortage of reserves, and whatever the troops the Nazi Command managed to muster moved very slowly along widely extended communications. Besides, Soviet partisans operating in the enemy rear knew why German troops were hurrying south and did all they could to obstruct their movement. Braving Nazi terror and disregarding all German precautions, our valiant patriots derailed dozens of troop trains.

Time passed, but the Nazis failed to mass a large enough force for a relief operation and a new defence perimeter. Fearing his Stalingrad armies were doomed, Hitler hurried Manstein to start the operation before the build-up was completed.

Manstein initiated this operation on December 12 but only from the Kotelnikovo sector and along the railway line.

His Kotelnikovo group consisted of the 6th, 23rd and 17th Panzer divisions, a Panzer battalion of Tiger tanks, four infantry divisions and several supporting formations, and two Romanian cavalry divisions. After three days of heavy fighting, the enemy had thrust 45 kilometres forward to Stalingrad and even crossed the River Aksai-Yesaulovsky.

A fierce battle unfolded in the Verkhne-Kumsky sector taking a heavy toll on both sides. But despite heavy losses, the enemy continued to drive forward to Stalingrad. Battle-seasoned Soviet forces doggedly contested their defence lines. Only when the 17th Panzer Division returned and aerial bombardment was intensified did units of the 51st Army and General Shapkin's Cavalry Corps retreat across the River Myshkova.

The enemy was only 40 kilometres from Stalingrad and apparently believed victory was within reach. But these hopes were premature. In conformity with orders from the Supreme Command, Vasilevsky moved into action the 2nd

Guards Army under General R. Ya. Malinovsky, well reinforced with tanks and artillery; it reversed the tide of the
battle in favour of the Soviet forces.

On December 16 the troops of the South-Western Front
and the 6th Army of the Voronezh Front struck out to crush
the German concentration along the middle reaches of the
Don and emerge in the rear of the enemy's Tormosin grouping.

After defeating the 8th Italian Army, the lst Guards Army
under Lieutenant-General V. I. Kuznetsov, the 3rd Guards
Army under Lieutenant-General D. D. Lelyushenko (by this
time the lst Guards Army was divided into two guards armies —
the lst and the 3rd), and the 6th Army under Major-General
F. M. Kharitonov (attached to the South-Western Front
and reinforced by the 17th Armoured Corps under
P. P. Poluboyarov) raced ahead in the general direction of
Morozovsk.

The first wave smashing through enemy resistance involved
the 24th and 25th Tank corps and the 1st Guards Mechanized
Corps. Meanwhile, the 17th and 18th Tank Corps came up
on the right, in the neighbourhood of Millerovo.

The rapid thrust of the South-Western Front in this
direction compelled Manstein to bring into battle forces that
had earlier been intended to strike from the Tormosin Sector
in the direction of Stalingrad. Those forces turned against
the South-Western Front's troops which were emerging on
the flank and rear of Army Group Don.

In his December 28 report to the Supreme Command,
Vatutin, Commander of the South-Western Front, covering
the progress of the offensive, described the situation in the
following cable on the Baudaut printer.

"All forces facing our Front (around 17 divisions), have
been wiped out and their stocks captured. We have taken more
than 60,000 prisoners, about the same number have been
killed. The few remaining forces are hardly offering any
resistance, except on rare occasions.

"Ahead of us, the enemy continues stubborn resistance
along the Oblivskaya and Verkhne-Chirskaya line. Today in
the vicinity of Morozovsk we took prisoners from the 11th
Panzer Division and the 8th Air Field Division which had
previously faced Romanenko's army. The greatest resistance

to Lelyushenko's army and to our mobile forces is coming from the enemy formations which moved from the Kotelnikovo sector across the Don and to the line extending from Chernyshkovsky, through Morozovsk, and Skosyrskaya to Tatsinskaya. These troops are trying to dig in to obstruct the further advance of our mobile units and thus give their own forces a chance to retreat. Given favourable circumstances, the enemy may attempt to hold the entire salient with the aim of further rescuing its encircled grouping. He will get nowhere though. Every effort will be made to cut off that salient.

"Every day air reconnaissance spot detraining of enemy troops near Rossosh, Starobelsk, Voroshilovgrad, Chebotovka, Kamensk, Likhaya and Zverevo. Though it is hard to tell what the enemy plans to do, evidently he is establishing his main line of defence along the Seversky Donets. The enemy is compelled primarily to fill in the 350-kilometre-wide breach our troops have made. It would be a good idea to continue to strike at the enemy without affording any respite. However, that calls for reinforcements as the forces available here are busy finishing up the Small Saturn Operation. Additional forces are required to initiate Big Saturn."

The Supreme Commander and myself were present when the telegram came through. This is what Stalin replied:

"Your primary task is to prevent the defeat of Badanov's corps and send him Pavlov's and Russiyanov's forces for relief as soon as you can. You were right to permit Badanov to leave Tatsinskaya if absolutely necessary. It's advisable to use some infantry formation to bolster your blow at Tormosin with the 8th Cavalry Corps. You were right to dispatch the 3rd Guards Cavalry Corps and the rifle division to Tormosin via Suvorovsky.

"To develop Small Saturn into Big Saturn we have already sent you the 2nd and 23rd Tank corps. In a week you will get two more armoured corps and three or four rifle divisions... We have doubts about your plans to send the 18th Tank Corps to Skosyrskaya; better keep it at Millerovo and Verkhne-Tarasovskoye together with the 17th Tank Corps. Generally, bear in mind that it is safer to send two armoured corps at a time on long-range missions to prevent a repetition of Badanov's plight."

Then I inquired of Vatutin, "Where is the 18th Tank Corps at the moment?"

"It's directly east of Millerovo and won't be isolated," Vatutin replied.

"Keep Badanov in mind all the time. Rescue him at any cost," I instructed.

"I will do absolutely everything possible to rescue Badanov," Vatutin assured us.

We had good reason to discuss the 24th Tank Corps under V. M. Badanov. Here is what happened.

Entering the breakthrough north-west of Boguchar at 18:30 hours on December 17, the 24th Corps advanced some 300 kilometres fighting every inch of the way, and destroying en route to the Tatsinskaya Railway Station 6,700 enemy troops and capturing a great deal of hardware. Coming up to this station the morning of December 24, the corps swung into the attack from marching orders, assaulting the station from various sides. A group under Guards Captain I. A. Fomin crossed the railway line Likhaya-Stalingrad and burst into the station. Mowing down the enemy guard the group captured a trainload of disassembled aircraft. I very much regret that the brave Captain Fomin was killed in this operation.

At the same time Captain M. E. Nechayev's tanks roared on to the airfield where more than 200 German transport aircraft stood ready to take off, and crushed the whole lot under their treads. For five whole days the armoured corps held Tatsinskaya, putting up fierce resistance to encircling enemy reserves. The morning of December 29, under orders from Vatutin, the corps broke out of the encirclement thanks to the men's courage and Badanov's skilled guidance of the battle. They subsequently retreated in full fighting order to Ilyinka. Several days later this same formation successfully attacked Morozovsk.

In token of its signal contribution to the enemy rout in the Volga-Don area, the 24th Corps was renamed the 2nd Guards Tatsinskaya Tank Corps, while its commander, Badanov, was the first in the USSR to be decorated with the Order of Suvorov, 2nd Class. Many of his officers, political instructors and men were also decorated.

The successful blows struck by the troops of the South-

Western and Stalingrad Fronts on the Kotelnikovo and Morozovsk sectors sealed the fate of Paulus's encircled troops
at Stalingrad.

Having brilliantly accomplished their mission of routing the
enemy at great speed, the troops of the South-Western and
Stalingrad Fronts disrupted Manstein's plan of affording
Paulus relief. In early January, Vatutin's troops reached the
line running from Novaya Kalitva through Krizskoye-Chert-
kovo-Voloshino and Millerovo to Morozovsk, now directly
menacing the entire German grouping in the Caucasus.

By the end of December the remnants of the Germans'
Kotelnikovo group had rolled back to a line running through
Tsimlyanskaya, Zhukovskaya, Dubovskoye and Zimovniki,
while the decimated Tormosin group had retreated to the
Chernyshevskaya-Loznoi-Tsimlyanskaya line.

Thus, the attempt made by General Field-Marshal Manstein,
Commander of Army Group Don, to break through our
exterior perimeter and lead Paulus out of encirclement was
a total failure.

This was understood by both the officers and men of the
trapped forces, who sought in their despair to avoid the
imminent disaster. When they lost all hope of salvation they
became embittered.

After the failed attempt to break the ring holding the
doomed encircled troops, the military and political leadership
of Nazi Germany sought not to relieve them, but to get them
to fight on for as long as possible so as to tie up the Soviet
forces. The aim was to win as much time as possible to withdraw
forces from the Caucasus and to rush troops from other
Fronts to form a new front that would be able in some measure
to check our counter-offensive.

Meanwhile, the Soviet Supreme Command took steps to
finish off the trapped grouping as soon as possible, and thus
release the two Fronts engaged here for the quicker destruction
of Nazi forces retreating from the Caucasus, and those in
the south.

The Supreme Commander kept hurrying the Front commanders.

In late December the State Defence Committee met to
discuss further action.

The Supreme Commander suggested: "Only one man should direct operations to destroy the encircled enemy grouping. The fact that there are two Front commanders is interfering with this."

The committee members present agreed.

"Who gets this mission?"

Somebody suggested K. K. Rokossovsky for the job.

"Why aren't you saying anything?" the Supreme Commander turned to me.

"I think both commanders are worthy," I said. "Yeremenko will be offended if we put the forces of the Stalingrad Front under Rokossovsky."

"This is no time to be getting offended," Stalin retorted curtly. Then he ordered, "Call Yeremenko and notify him of the State Defence Committee's decision."

I phoned Yeremenko on the H F line that same evening and said: "Comrade Yeremenko, the State Defence Committee has decided to give Rokossovsky the job of snuffing out the enemy's Stalingrad grouping. Therefore, you are to place the 57th, 64th and 62nd armies of the Stalingrad Front under the Don Front."

Yeremenko asked, "What's the reason?"

I explained.

I could feel that Yeremenko was upset; I did not think he could continue the conversation calmly and so I suggested he call me back later. He did so in fifteen minutes.

"Comrade General, I just can't understand," he said, "why the preference for the Don Front Command? Please tell Comrade Stalin I want to stay here until the enemy is completely destroyed."

When I suggested he call up the Supreme Commander himself, Yeremenko said, "I already tried, but Poskrebyshev told me Comrade Stalin had said to address all my questions to you."

I put a call through to the Supreme Commander to tell him what Yeremenko had said. Stalin was none too pleased and said a directive should be issued at once to place three armies of the Stalingrad Front under Rokossovsky. This directive was issued on December 30, 1942.

The Staff of the Stalingrad Front was ordered to head

the group of armies operating on the Kotelnikovo Sector and to continue the destruction of enemy forces in the Kotelnikovo area. Shortly afterwards, the Stalingrad Front was renamed the Southern Front and was operating on the Rostov-on-the-Don sector.

By order of the Supreme Command, as of December 30, 1942, the 62nd, 64th and 57th armies of the Stalingrad Front were placed under the Don Front.

By January 10, 1943, the Don Front had a total operational strength of 212,000 officers and men, some 6,900 guns and mortars, over 250 tanks and up to 300 combat aircraft.

Vasilevsky was mainly occupied in late December with the task of destroying German troops at Kotelnikovo, Tormosin and Morozovsk. The Supreme Command appointed to the Don Front as its representative General N. N. Voronov, who in collaboration with the Front Military Council put forward a plan for destroying the trapped German grouping, known under the code name of Ring.

After analyzing this plan, the Supreme Command and the General Staff pointed out to General Voronov:

"The main shortcoming of your Ring plan is that the major and secondary assault forces strike in differing directions and do not link up anywhere; therefore, the operation's success is doubtful.

"The Supreme Command believes your prime mission in the first stage of the operation is to cleave through and destroy the western grouping of the encircled enemy forces in the Kravtsov-Baburkin-Marinovka-Karpovka area, so that our main attack mounted from the Dmitrievka-State Farm No. 1-Baburkin area wheel south to the Karpovskaya Railway Station area, while the secondary attack mounted by the 57th Army from Kravtsov and Sklyarov area drive towards the direction of the main assault and accomplish a link-up in the Karpovskaya Railway Station area.

"Simultaneously, it's advisable that an assault by the 66th Army through Orlovka be organized in the direction of the Krasny Oktyabr settlement. The 62nd Army meanwhile will attack from the opposite direction in order to link up with the 66th Army and thus cut off the industrial zone from the main enemy grouping.

"The Supreme Command hereby orders you to revise the plan as specified. The date you suggest for starting the operation has been approved.

"The first stage of the operation is to be completed within five or six days.

"The operational plan for the second stage is to be delivered through the General Staff by January 9. The results obtained during the first stage should be given due consideration.
"J. Stalin
"G. Zhukov

"January 28, 1942"

In January 1943, the exterior perimeter in the Don area advanced between 200 and 250 kilometres westward due to the efforts of the South-Western and Stalingrad Fronts. The hemmed-in German force was in a catastrophic position. These forces had no prospect of relief, stocks had run out, troops were on starvation rations, hospitals were packed, and the death rate from injury and disease was steep. The catastrophe was imminent.

To stop the bloodshed, the Supreme Command ordered the Don Front Command to present the 6th Army with a surrender ultimatum on generally accepted terms. Despite the inescapable defeat, the Nazi Command ordered its troops to reject the ultimatum and fight to the last ditch. Meanwhile, it held out promised relief that it never intended to provide, and the German rank and file knew it.

On January 10, 1943, after an intensive artillery bombardment, the Don Front launched an offensive to split up the enemy grouping and destroy it piecemeal. However, they fell short of their objectives.

On January 22, after additional preparation, the Don Front launched a fresh offensive. The enemy buckled and began rolling back. In the fighting General Tolbukhin's 57th Army and General Zhadov's 66th Army did remarkably well.

This is how an intelligence officer of Paulus's 6th Army described the Soviet-compelled German retreat in his reminiscences:

"We were forced back along the entire front... Our withdrawal was more like a flight... There was downright panic in places... The road of retreat was strewn with corpses, which blizzards, seemingly out of compassion, soon blanketed with snow... We were retreating without order." And further: "Out-racing death, which easily caught up to pluck out whole batches of victims, the army rolled back on to a small scrap of land that was an inferno."[1]

The southern group of German forces was snuffed out on January 31, its remnants, led by General Field-Marshal Paulus, commander of the 6th Army, surrendered. The remnants of the northern group capitulated on February 2. The great battle on the Volga was over; a major grouping of forces of Nazi Germany and its satellites ceased to exist.

The Stalingrad battle was extremely fierce, one that I personally can compare only to the battle at Moscow. Between November 19, 1942, and February 2, 1943, 32 divisions and 3 brigades were destroyed and the other 16 divisions lost from half to three-quarters of their effective strength.

Total enemy losses in the Volga-Don-Stalingrad area ran into some 1.5 million men, 3,500 tanks and assault weapons, 12,000 guns and mortars and 3,000 aircraft and large amounts of other equipment. This crippling toll had a telling effect on the overall strategic situation, shaking Nazi Germany's entire war machine to its foundations.

What were the causes of the German debacle at Stalingrad and our epoch-making victory?

The Nazis's strategic plans for 1942 failed because they underestimated the forces and potential of the Soviet state and the indomitable spirit of the people, and because they overestimated their own forces and capabilities.

Skilful utilization of the surprise factor, correct selection of the directions of the main effort, accurate detection of weak points in the enemy defences led to the defeat of the German troops in the operations code-named Uranus, Small Saturn, and Ring. Also of great importance was the correct calculation of the required manpower and materiel for the quickest possible breakthrough of tactical defences, as well as

---

[1] J. Wieder, *Die Tragödie von Stalingrad*, op. cit., pp. 59, 64.

full-scale exploitation of an operational breakthrough with the object of enveloping the enemy main grouping.

The actions of the armoured, mechanized and air forces were decisive in swiftly enveloping and routing the enemy.

The commanders and staff officers left nothing to chance; they meticulously thought out every detail in preparing the counter-offensive. And during the offensive, control of the troops in all echelons was marked by clarity of purpose, firmness and foresight.

The party-political work conducted by the military councils, political bodies, Party and YCL organizations and commanders, fostering in soldiers confidence and bravery and encouraging mass heroism on the battlefield, contributed significantly to the enemy defeat.

The Stalingrad victory turned the tide of war in favour of the Soviet Union and launched the massive efforts to drive the enemy off Soviet territory. After the battle the Soviet Supreme Command took possession of strategic initiative and held in until the war was over. It was a jubilant, though hard-won victory not only for the fighting forces directly destroying the enemy, but also for the Soviet people working day and night to provide the army with the wherewithal to successfully rout the enemy. Patriots of Russia, the Ukraine, Byelorussia, the Baltic republics, the Caucasus, Kazakhstan and Central Asian republics earned immortal fame by their staunchness and mass-scale heroism.

Henceforth, enemy officers and generals and the German people generally began showing more openly their aversion to Hitler and the entire Nazi leadership. They had come to realize that Hitler and his entourage had embroiled the nation in what was an out-and-out gamble and that the victories he had promised had evaporated with their troops in the catastrophe on the Don and the Volga and in the Northern Caucasus.

"The Stalingrad defeat," Lieutenant-General Westphal observed, "came as a deep shock to both the German nation and their army. Never before in all of Germany's history had there been so fearful an end of so large a force."

Because of the rout of the German, Italian, and Romanian armies in the Volga and the Don area and later of the Hungarian armies in the Ostrogozh-Rossosh operation, Germany's influence on its allies declined drastically. Discord and friction set in when the allies lost faith in Hitler's leadership and wanted to break out of the web of war in which he had enmeshed these countries.

The German debacle at Stalingrad had a sobering effect on the neutral countries and those still pursuing a wait-and see policy, compelling them to acknowledge the USSR's superb power and the inevitable defeat of Nazi Germany.

It is common knowledge that news of the Nazi debacle at Stalingrad prompted jubilation around the world. It was a tremendous inspiration to peoples to further their efforts against Nazi occupation.

For myself personally, the defence of Stalingrad, the preparation of the counter-offensive and participation in deciding the main aspects of operations in the south were of special importance as now I had accumulated far more experience in mounting a counter-offensive than I had at Moscow in 1941 where limited forces did not permit a counter-offensive with the aim of encircling an enemy grouping.

For successful general leadership of the counter-offensive at Stalingrad and the major results, along with others I was decorated with the Order of Suvorov 1st Class (No. 1).

I regarded this decoration not only as a great personal honour, but also as a summons to work still harder to bring nearer the hour of the complete rout of the enemy, the hour of total and final victory. Vasilevsky, Voronov, Vatutin, Yeremenko, Rokossovsky were also awarded the Order of Suvorov 1st Class. Many generals, officers, sergeants and soldiers also received high government decorations.

The successful defeat of the German forces at Stalingrad, on the Don and in the Caucasus opened the door to a stepped-up offensive on the South-Western Direction by all the Fronts.

After smashing the enemy in the Don-Volga area, successful operations were conducted in the Ostrogozh-Rossosh and the Voronezh-Kastornoye sectors. Soviet troops forced ahead moving further west and taking Rostov, Novocherkassk, Kursk, Kharkov and a number of other key areas. The overall operational and strategic situation along the entire Soviet-German front had swung steeply against the Nazi forces.

CHAPTER 4

The Crushing Defeat of the Nazi Troops in the Kursk Bulge

The battle of Stalingrad was a real landmark in the campaign of the winter of 1942/1943, an event of tremendous international importance. Once the enemy had been annihilated in the Demyansk area on the North-Western Front, our troops advanced to the River Lovat. The enemy was driven out of the Rzhev-Vyazma region by the forces on the Western Front and the Dukhovshchina-Spas Demensk line was taken.

By the middle of March 1943 the wind of change was blowing in favour of the Soviet Union on all Fronts. After the crushing defeat of the German, Romanian, Italian, and Hungarian troops in the Volga and Don regions and in the North Caucasus, the enemy, having sustained heavy losses, had withdrawn to the Sevsk-Rylsk-Sumy-Akhtyrka-Krasnograd-Slavyansk-Lisichansk-Taganrog line by mid-March.

From the moment the Soviet forces started the counter-offensive near Stalingrad in November 1942 until March 1943, all in all, they routed more than one hundred enemy divisions. Naturally, these great victories were won at great cost to our fighters and the Soviet people, for we also sustained heavy losses.

A lull followed on the Fronts except for sectors of the Voronezh, South-Western and Southern Fronts and in the Kuban area where bitter fighting continued.

To prevent the situation of its forces on the southern flank of the Front from further deteriorating, after obtaining reinforcements, the German High Command organized a counter-offensive on the South-Western Front. This operation was to push our forces back beyond the River Seversky Donets, and then, under the cover of the defences, to attack the forces on the Voronezh Front and capture Kharkov and Belgorod.

As was later discovered from captured documents, if the situation had been in their favour, the Nazi Command had intended to step up operations and eradicate the Kursk Salient.

At the beginning of March, from the Lyubotin area, the enemy dealt a telling counterblow at the forces on the left flank of the Voronezh Front; owing to their losses, our troops were compelled to withdraw. The enemy seized Kharkov again on March 16 and began to mount an offensive on the Belgorod sector.

A representative of the Stavka at that time, I was on the North-Western Front, which was under the command of Marshal Timoshenko. Having reached the River Lovat, our forces were preparing to force a crossing.

Stalin rang the command post of the North-Western Front on either the 13th or 14th of March.

I described to the Supreme Commander the situation on the River Lovat and told him that the river had become impassable owing to the early thaw and that the troops of the North-Western Front would evidently have to cease their offensive operations for a while.

Stalin agreed. After he had put a few more questions to me regarding the possible course of events on the North-Western Front, Stalin ended up by informing me that V. D. Sokolovsky had been made Commander of the Western Front.

I suggested that Konev, who had commanded the Western Front before that, should be appointed Commander of the North-Western Front and that Timoshenko should be sent to the south as a representative of the Stavka to assist the commanders on the Southern and South-Western Fronts. He knew these regions well, and in the last few days events there had turned to our disadvantage.

"All right," said Stalin, "I'll tell Poskrebyshev to get Konev to ring you. You give him all your instructions, and you yourself can set out for the General Headquarters tomorrow. We must discuss the situation on the South-Western and Voronezh Fronts. You may," he added, "have to go to the Kharkov area."

Some time later, Konev telephoned me.

"The Supreme Commander has ordered that you should be appointed Commander of the North-Western Front instead of Timoshenko, who is to be sent to the southern flank of our Front as a representative of the Stavka," I told him.

Konev thanked me and said he would leave for his new appointment on the following morning.

The next morning I set out for the General Headquarters.

I arrived in Moscow late in the evening on that same day. I was extremely tired as we had had to travel by jeep along extremely rough roads.

Poskrebyshev told me by telephone that Stalin had got together a large number of people to discuss fuel supplies for metal production and electricity generation and for the aircraft and tank works. I was ordered to attend the meeting immediately, so after a quick bite I set out for the Kremlin.

Gathered in the study of the Supreme Commander, besides the members of the Politbureau, were department heads, designers, and managers of the biggest factories. Their reports clearly revealed the grave situation that still persisted in industry. There were hold-ups in the aid under Lend-Lease from the USA.

It was at least three o'clock in the morning before the meeting came to an end. All those who had attended it left either for the Central Committee, or the Council of People's Commissars or Gosplan (State Planning Committee) in the quest for resources and the enforcement of urgent measures to make industry more efficient.

Stalin came up to me after the meeting and asked, "Have you had dinner?"

"No."

"Well, then come over to my place and we can talk about the situation in the Kharkov area at the same time."

While we were eating, a map showing the sectors on the South-Western and Voronezh Fronts arrived from the General Staff. The General Staff officer, who was charged with keeping abreast of the situation on the Voronezh Front, said that it had seriously deteriorated by March 16. A difficult situation had ensued to the south-west of Kharkov after the enemy's armoured and motorized units, which had mounted an offensive from the Kramatorsk area, forced back the units on the South-Western Front beyond the River Donets.

At the same time, the enemy units had launched an offensive from the Poltava area and Krasnograd. N. F. Vatutin drew off the units of the 3rd Tank Army and the 69th Army, which had managed to rush ahead and organized more closely deployed formations to the west and south-west of Kharkov. The troops on the Voronezh Front, which was commanded by Colonel-General F. I. Golikov, were not withdrawn.

"Why didn't the General Staff suggest that they should withdraw?" asked the Supreme Commander.

"We did advise them to," replied the officer.

"The General Staff should have intervened in affairs on that front," Stalin remarked insistently. Then, after a moment's thought, he turned to me, "You're going to have to fly out to the front in the morning."

The Supreme Commander immediately telephoned the member of the Military Council on the Voronezh Front, Khrushchev and reprimanded him because the Military Council had not taken measures to combat the enemy's counter-offensives. Having dismissed the officer, the Supreme Commander said, "But we must finish our dinner all the same."

It was five o'clock in the morning by that time...

After dinner, which really was more like breakfast, I requested permission to go to the People's Commissariat for Defence to get ready for the flight to the Voronezh Front. At seven o'clock in the morning I left the Central Aerodrome for the headquarters of the Voronezh Front. The moment I got into the plane I fell fast asleep, and was only awakened by the jolt as the aircraft landed.

That very day I rang Stalin over the HF and informed him of the state of affairs on the Voronezh Front which was worse than that described by the General Staff officer that morning. After they had captured Kharkov, the enemy units, not hindered by any particular resistance, advanced on the Belgorod sector and took Kazachya Lopan.

"All available forces from the Stavka's reserves must," I reported to the Supreme Commander, "be deployed here; otherwise, the Germans will capture Belgorod and continue their offensive on the Kursk sector."

During a conversation with Vasilevsky an hour later I learned that a decision had already been taken by the Supreme Commander and instructions issued to the effect that the 21st Army, the 1st Tank Army and the 64th Army were to be transferred to the Belgorod area. The tank army formed part of my reserve.

Belgorod was taken by the SS Panzer Corps on March 18, but the enemy was no longer able to break through further to the north.

From the report made to me by the Commander of the 52nd Guards Division, N. D. Kozin, I discovered the following: the army vanguard under Commander of the 155th Guards Rifle Regiment, Lieutenant-Colonel G. G. Pantyukhov, had, on the orders of the Commander of the 21st Army, General I. M. Chistyakov, been sent to Belgorod to come into contact with the enemy and take prisoners.

As it advanced towards Belgorod, the army vanguard spotted the enemy and ambushed him not far from Shapino, north of Belgorod, taking prisoners from the Panzer Division Totenkopf. It was discovered that the enemy detachment was heading for Oboyan.

By the end of the day on March 18, the 52nd Division's main forces had occupied defensive positions to the north of Belgorod and advanced battle outposts. From then on, no matter how the enemy tried to dislodge our troops, he failed. The 67th Guards Rifle Division took up defensive positions to the right of the 52nd Division, and the 375th Rifle Division to the left of it.

Lieutenant-Colonel P. S. Babich, Commander of the 153rd Regiment, Lieutenant-Colonel I. S. Voronov, the head of the division's political department, and the Commander of the 151st Rifle Regiment, Lieutenant-Colonel I. F. Yudich, had, according to the report submitted by the Commander of the 52nd Division, distinguished themselves in the fighting to the north of Belgorod. I presented decorations to many of the fighters in this division on March 20.

The main forces of the 21st Army spent March 20 and 21 setting up sufficiently impregnable defences to the north of Belgorod, and the forces of the 1st Tank Army were concentrated to the south of Oboyan.

At the end of March, the Nazi forces' repeated attempts to break through our troops' defences near Belgorod and the Seversky Donets, where the 64th Army was entrenched at that time, ended in failure. Having sustained great losses, the enemy dug himself in along the line he had reached.

From that moment on, the situation became stable on the Kursk Bulge, both sides preparing for a decisive encounter.

The Supreme Commander ordered that Colonel-General Vatutin should be appointed Commander of the Voronezh Front to further assist in its supervision. Once he had taken command, with his usual energy Nikolai Vatutin got down to building up the forces on the front and setting up defence formations well disposed in depth.

At the end of March and the beginning of April, Vatutin and I visited almost all the units of the Front. With the commanders of the units and formations we appraised the situation, defined the tasks to be tackled and measures to be taken more precisely, should the enemy launch an offensive. I visited the sector of the defences held by the 52nd Guards Rifle Division twice as I was very anxious about it. I was of the opinion that this division would be the recipient of the enemy's main blow. The other commanders of the Front and the army concurred, and we resolved to reinforce this all-important sector with artillery by every means.

The time had come to get down to planning the battle for Kursk.

As agreed with the Chief of General Staff, Vasilevsky, and the commanders of Fronts, we took a series of measures to arrange thorough reconnaissance of enemy positions on the sectors of the Central, Voronezh and South-Western Fronts.

Vasilevsky gave the intelligence division and the Central Headquarters of the partisan movement the assignment of discovering the extent and distribution of the enemy's reserves in depth, the regrouping and concentration of troops moved in from France, Germany, and other countries.

In general, the impact of our offensive operations against the enemy was significantly intensified by the activities of the partisans which were arranged and directed from the centre by means of the constant and indefatigable efforts of local underground party organizations. The actions of the partisans were coordinated with those of the regular army, which they assisted in obtaining data on the enemy, while destroying his reserves, cutting his communications, and hampering the redeployment of his forces and weapons.

In 1942, the Nazis already had to pit almost ten per cent of their ground forces on the Soviet-German front against the partisans. In 1943, SS and SD police forces, 500,000 soldiers from auxiliary units and more than 25 divisions from the army in the field were being employed for these purposes.

The Communist Party carefully supervised the patriotic struggle of the people against the Nazi invaders, thereby rendering valuable assistance to our regular forces. Communists in partisan detachments not only took up arms in the struggle, but also did much to enlighten the population politically by circulating leaflets, making appeals, disseminating reports from the Soviet Information Agency and exposing the mendacious propaganda put out by the enemy. The partisans' efforts did much to undermine the morale of the enemy forces.

The forces on the fronts carried out intensive reconnaissance both from the air and on the ground, within their own sectors. Consequently, by the beginning of April we had sufficiently detailed information on the deployment of the enemy forces around Orel, Sumy, Belgorod, and Kharkov. Once I had analyzed these data and also those we had managed to obtain from the wider theatre of operations and had discussed them with the commanding officers of the Voronezh and Central Fronts, and then with the Chief of General Staff, Vasilevsky, I sent the Supreme Commander the following report:

"To Comrade Vasilyev[1]

"5:30 a. m., April 8, 1943

"I hereby state my opinion on the possible movements of the enemy in the spring and summer of 1943 and our plans for defensive actions in the coming months.

"1. Having suffered serious losses in the winter campaign of 1942/43, the enemy would not appear to be able to build up big reserves by the spring to resume the offensive on the

---

[1] Stalin's code name.— *Author*.

Caucasus and to push forward to the Volga to make a wide enveloping movement around Moscow.

"Owing to the inadequacy of large reserves, in the spring and first half of the summer of 1943 the enemy will be forced to launch offensive operations on a smaller front and resolve the task facing him strictly in stages, his main aim being the taking of Moscow.

"Proceeding from the fact that, at the given moment, there are groupings deployed against our Central, Voronezh and South-Western Fronts, I believe that the enemy's main offensives will be spearheaded at these fronts, in order to rout our forces on this sector and to gain freedom for his manoeuvres to outflank Moscow and get as close to it as possible.

"2. At the first stage, having gathered as many of his forces as possible, including at least 13 to 15 tank divisions and large air support, the enemy will evidently deal the blow with his Orel-Kromy grouping in the enveloping movement around Kursk from the north-east and likewise with the Belgorod-Kharkov grouping from the south-east.

"An additional attack on Kursk from the south-west aimed at dividing our front must be expected from the west, from the area around Vorozhba between the rivers Seim and Psyol. The enemy will attempt by means of this operation to defeat and surround our 13th, 70th, 65th, 38th, 40th, and 21st armies, his ultimate purpose at this stage being to reach the River Korocha-Korocha-Tim-River Tim-Droskovo line.

"3. At the second stage, the enemy will attempt to come out on the flank and in the rear of the South-Western Front, his general direction being through Valuiki-Urazovo.

"To counter this offensive, the enemy may deal a blow at the Lisichansk area on a northern, Svatovo-Urazovo sector.

"In the remaining sectors the enemy will strive to reach the Livny-Kastornoye-Stary and Novy Oskol line.

"4. At the third stage, after the corresponding regrouping, the enemy will possibly try to reach the Liski-Voronezh-Yelets front and, taking cover in a south-eastern direction, may launch an offensive as part of the wide enveloping movement around Moscow from the south-east via Ranenburg-Ryazhsk-Ryazan.

"5. In his offensive operations this year the enemy may

be expected to count chiefly on his tank divisions and air force since his infantry is at present considerably less well prepared for offensive action than it was last year.

"At the present time, the enemy has as many as 12 tank divisions lined up along the Central and Voronezh Fronts and, by taking in three or four tank divisions from other sectors, he could pitch as many as 15 or 16 tank divisions with some 2,500 tanks against our Kursk grouping.

"6. If the enemy is to be crushed by our defensive formations, besides measures to build up the anti-tank defences on the Central and Voronezh Fronts, we must get together 30 anti-tank artillery regiments from the passive sectors as rapidly as possible and redeploy them as part of the Supreme Command's reserves in the areas threatened; all the regiments of the self-propelled artillery must be concentrated in the Livny-Kastornoye-Stary Oskol sector. Even now it would be desirable for some of the regiments to be placed under Rokossovsky and Vatutin as reinforcements and for as many aircraft as possible to be transferred to the Supreme Command's reserves to smash the shock groupings with massed attacks from the air coordinated with action by tank and rifle formations and to frustrate the plan for the enemy's offensive.

"I am not familiar with the final location of our operational reserves; therefore I believe it expedient to propose their deployment in the Yefremov-Livny-Kastornoye-Novy Oskol-Valuiki-Rossosh-Liski-Voronezh-Yelets area. The deeper reserve echelon should be deployed around Ryazhsk, Ranenburg, Michurinsk, and Tambov.

"There must be one reserve army in the Tula-Stalinogorsk area.

"I do not believe it is necessary for our forces to mount a preventive offensive in the next few days. It will be better if we wear the enemy out in defensive action, destroy his tanks, and then, taking in fresh reserves, by going over to an all-out offensive we will finish off the enemy's main grouping.

"Konstantinov "[1]

---

[1] Zhukov's code name.— *Author.*

Our forecasts did not differ in the main from what the Nazi commanding officers had in fact intended to do.

The orders issued by Hitler on April 15, 1943, read as follows:

"General Headquarters of the Führer

"April 15, 1943

"Top Secret

"For Commanding Officers Only

"As soon as weather conditions permit, I have decided to launch the Citadel offensive, the first offensive operation this year.

"Decisive importance is attributed to this offensive. It should be carried out rapidly and with definite success. The offensive should give us the initiative for the whole of the spring and summer of this year.

"In this connection, all preparatory measures should be implemented with the greatest of care and energy. The best formations, the best armaments, the best commanding officers and a large amount of ammunition should be used where the main thrusts are being made. Each commanding officer, every soldier of the line must become thoroughly aware of the decisive significance of this offensive. The victory near Kursk should be a torch for the whole world.

"I hereby give the following orders:

"1. The aim of the offensive is a concentrated thrust carried out decisively and rapidly by the forces of one main attack force from the area around Belgorod and of another from the area to the south of Orel to surround the forces in the Kursk area by a concentric offensive and destroy them.

"2. It is necessary:

"a) to take every possible advantage of the surprise factor and to keep the enemy in ignorance above all with regard to the deadline for the offensive to begin;

"b) to ensure maximum concentration of the striking forces on a narrow sector in order to break through the enemy defences, taking advantage of the overwhelming superiority in all means of attack in that area (tanks, assault equipment, artillery, mortars, and so forth), with a single thrust, unite both the attacking armies and thereby close the encirclement.

"In both army groupings, the newly arrived formations, which had joined up with the main attack army, should not have any radio communication...

"7. For the purposes of secrecy, only those persons whose involvement is absolutely necessary, should be informed of the plans for the operation."

Thus, having appraised the situation correctly, before the German offensive was launched, the Soviet commanding officers had precisely determined the probability and direction of the Nazi forces' manoeuvres in the Kursk Bulge area.

On April 9 or 10, I don't remember exactly, Vasilevsky arrived at the headquarters of the Voronezh Front. Once again he and I discussed my report in detail, the situation obtaining, the plans for disposition of the operational and strategical reserves and the nature of the forthcoming operations. We concurred on all questions.

Having drawn up a draft for the Supreme Command directive regarding the disposition of the Supreme Command reserves and the setting up of the Steppe Front, we sent it to the Supreme Commander bearing our signatures.

This document envisaged the disposition of the armies and the means of reinforcements on the Fronts. It was proposed that the Steppe Front headquarters should be established in Novy Oskol, to have a command post of the Front in Korocha, and the Front's auxiliary troop control post in Veliky Burluk. As was always the case in preparing big operations, the Fronts' commanding officers and the headquarters were to communicate their considerations and suggestions regarding the nature of the operations to the General Staff.

As some of the accounts of the organization of defences and the counter-offensive in the area around Kursk in 1943 are incorrect, I believe it is necessary here to quote from the relevant documents that were filed at the General Headquarters and the General Staff. I thereby note that no other documents were delivered to the General Headquarters.

Here is the report of April 10, sent on the orders of the General Staff, by the Chief of Staff of the Central Front, Lieutenant-General M. S. Malinin.

"From the Central Front, April 10, 1943

"To the Operations Chief, General Staff of the Red Army

"Colonel-General Antonov[1]

"...4. The objective and most probable directions of the enemy offensive in the spring and summer period of 1943:

"a) Taking into account the forces and means and, what is most important, the outcome of the offensives in 1941 and 1942, in the spring and summer period of 1943 an enemy offensive is to be expected solely in the Kursk and Voronezh operational direction.

"There is hardly likely to be an enemy offensive on other sectors.

"The general strategical situation being as it is at this stage in the war, it would be to the Germans' benefit to ensure a firm hold on the Crimea, the Donbass and the Ukraine and, for that purpose, to advance the front to the Shterovka-Starobelsk-Rovenki-Liski-Voronezh-Livny-Novosil line. To achieve this, the enemy will require no less than 60 infantry divisions with the corresponding air, tank and artillery support.

"The enemy cannot concentrate such forces and means on the given sector.

"This is why the Kursk-Voronezh operational direction is acquiring paramount importance.

"b) Proceeding from these operational suppositions, the enemy is expected to direct his main efforts simultaneously along inner and outer radii of action:

"— along the inner radius — from the Orel area via Kromy to Kursk and from the Belgorod area to Kursk via Oboyan;

"— along the outer radius — from the Orel area via Livny to Kastornoye and from the Belgorod area to Kastornoye via Stary Oskol.

"c) If we do not take measures to counter the intended enemy offensive, his successful operations on these sectors could lead to the rout of the forces of the Central and Voronezh Fronts, to the capture by the enemy of the vital Orel-Kursk-Kharkov railway line and to the attainment by his forces of an advantageous line to his firm hold on the Crimea, the Donbass, and the Ukraine.

"d) The enemy cannot set about regrouping and concentrating his forces in the probable directions of his offensive

---

[1] The first three points have been omitted as they merely contain a list of the confronting enemy forces.— *Author*.

and also building up the necessary reserves until the end of spring when the roads have improved and the floods ended.

"Consequently, the enemy may be expected to go over to a decisive offensive in the second half of May 1943.

"5. In the circumstances obtaining in the given operational situation the following measures are deemed expedient:

"a) To destroy the enemy Orel grouping by the joint efforts of the forces of the Western, Bryansk, and Central Fronts, thereby depriving him of the opportunity of dealing a blow at Kastornoye from the Orel area via Livny, of seizing the Mtsensk-Orel-Kursk railway, which is vital to us, and preventing the enemy from using the Bryansk network of railways and dirtroads.

"b) To foil the enemy offensive operations, the forces on the Central and Voronezh Fronts must be reinforced with aircraft, mainly fighters, and anti-tank artillery, not less that 10 regiments being sent to each front.

c) For this purpose, it is desirable to have strong Supreme Command reserves in the Livny-Kastornoye-Liski-Voronezh-Yelets area.

                              "Lieutenant-General Malinin
                              "Chief of Staff, Central Front."

The commanding officers of the Voronezh Front also presented their suggestions.

"To the Chief of General Staff
"of the Red Army, April 12, 1943
"At the present time, it has been established that the Voronezh Front is confronted by:

"1. Nine infantry divisions in the first line (26th, 68th, 323rd, 75th, 255th, 57th, 332nd, 167th and one unidentified). These divisions are positioned along the Krasno Oktyabrskoye-Bolshaya Chernetchina-Krasnopolye-Kazatskoye front. According to the information furnished by prisoners, the unidentified division is advancing towards the Soldatskoye area and is to replace the 332nd Infantry Division.

"These data are being checked. Information is available but has not been checked that there are six infantry divisions in the second echelon. Their position has not yet been established, and these data are also being verified.

"According to radio intelligence, the headquarters of a Hungarian division has been located in the Kharkov area, which may be moved forward in a secondary direction.

"2. At present, there are only six tank divisions (Gross Deutschland, Adolf Hitler, Totenkopf, Reich, the 6th and the 11th). Of these three are in the front line and the other three (Gross Deutschland, the 6th and the 11th) in the second line. According to radio intelligence, the headquarters of the 17th Panzer Division has moved from Alekseyevsky to Tashchagovka, which indicates that this division is moving northwards. With his present forces, the enemy can bring as many as three more tank divisions into the Belgorod area from the South-Western Front sector.

"3. Thus, the enemy is likely to set up a shock group of up to ten tank divisions and not less than six infantry divisions, all in all as many as 1,500 tanks to counter the Voronezh Front; this concentration of forces may be expected in the Borisovka-Belgorod-Murom-Kazachya Lopan area. This shock group may have air support with an effective strength of approximately as many as 500 bombers and no less than 300 fighters.

"It is the enemy's intention to strike blows concentrically from the Belgorod area to the north-east and from the Orel area to the south-east in order to surround our forces deployed to the west of the Belgorod-Kursk line.

"Subsequently an enemy offensive is to be expected on the south-eastern sector at the flank and rear of the South-Western Front with the objective of eventually pushing northwards.

"It is not out of the question, however, that the enemy will decide not to launch an offensive to the south-east this year and will put another plan into effect, namely, after the attacks made concentrically from the Belgorod and Orel areas, he will pursue an offensive to the north-east for the purpose of a wide enveloping movement around Moscow.

"This possibility must be taken into account and the reserves prepared accordingly.

"Thus, opposite the Voronezh Front, the enemy will probably spearhead his main offensive from the Borisovka-Belgorod area on the Stary Oskol sector, with part of his forces moving towards Oboyan and Kursk. Additional attacks are to be expected on the Volchansk-Novy Oskol and Sudzha-Oboyan-Kursk sectors.

"The enemy is not yet ready to launch a big offensive. The offensive is not expected to begin earlier than April 20, but most likely in early May.

"However, individual attacks may be expected at any time. Therefore, we demand that our forces be in a constant state of full combat readiness.

"Fedorov, Nikitin, Fedotov"[1]

Consequently, the Supreme Command did not come to a definite decision until April 12 as to our forces' operations in the spring and summer period of 1943 in the Kursk Bulge area.

At that time, no offensive from the Kursk area was planned. Nor could things have been done differently for our strategical reserves were just being formed, and the Voronezh and Central Fronts, which had sustained losses in the previous battles, needed reinforcements of men, armaments and materiel.

Precisely owing to this situation, the commanding officers on the Fronts received instructions from the Supreme Command to the effect that the Fronts should go over to defensive positions.

The Supreme Command made me responsible for the general supervision of the forces on the Central and Voronezh Fronts on the spot and ensuring that the Supreme Command instructions were carried out.

On April 10, the Supreme Commander rang me in Bobryshevo and ordered me to be in Moscow on April 11 to discuss the plan for the summer campaign of 1943, and in particular with regard to the Kursk Bulge.

Late in the evening on April 11, I returned to Moscow. Vasilevsky told me that Stalin had given orders that a map detailing the situation, the necessary calculations and proposals should be made ready by the evening of April 12.

---

[1] Code names of Vatutin (Fedorov), Khrushchev (Nikitin), and Korzhenevich (Fedotov).— *Author*.

Vasilevsky, his deputy A. I. Antonov, and I spent the whole day on April 12 preparing the necessary information for the report to the Supreme Commander. The three of us got down to the work we had been commissioned to do early in the morning, and since we were fully in accord with one another, everything was ready by the evening. Besides all his other merits, Antonov had a brilliant gift for putting material into shape, and while Vasilevsky and I drafted the report for Stalin, he quickly drew up a map detailing the situation, a chart of operations on the Fronts in the Kursk Bulge area.

We all believed that, proceeding from political, economic, and military and strategical considerations, the Nazis would attempt, at any price, to retain their hold on the front stretching from the Gulf of Finland to the Azov Sea. They could fit out their own forces well in one of the strategical directions and make ready for a big offensive operation in the Kursk Salient area in an attempt to rout the forces of the Central and Voronezh Fronts there. This could change the general strategical situation in favour of the German forces, not to mention the fact that, in these circumstances, the overall length of the front would be considerably shortened and the general operational density of the German defence positions would be increased.

The situation in this sector would make possible a two-pronged movement towards Kursk, one thrust from the area south of Orel, and the other from the Belgorod area. It was assumed that the German commanding officers in the remaining sectors would carry out defensive operations as, according to our General Staff, there the Germans did not have necessary forces for offensive operations.

In the evening of April 12, I went to the GHQ with Vasilevsky and Antonov.

The Supreme Commander listened to our views more attentively than ever before. He agreed that the main forces should be concentrated in the Kursk area, but, just as before, he was anxious about the Moscow sector.

When discussing the plan for the operations at the Supreme Command GHQ, we came to the conclusion that it was imperative to build up stable defences, well organized in depth on all the most important sectors, and above all, in the Kursk Bulge area. In this connection, the commanding officers at the fronts were given the necessary instructions. The forces set about deeper entrenchment. It was decided not to involve in the operation for the time being the Supreme Command's strategical reserves that had been built up and got ready, but to concentrate them closer to the most dangerous sectors.

Thus, by mid-April the Supreme Command had already taken a preliminary decision on deliberate defence. (The italics are mine — *G. Zh.*) True, we repeatedly returned to that question but the final decision on deliberate defence was taken by the Supreme Command at the beginning of June 1943. At that time, the enemy's intention of launching a mighty offensive against the Voronezh and Central Fronts was in actual fact known; it was to involve the biggest tank groupings using the new Tiger and Panther tanks and the self-propelled Ferdinand guns.

The Supreme Command considered the Voronezh, Central, South-Western and Bryansk Fronts to be the main ones involved in the action at the first stage in the summer campaign. According to our calculations, this was to be the main scene of action. We wanted to counter the expected offensive of the German forces with a powerful defence, to defeat them, and, above all, to crush the enemy tank groupings, and then, going over to a counter-offensive, to rout the enemy at long last. Simultaneously with the plan for deliberate defence and counter-offensive, it was also decided to work out a plan for offensive operations, without waiting for the enemy offensive if he should postpone it for a long period.

Thus, our forces' defences were in no way necessitated, but purely deliberate ones, and depending on the situation, the Supreme Command was to choose the moment for going over to the offensive. It was borne in mind that things should not be done in too much of a hurry, nor should they be dragged out too much either. (The italics are mine.— *G.Zh.*)

At the same time it was decided in which sectors the Supreme Command's main reserves should be concentrated. It was intended to deploy them in the Livny-Stary Oskol-Korocha area where defences were to be organized should the enemy break through in the Kursk Bulge area. Other reserves were to be stationed behind the right flank of the Bryansk Front in the Kaluga-Tula-Yefremov area. The 5th Guards Tank Army and a number of other formations of the Supreme Command's reserves were to prepare for action beyond the junction of the Voronezh and South-Western Fronts, in the Liski area.

Vasilevsky and Antonov were ordered to set about drawing up all the documents needed regarding the plan adopted, in order to discuss it yet again at the beginning of May.

I was instructed to fly to the North Caucasian Front. Heavy action was being conducted there to annihilate the enemy's Taman grouping, the core of which was formed by the well-equipped 17th Army of the German forces.

The elimination of the enemy on the Taman Peninsula was of great significance to the Soviet Command. Besides destroying a big enemy grouping of 14 to 16 divisions, numbering approximately 180,000-200,000 men in this sector, as a result of this operation, we liberated Novorossiisk. Since the first half of February the heroic detachment of men of the 18th Army and the sailors of the Black Sea Fleet had been fighting here on a small bridgehead.

People's Commissar for the Navy N. G. Kuznetsov, Air Force Commander A. A. Novikov, General S. M. Shtemenko of the General Staff and I arrived at General Leselidze's 18th Army.

Once we had familiarized ourselves with the situation, forces and resources of the army and the sailors of the Black Sea Fleet, we all came to the conclusion that it was impossible at that time to take any kind of big measures to extend the Novorossiisk bridgehead, which the troops used to call the Little Land.

Indeed, that bridgehead was no more than 30 square kilometres in area all in all. At that time there was one question that particularly worried us, namely whether the Soviet fighters would hold out in the face of the ordeals falling to their lot in an unequal struggle with the enemy who made air attacks on and subjected to artillery fire the defenders of this little bridgehead day and night.

We wanted to ask the advice of the head of the political department of the 18th Army, L. I. Brezhnev, about this; Brezhnev had been here numerous times and was familiar with the situation, but at that moment he was on the Little Land where extremely fierce fighting was going on.

From what the Commander of the Army Leselidze told us, it was clear that our forces were completely determined to fight the enemy until he was ultimately defeated and not allow themselves to be pushed into the sea.

Having told Stalin my views, Shtemenko and I set out for the 56th Army on the North Caucasian Front which was commanded by General A. A. Grechko at that time.

At that moment, another offensive was planned in the area of the Cossack village of Krymskaya, but the army's commanding officers considered that they were not sufficiently prepared for it. They decided to postpone the attack, to bring up the ammunition and the artillery from the passive sectors of the front, and planned the best ways of using the aircraft and the special People's Commissariat of Internal Affairs Division from the Supreme Command's reserves.

At the same time, we also worked together with the commanding officers of the 18th Army. This army's landing party needed the support of the fleet and air attacks at Myskhako on the enemy who confronted the heroic members of the landing party.

Before this, the 56th Army had fought a number of brilliant battles in which it had liberated the area around the River Kuban. Now it was to smash the enemy defences of the 17th Army in the area around Krymskaya and take the enemy's Novorossiisk grouping in the rear. It was further planned to combine the efforts of the forces on the front to eliminate the enemy's Taman bridgehead.

The rout of the enemy on the approaches to Krymskaya and its capture were assigned to the 56th Army alone, but its forces were limited, and neither the Supreme Command nor the Front were seriously in a position to provide it with reinforcements. The army had to break through the strongly fortified defences that the German forces had set up on the approaches to the village. Grechko planned and made preparations for the operation expertly and with great foresight.

The 56th Army's offensive on Krymskaya began on April 29. In spite of the scarcity of its forces, especially aircraft, tanks, and artillery, skilfully manoeuvring the means available, the army's commanding officers crushed the sustained resistance of the enemy defence. The troops of the 56th Army captured the village, an important railway junction and pushed the enemy back beyond Krymskaya.

Owing to the lack of resources, the 56th Army, like the other armies on the front, had to call off any further offensive. The offensive operations of the forces on the North Caucasian Front in the area the Stavka had to postpone until a more auspicious moment presented itself.

* * *

The Party's Central Committee, the State Defence Committee, the Supreme Command and the General Staff tackled an enormous amount of work in the spring of 1943 when preparing the Red Army for the summer campaign. The Party rallied the country around it to wreak a crushing defeat on the enemy.

The extensive action being effected on the front meant that a number of measures had to be taken to improve the organization of the forces and re-equip them with the latest technology. The necessary measures to further improve the structure of the Red Army were being carried out at the General Staff. The fronts' and armies' organizational forms were being subjected to revision and improvement. The forces were reinforced with artillery, anti-tank and mortar units and got further backing in better communications. The rifle divisions were supplied with the most up-to-date, automatic, anti-tank weapons and united into rifle corps in order to improve the command of the field armies and boost their might.

New artillery formations armed with more efficient systems were built up. Artillery breach brigades, divisions, and corps were formed from the reserves of the Supreme Command and were intended to create high fire density on the main sectors in major offensive operations. Anti-aircraft divisions began to be put at the disposal of the Fronts and the country's anti-aircraft defence, greatly improving its capacity.

The Party's Central Committee and the State Defence Committee were particularly concentrating on the production of tanks and self-propelled guns.

By the summer of 1943, besides independent mechanized and tank corps, we had set up and fitted out five tank armies of new structure, which did, as a rule, incorporate two tank and one mechanized corps. Moreover, 18 heavy tank regiments were set up to ensure a breach in the enemy's defences and reinforce the armies.

Much was done to reorganize the air force as well which was equipped with aircraft of improved construction such as the LA-5, YaK-9, PE-2, TU-2, IL-4 aeroplanes. By the summer almost all our aviation had been re-equipped with new materiel and a number of additional air-force units had been formed as part of the Supreme Command's reserves, including eight air corps capable of long-range operations.

Our air force was already superior to that of the Germans in the number of aircraft at its disposal. Each Front had its own air army numbering 700 to 800 aircraft.

Much of our artillery was motorized. The engineer units and communications troops were supplied with Soviet-made vehicles and Studebeckers. The rears of all major Fronts were provided with considerable numbers of motor vehicles. The Red Army's Logistics Division had at its disposal dozens of new motorized battalions and regiments which greatly improved the manoeuvrability and efficiency of all the rear services.

Much attention was paid to training personnel. In 1943, hundreds of thousands of men underwent primary and refresher training at various training centres, large strategic reserves were being formed and strengthened. By July 1, the Supreme Command reserves included several field armies, one air and two tank armies.

By July 1943 our fighting forces numbered more than 6,600,000 people, equipped with 105,000 guns and mortars, approximately 2,200 combat field mounts of rocket artillery, more than 10,000 tanks and self-propelled gun mounts and nearly 10,300 combat aircraft.

The tremendous amount of work done by the State Defence Committee, and the Party to strengthen and retrain the

Soviet troops on the basis of the battle experience accumulated, greatly boosted the forces' fighting efficiency at the Fronts.

The Communist Party as always paid great attention to improving the standard of Party-political work among the troops. Thousands of Communists joined the forces, and their efforts helped to raise the morale among the brave Red Army men. By the end of 1943, there were already 2,700,000 Communists in the Soviet Armed Forces and approximately the same number of Komsomol members.

The political bodies and Party and Komsomol organizations put all their efforts into improving the moral qualities and political awareness of army personnel. This was facilitated by the restructuring of the army political organizations which was executed in accordance with the resolution of the Central Committee of the Communist Party of May 24, 1943, "On the Reorganization of the Structure of Party and Komsomol Organizations in the Red Army and Raising the Role of Front, Army and Division Newspapers".

In accordance with this resolution, Party organizations started to be set up in the battalions instead of in the regiments. Regimental Party bureaux became equated to Party committees. This arrangement of the Party organizations made it easier for the Communists to supervise the grass-roots organizations in a more specific manner. The Party-political work done by the commanders, the political activists, Party and Komsomol organizations, based on the May resolution was one of the major factors boosting the Soviet Armed Forces' combat readiness on the eve of the great and fierce battles with the enemy that ensued in the summer and autumn campaigns of 1943.

By the summer of 1943, just before the battle for Kursk, our Armed Forces were, on the whole, both numerically and qualitatively superior to the Nazi Armed Forces.

Now the Soviet Supreme Command had all the necessary means to crush the enemy forces, to decisively and firmly retain the strategic initiative in all the key directions and dictate its terms to the enemy.

The enemy was preparing to wreak vengeance for the defeat at Stalingrad.

When they realized that their Armed Forces had lost their former superiority over the Red Army, the Nazi military and political leadership took total measures to send their best forces to the Soviet-German front.

Picked troops were moved in from the West in large numbers. Working round the clock, the war industry hastened to produce the new Tiger and Panther tanks and the heavy self-propelled Ferdinand guns. The air force was supplied with Focke-Wulf-190A and Heinkel-129 aircraft. The German forces were considerably reinforced with personnel and materiel.

On the Soviet-German front Germany and its allies had 232 divisions, more than 5,300, 000 men, more than 54,000 guns and mortars, 5,850 tanks and assault weapons, and approximately 3,000 combat planes. Staffs at all levels were intensively working on the plans for the forthcoming offensives.

To conduct the operation planned against the Kursk Salient, the Nazi Command concentrated 50 of its best divisions, including 16 tank and motorized divisions, 11 tank battalions and assault weapon divisions comprising up to 2,700 tanks and assault weapons and more than 2,000 aircraft (almost 69 per cent of all the combat planes on the Eastern Front). More than 900,000 men were ready for battle.

The German commanding officers felt convinced of success. Nazi propaganda launched an all-out campaign to raise morale among the troops by promising certain victory in the impending battles...

In the first half of May I returned to the GHQ from the troops of the North Caucasian Front. At that time, the planning of the summer campaign at the General Staff was in the main being completed. The Supreme Command had carried out thorough intelligence and aerial reconnaissance, which had gained reliable information on the enemy flows of troops and ammunition towards the Orel, Kromy, Bryansk, Kharkov, Krasnograd and Poltava sectors. This confirmed the correctness of our forecasts in April. The Stavka and General Staff became increasingly of the opinion that the German forces might mount an offensive in the next few days.

The Supreme Commander demanded that the Central, Bryansk, Voronezh, and South-Western Fronts be alerted to the fact that the forces on the fronts should be completely ready to meet an enemy offensive. On his orders, a Supreme Command's directive was issued in which provisions were made in the case of intensive enemy action. The expected offensive was to be halted by aircraft and artillery counter-preparation.

In response to the Stavka's warning, the commanding officers at the fronts effected a series of fresh measures to intensify the system of fire and anti-tank defences, and artificial obstacles.

Here is one of the reports regarding this question sent in by the Command of the Central Front:

"Stavka of the Supreme Command

"For Comrade J. Stalin

"Re Supreme Command directive of May 8,1943, I hereby report:

"1. On receiving the Supreme Command directive, all the armies and independent corps on the Central Front were ordered to have their troops ready for battle by the morning of May 10.

"2. Throughout May 9 and 10:

"a) The troops were told of the likelihood of an enemy offensive within the next few days;

"b) Units of the lst and 2nd echelons and of the reserve were made completely ready for battle. The commanding officers and staffs are inspecting troop readiness on the spot;

"c) Army reconnaissance and fire have been intensified within the army zones, especially on the Orel sector. In units of the first echelon the reliability of coordinated fire is being checked in practice. The units of the second echelon and the reserve are doing additional reconnoitring in the directions of possible action and are defining more precisely aspects of coordination with units of the first echelon. The ammunition stocks are being replenished at firing positions. Fortifications have been strengthened, especially on sectors where tanks may be used. Mines are being laid in depth in defence zones. The technical communications have been checked and found to operate faultlessly.

"3. The 16th Air Army has stepped up aerial reconnaissance and is keeping the enemy under careful observation in the

Glazunovka-Orel-Kromy-Komariki area. Air formations and
army units are ready to counter enemy air attacks and put a stop
to any possible enemy offensive operations.

"4. To frustrate a possible enemy offensive on the Orel-Kursk
sector, counter-preparations have been made involving the
artillery of the 13th Army and the aircraft of the 16th Air Army.

"Rokossovsky, Telegin, Malinin"

Very similar reports arrived from the other Fronts.

General of the Army Vatutin regarded the situation taking
shape somewhat differently. Although he was not opposed to the
defence measures, he suggested to the Supreme Commander
that a forestalling blow should be struck at the enemy's Belgorod-Kharkov grouping. In this, he had the full support of
the Military Council Member Khrushchev.

Chief of the General Staff Vasilevsky, Antonov and other
General Staff officers were not in favour of this proposal of
the Voronezh Front Military Council. I concurred completely
with the opinion of the General Staff and reported this to
Stalin.

The Supreme Commander himself was not yet certain whether
it was better to counter the enemy with defensive operations or
to deal a forestalling blow at him. Stalin was afraid that our
defences could not take the German forces' blow, as had been
the case several times in 1941 and 1942. At the same time, he
was not sure that our troops were in a position to defeat the
enemy in offensive action.

After repeated discussions, the Supreme Commander resolved to counter the German offensive with all kinds of depth-
echeloned defences, with mighty attacks from the air, and
counterblows from operational and strategic reserves; then,
once the enemy was exhausted and drained of his life blood,
to strike at him with a telling counter-offensive on the Belgorod-Kharkov and Orel sectors, followed by deep thrusts on
all the major sectors.

After defeating the Germans in the Kursk Bulge area, the
Supreme Command intended to liberate the Donbass, the
whole of the Left-Bank Ukraine, to eliminate the enemy's
bridgehead on the Taman Peninsula, liberate the eastern areas
of Byelorussia and create conditions for driving the enemy out
of our territory completely.

The Supreme Command planned to destroy the enemy's main forces in the following manner. As soon as the final concentration of the enemy's main groupings in the assault positions was established, powerful fire was to be opened on him suddenly with all types of guns and mortars, and our aviation was simultaneously to strike at him with all the means at its disposal. It was resolved to continue the aerial onslaught throughout the defensive fighting, using the aircraft from the neighbouring Fronts for this purpose and also the Supreme Command's long-range aviation.

When the enemy went over to the offensive, the forces on the Voronezh and Central Fronts were to doggedly defend every position, every line, with fire, counterattacks and counterblows from the depth. The moving up of reserves incorporating tank corps and armies from operational depth to the threatened sectors was envisaged for this purpose.

Once the enemy had been weakened and brought to a halt, the forces on the Voronezh, Central, Steppe, and Bryansk Fronts, and the left flank of the Western Front and the right flank of the South-Western Front were to go over to a counter-offensive immediately.

In accordance with the decision taken, the Supreme Command issued a directive setting the following assignments:

The Central Front was charged with defending the northern part of the Kursk Salient, in order to exhaust and drain the enemy of his strength in the course of defensive operations; after this, it was to launch a counter-offensive and, in coordination with the Bryansk and Western Fronts, smash the German grouping in the Orel area.

The Voronezh Front, which was charged with defending the southern part of the Kursk Salient was also to wear down the enemy and bleed him white and then to go over to a counter-offensive in coordination with the Steppe Front and the right flank of the South-Western Front and rout the enemy completely in the Kharkov and Belgorod areas. The main forces on the Voronezh Front were to concentrate on the left flank, on the section where the 6th and 7th Guards armies were deployed.

The Steppe Front, which was located beyond the Central and Voronezh Fronts on a line stretching from Izmalkovo, Livny, the River Kshen to Bely Kolodez, was charged with preparing the defences along the above-mentioned line and countering possible breakthroughs by the enemy from the Central and Voronezh Fronts, and was also to be prepared to start offensive operations.

It was the job of the troops on the Bryansk Front and the left flank of the Western Front to help the Central Front in frustrating the enemy offensive and also to be ready to mount an offensive on the Orel sector.

The Central Staff of the partisan movement was set the task of organizing sabotage on a large scale in the enemy rear to wreck all the enemy's vital lines of communication in the Orel, Kharkov and other regions and also to collect and dispatch to the Stavka all the important intelligence information regarding the enemy.

Independent offensive operations were envisaged on a number of sectors in the country's south and on the North-Western Direction to pin down the enemy's forces and prevent him manoeuvring with his reserves.

In May and June the Soviet troops were getting ready for the impending battles in the Kursk area. I myself had to spend both these months with the troops on the Voronezh and Central Fronts, making a study of the situation and our troops' preparations for the forthcoming operations.

Here is one of the typical reports to the Stavka of the Supreme Command at that time:

"May 22, 1943, 04:48

"For Comrade Ivanov[1]

"I hereby report on the situation obtaining on the Central Front on May 21, 1943.

"1. On May 21, it was established by all types of reconnaissance that the enemy has 15 infantry divisions in the first line of defence opposite the Central Front; 13 divisions, including three tank divisions in the second line and in reserve.

"There is, moreover, information that the 2nd Tank Division and the 36th Motorized Division are concentrated to the south of Orel. The intelligence on these two divisions needs to be checked.

---

[1] Stalin's code name.— *Author*.

"The enemy's 4th Tank Division, which was formerly deployed to the west of Sevsk has been moved somewhere. In addition, there are three divisions in the Bryansk and Karachev areas, two of them tank divisions.

"Consequently, as of May 21, the enemy can release 33 divisions, six of them tank divisions, against the Central Front.

"The Front's instrumental and visual reconnaissance has discerned 800 guns, mainly 105-mm and 150-mm ones.

"The enemy has deployed most of his artillery against the 13th Army, the left flank of the 48th Army and the right flank of the 70th Army, i. e. in the Trosno and Pervoye Pozdeyevo sector. Some 600 to 700 tanks are in position behind this main artillery grouping along a line from Zmiyevka to Krasnaya Roshcha. Most of them are concentrated to the east of the River Oka.

"The enemy has concentrated 600 to 650 aircraft in the Orel, Bryansk and Smolensk areas, the main grouping being in the Orel area.

"Over the last few days the enemy has remained passive both on the ground and in the air, restricting himself to minor aerial reconnaissance and occasional air raids.

"The enemy is doing trench work on the front line and in tactical depth and is building up particularly strong defences opposite the 13th Army and in the Krasnaya Slobodka and Senkovo sector where he has already constructed a second line of defence beyond the River Neruch. According to observations, the enemy is setting up a third line of defence on this sector three to four kilometres north of the River Neruch.

"Prisoners have told us that the Nazi Command knows of our grouping to the south of Orel and that we are preparing an offensive, and that German units have been warned about it. Captured airmen assert that the Nazi Command is itself preparing for an offensive and that aircraft are being amassed for this purpose.

"I personally have visited the front lines of the 13th Army, have examined the enemy defences from various points, have observed his actions, talked to the divisional commanders of the 70th and 13th armies and to Commanders Galanin, Pukhov, and Romanenko, and have come to the conclusion that the enemy is not directly prepared for an offensive on the front line.

"Perhaps I am mistaken, and the enemy is camouflaging his preparations very skilfully but, having analyzed the position of his tank units, the insufficient density of the infantry formations, the fact that there are no heavy artillery groupings, and also the scattered nature of the reserves, I believe that the enemy cannot launch an attack before the end of May.

"2. Our 13th and 70th armies' defences are correctly organized and spaced in depth. The 48th Army's defences are sparsely arranged and have a very weak artillery density, and, should the enemy strike at Romanenko's Army and attempt to bypass Maloarkhangelsk from the east in order to go round the main Kostin[1] grouping, Romanenko would fail to withstand the enemy's thrust. The reserves of this front are mainly deployed behind Pukhov and Galanin and would not be able to render Romanenko assistance in time.

"I think that reinforcements should be sent to Romanenko's Army from the Supreme Command reserves in the form of two rifle divisions, three tank regiments with T-34 tanks, two anti-tank regiments and two mortar or artillery regiments from the reserves of the Supreme Command. If Romanenko is supplied with these, he will be able to build up good defences and, should it become necessary, attack with a dense grouping.

"The main shortcomings in the defences of Pukhov's, Galanin's and the Front's other armies is the lack of anti-tank regiments. At the present moment, the Front has only four anti-tank regiments, two of them immobilized in the rear zone of the Front.

"The first echelons' and front lines' anti-tank defences are badly organized owing to the great shortage of 45-mm guns at battalion and regiment level.

"I consider that Kostin should be sent four anti-tank regiments (six altogether with Romanenko) and three regiments of self-propelled 152-mm artillery as soon as possible.

"3. Kostin has not completed preparations for an offensive. When Kostin, Pukhov and I worked this question out on the spot, we came to the conclusion that the breakthrough sector should be shifted two to three kilometres west of the sector chosen by Kostin that is as far as and including Arkhangels-

---

[1] Rokossovsky's code name.— *Author.*

koye, and one reinforced corps should be deployed in the assault echelon and a tank corps to the west of the railway line.

"The breakthrough planned by Kostin cannot be carried out with an artillery grouping since the enemy has considerably reinforced his defences on this sector and extended them in depth.

"If the breakthrough is going to be a success, Kostin probably needs to have one more artillery corps transferred to him.

"As regards ammunition, the front does, on average, have a 1.5 .fire unit.

"I request that Yakovlev be obliged to supply the front with three fire units for the main calibres within two weeks.

"4. At the present moment, Pukhov has 12 divisions, six of them integrated into two corps and six divisions commanded by Pukhov himself. For the benefit of our cause, I request that orders be given for two corps commands to be formed urgently and transferred to Pukhov and one corps command to be formed and transferred to Galanin, who has five independent divisions at present, besides a rifle corps.

"I await your decision.

"Yuryev"[1]

I studied the situation on the Voronezh Front in a similar manner and immediately sent a report in to the Stavka. The commanding officers on the Fronts and their staffs were, in their turn, keeping track of the enemy's every move, summing up the situation and also making immediate reports to the General Staff and the Stavka.

After witnessing the efforts made by the staffs of the army units and the Fronts, I must say that their indefatigable activity played a vital part in the battles of that summer period. Day and night the staff officers painstakingly collected and analyzed information on the enemy troops, their capabilities and intentions. Summaries of the information were submitted to the command so that the latter could make basic decisions.

In order to work out a plan of action for the troops in the

---

[1] Zhukov's code name.— *Ed.*

Kursk Bulge area, the Supreme Command and the General Staff had to organize thorough reconnaissance to gather intelligence on the deployment of enemy troops, the regroupings of the armoured and artillery formations, bombers and fighters, and, what was most important, to get information about the intentions of the enemy command.

Anyone who is familiar with the scope and method of preparing large-scale operations can appreciate the complexity and multiformity of the work done by the commands and staffs in preparing for the Battle for Kursk.

When processing the information obtained, the General Staff had to make an in-depth analysis of it, to draw the appropriate conclusions from all the numerous reports, among which there could be mistaken and misleading ones. It is common knowledge that such many-sided work is carried out by thousands of people, members of the intelligence and reconnaissance services, partisans and people supporting our cause.

When preparing for action, the enemy put into effect a system of special measures to camouflage his intentions such as false regroupings and similar deceptive moves. In such cases, higher staffs had to be able to understand what was going on and distinguish the true from the false.

An operation like this can only be arranged on a large scale if there is centralized direction and pooling of all efforts, and not on the basis of certain individual ideas or assumptions.

Mistakes do, of course, occur even with a system like that.

Thus, the Stavka and the General Staff thought that the enemy was setting up his most powerful grouping in the Orel area to launch an offensive against the Central Front. In actual fact, the strongest grouping was disposed against the Voronezh Front and included eight tank and one motorized divisions, two individual battalions of heavy tanks and one division of assault equipment. They numbered as many as 1,500 tanks and assault weapons. The enemy's tank grouping against the Central Front had only 1,200 tanks and assault weapons. This largely explains the fact that the Central Front was able to repulse the enemy offensive more easily than the Voronezh Front.

How were the main groups of troops disposed when the battle began?

The 6th Guards Army commanded by General Chistyakov and the 7th Guards Army under the command of General Shumilov were defending the most dangerous sectors in the Belgorod area. Right behind the 6th Army, in the second echelon on the Oboyan sector the 1st Tank Army was stationed, command-ed by General Katukov. The 69th Army was disposed beyond the junction between the 6th and 7th armies, covering the sector on Korocha and Prokhorovka. The front reserves — the 35th Guards Rifle Corps and the 2nd Guards Tank Corps — were deployed in the Korocha area, and the 5th Guards Tank Corps to the south of Oboyan.

The 1st Tank Army prepared a line of defences and other dug-in fortifications for all units so that the enemy troops could be countered from stationary positions with tank and all other types of artillery fire, should it prove necessary.

Thanks to the efforts of the troops, a carefully coordinated fire system had been worked out with the neighbouring troops, both along the front line and in depth, as well as air-ground copperation.

The most dangerous sector of the Central Front near Ponyri was defended by the 13th Army under the command of General Pukhov. Beyond the junction between this army and General Galanin's 70th Army, the 2nd Tank Army under the command of General Rodin was disposed in operational depth.

The 9th and 19th Tank corps and several anti-tank artil-lery units comprised the reserves at the front. General S. I. Rudenko's 16th Army was providing the air cover.

I would just like to say a few words about our reserves. When making preparations for the Kursk operation, the Supreme Command put great effort into ensuring that they had large reserves at their disposal.

The troops of the Steppe Front were concentrated on the Livny-Stary Oskol line, and it was their job to counter any surprise attacks and to act as a strong front grouping in the overall counter-offensive. The Steppe Front was comprised of General A. S. Zhadov's 5th Guards Field Army, the 27th, 53rd and 47th field armies, the 5th Guards Tank Army, the

1st Guards Mechanized Corps, the 4th Guards Tank Corps, the 10th Tank Corps, and the 3rd, 5th, and 7th Cavalry corps. The Steppe Front was supported by the 5th Air Army. The Commander of the Front was Colonel-General Konev, the member of the Military Council was Lieutenant-General Susaikov, and the Chief of the Front's Staff was Lieutenant-General Zakharov.

The Steppe Front was allotted a major part in the operation. It was to stop the advancing enemy from making deep thrusts into our lines, and during the counter-offensive its task was to intensify the impact of the blow by striking out with our forces from depth. As the forces on that front were deployed at a considerable distance from the enemy, they were ensured freedom of manoeuvring.

The Steppe Front fundamentally differed in its composition and purpose from the Reserve Front, which had been in operation on the approaches to Moscow in the autumn of 1941. At that time, the Reserve Front was essentially a second operational echelon deployed by the main forces on the rear lines of the Western Front.

The situation finally became clear in the last few days of June, and we realized that the enemy would mount an offensive in the coming days precisely here in the Kursk area and nowhere else.

Stalin telephoned me on June 30. He ordered me to remain on the Orel sector to coordinate the operations of the Central, Bryansk, and Western Fronts.

"Vasilevsky is in command on the Voronezh Front," said the Supreme Commander.

At the time, I was on the Central Front where Rokossovsky and I were working with the troops of the 13th Army, the 2nd Tank Army and the reserve corps. In the section covered by the 13th Army, where the enemy was expected to spearhead his main thrust, provision was made for exceptionally dense artillery fire. The 4th Artillery Corps of the Supreme Command reserve, which was provided with 700 guns and mortars, was disposed near Ponyri. All the main forces of the front's artillery units were deployed here, as well as the Supreme Command reserve. The density of the artillery was brought up to 92 guns and mortars per kilometre of the front line.

To repel a large-scale tank thrust, anti-tank defences on both fronts were constructed in full troop deployment depth and supplied with artillery, tanks, and artificial obstacles and mines.

The strongest anti-tank defences on the Central Front were made ready in the 13th Army's zone and the flanks of the 48th and 70th armies adjacent to it. The anti-tank artillery defences in the 13th Army zone of the Central Front comprised more than 30 pieces per kilometre of the front line.

On the Voronezh Front it comprised 15.6 guns per kilometre of the front line in the zones of the 6th and 7th Guards armies, and as many as 30 pieces if we take into account the means at the disposal of the second echelon. The anti-tank defences on this section were, moreover, reinforced by two tank regiments and one tank brigade.

The defences consisted of anti-tank strong points and tank-proof localities on all sectors where tank attacks were likely to be made. Besides the employment of artillery and tanks, the sections were extensively mined, anti-tank ditches were dug and scarps and other artificial obstacles were created. Mobile obstacle detachments and anti-tank reserves were extensively used as well.

All these anti-tank measures were sufficiently effective, for we had gleaned the tremendous experience in the previous hard fighting. The enemy tank troops were sure to be defeated and this would help to promote the complete rout of the invaders.

The following was established from documents captured and from intelligence information: aviation comprised of the 1st, 4th and 8th Air corps with a total number of more than 2,000 combat planes, under the command of General Field-Marshal Richthofen, was in the field against the Central and Voronezh Fronts.

Since March, the enemy air forces had gradually been stepping up their raids on railway junctions, roads, towns and key targets in the rear and, in June, they started bombing our fighting forces and rear zones increasingly more often.

Cover for the troops and the whole of the Kursk Salient was provided by the 2nd, 5th and 16th air armies and two fighter divisions of the country's Anti-Aircraft Defence. As an enemy offensive was expected, the Fronts were considerably reinforced with anti-aircraft resources which allowed them to cover a large number of objects with two-, three-, four- and five-layer barrage.

The anti-aircraft artillery defences operated in coordination with fighter aircraft and the whole of the observation, warning and guidance service. The carefully and well organized anti-aircraft defence on the fronts and the whole of the Kursk Salient provided reliable cover for our troops and caused the enemy air forces to sustain heavy losses.

The depth of fortifications along the fronts was more than 150 kilometres and, counting the Steppe Front, the overall depth was 250-300 kilometres. Very much was done to provide the troops with ample engineering facilities and effective means of destroying the advancing enemy.

A truly enormous amount of work was done by the logistical service of the Fronts, armies and formations. Unfortunately, little has been written here about the rear services and its officers, who, through their diligence and initiative, greatly helped the troops and commanding officers of all levels to combat the enemy, crush him and put an end to the war with a world-wide historic victory.

In general, a battle cannot be won today without an efficient, accurately functioning logistical service. Lack of the appropriate materiel and supplies during an operation cannot help but result in setbacks.

"Without logistical facilities thoroughly organized on the basis of precise mathematical calculations, without sufficient supplies of everything required for operations, without very accurate estimation of the volume of logistical transportation, without proper evacuation arrangements, any proper and rational conducting of any large combat operation is out of the question," M. V. Frunze said.

On the Central Front the chief of the logistics was General N. A. Antipenko. At the time of the battle for Moscow he had been chief of the logistics of the 49th Army on the Western Front. Even at that time he displayed outstanding organizational abilities. Excellent work was also done by the Chief of the Logistics of the 1st Ukrainian Front, General N. P. Anisimov, who was of great assistance in providing the troops fighting in difficult conditions with materiel. Ani-simov commanded well deserved respect among the troops and in the logistical service. I especially recall the Proskurovo-Chernovtsy operation when he coped splendidly with organiz-ing the Front's logistical facilities in spite of the completely impassable roads in spring.

A really concerted effort was needed to provide materiel for the forthcoming operations so that the actions planned by the Supreme Command on the Fronts could be made pos-sible. On the Central and Voronezh Fronts alone 1,336,000 men, 3,444 tanks and self-propelled pieces of artillery, 19,100,000 guns and mortars, and 2,900 aircraft (taking into account the long-range aircraft and the South-Western Front's 17th Air Army) are known to have been involved in the fighting.

In spite of the bad weather, the great difficulties in transportation and the enemy's attempts to frustrate by air raids deliveries of all that was needed for the imminent operations, logistical services provided us with supplies not only during our defensive engagement, but even after we had rapidly gone over to a counter-offensive.

It is hard for me to say which Front's logistical services were best prepared, but since it took less time for the Central Front to begin the counter-offensive I think the logistical services here were the most efficient both before and during the operation. Of course, this was significantly affected by the scale of the Fronts' defensive and offensive operations.

I ought to mention that the Fronts' Military Councils took much time and trouble over the logistics.

The local population in the Kursk Bulge area gave great help to the logistical services and the forces there. In-dustrial enterprises in the areas near the front lines did repairs to tanks, aircraft, motor vehicles, and artillery and other equipment. They produced large amounts of army and hospital wear. The local inhabitants also did an enormous amount of work, constructing lines of defences and building and repairing roads.

It may be said that the front and the rear here had genuinely merged to form a single whole. Each person did everything he or she possibly could to contribute to victory. The community of the goals of our people and the Armed Forces in the fight to save their socialist Motherland was thereby manifested.

General Vatutin and General Rokossovsky dealt with many logistical questions themselves and this was largely the reason why our troops were so well provided with materiel by the beginning of the battle.

In May and June intensive preparations were being made for battle amongst all the troops serving on the ground and in the air, every single man and officer getting ready to meet the enemy.

And this encounter soon took place...

By means of all kinds of reconnaissance, the Supreme Command and the Fronts managed to establish the exact time when the enemy would mount his offensive. On July 2, the Stavka warned the commanders of the Fronts that the enemy's offensive was anticipated between July 3 and July 6.

Now our most pressing task was that of making powerful artillery and air counter-preparations among the Soviet troops.

I was at Rokossovsky's headquarters in the evening of July 4. From an HF telephone call to Vasilevsky, who was at Vatutin's headquarters, I had already learned the outcome of the engagement with the enemy's advanced detachments in the Belgorod area. I found out that the information obtained that very day from a captured private of the 168th Infantry Division, that the enemy was to mount his offensive at dawn on July 5, had been verified, and the Voronezh Front was to make artillery and air counter-preparations as envisaged by the Supreme Command's plan.

I immediately passed this information on to Rokossovsky and Malinin.

Somewhere between two and three in the morning, the Commander of the 13th Army, General Pukhov, rang Rokossovsky to tell him that a captured sapper of the 6th Infantry Division had informed him that the German troops were ready to begin an attack. This was to happen at approximately 3 a.m., on July 5.

Rokossovsky asked me, "What shall we do? Shall we report to the Stavka or give orders for counter-preparations to begin?"

"We won't waste time. Give the order as stipulated in

the plan of the Front and the Stavka, and I'll ring Stalin right away."

They put me through to the Supreme Commander immediately. He was at the General Headquarters and had only just finished talking to Vasilevsky. I told him about the information we had received and the decision taken to make counter-preparations. Stalin agreed with this decision and ordered that he be kept informed more regularly.

"I shall wait at the General Headquarters to see how events develop," he said.

I sensed that Stalin was feeling anxious. Indeed, all of us were very worried and extremely keyed up in spite of the fact that we had managed to set up defences in depth and we now had at our disposal powerful means for striking at the German troops. It was well into the night, but we could not sleep a wink.

As always happened in such cases, Rokossovsky and I moved to the Front headquarters. I had been acquainted with the Chief of Staff of the Central Front, Malinin, since the time of the battle for Moscow; at that time he was chief of staff of the 16th Army. He was a thoroughly trained, top-class staff officer. He made an excellent job of fulfilling the obligations with which the headquarters were charged. The Operations Chief General Boikov had greatly assisted him. A modest, diligent and enterprising fellow was like the right hand of the Front's Chief of Staff. And even now when the telephones were ringing all the time, and he was inundated with impatient questions and inquiries, he remained as calm as ever.

Colonel G. S. Nadysev, Chief of Staff of the Front artillery, was here, too. He went backwards and forwards, negotiating with the commanders of the artillery formations from the Supreme Command reserves and talking with the commanding officer of the Front artillery, General V. I. Kazakov, who was with the 4th Artillery Corps at that time.

It should be mentioned that the artillery staffs and all the commanding officers of the Front artillery, of the armies and formations made an excellent and well thought-out job of organizing the artillery defences and the counter-preparations.

At 2:20 a.m., the order was issued to begin the counter-preparations. Everyone raced round and round, twisting and twirling, a terrible rumbling was heard and a very great battle began in the Kursk Bulge area. The sounds of the heavy artillery, the explosions of bombs and the M-31 rocket projectiles, the outbursts of the Katyushas and the constant hum of the aircraft engines merged into what was like the strains of a "symphony" from hell.

The distance between our headquarters and the enemy troops was no more than 20 kilometres as the crow flies. We could hear and feel the hurricane-like fire and could not help conjuring up the terrible picture on the enemy's initial bridgehead, as he was suddenly hit by the whirlwind of counter-preparation fire. Taken unawares, the enemy officers and men probably pressed themselves to the ground or threw themselves into the first convenient hole, ditch or trench, any crack, to protect themselves somehow or other from the frightful explosions of the bombs, shells and mines...

At 2:30 a.m., when the counter-preparation was going ahead everywhere, the Supreme Commander rang me.

"Well, how's it going? Have you begun yet?"

"Yes, we have."

"What's the enemy doing?"

I told him that the enemy was attempting to retaliate from separate batteries, but had soon been quelled.

"All right," said Stalin, "I'll ring you again later."

At that moment, it was hard to determine the outcome of our counter-preparation, but the offensive mounted by the enemy at 5:30 a.m. which was poorly organized and ragged indicated that the enemy had suffered heavy losses.

Prisoners taken during the fighting said that our offensive had been completely unexpected. From what they told us, it appeared that the artillery had been hard hit, and communications, the system of observation and control had been disrupted almost everywhere.

It should, however, be mentioned that when the enemy began his operation, our plan for counter-preparation had not been worked out to the last detail. We had not determined precisely the initial positions of the assault concentrations and the specific distribution of the targets on the night of July 4.

Although it was not easy to define the location of the targets precisely with all the means of intelligence we had at our disposal at that time, all the same, considerably more could have been done to achieve this.

Consequently, in a number of cases we had to aim our fire at an area at large and not at specific targets. This is why the enemy did not suffer heavy losses. He was able to go over to the offensive two-two and a half hours later and advanced three to six kilometres on the first day, in spite of the unprecedented density of the fire by our defences. This would not have occurred if the counter-preparation had been better organized, and the enemy would have sustained considerably greater losses.

True, it should not be forgotten that the counter-preparation took place at night, as a result of which the air force made an insignificant, and to be quite honest, ineffective contribution; raids on enemy aerodromes at dawn did not fulfil their purpose in any way at all as the German Command had its aircraft in the air by that time to assist its ground troops.

Our air force managed to be considerably more effective, striking at tactical battle arrays and enemy columns, which were regrouping during the fighting.

Naturally, the artillery counter-preparation did inflict heavy losses on the enemy and disorganized the troop control in the course of the offensive but, all the same, we had expected that its impact would be greater. When observing the course of the fighting and questioning prisoners, I came to the conclusion that the Central and Voronezh Fronts had started the counter-preparation too early. The German soldiers were still asleep in the trenches, dug-outs, and ravines, and the tank units were under cover in the waiting areas. It would have been better to have begun the counter-preparation approximately 30-40 minutes later.

Somewhere between half past four and five in the morning of July 5, enemy aircraft appeared and at the same time, the enemy opened artillery fire on the defences of the Central Front, and the troops of the 13th Army were shelled particularly intensively. Half an hour later, the German forces began their offensive.

The enemy's front line in the attack comprised three tank and five infantry divisions. The 13th Army and the flanks of the

48th and 70th armies adjacent to it bore the brunt of the blow. The attack was countered by powerful fire from the entire system of our defences and the Nazi troops were repelled with heavy losses.

All day long on July 5, the enemy launched five fierce attacks in an attempt to break through our forces' defences, but he was not able to make any substantial progress. Our troops dug in on almost all sectors of the front, and it seemed that no force could dislodge them. It was not until the very end of the day that the enemy drove a wedge into our defences to a depth of from three to six kilometres in the Olkhovatka area.

The men of the 13th Army fought particularly bravely, including General A. B. Barinov's 81st Division, Colonel V. N. Janjgava's 15th Division, General M. A. Yenshin's 307th Division, and Colonel V. N. Rukosuyev's 3rd Anti-Tank Artillery Brigade. Captain G. I. Igishev's battery, which destroyed 19 enemy tanks in one day, took a heavy blow. Although all the men in this battery died heroically in battle, they did not allow the enemy to get through.

The 70th Army commanded by General Galanin which was made up of frontier guards from the Far East, the Trans-Baikal area and Central Asia, fought valiantly.

In the evening a decision was taken to move the 2nd Tank Army and the 19th Tank Corps into action the next morning, that is, on July 6, which were in close coordination with the troops of the 13th Army to strike a counterblow and push the enemy back to his initial positions, thereby restoring the whole system of defences in the 13th Army's sector.

Particular valour was displayed by the 17th Guards Rifle Corps. On July 6, the 203rd Guards Rifle Regiment of the 70th Guards Division, commanded by Major V. O. Konovalenko repulsed about 16 attacks by the enemy and inflicted heavy losses upon him.

However, in spite of the well-organized defences and the very great courage and mass heroism of our troops, at a cost of great losses, on July 5 and 6 the enemy did, nevertheless, manage to advance as much as 10 kilometres in some sectors. Both days, in spite of the enormous losses it had sustained, the enemy air force raged overhead. But even so, the enemy was not able to break through our tactical defences.

Once he had regrouped his shock tank units, on the morning of July 7, the enemy mounted a fierce attack on Ponyri. The defence line there was held by the 307th Rifle Division commanded by Major-General Yenshin, reinforced with the 5th Artillery Division, the 13th Anti-Tank Artillery Brigade, and the 11th and 22nd Mortar Brigades.

The din of fierce fighting on the ground and in the air continued unabated all day long around Ponyri. The enemy hurled more and more tank units into battle, but he did not manage to break through the defences here either.

On July 8, the attacks were stepped up on the Olkhovatka sector. Here, once again the enemy came up against the heroic staunchness of the Soviet men. The artillerymen of the 3rd Anti-Tank Artillery Brigade commanded by Colonel Rukosuyev particularly distinguished themselves. Greatly outnumbered, the brigade fought an unequal battle against 300 enemy tanks.

Nor did the enemy have any success in subsequent attempts to break through the Soviet forces' defences.

Thus, having lost a considerable part of their tanks, on which Hitler had mainly staked, the German troops were not able to advance before July 10.

During the above battle, Stalin rang me in the small hours of July 9 at the command post of the Central Front and, once he had learned of the situation, he said:

"Don't you think it's time to move the Bryansk Front and the left flank of the Western Front into action, as was envisaged in the plan?"

"Here, on the sector of the Central Front, the enemy no longer has at his disposal forces capable of breaking through our forces' defences," I replied. "We must attack immediately with all the forces on the Bryansk Front and the left flank of the Western Front, without which the Central Front can't carry out the planned counter-offensive successfully, before the enemy gets a respite to organize his defences, which is something he will be forced to do."

"All right. Go and see Popov and get the Bryansk Front into action. When will the Bryansk Front be able to begin the offensive?"

"On the twelfth."

"That's settled then."

I did not trouble to ask the Supreme Commander about the state of affairs on the sectors of the Voronezh Front, since I was directly in contact with Vasilevsky and with the General Staff and knew that there had been extremely fierce fighting there just as on the other sectors of the Central Front.

Allow me to give a brief account of the events on the first day of the battle on the section of the Voronezh Front of which I had learned from a report to the Stavka from the Front Command.

At 16:10 on July 4, the enemy's advanced detachments began offensive operations. The aim of these operations was apparently reconnaissance. On July 5, following artillery and air bombardment, the enemy launched an offensive from the Streletski-Tomarovka-Zybino-Trefilovka area, with no less than 450 tanks.

The first attack was repulsed.

In the afternoon, after moving heavy Tiger tanks into action, the enemy again went into the attack. This time he succeeded in crushing the resistance offered by the 52nd Guards Rifle Division, which was commanded by Colonel I. M. Nekrasov, and in taking a number of villages, among them Berezov, Gremuchi, Bykovo, Kozma-Demyanovka, and Voznesenski. Hard-pressed, the neighbouring 67th Guards Rifle Division under the command of Colonel A. I. Baksov, abandoned Cherkasskoye and withdrew to Krasny Pochinok.

On that day, the Nazi troops sustained tremendous losses, but the Front's troops also lost 60 tanks, 78 aircraft, and a considerable number of men.

From an analysis of the enemy offensive it became obvious that more enterprising and experienced generals were directing his troops in the Belgorod area. This was indeed the case. General Field-Marshal Manstein had taken over command of the grouping.

But what was happening on the Bryansk Front?

On the evening of July 9, as instructed by the Supreme Commander, I was at the Front headquarters where I met Commander M. M. Popov, Member of the Military Council L. Z. Mekhlis and Chief of Staff of the Front, L. M. Sandalov. They had already received orders from the Stavka to go over to the offensive.

I should mention how exceptionally well versed in tactics General Sandalov, Chief of Staff, was, his ability to plan offensive operations precisely and to organize a system of troop control. I had been acquainted with him since the battle for Moscow when he had been the 20th Army's chief of staff. He was one of the most capable of our chiefs of staff with a real understanding of strategy and tactics.

The offensive had been planned and the armies were well prepared. Exceptionally talented and experienced generals were in command of the armies. The 3rd Army was commanded by General A. V. Gorbatov, the 61st Army by General P. A. Belov, the 63rd Army by General V. Ya. Kolpakchi, the 3rd Guards Tank Army by General P. S. Rybalko, and the 11th Guards Army of the Western Front, which was to attack at the same time as the Bryansk Front, was under the command of General I. Kh. Bagramyan.

I visited all these armies of the Bryansk and Western Fronts and gave their commanding officers help and advice as best I could.

I particularly had to go into detail in the army under Bagramyan, with whom I had long had working and comradely contacts. At that time, the Commander of the Western Front General V. D. Sokolovsky, and the representative of the Stavka, General N. N. Voronov, who was supervising artillery matters, were with Bagramyan.

When discussing the method of artillery fire reported by Artillery Commander of the 11th Guards Army, General P. S. Semyonov, the idea was conceived of confronting the enemy with some kind of new method, unknown to him.

After lengthy talks we all decided not to begin our attack after artillery preparation as was customary, as this helped the enemy to tell when our troops would launch an attack, but in the course of artillery preparation itself at the moment when its rate and volume was being stepped up. This method proved to be well worthwhile.

On July 12, the Bryansk Front and the reinforced 11th Guards Army of the Western Front went over to the offensive and, in spite of the well-ramified defences disposed in depth and the enemy's dogged resistance, broke through them and started to move forward in the general direction of Orel.

As was expected, the enemy yielded on the Orel bridgehead and began to take his troops from the grouping operating against the Central Front and to send them into action against the Bryansk Front and the 11th Guards Army on the Western Front. The Central Front immediately took advantage of this and went over to a counterattack on July 15.

So, here in the Orel area the general offensive the Nazis had prepared for so long, ultimately ended in failure. The German troops now had to experience the bitterness of crippling defeat and to feel the power of Soviet arms, which rained down upon them, the much-hated enemy, with all their might.

In the Belgorod area, however, the enemy was still dealing very powerful blows. On July 6, extremely bloody fighting broke out on the Oboyan sector. On both sides, many hundreds of aircraft, tanks and self-propelled guns were involved in the action simultaneously. But the enemy could not overthrow the formidable defences put up by our troops. The tank crews, artillerymen and the units that had withdrawn from the front line courageously repelled the enemy's repeated attacks. On July 6 alone, the enemy lost more than 200 tanks here, tens of thousands of men, and approximately 100 combat aircraft.

After moving up reserves and regrouping his forces, at dawn on July 7, the enemy sent another strong grouping of tanks into action. The bulk of them attacked the 6th Guards Army and the 1st Tank Army on the Oboyan-Prokhorovka sector, and more than 200 tanks were sent against the 7th Guards Army commanded by Shumilov on the Korocha sector.

On the night of July 7, our 6th Guards Army and 1st Tank Army received urgent reinforcements from front reserves.

Fierce enemy attacks began again on the morning of July 7. The incessant roar of the battle, the gritting noise of the tanks and the raving of engines resounded unabated in the air and on the ground.

The troops on the Voronezh Front which had fought with powerful air cover did not allow the enemy to break through the second defence zone, but in some places he did manage to drive in a wedge.

At that time, the Front Command sent the 2nd and 5th Guards Tank corps, and also several rifle divisions and ar-

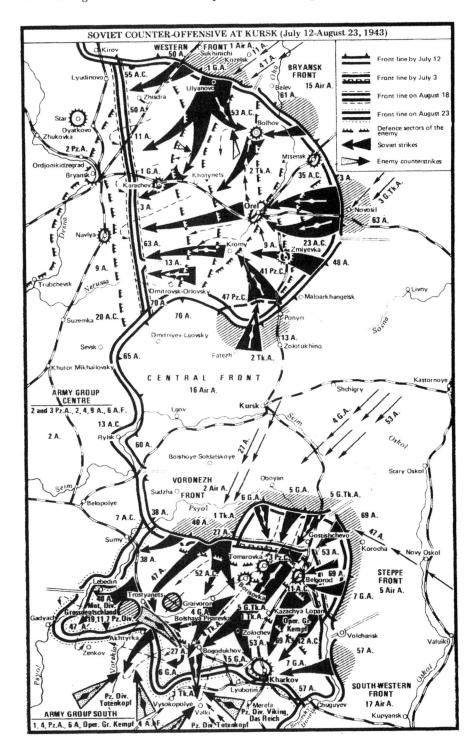

SOVIET COUNTER-OFFENSIVE AT KURSK (July 12-August 23, 1943)

tillery units moved up from other directions, into this sector, which had now become dangerous.

In two days, the enemy lost at least another 200 tanks and a great deal of other materiel. His infantry units were already half their original size. Having regrouped his main forces in a narrower sector throughout July 10, the enemy hurled them into the attack once again on the Prokhorovka sector, counting on crushing our weakened troops here. Fierce fighting continued on the Prokhorovka sector throughout July 11.

By the end of the day a dangerous crisis was apparent in the sector of the Voronezh Front. In accordance with the previously worked out plan, the Supreme Command brought up the 5th Guards Field Army and the 5th Guards Tank Army from its reserves into the Prokhorovka area and sent them into action on the morning of July 12. When it went into action, the 5th Guards Tank Army had more than 800 tanks and self-propelled gun mounts. All in all, the enemy had as many tanks on the Oboyan and Prokhorovka sectors, but the fighting spirit of his troops had already been dampened in the previous encounter with the 6th Guards Army, the 1st Tank Army, and the 7th Guards Army.

There was extremely fierce fighting on the Voronezh Front throughout July 12, which was especially bitter on the Prokhorovka sector where the 5th Guards Tank Army under the command of General P. A. Rotmistrov, was making the greatest headway.

On that day, the Supreme Commander telephoned me at the command post of the Bryansk Front and ordered me to fly out to the Prokhorovka area immediately and take charge of coordinating operations on the Voronezh and Steppe Fronts.

I arrived at the command post of the Voronezh Front on July 13, and the Commander of the Steppe Front, General Konev, was also there. On the evening of that day I met Vasilevsky at the command post of the 69th Army. The Supreme Commander had sent him to the South-Western Front to organize the offensive operations there which were to begin when the Voronezh and Steppe Fronts went over to the counter-offensive.

Once we had familiarized ourselves with the situation and the operations being conducted by the enemy and our forces, we came to the conclusion that the counterblow initiated should be continued even more vigorously, in order to seize the enemy-held lines in the Belgorod area on the heels of the enemy as he withdrew. After that, once the troops had undergone swift preparation, we would go over to a decisive counter-offensive with all the forces of the two Fronts.

Fierce, bloody battles were being fought on all sectors of the Front, and hundreds of tanks and self-propelled guns were going up in smoke. Clouds of dust and smoke hung above the battlefield. This was the turning point in the fighting on the Belgorod sector. Drained of their life blood and having lost their faith in victory, the Nazi forces gradually changed over to defensive operations. On July 16, the enemy finally halted the attack and began to withdraw his troops in the rear to Belgorod. On July 17, the withdrawal of the enemy troops was discovered; however, units still engaged with our forces offered a dogged resistance.

On July 18, Vasilevsky and I were in the sector where the units of the 69th Army under the command of Lieutenant-General V. D. Kryuchenkin, the 5th Guards Army commanded by Lieutenant-General A. S. Zhadov, and the 5th Guards Tank Army commanded by Lieutenant-General P. A. Rotmistrov were in action.

We personally happened to watch the fierce battles near the Komsomolets State Farm and Ivanovskiye Vyselki where the 29th and 18th Tank corps were in action. Here the enemy offered powerful fire resistance and even went over to counterattacks. Over July 18, the armies of Rotmistrov and Zhadov only managed to force the enemy back a mere four to five kilometres, and Chistyakov's 6th Guards Army only occupied the height near Verkhopenye. You could feel how extremely exhausted the troops in Chistyakov's army were. They had had neither sleep nor rest since July 4. Additional forces were needed to prevent the planned withdrawal of the German units. This meant that we needed to send into action Major-General B. S. Bakharov's 18th Tank Corps, and Major-General I. F. Kirichenko's 29th Tank Corps and also part of the forces of I. M. Managarov's 53rd Army.

Some people think that the command of the Voronezh Front, unlike that of the Central Front, was not able to determine precisely the direction in which the enemy would deal his main blow, and therefore it did, as it were, dissipate forces over a 164-km-wide zone, and did not amass forces and means in the direction of the enemy's main thrust. Neither is this correct nor the assertion that the 6th Guards Army whose defences were assailed by the main grouping moving towards Kursk from the south had a wider line of defence (64 km) than its neighbours, who had 50 km each. The average density of the artillery in this army's sector was 25.4 pieces and 2.4 tanks per kilometre of front line, whereas throughout the entire front zone it was 35.6 pieces and 6.9 tanks.

When analyzing the situation, the Stavka, the General Staff, and the command of the Voronezh Front considered that the enemy would deal his main blow not at the 6th Guards Army alone, but at the 6th and 7th Guards armies. As far as the assertions regarding the width of the defence zones are concerned, the line of defence of the 6th and 7th Guards armies, where the German troops' main thrust was anticipated, was 114 kilometres, and that of the other two armies — 130 kilometres. The average density of the artillery and tanks was not estimated accurately enough, namely, in the sectors of the 38th and 40th armies the artillery density was negligible, and these armies had very few tanks.

At the same time, almost all the artillery units and formations from the Supreme Command reserves, all the tank units and formations and all the Front reserves were concentrated in the zone of the 6th and 7th Guards armies. Moreover, the 1st Tank Army with its well organized defence line was disposed in operational depth behind the 6th Guards Army's defences, while the 69th Army was holding another prepared defence line beyond the junction between the 6th and 7th Guards armies in depth. In the operational zone behind the 6th and 7th Guards armies, moreover, there were the Front reserves — the 35th Guards Rifle Corps, and the 2nd and 5th Guards Tank corps.

Hence, the criticism of the command of the Voronezh Front is founded on a lack of knowledge of affairs there, on an inaccurate estimation of the forces, means and specific conditions of the operational situation. Only the density of the strength and means of the armies has been calculated, disregarding the artillery from the Supreme Command reserves which was disposed in the zone of the 6th Guards Army. As far as the density of the tanks is concerned, the Front Command staked chiefly on the lst Tank Army and on the 2nd and 5th Guards Tank corps.

To determine the strength of the defences in big battles, not only must the means and strength of tactical defence be taken into account, but also the forces in operational depth, then no mistake will be made.

As for the results of the defensive fighting on the Fronts, it should not be forgotten that on the first day the enemy dealt his blow at the 6th and 7th Guards armies on the Voronezh Front with almost five corps (the 2nd SS Tank Corps, the 3rd Tank Corps, the 48th Tank Corps, the 52nd Army Corps, and part of the Raus Corps), while he attacked the Central Front with only three corps. The difference in the impact of the blows dealt by the German forces from the Orel direction and from the Belgorod area can easily be understood.

As for Vatutin's ability to deal with strategic and operational questions, I must state with complete impartiality that Vatutin, the Commander of the Voronezh Front, was a highly erudite and steadfast commander.

As I have already mentioned, the counter-offensive in the Kursk Bulge area had been prepared long before the enemy went over to the offensive. Back in May the Supreme Command had considered a plan for a counter-offensive on the Orel sector code-named Kutuzov. Its purpose was for the forces of the Central and Bryansk Fronts and the left flank of the Western Front to deal a blow at the Orel grouping on three sides along the converging directions.

It has already been noted that the troops on the Bryansk and Western Fronts started to mount an offensive on July 12, and those of the Central Front on July 15. Thus, a mighty offensive was launched on three fronts in the Orel area, the immediate object of which was to defeat the enemy's Orel grouping.

The counter-offensive started here and also the great exhaustion of the enemy troops in the Belgorod area forced the Nazi Command to acknowledge that the widely thought out Plan Citadel had ended in failure. To prevent their forces from completely being destroyed, the enemy command decided to withdraw General Field-Marshal Manstein's troops back to the lines of defences where the offensive had been started.

The enemy succeeded in doing this owing to the extreme exhaustion of our lst Tank and 6th and 7th Guards armies. By July 23, the enemy's main forces had been pulled back to the Belgorod line of defences.

Having reached the front line of the German defences by July 23, the troops of the Voronezh and Steppe Fronts, were not able to mount a counter-offensive immediately, although the Supreme Commander required it of them. They needed fresh supplies of fuel, ammunition, and other kinds of materiel, to organize the coordination of all types of troops, careful reconnaissance and to effect some regrouping of the troops, especially of artillery and tanks. At least eight days were needed for this according to the most rigid calculations.

After repeated talks, the Supreme Commander reluctantly approved our decision, since this was the only way.

The operation was planned in great depth and required careful preparation and all-round provisioning, otherwise it might end in failure for us. A well calculated and prepared offensive should guarantee a definite breakthrough of the enemy's defences in tactical and operational depth, and such an assault should also provide the right conditions for subsequent offensive operations.

However, the Supreme Commander was pressing us to start the operation. It took Vasilevsky and myself a great deal of trouble to persuade him that the action should not be launched in a hurry, and that the operation should only be mounted when everything was completely ready and all the materiel was at hand. The Supreme Commander concurred with us.

After Stalin's death, the idea became current that he alone took decisions on questions of a military and strategic nature. I cannot agree with this. I have already mentioned above that when someone who had a good knowledge of the matter made a report to him, he would take notice of it. I even know of cases when he changed his mind with respect to decisions previously taken. This was the case in particular, to the schedule of many operations.

The battle fought in the Kursk, Orel, and Belgorod area was one of the most important engagements of the Great Patriotic War and the Second World War as a whole. Not only were the picked and most powerful groupings of the Germans destroyed here, but the faith of the German Army and the German people in the Nazi leadership and Germany's ability to withstand the growing might of the Soviet Union was irrevocably shattered.

The defeat of the main grouping of German troops in the Kursk area paved the way for the subsequent wide-scale offensive operations by the Soviet forces to expel the Germans from our soil completely, and then from the territories of Poland, Czechoslovakia, Hungary, Yugoslavia, Romania, and Bulgaria and ultimately to crush Nazi Germany.

What was the decisive factor in the enemy's defeat near Kursk? What caused his powerful, long prepared offensive to fall through?

Above all, when the defensive engagement was started, the Soviet troops were superior to their enemy both in numbers and especially in quality.

The increased might of the Soviet Air Force, the armoured forces and artillery allowed shock groupings to be formed in a short space of time which hastily smashed the resistance offered by the enemy forces. This also provided the Soviet military leadership with the opportunity to prepare for and confidently bring about the defeat of the enemy troops in the Kursk Bulge area and foil Hitler's far-reaching plan for offensive operations in 1943.

Why did the enemy decide to mount his general offensive in the Kursk area?

The point is that the operational disposition of the Soviet troops in the Kursk Salient, which curved inwards towards the enemy appeared extremely promising to the Nazi Command. Here two key Fronts could be surrounded immediately, as a result of which a considerable breach would be made, allowing the enemy to conduct major operations in the Southern and North-Eastern directions.

In their appraisals of the situation and of possible enemy decisions, the Stavka, the General Staff and the command of the Front proceeded precisely from this assumption, which turned out to be correct.

Remarkably, the entire Soviet strategic command was in the main unanimous in its appraisal of the impending enemy action. The improved skill of our staffs and commands on an operational and strategic scale was evident more than ever before in this unity of views founded on an in-depth analysis of all the conditions involved.

This could certainly not be said of the German forces' command, which had failed to appraise the situation correctly and thoroughly and did not concur in their plans for the imminent operations and ways of conducting them. As it had lost the strategic initiative, it could not cope with the difficulties that arose and things were made even more complicated by the sharp lowering of fighting spirit among the troops.

As I have already mentioned, in the battle near Kursk the forces of the Central and Voronezh Fronts slightly outnumbered the enemy in strength and materiel. To be more specific, we had a 40 per cent superiority over the enemy in manpower, 90 per cent in guns and mortars, 20 per cent in tanks, and 40 per cent in aircraft. But, in relying mainly on tanks and motorized troops, the Nazi Command deployed them in narrow sectors, creating considerable superiority over the Soviet troops which held the tactical defence zone, in the early days of the battle.

But when our troops, which were disposed in operational depth went into action, the superiority became that of the Soviet forces.

In this case, the Nazi High Command overestimated the combat strength of its own troops and had very greatly underestimated the possibilities of the Soviet forces. This time the enemy had particularly relied on his Tiger and Panther tanks and the Ferdinand assault guns, apparently believing that these systems would stun the Soviet troops and they would not withstand their ramming impact. But this did not occur.

In spite of the fact that Nazi Germany was still continuing to draw support from the economies of most of the European countries, after such fierce engagements on the Eastern Front, it could no longer compete with the growing economic and military might of the Soviet state.

Western bourgeois political and military historians are trying to prove that the Red Army only achieved its superiority in materiel thanks to the material assistance rendered by the USA and Britain.

I do not wish to deny this completely and make out that this aid did not exist. It did help the Red Army and the war industry to a certain extent, but, all the same, it should not be regarded as more significant than it actually was.

Our material superiority over the enemy was gained thanks to the advantages of the Soviet social system, the heroic struggle of the Soviet people, guided by the Party, at the front as well as in the rear.

So, the Nazis lost a very great battle for which they had prepared themselves, bending every effort and possibility to take their revenge for the destruction of their forces near Moscow in 1941 and in the winter of 1942/1943 on the Volga and near Leningrad.

As he always did in such cases, Hitler, vexed by these failures and exceptionally big losses, blamed his generals and field-marshals entirely for the failure of the Citadel offensive operation. He removed them from their posts and replaced them with new ones. Hitler did not understand that the failure of a big strategic operation depended not only on the commanding officers but was chiefly determined by the big sum total of military and strategic, political, moral and material factors.

The basic plan for the Soviet forces' counter-offensive in the Kursk Bulge area which was worked out and approved by the Supreme Command back in May, as we have already mentioned, was amended in the course of the defensive engagement and repeatedly discussed at the General Headquarters. This was a plan for the second stage in routing the enemy in the Orel, Belgorod and Kharkov areas and formed part of the plan for the whole of the 1943 summer campaign.

The first stage, the defensive engagement in the battle near Kursk was completed by our forces on the Central Front on July 12, and on July 23 on the Voronezh Front. The difference in the time it took to complete the defensive operations on these Fronts can be explained by the scale of the fighting and the losses sustained. It should also be taken into account that on July 12, the Central Front was rendered considerable assistance by the Bryansk and Western Fronts, which had mounted an offensive against the enemy's Orel grouping. This compelled the Nazis to move in seven divisions urgently from its forces fielded against the Central Front.

The second stage, the counter-offensive, also began at different times.

So, it began on August 3 in the Belgorod area, i. e. 20 days after the Central, Bryansk, and Western Fronts had gone over to the offensive; it did not take the latter so long to prepare for the offensive, since the planning of the counter-offensive and its comprehensive provisioning had on the whole been worked out earlier and defined more precisely in the course of the defensive engagement.

More time was needed for preparations in the Belgorod area, since the counterattacking troops from the Steppe Front did not have a completely elaborated plan of action in advance. As they had been part of the Supreme Command's reserves, they could not yet be aware of the specific assignments, the initial positions for the counter-offensive of the enemy against whom they were to be in action.

In the course of the preparations and conducting of the counter-offensive, I mainly had to work among the troops of the Voronezh and Steppe Fronts, but on July 30-31, on the orders of the Supreme Commander, I flew out to the troops on the Western Front, to visit the sector held by the 4th Tank Army.

In accordance with the plan for the operations by the Voronezh and Steppe Fronts which bore the code name Rumyantsev, the main thrust was to be made from the Belgorod area by the combined flanks of these two Fronts in the general direction of Bogodukhov-Valki-Novaya Vodolaga bypassing Kharkov from the west. As soon as our troops approached Kharkov, the forces of the South-Western Front were to mount an offensive. Its 57th Army commanded by General N. A. Gagen was to strike the blow, enveloping Kharkov from the south-west.

The counter-offensive was to be launched by the forces of the Voronezh Front in more difficult conditions than in the Orel area. During the defensive engagement they had sustained great losses in men, armaments, and materiel. Withdrawing to his previously prepared line of defences, the enemy occupied them in time and made ready quite well to counter our offensive. It was established by reconnaissance that the Germans had hastily brought up tank and motorized divisions from other directions to reinforce the Belgorod-Kharkov grouping.

Everything indicated that there would be fierce fighting here, especially involving the troops of the Steppe Front, which, owing to circumstances, was forced to attack the well-fortified Belgorod defence zone.

The Supreme Command used the Steppe Front correctly. If its forces had not been sent into action in the course of the defensive engagement to reinforce the Voronezh Front, the latter might have found itself in an extremely perilous situation. In no way could we have allowed events to turn out like that, for it is not hard to guess what the outcome would have been.

As regards the counter-offensive to be launched by the Steppe Front using all the forces on the Belgorod sector simultaneously, it should be recalled that when the armies of the Steppe Front were sent to reinforce the Voronezh Front, conditions were not yet ripe for putting all the forces of the Steppe Front into action. It only became quite obvious that circumstances were right for going over to the counter-offensive by July 20, and the actual changeover to the counter-offensive could only be brought about after the comprehensive preparation of both Fronts, which required a considerable period of time.

On July 23, hot on the heels of the enemy, Soviet troops reached the line to the north of Belgorod and on the whole seized the defence positions that had been held by the Voronezh Front until July 5.

Having discussed the situation with the Front Command, the General Staff, and the Supreme Commander, we resolved to halt the troops and thoroughly prepare them for an all-out counter-offensive.

After all, before going over to the offensive, the Fronts needed to do the following:

—regroup their forces and materiel;

—make thorough reconnaissance of targets for air and artillery attack;

— reinforce the troops, who had sustained losses; this particularly applied to the 6th and 7th Guards armies, the 1st Tank Army, and a number of artillery units;

—stock up with fuel, ammunition, and everything needed for an offensive operation conducted in depth.

But, besides this, the Steppe Front still had to work out a detailed plan for the counter-offensive and its comprehensive provisioning.

The general idea of launching a counter-offensive near Belgorod was the following.

The Voronezh Front was to deal its main blow with the forces of the 5th and 6th Guards armies, the 5th Guards Tank and 1st Tank armies in the general direction of Valki and Novaya Vodolaga. The artillery density in the sector where the 5th and 6th Guards armies were to make a breakthrough was brought up to 230 guns and mortars per kilometre, while tank density was increased to 70 per kilometre. The divisions were assigned three-kilometre-wide sectors to make their breakthrough.

This mass concentration of breakthrough means was needed because on the very first day of the counter-offensive it was planned to bring two tank armies into the breach. To the right, the 40th and 38th armies went over to the offensive in the general direction of Graivoron and further on to Trostyanets. General S. A. Krasovsky's 2nd Air Army provided air cover.

The Steppe Front commanded by Colonel-General Konev and comprised of the 53rd, 69th and 7th Guards armies and the 1st Mechanized Corps, had as its immediate objective the taking of Belgorod and mounting an attack on Kharkov, cooperating with the main forces of the Voronezh Front. Air support for the troops of the Steppe Front was to be provided by General S. K. Goryunov's Air Army.

When preparing the operation for the troops of the Steppe Front I became acquainted with the Commander of the 53rd Army, General Managarov, with whom I had had little contact earlier.

Managarov made a very good impression on me, although I had to work hard to help him plan the offensive for his army. But when the work was over and we sat and had supper together, he took up an accordion and played several cheering pieces beautifully. My tiredness disappeared immediately. I glanced at him and thought that the men particularly liked this type of commander and would follow him through fire and water...

I thanked Managarov for his excellent performance on the accordion (something which I had, incidentally, always wanted to do myself) and expressed the hope that he would give just as good a performance of artillery music for the enemy on August 3.

Managarov grinned and said: "We'll try, we do have something to play on."

I also liked the Commander of the Artillery, Lieutenant-General N. S. Fomin, who possessed an excellent knowledge of methods of using large masses of ordnance in artillery offensives. He and Colonel-General of the artillery Chistyakov, who was the Stavka representative, made a very good and helpful job of distributing the artillery, supplying it with ammunition, in training the men and getting everything ready for an effective artillery assault.

The counter-offensive in the Belgorod area began on the morning of August 3. The artillery and aviation of the Voronezh Front dealt a powerful blow, as a result of which the troops of the 5th and 6th Guards armies, which had gone over to the offensive and had been reinforced with a large number of tanks soon broke through the main line of the enemy's defences. In the afternoon the 1st and 5th Guards Tank armies took advantage of the breach to move their vanguards forward 30 to 35 kilometres by the end of the day, completely destroying the whole of the tactical defence line in this sector.

The Steppe Front did not have such powerful means as the Voronezh Front to make a breakthrough, and the offensive went ahead somewhat more slowly here. By nightfall the vanguards had advanced up to 15 kilometres, but even that we considered a great achievement, all the more so since the armies of the Steppe Front had stronger and deeper enemy defences to overcome.

The next day the enemy put up greater resistance, and the Steppe Front's offensive on August 4 progressed considerably more slowly. But we were not troubled by this too much as the shock group of the Voronezh Front had been able to push ahead, gaining the flank of the enemy's Belgorod grouping. Here, fearing that they might be surrounded, the Nazi Command began to withdraw their troops by the end of the day on August 4, which allowed the troops of the Steppe Front to move ahead more quickly.

At six o'clock on the morning of August 5, the 270th Guards Rifle Regiment of the 89th Guards Rifle Division and

also units of the 305th and 375th Rifle divisions were the
first to break into Belgorod. The 93rd, 94th Guards and the
111th Rifle divisions fought well; the 89th Guards and the
305th Rifle divisions had the honorary name of Belgorod Divisions conferred upon them.

Once they had cleared the remaining enemy troops out of
the city, the armies of the Steppe Front, in coordination with
the forces of the Voronezh Front, rapidly forged ahead.

In the evening of August 5, in Moscow, the capital of our
Motherland, a salute resounded in honour of the valiant troops
of the Bryansk, Western, and Central Fronts who had taken
Orel, and the troops of the Steppe and Voronezh Fronts who
had taken Belgorod. This was the first artillery salute during
the Great Patriotic War fired to honour the martial prowess
of the Soviet forces.

Morale among the troops sharply improved, faces were
aglow with joy, courage and confidence in our forces.

Having appraised the course of events, on August 6 the
commanding officers of the Steppe Front and I sent proposals
to the Supreme Commander regarding the further development
of the operation on the Belgorod-Kharkov sector.

"From the army in the field, August 6, 1943.
"To Comrade Ivanov.[1]
"We report:
"In view of the successful breach of the enemy front and
the progress of the offensive on the Belgorod-Kharkov sector,
the operation will further be conducted according to the following plan:
"1. The 53rd Army with the Solomatin[2] Corps will advance
along the Belgorod-Kharkov highway, striking the main blow
in the direction of Dergachi.

"The army should reach the Olshany-Dergachi line and replace Zhadov's units there.

"The 69th Army is to advance to the left of the 53rd
Army in the direction of Cheremoshnoye. When it reaches

---

[1] Stalin's code name.— *Author.*

[2] Lieutenant-General of the Armour, M. D. Solomatin, Commander of
the 1st Mechanized Corps.— *Author.*

Cheremoshnoye, the army, after placing several of its best divisions under Managarov, is itself to remain in the Front's reserve to be brought up to full complement in the Mikoyanovka-Cheremoshnoye-Gryaznoye area.

"The 69th Army needs to be replenished with 20,000 men as soon as possible.

"The 7th Guards Army will presently advance from the Pushkarnoye area to Brodok and then to Bochkovka, dislodging the enemy front from north to south.

"From the Cheremoshnoye and Ziborovka line the 7th Guards Army will strike the main blow at Tsirkuni and come out on the Cherkasskoye-Lozovoye-Tsirkuni-Klyuchkin line.

"It will advance on Murom with part of its forces from the Ziborovka area, and then on Ternovaya, to help the 57th Army force the River Seversky Donets near Rubezhnoye and Stary Saltov.

"2. It would be advisable for the 57th Army of the South-Western Front to be handed over to and made subordinate to the Steppe Front and preparations should now begin for the 57th Army's thrust from the Rubezhnoye-Stary Saltov line in a general direction towards Nepokrytaya and then on to the Frunze State Farm.

"The 57th Army must be brought out to the Kutuzovka State Farm-Frunze State Farm-Rogan (northern) line.

"Should the 57th Army remain subordinated to the South-Western Front, the moment Shumilov[1] approaches the Murom sector, it must be ordered to conduct an offensive in the above-mentioned direction.

"3. To perform the second stage, that is the Kharkov operation, the 5th Guards Tank Army, which is to come out at the Olshany-Stary Merchik-Ogultsy line, must be placed under the Steppe Front.

"We suggest that the Kharkov operation should tentatively be arranged according to the following plan:

"a) The 53rd Army in coordination with Rotmistrov's army is to envelop Kharkov from the south and south-west.

---

[1] Lieutenant-General M. S. Shumilov, Commander of the 7th Guards Army.— *Author.*

"b) Shumilov's army is to advance from the north southwards from the Tsirkuni-Dergachi line.

"c) The 57th Army is to advance from the east from the Frunze State Farm and Rogan line, enveloping Kharkov from the south.

"d) If the 69th Army has been replenished by this time, it is to fan out at the junction between Zhadov's and Managarov's armies in the Olshany area and is to advance southwards to provide support for the Kharkov operation from the south.

"The 69th Army is to come out on the Snezhkov Kut-Minkovka-Prosyanoye-Novoselovka line.

"e) The left flank of the Voronezh Front must be brought to the Otrada-Kolomak-Snezhkov Kut line.

"Zhadov's army and the left flank of the 27th Army are charged with this mission.

"It would be advisable to have Katukov's[1] army in the Kovyagi-Alekseyevka-Merefa area.

"The South-Western Front must strike a blow from the Zamostye area in the general direction of Merefa, moving forwards along both banks of the River Mzha; part of its forces are to advance to Osnova via Chuguyev; part of its forces must clear the forests of the enemy to the south of Zamostye and emerge at the Novoselovka-Okhochaye-Verkhny Bishkin-Geyevka line.

"4. To conduct the Kharkov operation, besides the 20,000 extra men, we need another 15,000 men for the divisions of the 53rd and 7th Guards armies; 200 T-34 and 100 T-70 tanks, besides 35 KV tanks to bring the tank units' front line up to full complement. Four self-propelled artillery regiments and two engineer brigades need to be moved up.

"The air forces on the Front should be brought up to full complement with assault and combat aircraft and bombers in the following numbers: 90 fighters, 40 PE-2 and 60 IL-2 planes.

"Please endorse.

"Zhukov, Konev, Zakharov"

---

[1] Lieutenant-General of the Armour, M. Ye. Katukov, Commander of the 1st Tank Army.— *Author.*

Meanwhile, the action was still going on. On August 7, the 1st Tank Army and the advanced units of the 6th Guards Army of the Voronezh Front seized the town of Bogodukhov. The enemy no longer had a single solid front. His 4th Army was operating in considerable isolation from the Kampf group, and he had no forces to close the gap.

The group of enemy forces which was withdrawing westwards from Graivoron and comprised three infantry divisions and the 19th Tank Division was attacked by a big group of aircraft from the 2nd Air Army and then destroyed by General Trofimenko's 27th Army which complicated the situation of the enemy's 4th Army even more.

On August 11, the units of the 1st Tank Army crossed the Kharkov-Poltava railway line.

To save the 4th Army from inevitable disaster, German Army Group South hastily moved its last reserves to the Akhtyrka area.

Fearing that his Kharkov grouping would be surrounded, the enemy rallied his troops comprising three tank divisions (Totenkopf, Viking and Reich) and on August 11 struck a counterblow at the 1st Tank Army and the units of the 6th Guards Army. The debilitated units of the 1st Tank Army and the 6th Guards Army, unable to withstand the blow, began to retreat to more advantageous lines.

At that time, General Rotmistrov's 5th Guards Tank Army was rushed to their help. Fierce fighting ensued and lasted for several days. By nightfall on August 16, the enemy had been halted by joint efforts.

The enemy dealt a counterblow from the Akhtyrka area on August 18. To destroy him, the 4th Guards Army from the Supreme Command reserves was sent into action in addition. It was commanded by General G. I. Kulik. Unfortunately, he coped badly with his duties and soon had to be removed from command.

The armies of the Steppe Front moved right up to Kharkov, engaging in combat in its environs. Managarov's 53rd Army was energetic in action, and particularly its 89th Guards Rifle Division commanded by Golonel M. P. Seryugin and the 305th Rifle Division under the command of Colonel A. F. Vasilyev.

In action day and night, the units of the 53rd Army tried
to make the breakthrough in the defences on the approaches
to the city more quickly. The fiercest battle was fought for
Height 201.7 in the Polevoi area which was taken by a combined
company of 16 men from the 299th Rifle Division commanded
by Senior Lieutenant V. P. Petrishchev.

When only seven of the men still remained alive, the commander addressed his men with the words:

"Comrades, let us stand our ground on this height just as
the Panfilov Division stood at Dubosekovo. We may die, but we
shall not retreat!"

Nor did they retreat. The heroic fighters held the height
until the units of the division reached it. For their valour and
heroism by decree of the Presidium of the Supreme Soviet
of the USSR, Senior Lieutenant V. P. Petrishchev, Junior
Lieutenant V. V. Zhenchenko, Senior Sergeant G. P. Polikanov
and Sergeant V. E. Breusov had the title of Hero of the Soviet
Union conferred upon them. The rest of the men were decorated
with orders.

The formations of the 20th Guards Rifle Corps commanded
by General N. I. Biryukov, troops commanded by General
M. G. Mikeladze, Guards Lieutenant-Colonel O. S. Gudemenko,
and Colonel O. S. Dobrov, and also the 4th Guards Tank
Corps particularly distinguished themselves in the fierce fighting.

By August 22 the Soviet troops' offensive near Kharkov
had increasingly been stepped up. To prevent his forces from
being surrounded, on August 22 the enemy began to withdraw
from Kharkov. The next morning his last rearguard units pulled
out, and the troops of the Steppe Front went into the city
where they were enthusiastically welcomed by the inhabitants.

A big rally took place in Kharkov which was attended by
representatives of Party and Soviet organizations of the Ukraine
and of the Red Army. The rally was held amidst great
jubilation. The working people of Kharkov rejoiced, in Moscow
a salute was fired in honour of the valiant warriors, who had
liberated this big Ukrainian city.

At that time, the troops of the Steppe Front were fighting
to the south of Kharkov, advancing in the Merefa sector.

Having thrust back the enemy's counterattacking groupings
around Bogodukhov and Akhtyrka, on August 25, the Voronezh

Front had dug itself firmly in along the Sumy-Gadyach-Akhtyrka-Konstantinovka line and was now preparing offensive operations to get to the middle reaches of the Dnieper. The Steppe Front was given a similar mission.

On the Orel sector the aim of the counter-offensive plan was to defeat the German 9th and 2nd Panzer armies and to promote a thrust in the general direction of Bryansk.

The troops on the left flank of the Western Front were charged with destroying, in coordination with the forces of the Bryansk Front, the Bolkhov group of the enemy's forces and then to press on to Khotynets and cut off the enemy's line of retreat from the Orel sector.

To begin with, the Western Front conducted its offensive with the 11th Guards Army commanded by General Bagramyan, reinforced with a tank corps and four tank brigades. In action the troops of this group received support from the 1st Air Army commanded by General M. M. Gromov. Several days later, this group was reinforced with the 11th Army commanded by General I. I. Fedyuninsky and the 4th Tank Army under General B. M. Badanov.

The Bryansk Front was operating with the 61st, 3rd, and 63rd armies, and at that time it also included the 3rd Guards Tank Army commanded by Rybalko which had been brought up to full complement in the Gorbachevo Station sector. The troops' operations on the front were supported by General N. F. Naumenko's 15th Air Army.

The Central Front went into action with the 48th and 13th armies and the right flank of the 70th Army, the 2nd Tank Army and all the formations taking part in the defence engagement and the counterblow.

By this time, to prevent the forces of the Bryansk and Western Fronts forging a breach in his forces, the enemy moved up several panzer and infantry divisions from the sector fielded against the Central Front, thereby considerably weakening his defences to the south of Orel. As a result the Central Front had more favourable conditions for conducting its offensive operations.

The offensive launched by the Western and Bryansk Fronts progressed more slowly than expected. It went ahead somewhat better on the left flank of the Western Front. Nor did the counter-offensive started by the Central Front on July 15 speed up the general offensive.

Later, when analyzing the reasons for the slow development of events, we came to the conclusion that the main cause was that the Stavka had been in rather a hurry when going over to the offensive and had not set up a stronger grouping in the left flank of the Western Front; the existing flank had to be greatly reinforced during the fighting. The troops of the Bryansk Front had to make a frontal assault on the deeply echeloned defences to break them down.

I think it would have been better if Rybalko's army had not been put into action on the Bryansk Front, but together with Bagramyan's army. The Stavka waited a bit too long before putting General Fedyuninsky's 11th Army and also General Badanov's 4th Tank Army into the field.

The Central Front started its counter-offensive at the point where it completed its counterblow and moved in a broad front, making a head-on assault on the main enemy grouping. The Central Front's main thrust should have been made somewhat further to the west, bypassing Kromy.

Unfortunately, this was not done. We were in too much of a hurry. At that time, we all thought that we needed to destroy the enemy as quickly as possible before he managed to entrench himself firmly in the defences. But this reasoning was not correct. All this taken together resulted from the fact that we had underestimated the enemy's defence potential.

In the next few days, the counter-offensive on the Orel sector progressed at a slow rate just as it did earlier.

On August 5, the troops of the Bryansk Front liberated Orel. The 5th, 129th and 380th Rifle Divisions particularly distinguished themselves in these battles.

When Antonov, Vasilevsky and I reported to the Supreme Commander that we might be able to surround the enemy grouping in the Orel area, for which purpose we would need to considerably reinforce the left flank of the Western Front, Stalin said:

"It is our job to drive the Germans out of our territory as soon as possible and we shall surround them when they become more debilitated..."

We did not insist on our point of view, but that was a

mistake. We should have insisted that we were right: at that time our troops could already have conducted the operation of encirclement and annihilation.

The 3rd Army commanded by General A. V. Gorbatov, who coped excellently with commanding his army throughout the war, was the most active among the troops of the Bryansk Front.

The slow development of the counter-offensive on all three fronts gave the enemy the opportunity to regroup his troops, move in fresh forces from other areas and withdraw the troops from the Orel area.

Subsequently, these Fronts moved forward at a slow pace as well and did not exceed more than four kilometres a day on average. On August 18, the counter-offensive operation was completed along a line from the east of Lyudinovo, 25 kilometres east of Bryansk, to Dmitrovsk-Orlovsky.

This major battle of the Great Patriotic War ended in the taking of Kharkov on August 23, 1943. It was concluded with the rout of the main grouping of German troops, in whom Hitler had placed so many of his military and political hopes.

But what was the outcome of the battle of Kursk?

This very great battle between our forces and the Nazi troops lasted 50 days. It culminated in a victory for the Red Army, which destroyed 30 picked German divisions, including seven panzer divisions. These divisions lost more than half of their men.

The overall losses sustained by the enemy amounted to approximately 500,000 men, 1,500 tanks, including a large number of Tiger and Panther tanks, 3,000 guns, and more than 3,700 aircraft. The Nazi leadership could no longer compensate for such losses with any kind of total measures.

The outstanding victory of our forces near Kursk was an indication of the growing might of the Soviet state and its armed forces. The victory was forged at the front and in the rear by the efforts of all Soviet people under the leadership of the Communist Party. Our troops displayed exceptional courage, mass heroism and military skill in the fighting near Kursk. The Communist Party and the Government highly appreciated the military prowess of the troops by awarding more than 100,000 generals, officers, and men with orders and medals and conferring on many of them the title of Hero of the Soviet Union.

The defeat of the Nazi troops near Kursk was of vital international significance and raised the authority of the Soviet Union even higher.

The spectre of inevitable disaster now arose before Nazi Germany. The defeat of the German troops in the summer of 1943 had forced the Nazis to move 14 divisions and other reinforcements to the Soviet-German front from other fronts, thereby draining the strength of its forces in Europe.

Hitler's attempt to wrest the strategic initiative from the Soviet Command ended in failure. This proved how exhausted Germany was. Nothing could save her now. It was just a question of time.

The Soviet strategic and tactical command had become considerably more qualified and skilled in the art of warfare.

Unlike the counter-offensive near Moscow and Stalingrad, the counter-offensive in the Kursk Bulge area was a premeditated and well backed-up deep thrusting operation.

Considerably larger forces than in the previous big counter-offensive operations were involved here. For example, 17 small field armies without tank formations were in the field near Moscow, and 14 field armies, one tank army and several mechanized corps around Stalingrad. Twenty-two powerful field armies, five tank and six air armies and the biggest long-range air armies were involved in the counter-offensive near Kursk.

In the course of the counter-offensive in the battle near Kursk tank and mechanized formations were widely used for the first time, and, in a number of cases, these were a decisive factor in operational manoeuvring, a means of making swift thrusts in depth and of striking at enemy groupings in the rear.

The tank armies, artillery divisions and corps, and the Fronts' powerful air armies substantially enhanced our potential and consequently changed the nature of the operations on the Fronts, both in their scale and aims. The Soviet troops were now much more mobile than they were during the early period of the war. This greatly increased their manoeuvrability and the daily rate of advance. The density of artillery and mortar fire and of tanks had been radically boosted. In the offensive campaigns in the summer of 1943, we were able to create a density of between 150 and 200 guns and between 15 and 20 tanks per kilometre of front line.

The victory of the Soviet forces near Belgorod, Orel, and Kharkov was in many ways facilitated by the partisans who were active in the enemy's rear. Especially the partisans of Byelorussia, of the Smolensk and Orel regions and the area along the Dnieper derailed many enemy trains.

One of the decisive factors contributing to the victory in the Kursk Bulge was the high morale and level of political awareness of the Soviet troops. The commanders, political workers, Party and Komsomol organizations worked intensively and pain-stakingly both during the preparations for the battle and during the battle itself. They put a great deal of effort into raising the fighting capacity of the troops....

On August 25, 1943, I was summoned to the General Head-quarters to discuss the situation and the further tasks to be tackled in the overall offensive of the Soviet troops which was now snowballing after the rout of the German troops in the Kursk Bulge area.

CHAPTER 5

Fighting for the Ukraine

Before my return to Moscow in August 1943, during the counter-offensive on the Voronezh and Steppe Fronts, we were twice visited by Antonov, Deputy Chief of General Staff, who flew in to report on the revisions made by Stalin to the plan for the completion of the 1943 offensive operations and the General Staff's blueprints for the autumn campaign.

Antonov was a peerlessly able general and a man of great culture and charm. It always delighted me to hear him present the strategic and tactical ideas of the General Staff. He set forth and explained the capacities of the German forces after their rout at the Kursk Salient with the utmost clarity and conviction.

The General Staff felt that the Nazi High Command still had considerable forces to carry on the war against the Soviet Union, especially so since Britain and the United States seemed hardly inclined to launch any large-scale offensive in Europe. The landing of their troops in Southern Italy (Sicily) made no substantial changes in the deployment of German forces on the various strategic directions, although the Nazi leadership was, of course, forced to face additional pressure.

The General Staff felt — with the concurrence of the Supreme Commander — that on the Eastern Front, Germany was no longer in a position to conduct large-scale offensive action. However, it did have sufficient manpower and material supplies for active defensive operations. This, in fact, was amply illustrated by the fighting in the areas of Bogodukhov, Akhtyrka and Poltava, where the German forces battled fiercely and dealt us some rather telling counterblows, sometimes with temporary success.

I fully agreed with Antonov's conclusions, and also believed that the Nazi High Command would exhort its forces to put up a stiff defence so that it could hold on to the Donbass and the area of the Ukraine east of the Dnieper.

The draft directives drawn up by the General Staff, and in part already issued to the fronts, called for a wholesale offensive on all fronts of the Western and South-Western directions with a view to reaching the eastern areas of Byelorussia and the River Dnieper so as to capture bridgeheads and thus help liberate the area of the Ukraine west of the Dnieper.

From Antonov's report I gathered that Stalin was urging for the immediate development of the offensive so as to give the enemy no chance to organize a defence on the approaches to the Dnieper. I personally agreed with this general plan, though I disagreed with the form our offensive operations were to take, according to which our Fronts from Velikiye Luki to the Black Sea were supposed to mount frontal blows.

After all, there was, I felt, every opportunity (after certain regroupments) to execute operations to cut off and encircle sizable enemy forces, thus facilitating further military successes. What I specifically had in mind was the southern enemy group in the Donbass, which could be cut off by a powerful blow from the Kharkov-Izyum area in the general sector of Dnepropetrovsk and Zaporozhye.

Antonov told me that he himself shared my view, but the Supreme Commander was demanding that the enemy be pushed back immediately by means of frontal blows.

Before Antonov flew back to Moscow I again asked him to report my observations to the Supreme Commander, and to communicate a request from the fronts for the replenishment of our tank units with materiel and trained effectives since the bitter fighting had severely undermanned them.

Several days later Stalin phoned to say he had ordered tanks and replacements to be sent to Vatutin and Konev. Then he remarked that he did not share my view on the expediency of striking at Zaporozhye by means of the South-Western Front troops from the Izyum area because it would take too long.

I did not bother to argue, since I knew that so far Stalin was generally disinclined for several reasons to contemplate any large-scale encirclement operations.

In conclusion, Stalin demanded steps to ensure the rapid advance of our forces to the Dnieper.

So, as I have already mentioned, on August 25, Antonov and I arrived at the General Headquarters. Stalin had just ended a conference with the members of the State Committee for Defence which had heard a report on the plan for the production of aircraft and tanks in the second half of 1943.

Thanks to the tremendous efforts by the Party and the people, our economy, and especially the war industry, were by that time already capable of supplying the fronts with all that was necessary. The accelerated development of the Second Baku, the heroic labour of the workers at the Kuznetsk and Magnitogorsk metallurgical combines, the construction of blast-furnaces, power stations and mines in the liberated areas ahead of time, the rising production at the non-ferrous metal and iron-and-steel plants in the Urals, Siberia, and Kazakhstan, the introduction of the conveyor method at the plants manufacturing military supplies, the tremendous creative work on modernizing our military equipment and production technology — all gave us new possibilities for crushing the enemy.

In 1943 our industry produced 35,000 high-class war planes, 24,000 tanks and self-propelled artillery pieces. In this respect we were already far ahead of Germany, both in quality and quantity. The Nazi High Command issued a special order to avoid meeting engagements with our heavy tanks...

After several questions about the situation on the Voronezh and Steppe Fronts, the Supreme Commander asked whether we had received the directive on continuing the advance towards the Dnieper, and inquired how the Fronts were assessing their capabilities. I reported that the troops of the Fronts had sustained considerable losses, and should be replenished with sizable replacements in manpower and materiel, especially tanks.

"All right," Stalin said, "we'll talk about that later; right now let's listen to what Antonov has to say about the offensive in other directions."

Antonov spread out his maps illustrating the situation in the western and south-western strategic directions; as always, the maps had been most artistically prepared by the Operations Division of the General Staff. I have to admit that a graphically well-finished map is a great help in visualizing the general situation and elaborating the necessary decisions.

Antonov also presented a report on the enemy forces. It was clear from what he said that the enemy was doing all he could to check the initiated offensive on the Kalinin, Western, Bryansk and South-Western Fronts. According to intelligence reports the enemy had attempted to put up a defence on the following sector: the River Narva-Pskov-Vitebsk-Orsha-the Rivers Sozh, Dnieper and Molochnaya. Nazi propaganda was making the most of this defensive line, calling it the Eastern Wall against which the Red Army would break its head.

Reporting on the progress of the so-called Smolensk offensive launched by the Western Front and the left wing of the Kalinin Front, Antonov pointed out that the troops had encountered formidable obstacles. First there was the difficult wooded and marshy terrain and, second, there was the heightened resistance of the enemy troops which were being reinforced with units moved up from the Bryansk area.

Stalin asked: "What tasks are the partisan detachments carrying out?"

"Their major tasks," Antonov replied, "are to frustrate railroad transportation in the Polotsk-Dvinsk, Mogilev-Zhlobin, and Mogilev-Krichev sectors."

"What is happening on the South-Western Front?"

"The forces of the South-Western Front," answered Antonov, "having mounted an offensive in the Front's centre had no success. The situation is better on the Front's left wing where the 3rd Guards Army under General Lelyushenko is in contact with the enemy."

I no longer remember every minute detail of that conference, but what I do recall very well is that Stalin demanded urgent measures to capture the Dnieper and the River Molochnaya so as to prevent the enemy from completely devastating the Donbass and the area east of the Dnieper.

His reasoning was quite correct, since in their savage fury the retreating Nazis were burning and destroying everything of value. They were blowing up factories and plants, reducing towns and villages to ruins, destroying power stations, blast- and open-hearth furnaces, razing schools and hospitals, and killing thousands of children, women and old people.

After giving Antonov his instructions, Stalin told me as well as Ya. N. Fedorenko and N. D. Yakovlev to find out what could be done for the Voronezh and Steppe Fronts. Considering the important tasks that these two Fronts were to execute, I reported to Stalin that evening on the number of men, tanks, artillery and ammunition which should immediately be set aside for them.

Stalin looked through the table of available supplies and my request for some time. Then, taking a blue pencil as he usually did, he slashed my figures by almost 30 to 40 per cent.

"We'll give you the rest," he said, "when the Fronts reach the Dnieper."

The same day I set off by plane for the combat zone, where the offensive was going to be continued according to the directive of the Supreme Command.

Somewhat later, on September 6, a new directive was issued by the Supreme Command. The fronts under my command were to continue advancing to the middle reaches of the Dnieper and to capture a bridgehead there. The Voronezh Front under Vatutin was to push forward for Romny, Priluki and Kiev. Meanwhile the Steppe Front under Konev was to advance on the Poltava-Kremenchug sector.

It was impossible for us to make any thorough preparations for the advance towards the Dnieper. The troops of both Fronts were very tired after non-stop fighting. Problems of material and technical supplies were also making themselves felt. Even so, from marshal down to the last soldier, we all burned with a desire to drive the enemy out of our land as swiftly as possible and to liberate the long-suffering Ukrainian people from the odious yoke of the invaders who were taking revenge on the Soviet people for their military setbacks, showing no mercy to either children or aged alike.

It did not take us long to elaborate the operational and tactical decisions, since by then the troops and staffs had accumulated a wealth of experience and skills in swiftly analyzing the situation, taking decisions and giving the troops brief and precise orders.

As for the commanders and Front headquarters, they had become expert in organizing and conducting operations, and it was easy to work with them. We seemed to understand each other with hardly a word passing between us.

At this time I continued to keep in touch with Vasilevsky, who was then coordinating the actions of the South-Western and Southern Fronts. We were fully cognizant of the formidable enemy group opposing our Fronts in those areas. Although our forces had a certain edge in manpower, this could not eliminate the great adversities that beset their offensive operations, especially so since our Fronts had almost no quantitative superiority in tanks and combat aircraft.

The offensive launched by the Fronts under my control was developing very slowly.

The enemy was putting up stiff resistance, particularly in the Poltava area. However, in the first half of September, after heavy losses, he began a withdrawal from the Donbass and the Poltava area. The 3rd Guards Tank Army under Rybalko which had arrived from the Supreme Command reserve and had been committed on the Voronezh Front's sector began to resolutely follow the enemy in the Dnieper sector.

Besides the 3rd Guards Tank Army, the Voronezh Front was also reinforced with the 13th and 60th armies commanded by Generals Pukhov and Chernyakhovsky from October 5, 1943. Regroupings took place on other fronts as well. The Steppe Front had been given from the Voronezh Front the 52nd and 5th Guards armies under Generals Koroteev and Zhadov.

No longer strong enough to withstand the onslaught of our forces, the German troops began withdrawing to the Dnieper. The Fronts did everything they could to capture bridgeheads on the river, and begin forcing this major water obstacle in hot pursuit of the retreating enemy forces.

To demoralize the enemy troops we committed all of the Fronts' available aircraft. As they pursued the enemy, our formations established improvized mobile detachments which were to move swiftly to rear sections of the roads so that they could capture and hold those positions that the enemy might want to occupy to build up a defence.

To raise our troop morale even higher in force-crossing large rivers, on September 9, 1943 the Supreme Command issued an order under which commanding officers were to be awarded the Order of Suvorov for forcing major rivers like the Desna, and the title of Hero of the Soviet Union for forcing the Dnieper.

The military councils, political organs and commanders

of all ranks began an extensive campaign to explain the importance of the swift capture of the western banks of the Dnieper
and Desna. Everyone whom we talked with about the forthcoming mission and methods of executing it showed themselves
fully aware of the importance of capturing the Dnieper and its
swift crossing, particularly the significance of liberating Kiev,
the capital of the Ukraine.

After capturing Poltava on September 23 the Steppe Front
was approaching the Dnieper with the advance units of its left
flank.

Mechanized units of the 3rd Guards Tank Army and units
of the 40th and 47th armies captured a bridgehead on the
Dnieper in the Veliky Bukrin area. They were supposed to widen
it quickly in order to secure the commitment of the main group
of the Voronezh Front to outflank and envelop enemy forces
in Kiev from the south and south-west.

The German High Command immediately threw into action
against our bridgehead a sizable force made up of the 24th and
48th Panzer corps with up to five infantry divisions; they struck
out at our forces and held them in check on the Bukrin
bridgehead.

In the Lyutezh area to the north of Kiev, units of General
N. Ye. Chibisov's army crossed the Dnieper on the march.
The first to reach the far bank were men from the 842nd Rifle
Regiment of the 240th Division. An assault group commanded
by Sergeant P. P. Nefedov displayed particularly meritorious
action. For his heroism and gallantry in the capture and
holding of the bridgehead, the title of Hero of the Soviet
Union was conferred on Nefedov, the others were awarded military orders.

The troops which forced the Dnieper exhibited outstanding
staunchness and courage.

In general, they pushed onward as soon as they reached the
river; without waiting for pontoons or other heavy bridge-
building equipment, they used anything that came to hand —
timber rafts, ferries, fishermen's row-boats and motor-boats.
Everything that happened to be there was used. On the opposite
bank there was fierce fighting for bridgeheads. Having no
time to dig in, our troops immediately engaged the enemy, who
did everything they could to force them back into the river...

During the Dnieper crossing, fierce fighting culminated in a major success on the sector of the Steppe Front in the areas of Dneprovokamenka and Domotkan. There, particular gallantry was displayed by units of General G. B. Safiulin's 25th Guards Rifle Corps which, beating off repeated enemy attacks, ensured the successful crossing of the Dnieper by the 7th Guards Army. At the same time units of General M. N. Sharokhin's 37th Army also successfully forced the Dnieper. The first of that army to force the Dnieper southeast of Kremenchug were units of Colonel I. N. Moshlyak's 62nd Guards Division.

Contributing to success of the Fronts' forces were their aviation and long-range air units which solidly ensured our domination of the air through concerted air strikes at airfields and enemy defences and reserves.

By the end of September, after overrunning the enemy defences, our troops had crossed the Dnieper on a 700-km sector from Loyev to Zaporozhye, seizing several important bridgeheads from which the offensive was scheduled to be developed further west.

For successfully crossing the Dnieper and heroism, gallantry and combat skill, and for successfully storming enemy defences on the river, over 2,500 generals, officers, NCO's and enlisted men were awarded the title of Hero of the Soviet Union.

Between October 12 and December 23, the troops of the Voronezh Front,[1] carried through the Kiev strategic operation.

It had initially been planned to smash the Kiev grouping and regain Kiev by a main blow from the Bukrin bridgehead. This plan later had to be abandoned as the enemy concentrated the main forces of the Kiev grouping at that point. This direction was stated for subsidiary action, while the main blow was shifted to the Lyutezh bridgehead, north of Kiev, where the Nazis had weakened their northern sector.

The new plan for the liberation of Kiev and the continuation of the offensive towards Korosten-Zhitomir-Fastov

---

[1] On October 20, 1943, the Voronezh Front was renamed the Ist Ukrainian Front, and the Steppe Front — the 2nd Ukrainian Front.— *Author*.

was submitted to the Supreme Commander. After being considered by the General Staff and coordinated with the Central Front, it was endorsed by the Supreme Command.

On October 25 the 3rd Guards Tank Army began to regroup from the Bukrin bridgehead. It was supposed to cover about 200 kilometres along the Dnieper, which in fact meant a manoeuvre along enemy lines. Fortunately for us, the weather was unfit for flying; so during this manoeuvre, enemy air reconnaissance was almost totally inactive.

The 7th Artillery Assault Corps was also regrouped from the Veliky Bukrin area.

All measures of camouflage and radio deception were taken. Some of the movement to the Lyutezh bridgehead was carried out at night. To concentrate enemy attention on the Bukrin bridgehead, the troops at that point resorted to vigorous action, and used various ruses to trick the enemy. The enemy failed to detect the regroupment of our tank army and artillery corps, and so still believed that our main blow would come from this area.

By November 1, the 38th Army under General K. S. Moskalenko, 3rd Guards Tank Army under General P. S. Rybalko, 5th Guards Tank Corps under General A. G. Kravchenko, 7th Artillery Assault Corps and a large number of artillery and other units had been concentrated at the Lyutezh bridgehead.

All in all, about 2,000 guns and mortars and 500 Katyusha rocket mortars were brought together for the operation. By the time it began our forces on the Kiev sector had gained a considerable superiority over the enemy.

In the early morning of November 3 — and quite unexpectedly for the Nazi forces — the assault on Kiev began, supported by the 2nd Air Army.

To contain the enemy in the area of the Bukrin bridgehead, the 27th and 40th armies of the front had moved onto the offensive on November 1. The enemy assumed this attack was the main blow, and to counter it, brought in additional forces, including the SS Reich Panzer Division from General Field-Marshal Manstein's reserve. That was exactly what we wanted.

However, on November 3 and 4 the advance of the 38th

Army towards Kiev proceeded at a slow pace. To make a decisive impact on the course of the operation it was decided to commit the 3rd Guards Tank Army. By the morning of November 5, it had cut the Kiev-Zhitomir road, thereby creating favourable conditions for the troops advancing on Kiev.

General Moskalenko's 38th Army (Major-General A. A. Yepishev, member of the Military Council) reached the outskirts of Kiev by the end of November 5; at 4 a.m. on November 6 it captured Kiev, along with the Tank Corps of General A. G. Kravchenko.

A cable was immediately sent to the Supreme Commander. It read: "Immensely happy to report that the task set by you to liberate our beautiful city of Kiev, capital of the Ukraine, has been accomplished by the troops of the 1st Ukrainian Front. The city of Kiev has been completely cleared of the Nazi invaders. The troops of the 1st Ukrainian Front are continuing to execute the tasks given them."

General of the Army Vatutin, Commander of the Front, and Major-General K. V. Krainyukov, member of the Military Council, played a key role in the successful completion of that operation.

Extensive and important work in elaborating and organizing the operation to liberate Kiev and rout the enemy grouping was done by the Military Council of the 38th Army.

Taking part in the fighting for Kiev was the Czechoslovak Brigade commanded by Colonel Ludvik Svoboda. One hundred and thirty-nine officers and enlisted men of this heroic brigade were awarded Soviet orders.

The Soviet people will remember with gratitude the role of Czechoslovak officers and men in defeating the Nazi forces in the Great Patriotic War.

At 9 in the morning members of the Front's Military Council and I arrived in Kiev. Its residents, who had been hiding from the brutal reprisals meted out by the vicious enemy, were streaming towards the city. A crowd of people quickly gathered around our cars.

The first thing that struck the eye was that the great majority of the people were so thin. But their eyes shone, for they were seeing their liberators, their brothers — the Soviet soldiers — not in their dreams but in the flesh. They were overcome with joy, and could not contain their tears. Everyone wanted to voice his innermost thoughts and feelings...

As I drove along the Kreshchatik, once a beautiful avenue, that I had known so well, I could recognize nothing: everything was in ruins. This was what our ancient city of Kiev looked when the fascists left it.

After liberating Kiev, the Front's troops drove the enemy even further west, and gained control of Fastov, Zhitomir and several other towns.

Fearing total disaster, the German High Command hastily concentrated a counter-assault force in the Zhitomir area comprising 15 divisions, including 8 Panzer and motorized, with which it struck a powerful blow at the troops of the 1st Ukrainian Front on November 13. As a result, the enemy was able to recapture Zhitomir and to press 30 to 40 km forward. But the situation was soon remedied with the arrival of our reserves. Our front-line defences now passed 150 km west and 50 km south of Kiev.

Let us now take a retrospective look to reconstruct the situation during this period in the sector of the 2nd Ukrainian Front (formerly the Steppe Front), which I was only able to visit sporadically since the combat situation required that I be present on the Kiev sector.

On September 30 the troops of the 2nd Ukrainian Front forced the Dnieper and siezed a bridgehead on the western bank with a frontage of 30 km and a depth of 15 km.

A bridgehead of this size was fully adequate for further continuing the thrust by the main task force.

At the time the Dnieper was crossed I managed to be present in the sector of the 53rd Army commanded by General Managarov. As previously during the Belgorod offensive, he displayed great skill in controlling his army, and appeared far more experienced than he had been prior to the counter-offensive at the Kursk Salient. This observation also fully applied to most of the men making up the command echelons of the Army's units and formations. All the staffs had heightened their organizing abilities and troop control as well as their reconnaissance services, and — most important — the staffs and chains of command had now mastered the art of swiftly and profoundly analyzing the situation.

As I talked to Army Commander Managarov, I kept watching Konev. Formerly, he had usually broken in to correct or elaborate reports presented by his subordinates. But now, listening to Managarov's crisp and succinct report, he was silent and registered his pleasure with a smile. I was also exceptionally pleased by the alacrity and efficiency displayed by Managarov and his staff.

Taking my leave of Managarov, I remarked jokingly: "Everything's fine. The only thing missing is an accordion." With a laugh Managarov said his accordion was in the rear, and he had not played it since the time I had visited him during preparations for the Belgorod counter-offensive.

...The liberation of Kiev, as well as the capture and broadening of the bridgeheads on the Dnieper in the areas of Kiev, Cherkassy, Kremenchug, Dnepropetrovsk and Zaporozhye, drastically worsened the situation for the German forces in the Ukraine. The Dnieper gave the enemy the chance to organize an almost impregnable defence, and the Nazis had pinned great hopes on being able to stop the Soviet troops in front of this natural obstacle.

The Supreme Command had received information from the intelligence service that Hitler himself had visited the headquarters of Army Group South, where he had given his troops the categoric order to fight for the Dnieper to the last man and to hold it at all costs.

The Nazis fully understood that the loss of the Ukraine would entail the final collapse of their front in the south of our country, the loss of the Crimea, and the further prospect of Soviet forces reaching the Soviet border. Then the general situation in the fascist camp would become even more critical.

But despite the rigid and absolute demands of both Hitler and General Field-Marshal Manstein, the battle for the Dnieper was lost, although the German forces did attempt once again to reconstitute their defences in the area of Kremenchug, Dnepropetrovsk and Zaporozhye.

By October 23 the strike force of the 2nd Ukrainian Front, which included the 5th Guards Tank Army reassigned from the Supreme Command reserve, reached the approaches to

Krivoi Rog and Kirovograd. To eliminate the imminent danger the Nazi High Command put together a powerful force and hurled it against the units of the 2nd Ukrainian Front.

At the very height of the fierce fighting I arrived at Konev's command post four kilometres from the battlefield. It was possible to observe some of the actual fighting through the stereotelescope.

Konev was concerned that the troops of his front, seriously undermanned and weary as a result of previous action, might not be able to hold out against strong enemy pressure. To ensure an effective strike at enemy units he had had to throw in his entire air force, and reinforce his units with artillery reassigned from other sectors of the Front. In turn, the Nazi Command sent wave after wave of bombers which struck telling blows at our forces.

As October 24 drew to a close, our troops were forced back on several sectors, initially pulling back as much as ten kilometres, and then under further pressure, another 25 km. They then firmly entrenched themselves on the River Ingulets. Nothing the enemy could do proved capable of pushing them further back. After heavy losses, the enemy was compelled to abandon further attempts to attack and passed to the defensive.

As they were not strong enough to continue their offensive on the Krivoi Rog sector, the troops of the 2nd Ukrainian Front likewise took up a defensive position.

On the right flank of the Front, however, the fighting continued with unabating intensity. Here, General K. A. Koroteyev's 52nd Army, working closely with partisan detachments, successfully forced the Dnieper, and on December 14 captured a bridgehead and the town of Cherkassy.

In the course of fierce battles the troops of the 3rd Ukrainian Front captured the enemy bridgehead at Zaporozhye. Our forces liberated Dnepropetrovsk.

By the end of December a strategic bridgehead was established on the sector of the 2nd and 3rd Ukrainian Fronts with a frontage of 400 km and a depth of 100 km; this made it possible to mount further offensive operations in the immediate future.

As I was utterly engrossed in coordinating the actions of the 1st and 2nd Ukrainian Fronts, I was unable to keep in touch with all the ramifications of the action in the sectors of the 3rd and 4th Ukrainian Fronts. I did know from telephone conversations with the Supreme Commander, the General Staff and Vasilevsky that the 4th Ukrainian Front, which had smashed the enemy on the River Molochnaya, had successfully thrust forward, seizing a bridgehead on the Perekop Isthmus and trapping the German forces in the Crimea.

In mid-December I was summoned to the GHQ for a more detailed examination of the general situation and for the scrutiny and final revision of the plan for the further offensive. Vasilevsky was also there, and as soon as I met him at the General Staff we exchanged views about the results of 1943 and the prospects for the immediate future.

Vasilevsky looked tired. Like me, he had been continuously on the move since April either airborne or driving along front-line roads. The situation at the time was fairly complex and tense, abounding with kaleidoscopic alternations between momentous successes and disappointing setbacks. All this taken together, plus the continuous lack of sleep and physical and mental tension, had an extremely telling effect, particularly when we found ourselves in Moscow, in the quiet of city offices, where neither the sound of air raids or artillery bombardment, nor alarm-filled reports from dangerous sectors of the front, could be heard.

Present at a Supreme Command December conference were the majority of the other members of the State Committee for Defence. This was in effect a meeting of the State Committee for Defence, attended by several members of the Stavka of the Supreme Command.

The conference continued for quite some time. Vasilevsky and Antonov contributed to the discussion of the outcome and experience of the fighting at the fronts and of the general situation and prospects of the war. A report on questions of the economy and war industry was presented by Voznesensky. Stalin spoke on international events and the likelihood of our allies opening a second front.

According to figures presented by the General Staff, by the end of 1943 the Soviet Armed forces had liberated over half the territory captured by the German forces in 1941-1942. Since the Stalingrad counter-offensive, the Soviet troops had completely routed or taken prisoner 56 divisions, and inflicted devastating losses on 162 divisions. These latter had to be either seriously replenished or completely remanned. In this period over 7,000 tanks had been destroyed, along with more than 14,000 planes, and up to 50,000 guns and mortars. The German forces had lost many of their crack generals, officers, NCOs and privates.

At the same time, despite initial difficulties, the Communist Party and Government had managed to successfully overcome the problem of training skilled officers by the end of 1943. Not only were the requirements of the front satisfied, but in addition, large reserves were formed. Even before the great offensives of 1943, we had over 100,000 officers in reserve, who already had extensive war experience and the necessary military and technical training. That year the number of generals in our armed forces doubled.

In the second period of the war Germany had been bled on the Eastern Front to the extent that it was no longer able to wage offensive warfare on a large scale. But it did have sufficient strength to wage active defence. By the end of 1943, to strengthen the front-line troops which had taken a severe battering during the latter half of the war, the Nazi High Command brought up from the west another 75 divisions with large quantities of materiel, armament, and material supplies.

Our armed forces continued to build up their combat strength. In 1943, 78 new divisions were formed. By the end of the year we had a total of five new tank armies, 37 tank and mechanized corps, 80 independent tank brigades and 149 tank and self-propelled artillery regiments. Also, six artillery corps, 26 artillery divisions, 7 Guards rocket mortar divisions and dozens of other artillery units had been newly manned.

With the final shift in the war situation in favour of the Soviet Union, the Allied landings in Italy and Italy's defeat, and the powerful upsurge of the resistance movement throughout Europe, Hitler's satellite countries were now confronting a highly critical situation. Popular wrath was gathering momentum and turning against Nazi Germany, and there was a universal desire to end the war as soon as possible. In Poland, Yugoslavia, Czechoslovakia, and in Germany itself, the fearful defeats on the Soviet-German front, the newly looming economic problems and the acute shortage of manpower to make up for losses led to growing disbelief in the victory of German forces. This sentiment spread to sizable sections of the working people of the occupied countries and of the countries of the fascist bloc. A wave of national liberation movement against Nazi occupation has swept Greece, France and other European countries.

In our country the latest important victories inspired the people with complete assurance that the war was going to be won. It goes without saying that everyone grieved at the loss of sons, brothers, fathers, sisters and mothers, but our people grimly bore these losses with a high sense of duty to their country.

By the end of 1943 the command elements had gained a wealth of new experience in the art of strategy and tactics. The organization of large-scale operations by Fronts and groups of Fronts, and their triumphant execution, enabled the Supreme Command, the General Staff and the Fronts themselves to acquire a better understanding and a better mastery of the most effective methods of smashing enemy forces with the least possible losses in men and materiel.

Within the General Staff a large team of experienced operations experts, troops organizers and intelligence specialists had emerged. Indeed, the Supreme Command itself had achieved new heights in mastering the methods and means of waging modern warfare. We all found it far easier to work together and understand one another. This is what we had previously lacked — and this is what had been partially responsible for some of our earlier misfortunes.

The successful actions of the Soviet troops were largely due to better Party-political work—the military councils summing up the results of operations, depicting in talks to the personnel the vivid examples of gallantry and heroism displayed by all ranks, and popularizing the best methods of carrying out major combat assignments.

I would like to say that in general, through these military councils of Fronts, armies and fleets, the Party was able to flexibly combine both military and political leadership.

Generals and officers were now seen more often in the smaller units, where they met and talked with the NCOs and enlisted men. The chiefs of political organs and instructors also improved the direction of Party-political work.

In this regard I would like to pay special tribute to the work of the political departments of the 1st Ukrainian Front headed by General S. S. Shatilov, and of the 1st Byelorussian Front headed by General S. F. Galajev. Great assistance was provided to the troops by leading Party and government officials of the Ukraine and Byelorussia.

According to the Central Headquarters of the partisan movement, the partisan forces doubled their strength in 1943. Many partisan detachments merged and formed organized units and formations which could execute large-scale operations behind enemy lines, thus diverting sizable enemy forces. In effect, a formidable front of people's avengers driven by bitter hatred for the German invaders emerged inside enemy-held territory.

Especially strong partisan forces operated in Byelorussia and the Ukraine. The most significant in 1943 were the partisan detachments under V. E. Samutin, F. F. Taranenko, V. I. Kozlov, A. F. Fyodorov, A. N. Saburov, Z. A. Bogatyr, P. M. Masherov, S. A. Kovpak, M. I. Naumov, I. E. Anisimenko, Ya. M. Melnik, D. T. Burchenko and F. F. Kapusta.

In all their plans and actions, the Soviet Command took serious account of their formidable strength and increasing significance, especially since tactically, the art of partisan warfare had reached a higher stage.

The actions of these guerilla units and formations were now mainly coordinated and planned by the military councils of the Fronts and by the leaders of the Party Central Committees of the Ukraine and Byelorussia. Underground YCL organizations headed by the Byelorussian CC YCL Secretaries K. T. Mazurov and F. A. Surganov, who remained permanently in enemy-occupied territory, greatly assisted the Party in organizing partisan detachments. In 1943 the partisans blew up 11,000 trains, damaged or put out of action 6,000 locomotives and about 40,000 coaches and flatcars, and destroyed over 22,000 motor vehicles and over 900 railway bridges. These operations were organized and directed by local underground Party organizations.

The entire Soviet rear area had drastically changed. In 1943 there was a sharp increase in the production of armaments and ammunition. Several vital decisions on economic recovery in the liberated areas were passed in August 1943. In the last quarter of that year, 6.5 million tons of coal, 15,000 tons of oil and 172 million kwh of electricity were produced in the liberated areas alone. The rear of the Soviet Armed Forces was now able to supply the troops with everything needed for a successful armed struggle much more efficiently.

Our country had now fully switched on its entire colossal might. In 1943, our relationships with the Allies improved somewhat. We received a bit more material aid from the United States than in 1942, but it was still far short of what had been promised. By the end of the year this material aid was even cut back slightly. As an excuse, the US Government continued to cite its requirements in connection with the forthcoming Second Front and its commitments to Britain.

By the end of 1943 we had finally overcome our grave situation and, now, with formidable strength and means of war at our disposal, firmly held the strategic initiative; generally speaking, we no longer required a second front in Europe as badly as we had during the earlier two grim years. However, as we wanted to see Nazi Germany defeated as soon as possible, and the earliest possible termination of the war, we all looked forward to the Second Front being opened in the immediate future.

Of course, we all rejoiced in the victories in Italy, at El Alamein, in Tunisia and elsewhere, yet all this fell short of what we had been waiting from our Allies for so long so that we could feel their worthy contribution to victory.

On his return from the Teheran Conference, Stalin said:

"Roosevelt has given his word that extensive action will be mounted in France in 1944. I beleieve he will keep his word. But even if he does not, our own forces are sufficient to complete the rout of Nazi Germany."

Until now I have said nothing about the situation in our Western and North-Western directions. This is not at all because of any lapse of memory, but because throughout 1943 I was wholly engrossed in the fighting at the Kursk Salient, on the approaches to the Dnieper and in the fighting for the Dnieper and its right bank. As for the Western and North-Western directions, in 1943 they were the personal responsibility of the Supreme Commander and the General Staff, while we would sometimes merely be asked by the Supreme Commander to offer our observations or suggestions.

By the end of 1943 important successes had also been achieved in these directions. Soviet troops had pushed the enemy out of the last part of the Kalinin Region, and liberated the Smolensk Region and a goodly chunk of Eastern Byelorussia. By the end of the year following the successful advance of our forces, the front line in the North-Western and Western directions passed through Lake Ilmen, Velikiye-Luki, Vitebsk and Mozyr.

In the South-Western and Southern directions the front line passed at that time, from Polessye, through Zhitomir, Fastov, Kirovograd (exclusively), Zaporozhye and Kherson. The Crimea was still in German hands. Around Leningrad and in the north, the situation was vastly better, and Leningraders could now breathe a lot easier.

The members of the State Committee for Defence and we of the Stavka of the Supreme Command, believed that even though we had scored some signal successes and the enemy was now significantly weaker, he was still sufficiently strong. The fact that there was no second front in Europe provided the enemy with the opportunity to wage a stubborn defensive battle in 1944.

By the beginning of 1944, Germany and her satellites had an army of some five million men, with 54,500 guns and mortars, 5,400 tanks and assault guns, and more than 3,000 planes.

The Soviet Armed Forces had a 30 per cent superiority over the enemy in manpower, 70 per cent in artillery, and 230 per cent in aircraft. This quantitative advantage, coupled with excellent qualitative characteristics of the weapons, was boosted even further by the high morale of our troops and the improved tactical and strategic skills of the command echelons.

After an in-depth and comprehensive analysis, the Supreme Command decided in the winter campaign of 1944 to mount an offensive on a front running from Leningrad all the way down to the Crimea.

According to our plan, the major offensive operations were to be launched in the South-Western theatre of war in order to liberate the entire Ukraine west of the Dnieper, and the Crimea. It was decided to totally smash the siege of Leningrad, and to push the enemy out of the entire Leningrad Region. On the North-Western Direction the troops were to reach the boundaries of the Baltic Republics. The Western Direction was ordered to liberate as much of Byelorussia as possible.

When the actions of Soviet forces in the winter of 1944 were planned, it was also decided to concentrate the principal effort on the 1st, 2nd, 3rd and 4th Ukrainian Fronts so as to build up a greater superiority over the enemy in those sectors and to swiftly smash the forces of Army Groups South and A.

As for the other Fronts in the north, north-west and west, the Supreme Command decided to deploy fewer forces so as not to divert them from the main sections of the front.

After the Supreme Command conference, Vasilevsky and I spent another five days or so working with the General Staff to specify the tasks of the individual fronts. The Supreme Commander twice invited us to dinner in his Kremlin apartment.

Once when I was in Stalin's apartment, I made one more attempt to raise the question of encirclement operations. This time Stalin said:

"We are now stronger, and our troops more experienced. Now we can and must carry out operations aimed at encircling the German forces."

Present at one dinner I attended were A. A. Zhdanov, A. S. Shcherbakov and other members of the Politbureau. Zhdanov described the heroic deeds and outstanding gallantry of the workers of Leningrad who ignored dangers and, though hungry most of the time, operated their machine-tools and machinery at factories and plants for 14 to 15 hours a day, doing everything they could to aid the troops. Zhdanov requested an increase in food rations for the Leningraders.

Stalin immediately gave instructions to comply with Zhdanov's request, and then added:

"Let us drink to the Leningraders. They are indeed gallant heroes of our people."

Once the tasks of the Fronts were finally worked out, Vasilevsky and I immediately went to the Fronts, which we were responsible for, where we had been assigned to carry out the further coordination of our actions. I went to coordinate the actions of the Fronts under Vatutin and Konev, and Vasilevsky those of the Fronts under R. Ya. Malinovsky and F. I. Tolbukhin.

I decided to begin by visiting the 1st Ukrainian Front to inform them of the Supreme Command decision and help plan the forthcoming operations on that Front.

As already mentioned, Vatutin was an outstanding staff officer, who had the enviable ability of setting forth his ideas succinctly and precisely — and in beautiful handwriting. He himself wrote out most of the important orders, directives, or dispatches to the Supreme Command. When I arrived, he was drawing up a directive for an attack by the major group of the Front's troops in the general direction of Vinnitsa.

Vatutin was working in an overheated peasant house, with a warm cape over his shoulders. One look at him, and I realized he was obviously unwell.

Briefly acquainting him with the Supreme Command plan for the coming period and having heard his latest observations regarding the actions of his Front, I suggested that he go to bed immediately and sweat out his illness, so that he would be completely operative by the start of the offensive. This he consented to do.

After downing a glass of strong tea with dried raspberries, and swallowing a couple of pills, Vatutin went to his room. A. N. Bogolyubov and I set out for the Operations Division of the Staff where we could get a further look at the situation and to check the readiness of the troops.

Less than ten minutes after we arrived, the telephone rang. Bogolyubov picked up the receiver. It was Vatutin calling Bogolyubov to his quarters. I decided to accompany Bogolyubov. We caught Vatutin poring over a map of the forthcoming offensive. Turning to him, I said:

"You told me you were going to bed, and here you are again at your map."

"I want to write a dispatch to the GHQ about preparations for the offensive," replied Vatutin.

Virtually dragging him out of the room, I proposed that the chief of staff do the work, especially as it was in his direct line of duty.

Vatutin was a restless man indeed. His feeling of responsibility for his job was far stronger than any sense of concern for his own welfare.

As I was pretty hungry, I dropped in to see Khrushchev, knowing I could always expect to get a good bite of something there. I found Khrushchev with General N. T. Kalchenko, the member of the Front's Military Council reponsible for material supplies, and M. S. Grechukha, a representative of the Ukrainian Party Central Committee. They all asked for the latest news from Moscow.

I gave them a detailed account of the Supreme Command decision to drive the enemy out of the Ukraine, west of the Dnieper, and of the specific responsibilities assigned to the 1st Ukrainian Front. Grechukha told us about the heinous atrocities committed by the Nazis just before the German retreat.

"So far," he said, "we haven't really discovered even a tenth of the bloody deeds of the Nazi murderers on Ukrainian soil..."

At that time, the 1st Ukrainian Front was confronted by an enemy force of 30 divisions, including 8 Panzer and one motorized. The forces were commanded by Panzer General E. Rauss. The enemy High Command still dreamed of smashing the Soviet forces by capturing an extensive bridgehead west of the Dnieper and the city of Kiev.

As I have already said, in the second half of November the enemy captured Zhitomir and made repeated attempts to oust the formations of the 1st Ukrainian Front and break through to Kiev. But no success came of these stubborn attempts. What is more, their recklessness was costing the German forces heavy losses; in some divisions they amounted to 60-70 per cent in manpower and materiel. Lacking strength and utterly exhausted, the German troops stopped offensive action, yet not abandoning hopes of recapturing Kiev and reaching the Dnieper.

The Supreme Command instructed the 1st Ukrainian Front to prepare and execute the Zhitomir-Berdichev operation to smash the opposing enemy 4th Panzer Army and thrust it back to the Southern Bug. To strengthen the 1st Ukrainian Front, the Supreme Command assigned the 18th Army, the 1st Tank Army, the 4th Guards and 25th Tank corps to it.

At the time the operation was to begin, the 1st Ukrainian Front comprised the 1st Guards, 13th, 18th, 27th, 38th, 40th and 60th field armies, the 1st and 3rd Guards Tank armies. Its total strength was 63 infantry divisions, 6 tank, 2 mechanized corps and 3 cavalry divisions.

The plan for the offensive by the Front envisaged the defeat of the enemy in the Brusilov area, and an advance to a line running through Lyubar, Vinnitsa and Lipovaya.

General I. D. Chernyakhovsky's 60th Army, reinforced by the 4th Guards Tank Corps, was given the responsibility of advancing from the Malin area to the River Sluch on a sector between Rogachev and Lyubar. General Pukhov's 13th Army was ordered to advance towards Korosten and Novograd-Volynsky. The 40th and 27th armies were to thrust towards Belaya Tserkov and further on towards Khristinovka, where they were to join the troops of the 2nd Ukrainian Front.

General S. A. Krasovsky's 2nd Air Army was to provide air support.

On the morning of December 24, after a 50-minute artillery and air bombardment, the troops of the main group of the front went onto the offensive. The enemy defences were unable to withstand the blow and the German forces began to hastily withdraw. Favourable circumstances enabled the 1st and 3rd Guards Tank armies to be committed to battle in the afternoon. By the end of December 30 the frontage of the thrust had been expanded to 300 km with a depth of over 100 km. Our forces captured Korosten, Brusilov, Kazatin, Skvira and many other towns and communities.

The advancing troops engaged the enemy on the approaches to Zhitomir, Berdichev and Belaya Tserkov. The Nazi High Command was compelled to take emergency measures in order to close the gap, and to do so moved up 12 divisions from other army groups (North, Centre and A).

On December 31, Zhitomir was again liberated. Heavy fighting continued for Berdichev, a major railway and road junction. Units of General Katukov's lst Guards Tank Army and General Leselidze's 18th Army operated on this sector. Poor organization cost the lst Guards Tank Army losses without any compensating success, and it was not until January 5, after Vatutin personally intervened, that Berdichev was taken.

Participating in the battle for Belaya Tserkov was the lst Czechoslovak Brigade under General L. Svoboda. The collected manner and intelligent reasoning of this rugged, handsome man evoked in all of us a feeling of profound respect and complete confidence. And no one ever regretted our opinion of him. To the very end of the war Svoboda successfully commanded the Czechoslovak forces, and his heroic deeds were a worthy contribution to the rout of the enemy, whom he hated just as much as we Soviet people did.

The blows of the lst Ukrainian Front thrust the enemy back to the west. This prompted the Nazi Command to assemble troops in the areas of Vinnitsa and Uman in order to strike a counterblow at the 38th, 40th and lst Guards Tank armies. A major battle ensued.

Our troops passed to the defensive and tried to neutralize the enemy by direct artillery fire and air strikes. However, they were unable to withstand the enemy pressure, and were forced about 30 km back, where they finally dug in.

As a result of the Zhitomir-Berdichev operation, the troops of the lst Ukrainian Front advanced 200 km, completely liberating the Kiev and Zhitomir regions, as well as several districts of the Vinnitsa and Rovno regions. The left flank of the front enveloped the entire enemy group and occupied a large bridgehead in the area of Kanev and Korsun-Shevchenkovsky, thus creating an advantageous situation for the Korsun-Shevchenkovsky operation.

In mid-January the lst Ukrainian Front had reached a position along a line running through Sarny, Slavuta, Kazatin and Ilyintsy. From there the Front angled towards the Dnieper running as far as the area of Rzhishchev and Kanev where a large German force was solidly entrenched. In the hope of recapturing Kiev, the Nazi High Command probably failed to realize it was letting itself into a trap, which in effect was soon sprung in the Korsun-Shevchenkovsky area, and will be described further on.

Let us now look at the 2nd Ukrainian Front.

The 2nd Ukrainian Front, headed by Generals Konev, Zakharov and Susaikov, had like Vatutin's Front, received sizable reinforcements in tanks and self-propelled artillery by the end of December. The reinforced 5th Cavalry Corps and several artillery units had also been reassigned to it. This did strengthen the troops somewhat, but was far short of their requirements. Combined formations, without which no operation can be successful, were desperately lacking.

The 2nd Ukrainian Front was assigned to prepare and execute the operation involving the main blow towards Pervomaisk via Kirovograd. The Front was to have part of its forces advance in the general direction of Khristinovka where, joining up with the 1st Ukrainian Front, it was to defeat the enemy in the area of Zvenigorodka-Kanev.

It was not until January 7 that I was able to visit the 2nd Ukrainian Front, as I had to devote my entire attention to the troops under Vatutin, as the situation there was full of problems and dangers. On January 7 I flew up to the headquarters of the 2nd Ukrainian Front. At the time Konev was in the Kirovograd area, at his command and observation post.

At Front Headqarters I encountered Zakharov, the Chief of Staff of the Front, who briefed me on all the details of the situation.

I had known Zakharov since the time he had served in the Byelorussian Military District, where he had been Chief of the Operations Division of the District Staff. The District had then been under the command of Army Commander 1st Grade I. P. Uborevich, from whom one could always learn a great deal.

I must say that the Operations Division of the District Staff headed by Zakharov stood out among most of the frontier districts, and was distinguished for its team-work and masterful skill. Somewhat later Zakharov successfully commanded an infantry regiment at Bobruisk. As head of staff of the 2nd Ukrainian Front, Zakharov was certainly a good aide to Front Commander Konev.

After a brief examination of the situation at Front Headquarters and a phone conversation with Konev, I set out for his observation post.

Approaching the command post, I heard the sound of artillery fire, the explosion of aerial bombs and the roar of aircraft — all of which bore witness to the fierce battles raging in the air and on the ground.

Greeting Konev, I asked him how things were.

"We're beating the hell out of the enemy, but he hasn't given up Kirovograd yet," he replied.

From Konev's situation map and his description of what was happening, I realized the enemy would never be able to hold on to Kirovograd. By the end of January 7 not only was he enveloped by the troops of the Front; he barely managed to cling on to the town's southern outskirts where the offensive was being mounted by the 29th Tank Corps and the 29th and 50th Rifle divisions.

The armies under General Zhadov and General Shumilov had achieved special success. I knew both of these army commanders well. Since the beginning of the war they had travelled a long and difficult road. They had stood their ground out in gruelling battles with the enemy, and now, enriched by the experience of successful operations, they had come to Kirovograd at the head of armies as able and proficient war leaders.

Kirovograd was taken by the morning of January 8. Under heavy pressure the enemy was thrust westwards.

On the right flank of the Front, the offensive of the 53rd Army and the 4th Shock Army achieved nothing. Their advance was checked by powerful enemy counterattacks on the Smela-Kanizh line.

Suspending the offensive and taking up defensive positions, west of Kirovograd, the Front command regrouped the 5th Guards Tank Army under General Rotmistrov to the Front's right flank. But the move did not shift the balance in our favour.

Because more fundamental preparations were needed for further operations, the offensive of the 2nd Ukrainian Front was suspended in all directions. I returned to the lst Ukrainian Front to start getting ready for the Korsun-Shevchenkovsky operation.

Once the purposes and tasks of the operation had been discussed, Vatutin decided to form a group consisting of F. F. Zhmachenko's 40th Army, S. G. Trofimenko's 27th Army and the 6th Tank Army under General of the Armour A. G. Kravchenko, who had distinguished himself in the battle for Kiev.

According to a captured German map of January 24, 1944, the Korsun-Shevchenkovsky Salient, whose peak reached out all the way to the Dnieper, contained nine infantry, one panzer and one motorized divisions of the German lst Panzer and 8th armies.

This rather strong enemy group was obstructing the westward-aimed operations of the lst and 2nd Ukrainian Fronts, as it was located on the flanks of both of them.

On January 11, I outlined my views to the Supreme Commander on the plan to cut off, encircle and smash the entire Korsun-Shevchenkovsky group. He endorsed my proposal, and on January 12 confirmed the decision in a Supreme Command directive.

The directive provided for the two Fronts to strike pincer blows at the foot of the salient and to join up in the Zvenigorodka area. Before the operation began, the Supreme Command, at my request, reinforced the lst Ukrainian Front with the 2nd Tank Army.

Konev decided to strike out from the Verbovka and Krasnosilka areas with the 4th Guards Army, the 53rd and the 5th Guards Tank armies. To build up striking groups the Fronts had to considerably redistribute forces and materiel. Air support for the Front's strike groups was to come from the 2nd and 5th Air armies.

All in all, 27 rifle divisions, four tank, one mechanised and one cavalry corps, comprising 370 tanks and self-propelled guns, were mobilized to take part in smashing the Korsun-Shevchenkovsky group.

Our group had a 70 per cent superiority over the enemy

in infantry, 140 per cent in guns and mortars, 160 per cent in tanks and self-propelled guns.

Without question, this was sufficient to encircle and rout the enemy, but there was an untimely thaw with wet snow which played havoc with the roads. The weather also restricted air operations to the barest minimum. This meant that the troops were unable to fully build up material reserves. However, the operation could not be put off any longer.

The Korsun-Shevchenkovsky operation began on January 24 with assault by the 2nd Ukrainian Front in the general direction of Zvenigorodka. The 1st Ukrainian Front launched its offensive one day later. The enemy forces put up stiff resistance, fighting back with fire and counterattack; even so, they were unable to repulse the blows of the two Fronts.

On January 27, to try and close the gap, the enemy began a counterattack against units of the 2nd Ukrainian Front; they hoped to seal off the breach and cut off our advance elements of the 20th and 29th Tank corps of the 5th Guards Tank Army. Here they were partially successful.

However, the 20th Tank Corps under Lieutenant-General of the Armour I. G. Lazarev made a swift thrust forward and that same night captured the town of Shpola, ignoring the fact that the enemy had temporarily cut off his rearward communication lines.

I knew General Lazarev from the old days in the Byelorussian Military District where I had met him several times at manoeuvres and major district exercises during which he had received some excellent field training under Uborevich.

As I knew that Lazarev was proficient, I was certain he would acquit himself well and in this complex period would firmly lead his corps towards the assigned objective. On January 28 Lazarev's corps reached the area of Zvenigorodka, while the enemy had in the meantime closed the gap and was trying to repulse the attacks of the 2nd Ukrainian Front.

Taking the offensive, the striking force of the 1st Ukrainian Front smashed through the enemy defences but encountered fierce resistance in the depth of the enemy positions.

Aware that the enemy had succeeded in closing the gap, Front Commander Vatutin moved a strong advance force of

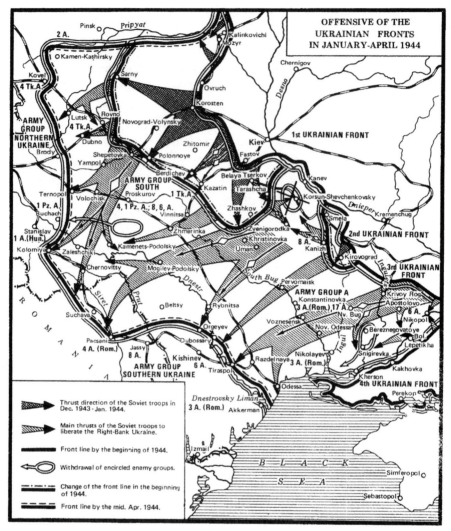

his Front into the Zvenigorodka area to reinforce the 20th and 29th Tank corps of the 2nd Ukrainian Front. The group was commanded by M. I. Savelyev, a gallant and able general, and consisted of the 233rd Tank Brigade, the 1228th Self-Propelled Artillery Regiment, a motorized rifle battalion and an anti-tank artillery battery.

Ably manoeuvring, this force boldly broke through the enemy units in the area of Lisyanka; on January 28 it joined up with the 20th Tank Corps in the town of Zvenigorodka, cutting off the major rearward communication lines of the enemy's Korsun-Shevchenkovsky group.

On the sector of the lst Ukrainian Front the German forces were putting up stubborn resistance. The first day General Zhmachenko's 40th Army scored small successes. Units of General Trofimenko's 27th Army, particularly the 337th Rifle Division under General G. O. Lyaskin and the 180th Rifle Division under General S. P. Merkulov were rather more successful. This success was extended by a rapid thrust by the 6th Tank Army towards the enemy's rearward communication lines, and this had a significant impact on the entire operation.

By January 30, committing additional forces, including the second echelon of the 5th Guards Tank Army, the 18th Tank Corps and the Cavalry Corps under General A. G. Selivanov, Konev's forces were able to drive the enemy back and create a new gap in his defences.

Moving forward, the troops of both Fronts trapped the Korsun-Shevchenkovsky group and began to compress it towards the centre of the ring. At the same time the two Fronts built up an outer combat position so as to prevent the enemy carrying out rescue operations from the Uman area.

To commemorate the breakthrough and the link-up of the lst and 2nd Ukrainian Fronts, a T-34 tank has been mounted on a pedestal in the centre of the town of Zvenigorodka. The inscription on the pedestal reads:

"Here on January 28, 1944, the ring around the German invaders encircled in the Korsun-Shevchenkovsky area was closed. The crew of a tank belonging to the 2nd Ukrainian Front 155th Red Banner Zvenigorodka Tank Brigade under Lieutenant-Colonel Ivan Proshin and including Lieutenant Evgeny Khokhlov, driver-mechanic Anatoly Andreyev and turret commander Yakov Zaitsev shook hands with tank-men of the lst Ukrainian Front. Glory to the heroes of our country!"

It is certainly a wonderful thing that heroic exploits are not forgotten. It is, however, unfortunate that the authors of the inscription did not mention the tank-men of the lst Ukrainian Front. This oversight should be rectified, and the names of the heroes from the lst Ukrainian Front who broke through to Zvenigorodka added...

Clinging to every possible line of defence, to every inhabited locality and every forest and dale, the surrounded German forces continued to put up stubborn resistance.

What we needed to drive the enemy out of his positions was powerful artillery fire, but road conditions made this impossible to provide. To build up even a minimum stock of shells, mines and tank fuel, all supplies had to be carried on bullocks, on foot, in sacks or on stretchers — in short, as best we could. Local Ukrainian villagers gave us great help in getting ammunition, fuel and food to the troops.

To save the troops inside the "cauldron" from imminent rout, the German Command decided to concentrate its forces against our outer front. On January 27, the 3rd, 11th and 4th Panzer divisions appproached the Novo-Mirgorod area, and were followed two days later by the 13th Panzer Division. Then the 16th and 17th Panzer divisions began assembling in the area of Rizino.

Every one of us involved in this operation to encircle the forces of the 1st and 8th German armies fully realized that the Nazi High Command was going to strike a blow from the outside to save the encircled forces.

To build up an outer front that could ensure the successful rout of the encircled troops, we committed the 6th Tank Army of the 1st Ukrainian Front reinforced by the 47th Rifle Corps, and the 5th Guards Tank Army of the 2nd Ukrainian Front reinforced by the 49th Rifle Corps and the 5th Engineer Brigade. The flanks of this outer front were secured by the 40th and 53rd armies.

In contrast to the actions of the enemy troops surrounded at Stalingrad, which remained on the defensive in the hope of being rescued by Manstein's group from Kotelnikovo, the enemy troops surrounded in the Korsun-Shevchenkovsky area themselves tried to break out of the ring by striking towards the rescue force operating outside it.

In the first days of February 1944, the enemy attempted to commit part of his panzer units in order to breach the outer front on the sector of the 2nd Ukrainian Front in the area of Novo-Mirgorod, but all the attempts were beaten back. Regrouping forces on the sector of the 1st Ukrainian Front, on February 3 and 4 the enemy struck two powerful blows in the Rizino and Tolmach-Iskrennoye areas, where he committed three more panzer divisions.

In the Rizino area the enemy was able to dent our defences. The enemy command was sure that this time a successful breakthrough was absolutely certain. General Hube, Commander of the German 1st Panzer Army, was lavish in his promises. We intercepted one of his notable radiograms reading: "I shall rescue you. Hube."

Counting on General Hube's formidable tank group, Hitler wrote in a cable to General Stemmermann, Commander of the surrounded troops: "You can rely on me like you would on a wall of stone. You will be freed from the ring. For the time being, hold on."

To prevent a breakthrough we hastily moved General S. I. Bogdanov's 2nd Tank Army, comprising two tank corps, from the Front reserve into the danger sector. Deploying for battle, the 2nd Tank Army struck a counterblow. The enemy was checked and partially thrown back to the areas he had attempted to leave. However, he still refused to abandon his intention of breaching our outer front. Pulling up one more tank division, one heavy tank and two assault gun battalions, and regrouping a sizable force of tank divisions in the Yerki area, the enemy launched a formidable offensive.

On Februbary 9, I sent a code message to Stalin, which read in part:

"... According to information received from pows, during battles in encirclement enemy troops have sustained heavy losses and their officers and men are now in a state of confusion bordering on panic.

"According to intelligence reports surrounded enemy forces have concentrated bulk of their troops in Steblev-Korsun Shevchenkovsky area. The enemy is apparently preparing for last attempt to break out towards Panzer group advancing on Malaya Boyarka. To secure this direction we intend by morning of February 9 to bring up one tank brigade from Rotmistrov to Lisyanka area and 340th Rifle Division from Zhmachenko to area of Krasnogorodok and Motayevka.

"Armies of Koroteyev, Ryzhov and Trofimenko have been continuing offensive throughout February 9.

"On February 8 at 15:50 hours our truce envoys delivered ultimatum to surrounded enemy through commander of Steblev combat sector, Colonel of the German Army Fukke.

"Truce envoys reported on their return that a reply will be given by German command on February 9 at 11:00 hours.

"Zhukov."

The Ultimatum was as follows:

"All those wounded or ill shall be accorded medical assistance.

"All officers, NCOs and men who surrender shall be immediately guaranteed nourishment.

"Your reply shall be expected at 11:00 a. m. on February 9, 1944, Moscow time, in written form, to be passed on through your personal representatives, who must come in a car with a white flag attached, along the route from Korsun-Shevchenkovsky through Steblev to Khirovka.

"Your representative will be met by a designated Russian officer near the eastern section of Khirovka on February 9, 1944, at 11:00 a. m. Moscow time.

"If you decline our offer to give up your weapons, the troops of the Red Army and air force will begin actions to destroy your encircled troops, and you will suffer the responsibility for their destruction.

"Deputy Supreme Commander-in-Chief
"Marshal of the Soviet Union G. Zhukov

"Commander of the Forces   Commander of the Forces of
   of the 1st Ukrainian Front   the 2nd Ukrainian Front
"General of the Army N. Va-   General of the Army I. Ko-
tutin   nev"

Leaflets with the following message were scattered among enemy troops displacements:

"To all the officer corps of the German troops encircled in the Korsun-Shevchenkovsky area.

"The 42nd and 11th Army corps are completely surrounded. The troops of the Red Army have encircled this group in a ring of iron. This ring of encirclement is getting tighter and tighter. All your hopes of being saved are in vain...

"The attempts by air transport to come to your assistance with ammunition and fuel have failed abyssmally. In just two

days, the 3rd and 4th of February, the air and ground forces of
the Red Army have shot down more than 100 Ju-52s.

"You officers of surrounded units should fully realize that
there is no real possibility of breaking out of encirclement.

"Your situation is hopeless, and resistance is totally senseless.
It will lead only to an enormous number of victims in officers and
men.

"To avoid a useless bloodbath, we propose that the following
terms of capitulation be accepted:

"1. All encircled German forces headed by you and your
staffs immediately cease military action.

"2. You put at our disposal your personnel, weapons, all
your military equipment, means of transport and all materiel
in good working order.

"To all officers and men who have ceased to resist, we
guarantee life and safety, and after the end of the war, return
to Germany or to any other country personally chosen by the
prisoner of war.

"All personnel who have surrendered will retain their military uniforms, military distinctions and orders, and personal
property and valuables; members of the senior officer corps, in
addition, will be allowed to retain their side-arms."

At noon on February 9, General Stemmermann's headquarters informed us that it had rejected our ultimatum.

At the same time the Germans launched fierce attacks on
the inner and outer fronts. February 11 saw particularly heavy
fighting. Our forces battled with exceptional staunchness. At
the cost of heavy losses, enemy Panzer divisions succeeded in
pressing forward to Lisyanka, but lack of strength forced the
enemy to pass over to the defensive.

In the early hours of February 12 the surrounded enemy
group massed all its available strength on a narrow sector
and attempted to break through to Lisyanka through Steblev,
seeking to join up with the Panzer divisions, but were unable
to. The enemy's further advance was checked. Even though
distance between the surrounded group and the rescue force
shrank to 12 kilometres, we could feel that the enemy simply
did not have the strength to effect a link-up.

In the early hours of February 12, I reported to the GHQ:

"Opposing Kravchenko is an enemy force of up to 160 tanks,

along with motorized infantry which is waging offensive along front running through Rizino, Chemerisskoye and Tarasovka in the general direction of Lisyanka and which, breaking through first line of 47th Rifle Corps, has thrust ten kilometres inside our defences.

"Further enemy advance has been checked on River Gniloi Tkich by units of 340th Rifle Division and 5th Mechanized Corps, making up second line of defence together with reserve regiments of S-P-85.

"Because of lack of communication with commander of 47th Rifle Corps, situation on left flank of army in sector of Zhabinka, Rizino, Dubrovka now being verified.

"Kravchenko possessed sufficent men and materiel to repulse enemy attacks, but during breach of our first-line defence lost control over some army units.

"Have ordered Nikolayev[1] to urgently deploy 27th Army command element in Jurzhentsy and to subordinate Kravchenko to Trofimenko in operations.

"Bogdanov's army to be concentrated by morning of 12.2 in area of Lisyanka, Dashukovka and Chesnovka; 202nd Rifle Divison to be deployed for battle on Khizhintsy-Jurzhentsy line. Fully manned brigade under Katukov to be pulled up to same area.

"Stepin[2] is ordered to have two brigades from Rotmistrov in Lisyanka by morning and to take up defensive positions, primarily anti-tank, along River Gniloi Tkich on Lisyanka-Murzintsy sector.

"On Stepin's sector:

"Rotmistrov's army has today beaten back attacks by up to 60 enemy tanks from Yerki towards Zvenigorodka. Intelligence has detected movement of up to 40 tanks from Kapustino to Yerki. Enemy may be pulling up tanks to Zvenigorodka sector from Lebedinsk sector.

"As of morning of February 12 Stepin has been moving 18th Tank Corps to Mikhailovka (east of Zvenigorodka) and 29th Tank Corps to Knyazhye-Lozovatka area.

"Smirnov's army has been waging battle for Miropolye, Kozhak, Glushki.

---

[1] Vatutin's code name.— *Author.*

[2] Konev's code name.— *Author.*

"For convenience of control, from noon on 12.2 Trofimenko's 180th Rifle Division is being reassigned to 2nd Ukrainian Front.

"Have ordered Stepin on February 12,1944 to employ main forces of Koroteyev's and Smirnov's armies to strike blow from east at Steblev and in rear of main group of encircled enemy which is preparing to thrust forward towards advancing tank group.

"All night aviation of Fronts active in area of Steblev.

"Zhukov"

On the morning of February 12 I had an attack of the flu and a high temperature, and was put to bed. Feeling very warm I fell into a deep sleep. I don't know how long I slept, but suddenly I felt my Adjutant General L. F. Minyuk, shaking me as hard as he could to wake me up.

"What's the matter?" I asked.

"Stalin is on the phone," he replied.

Jumping up, I took the receiver. The Supreme Commander said:

"I was just told that during the night the enemy broke through in Vatutin's sector from the Shanderovka area to Khilki and Novaya Buda. Do you know anything about it?"

"No, I don't," I answered.

"Check it and report to me."

I immediately called Vatutin and learned that the enemy had indeed attempted to take advantage of the blizzard to break out of encirclement, and had succeeded in pressing two or three kilometres forward and occupying Khilki where he was stopped.

After a few words with Vatutin and deciding on several additional measures, I phoned the Supreme Commander and told him all I knew about the situation on Vatutin's sector.

Stalin said:

"Konev has proposed that total control over the troops charged with smashing the Korsun-Shevchenkovsky group be transferred to him, and command of the outer front concentrated in Vatutin's hands."

The final rout of the enemy group inside the cauldron," I replied, "is a matter of three or four days. Transfer of control over the 27th Army to the 2nd Ukrainian Front can only retard the progress of the operation."

"Let Vatutin personally supervise the operations of the 13th and 60th armies in the Rovno-Lutsk-Dubna area, while you assume responsibility for preventing a breakthrough by the enemy striking force from the Lisyanka area." With that the Supreme Commander hung up.

A couple of hours later we received a directive which read as follows:

"To the Commander of the lst Ukrainian Front

"To the Commander of the 2nd Ukrainian Front

"To Comrade Yuryev[1]

"Given that the elimination of the Korsun enemy group requires the joint effort of all forces charged with this task, and since most of these forces belong to the 2nd Ukrainian Front, the Stavka of the Supreme Commander-in-Chief hereby orders:

"1. Control of all forces operating against the Korsun enemy group shall be assigned to the Commander of the 2nd Ukrainian Front with the task of destroying the Korsun German group within the shortest possible time.

"Accordingly, the 27th Army comprising the 180th, 337th and 202nd Rifle divisions of the 54th and 159th Fortified Districts and all available reinforcement units shall be reassigned as of midnight of February 12, 1944 to the operational command of the Commander of the 2nd Ukrainian Front. The lst Ukrainian Front shall continue to be responsible for all supplies for the 27th Army.

"Pending the establishment of direct communications the Commander of the 2nd Ukrainian Front shall maintain contact with the 27th Army Headquarters through the Headquarters of the lst Ukrainian Front.

"2. Comrade Yuryev shall be released from supervision of the elimination of the Korsun German group and charged with coordinating the operations of the lst and 2nd Ukrainian Fronts with the task of preventing an enemy breakthrough from Lisyanka and Zvenigorodka to link up with the Korsun enemy group.

" Report on fulfilment.

---

[1] Zhukov's code name.— *Ed.*

"Headquarters of Supreme
"Commander-in-Chief
"J. Stalin
"A. Antonov
"February 12, 1944"

Vatutin was an extremely emotional man. Having received this directive he immediately called me and, thinking that I was fully responsible for it all, said with overtones of chagrin:

"Comrade Marshal, you of all people surely know I've had no sleep for several days on end and given every ounce of strength to the Korsun-Shevchenkovsky operation. Why then have I now been brushed aside from the completion of this magnificent operation? I am proud of my troops too and I want Moscow to salute the soldiers of the 1st Ukrainian Front."

"Nikolai Fedorovich, this is an order from the Supreme Commander. You and I are soldiers, so let us carry out our orders without argument."

"The order will be obeyed."

After February 12, despite all his attempts the enemy was never able to break through from Shanderovka area to Lisyanka.

On February 14, the troops of the 52nd Army of the 2nd Ukrainian Front occupied the town of Korsun-Shevchenkovsky. The ring around the surrounded enemy troops continued to press inwards. The German generals, officers and men realized that the promised rescue would never materialize, and they would now have to rely on their own strength alone. According to prisoners of war, their units were overwhelmed by utter desperation, especially when they learned that many of their division commanders and staff officers had fled by plane.

On the night of February 16 there was a heavy snow storm. Visibility was reduced to 10-20 m. This blizzard gave the Germans a glimmer of hope, and they attempted to break through to Lisyanka in order to join up with Hube's group. The attempt was stymied by Trofimenko's 27th Army and the 4th Guards Army of the 2nd Ukrainian Front.

A particularly heroic fight was put up by the cadets of the school battalion of the 41st Guards Rifle Division under Major-General K. N. Tsvetkov. Throughout the morning of February 17, a fierce battle raged to crush the thrusting columns of German forces, and most of them were routed and captured.

Only a few tanks and armoured personnel-carriers carrying generals, officers and some SSmen, managed to break out of the ring.

As we had expected, it was all over for the surrounded group by February 17. According to the information presented by the 2nd Ukrainian Front, 18,000 men and the entire materiel of the group were captured.

On February 18 Moscow saluted the troops of the 2nd Ukrainian Front. Not a word was said about the troops of the lst Ukrainian Front. I feel that was a mistake on the part of the Supreme Commander.

There is no denying that success in surrounding and destroying an enemy group depends on the action of both the inner and outer Fronts; in this instance, equal success was achieved by the brilliant action of both Fronts — Vatutin's and Konev's.

By the end of February 1944 the successful operations of the two Ukrainian Fronts had created a favourable situation for completely expelling enemy forces from the entire territory of the Ukraine west of the Dnieper. The 1st Ukrainian Front, whose right flank had captured the Lutsk, Shumskoye and Shepetovka areas, emerged to face the flank of the Proskurov-Vinnitsa enemy group, while the 2nd Ukrainian Front established departure positions for a blow through Uman on the Mogilev-Podolsk sector. The 3rd Ukrainian Front reached the line of Krivoi Rog, Shirokoye and Kochkarovka, ready to strike on the Tiraspol-Odessa sector.

Between February 18 and 20 I was at the GHQ where I reported to the Supreme Commander on the plan of further operations. Stalin ordered me to resume coordination of the actions of the lst and 2nd Ukrainian Fronts, and to immediately begin an offensive.

On February 21 I arrived at the headquarters of the lst Ukrainian Front and immediately passed on to Vatutin and the members of the Front's Military Council the instructions I had received from the Stavka.

After rechecking the situation and the tasks approved by the Supreme Command, the Fronts began to accelerate the preparations for new offensive operations and their material support which, because of the spring thaw in the Ukraine, presented enormous difficulties. It was particularly hard to stock up shells, mines, bombs, fuel and food supplies directly in the units.

Considering the muddy and waterlogged terrain, the Nazi High Command believed the Soviet Forces would never be able to advance in such conditions, and it would therefore have ample time to regroup its troops and fortify its defences. We decided to capitalize on this miscalculation and strike a series of crushing blows when the enemy least expected them.

Briefly, we once again decided to employ the stratagem of operational suddenness, which the Soviet Command elements had now firmly mastered.

In accordance with the plans of the Supreme Command, the lst Ukrainian Front was to mount its major blow from the area of Dubno, Shepetovka and Lyubar on the general sector of Chernovtsy so as to smash the Proskurov-Vinnitsa-Kamenets Podolsky group of enemy forces.

Once it reached the Carpathian foot-hills the plan was to slash the strategic front of the enemy and thus deprive him of any chance for manoeuvring along the shortest possible routes. Provided this operation was successful, the entire southern group of German forces would have to utilize communication lines solely through the Focşani Gates, through Romania and Hungary, and this involved great distances.

The 2nd Ukrainian Front was to conduct an operation in the general direction of Beltsy-Yassy, and part of its forces was to advance on Khotin in cooperation with the left flank of the lst Ukrainian Front. The 3rd Ukrainian Front was ordered to be ready to strike at Odessa and Tiraspol to liberate the maritime areas, reach the Dniester, and secure a bridgehead there.

During the day of February 28 I dropped in to see Vatutin at front headquarters, as I wanted to have another discussion on questions relating to the forthcoming operation. After we had been going over things for about two hours, he said to me:

"I am thinking of going to the 60th and 13th armies to see how they're handling problems of liaison with the air force and to check whether they will have all material supplies ready by the start of the operation."

I advised him to send some other responsible officers so

that he himself could begin examining the decisions taken by the army commanders, and once again check cooperation with the air force and attend to the problems of the Front's service area. Vatutin nonetheless insisted on going, pointing out that he had not been to the 60th and 13th armies for a long time. I ultimately consented, thinking that in the meantime I myself could deal with problems of the Front headquarters and coordinate the actions of the various service commanders.

Unfortunately, what I feared above all happened. On February 29 I received a telephone call from the field aerodrome, and was told that Front Commander Vatutin had just been brought in seriously wounded.

As is clear from the documents, Vatutin was wounded in the following circumstances.

General Vatutin and Front Military Council Member Major-General Krainyukov, guarded by eight men, left the headquarters of the 13th Army (Rovno area) at 4:30 p.m. on February 29 for the 60th Army (Slavuta area) along the Rovno-Gosha-Slavuta route.

At 7:40 p.m. Vatutin and his group saw, near the north part of the village of Milyatyn, a crowd of about 250-300 people and at the same time heard a few shots coming from the crowd.

Vatutin ordered the cars to stop so they could find out what was happening. Suddenly, the cars were fired on from the windows of nearby houses by Bandera groups inside.

Vatutin and those accompanying him rushed out of the cars, and Vatutin was wounded in the leg.

Quickly turning one of the cars, three soldiers lifted Vatutin up, put him into the car, took the documents, and drove off in the direction of Rovno. Krainykov left with them.

Vatutin was hit above the knee. They were only able to bind the wound up in the village of Gosha, and he had lost a lot of blood.

He was taken to military hospital in Rovno, and then moved to Kiev.

Issuing the necessary instructions to the chief of the Front's medical service, I took over the duties of Front Commander. I also immediately phoned Stalin to report Vatutin's wound and evacuation. The Supreme Commander endorsed my decision to take control of the Front during the forthcoming important and complex operation.

Leading specialists were summoned to Kiev, including the illustrious surgeon Burdenko, but despite everything Vatutin's life could not be saved. He died on April 15. On April 17 he was buried in Kiev. Moscow, the capital of our country, paid the final military tribute to this loyal son of his people and brilliant military leader with a salute of 20 artillery salvoes.

To conduct the operation we had to quickly carry out large troop regroupments from the left flank of the front, moving them closer to the right flank. The 3rd Guards Tank Army had to be moved from Berdichev to the Shumskoye area (a distance of about 200 km), and the 4th Tank Army had to cover 350 km. Roughly the same distance had to be covered, during the spring thaw, by large numbers of artillery and engineer units and the logistical service echelons.

Despite all the difficulties, the regroupment plan went according to schedule. Most important, enemy reconnaissance failed to detect these regroupments which went on mainly under cover of darkness, or during the day if the weather made flying impossible.

On March 1 a Supreme Command directive appointed me Commander of the 1st Ukrainian Front. From that day I was given full responsibility for the success of the forthcoming operation of my Front. In view of this I was relieved of all responsibility for the actions of the 2nd Ukrainian Front, and the Supreme Command itself assumed control of it.

On March 4, 1944, the 1st Ukrainian Front began the offensive. The enemy defences were breached on the sector between Shumskoye and Lyubar, and the 3rd Guards and 4th Tank armies swept into the gap. By March 7 these two tank armies had overrun enemy positions, reached the Ternopol-Proskurov line, and severed the important Lvov-Odessa railway. Fearing that Proskurov-Vinnitsa-Kamenets-Podolsky group would be encircled, the Nazi High Command concentrated additional 15 divisions against the 1st Ukrainian Front.

On March 7 a fierce battle began, the kind of battle we had not seen since the Battle of the Kursk Salient.

For eight days the enemy did everything he could to throw our forces back to their lines of departure, but without success.

Having exhausted and weakened the counterattacking enemy forces, our troops on the main-blow sector, reinforced by Front reserves, including the lst Tank Army, broke enemy resistance on March 21, and began a swift advance southward.

The formations of the lst Tank Army made especially rapid progress. At the same time the other armies of the Front advanced rapidly from the east, north-east and north. Smashing enemy units, the 1st Tank Army captured the town of Chertkov on March 24, while the 8th Guards Corps of the Army commanded by General I. F. Dryomov reached the bank of the River Dniester that same morning. The 1st Guards Tank Brigade under Colonel V. M. Gorelov and the 20th Motorized Rifle Brigade under Colonel A. Kh. Babadjanyan reached the area of Zaleshchiki and the Dniester, as did units of the 11th Guards Tank Corps under General A. L. Getman.

On the night of March 24 the 64th Tank Brigade under Colonel I. N. Boiko broke into the Mosha railway station on the approaches to Chernovtsy, where a trainload of tanks and ammunition was being unloaded. Our tank-men captured it. On March 28 our tanks overran Chernovtsy airfield where preparations were in progress to get dozens of enemy planes airborne. But this was never to be.

On March 29 units of the 11th Guards Tank Corps under General Getman and the 24th Rifle Division liberated the town of Chernovtsy from the German invaders. The residents of the town joyfully welcomed the Soviet troops.

At their request the Military Council of the lst Tank Army placed the tank commanded by Lieutenant P. F. Nikitin on a pedestal in the town. The inscription on the memorial plaque reads: "This tank commanded by Guards Lieutenant P. F. Nikitin was the first to break into the town when it was liberated from the Nazi invaders on March 25, 1944." A street in the town was also named after Nikitin.

By the end of March the enemy group numbering 23 divisions, including ten Panzer, one motorized and one artillery, was for the most part surrounded.

Moving in for the kill against the surrounded enemy group from the east were the 18th and 38th armies; some units of the 1st Guards Army and the 1st and 4th Tank armies (excluding the 8th Mechanized Corps) crossed the Dniester and cut the enemy's southern communication lines. At the critical moment, our troops operating on the inner front found themselves seriously undermanned, short of artillery and ammunition, which could not be brought up quickly enough because of the bad roads. The 3rd Guards Tank Army, which had sustained heavy losses, was ordered by the Supreme Commander to withdraw and await reserves. By the end of March the 4th Tank Army was in the Kamenets-Podolsky area, and also severely undermanned.

All these factors taken together meant that no vigorous action was taken to split up the surrounded enemy group. As I retrospectively analyze the whole operation today, I think that the 1st Tank Army should have been turned from the Chertkov-Tolstoye area to the east to strike at the surrounded group. But we had reliable intelligence from various sources that the surrounded enemy intended to attempt a breakthrough southward across the Dniester to the Zaleshchiki area. At the time this seemed an extremely reasonable and likely way of action.

In this event, the enemy could cross the Dniester and easily occupy its southern bank, where it could organize a defensive. Making this easier was the fact that the 2nd Ukrainian Front's 40th Army on the right flank had still not reached Khotin by March 30.

Given the situation, we felt it necessary to envelop the enemy with the 1st Tank Army as deeply as possible by moving its main forces to the other side of the Dniester so it could capture the area of Zaleshchiki, Chernovtsy and Kolomiya. However, when the German Command of Army Group South learned that our troops had severed the southward lines of retreat, it ordered the encircled forces to try and break through not to the south, but to the west through Buchach and Podgaitsy.

As we subsequently found out from captured documents, the command of Army Group South assembled a task force, including the 9th and 10th SS Panzer divisions; on April 4 it struck a powerful blow at our outer front from the Podgaitsy area. The enemy Panzer group overran the defences of the 18th Corps and the 1st Guards Army and swept on towards Buchach, where it met its units which were breaking out of the ring.

Neither I nor the Front headquarters were able to absolutely ascertain the numbers of the units that broke out.. Various figures were cited, but the final count was probably a great many more than the several dozen infantry-carrying tanks our troops reported at the time.

During the heavy fighting the surrounded troops of the 1st Panzer Army lost well over half their forces and their entire artillery, along with the bulk of their tanks and assault guns. Of some formations, nothing but headquarters remained.

On April 12 the enemy group surrounded in Ternopol was attacked in strength; two days later it was completely routed. On April 14 Ternopol was captured by the 15th and 94th Rifle and the 4th Guards Tank corps.

Completing the operation, the forces of the Front took up defensive positions along the Torchin-Berestechko-Kolomiya-Kuta line.

We still could not envelop the Proskurov-Kamenets Podolsky grouping because during that operation we failed to redeploy our troops as required.

Since the beginning of the operation, the troops of the Front had advanced about 350 km. The enemy's defences were smashed to their very foundations, and a vast gap had been made in his front from the town of Ternopol to Chernovtsy. To close this gap, the German High Comand hastily moved sizable forces from other fronts — Yugoslavia, France, Denmark and Germany. The 1st Hungarian Army was also brought up.

The forces of our Front liberated 57 towns, 11 railway junctions, many hundreds of settlements, and the regional centres — Vinnitsa, Proskurov, Kamenets-Podolsky, Ternopol and Chernovtsy; they reached the foot-hills of the Carpathians, slashing the entire strategic front of the enemy's Southern group in two. From then on, the enemy had no lines of communication other than through Romania.

The Soviet forces again displayed their great combat skills and scored outstanding successes. Our victories were achieved not only due to the superiority of organization and material equipment, but also because of our patriotic spirit and mass heroism. For meritorious service to their country many thousands of enlisted men, NCOs, officers and generals were awarded government decorations. I received the Order of Victory No. I.

From information sent by the General Staff I learned that by the end of April and the beginning of May the troops of the 2nd and 3rd Ukrainian Fronts had smashed the opposing enemy troops and reached the line of Suchava, Yassy, Dubossary, Tiraspol, Akkerman, and the Black Sea coast. An offensive by the 4th Ukrainian Front, the independent Maritime Army and the Black Sea Fleet culminated in the complete rout of the Crimea group of enemy forces. On May 9 the Hero City of Sebastopol was freed, and on May 12 the operation to liberate the Crimea was completed.

On April 22 I was summoned to Moscow and the Supreme Command GHQ to discuss the summer and autumn campaign.

Even though throughout the winter and spring campaign, the actions of our forces had resulted in signal victories, I felt the German troops were still strong enough to put up a stiff defence on the Soviet-German front. As far as the strategic proficiency of their High Command and the local army group commands was concerned, after the disaster in the Stalingrad area and particularly after the Kursk battle, it had drastically declined.

Unlike the first phase of the war, the Nazi Command had become sluggish and lacked ingenuity, particularly in critical situations. Their decisions betrayed the fact that they were unable to correctly assess the capacities of either their own troops or those of the enemy. The Nazi Command would often be too late in withdrawing its forces from under the threat of flanking blows or encirclement — and this, of course, placed these in a hopeless position.

Reading post-war memoirs of German generals and field-marshals, one is simply astounded by their interpretations of the reasons for their setbacks, miscalculations and blunders and their oversights in directing their troops.

Most point the finger at Hitler as the prime reason. They point out that after assuming personal control over Germany's Armed Forces in 1941, and being wholly inept in matters of strategy and grand tactics, he directed the armed struggle dictatorially, without heeding the advice of his generals and field-marshals. I myself feel there is some measure of truth in this — perhaps even a large measure — yet the basic reasons for the German defeats are not to be found here.

After losing the initiative following the defeat on the Volga and particularly at the Kursk Salient, the Nazi High Command were compelled to face new factors and methods of strategic and tactical troop control which they were not prepared for. Encountering serious problems during forced withdrawals and in conducting strategic defence operations, the Nazi Command elements were unable to readjust.

The German troops quickly lost their morale. This factor plays a key role in defensive operations.

The Nazi High Command also failed to take into account the fact that the Red Army, Navy and Air Force, both quantitatively and, more important, qualitatively were now totally different from what they had been in the initial stage of the war; that our command elements had taken a giant step forward on the strategic and tactical level and that they had steeled themselves in the grim conditions of armed struggle.

Aboard a Moscow-bound plane I studied the latest reports furnished by the Fronts. Once again they confirmed my belief that the Stavka had made the correct decision on April 12, 1944, when routing the German forces in Byelorussia was given top priority. To draw a maximum of German strategic reserves from Byelorussia, it was first necessary to deliver a series of powerful blows against other sectors.

Success here was certain: first, the operational deployment of the troops of Army Group Centre, whose front lines were bent outwards towards our troops, created advantageous conditions for deep enveloping blows at the foundations of the bulge; second, we were now in a position to muster overwhelming superiority over the enemy in the directions of the main blows we had contemplated.

I was very familiar with Byelorussia, especially those areas held by Army Group Centre.

The first thing I did when I arrived in Moscow was to call on Antonov at the General Staff. At that time he was busy preparing a situation map for the Supreme Commander. Antonov briefed me on the course of the fighting to liquidate the enemy group in the Crimea and on the mobilization of new reserve troops and material supplies for the summer campaign. He warned me not to let Stalin know that he had told me about the supply situation — Stalin had forbidden such information to be divulged to anyone so that we should not ask the Stavka for these supplies before the time came.

Here I must point out that the Supreme Commander had recently begun to take a more economical approach to the distribution of human and material resources at the disposal of the GHQ. Now he would assign them first of all only to those Fronts which were really involved in key operations. Other Fronts received reasonably limited supplies.

Writing in *Voyenno-Istorichesky Zhurnal* (Journal of Military History), one former Front commander, voicing his views on the work of the special representatives of the Stavka, has stated that "most manpower and material supplies were always sent wherever the actions of Fronts were coordinated by representatives of the Stavka, to the detriment of other Fronts".

But what else could have been done? Stavka representatives coordinated operations precisely where the main action was being played out, and it was these operations that required top priority in material supplies. This practice was fully justified.

From Antonov's office I phoned the Supreme Commander. My call was taken by Poskrebyshev, who suggested I have a little rest, and he would call me back as soon as Stalin was free. This was certainly a useful and attractive suggestion, as I had usually been getting no more than four or five hours sleep a day, and in cat-naps at that...

Finally Stalin made an appointment for 5:00 p. m.

I then called Antonov and found out he had also been summoned to the Supreme Commander. Stalin had decided to familiarize himself with the latest situation and with the observations of the General Staff.

When I entered Stalin's office there were Antonov; the Commander of the Armoured Forces, Marshal Ya. N. Fedorenko; the Commander of the Air Force, Colonel-General A. A. Novikov; as well as Deputy Chairman of the Council of People's Commissars, V. A. Malyshev.

After greeting me Stalin inquired whether I had been to see Shvernik.

I said that I had not.

"You must go and receive your Order of Victory".

I thanked the Supreme Commander for the high award. Turning to Antonov Stalin asked: "How do we begin?"

"Allow me to make a brief report on the situation on the Fronts as of noon today," said Antonov.

After a quick review of the events on all strategic directions, Antonov set forth the General Staff's predicitions regarding possible German actions in the summer campaign of 1944. As far as suggestions about the possible actions of Soviet forces during the summer period were concerned, Antonov made no mention of them. I realized that he had decided to voice his opinion only whenever the Supreme Commander himself would directly ask for them.

Addressing the Air Force Commander, General Novikov, Stalin inquired about the state of the Air Force, and asked specifically, whether the aircraft supplied by the industry would be sufficient to provide adequate replacements for the Front air armies and for the long-range aviation. After hearing Novikov's replies, which were extremely optimistic, the Supreme Commander suggested that Marshal Fedorenko report on the state of the armoured troops and the chances of their being fully manned by the beginning of the summer campaign.

Throughout it all I felt Stalin knew all the figures beforehand, but probably wanted to brief all those in attendance through those who were directly responsible before asking us what we thought. We were already accustomed to this method that Stalin employed for discussing problems.

Stalin casually packed his pipe, put a match to it and started it going. Then taking a deep puff and exhaling, he said:

"Now let's hear what Zhukov has to say." And with that he approached the map which Antonov had used in his report.

Taking my time, I spread out my own map, which was somewhat smaller than the General Staff map, although equally well detailed. The Supreme Commander walked up to my map and perused it with the utmost attention.

I began by agreeing with Antonov's basic observations regarding the most likely actions by the German troops and the problems they would have to encounter on the Soviet-German front in 1944.

At this point Stalin interrupted me and said:

"These will not be the only problems. In June the Allies intend to finally conduct a major landing operation in France. Our allies are in a hurry," Stalin smiled. "They are afraid that we will rout Nazi Germany without them. Of course, it is in our interests to see Germany finally beginning to fight on two fronts. This will make things even more difficult for them, and they will not be able to overcome them."

In outlining my suggestions for the plan of the summer campaign of 1944, I made a point of drawing Stalin's notice to the enemy group in Byelorussia; once it was defeated, the enemy defences on the entire western strategic direction would collapse.

"What does the General Staff think about that?" Stalin asked Antonov.

"I agree," he said.

I did not see Stalin press the buzzer which summoned Poskrebyshev. He entered the office and stopped, awaiting orders.

"Put me through to Vasilevsky," said Stalin.

A couple of minutes later Poskrebyshev reported that Vasilevsky was on the line.

"Good day," Stalin began. "Zhukov and Antonov are here with me. Do you think you could fly in for consultations about the plan for the summer? ... What is the situation at Sebastopol? ... Very well, stay where you are then, but send your suggestions for the summer period to me personally."

Replacing the receiver, the Supreme Commander said: "Vasilevsky has promised to finish off the enemy group in the Crimea in about 8 or 10 days. He then went on to say: "But don't you think it might be better to begin our operations with the 1st Ukrainian Front so as to envelop the Byelorussian group to an even greater extent and lure the enemy's reserves from the central direction to this sector?"

Antonov pointed out that in this case the enemy would find it easy to manoeuvre between the adjacent fronts. It would be better to start in the north and then conduct an operation against Army Group Centre to liberate Byelorussia.

"Let's see what Vasilevsky suggests," said Stalin. "And call the Front commanders. Have them report their own ideas for actions by their fronts in the immediate future..." Then turning to me, the Supreme Commander continued: "You and Antonov can attend to the draft plan for the summer period. We'll talk again when you are ready."

Two or three days later the Supreme Commander again summoned Antonov and myself. After discussing the plan we decided on the following: the first offensive operation was to be carried out in June on the Karelian Isthmus and the Petrozavodsk sector, and then in the Byelorussian strategic direction.

On April 28, after more work with the General Staff, I returned to the 1st Ukrainian Front. At the beginning of May, when the liberation of the Crimea was drawing to a close, I sent the Supreme Commander my suggestion that the command of the 1st Ukrainian Front be transferred to Konev so that I could immediately begin preparing the operations to liberate Byelorussia.

Stalin agreed, but told me that the 1st Ukrainian Front was still my responsibility.

"The Byelorussian operation is to be followed by an operation on the sector of the 1st Ukrainian Front," he said.

Not to lose any time I decided not to wait for Konev to arrive, and instructed the Front Chief of Staff, V. D. Sokolovsky, to communicate to him my views and suggestions for further action by the Front.

During the time I commanded the 1st Ukrainian Front I was able to make an in-depth study of the higher command elements, and I would like here to make special mention of the officers and generals at Front headquarters who, through their great sense of duty and proficiency, furnished able assistance to the Front command in organizing offensive operations. The rear services of the Front worked well. In even the most critical situations, the service echelons of the 1st Ukrainian Front always did everything they were asked, and the combat troops were deeply grateful to the tireless personnel of the rearward services for their all-embracing solicitude.

When I returned to the GHQ I met Vasilevsky, who was preparing to coordinate the actions of the lst Baltic and 3rd Byelorussian Fronts. It was natural that we had to discuss things together.

CHAPTER 6

Liberation of Byelorussia and the Ukraine

The Byelorussian people languished under the yoke of enemy occupation for three years. The Nazis robbed or destroyed almost all public property, ravaged cities, burned 1,200,000 buildings in villages, destroyed 7,000 schools and killed over 2,200,000 civilians and prisoners of war. Nearly every family suffered from the war. But despite all the trials, Byelorussia did not submit to the Germans; her people did not lose heart, and did not stop their fight against the invaders.

The Byelorussian partisans were aware that the Red Army had routed the German troops in the Ukraine and driven them far to the west, and were preparing for decisive operations.

By the summer of 1944, nearly 143,000 well-armed partisans, organized in large detachments, units and formations, were operating in Byelorussia.

A few days before the Red Army initiated operations to liberate Byelorussia, partisan units directed by the republican and regional bodies of the Party carried out extensive actions, demolishing railways, highways and bridges and thus paralyzing the enemy's rear at the most crucial moment.

In the preceding chapter, I alluded to a small conference held in April by the Supreme Command, which in principle adopted the plan of operations for the summer period. I would now like to describe in greater detail how the plan of the Byelorussian operation was prepared.

Shortly after the conference at the General Headquarters, Vasilevsky submitted to Stalin a summary of the general situation and basic proposals for the 1944 summer period.

What was our progress on the eve of the summer campaign of 1944?

The Red Army was still fighting the main forces of fascist Germany and its satellites all by itself. In winter 1944 it inflicted a serious defeat on the German fascist troops. Thirty divisions and six brigades were totally destroyed. One hundred and forty two divisions and one brigade lost from 50 to 70 per cent of their combat strength. To bolster up its Fronts, the German Command had to shift 40 divisions and four brigades from Germany and other countries of Western Europe to the Soviet-German front. The Red Army liberated a vast area — about 330,000 square kilometres. Almost 19 million people had lived there before the war.

The German fascist troops, however, were still a formidable force.

In July 1944, Germany's industry reached its wartime peak. During the first half of the year Germany manufactured over 16,000 aircraft and 8,300 heavy and medium tanks and assult guns.[1]

In a feverish attempt to put off its inevitable defeat, the Nazi leadership was squeezing out the last strength from the country and the people. It carried out one mobilization after another, thereby uprooting the German nation with its own hands. The German army comprised 324 divisions and 5 brigades.

Most of the combatant troops remained on the Soviet-German front. We were confronted with 179 German full-strength divisions and 5 brigades, as well as 49 divisions and 12 brigades of the satellites. There were 4.3 million people armed with 59,000 artillery pieces and mortars, 7,800 tanks and assault guns, and nearly 3,200 combat aircraft.

The Red Army had nearly 6.6 million officers and men in its ranks. The Fronts had 98,100 guns and mortars, 7,100 tanks and self-propelled artillery mountings and about 12,900 combat aircraft.

Never before in history had a country waged tremendous liberation battles and simultaneously rebuilt a war-ravaged economy so quickly and on such a scale. In the winter and summer of 1944, the economic strength of the Soviet Union was steadily

---

[1] See: *A History of the Second World War, 1939-1945*, Vol. 8, Voenizdat, Moscow, 1977, p. 415 (in Russian).

building up. In the first half of the year 16,300 aircraft were built, along with 10,200 medium and heavy tanks and self-propelled artillery mountings, over 119 million shells, bombs and mines. The people, led by the Party, concentrated totally on supplying the army with everything it needed to defeat the enemy.

At the end of April, the Supreme Command made the final decision on the summer campaign, including the Byelorussian operation; it instructed Antonov to ensure the preparation of the plans for front operations and to begin concentrating the troops and materiel for the Fronts that would take part.

The 1st Baltic Front was given the 1st Tank Corps, while the 3rd Byelorussian Front was reinforced by the 11th Guards Army and the 2nd Guards Tank corps. The 28th Army, the 9th and 1st Guards Tank corps, the 1st Mechanized and the 4th Guards Cavalry corps were concentrated on the right wing of the 1st Byelorussian Front. The 5th Guards Tank Army—a reserve of the Supreme Command—was being concentrated in the area of the 3rd Byelorussian Front.

Vasilevsky returned to Moscow in mid-May. At that time the General Staff was completing all the draft documents for the plan of Operation Bagration (code name for the Byelorussian action), including logistic support.

On May 20, the Supreme Commander called in Vasilevsky, Antonov and myself in order to finalize the Supreme Command decision on the plan for the summer campaign. As I have said, it required that an offensive be launched first in the Karelian Isthmus by the troops of the Leningrad Front and the Baltic Fleet, and then another to begin later, in the latter half of June, in Byelorussia.

After considering the Bagration plan at the Stavka, the Supreme Commander ordered Front Commanders Bagramyan, Chernyakhovsky and Rokossovsky to report their suggestions so that he could give specific directions for the plans of the Fronts.

The Supreme Commander received Vasilevsky, Antonov, Rokossovsky and Bagramyan in my presence on May 22, and Chernyakhovsky on May 25. The Front Commanders had been briefed by the General Staff on the planned operations, and came with draft plans for their troops.

Since the plans had been elaborated in parallel by the General Staff and the Front Headquarters, and since the Front Commands, the General Staff and the Deputy Supreme Commander maintained close contact, the draft plans fully conformed with the intentions of the Stavka and were immediately approved by the Supreme Commander.

Vasilevsky and I were then ordered to supervise the coordination of the actions of certain fronts. He was responsible for the 1st Balitic and the 3rd Byelorussian Fronts, and I for the 1st and 2nd Byelorussian Fronts. The Supreme Command sent General Shtemenko, Chief of Operations, and a group of officers, to the 2nd Byelorussian Front to help me.

On June 4, Vasilevsky left for the front to prepare for Operation Bagration on the spot: a day later, at 8:00 on June 5, I arrived at the command post of the 1st Byelorussian Front.

It must be pointed out that the version prevalent in certain military circles, i.e., that Rokossovsky had urged the Supreme Commander to accept the idea of "two main blows" in the Byelorussian direction with the forces of the 1st Byelorussian Front, is without foundation. Both blows planned by the Front had been proposed by the General Staff and were approved by Stalin as early as May 20, before the Commander of the 1st Byelorussian Front arrived at the GHQ.

It would also be pertinent to mention that Soviet military theorists have never favoured the concept of two main blows made by one Front; when both blows are equal in force and significance, they have usually been designated "powerful blows" or "striking groupings". I stress this to avoid confusion in military-strategic terminology.

Based on the approved operational-strategic plan of the Bagration action and the representations of the Fronts, the General Staff finally considered and coordinated the plan of logistic support; participating in this were A. A. Novikov, N. N. Voronov, N. D. Yakovlev, A. V. Khrulev, I. T. Peresypkin, Ya. N. Fedorenko and other leading military experts and commanders. On May 31, the Front Commanders received the Supreme Command directive, and in accordance with it detailed preparation of the troops commenced.

The Supreme Command's plan envisaged three powerful blows:

— by the 1st Baltic and 3rd Byelorussian Fronts in the general direction of Vilnius;

— by the 1st Byelorussian Front in the direction of Baranovichi;

— by the 2nd Byelorussian Front in conjunction with the left-flank grouping of the 3rd Byelorussian and the right-flank grouping of the 1st Byelorussian Fronts in the general direction of Minsk.

The immediate task of the 1st Baltic and the 3rd Byelorussian Fronts was to defeat the enemy Vitebsk formation, bring armoured and mechanized troops into the breach, and exploit the main blow westward in order to envelop the Borisov-Minsk group of German troops with the left-flank grouping.

The 1st Byelorussian Front was to crush the Zhlobin-Bobruisk formation, bring mobile troops into action, and exploit the main effort directed at Slutsk and Baranovichi, enveloping the Minsk grouping of enemy troops from the south and southwest.

The 2nd Byelorussian Front was to strike on the Mogilev-Minsk sector.

At the outset of the offensive the front line of the German defences of the Army Group Centre stretched from Polotsk to Vitebsk and further along the line Orsha, Zhlobin, Kapatkevichi, Zhitkovichi and along the Pripyat River. Polotsk, Vitebsk, Orsha and Mogilev were then in German hands.

These big towns and the rivers Dnieper, Drut, Berezina and Svisloch, as well as several small, boggy rivers and rivulets, formed the solid basis of a deeply echeloned enemy defence in the vital Warsaw-Berlin strategic direction. Although the Stavka had concentrated considerable forces against the Army Group Centre, we felt that special care should be given to the preparation of the troops to take part in Operation Bagration so that its success would be ensured.

Before Vasilevsky and I left for the front, we met to discuss in minute detail all the strong and weak points of the enemy defence and the measures to be carried out at the various headquarters and among the troops. I reached agreement with Antonov on the ways to control the concentration of troops, material supplies and the Supreme Command reserves, as well as on questions of communication and information on the actions of the Supreme Command on other sectors.

Within a very short time the fronts had to be supplied with immense quantities of materiel and equipment.

According to the General Staff's estimates the troops that were to take part in Operation Bagration needed nearly 400,000 tons of ammunition, 300,000 tons of fuel and lubricants, up to 500,000 tons of food and fodder. Five combined armies, two armoured, one air army and the units of the 1st Army of Wojsko Polskie had to be concentrated. Besides, from its reserves the Stavka allocated to the fronts four combined armies, two armoured armies, 52 rifle and cavalry divisions, 6 detached armoured and mechanized Corps, 33 air divisions, more than 210,000-strong replenishment and 2,849 artillery pieces and mortars.

All these movements had to be done with great caution to prevent the enemy from detecting the preparations for the offensive. This was especially important since our reconnaissance reports showed that the German High Command expected us to strike the first blow of the summer campaign in the Ukraine, not Byelorussia. It evidently believed that the wooded and boggy terrain would not allow us to move to Byelorussia and employ to best advantage our four tank armies now located in the Ukraine.

According to the Supreme Command plan, the troops of the 1st Ukrainian Front were to move into action in the second phase of the Byelorussian operation, when the troops of the right flank of the 1st Byelorussian Front had smashed the Bobruisk-Minsk-Slutsk enemy formation and reached the Volkovysk-Pruzhany line.

The Supreme Command attached great importance to this operation by the 1st Byelorussian Front, and concentrated its main forces and materiel there.

Since I was responsible for coordinating the actions of the 1st and 2nd Byelorussian Fronts and, in the second stage, also of the 1st Ukrainian Front as well, I concentrate here primarily on the operations of these three Fronts.

Early in the morning of June 5, I arrived on directions of the Supreme Commander at the command post of the 1st Byelorussian Front at Durevichi, where I met Rokossovsky,

Member of the Military Council Bulganin, and Chief of Staff Malinin.

After examining questions relating to the plan of the operation, Rokossovsky and I had a detailed discussion of the situation on the right flank of the front with the field army commanders, commander of the air army General Rudenko, commander of the front artillery General Kazakov and commander of the armoured and mechanized troops General Orel, reached agreement on the planning and practical steps in preparing the operation.

Special attention was given to a meticulous study of the terrain in the battle area and to the reconnaissance of the enemy defence system, as well as to the preparation of the troops, headquarters and logistic support for the commencement of the operation.

During the next two days, June 6 and 7, Rokossovsky and I along with the Supreme Command representative Yakovlev and General Kazakov, carefully studied the situation in the Rogachev-Zhlobin area which was the sector of the 3rd and 48th armies. Here, at the observation post of Army Commander Gorbatov we heard reports from General Zholudev commanding the 35th Rifle Corps and Commander of the 41st Rifle Corps Urbanovich.

On June 7, similar work was done in the sector of the 65th Army commanded by General Batov. We gave particular attention to a study of the terrain and the enemy defences in the area of the 69th and 44th Guards Rifle divisions of the 18th Rifle Corps where our main strike was planned.

In accordance with the plan of the Supreme Command, the Front Commander, General Rokossovsky, conducted detailed additional reconnaissance and decided to penetrate the enemy defence by two striking forces north of Rogachev and south of Parichi. Their immediate task was to rout the confronting enemy, surround the Zhlobin-Bobruisk group by converging thrusts, and eliminate it.

Once Bobruisk was liberated, the bulk of the front's troops were to advance via Slutsk in the general direction of Baranovichi. Part of the forces were to strike at Minsk via Osipovichi and Pukhovichi in conjunction with the 2nd Byelorussian Front. According to our estimates, the 1st Byelorussian

Front had sufficient troops and materiel to carry out this operation.

The Rogachev attack group included the 3rd Army commanded by Lieutenant-General A. V. Gorbatov, the 48th Army commanded by Lieutenant-General P. L. Romanenko, and the 9th Armoured Corps under Major-General B. S. Bakharov.

The Parichi group consisted of the 65th Army commanded by Lieutenant-General P. I. Batov, and the 28th Army commanded by Lieutenant-General A. A. Luchinski. A mechanized cavalry group under Lieutenant-General I. A. Pliev and the 1st Guards Tank Corps under the command of Major-General M. F. Panov were to enter the breach made by the southern Parichi grouping.

The striking groupings were supported by the 16th Air Army commanded by Colonel-General S. I. Rudenko. The Front also had operational control over the Dnieper Flotilla commanded by Captain V. V. Grigoriev.

The main problem in the offensive of the 1st Byelorussian Front, especially its southern Parichi grouping, was to negotiate the difficult wooded and boggy terrain.

I knew the area well, as I had served there for more than six years and had walked the length and breadth of the country. I had done quite a bit of duck shooting in the swamps near Parichi which abounded in water and forest game.

As we had thought, the German Command did not expect us to attack in that area, so our troops faced isolated pockets of resistance, and no solid defence lines.

In the Rogachev area the German defences were stronger, with the approaches covered by enemy fire.

As I have said, the 2nd Byelorussian Front, then commanded by Colonel-General Zakharov (Member of the Military Council Mekhlis, Chief of Staff Lieutenant-General Bogolyubov), was to strike a secondary blow on the Mogilev-Minsk sector. It did not have sufficient means to break through and conduct an offensive simultaneously with all the armies of the first echelon; and to push the enemy out of the region east of Mogilev before the striking forces of the 1st and 3rd Byelorussian Fronts had reached the deep rear of the Army Group Centre was of no use.

At the decision of General Zakharov, the blow on the

Mogilev sector was to be made by the reinforced 49th Army under General I. T. Grishin. The other armies (33rd and 50th) were to immobilize the enemy and to assume the offensive at a later stage, when enemy resistance on other sectors had been broken.

On June 8 and 9, I, together with Generals Yakovlev and Shtemenko, plus the Front commanders, checked the preparedness of the 2nd Byelorussian Front for a strike on the Mogilev-Minsk sector. General Shtemenko did a great deal to help General Zakharov, who had just recently assumed command of the Front.

When we arrived at General Zakharov's headquarters, he gave well-grounded reasons for his decision on the way to conduct the operation. We also received suggestions and decisions from air army commander K. A. Vershinin and the heads of other arms of the service.

To the best of my memory, there were no major objections to the planning of the operation with regard to its various targets, tasks and groupings.

I decided to go with Front Commander Zakharov, Yakovlev and Shtemenko to the 49th Army of Grishin on the morning of June 9 to get a close-up look at the enemy's forward line of defence and its depth. First we called at the observation post of General V. G. Terentiev, Commander of the 70th Rifle Corps, who gave a detailed and comprehensive account of the situation, and also offered suggestions.

By the end of the day we were able to formulate the final tasks for reconnoitring the enemy fire system, planning the artillery and air offensive, and the operational and tactical formation for the attack and offensive.

I decided to make representative of the General Staff General Shtemenko responsible for the operation of the 2nd Byelorussian Front. I myself concentrated on preparing the 1st Byelorussian Front, which was to play the key role.

When we returned to the 3rd Army of General Gorbatov we met the Front Commander and his assistants. I telephoned the Supreme Commander and reported on the preparation of the Fronts. I pointed out that the schedule of troop and cargo transportation was not being fulfilled, and asked him to instruct the People's Commissar of Means of Communications and Khrulev to look into the matter; otherwise the operation would have to be put off.

I also proposed that all the long-range aviation be employed in the Byelorussian action, and its operation against targets on German territory be put off until a later time. The Supreme Commander agreed, and immediately ordered Air Marshal A. A. Novikov and Air Marshal A. E. Golovanov, who was in charge of the long-range aviation, to report to me. I had worked with both of these capable commanders in all major previous operations, and they had given the ground troops valuable assistance.

Novikov, Golovanov, Rudenko, Vershinin and I thoroughly discussed the situation — the tasks and operational plans of the various air armies and their cooperation with the long-range aviation, which was to strike at enemy headquarters, communication centres of operational formations, reserves and other key targets. We also discussed the manoeuvres of the air forces of the individual Fronts in the common interest. Vasilevsky was given 350 heavy long-range aircraft to support the actions of the 3rd Byelorussian Front.

On June 14 and 15, the Commander of the 1st Byelorussian Front conducted a rehearsal of the operation in the 65th and 28th armies. Generals from the GHQ were in attendance with us.

Also present were corps and division commanders, as well as officers in charge of artillery and other arms. The purpose of the exercise was to clear up all details regarding the tasks of the infantry and armoured formations, the plan of the artillery offensive, and its cooperation with the aviation. Special attention was given to the details of the terrain in the zone of future action, the organization of the enemy defence, and ways of quickly reaching the Slutsk-Bobruisk road, of reaching and capturing Bobruisk, and of blocking the withdrawal routes of the Zhlobin-Bobruisk formation.

During the next three days similar exercises were conducted in the 3rd, 48th and 49th armies. We were able to better acquaint ourselves with the officers who were to lead the troops to rout a major enemy grouping which was holding on to a strategic position — the Army Group Centre. Theirs was a great responsibility since the defeat of the Army

Group Centre spelled the complete expulsion of the enemy from Byelorussia and Eastern Poland.

At the same time, intensive training and political studies were being conducted in the units of both Fronts to elaborate the fire tasks and the tactics and techniques of attack and offensive in conjunction with tanks, artillery and aviation; the tasks facing the troops were explained. This kind of training had been made compulsory before any major operation, and produced very gratifying results. The troops' actions were thus better coordinated and more effective, and losses were smaller.

The headquarters of units, formations and armies adjusted the details of control and communication. Command and observation posts were thrust forward and dug in, and observation and communication systems established; the procedure of moving them forward and directing the troops while pursuing the enemy was worked out in detail.

The reconnaissance units of the Fronts, armies and smaller formations once again studied the enemy fire system and the location of his tactical and operational reserves. They made final corrections in the maps and sent them to the units.

The logistic services of the Fronts performed like titans. Despite the enormous difficulties materiel, ammunition, fuel and food were promptly and secretly supplied to the troops. During the offensive the troops of the two Fronts had everything necessary for combat action brought up in time across a really difficult terrain.

On June 22, the two Fronts conducted reconnaissance in force, ascertaining the pattern of the enemy fire system in his forward line of defence and the location of previously unknown batteries.

All in all, the Byelorussian operation was to cover a vast area along a front stretching for more than 1,200 km from Lake Neshcherdo to the Pripyat, and 600 km deep — from the Dnieper to the Vistula and the Narew. In fierce battle, our troops would have to engage 200,000 enemy soldiers and officers armed with 9,500 artillery pieces and mortars, 900 tanks and assault guns and 1,350 combat aircraft. The prearranged defences, 250-270 kilometres deep, also had to be overcome.

The Soviet offensive in Byelorussia coincided with the third anniversary of the war. The three war years had seen events of historic importance. The USSR had beaten the Nazi troops in several major battles and was completing the liberation of its territory. On the eve of the new clash against the enemy, our men were confident of defeating the Army Group Centre.

They were undoubtedly encouraged by the fact that on June 6, 1944, our allies had landed in Normandy and opened a second front in Europe. Although the fate of Nazi Germany had been virtually sealed, Soviet soldiers enthusiastically welcomed the Second Front, which brought the downfall of fascism and the end of the war closer.

The general offensive was initiated on June 23 by the 1st Baltic Front (commander Colonel-General Bagramyan, member of the Military Council General Leonov, Chief of Staff General Kurasov); the 3rd Byelorussian Front under Colonel-General Chernyakhovsky (member of the Military Council General Makarov, Chief of Staff General Pokrovsky); and the 2nd Byelorussian Front under Colonel-General Zakharov. The 1st Byelorussian Front under General of the Army Rokossovsky joined the offensive on the following day.

Behind enemy lines, partisan detachments, units and formations began active operations, coordinating them, as previously arranged, with the actions of the Fronts. Front headquarters had special departments for the guidance of the partisan movement; these were responsible for communications, provision of materiel and supplies and coordination with the partisan detachments. Partisan units and detachments were very active in the Byelorussian operation. This was facilitated by the wooded terrain. More Soviet officers and men had been left behind there when our troops retreated in 1941 than anywhere else.

The initial days of the Byelorussian offensive saw fierce fighting on the ground and in the air on all sectors, although weather conditions somewhat restricted aviation on both sides — I soon learned from the General Staff that Vasilevsky was successfully breaking through the enemy defences. That was wonderful news for all of us.

Things were also going well on the 2nd Byelorussian Front,

where the 49th Army of General Grishin had smashed through the enemy defences on the Mogilev sector and secured a bridgehead on the River Dnieper on the march.

The 1st Byelorussian Front was pushing ahead towards Parichi according to plan. On the very first day the 1st Tank Corps of General Panov entered the gap and deepened it by 20 kilometres towards Bobruisk; this made it possible to bring General Pliev's mechanized cavalry group into action on the following day.

On June 25, Pliev's group and Panov's corps knocked out the rear guard units of the retreating enemy and began to advance rapidly. The 28th and 65th armies were also advancing steadily. The armoured and artillery units moving towards Parichi ploughed up the wooded and boggy terrain so thoroughly that even tractors could hardly get across.

Inspired by the successful breakthrough, the engineer units and men of all arms did all they could to quickly build a corduroy road which greatly facilitated logistic support.

At the same time, however, the strength of the enemy defence on the Rogachev-Bobruisk sector had been underestimated due to inadequate reconnaissance. As a consequence, the 3rd and 48th armies were assigned excessively large penetration areas. Besides that, the two armies did not have sufficient means for a successful breakthrough. I failed in my duty as a representative of the Supreme Command to correct the Front commanders.

There was another circumstance hindering our progress in that area. When preparations were being made for the breakthrough, the commander of the 3rd Army, Lieutenant-General Gorbatov, proposed that a strike be made with an armoured corps under Bakharov from a more northerly point, a wooded and boggy area where he knew the enemy defence was very weak. His proposal was rejected, and Gorbatov was ordered to plan a breakthrough at a sector assigned by the Front Command, since an alternative decision would result in the main blow of the 48th Army being shifted northwards as well.

When the battle began, the breakthrough was painfully slow. In view of the delay Gorbatov asked to be permitted to implement his original plan and strike with an armoured corps at a point further north. I supported his request. The operation was a success, the enemy was crushed and General Bakharov's tankmen overran the enemy flank in their dash towards Bobruisk, cutting off the only route of retreat across the River Berezina.

After this successful manoeuvre the Germans began to roll back from the Zhlobin-Rogachev line, but too late — the only bridge near Bobruisk was captured by Bakharov's tankmen on June 26.

Panov's armoured corps reached an area north-west of Bobruisk and cut off all routes of withdrawal for the Germans in that town.

Thus on June 27, two "pockets" had been made in the Bobruisk area; trapped in them were the German 35th Army Corps and 41st Panzer Corps, in all nearly 40,000 men.

I was not able to see the liquidation of the enemy in Bobruisk, but witnessed the rout of the Germans south-east of the city. Hundreds of bombers of Rudenko's 16th Air Army, coordinating missions with the 48th Army, struck blow after blow at the enemy group. Scores of lorries, cars and tanks, fuel and lubricants were burning all over the battlefield. More and more bomber echelons took their bearings from the blazing fires, and kept dropping bombs of various weights.

The terror-stricken German soldiers scattered in every direction; those who did not surrender were killed. Thousands of Germans who had been taken in by Hitler who had promised them a victorious *Blitzkreig* against the Soviet Union were dying in the fields of Byelorussia. One of our prisoners was General Lützow, Commander of the 35th Army Corps.

The 48th Army under Romanenko and the 105th Rifle Corps of the 65th Army had the job of finally eliminating the enemy troops in the Bobruisk area. The 3rd and 65th armies with the 9th and 1st Guards Tank corps were ordered not to halt in the Bobruisk area, but to proceed rapidly in the general direction of Osipovichi, which was liberated on June 28. On June 29 our troops totally cleared Bobruisk of the enemy.

The 28th Army of General Luchinski and the mechanized cavalry group of General Pliev were thrusting towards Slutsk.

After the enemy's defeat in the Vitebsk-Bobruisk area,

the flank groupings of our troops made considerable headway, and threatened to surround the Army Group Centre.

As we observed and analyzed the actions of the German troops and their High Command at that time, we were somewhat surprised by their blunders, which resulted in catastrophic consequences. Instead of quickly withdrawing to the rear lines and reinforcing their flanks, which were threatened by the Soviet striking forces, the German troops engaged in prolonged frontal battles east and north-east of Minsk.

On June 28, after consultation with Vasilevsky, myself and the Front commanders, the Stavka of the Supreme Command specified the further tasks of our troops.

The 1st Baltic Front was ordered to liberate Polotsk and advance towards Glubokoye. The 3rd and 2nd Byelorussian Fronts were to liberate Minsk, capital of Byelorussia. The 1st Byelorussian Front was instructed to advance with its main forces towards Slutsk and Baranovichi; part of its forces were to exploit the strike at Minsk, envelop it from the south and south-west. The tasks set by the Stavka stemmed from the overall objective of the operation — to surround and rout all troops of the Army Group Centre. The strength and disposition of our troops fully corresponded to that objective.

The success of the operation testified to the foresight and the growing maturity of the Soviet commanders who had mastered the art of operations and strategy.

It is unfortunate that I was unable to communicate directly with Vasilevsky so that we could agree on further cooperation between General Gorbatov's 3rd Army and the 2nd and 3rd Byelorussian Fronts, whose object was to take Minsk and shut off the withdrawal routes of a major German force. The 2nd Byelorussian Front was pressing hard on the grouping, preventing it from breaking away — a positive factor in parallel pursuit.

The entire German 4th Army was almost completely surrounded. How would the German High Command act at that critical moment? It was a very important question for our Supreme Command, the General Staff and all of us who were conducting this important operation.

As is the rule in such conditions, the echelons of command concentrated on reconnaissance to find out the enemy's general plan and practical steps. But no matter how hard we tried to discover the main features of the operational strategy of the German Command, we found nothing beyond the reinforcement of the sectors considered most dangerous.

The Byelorussian partisans operating in the Minsk area informed us that the Government House, the buildings of the republican Party Central Committee and the Officers' House were being hastily mined for demolition before retreat. To save the city's biggest buildings we decided to accelerate the advance of our armoured troops and send along engineers for de-mining. Their task was to fight their way into the city — avoiding engagement with the enemy on the approaches — and seize the government buildings.

The action was performed successfully, and the important buildings were cleared of mines and saved.

At dawn on July 3, the 2nd Guards Tank Corps of A. S. Burdeiny burst into Minsk from the north-east; the advanced units of the 5th Guards Tank Army under Marshal Rotmistrov approached the city from the north. At mid-day the 1st Guards Tank Corps of the 1st Byelorussian Front commanded by General Panov entered the city. The 3rd Army of General Gorbatov followed Panov's Tank Corps into the Minsk area. Other Soviet troops went south-west and north-west of Minsk, throwing back to the west the reserves the enemy was bringing up.

By the end of July 3, a major group of formations of the German 4th Army was cut off from withdrawal routes and encircled east of Minsk. It included the 12th, 27th and 35th Field corps and the 39th and 41st Tank corps — more than 100,000 officers and men in all.

By the evening of July 3, all of Minsk was liberated.

The capital of Byelorussia was barely recognizable. I had commanded a regiment there for seven years and knew well every street, and all the main buildings, bridges, parks, stadiums and theatres. Now everything was in ruins; where whole apartment buildings had stood, there was nothing but heaps of rubble.

The people of Minsk were a pitiful sight, exhausted and haggard, many of them in tears...

By July 11, the surrounded German troops, in spite of their

resistance, were killed or taken prisoner. Among the 35,000 prisoners were 12 generals, including three corps commanders and nine division commanders. Our men spent several days more tracking down groups of German officers and men trying to join their troops, but the enemy was rolling back so rapidly that this was not easy. The local population and the partisans, the real masters of the Byelorussian forests, helped us immensely in clearing the territory of the enemy.

Since a gap had been made in the enemy defence on the Western sector, on July 4 the Supreme Command ordered to continue the offensive. The Fronts were ordered:

— the 1st Baltic Front to advance in the general direction of Siauliai with its right flank moving towards Daugavpils and its left flank thrusting for Kaunas;

— the 3rd Byelorussian Front to move towards Vilnius, part of its forces advancing towards Lida;

— the 2nd Byelorussian Front to move to Novogrudok, Grodno and Belostok;

— the 1st Byelorussian Front to advance to Baranovichi and Brest and establish a bridgehead on the Western Bug.

On July 7, when our troops were completing the elimination of the encircled enemy grouping east and south-east of Minsk, and the advance echelons of the 1st and 3rd Byelorussian and the 1st Baltic Fronts had advanced far west of the Minsk meridian and were fighting in the area of Vilnius, Baranovichi and Pinsk, Stalin telephoned to summon me to the GHQ.

Early in the morning of July 8, I was still in the Baranovichi area. The troops of the 65th and 48th armies were already engaged in fighting for the city, and several hours later it was liberated. On that day I flew to Moscow, put myself in order, and went to the General Staff.

Before meeting the Supreme Commander I wanted to study the latest developments in greater detail.

Antonov, precise as usual, analyzed the situation and informed me of the General Staff's opinion of probable developments in the immediate future. As I listened to Antonov I was pleased to note that the General Staff and its leadership had greatly improved their strategic and operational skills.

At about 13:00 Stalin called Antonov and asked about me.

After a few more questions he told Antonov and me to report at his summer house. We arrived at 14:00 sharp. Stalin was in good humour and joked.

During our talk Vasilevsky called over the radiotelephone and reported on the latest developments on the 1st Baltic and 3rd Byelorussian Fronts. The news must have been good, for Stalin's gaiety increased.

"I haven't had breakfast yet," he said, "let's go to the dining room and talk."

Although Antonov and I had had breakfast, we did not decline the invitation.

During breakfast we talked about Germany's capacity to wage war on two fronts, against the Soviet Union and the Allied expeditionary forces which had landed in Normandy, and about the role and tasks of the Soviet troops at this concluding phase of the war.

From the precise manner in which Stalin expressed his ideas it was obvious that he had thought out all these matters very carefully. Although he believed that we were strong enough to finish off Nazi Germany single-handed, Stalin sincerely welcomed the opening of the Second Front in Europe, which brought closer the end of the war, so much desired by the Soviet people who were extremely exhausted by the war and privations.

No one had any doubt that Germany had definitely lost the war. This was settled on the Soviet-German front in 1943 and the beginning of 1944. The discussion now centred on how soon and with what political and military results the war would end.

Molotov and other members of the State Committee for Defence joined us.

In discussing Germany's ability to continue the armed struggle, we all agreed that her main problem would be the exhaustion of her manpower and resources at a time when the Soviet Union would receive reinforcements from partisan units and the people who had remained in occupied territory, now that the Ukraine, Byelorussia, Lithuania and other areas had been liberated. Besides, the opening of the Second Front compelled Germany to strengthen her forces in the west.

The question was what Hitler's military leaders could hope for in the given situation.

Stalin's answer was: "They are like a gambler betting his last coin. All their hopes were pinned on the British and Americans. In deciding to wage war against the Soviet Union, Hitler took into account the imperialist circles in Britain and the USA, who totally shared his thinking. And not without reason: they did everything they could to direct the military actions of the Wehrmacht against the Soviet Union."

Molotov added that Hitler would probably attempt at any cost to make a separate agreement with the US and British government circles.

"That is true," said Stalin, "but Roosevelt and Churchill will not agree to a deal with Hitler. They will try to attain their political aims in Germany by setting up an obedient government, not through collusion with the Nazis, who have lost all the trust of the people."

Then Stalin asked me: "Can our troops begin liberating Poland, reach the Vistula without a stop, and in what sector can we commit the 1st Polish Army which has now become an effective fighting force?"

"Not only can our troops reach the Vistula," I replied, "but they have to secure good bridgeheads beyond it which are essential for further offensive operations in the strategic direction of Berlin. As for the 1st Polish Army, it should be directed towards Warsaw."

Antonov completely agreed with me. He also reported to the Supreme Commander that the German Command had brought up a large group of troops, including armoured formations, to plug the gap which had been formed as a result of the actions of our western fronts. As a result, the enemy's strength in the sector of the 1st Ukrainian Front was considerably weakened.

Antonov went on to report on the concentration of materiel and replacements on the 1st Ukrainian Front and the left flank of the 1st Byelorussian Front, which were getting ready to assume the offensive in accordance with the previously adopted plan.

"You will now have to undertake the coordination of the 1st Ukrainian Front," Stalin told me. "Give special attention to the left flank of the 1st Byelorussian Front and the 1st

Ukrainian Front. You know the general plan and the tasks of the 1st Ukrainian Front. No changes have been made in the Supreme Command's plan, and you can acquaint yourself with the details at the General Staff."

Next we discussed the capacities of the troops coordinated by Vasilevsky.

I told the Supreme Commander it was advisable to considerably strengthen Vasilevsky's group of fronts and the 2nd Byelorussian Front, and ask Vasilevsky to cut off the German Army Group North and occupy East Prussia.

"Are you in cahoots with Vasilevsky?" asked Stalin, "because he also asks for his fronts to be reinforced."

"We are not," I replied, "but if that is his opinion, he is correct."

"The Germans will fight for East Prussia till the very end," Stalin said, "and we may get stuck there. We should first of all liberate the Lvov Region and the eastern part of Poland. Tomorrow you will meet Bierut, Osubko-Morawski and Rola-Zimerski at my place. They represent the Polish National Liberation Committee and they intend to issue a manifesto to the Polish people after the 20th of this month. We will send Bulganin as our representative to the Poles, and leave Telegin as Member of the Military Council at Rokossovsky's headquarters."

That evening I was invited to Stalin's country house; Bierut, Osubko-Morawski and Rola-Zimerski were already there. Our Polish comrades spoke about the difficult situation of their people, who had suffered five years of occupation. The members of the Polish National Liberation Committee and the Krajowa Rada Narodowa dreamt of liberating their native land as soon as possible. It was already agreed jointly that the Krajowa Rada Narodowa would begin its first organizational activities in Lublin.

On July 9, Stalin once again considered the plan of the Kovel offensive (1st Byelorussian Front). It provided for:

— the routing of the Kovel-Lublin enemy grouping;
— the capture of Brest in conjunction with the Front's right-wing troops;
— reaching the Vistula on a broad front, and securing a bridgehead on its western bank.

On July 10, I was already back with the troops, where Rokossovsky, Novikov and I worked out the plans for the operations on the left flank of the 1st Byelorussian Front.

On July 11, I left Rokossovsky's headquarters by plane for the 1st Ukrainian Front.

The task of the 1st Ukrainian Front was to strike two powerful blows, one in the direction of Lvov and the other in the direction of Rava-Russkaya and Stanislav with part of the forces. The depth of the operation was about 220-240 kilometres, its frontage 100-120 kilometres.

Concentrated in that sector were 80 divisions, 10 armoured and mechanized corps, 4 separate armoured and self-propelled artillery brigades, 16,100 guns and mortars, 2,050 tanks and self-propelled guns and 3,250 aircraft.

Total troop strength was 1,110,000 — this was more than enough for such an action. I thought it expedient to allot some of the forces of the 1st Ukrainian Front to strike at East Prussia. For some reason, however, the Supreme Commander was against it.

I set up my command post in the area of Lutsk so that I could be closer to the Kovel grouping of the 1st Byelorussian Front and to the troops of the 1st Ukrainian Front.

After the destruction of the encircled enemy in the Minsk area, our offensive developed satisfactorily. On some sectors the Germans tried to put up resistance, but were swept away and forced to retreat all along the front to Siauliai, Kaunas, Grodno, Belostok and Brest.

The offensive of the 1st Ukrainian Front began on July 13 on the Rava-Russkaya sector and proceeded according to plan. The 3rd Guards Army under General Gordov and the 13th Army of General Pukhov did particularly well.

On the Lvov sector, the offensive started on July 14, but for a number of reasons the enemy defence could not be immediately broken. Furthermore, the enemy launched a counter-offensive in the Zolochev area against the 38th Army and forced it to move back. Things improved when the 3rd Guards Tank Army of Rybalko went into action on July 16 in rather difficult conditions.

On July 17, the 4th Armoured Army under Lelyushenko followed the 3rd Guards Tank Army onto the offensive and consolidated the initial success. By the joint efforts of the 60th and 38th Field armies and the 3rd Guards and 4th Tank armies the enemy troops were also pressed back on the Lvov sector. However, our troops advanced slowly.

As July 18 drew to a close, the troops of the 1st Ukrainian Front had penetrated the Germans' defence and advanced from 50 to 80 kilometres; in doing so they had encircled an enemy group of up to eight divisions in the area of Brody.

On that memorable day the troops of the 1st Byelorussian Front's left flank began an offensive from the area of Kovel towards Lublin. All the armies of the Front moved into action. I must give credit to the command, headquarters and logistic agencies of the 1st Byelorussian Front for their able and well-organized guidance of the troops and their timely supply of everything required for the operation.

The four Fronts struck powerful blows at the Army Group Centre, crushing the German 3rd Panzer Army and the 4th and 9th Field armies. A breach of up to 400 kilometres wide and up to 500 kilometres deep was made in the enemy strategic front, and the German Command had nothing which could enable it to quickly close the gap.

At this stage of the Byelorussian operation, the East Prussian bastion of the German defence was the main obstacle confronting us. This large enemy group was protected by the natural terrain, and the strong engineering works. To successfully advance on Berlin, we had to break through the enemy defensive in East Prussia on the march without a break in the rhythm of the Fronts.

This would be possible if the advancing troops were to receive reinforcements when required. We estimated that the 1st Byelorussian Front had to get additionally 300-400 tanks and self-propelled guns, and the 2nd Byelorussian Front had to receive a field and a tank army, one rifle corps, and several tank and self-propelled artillery regiments. They also had to receive better air support.

Once these reinforcements had come, all the three Byelorussian Fronts, in my opinion, would be able to seize East Prussia and reach the Vistula up to the Bay of Danzig inclusively, or at the very least, by simultaneously reaching the Vistula, to cut off East Prussia from Central Germany.

After meticulously drafting the possible directions of our offensive and the required forces, I reported my proposals to the Supreme Command in the early hours of July 19:

"To: Comrade Stalin.

"Copy to Antonov.

"In view of our troops' imminent approach to the state border, I present my considerations for the operations of the Byelorussian Fronts in the immediate future:

"1) The main strategic objective of the 1st, 2nd and 3rd Byelorussian Fronts in the immediate stage must be: to reach the Vistula up to the Bay of Danzig inclusively and seize East Prussia, or at the very least, by simultaneously reaching the Vistula, to cut off East Prussia from Central Germany.

"2) Because of its fortified belts, engineering works and natural terrain, East Prussia is a very serious obstacle. The approaches to Koenigsberg are protected by five fortified belts to the south-east and south, and from the east, besides that, the west of Insterburg has been prepared to be flooded.

"The best possible directions for the offensive in East Prussia are:

"**first direction** — from the Tilsit area along the coast in the general direction of Koenigsberg via Libocz.

"**second direction** — from the Kaunas-Alitus area via Gumbinnen to Koenigsberg, making absolutely sure to skirt the flooded area and Letzen fortified area from the south.

"**third direction** — from the Mlawa area via Hohenstein-Allenstein to Braunsberg.

"Besides this, a powerful force should be brought up east of the Vistula in the general direction of Marienburg to cut off East Prussia from the Danzig area.

"First direction — the blow from the Tilsit area must only come once the Germans have been driven out of Lithuania.

"In the development of the offensive by the 3rd and 2nd Byelorussian Fronts the 2nd and 3rd directions can be utilized.

"3) The blow against Gumbinnen can be delivered by Chernyakhovsky, and he must launch an offensive with part of his troops north of the August forest via Suwalki towards Goldap.

"The blow from the Mława area must be delivered by the 2nd Byelorussian Front in the following directions:

"a) one group in the direction of Allenstein;

"b) one group in the direction of Marienburg to reach the Bay of Danzig;

"c) one group must reach the Vistula in the Grudziadz--Nishava sector, where it is to dig itself in.

"To the left, the 1st Byelorussian Front must reach the line of the 1st Ukrainian Front, and along with this Front, seize propitious bridgeheads on the western bank of the Vistula.

"4) The forces of the 1st Byelorussian Front are sufficient to fulfil the above tasks. They should be allocated an additional 300 tanks and 100 self-propelled guns.

"The 2nd Byelorussian Front will require one army of nine divisions, one infantry corps of three divisions, two-three tank corps or a tank army, four heavy tank regiments, and four regiments of 152-mm self-propelled artillery pieces, plus air reinforcement.

"5) To avoid superfluous regrouping in the future, I wish the following dividing lines to be recognized:

"a) between Chernyakhovsky and Zakharov: Grodno-Likk-Heilsberg (all for Chernyakhovsky);

"b) between Zakharov and Rokossovsky: Belostok-Ostrolenka-Nishava (all for Zakharov).

"6) I consider it expedient for the future operation to consult with you personally and it would be good if you summon Vasilevsky.

"G. Zhukov."

Soon afterwards I was called to Moscow for discussions with Stalin. However, he refused to accept my plan, and did not agree to reinforce the Fronts on the East Prussian sector nor was the Supreme Command able to assign reserves to the Byelorussian Fronts. I think Stalin made a really serious mistake here, as what was involved was the very complex and bloody East Prussian operation.

In the latter part of July the German High Command found itself in a difficult position, which was further complicated by the offensive begun by the 2nd and 3rd Baltic Fronts and the pressure of the Allied expeditionary forces in the West.

German General Buttlar wrote in this connection: "The rout of the Army Group Centre put an end to the organized resistance of the Germans in the East."

Nevertheless, the command of the Army Group Centre found the best possible mode of action in the extremely difficult circumstances. Since it had no solid line of defence and could not form one as the forces were unavailable, the German Command decided to delay the advance of our troops by swift counterblows. These tactics enabled the Germans to deploy in the rear lines troops dispatched from Germany and other sectors of the Soviet-German front.

The striking forces of the 1st Byelorussian Front's left flank included the 47th Army, the 8th Guards Army, the 69th Army and the 2nd Guards Tank Army, supported by the 6th Air Army. The 1st Army of Wojsko Polskie under Lieutenant-General Berling also operated there. The troops of the 1st Byelorussian Front forced the River Bug and entered Eastern Poland, initiating the liberation of the Polish people from the German occupation.

On July 22, the troops of the 1st Byelorussian Front liberated Holm. This created a breach, and on July 24, the 2nd Tank Army (under General A. I. Radzievsky, who took charge of the Army after General S. I. Bogdanov had been wounded) liberated Poland's key administrative centre of Lublin. On July 25, continuing the advance, army units reached the Vistula in the area of Deblin.

Our troops liberated the prisoners of the Maidanek death camp, where the Nazis had murdered one and a half million people, including old men, women and children. What the eyewitnesses told me was terrifying. The fascist atrocities later were made known to the whole world, and were declared grave crimes against humanity.

On July 28, the troops of the 1st Byelorussian Front crushed the Brest grouping of the Germans and liberated the city of Brest and the legendary Brest Fortress, whose defenders had been among the first to encounter the enemy attack in 1941 and won immortal glory by their mass heroism.

The routing of the German Army Group Centre was carried out in close cooperation with the partisans. During our offensive, Byelorussian guerillas blew up roads and railways, destroyed bridges and other important railway structures. A total of 230 trains with troops and materiel were derailed in the month of July alone. The active operations of the partisans behind enemy lines paralyzed his supply and transport agencies, and further undermined the morale of the German officers and men.

The 8th Guards Army and the 69th Army followed the 2nd Tank Army and other mobile formations; on July 27, they reached the Vistula and began crossing it near Magnuszew and Puławy; these were later to play a historic role, during the liberation of Poland in the Vistula-Oder operation.

The German Command realized the importance of the bridgeheads that the Soviet troops had captured on the Vistula and brought considerable forces into action, including the Hermann Goering SS Panzer Division, against the 8th and 69th armies. During the fierce fighting for the bridgeheads, all the German attacks were beaten back with heavy losses.

I must mention here the skill and determination displayed by General Kolpakchi, commanding the 69th Army, and General Chuikov, who commanded the 8th Guards Army; these two commanders conducted the battle for the seizure and retention of the Vistula bridgeheads with great skill and determination.

Those of our officers and men who first crossed the Vistula and landed on its western bank were real heroes.

At the Magnuszew bridgehead I talked with wounded men from the 220th Guards Rifle Regiment of the 79th Guards Rifle Division. Here is what one of them told me:

"Before dawn our company was ordered to cross the western bank of the Vistula. We were about fifty men, under the command of Lieutenant V. T. Burba. As soon as we landed on the opposite bank the Germans opened fire on us, and then attacked. We repulsed the first attack, but a second and third followed. The next day we were attacked continuously by infantry and tanks. After the last and the most fierce attack, there were only twelve men left in our company.

"Just before the last attack began Lieutenant Burba said: 'Boys, there are not many of us left. Reinforcements will come only in the evening; until then we are going to fight to the last drop of our blood but we won't give up our position.'

"Soon we were attacked by tanks and infantry, almost a whole company. When several tanks came close to us our commander threw a bunch of grenades and stopped one; with a bunch of grenades in his hand he hurled himself under another. We beat back the attack, but our commander was killed. Of one entire company, only six men were left. Soon we received reinforcements. The bridgehead remained ours..."

The soldier could not contain his tears as he spoke of his commander's death. I couldn't listen to him without being deeply moved; it was painful to know that such fine men were dying for our country. Lieutenant V. T. Burba was posthumously awarded the title of Hero of the Soviet Union.

Another act of heroism was performed by soldier P. A. Khlyustin, member of the Young Communist League, from the 4th Company of the same 220th Regiment. Like Lieutenant Burba, he threw himself under a German tank with a bunch of grenades, thus halting an enemy attack at the price of his life. Komsomol member Khlyustin was also posthumously awarded the title of Hero of the Soviet Union.

Both at the initial stage of the war, and now, when it was drawing to a close, the Soviet citizen would readily sacrifice his life for the sake of his Motherland...

The successful actions by the Kovel striking forces of the 1st Byelorussian Front, which reached the Vistula in such a short time, were crucial to the outcome of the Lvov-Sandomierz operation, which initially did not proceed as well on the Lvov sector as the Front Command and the GHQ had expected.

Here I would like once again to allude to reconnaissance, the importance of reconnaissance in warfare. Military experience has shown that intelligence data and the correct analysis of it should be the basis for appraising the situation, making decisions and planning operations. If the intelligence data is wrong or misinterpreted, the reasoning of all command echelons is inevitably affected, and the operation will not develop as planned.

When preparations were being made for the operation on

the Lvov sector, the intelligence agencies of the 1st Ukrainian Front failed to disclose the enemy's entire defence system and to locate the operational reserves of the German Command, first of all its armoured troops. The result was that the Front Command could not foresee the possible counter-manoeuvre by the enemy when his defence was penetrated. Artillery preparation and air support were poorly planned due to inadequate sludy of the enemy fire layout.

Artillery fire and bombardment are most effective when shelling or bombing is carried out against very specific targets, not at areas or probable targets. Area shelling or bombing cannot destroy an enemy defence system; this is what happened on the Lvov sector — a lot of shelling and bombing, but almost no real results.

Another important factor in understanding mistakes made in preparing for the operation is the armour's support of the infantry's attack and offensive.

Advancing infantry is naturally vulnerable to enemy fire. All fire emplacements surviving the artillery preparation — a machine-gun, a gun, a dug-in tank, a pillbox, etc. can "pin down" the advancing infantry and retard its progress. In these conditions, tanks can be of tremendous value when they accompany the infantry, and their fire neutralizes the enemy weapons not silenced by the artillery preparation.

All this postulate was totally ignored in this instance. I cannot see why these mistakes are never mentioned when the Lvov-Sandomierz operation is discussed by historians. They must be analyzed and explained to our young people, so that the necessary conclusions can be drawn from the past.

The defeat of a large German grouping in the area of Brody and the successful advance of the 1st Byelorussian Front's left wing on the Lublin sector and the 1st Ukrainian Front's right wing on the Rava-Russkaya sector enabled the command of the 1st Ukrainian Front to send Rybalko's Tank Army to envelop Lvov from the north and northwest. The aim of the turning manoeuvre was to sever the routes of withdrawal of the enemy's Lvov grouping on the River San, capture Peremyshl, and by delivering a blow from the west to help the 38th, 60th and 4th Tank armies capture Lvov. At that time the troops of the Front's right wing were continuing to advance in the general direction of Sandomierz.

During my talk with Konev on July 22, we agreed that the seizure by the 3rd Tank Army of the rear communications on the River San would force the enemy to leave Lvov. In fact we both came to the conclusion that the surrender of Lvov by the Germans was practically a *fait accompli,* and one day sooner or later did not matter much.

But at dawn of July 23, Konev got me on the phone and said that Stalin had just called him. "What is your and Zhukov's grand idea about Sandomierz?" he asked. "We first have to take Lvov and only then think of Sandomierz."

"And what was your reply?" I asked Konev.

"I reported that the 3rd Tank Army is striking at the enemy's Lvov grouping from the rear, and that Lvov would soon be taken."

Konev and I agreed that during the day I would phone the Supreme Commander, while the Front's troops would continue operations on the sectors assigned to them.

When I learned that Lublin had been liberated by the 2nd Tank Army of the 1st Byelorussian Front, I rang up the Supreme Commander. He was still at his flat, and had already heard about it.

After listening to my report on the actions of the 1st Ukrainian Front, the Supreme Commander asked: "When do you expect Lvov to be taken?"

"Not later than in two to three days," was my reply.

Stalin said: "Khrushchev phoned, and he does not agree with the assignment given to Rybalko's army. The army is not taking part in the offensive on Lvov, and he thinks that that can hold things up. You and Konev are in a rush to get to the Vistula. It won't run away from you. Get Lvov quickly over with first."

All I could do was to tell the Supreme Commander that Lvov would be taken before our troops reached the Vistula. I did not want to upset Konev with the details of the talk.

As a result of a brilliant 120-km enveloping manoeuvre by General Rybalko's Tank Army, the push from the east by the 38th and the 60th armies, and the fighting by the 4th Tank Army in the southern part of Lvov, the enemy retreated from Lvov to Sambor. On July 27, Lvov was liberated by the Soviet troops.

Belostok was liberated on July 27. On that day a Supreme Command directive approved our decision to exploit the blow of the 1st Ukrainian Front in the direction of the Vistula and to secure a bridgehead there as the 1st Byelorussian Front had done. The general purpose of this operation was to ensure a subsequent offensive aimed at completing the liberation of Poland.

On receiving the Supreme Command directive, on July 28, Front Commander Konev ordered the 3rd Armoured Army to make a dash towards the Vistula, by the close of the day seize a bridgehead as it proceeded ahead and then take Sandomierz. The 13th Army of Pukhov was ordered to reach the line between Sandomierz and the mouth of the Visloka and secure a bridgehead on the Konary-Polaniec Front. The 1st Guards Tank Army of General Katukov was to strike at Baranów and reach the area of Bogoria.

The 5th Guards Army under Lieutenant-General Zhadov was also advancing towards Sandomierz.

One must not ignore the exceptional bravery, initiative and cooperation of all arms of the service of the 1st Ukrainian Front involved in the difficult crossing of the broad and deep Vistula. I did not witness it myself, but what I heard from officers and generals was astounding. The engineers showed particular courage and organization.

The German Command had exhausted its reserves in the Byelorussian and then Lvov-Sandomierz operations, and was unable to put up any real resistance to the troops of the 1st Ukrainian Front crossing the Vistula. Marshal Konev's troops firmly established themselves on the Sandomierz bridgehead.

On July 29, the Supreme Commander phoned and congratulated me by saying I had been awarded a second Gold Medal of Hero of the Soviet Union. Then came a ring from Kalinin, who also extended his congratulations.

"Yesterday the State Committee for Defence, acting on Stalin's proposal, decided to decorate you for the Byelorussian operation and the liberation of the Ukraine."

On that memorable day I received many telegrams and

words of congratulation from friends and comrades. But my
greatest joy was the fact that the Soviet Army had taken a firm
stand on the western bank of the Vistula and was ready to
fulfil its liberation mission in Poland, and then to invade
Nazi Germany and crush it completely.

The German Command realized the value of our bridgeheads
on the Berlin sector, and did everything it possibly could
to wipe out the Magnuszew, Puławy and Sandomierz bridgeheads. The enemy brought in large forces, including
armoured and mechanized divisions, but it was all too late.

The 1st Byelorussian and the 1st Ukrainian Fronts had
concentrated so many troops and weapons in those areas that
the Germans could not throw us back across the Vistula.

In these two months the Soviet troops had routed two
powerful strategic groupings of Germans, liberated Byelorussia,
completed the liberation of the Ukraine, and freed much of
Lithuania and Eastern Poland.

In these battles the 1st, 2nd and 3rd Byelorussian Fronts
and the 1st Baltic Front routed about 70 German divisions;
30 of them were surrounded and taken prisoner or destroyed.
Over 30 divisions were routed and eight divisions completely
wiped out in the offensive by the 1st Ukrainian Front on the
Lvov-Sandomierz sector.

The Byelorussian operation vividly demonstrated the ability
of Soviet commanders of all levels to quickly encircle and
destroy large enemy formations. The skill of the commanders,
coupled with the competent actions and valour of the troops,
resulted in the collapse of the Germans' strongest grouping
in the Berlin strategic direction.

The defeat of the Army Groups Centre and Northern
Ukraine, the capture of three major bridgeheads on the
Vistula, and the reaching of Warsaw brought our striking
Fronts closer to Berlin. It was now only 600 kilometres away.

The routing of the Iasi-Kishinev group by the 2nd and
3rd Ukrainian Fronts and the liberation of Moldavia created
the conditions for the withdrawal of Romania and Hungary from
the war

All this brought nearer the collapse of the fascist bloc
and the defeat of Nazi Germany.

In the Western strategic direction, the front line had

advanced 600 kilometres. By the end of August, it ran west of Jelgava, Siauliai, Suwałki, Ostrolenka, Pultusk, Praga (a Warsaw suburb), Magnuszew, Sandomierz, Sanok, Drogobych and Chernovtsy, where it joined the line of the 2nd Ukrainian Front.

On the North-Western sector, the Baltic Fronts, along with the Leningrad Front and Baltic Fleet, were preparing an offensive blow against the Army Group North, in order to liberate all the Baltic Republics as soon as possible, and to defeat another powerful German force which had been pressed against the sea.

In the Western theatre, the military situation was also unfavourable for Germany. After heavy losses in the fighting in Normandy and unable to move troops in from other fronts to strengthen their forces in Northern France, the Germans began to rapidly retreat all along the front towards the German border and the Siegfried Line.

The Allied troops were pursuing the enemy on all sectors. After capturing Rome, the Allies intended to continue their offensive in Northern Italy. Liberation movements quickly spread all over Europe and the Balkans. The Germans felt them, especially in Yugoslavia, Poland, Albania, Greece and France. The German High Command was forced to detail considerable troops to fight the Resistance and the national liberation forces.

The Allied and Soviet air forces were at the same time inflicting heavy damage on key industrial facilities in Germany, thus aggravating the economic, military and political situation.

It appeared that the German High Command would quickly withdraw its Army Group North (60 divisions, over 1,200 tanks and 7,000 guns) in order to save the troops and build up deep defences on a more narrow front both in the east and in the west.

However, the German Command could not rise above considerations of political prestige, thus bringing closer Germany's collapse. Hitler still evidently believed that an agreement could be reached with Western reactionary forces, so that they could jointly wage a battle against the "Communist menace" in the future. In general, however, in the battles for the Ukraine, Byelorussia and the Baltic Republics, Hitler's military and political leaders proved unable to understand the situation and find the correct solution at that crucial moment.

A characteristic of the 1944 summer campaign was the further build-up of the combat strength of the Soviet Armed Forces and the increasing operational and strategic skills of our high command and headquarters.

In the summer of 1944 the Soviet troops carried out seven major operations to surround and smash groups of German troops. This was many more than in previous campaigns. The more important of them were the Byelorussian, Iasi-Kishinev and Lvov-Sandomierz operations in which 147 enemy divisions were crushed. As a result the German defensive front was broken over a 2,200-km stretch from the Western Dvina to the Black Sea. On some sectors our troops advanced up to 700 kilometres.

All twelve Fronts, as well as the Northern, Baltic and Black Sea Fleets, and all lake and river flotillas took part in the offensive operations in the summer campaign of 1944.

On August 22, I was phoned from Moscow and told that I had been ordered by the Supreme Commander to report at General Headquarters immediately. I was informed that I was to go on a special mission for the State Committee for Defence.

I bid farewell to my friends and comrades-in-arms and flew to Moscow on August 23, I arrived in the capital in the evening and immediately went to the General Staff.

*   *   *

The special mission of the State Committee for Defence was as follows. I was to fly to the 3rd Ukrainian Front to prepare the Front for war against Bulgaria, whose monarchial government continued to cooperate with Nazi Germany.

Stalin advised me to see Georgi Dimitrov before leaving so I could learn more about the general political situation in Bulgaria, the activities of the Bulgarian Workers' Party, and armed actions of Bulgaria's anti-fascist forces.

Dimitrov impressed me very much. He was an exceptionally unassuming and warm-hearted man. From his reasoning and conclusions, one could see that he was also a man of great intellect and political acumen. Our meeting was very friendly, and he told me at length about everything that would be useful for me to know. It was obvious that he had very effective communication channels with the underground organizations of the Bulgarian Workers' Party (Communists).

Dimitrov said to me:

"Although you are going to the 3rd Ukrainian Front to prepare the troops for war against Bulgaria, I can assure you there will be no war. The Bulgarian people are waiting impatiently for the Red Army so as to overthrow with its help the monarchical government of Bagryanov and establish the power of the People's Liberation Front.

"The Soviet forces will not be met," Dimitrov continued, "with artillery and machine-gun fire from the Bulgarians, but with bread and salt — according to our old Slav custom. I don't think the Bulgarian troops will risk engaging the Red Army. As far as I know, our people are doing a great deal of work in almost every army unit. There are extensive guerilla forces in the mountains and in the forests. They are not sitting there doing nothing, but are ready to come down from the mountains and take part in a popular uprising."

He sat silent for a moment, then said:

"The successes of the Soviet troops have greatly activated the popular liberation movement in Bulgaria. Our Party is leading this movement, and is determined, with the Red Army approaching, to initiate an armed uprising."

I thanked Dimitrov for talking to me, and returned to the General Staff to complete the elaboration of the plan of the future operation in Bulgaria. I was almost certain there would be no military action, but then we are military men, and when our political leadership gives us an assignment, we have to carry it out with the greatest precision.

At that time the Bulgarian Royal Army numbered over 510,000. Part of this force confronted the troops of the 3rd Ukrainian Front.

At the end of August, I flew to where the 3rd Ukrainian Front Headquarters was stationed — the town of Pitesti, not far from the Černavoda Bridge, which our aviation had bombed repeatedly during the war to disrupt freight traffic between the port of Constanta and Romania's main regions.

Marshal Tolbukhin was in command of the 3rd Ukrainian Front. By this time, his troops had reached the line stretching from Ruse (Ruschuk), along the banks of the Danube down to the Black Sea. The Front included the 37th, 46th and 57th Field armies and the 17th Air Army. The Black Sea Fleet and the Danube Flotilla were in Marshal Tolbukhin's operational control. Marshal Timoshenko was coordinating the actions of the 2nd and 3rd Ukrainian Fronts. I met them at Piteşti to discuss operations of the Fronts.

In the entire Southern theatre, operational and strategic situations were developing favourably. After totally routing the Iasi-Kishinev enemy grouping and liberating most of Romania, the troops of the 2nd Ukrainian Front were rapidly moving west over the Walachia plain. They split the German forces in two, cutting off the troops in Transylvania and the Carpathians from the forces in Greece, Yugoslavia and Albania. The Black Sea Fleet controlled the Black Sea, while the Soviet Air Force had command of the air.

According to the planned offensive of the 3rd Ukrainian Front, the 46th Army was to advance in the general direction of Yesek-Kubrat; the 57th Army, towards Kochmar-Shumen; the 37th Army, towards Dobrich-Provadia; while the 7th and 4th Guards Mechanized corps were to advance towards Karno-bat-Burgas, and reach these points on the second day of operations.

Since the pro-fascist government of Bulgaria continued, despite repeated warnings from the Soviet Government, to violate its commitments of neutrality and actively collaborate with Nazi Germany, the Soviet Government declared war on Bulgaria on September 5; on September 6, the Supreme Command ordered the 3rd Ukrainian Front to begin military operations.

On the morning of September 8, everything was ready to open fire, but from our observation posts we did not see any targets we could shell...

Through stereotelescopes, binoculars and with the naked eye, we could observe the ordinary flow of peaceful life — smoke was billowing from the chimneys, and people were going about their daily chores. We could detect no military units.

Marshal Tolbukhin ordered the advance detachments forward. In less than half an hour, the 57th Army commander reported that a Bulgarian infantry division was lined up on both sides of the road, welcoming our troops with unfurled red banners and military music. Similar reports soon came in from other directions. Army commanders informed me that Soviet troops were spontaneously fraternizing with Bulgarians.

I immediately phoned Stalin. He told me:

"Don't disarm the Bulgarian troops. Let them be while they are waiting for orders from their government."

This simple act by the Supreme Command reflected our full confidence in the Bulgarian people and army, who gave a fraternal welcome to the Red Army as their liberator from German occupation and from the pro-fascist monarchy.

As our troops moved deeper and deeper into the country, they were hailed warmly everywhere. Soon we linked up with the guerilla detachments which were well-armed, and had seized several towns and military targets.

In view of the imminent danger posed by the German forces which could strike from the area south of Niš towards Sofia, the Supreme Command ordered a reinforced infantry corps to be moved into the Bulgarian capital.

On September 8, we entered Varna, and on the following day Burgas and other areas. As our Black Sea naval force was approaching Bulgarian ports and Soviet paratroops were landed, the Germans sank their ships, and their troops were subsequently captured by our sailors.

On September 9, the Bulgarian people, led by the Workers' Party, overthrew the pro-fascist government and proclaimed a democratic government of the Fatherland Front, which proposed an armistice to the Soviet Government.

The State Committee for Defence immediately instructed the Supreme Command to halt the advance of our troops in Bulgaria.

On orders from the Supreme Command, the troops stopped their advance at 21:00, September 9, and were deployed in assigned areas. It was gratifying to know that in this so-called war there had been no casualties on either side. All these events were a graphic example of how the Soviet Armed Forces were carrying out their liberating mission. They also demonstrated the real force, of the masses in abolishing anti-popular regimes.

Circumstances did not permit me to travel in Bulgaria at that time, a country with which our people are bound by age-old ties of friendship born in common battles against oppression.

Vacationing in Varna after the war, my wife and I travelled almost all over Bulgaria. As a Lieutenant-Colonel in the medical service and a physician at the Burdenko Chief Military Hospital, my wife was especially interested in the organization of public health in Bulgaria, while I was interested in military aspects.

Everywhere we went, we saw that the Bulgarians cherished the memory of the Russian soldiers who had given their lives for the better future of the Bulgarian people. It was especially gratifying to see the enthusiasm of the working class, peasants and intellectuals who, led by their Communist Party, were remaking their country along socialist lines.

CHAPTER 7

From the Vistula to the Oder

At the end of September 1944 I returned to General Headquarters from Bulgaria. A few days later the Supreme Commander instructed me to promptly go to the area of Warsaw and the sectors of the 1st and 2nd Byelorussian Fronts.

First of all I wished to find out how things were in Warsaw itself whose residents had not long before staged an uprising against the fascist aggressors. The German Command dealt ruthlessly with the insurgents and subjected the population to brutal reprisals. The city was razed to the ground. Thousands of civilians perished in the wreckage.

As was established later, neither the command of the Front nor that of Poland's 1st Army had been informed in advance by Bor-Komorowski, the leader of the uprising, about the forthcoming events in Warsaw. Nor did he make any attempt to coordinate the insurgents' actions with those of the 1st Byelorussian Front. The Soviet Command learned about the uprising after the event from local residents who had crossed the Vistula. The Stavka had not been informed in advance either.

On instructions by the Supreme Commander, two paratroop officers were sent to Bor-Komorowski for liaison and coordination of actions. However, Bor-Komorowski refused to receive the officers.

To assist the Warsaw insurgents, Soviet and Polish troops crossed the Vistula and seized a section of the Warsaw Embankment. However, Bor-Komorowski again made no attempt to make any reciprocal move in our direction. In a day or so the Germans brought up considerable forces to the Embankment and began pressing our troops. A serious situation developed, and our troops suffered heavy losses. Having considered the situation, and being convinced of the impossibility of capturing Warsaw, the command of the Front decided to withdraw the troops from the Embankment to its bank.

I have ascertained that our troops did everything they possibly could to help the insurgents, although the uprising had not been in any way coordinated with the Soviet Command.

All that time — both before and after our troops' forced withdrawal — the 1st Byelorussian Front continued to furnish assistance to the insurgents by air-dropping provisions, medicines and ammunition. I remember there were many false reports on the matter in the Western press which could have misled public opinion.

At the beginning of October, I went to the 47th Army under General F. I. Perkhovich, which was conducting offensive operations between Modlin and Warsaw. Advancing on flat terrain this army, almost utterly worn out and depleted, was sustaining great casualties. Things were no brighter with the neighbouring 70th Army which was fighting in the zone between Serock and Pułtusk.

I did not understand the operational aim of this offensive, which was draining our strength. Rokossovsky saw it the way I did, but the Supreme Commander required the 47th Army to reach the Vistula in the area between Modlin and Warsaw, and to expand the bridgeheads on the River Narew.

I called up the Supreme Commander and, having reported the situation, asked him for orders to halt the offensive in the zone of the 1st Byelorussian Front, because it led us nowhere, and for the right wing of the 1st, and for the left wing of the 2nd Byelorussian Fronts to assume the defensive so as to give them a respite and the opportunity to move up reinforcements.

"Fly in with Rokossovsky to General Headquarters tomorrow for a discussion," Stalin replied. "Good-bye."

The following afternoon, Rokossovsky and I were at General Headquarters.

Antonov, Molotov and Malenkov were there with Stalin. Greeting us, he said:

"Well, let's hear your report."

I spread out my map and began explaining the situation. I saw that Stalin was restless; he would come up to look at the map, then step back, then approach again, eyeing me, the map and Rokossovsky in turn. He even put his pipe aside, which was a sure sign that his composure was slipping and that he was displeased with something.

"Comrade Zhukov," Molotov interrupted me, "you are suggesting that the offensive be stopped now that the defeated enemy is unable to stand up to our pressure. Is that sensible?"

"The enemy has already had time to organize his defence and bring up reserves," I countered. "He is now successfully holding us back. We are suffering unjustifiably heavy losses."

"Do you share Zhukov's opinion?" Stalin asked, turning to Rokossovsky.

"Yes, I believe the troops need a respite to organize themselves after their long and strenuous period of fighting."

"I suppose the enemy could use a respite to no less advantage than we would," the Supreme Commander said. "And, what if we support the 47th Army with aviation and reinforce it with artillery and tanks—will it be able to break through to the Vistula between Modlin and Warsaw?"

"That's hard to say, Comrade Stalin," Rokossovsky replied. "The enemy might also strengthen that sector."

Stalin turned to me and asked: "And what do you think?"

"My opinion is that this offensive will yield us nothing but casualties," I said. "From the operational viewpoint, we don't particularly need the area north-west of Warsaw. The city must be taken by skirting it on the south-west, and at the same time dealing a powerful splitting blow in the general direction of Łódź-Poznań. The Front does not now possess the forces for that, but they should be brought up. At the same time, the neighbouring Fronts in the Berlin zone of operations should be thoroughly prepared for joint action."

"Go and think over your suggestions some more," Stalin interrupted.

Rokossovsky and I went to the library and spread out the map again. But we had hardly sat ourselves down when we were again called into the Supreme Commander's office.

"We have considered it all, and decided to aggree to our forces moving onto the defensive," Stalin said. "As for future plans, we'll discuss them later. You may go now."

Rokossovsky and I parted silently, each preoccupied with his own thoughts. I headed for the Defence Commissariat, while

Rokossovsky went to prepare for the flight to the front.

The next day the Supreme Commander phoned me:

"What would you say to the Stavka taking over control of all the Fronts in future?"

I understood that he meant to abolish the post of the Supreme Command representatives for coordinating the Fronts.

"Yes, there are fewer fronts now," I replied. "I think that there is ample opportunity to control the Fronts directly from General Headquarters, since the overall frontage has shrunk, making control of them easier."

"You say this without feeling offended?"

"What's there to be offended about? I hope neither Vasilevsky nor I will find ourselves out of work," I joked.

That evening the Supreme Commander called me up and said:

"The 1st Byelorussian Front is operating on the Berlin sector. We propose to put you in charge of that Front."

I told him that I was ready to take command of any Front.

"You are also to continue as my deputy," Stalin said. "I'll talk to Rokossovsky right away."

Telling Rokossovsky of his decision, Stalin suggested that he be transferred to the 2nd Byelorussian Front.

At the end of October 1944, the Supreme Command, together with several representatives of the State Committee for Defence and the Chief of General Staff, discussed the final operations plan of the Great Patriotic War.

The Communist Party continued mobilizing the people's efforts to achieve the main objective—to ensure an early victory over the enemy. At the same time, it was increasingly concerned with creating conditions for comprehensive post-war economic recovery and the rapid transition to peaceful construction.

Fuel-and-power problems were being decided successfully. There was a sharp increase in the production of pig-iron, rolled steel, tools and tractors. Many dozens of blast- and open hearth furnaces, and powerful rolling mills were being put into operation.

The people in the rear, rejoicing at the victories on the front, were doubling and trebling their efforts. It was with exceptional enthusiasm that the people were rebuilding the plants, factories and transport which had been reduced to ruins. Flooded shafts were being restored. Sowing was done on the land which had not yet cooled after the flames of battle, and was still saturated with people's blood.

The Red Army was increasingly relying on the expanding national economy. There was a rise in the scope of military operations and the tempo of the offensive. There were greater requirements for military production, and they were being promptly met.

In 1944, the country manufactured 29,000 tanks and self-propelled artillery guns, and more than 40,000 aircraft. There was a two-to-three-fold increase in the output of IS-2 heavy tanks with 122-mm guns, T-34 modernized medium tanks, YaK-3 fighters, IL-10 assault planes and TU-2 highspeed bombers.

All that combat materiel was of first-class quality, created by talented designers. It was produced on a mass scale, and its tactical and technical characteristics were superior to German and many foreign war machines.

Soviet economic progress made it possible not only to fully meet the requirements of the Soviet Armed Forces, but also to provide arms for the peoples of Central and South-Eastern Europe to use in their liberation struggle. As an example, the Wojsko Polskie was supplied with, 8,340 guns and mortars, 630 aircraft, 670 tanks and self-propelled artillery pieces, over 406,000 rifles and submachine-guns, and many motor vehicles and other equipment. The Yugoslav troops received 5,800 artillery pieces and mortars, about 500 aircraft, 69 tanks, over 193,000 pistols, rifles and submachine-guns, and more than 15,500 machine-guns.

By that time the Soviet Armed Forces had driven out the Nazi forces from Soviet territory, re-established the state border (except in Courland), and were partially fighting on the territory of Nazi Germany and in East European countries.

The lines of the 2nd and 1st Baltic Fronts ran through Tukums, Mémele (exclusive), the River Neman and up to Jurburg.

The 3rd and 2nd Byelorussian Fronts held positions along the Jurburg-Augustow Canal-Lomza-Serock line, and had two bridgeheads on the River Narew.

The 1st Byelorussian and the 1st Ukrainian fronts stood on the Praga (Warsaw suburb)-Vistula-Jaslo line.

These two Fronts had three large bridgeheads — in the areas of Magnuszew, Pulawy and Sandomierz.

Farther on the lines of the Soviet front extended from Levice through Esztergom and Lake Balaton to Pécs.

Still farther were the lines of the Bulgarian Army. The Yugoslav People's Liberation Army headed by Marshal Josip Broz Tito had moved out to the Vukovar-Čačak-Split line, up to the Adriatic Sea.

After liberating France, Belgium and part of Holland, the American, British and French forces had advanced to the line running from the Maas estuary in Holland down to the German border up to Switzerland. They had thus moved up to the fortified area known as the Siegfried Line.

Fascist Germany was hard pressed. Towards the end of 1944 the production of armaments began to decline sharply. The stranglehold on Germany was being tightened in the east, south-east and west. It can be said that by the end of 1944 Germany found itself in strategic encirclement with practically no way out. Hopes of aid and support from Western imperialist circles dissipated, and the strength of the Red Army grew from day to day.

Not a single one of the Germans we 'had captured and interrogated during that period believed in Germany's victory. "*Deutschland kaput*", "*Hitler kaput*", they all declared. However, Hitler decreed one general call-up after another. The fascists mercilessly suppressed the slightest opposition to the regime. The Gestapo's persecutions became especially cruel after the attempt on Hitler's life on July 20, 1944.

The German Gvernment's decree on the formation of the Volkssturm (people's militia), involving men between 18 and 60, became effective on October 18. That force, under Himmler's command, was to serve as a reserve army.

We were well aware that the Volkssturm would not be able to stand up to our battle-tried and well-armed regular troops. The Hitlerites even formed a women's auxiliary corps. All those measures fully indicated to us that Germany was desperate—it was straining its last strength in an attempt to put off the inevitable collapse.

However, by the end of 1944 the German High Command was still capable of conducting defensive operations and offering active resistance. Its armed forces still had 9,400,000 men, including 5,400,000 men in the field army. The Nazi Command still kept the bulk of its forces at the Eastern Front: 3,700,000 men, over 56,000 artillery pieces and mortars, more than 8,000 tanks and assault guns, 4,100 combat aircraft.

It should be noted that the length of the Soviet-German front was nearly halved, and the enemy's defence density was, therefore, high.

At that time the Soviet forces outnumbered the enemy on all counts. By late 1944 our strength in the field was 6.7 million. We had 107,300 artillery pieces and mortars, 2,677 rocket launchers, 12, 100 tanks and self-propelled artillery pieces and over 14,700 combat planes.

It was only thanks to the far-sighted policies and confident leadership of the Party, the advantages of the socialist system, the selfless labour and the colossal strain of the Soviet people, that such a powerful army could be built to drive the enemy from Soviet territory. It was not easy for our people to achieve this victory—to achieve definitive military superiority over the enemy.

Our combat power was boosted at the time by the Polish, Czechoslovak, Romanian and Bulgarian troops which were crushing the fascists successfully. Towards the beginning of 1945 their total number was 347,000 men, 4,000 artillery pieces and mortars, and about 200 tanks.

The valourous French air regiment, Normandy-Neman, fought as part of the 3rd Byelorussian Front's forces.

In the west the American, British and French forces had 76 full-strength, well-equipped divisions and 15 detached brigades, 16,100 tanks and self-propelled artillery pieces, and over 16,700 cambat planes. The German Command had concentrated against those forces only 74 short-strength and poorly trained divisions and three detached brigades, 3,500 tanks and assault guns, and up to 2,700 combat planes.

Consequently, soon after the opening of the Second Front, the Allies had twice the number of men, four times the number of tanks, and six times the number of aircraft that the enemy had.

In Italy, the Germans had 31 short-strength divisions against 22 Allied divisions.

After an all-round assessment of the situation and capabilities of the warring parties, the Supreme Command decided to prepare and conduct powerful offensive operations in early 1945 in all the strategic directions with the following general aims:

— to rout the East Prussian grouping and occupy East Prussia;

— to defeat the enemy in Poland, Czechoslovakia, Hungary and Austria;

— to move out to the line running through the Vistula mouth, Bromberg (Bydgoszcz), Poznań, Breslau (Wrocław), Moravská Ostrava and Vienna.

The Warsaw-Berlin line of advance — where the zone of the 1st Byelorussian Front was to be—was to be the direction of the main effort. The 2nd and 1st Baltic Fronts and the Baltic Fleet were assigned to rout the Courland enemy grouping (the 16th and 18th armies). They were also to prevent the enemy forces pressed to the Baltic Sea from being transferred to other fronts.

At that period the Supreme Command maintained effective contacts with the High Command of the Allied Expeditionary Forces in the West. We knew that American, British and French commands were preparing an offensive operation to defeat the Germans in the Ruhr and Saar areas and reach Germany's central parts. Secondary blows were planned in the Southern and South-Eastern strategic directions.

One very essential detail should be pointed out here: the Soviet and Allied forces were approximately the same distance away from Berlin. In his memoirs Sir Winston Churchill often mentions Berlin as an objective which he preferred the Allied forces to take, although under an agreement among the heads of government it was the mission of the Soviet forces to capture Berlin.

Coordination of action between the Soviet and Allied forces was effected mainly through mutual information passed between their high commands.

I must say that at that time Stalin trusted Eisenhower's reports. All information concerning current operations of our troops and our plans was transmitted by our General Staff via the US and British Military Missions. Besides, the heads of government regularly exchanged messages concerning fundamental actions.

Correspondence between Stalin and President Roosevelt reveals that they had attained a complete understanding as to the implementation of USSR-USA agreements, both on the Lend-Lease Act and military strategy.

The same could not be said about Winston Churchill. In his letters one could sense a lack of sincerity, secret intentions, and a persistent desire to seize Central Germany. Naturally, this compelled the Soviet Government to be somewhat on guard.

I do not think there is any need to cite correspondence between Churchill, Roosevelt and Stalin here, since it has been published. Reading it carefully today, one can see more clearly how Churchill nurtured his plans for the post-war reorganization of the central European states headed by pro-Western governments.

In late October and early November 1944, I did a great deal of work, as assigned to me by the Supreme Commander, elaborating the main aspects of the final campaign — primarily the plan of operations on the Berlin sector.

I can state with satisfaction that by then our General Staff's skill in planning large-scale offensive operations was on a very high level.

From an assessment of the situation, the General Staff concluded that the enemy would offer the greatest opposition on the Berlin sector. Proof of this was the scant results of the offensive operations by the 3rd, 2nd and 1st Byelorussian Fronts in October and the fact that they were forced to go onto the defensive in the Western strategic direction at the beginning of November.

My thinking was exactly that of the General Staff and its chief operations officers A. I. Antonov, S. M. Shtemenko, A. A. Gryzlov and N. A. Lomov, who at all stages of the work of the Operations Department proved themselves outstanding strategists.

In the opinion of the General Staff, the offensive would have to be initiated by our Southern Fronts on the Vienna sector.

This would inevitably compel the German Command to move considerable forces from our Western Fronts in order to reinforce their South-Eastern strategic direction, which was crucial for the fate of south and south-east Germany.

Planning an offensive on the Western sector involved a serious problem — that of East Prussia, where the enemy had considerable forces and well-organized defences, supported by permanent engineering installations, difficult terrain and strong stone structures in villages and towns.

It was a pity the Supreme Commander had shown a lack of understanding in summer when it was proposed to strengthen the troops of the Fronts operating on the East Prussian sector. With the Byelorussian offensive operation developing successfully, its momentum could have been employed to break the enemy defence. Now the enemy grouping in East Prussia could be a serious threat to our forces that were to advance on Berlin.

On either November 1, or perhaps November 2— I don't remember which — Antonov and I were summoned by the Supreme Commander for a discussion of the plan for the winter operations. Antonov presented a draft which I had approved. And once again, the Supreme Commander did not feel it possible to accept our joint proposal of strengthening the 2nd Byelorussian Front with one more army in order to knock out the East Prussian grouping. We suggested getting that army from the Baltic Fronts which, in our opinion, should have moved over to the defensive so it could contain the 16th and 18th armies of the Courland enemy grouping.

After the October Revolution holidays we and the General Staff began elaborating the offensive plan for the 1st Byelorussian Front.

By that time, the command and the staff of that Front had already submitted their major considerations to the General Staff on conduct of the operation, considerations basically reflecting the current situation. We had discussed them on several occasions with Rokossovsky and Malinin.

As I have already mentioned, I did not favour a frontal attack on Warsaw across the Vistula, and I made this known to the Supreme Commander. He approved my proposals.

On November 15, I left for Lublin, where I received an

order appointing me Commander of the 1st Byelorussian Front (with General Telegin as Member of the Front's Military Council), and Rokossovsky Commander of the 2nd Byelorussian Front. There, in Lublin, I met Bierut and other leaders of the Polish Workers' Party and of the National Liberation Committee.

On November 16, I assumed command of the Front, and that same day Rokossovsky left for the 2nd Byelorussian Front.

Until the end of November, the staff of the Front headed by Malinin continued working out the plan of the offensive and drawing up requests to the Supreme Command for reinforcements and supplies. The staffs of the Front and of the Front rear, and commanders of the fighting services had done a colossal amount of work calculating strength and supplies for the coming operation.

The plan was approved in late November. Although an exact time had not been fixed by the Supreme Commander for the beginning of the operation, he had tentatively fixed it for the period of January 15-20.

The tasks ahead of us and time limits for attaining combat readiness required extensive and complex work with the troops, command personnel, staffs and logistic agencies.

Preparations for the Vistula-Oder operation were very different from those of similar scale on Soviet territory. Before, we were fed with intelligence by guerilla detachments operating behind enemy lines. Now, there was none of this any more.

We could only gather intelligence through secret service agents and through aerial and ground reconnaissance. This important aspect of the situation was pointed out emphatically to all chiefs of staff.

Our supply routes along railways and motor roads now lay in Poland where, besides true friends and people loyal to the Soviet Union, there were enemy intelligence agents. The new conditions demanded special vigilance and secrecy of manoeuvres and deployment.

By that time the army Party organizations had carried out, on the instructions of the Party Central Committee, extensive explanatory work as to how our troops must conduct themselves abroad — they were to come as liberators, not conquerors. Thorough orientation was necessary in all units of the front so as to prevent, right from the outset, any irresponsible acts on the part of our officers and men in Poland.

We had established normal relations with local authorities and public organizations, and had their cooperation wherever possible. The troops, in turn, shared everything they had with the people. In this way, from the very beginning, we laid the foundation of fraternal friendship between the Soviet and Polish peoples who had lived through the horrors of Nazi occupation.

The Military Council of the Front decided to stage the future operation so as to conduct preparations with greater efficiency. All commanders of the armies, members of the military councils, chiefs of staff, commanders of detached corps, the deputy commander for logistics and heads of the fighting arms and services took part in the manoeuvre. The staff of the Front proved itself splendidly able to organize an interesting and instructive manoeuvre. Problems of logistical support stated by the logistics chief were given careful consideration.

The army commanders also held manoeuvres on the army scale. Staging the operations and discussing of the relevant problems helped the command personnel better understand each other's role in future combat, and cleared up matters of cooperation with their neighbours, the air force, mobile troops, artillery and engineers.

As the operation had to be launched from two comparatively small bridgeheads with tremendous troop concentrations, it was exceedingly difficult to organize logistical operations in the army and the immediate rear, especially since during the stepping-up period, logistical operations could be conducted only via the bridgeheads and their very inadequate dirt roads.

To establish closer cooperation between the bridgeheads, a war game was held on January 4 at the headquarters of the 69th Army under General Kolpakchi. The commanders of all units of that army took part. I had also invited Chuikov, commander of the 8th Army; Berzarin, commander of the 5th Army; Katukov and Bogdanov, commanders of the 1st and 2nd Tank armies, and their chiefs of staff.

At the end of December, I had to fly to General Headquarters to discuss a number of problems with the Supreme Commander prior to final approval of the general plan of closing operations.

At the end of November 1944, the Supreme Command finally evolved the concept of closing operations in the Western strategic direction. Timely adoption of a strategic plan gave the Fronts opportunity to carefully consider all operational, strategic, logistical and political problems.

Two large-scale offensive operations were planned in the Western strategic direction before we were to strike directly at Berlin: one — in East Prussia by the 3rd and 2nd Byelorussian Fronts; the other — on the Warsaw-Berlin sector.

Involved in the second were to be the 1st Byelorussian and 1st Ukrainian Fronts.

The 1st Byelorussian Front was to mount the offensive in the general direction of Poznán. The 1st Ukrainian Front was to reach the Oder (Odra) north-west Glogau (Głogow), Breslau (Wrocław) and Ratibor (Racibórz). The entire 2nd Byelorussian Front stood poised against the East Prussian enemy grouping. Up to the beginning of February the main forces of the Front were supposed to fight to tie up this grouping in East Prussia. The left flank armies of the Front having advanced to the lower Vistula north of Bromberg (Bydgoszcz) were to pass over to the defensive.

The immediate operational objective of the 1st Byelorussian Front was to break the crust of enemy defence in two different areas simultaneously and, having knocked out the Warsaw-Radom enemy grouping, to move out to the Lódź meridian. The subsequent plan of action was to advance towards Poznań up to the line running through Bromberg (Bydgoszcz)-Poznań and further south where tactical contact with the troops of the 1st Ukrainian Front was to be made.

The subsequent advance was not planned, as the Supreme Command could not know beforehand what the situation would be by the time our forces reached the Bromberg (Bydgoszcz)-Poznań line. The advance of the 2nd Byelorussian Front could be slowed, in which case the objective set by the Supreme Command of enveloping and sawing up the East Prussian enemy grouping would not be fulfilled. Then the 1st Byelorussian Front might have to move a considerable part of its forces north to help out the 2nd Byelorussian Front.

As for our neighbour on the left, we were certain that he would not lag behind: the strength of the 1st Ukrainian Front was almost as great as that of the 1st Byelorussian Front. Besides, both Fronts had practically adjacent zones of responsibility. For that reason we supposed we would not have to deploy our forces southward. Nor had the Supreme Command envisaged any south-westward or southward movement by the grouping of the 1st Byelorussian Front.

It was impossible to provide for any such movement when planning an operation for a depth of several hundred kilometres with the enemy command free to manipulate its reserves. For instance, the Germans could bring up reinforcements from the Western theatre, or draw off forces from the cut-off Courland grouping, or, finally, achieve sufficient troop concentration in one of their sectors by manoeuvring forces about the front so as to organize active resistance.

Thus the Supreme Command considered that the decision on subsequent action by the 1st Byelorussian Front after the forces of the Front gained the Bromberg (Bydgoszcz)-Poznań line should be taken later, depending on the situation.

Initially called Operation Warsaw-Poznań, but once the 1st Byelorussian Front approached the Oder in the area of Küstrin, it was renamed Operation Vistula-Oder.

The plan of the operation was as follows: the main attack was to be launched from the Magnuszew bridgehead by the 5th Shock, 61st and 8th Guards armies, and the 1st and 2nd Guards Tank armies. Besides, after crossing the River Pilica, from behind the right flank of the 61st Army under General Belov, elements of the 1st Army of Wojsko Polskie under General Stanislaw Poplawski were to attack Warsaw from the south.

After crossing the River Pilica, the 61st Army under General Belov was to skirt Warsaw, advancing towards Sochaczew with the idea of attacking Warsaw with part of its force from the west. General Berzarin's 5th Shock Army, after breaking the crust of enemy defence, was to press the attack in the general direction of Ozorków and further on towards Gniezno. The 8th Guards Army under General Chuikov, after breaking through the enemy lines, was to advance left of the 5th Army in the general direction of Łódź, and further on towards Poznań.

The 2nd Guards Tank Army under General Bogdanov was

to enter the breach in the 5th Shock Army zone and thrust forward to the area of Sochaczew and try to cut the withdrawal routes of the Warsaw grouping. After that the army was to advance on Kutno and Gniezno. The 1st Guards Tank Army under General Katukov was to enter the breach in the zone of the 8th Guards Army and intensify its thrust towards Łódź, and then move in the direction of Poznań.

The ground forces were to be supported by General Rudenko's 16th Air Army. The 2nd Guards Cavalry Corps under General Kryukov was to move out after the 2nd Guards Tank Army, and advance along the Vistula in the general direction of Bromberg (Bydgoszcz). The 3rd Shock Army of General Kuznetsov was to form the rear echelon of the Front.

The secondary attack was to be launched by the 69th and 33rd armies, from the Puławy bridgehead, reinforced by the 11th and 9th Tank corps, and then move in the general direction of Radom, and further on towards Łódź. After the breakthrough, part of the left-flank 33rd Army and the 9th Tank Corps were to knife towards Skarzysko-Kamienna and envelop and rout the Kielce-Radom enemy grouping. The 4th Tank Army of the 1st Ukrainian Front, commanded by General Lelyushenko, was to coordinate efforts with the 33rd Army.

The 7th Cavalry Corps under General Konstantinov, the Front reserve, was to advance in the rear echelon.

Twenty-four hours later, the 47th Army under General Perkhorovich, attacked northwest of Warsaw, where it was joined by the 2nd Division of the 1st Army of Wojsko Polskie.

The rout of the Warsaw-Radom-Łódź grouping and the seizure of Warsaw — the Front's initial objective — had been planned in great detail. The plan of the next mission was sketchy. As is usual with planning operations for a front, we expected to elaborate it as the initial mission was being fulfilled.

In our calculations, we had proceeded from the knowledge that we would have to fight a stubborn and then still strong enemy, whom we already knew well.

We had given much thought to improving the organization of artillery preparation and air support in order to effect a breakthrough for the entire tactical depth and send tank troops into the gap, on which we primarily relied, as early as possible.

While preparing the operation, we had taken great pains to mislead the enemy as to the scope of our offensive and directions of attacks, especially of the main attack. We had been working to make the enemy think that we were concentrating troops against Warsaw, on the east of the city.

However, we were not absolutely certain that the enemy had been deceived and had no idea of our true plans. We were afraid that having guessed our intentions he would withdraw his main forces from the forward positions into the depth, letting us fire hundreds of thousands of shells on empty lines.

Following a comprehensive analysis of the situation and a discussion of all the pros and cons with commanders of the fighting services, we decided to conduct, right before the main attack and after a powerful 30-minute artillery attack, a major reconnaissance effort. And if the enemy hesitated, we would immediately attack in full strength.

For this frontal attack each division detailed one or two infantry battalions with tanks and self-propelled mounts. Reconnaissance in force, besides artillery, was also to have air support.

The enemy did not sustain the probing attack, and began rolling back from the main line of resistance, apparently having taken it for the attack of the main Front forces. Having opened up with all their artillery and directed the bulk of the air force against targets in the depth of enemy defence, the armies of the Front then dashed forward with their attack echelons. On the first day of the operation at 13:00 the 11th Tank Corps was brought into battle.

From that moment on the breakthrough exploitation went according to plan, and we saved many thousand tons of ammunition, which came in handy later on in continuing the operation.

On the second day of the offensive the 1st and 2nd Guards Tank armies and the 9th Tank Corps were brought into action. Their thrust shook both the tactical and strategic defence systems of the enemy. When the 2nd Guards Tank Army, rolling swiftly, reached the Żyrardów-Sochaczew area, and the 47th Army seized a portion of the Vistula's southern bank north of Warsaw, the Germans began a hasty withdrawal from the city.

Leaving Warsaw, they demolished the Polish capital completely, and annihilated the people *en masse*.

Operating to the right of the 1st Byelorussian Front were

the 2nd and 3rd Byelorussian Fronts. Their mission was to knock out the East Prussian enemy grouping and take East Prussia.

The main grouping of the 2nd Byelorussian Front was to advance to the area of Marienburg and cut off the East Prussian grouping from East Pomerania, Danzig and Gdynia.

The Front was to launch its main attack from the Rózan bridgehead in the direction of Mława. The secondary blow was to be delivered from the Serock bridgehead in the general direction of Bielsk and Lipno. The 70th Army was to advance its left wing along the northern bank of the Vistula and prevent the enemy's retreat from the zone of operations of the 1st Byelorussian Front across the river.

The offensive began on January 13. The 2nd Byelorussian Front (Marshal Rokossovsky, Commander; General Subbotin, Military Council Member; General Bogolyubov, Chief of Staff) employing part of its forces, passed to the offensive simultaneously with the 3rd Byelorussian Front (General Chernyakhovsky, Commander; General Makarov, Military Council Member; General Pokrovsky, Chief of Staff). On the next day, Rokossovsky's main forces set out on the Mława sector.

The enemy resisted stubbornly. The breakthrough was being exploited very slowly, and it was not until January 19, after all the armoured and mechanized units of the Front were moved into battle, that the breakthrough was completed. The 2nd Byelorussian Front captured Mława, Przasnysz and Ciechanów. Advancing briskly south of the Vistula, the 47th Army and the 2nd Guards Tank Army had provided reliable protection for the 2nd Byelorussian Front's left flank.

The 1st Ukrainian Front (Marshal Konev, Commander; General Krainyukov, Military Council Member; General Sokolovsky, Chief of Staff), operating on the left of the 1st Byelorussian Front, started the offensive from the Sandomierz bridgehead on January 12. The mission which the Supreme Command had assigned to the 1st Ukrainian Front was to reach the Piotroków-Częstochowa-Miechów line on the 10th or 11th day of the operation, and then continue the offensive towards Breslau.

The offensive of the 1st Ukrainian Front was moving ahead successfully. The central line of resistance had been pierced on the first day and the attack echelons supported by sections

of the tank armies, advanced 20 km. The 3rd Guards Tank
Army under General Rybalko and the 4th Tank Army under
General Lelyushenko went into action and emerged into the operational space, destroying the enemy reserves which were
coming up.

In his memoirs on the Battle of Vistula German General
K. Tippelskirch gives the following description of the offensive:

"The blow was so strong that it toppled not only the 1st
echelon divisions but also the rather large mobile reserves
that had been drawn up quite close to the front lines on Hitler's peremptory orders. These reserves had already suffered
during the Russian artillery preparation, and later when the
general retreat started they could not be used as planned at all."[1]

To his account I can only add that those reserves could not
be used in any case, since they had been annihilated by
the forces of the 1st Ukrainian and 1st Byelorussian Fronts.

On January 17, Rybalko's 3rd Guards Tank Army and the
5th Guards Army under Zhadov captured Częstochowa, while
the 59th and 60th armies began engagements at the northern approaches to Cracow.

After six days of offensive operations the 1st Ukrainian
Front had advanced 150 km and reached the Radom-Często-
chowa-north of Cracow-Tarnów line. The situation was favourable for the Front to continue its advance towards the Oder.

The 1st Byelorussian Front, which had started the offensive
on January 14, was also successfully continuing the operation.

General K. Tippelskirch writes:

"By the evening of January 16 (i.e. the third day of the
offensive.— *Author*) there was no continued, organically connected German front in the sector between the Rivers Pilica
and Nida. The units of the 9th Army still holding on the Vistula
near Warsaw and south of it were in grave danger. There were
no more reserves."[2]

On January 17, the 1st Byelorussian Front and the 1st Ukrainian Front came abreast. That day the units of the 1st Army

---

of Wojsko Polskie took Warsaw. Along with them came elements of the Soviet 47th and 61st armies.

Just as happened after the German defeat outside Moscow, when Warsaw fell Hitler severely punished his commanding generals. Colonel-General Harpe, Commander of the Army Group A, was replaced by Colonel-General Schörner; and General Luttwitz, Commander of the 9th Army, by Infantry General Busse.

After the Military Council of the Front had looked over the ravaged city, it reported to the Supreme Commander:

"The fascist barbarians have destroyed Warsaw, capital of Poland. With sadistic cruelty the Hitlerites demolished one block of houses after another. The largest industrial enterprises have been razed to the ground. Houses have been either blown up or burnt down. The municipal economy is disrupted. Thousands upon thousands of civilians have been exterminated, the rest driven out. It is a dead city."

Listening to people from Warsaw tell about Nazi atrocities during the occupation and especially before the retreat, one found it hard to understand the psychology and moral character of the enemy

Polish officers and men took the destruction of the city especially hard. I saw battle-scarred Polish soldiers shed tears, and pledge then and there to take revenge on the fiendish foe. As for Soviet soldiers, we were all embittered and determined to aptly punish the enemy for the atrocities committed.

Boldly and swiftly breaking down all enemy resistance, our troops were rapidly gaining ground.

With the operation developing successfully, on January 17, the Supreme Command specified the tasks of the Fronts on the Oder sector:

The 1st Byelorussian Front was to reach the Bydgoszcz-Poznán line by February 2 or 4;

The 1st Ukrainian Front was to contain the offensive with its main force towards Breslau (Wroclaw), and not later than by January 30 to approach the Oder south of Leszno and establish a bridgehead on the left bank. Its left flank was to liberate Cracow by February 20-22.

To check the advance of the 1st Byelorussian Front the German High Command redeployed Panzer Division Gross

Deutschland, to the Lódz area from East Prussia, and five more divisions from the West. However, those forces were destroyed even before they could properly deploy for combat. Our thrust was so swift and so stunning that the Germans abandoned all hope of stopping the Soviet troops anywhere in Poland.

Lódz fell on January 19, and on January 23, the Front's right flank forces captured Bydgoszcz. On the morning of January 22, the units of the 1st Guards Tank Army commenced fighting at the approaches to Poznan. The 69th Army and then the 8th Guards Army soon drew up near Poznan. The left flank of the front reached the area of Jarocin and established tactical cooperation with the right wing of the 1st Ukrainian Front.

On January 25, the Supreme Commander called me up during the day, and, having listened to my report, asked what we were going to do next.

"The enemy is demoralized and unable to offer any considerable resistance," I replied. "We have decided to continue the offensive until we reach the Oder. Our main direction is towards Küstrin (Kostrzyn) where we will try to seize a bridgehead. Our right flank will turn north and north-west to face the East Pomeranian grouping which as yet presents no immediate serious danger."

"When you reach the Oder you will be separated from the 2nd Byelorussian Front by more than 150 kilometres," Stalin said. "We cannot afford that now. We will have to wait for the 2nd Byelorussian Front to finish its operation in East Prussia and move its forces out beyond the Vistula."

"How much time will that take?"

"Ten days or so. Besides," Stalin added, "right now the 1st Ukrainian Front will not be able to continue its advance and protect you on the left, because it will be engaged for some time liquidating the enemy in the area of Oppeln (Opole) and Katowice."

"I ask your permission not to stop the offensive," I said, "because later it will be more difficult for us to penetrate the Miedzyrzecz fortified line. It will suffice to give the front one more army to protect the right flank."

The Supreme Commander said he would think it over, but we did not hear from him that day.

On January 26, the reconnaissance group of the 1st Guards Tank Army reached the Miedzyrzecz fortified line, and captured a large group of officers and men. From prisoners' statements it appeared that the line was not yet manned in many places, and that units were just moving out to fill in the gaps. The Front Command decided to accelerate the advance of the main forces towards the Oder and to try and seize bridgeheads on the western bank on the march.

To protect the main forces of the Front moving towards the Oder from possible blows of the enemy forces in East Pomerania, we decided to turn the 3rd Shock Army, the 47th Army, the 61st Army, the 2nd Guards Cavalry Corps and the 1st Army of Wojsko Polskie to the front facing north.

Sections of the 8th Guards Army, the 69th Army and the 1st Guards Tank Army were left behind to deal with the garrison in Poznań. The 8th Guards Army under the command of General Chuikov was assigned to seize Poznań. It was then believed that surrounded in the city were 20,000 troops at most, but actually it turned out that there were over 60,000. So fighting in the fortified city dragged out until February 23.

According to our calculations, the enemy could not organize a counterblow from Pomerania before the Front forces reached the Oder. If any serious danger cropped up, we still had time to regroup part of the forces from the Oder to knock out the Pomeranian grouping. This is what later happened.

After further consultations, the Supreme Commander consented to the Front Command's plan, instructing us to take good care of our right flank. As for reinforcements, he refused us any. The Supreme Command's concern about our right flank proved absolutely correct. Subsequent events showed that the threat from East Pomerania was building up.

Our offensive was swiftly moving ahead. The main forces of the Front, having knocked out isolated enemy units and crushed the resistance on the Miedzyrzecz fortified line, reached the Oder between February 1 and 4, and seized a very important bridgehead on the western bank in the area of Küstrin (Kostrzyn).

Here it is impossible for me not to dwell at some length on the heroic deeds of the 5th Shock Army, headed by

Lieutenant-General Berzarin and Lieutenant-General Bokov, Member of the Military Council.

The advance detachment of the 5th Shock Army played a key role in seizing the bridgehead. The detachment was led by Colonel H. F. Yesipenko, Deputy Commander of the 89th Guards Rifle Division, and Lieutenant-Colonel D. D. Shaposhnikov, Representative of the Military Council of the 5th Army and deputy chief of the army's Political Department.

The detachment consisted of the 1006th Rifle Regiment of the 266th Rifle Division, the 220th Detached Tank Brigade under Colonel A. N. Pashkov, the 89th Detached Heavy Tank Regiment, a tank destroyer regiment, and the 489th Mortar Regiment.

By the morning of January 31, the advance detachment forced the Oder, and seized a bridgehead in the area of Kienitz, Gross, Neuendorf and Rehfeld.

The appearance of Soviet troops only 70 km from Berlin utterly astounded the Germans.

At the moment the detachment burst into the town of Kienitz, German soldiers were blissfully walking the streets, and officers were sitting at a restaurant. Trains on the Kienitz-Berlin line were running on schedule, and communications were operating normally.

Colonel Terekhin, infantry battalion commanders Kravtsov, Platonov and Cherednik, and artillery battalion commanders Zharkov and Ilyashchenko organized solid defences at the bridgehead. Both officers and men realized that the Germans would do everything they possibly could to drive the detachment back beyond the Oder.

In the morning of February 2, the enemy launched a sweeping artillery and mortar attack on the positions held by the detachment. Soon after that attack the Luftwaffe came. The bridgehead ground shook with the bursting of shells, mines and bombs. The hurricane of fire raged for about an hour. Then enemy troops, supported by armour, attacked our advance detachment from three directions.

Ignoring his heavy losses, the enemy pushed stubbornly ahead. His armour even succeeded in breaking through to our artillery positions and destroying several batteries. The situation was critical. Enemy tanks threatened to emerge into the detachment's immediate rear, and once that happened, it would hardly be able to hold out. Things reached the point that Captain Kravtsov's battery had only one anti-tank gun left. The gun crew under Senior Sergeant Belsky engaged eight enemy tanks.

There were only thirteen shells left.

Belsky counted them again — yes, only thirteen, and eight tanks.

"We'll fire point-blank to cinch it," Belsky told his men. "We've got to stop the enemy, even if we die doing it."

Senior Sergeant Belsky and his comrades, Kargin and Kcheryusov, were experienced soldiers. The outcome of the battle depended on their fortitude and skill.

They had rolled the gun into a barn, smashed a hole in the wall, and set the gun for direct fire. They were under cover, and could score broadside hits.

The clanging of tracks was already audible. Senior Sergeant Belsky was behind the gun. The leading tank was no more than 150 m away. The cross on its turret was plainly visible.

As coolly as he could, Belsky drew a bead on the tank and waited. Fire. The shell hit the fuel tank. At once red flames danced over the machine. The second shell also hit home — another tank spun helplessly with a broken track. A minute later, a third tank burst into flames. This was real precision firing.

Smoke was rising over the five enemy tanks which had been stopped dead before our lines. The remaining three had turned back.

For courage and valour displayed in that battle, Senior Sergeant Belsky received the Order of the Red Banner. The rest of the crew received other awards.

Following up the advance detachment, the 26th Guards Rifle Corps under Lieutenant-General P. A. Firsov (with Colonel D. N. Andreyev as Chief of the Political Department) began expanding the bridgehead.

The Corps' 94th Guards Division, commanded by Lieutenant-Colonel B. I. Baranov, and Chief of the Political Department Colonel S. V. Kuzovkov, forced the Oder. The 286th and 283rd Guards regiments engaged and overran the enemy at the bridgehead. The Division's 199th Guards Artillery

Regiment fought courageously in that battle (Lieutenant-Colonel I. F. Zherebtsov, commander, and Major V. I. Oryabinsky, his deputy for political affairs).

Senior Lieutenant Mironov's battery fought with particular skill. During an enemy attack, Battery Commander Mironov was wounded, and Senior Lieutenant Avelichev took over for him. Together with the infantry the battery beat off six enemy attacks that day. Senior Sergeant Shvetsov and Sergeant Volkov, leaders of the battery Party organizations, were especially dauntless.

The officers and men of the 2nd Battalion of the 1050th Rifle Regiment (Battalion Commander, F. K. Shapovalov; his deputy for political affairs, I. F. Osipov) displayed mass heroism. Under adverse conditions they beat off attack after attack by the enemy's infantry and armour.

The officers and men of the 3rd Battalion under A. F. Bogomolov were really magnificent. Although severely wounded, the commander refused to leave the battleground, and continued directing the action of his troops. Bogomolov died, and for heroism and valour was posthumously awarded the title of Hero of the Soviet Union.

All officers, NCOs and men of the 1st Battalion of the 1008th Rifle Regiment received orders or medals for that action. Battalion Commander M. A. Alexeyev and Senior Lieutenant Kulinur Usenbekov, battalion Party leader, were awarded the high title of Hero of the Soviet Union. The Order of Suvorov, 3rd Class was conferred on the 1008th and 1010th Rifle regiments of the 266th Division for mass heroism.

The men of the 1054th Regiment (the 301st Rifle Division) under Lieutenant-Colonel N. N. Radaev fought several days of sustained battles. Thanks to his advantageous positions on the heights and his earlier entrenchment in the brick houses of the area, the enemy was able to hold out against the advancing regiment. All the approaches to the enemy defences that Radaev's regiment was to break through were kept under heavy enemy fire from all sorts of guns. The Soviet troops had to wade across terrain waterlogged by melting snow.

At dawn, our guns opened fire along the whole sector. Soviet artillery fired on trenches and previously detected points and other Nazi firing positions.

And almost immediately afterwards, the regiment units went into attack. As always, Communists and Young Communist League members were in the front lines. Lieutenant I. F. Senichkin, Komsomol Organizer of the 3rd Rifle Battalion, who led his men into attack, fought with distinction.

During the attack our troops drove the enemy out of the trenches and eliminated two defensive positions. But the enemy troops soon regained their composure, concentrated their forces, and began a counter-attack. And in one sector they were even able to break through and push us back.

However, the Germans were unable to get very far. The 3rd Battalion struck a powerful blow, crushed them, and successfully continued the offensive. For courage and valour in this battle, Senichkin was awarded the Order of the Patriotic War 2nd grade.

In the history of the Great Patriotic War, there are hosts of similar episodes in which one can see the heroism of the Soviet soldier.

After many days of fierce fighting, the bridgehead was expanded. It was from that jumping-off position that the striking force of the 1st Byelorussian Front began its Berlin offensive.

Enemy resistance on the right flank of the front had become considerably stiffer by then. Air and ground reconnaissance detected the movement and concentration of considerable enemy forces in East Pomerania.

Swift and determined action was required to eliminate the threat from the north. On February 2, the Military Council of the Front had already ordered the 1st Guards Tank Army to leave its positions on the Oder to the neighbouring units to attend to, and to move out by forced march to the Arnswalde area. The 9th Tank and the 7th Guards Cavalry Corps were also redeployed there, and many artillery and engineer units and plentiful supplies streamed into the area.

The German counter-offensive from East Pomerania was becoming more imminent every day.

On January 31, the Military Council of the Front sent the following report to the Supreme Commander:

"1. Because of the sizable lag of the 2nd Byelorussian Front's left wing behind the right flank of the 1st Byelorussian Front, our attack frontage has reached 500 km, as of late January 31.

"If Rokossovsky's left flank continues to stand still, the enemy will undoubtedly take resolute action against the stretched-out right flank of the 1st Byelorussian Front.

"Ask you to order Rokossovsky to immediately begin advancing his 70th Army westward, even at the level of the rear echelon of the 1st Byelorussian Front's right flank.

"2. Ask for instructions to Konev to gain the Oder line as soon as he can.

"Zhukov, Telegin."

We received no prompt reply to this message, nor did we get any material help. It was only on February 8 that the Supreme Command ordered the 2nd Byelorussian Front to launch an offensive two days later from the Graudenz-Ratzeburg line to knock out the East Pomeranian grouping, capture Danzig, and gain the Baltic Sea coast.

On February 10, the 2nd Byelorussian Front began the offensive, but did not have the strength to be able to complete its mission. With the arrival of the fresh 19th Army from the Supreme Command Reserve, the 2nd Byelorussian Front resumed its offensive operations on February 24.

The 1st Byelorussian Front, whose chief striking force consisted of the 1st and 2nd Guards Tank armies, started the offensive on March 1. The powerful thrust of that force greatly facilitated the advance of the 2nd Byelorussian Front.

On March 4-5, the forces of the 1st Byelorussian Front gained the Baltic Sea coast, while the forces of the 2nd Byelorussian Front also reached the coast, and on March 4 captured Köslin (Koszalin), after which it turned east — towards Gdynia and Danzig (Gdańsk). By the Supreme Command order the 1st Tank Army of the 1st Byelorussian Front, which had advanced to the area of Kolberg (Kołobrzeg), was temporarily assigned to the 2nd Byelorussian Front to destroy the enemy in the Gdynia area. Meanwhile, the right wing of the 1st Byelorussian Front, mopping up the shattered enemy forces, was moving out to the Baltic coast and to the lower Oder.

Here I believe it is in place to examine at greater length an issue repeatedly brought up by some writers of memoirs, particularly Marshal Chuikov: why didn't the command of the 1st Byelorussian Front, after its forces had gained the Oder at the beginning of February, press the Supreme Command for permission to continue the advance on Berlin without stopping?

In his reminiscences Chuikov asserts that "Berlin could have been taken already in February. And that, of course, would have brought the end of the war nearer."

Several military experts have written articles opposing this viewpoint; however, Chuikov considers that "objections are being heard not from active participants in Operation Vistula-Oder but from either those who took part in working out orders for Stalin and for the Front to halt the Berlin offensive and launch an East Pomeranian operation, or from authors of some historical works".

I must say that there was more to the Berlin offensive than Marshal Chuikov appears to see.

When on January 26, it became clear that the enemy would not be able to sustain our attack on the fortified areas at the approaches to the Oder, we advanced a tentative plan of action to the Supreme Command. Its essence was as follows:

By January 30, the forces of the Front were to gain the Berlinchen (Barlinek)-Landsberg (Gorzów Wielkopolski)-Grätz (Grodzisk) line, bring up the rear, replenish supplies, and on the morning of February 1 or 2, resume the offensive so as to force the Oder on the march.

From there they were to heighten the offensive on the Berlin sector, directing their main effort towards skirting Berlin on the north-east, north and north-west.

The Supreme Command endorsed this plan on January 27.

On January 28, Marshal Konev, Commander of the 1st Ukrainian Front, submitted a similar plan to the Supreme Command. Basically, it involved knocking out the Breslau grouping, reaching the Elbe by February 25 or 28, and having the right flank forces in coordination with the 1st Byelorussian Front, capture Berlin.

That plan was also endorsed by the Supreme Command on January 29.

Chuikov is right when he says that at the time the enemy had limited strength at the approaches to Berlin, and his defences were rather weak. That was clear to us. As a result, the Command of the Front issued the troops the following orientation:

"Attention of Military Councils of all armies, commanders of fighting services and the chief of rearguard forces.

"Below are tentative calculations for the immediate future and a brief situation estimate:

"1. The enemy confronting the 1st Byelorussian Front has up to now no sufficiently large groupings for a counter-attack.

"The enemy has no permament line of defence either. He is now protecting a number of directions, and is trying to organize mobile defence in several sectors.

"According to preliminary information, the enemy has removed four tank divisions and five or six infantry divisions from his Western theatre, and is moving them over to the Eastern theatre. As the same time the enemy is continuing the troop transfer from the Baltic area and from East Prussia.

"In all probability, in the next six or seven days the enemy will deploy the incoming forces along the Schwedt-Stargard-Neustettin line so as to cover Pomerania, and deny us Stettin and access to the Pomeranian Bay.

"The forces being transferred from the West will evidently be deployed in the area of Berlin to cover approaches to the city.

"2. The task of the front forces is for the next six days to consolidate the gains by vigorous action; bring up everything that needs bringing up; replenish supplies, bringing them up to a double supply of fuel; and two ammunition sets; by sweeping assault to capture Berlin on February 15 or 16.

"To consolidate the gains (that is, between February 4 and 8) it is necessary:

"a)   for the 5th, 8th, 69th and 33rd armies to seize bridgeheads on the western bank of the Oder. Consequently, it is preferable that the 8th Guards and the 69th armies have a common bridgehead between Küstrin and Frankfurt. It would be good, if possible, if the bridgeheads of the 5th and 8th armies were merged;

"b) for the 1st Army of Wojsko Polskie, the 47th and 61st armies, the 2nd Tank Army and the 2nd Cavalry Corps to throw the enemy back beyond the Ratzeburg-Falkenburg-Stargard-Altdamm-River Oder line. After that they are to leave a covering force until the armies of the 2nd Byelorussian Front pull up, and then redeploy along the Oder for a breakthrough;

"c) to complete liquidation of the Poznań-Schneidemühl enemy grouping by February 7 or 8;

"d) to note that reinforcement means for the breakthrough will be the same as what the army possesses today;

"e) for tank and self-propelled artillery units to restore to service materiel now in running and medium repair by February 10;

"f) for the air force to complete deployment and to have at least six fuel refilling supplies at the airfields;

"g) for the front, army and immediate rear units to be in full readiness for the decisive phase of the operation by February 9 or 10.

"Zhukov, Telegin, Malinin."

However, as was pointed out before, the danger of a counter-blow from East Pomerania against the flank and rear of the Front's main force that was advancing towards the Oder began to loom large in early February. Here is what Field Marshal Keitel stated during an interrogation:

"...In February and March 1945 it was planned to launch a counter-offensive against the forces advancing on Berlin, using Pomerania as the jumping-off place. It was expected that having established cover in the area of Grudziądz (Graudenz) the Army Group Vistula would break through the Russian lines and, moving along the Warta and Netze river valleys, approach Küstrin from the rear."

This thinking is also confirmed by Colonel-General Guderian. In his *Memoirs of a Soldier* he writes: "The German Command was going to deliver a shattering counterblow with lightning speed by the Army Group Vistula before the Russians had time to bring up large forces or had guessed our intentions."

The cited testimony by military leaders of fascist Germany proves beyond all doubt that the danger from East Pomerania was very real. However, the Command of the 1st Byelorussian Front took the decisive counter-measures required.

Operating between the Oder and the Vistula in early February were the German 2nd and 11th armies, which had 22 divisions, including 4 tank and 2 motorized divisions; 5 brigades, and 8 combat groups. According to our intelligence, replacements kept coming up to the area.

Besides, the 3rd Panzer Army was deployed in the area of Stettin (Szczecin), which the German Command could use either to protect the Berlin direction, or to reinforce the East Pomeranian grouping (the latter, in fact, happened).

How could the Soviet Command take the risk of continuing the Berlin offensive with such a grave danger looming in the north?

Chuikov writes: "...As for risk, it has often to be taken in war. And in that particular instance, the risk was well worth taking — during Operation Vistula-Oder our troops had covered over 500 km, and only from 60 to 80 km stood between the Oder and Berlin."

Of course, we could have ignored the danger and let both tank armies, along with 3 or 4 field armies move straight in the direction of Berlin and come close to the city. But the enemy, striking from the north, could easily have broken through our cover and gained the passages across the Oder, putting our forces near Berlin in an extremely difficult position.

War experience shows that taking risks is advisable, but one should not overreach oneself. In this respect, the lesson learned by the Red Army during the Warsaw offensive in 1920 is very instructive, when its headlong, unprotected advance led, instead of success, to the overwhelming defeat of our Western Front.

"If we objectively estimate the strength of the Hitlerite grouping in Pomerania," Chuikov writes, "we see that any threat from it to our striking grouping on the Berlin sector could be successfully localized by the forces of the 2nd Byelorussian Front."

Facts upset this contention.

Initially, the task of routing the enemy in East Pomerania was supposed to be the sole responsibility of the forces of the

2nd Byelorussian Front. However, their strength proved to be totally insufficient. The offensive of that Front, begun on February 10, proceeded very slowly — its troops covered only 50 to 70 km in ten days.

At that moment the enemy launched a counter-attack south of Stargard and even succeeded in pressing our troops back, gaining some 12 km southward.

In view of the situation, the Supreme Command decided to move four field and two tank armies from the 1st Byelorussian Front in order to liquidate the East Pomeranian grouping, whose strength had by then grown to 40 divisions.

As is known, joint operations by the two Fronts to knock out the East Pomeranian grouping were completed only towards the end of March. You can see what a hard nut that grouping was.

Chuikov believes that the 1st Byelorussian and the 1st Ukrainian Fronts could detach from 8 to 10 armies, including 3 or 4 tank armies, to advance on Berlin in February 1945.

It is impossible to agree with this either. At the beginning of February, of the eight field and two tank armies of the 1st Byelorussian Front, only four short-strength armies were left on the Berlin sector the 5th Shock, half the 8th Guards, the 69th and 33rd armies.[1] The rest of the forces had been diverted to East Pomerania to crush the enemy grouping there.

As for the 1st Ukrainian Front, in the period between February 8 and 24, it was conducting an offensive operation north-west of Breslau (Wrocław). The main forces of that Front — four field, two tank and the 2nd Air Army — were engaged. The enemy had moved up considerable forces and was offering stubborn resistance.

In 17 days of the offensive, the 1st Ukrainian Front forces gained 100 km and reached the River Neisse. Attempts to force it and accelerate the offensive westward were unsuccessful; and the forces of the Front assumed the defensive along the east bank of the river.

It should also be borne in mind that our strength had been considerably sapped in the course of Operation Vistula-Oder. As of February 1, infantry divisions were, on the average,

---

[1] One corps from the 8th Guards and one from the 69th Army were fighting for Poznań.— *Author.*

5,500 strong, but, for instance, the 8th Guards had only from 3,800 to 4,800 officers and men. The number of tanks in the two tank armies was 740, an average of 40 per brigade, whereas in fact many brigades had only 15-20 tanks. Things were approximately the same with the 1st Ukrainian Front.

To top everything off, the fortress and the city of Poznan, deep in the rear of the front, were still held by the enemy. Chuikov's army did not take them until February 23.

The problem of logistical support should not be overlooked either. In 20 days, our troops advanced more than 500 km. Naturally, at this rate of advance, logistical establishments had fallen behind, and the troops were short of supplies, especially fuel. Similarly, the air force could not redeploy either because a rainy spell had turned all the airfields into bogs.

Chuikov, who had not analyzed all the complexity of the logistical situation, writes: "...Had General Hadquarters and Front HQs organized supplies properly, so as to have sufficient amounts of ammunition, fuel and provisions on the Oder, had the air force redeployed in time to airfields near the Oder, and the pontoon bridge-building units ensured passage across the Oder, four of our armies — the 5th Shock, the 8th Guards, the 1st and 2nd Tank — could in early February have stepped up the Berlin offensive further and, gaining another 80 or 100 km, completed that mammoth operation by taking the German capital on the march."

This "if so-and-so had..." kind of speculation on such an important point cannot be considered serious, even for a writer of memoirs. However, Chuikov's admission that supplies were disorganized and that the air force and pontoon bridge-building units had lagged behind points to the fact that in the circumstances it would have been utterly adventurist to launch a decisive offensive on Berlin.

It follows that neither the 1st Ukrainian nor the 1st Byelorussian Fronts could conduct the Berlin operation in February 1945.

Chuikov writes: "On February 4, the Commander of the 1st Byelorussian Front called army commanders Berzarin, Kolpakchi, Katukov, Bogdanov and myself to the headquarters of the 69th Army where he had just arrived, for a conference. We were already sitting at tables discussing the plan of the Berlin offensive when a call came over radiotelephone. I sat practically next to the RT set, and could hear the conversation well. It was Stalin calling. He asked Zhukov where he was and what he was doing. Marshal Zhukov replied that he was in conference with army commanders at the headquarters of Kolpakchi's army, planning the Berlin offensive with them.

"After listening to the report, Stalin told the Commander of the Front — and I understood it came as a surprise to him — to stop planning the Berlin offensive, and start working out an operation to deal with the German Army Group Vistula in Pomerania."

However, there was no such conference at the headquarters of the 69th Army on February 4. For that reason there could not either have been any RT conversation with Stalin, about which Chuikov writes.

On February 4 and 5, I was at the headquarters of the 61st Army which was deployed on the right wing of the front in Pomerania for action against the Pomeranian grouping. Nor could Commander of the 1st Guards Tank Army Katukov have been at that mythical conference either, because following a Front directive of February 2, 1945 (No. 00244) he had been, since the morning of February 3, conducting the redeployment of troops from the Oder to the area of Friedberg, Berlinchen and Landsberg.

As well, the Commander of the 2nd Guards Tank Army Bogdanov could not have been there either, because he was ill (General Radzievsky was then acting commander). As for Chuikov himself, on February 3 he was in Poznań, from where he sent me a message on the progress of fighting for the city and the fortress.

Chuikov's memory must have failed him.

It should be pointed out that only half the units of Chuikov's 8th Guards Army came up to the Oder. The rest were engaged in Poznań until February 23.

After some of the Front's forces were drawn off to Pomerania there were in fact three and a half armies left on the Oder on the Berlin sector and in early February the situation began to get complicated. On February 2 and 3, the Luftwaffe continually bombed the combat formations of Berzarin's 5th Shock Army at its bridgehead on the Oder. During those two days, the

German aircraft flew over 5,000 combat missions, inflicting heavy losses on the 5th Army.

The enemy was trying to eliminate the Küstrin bridgehead at whatever cost. Units were brought up from other fronts. The commander of the 5th Army Berzarin asked for more air support. However, the weather prevented our air force from active operations.

One of my telegrams to the Military Council of the 5th Army will provide an idea of the sutuation that had developed.

"Attention of the Military Council, Corps Commanders and Division Commanders of the 5th Shock Army:

"The 5th Shock Army has been assigned an especially important mission — that of holding the bridgehead on the west bank of the Oder and expanding it at least up to 20 km in frontage and 10 or 20 km in depth.

"I ask that you all understand your responsible historic role in carrying out your mission and, after explaining this to your men, to demand that they display the utmost fortitude and courage.

"Unfortunately, we cannot yet help you with aircraft, because all the airfields have turned into bogs and the planes cannot take off. Enemy planes are flying from Berlin aerodromes with concerete runways. I recommend:

"1) to dig in deep;

"2) to organize massive anti-aircraft fire;

"3) to move to night combat operations, launching each attack with a limited objective;

"4) to repulse enemy attacks during the day.

"In another two or three days the enemy will be washed out.

"I wish you and your troops historic success which you not only can, but must ensure.

"G. Zhukov."

Chuikov claims that it was he who first raised the issue of the possibility of capturing Berlin in February 1945 at a military science conference in Berlin later that year, but that the issue was not properly considered when he first raised it.

This question was certainly raised at the conference, only not by Chuikov, but by Major-General S. M. Yenyukov, representative of the General Staff. As far as I can remember, and as can be seen from the stenographic records of his report, Chuikov did not say a word on the subject.

But to get back to the events of March 1945.

The 2nd and 1st Byelorussian Fronts completed the East Pomeranian operation and wiped out the enemy grouping; by late March, they had occupied all of East Pomerania. In February and March, the 1st Ukrainian Front carried out two operations in Silesia, and by the end of March had reached the Neisse, coming abreast of the 1st Byelorussian Front forces which by then had gained the Oder.

As a result of Operation Vistula-Oder, most of Poland was liberated, and the fighting carried over to German soil. Sixty German divisions had been knocked out. To build up a new defence line on the Berlin sector, the German Command had to bring up 29 divisions and 4 brigades drawn off from other sections of the Soviet-German front, the Western Front, and from the Italian Front.

The Soviet offensive between the Vistula and the Oder is a brilliant example of a powerful strategic offensive operation, which proceeded without any pauses at an average rate of advance of 25-30 km a day and 45 km by tank armies (up to 70 km on some days).

This pace was the most rapid ever attained in the course of the Great Patriotic War.

The large scale of the strategic operation and its rapid pace were above all the result of the improved general situation on the fronts, the excellent fighting spirit of the Soviet troops, the favourably changing balance of forces, the further accumulation of combat, operational and strategic expertise.

The decisive role in exploiting the success after the breakthrough was played by tank armies and detached tank and mechanized corps. In cooperation with the air force, like a fast-moving ram of colossal power, they cleared the way for the field armies.

Once they entered the breach, tank armies and mechanized corps stepped up the offensive without a let-up day and night, giving the enemy no respite. Powerful advance detachments made deep thrusts, and did not engage in prolonged engagements with individual enemy groupings.

In close cooperation with the air force, tank armies and detached tank corps used swift thrusts to break the crust of enemy defence, cut his communication lines, seized passages and road junctions, demoralized the enemy, and disorganized his rear.

By striking deep into the enemy rear, the Soviet armour prevented the German troops from utilizing most of their permanent, solid defences. After his fortified lines on the Vistula were breached and until the time the Soviet forces reached the Poznań meridian, the enemy could not make a firm stand on even one of his deliberately organized positions.

The plan to deceive the enemy that had been worked out by the Soviet Command for Operation Vistula-Oder was totally successful, and the element of operational and tactical surprise was achieved. There are many statements by captured officers and men which show that the German Command had no idea whatsoever of our plans when our offensive began.

Here are some of those statements.

Captain Petzoldt stated:

"I am positive that even on January 14, 1945, the German command did not know even the direction of the Russian main effort. Nor did they know the Russian strength."

Senior Lieutenant Hans Wissenger stated:

"From our experience of past years, we were convinced that this year the Russians would also take the offensive in winter. The German Command counted on that. However, the start of the offensive showed that our command was, in any case, unaware either of the scope of this offensive, or its principal objective."

Senior Lieutenant Kosfeld stated:

"The German Command expected a Russian offensive at the end of December 1944. Later, officers often said it would start before January 15, 1945. The exact date of the offensive, however, was never known."

Each shot from our side made the enemy jump, of course. He was expecting us to strike, although he had no idea of the scope of our offensive, and evidently counted on our launching it from the bridgeheads, for there would hardly be anyone in favour of starting a major offensive with the forcing of a river as mighty and wide as the Vistula, and extending the initial phase. True, there were analogous suggestions coming from some of the front's operation officers. Those officers considered that the enemy had deeply-organized defences directly in front of our bridgeheads, whereas other sections on the Vistula were used only as covering.

But to adopt that plan would mean forcing a kilometre-wide river under utterly adverse conditions, where it was impossible to bring armour — that most important instrument of break-through — into action immediately. Mobile troops and most of the artillery could not then be ferried across fast enough to ensure a swift advance.

It goes without saying that jumping off from the bridgeheads involved a considerable disadvantage: enemy artillery and air force could punish us severely. But we had planned formidable counter-artillery and air strikes.

As far as supplies are concerned, Operation Vistula-Oder was organized well. The logistical agencies of the Front and armies had done an excellent job.

However, by the time our troops reached the Miedzyrzecz fortified line and the so-called Pomeranian Rampart, the armies began to run short of fuel and lubricants, and of the more urgently needed ammunition. There were several reasons for this, mainly that we were advancing twice as fast as had been envisaged. Rear communications lines stretched hundreds of kilometres while the main railway lines were still out of opera-tion because of the vast damage done to them, and there were no railway bridges across the Vistula.

From the information furnished by the Supreme Comman-der and the General Staff, I knew that during January, Februa-ry and March the troops of the 4th Ukrainian Front were ad-vancing in the Carpathians, assisting the 1st Ukrainian Front in carrying out its missions.

Meanwhile, in January, February and the first half of March, the forces of the 2nd and 3rd Ukrainian Fronts were fighting defensive battles, repulsing the enemy who tried to throw them back beyond the Danube and relieve his forces blockaded in Budapest and, thereby strengthen the Hungarian sector of his front.

In bitter fighting, the 2nd and 3rd Ukrainian Fronts inflicted a shattering defeat on the enemy striking forces, foiling all their attempts to reach the Danube; by mid-March they had created conditions enabling us to go onto the offensive on the Vienna sector.

Between March 16 and April 15 the forces of the 2nd and 3rd Ukrainian Fronts carried out the Vienna offensive operation, routing over 30 divisions of the Army Group South.

By mid-April, our troops had liberated all of Hungary and much of Czechoslovakia; they had entered Austria and liberated Vienna, gaining access to the central regions of Czechoslovakia. Germany finally lost its oil wells in Hungary and Austria, as well as many munitions and military supply factories.

Between January and April 1945, as a result of operations by the 2nd and 3rd Ukrainian Fronts, our southern strategic flank was brought forward abreast of the Fronts on the Berlin sector. Having reached the eastern bank of the Oder and the Neisse from the Baltic Sea down to Görlitz and protected the flanks, the Soviet troops had advantageous jumping-off positions for the final defeat of the Berlin grouping and the storming of Berlin.

On the left flank of the Soviet-German front our troops, after reaching the area of Vienna and south of it, took up advantageous positions for advancing deeper into Austria and the southern regions of Germany.

On the Western theatre, the armed forces of our Allies forced the Rhine in February and March, and surrounded a sizable German force in the Ruhr. On April 17, the encircled troops surrendered.

After the main German forces were destroyed on the Soviet-German front and the Allies had crossed the Rhine, Nazi Germany faced its doom. It had no strength left to continue fighting.

As the end of the war drew near, several political issues in our relations with the Allies became exacerbated. This should have come as no surprise.

The former sluggishness in the actions of the Anglo-American Command was replaced by utmost haste. The governments of Great Britain and the USA were prodding the command of the expeditionary forces in Europe to demand that the Allied troops advance faster into the central parts of Germany so as to occupy them before the Soviet Army moved in.

Churchill wrote to Roosevelt on April 1, 1945:

"The Russian armies will no doubt overrun all Austria and enter Vienna. If they also take Berlin will not their impression that they have been the overwhelming contributor to our common victory be unduly imprinted in their minds, and may this not lead them into a mood which will raise grave and formidable difficulties in the future? I therefore consider that from a political standpoint we should march as far east into Germany as possible, and that should Berlin be in our grasp we should certainly take it."[1]

I later learned that the British Command and several American generals had done everything to ensure that the Allied forces would capture Berlin and areas to the north and south.

In the course of the East Pomeranian operation, most likely on March 7 or 8, I had to urgently fly to the General Headquarters on order from the Supreme Commander.

Straight from the airfield I went to Stalin's country house where he was staying. He was not in the best of health.

Stalin asked me a few questions about the situation in Pomerania and on the Oder, heard out my answers, then said: "Let's stretch our legs a little, I feel sort of limp."

From the way he looked, talked and moved you could tell that he was extremely fatigued. After four years of war he was utterly overworked. He had worked overly hard and slept too little all that time, taking reverses, particularly those of 1941-1942, close to heart. All was bound to tell on his health and nervous system.

As we were strolling through the park, Stalin unexpectedly began telling me about his childhood.

We spent at least an hour chatting. Stalin then said:

"Let's get back and have tea; I want to talk something over with you."

On our way back I said: "Comrade Stalin, I've been meaning to ask you for a long time about your son Yakov. Have you heard anything about him?"

Stalin did not answer at once. We took a good hundred steps before he said in a kind of subdued voice:

"Yakov won't be let free. The fascists will shoot him first. From what we know, they are keeping him separate from

[1] Winston S. Churchill, *The Second World War*, Vol. VI, Cassel and Co. Ltd., London, 1954, p. 407.

the other POWs, and are putting pressure on him to betray
his country."

Stalin was silent for a minute, then said firmly: "No, Yakov wil prefer any kind of death to betrayal."

It was obvious that he was deeply worried about his son.
At the table, Stalin sat silent for a long time, not touching
his food.

Then, as though continuing his thoughts aloud, he said
bitterly:

"What a terrible war. How many lives of our people it has
carried away. There are probably very few families of us left
who haven't lost someone near to them... Only the Soviet
people, tempered in battle, and imbued with great spirit by
the Communist Party, could endure trials and tribulations
of this magnitude."

Stalin then told me about the Yalta Conference. I understood that he was pleased with the results, and thought very
highly of Roosevelt. Stalin said that he was still trying to get
the Allies to take the offensive so as to finish off Nazi
Germany more quickly. By the time of the Yalta Conference
our troops had reached the Oder and were fighting fierce
battles in East Prussia, in the Baltic, in Hungary and other
areas. Stalin had insisted that the Allies, who were 500 km
from Berlin, mount an offensive. An agreement was reached,
and after that the coordination of action between both sides
considerably improved.

Stalin told me at length about agreements with the Allies
concerning the administration of Germany after its capitulation, about "the control mechanism in Germany", the occupation zones its territory would be divided into, and what was
to be the link-up line for the Soviet and Allied forces.

He did not allude to the details of the organization of
"the control mechanism" or of the surpeme power in Germany. I was briefed on that much later.

Complete agreement had been reached as to Poland's
future western borders, which were to be along the Oder
and the Neisse (West). However, there was a great difference of
opinion on the composition of the future Polish government.

"Churchill wants the Soviet Union to share a border with
a bourgeois Poland, alien to us, but we cannot allow this to

happen," Stalin said. "We want to have, once and for all, a friendly Poland with us, and that's what the Polish people want too."

Somewhat later he added: "Churchill is out to groom Mikolajczyk who has spent over four years sitting it out in Britain. The Poles will not accept Mikolajczyk. They have made their choice..."

Poskrebyshev entered the room and handed Stalin some papers. After skimming through them, the Surpeme Commander said to me:

"You will now go to the General Staff and look through the calculations for the Berlin operation with Antonov. We'll meet here tomorrow at 13:00."

Antonov and I spent the rest of the day and a good half of the night in my office. He also told me many interesting things about the Yalta Conference.

Once again we considered the main points of the draft plan and the calculations for the Berlin strategic operation which was to be carried out by three Fronts. Since it had been discussed several times by the Supreme Command and at the General Staff, we only made those revisions that were necessary because of the extended operations in East Prussia, in the Danzig area and in the Baltic.

The next morning the Supreme Commander telephoned Antonov to tell us to come at 20:00 instead of 13:00.

At the discussion of the Berlin operation that evening were several members of the State Committee for Defence. Antonov made a report.

The Supreme Commander approved all of our proposals, and instructed us to issue necessary orders on the full preparation for the offensive operation in the Berlin strategic direction.

CHAPTER 8

The Berlin Operation

As the concluding operation of the Second World War in Europe the Berlin operation is particularly important. The taking of Berlin finally resolved many major military and political questions on which Germany's postwar settlement and its place in Europe's political life largely depended.

Preparing for the last battle with nazism the Soviet Armed Forces strictly adhered to the policy of Germany's unconditional surrender agreed upon with the Allies both in the military and economic and the political fields. At this stage in the war our main aim was completely to root out nazism in Germany's social and government system and strictly punish all major Nazi criminals for their atrocities, mass-sca e murders, destruction and outrages committed against the peoples in the occupied countries, particularly on our long-suffering land.

The plan of the Berlin operation basically shaped up at the Stavka in November 1944. It was specified in the course of the Vistula-Oder, East Prussian and Pomeranian operations.

In elaborating the plan of the Berlin operation account was taken of actions by the Allied Expeditionary Force which had reached the Rhine on a wide front in late March-early April 1945 and began to force it in order to launch a general offensive into the heart of Germany.

The Supreme Command of the Allied troops had set itself the immediate objective of routing the enemy group and occupying the Ruhr industrial area. Then it intended the US and the British troops to advance to the Elbe river on the Berlin sector. At the same time operations by US and French troops were developed in the southerly direction with the aim of capturing the Stuttgart and the Munich areas and reaching the heartlands of Austria and Czechoslovakia.

Despite the fact that the boundary of the Soviet occupation zone was to pass far to the west of Berlin acccording to the Yalta Conference agreements and that the Soviet forces were already on the Oder and the Neisse rivers (60-100 kilometres from Berlin) and were ready to launch the Berlin operation, the British Government with Winston Churchill at its head still dreamed of capturing Berlin ahead of the Red Army.

Although the US and the British politicians and military had not reached a consensus concerning strategic objectives in the concluding stage of the war, the Supreme Command of the Allied Expeditionary Force was not averse to taking of Berlin under favourable circumstances.

Thus, informing the Combined Chiefs of Staff about his decision regarding the final operations, on April 7, 1945, General Dwight D. Eisenhower said:

"If after the taking of Leipzig it appeared that I can push on to Berlin at low cost I am willing to do so." And further on: "I am the first to admit that a war is waged in pursuance of political aims, and if the Combined Chiefs of Staff should decide that the Allied effort to take Berlin outweighs purely military considerations in this theater, I would cheerfully readjust my plans and my thinking so as to carry out such an operation."

In the last days of March Stalin received Eisenhower's information on his intentions of reaching the agreed line on the Berlin sector through the US mission. It was clear from this message that it was intended to develop the offensive of the British and the US forces in the north-eastern direction to reach the Lubeck area and in the south-eastern direction to smash the enemy in the south of Germany.

Stalin was aware that the Nazi leadership had lately become very active in seeking separate agreements with the British and the US governments. In view of the hopeless situation of the German forces it was to be expected that the Nazis would stop resisting in the west and would open the way to Berlin for the US and the British forces so as not to give it up to the Red Army. On March 27, 1945, the Reuters correspondent with the 21st Army Group Campbell reported on the Anglo-American offensive that without encountering resistance on their way they were moving into the heart of Germany. In mid-April 1945 American radio commentator John Grover stated that the Western Front, in fact, did no longer exist.

How did the Anglo-American offensive actually proceed in the Rhine area?

The Nazis were known to have a weak covering force there. Having retired beyond the Rhine in their time the Germans could have organized serious resistance. However, this had not been done. And mostly because the main forces had been transferred to the east to fight against the Soviet troops. Even at a critical time for the Ruhr group the German High Command had reinforced the front in the east against the Soviet troops by drawing on its western forces.

At the beginning of the Anglo-American campaign the Germans had 60 extremely weak divisions in the west whose overall strength was equal to 26 complete divisions. The Allies had 91 full-strength divisions.

The Allies enjoyed a particular superiority in the air. They could suppress any resistance both on land and in the air practically in any point by means of air strikes.

So, the forcing of the Rhine by US and British troops took place in easy conditions, and the Rhine was taken practically without German resistance.

Not waiting for the German Ruhr group to be liquidated, the Allied Supreme Command rushed the main forces to the Berlin sector with the aim of reaching the Elbe.

It was learned from numerous talks after the war with US, British and French generals, including Eisenhower, Montgomery, de Lattre de Tassigny, Clay, Robertson, Smith and many others that the possibility of Allied forces taking Berlin was finally excluded only when German defences were shattered on the Oder and the Neisse by powerful Soviet artillery, mortar, and air force attacks and the joint onslaught of armoured units and infantry.

When Eisenhower's message that he had decided to launch two offensives — in the north-east and in the south of Germany — and that the US troops would stop at the agreed line on the Berlin sector was received by the Stavka, Stalin described Eisenhower as a man true to his word. However, that opinion proved to be premature.

During the Allies' landing and advance in France close contacts were maintained between the Red Army General Staff and the US and the British military missions, and we often exchanged information concerning enemy troop deployment. However, as the end of the war approached we began to receive information from our Allies which did not conform to the real state of affairs.

I would like to cite a letter of the Chief of General Staff A. I. Antonov to the head of the US military mission in the USSR, Major-General John R. Dean.

"Dear Sir:

"I would like you to inform General Marshall of the following:

"On February 20 of this year I received a message from General Marshall that the Germans were deploying two groups for a counter-offensive on the Eastern front: one in Pomerania for an attack against Torn and another in the Vienna — Moravska Ostrava area for an offensive towards Lodz. The southern group was to include the SS 6th Panzer Army. A similar report was received on February 12 from the head of the army section of the British military mission Colonel Brinkman.

"I am extremely grateful to General Marshall for the information intended to help attain our common goals which he so graciously offered us.

"At the same time I regard it as my duty to inform General Marshall that military actions on the Eastern front failed to confirm the information he communicated, because the fighting has shown that the main group of German troops, including the SS 6th Panzer Army, was deployed not in Pomerania and not in the Moravska-Ostrava area but in the Lake Balaton region from where the Germans advanced with the aim of reaching the Danube and force-crossing it south of Budapest.

"This fact shows that the information General Marshall has used did not correspond to the actual course of events on the Eastern front in the month of March.

"It is not to be excluded that certain sources of that information were specially intended to confuse both the Anglo-American and the Soviet commands and divert the Soviet Command's attention away from the area the Germans were preparing the main offensive operation on the Eastern front.

"Despite the above I request General Marshall, if possible, to continue communicating available information concerning the enemy.

"I regard it as my duty to send this message to General Marshall exclusively so he would be able to draw the relevant conclusions regarding the source of that information.

"Please convey my respect and acknowledgement to General Marshall.

"Yours truly, General of the Army Antonov
"Chief of Red Army General Staff

"March 30, 1945"

On March 29, summoned by the Stavka I arrived in Moscow again with the plan of the First Byelorussian Front for the Berlin operation. The plan had been elaborated by the Front HQ and Command during March; all questions of principle had been coordinated earlier with the General Staff and the Supreme Command. This enabled us to submit a plan worked out in detail to the Supreme Command for consideration and decision.

Late in the evening of the same day Stalin summoned me to his Kremlin office. He was alone. A conference with the members of the State Defence Committee had just ended.

Offering his hand in silence he then began to speak, as it always was, as if he were continuing a conversation just now interrupted:

"The German front in the west has collapsed completely and, apparently, the Hitlerites do not want to take measures to stop the advance of Allied troops. At the same time they are strengthening their groups on all the most important sectors against us. Here is the map, take a look at the latest data on German troops."

Lighting his pipe Stalin went on:

"I think it's going to be quite a fight..."

Then he asked my opinion of the enemy on the Berlin sector.

Producing my front reconnaissance map I laid it down before the Supreme Commander. Stalin began to examine the whole operational-strategic group of German troops in the Berlin strategic direction with great attention.

According to our data, the Germans had four armies there with no less than 90 divisions, including 14 panzer and motorized divisions, 37 separate regiments and 98 separate battalions.

Subsequently, it was learned that there were not less than a million effectives, 10,400 artillery pieces and mortars, 1,500 tanks and assault guns, 3,500 combat aircraft on the Berlin sector, and additionally a 200,000-strong garrison was being formed in Berlin proper.

"When will our troops be ready to attack?" asked Stalin.

I reported:

"The First Byelorussian Front can begin the offensive not later than in two weeks. The First Ukrainian Front will apparently also be ready by that time. The Second Byelorussian Front by all appearances will be delayed with the complete liquidation of the enemy in the Danzig and Gdynia area until mid-April and will be unable to begin the offensive from the Oder simultaneously with the First Byelorussian and the First Ukrainian Fronts."

"In that case, we will have to begin the operation without waiting for Rokossovsky's Front to act," said Stalin. "If he is a few days late, it's no tragedy."

Then he came up to his desk, leafed through some papers and picked up a letter.

"Here, read this."

The letter was from a foreign well-wisher. It told about clandestine talks between Nazi agents and official representatives of the Allies, from which it was clear that the Germans proposed to the Allies to stop fighting against them if they were to agree to a separate peace on any terms.

The letter also said that the Allies had allegedly rejected the German overtures. Nevertheless, it was not to be excluded that the Germans would open the way to Berlin for the Allied troops.

"What do you make of it?" asked Stalin. And without waiting for an answer, he remarked: "I think Roosevelt won't violate the Yalta accords, but as to Churchill, he wouldn't flinch at anything."

Approaching the desk again he called Antonov and ordered him to come immediately.

Fifteen minutes later Antonov was in the office of the Supreme Commander.

"How's Rokossovsky doing?"

Antonov reported on the situation and the course of military operations in the Danzig and Gdynia area, after which Stalin inquired about the state of affairs with Vasilevsky at Königsberg.

Antonov reported on the situation on the Third Byelorussian Front.

Stalin silently bid him read the letter he had just shown me.

Antonov said:

"This is further proof of backstage intrigues in which the Hitlerite and the British government quarters are engaging."

Addressing Antonov the Supreme Commander said:

"Communicate with Konev and order him to come to GHQ on April 1 with the plan of the operation for the First Ukrainian Front, and the next two days work on the general plan with Zhukov."

Next day Antonov showed me the draft strategic plan of the Berlin operation which completely included the plan of the offensive for the First Byelorussian Front. After I had carefully studied the plan of the Berlin operation elaborated by the Supreme Command I concluded that it had been well prepared and fully answered the operational and strategic situation obtaining at the time.

On March 31, Commander of the First Ukrainian Front Marshal Konev arrived at the General Staff and immediately joined in the study of the general plan of the Berlin operation, and then reported on the draft plan of the First Ukrainian Front's offensive.

As far as I can remember we were all unanimous at the time on all questions of principle.

On April 1, 1945, Antonov delivered his report on the general plan of the Berlin operation at the Supreme Command Stavka, then came my report on the plan of the First Byelorussian Front's offensive and Konev's report on the plan of the First Ukrainian Front's offensive.

The Supreme Commander refused to agree with the entire boundary line between the First Byelorussian and the First Ukrainian Fronts marked on the map of the General Staff. He hachured the line from the Neisse to Potsdam and drew the line only to Lubben (60 kilometres south-east of Berlin).

He told Marshal Konev right away:

"In case the enemy puts up stiff resistance on the eastern approaches to Berlin, which will undoubtedly happen, and the First Byelorussian Front is delayed, the First Ukrainian Front is to be ready to attack Berlin from the south with the tank armies."

There exists an incorrect idea that the 3rd and 4th Guards Tank armies were committed to the battle for Berlin allegedly not by a decision of the Supreme Command but on the initiative of the Commander of the First Ukrainian Front. In order to reconstruct how it really was I will quote Konev's words on the question at a meeting of the top-ranking commanding officers of the central army group on February 18, 1946, when everything was still fresh in our memories.

"When at about 24:00 hours on April 16 I reported that the offensive was proceeding successfully Comrade Stalin issued the following order: 'Comrade Zhukov is having it rather tough, turn Rybalko and Lelyushenko towards Zehlendorf, remember how we had agreed at General Headquarters.'"

It was decided to begin the offensive on Berlin on April 16 without waiting for the Second Byelorussian Front which, according to all precise estimates, could begin the offensive from the Oder not earlier than April 20.

In the early hours of April 2, in my presence, the Supreme Commander signed the directive for the First Byelorussian Front to prepare and carry out the operation with the aim of taking Berlin and instructions to reach the Elbe in 12-15 days.

It was decided to launch the main attack from the Küstrin bridgehead with four infantry and two tank armies. The latter were to be committed to battle after the enemy defence was breached bypassing Berlin from the north and north-east. The Front's second echelon (the 3rd Army commanded by Colonel-General A. V. Gorbatov) was also to be committed on the main sector.

In view of the changes in the boundary line and instructions for the Front to be ready to turn the tank armies from the south towards Berlin the Supreme Gommander signed the draft directive to the First Ukrainian Front a day later after he had made the necessary refinements.

The directive ordered the First Ukrainian Front to:

smash the enemy group in the Kottbus area and south of Berlin;

isolate the main forces of Army Group Centre from the Berlin group and thereby secure the offensive of the First Byelorussian Front from the south;

reach the Behelitz-Wittenberg line and further along the Elbe river to Dresden in 10-12 days (not later);

mount the front's main blow in the direction of Spremberg;

commit the 3rd and 4th Guards Tank armies after the breakthrough in the direction of the main blow.

In view of the fact that the Second Byelorussian Front was still heavily engaged with the German forces in areas south-east of Danzig and north of Gdynia, the Supreme Command decided to begin redeploying that Front's main forces to the Oder replacing the 1st Army of the Wojsko Polskie and the 61st Army of the First Byelorussian Front on the Kolberg-Swedt sector not later than April 15-18. Part of the forces of Rokossovsky's Front were ordered to remain in the Danzig and Gdynia areas for mopping-up operations.

The aims and the objectives of the Second Byelorussian Front were largely determined during discussions by the Supreme Command of the general plan of operations on the Berlin sector.

Since the Second Byelorussian Front was to launch the operation four days later Marshal Rokossovsky was not summoned to the General Headquarters to discuss the Berlin operation.

It turned out that in the first, most tense days the First Byelorussian Front was to advance with an open right flank without operational and tactical cooperation with the troops of the Second Byelorussian Front.

We seriously took into account not only the forced delay in the beginning of the Second Byelorussian Front's offensive, but also the difficulties it would inevitably encounter in forcing the Oder in its lower reaches. In the latter place the river has two main channels, the East and West Oder 150-250 metres wide and up to 10 metres deep. We believed that the Second Byelorussian Front would be able to force both channels rather quickly and secure the required bridgehead but not sooner than in two-three days. Therefore, its actual impact on the enemy north of Berlin would be felt around April 23-24, i.e. when the First Byelorussian Front was to be assaulting Berlin.

Of course, it would have been better to wait five or six days and begin the Berlin operation with three Fronts simultaneously but, as I have pointed out above, in view of the existing military-political situation, the Stavka could not put off the operation for a later date.

We had very little time left before April 16 and very many measures to be urgently taken. Troops were to be grouped, extensive logistical support provided for, and large-scale operational, tactical and special preparations of the Front carried out for an exceptionally important and unusual operation such as the taking of Berlin.

During the entire war I took a direct part in many large and important offensive operations but the coming battle for Berlin was a special, unprecedented operation. The forces of the Front were to break through a zone of strong solid defensive lines organised in depth beginning from the Oder and ending with strongly fortified Berlin. At the approaches to Berlin we would have to smash an enormous group of Nazi troops and capture the capital of Nazi Germany for which the enemy would undoubtedly wage a deadly struggle.

Pondering over the coming operation I repeatedly turned my thoughts to the outstanding Battle of Moscow when the strong enemy hordes at the approaches to the capital had been inflicting mighty blows on the Soviet forces in the defensive. I reconsidered separate episodes again and again analyzing the mistakes of the two sides. It was my desire to take into account the experience of that most involved battle to utilize the best in the coming operation to the most minute details, and try not to make any mistakes.

The Berlin operation was the final victorious act along the 3,000-km route of fighting by the heroic Soviet forces which had gained experience in major battles and been steeled in fierce combats. The men were eager to finish off the enemy as soon as possible and end the war.

In the evening on April 1, I called the Front Chief of Staff, Colonel-General M. S. Malinin, from Moscow and said:

"Everything has been approved without any special changes. We have very little time. Begin to take measures. I fly out tomorrow."

These short instructions were sufficient for Malinin immediately to begin implementing planned measures to prepare for the operation.

During the war we had not had any occasions to take cities as large and strongly fortified as Berlin. Its total area was nearly 900 square kilometres. A ramified network of underground communications enabled the enemy troops to carry out concealed manoeuvres.

Our reconnaissance planes photographed Berlin, all its approaches and defensive lines six times. The results of aerial photography, captured documents and prisoner interrogations were used to draw up detailed schemes and maps which were supplied to all the troops and commands down to companies.

Engineering units made a scale model of the city with its suburbs which was used in studying questions concerned with the organisation of the offensive, the general assault of Berlin and fighting in the city centre.

The conferences and command exercises with maps and Berlin's scale model between April 5 and 7, were effected very actively and in a creative spirit. Participating in these exercises were the army commanders, chiefs of staff, and members of military councils, the Chief of the Front Political Administration, artillery commanders of the armies and the Front, commanders of all separate corps and chiefs of the Front's arms of the service. The Front Logistics Chief was also present and carefully studied questions of the operation's logistical support. More detailed games and exercises were held between April 8 and 14 in the armies, corps, divisions and units of all the arms of the service.

Due to the Front's rear communications being extremely drawn-out as well as to diversion of large supplies for the East Pomeranian operation, the required supplies had not been secured by the beginning of the Berlin operation. Truly heroic efforts were needed on the part of the Front and army logistics personnel. They proved to be worth their duties.

In preparing the operation we all wondered what else to undertake in order to stun the enemy even more and smash him. Thus the idea originated of a night attack using searchlights.

It was decided to attack two hours before dawn. A hundred and forty anti-air searchlights were to light up suddenly enemy positions and objectives of the offensive.

During preparations for the operation the effectiveness of the searchlights was shown to its participants. All those present were at one favouring their use.

The question of using the tank armies was seriously discussed during the exercises when the breaching of the enemy tactical defences on the Oder was rehearsed. It was decided to commit the tank armies to battle only after the Seelow Heights were captured, on account of the strong tactical defences on these Seelow heights.

Naturally, we did not count on our tank armies gaining an opportunity for operational manoeuvring after the breaching of the tactical defences as had been the case, for example, in the previous Vistula-Oder, East Pomeranian and other operations. In the latter operations the tank armies had moved far ahead and created all conditions for the rapid movement forward by the field armies.

There were moments in the Vistula-Oder operation, for instance, when the 2nd Guards Tank Army was up to 70 kilometres ahead of the field armies. This was not envisaged in this operation, because the distance to Berlin along a straight line was not more than 60-80 kilometres.

Therefore the following was provided for. If the strength of the attack by the Front's first echelon was to prove insufficient to rapidly overcome the enemy tactical defences and the possibility of a delay was to arise, then both tank armies would be committed to smash the enemy defence. This would reinforce the attack of the infantry armies and help complete the breakthrough of the enemy tactical defences in the Oder and Seelow Heights area.

It was stipulated in the Supreme Command directive that both the 1st and the 2nd Guards Tank armies would be committed to battle for an attack on Berlin from the north-east and to outflank it from the north. However, during the rehearsal of the operation the commanding officers of the Front Staff and I had serious doubts that enemy defences would be successfully smashed in the offensive zone of the 8th Guards Army on the Front's main sector, particularly in the area of the strongly fortified Seelow Heights which were 12 kilometres from the forward line of the German defences.

Since the left-flank neighbour, the Second Byelorussian Front, would begin the offensive later than we, any delay in breaching the enemy defences could lead to a very unfavourable operational situation. To put the Front beyond the reach of chance, we decided to deploy the 1st Guards Tank Army commanded by General M. Ye. Katukov in home position behind Chuikov's 8th Guards Army so as to commit the former in the offensive zone of the 8th Guards Army in case of need.

Having assumed responsibility for the change in the deployment, as provided for in the Supreme Command's directive, I nevertheless reported in to the Supreme Commander.

After listening to my arguments Stalin said:

"Do as you think better, you're in a better position to judge on the spot."

What was happening in the meantime on the other side of the front lines?

The Nazi High Command was planning the battle for Berlin as the decisive battle on the Eastern front. Attempting to raise the morale of his troops Hitler wrote in an appeal on April 14:

"We have foreseen this attack and countered it with a strong front. The enemy is encountering the tremendous force of the artillery. Our infantry losses are being replenished by innumerable new formations, combined elements and units of the Volkssturm reinforcing the front. Berlin will remain German..."

Three groups of Nazi armies defended the main strategic directions on the Eastern front. Army Group Vistula along the Oder defended the approaches to Berlin from the north-east and the east. The central army group operated to the south defending Saxony and the approaches to Czechoslovakia's industrial areas from the north-east. The southern army group blocked the way to Austria and the south-eastern approaches to Czechoslovakia.

Initially, Army Group Vistula itself had been preparing to counterattack the forces of the First Byelorussian Front. But after it had been routed and lost the Pomeranian bridgehead the remaining troops retired beyond the Oder and began intense preparations to defend the Berlin sector. The Nazi Command continued to urgently form new units and formations, mostly SS, to reinforce Army Group Vistula. Thus, three divisions were formed in a short time in only one training camp in the Debritz area.

At first, Himmler headed the defence of the immediate approaches to Berlin, and all the top posts were given to SS generals. Thereby the Nazi Command emphasized that it was a particularly important moment. Nine divisions had been transferred to the Berlin sector from other sectors in March and April 1945.

During interrogations former Chief of the Nazi High Command Operations Department Headquarters, Colonel-General Jodl recalled:

"In order to provide the necessary reinforcements for the Eastern Front by the beginning of the decisive Russian offensive, we had to disband our entire reserve army, i. e. all the infantry, panzer, artillery and special reserve units, military schools and colleges, and send their personnel to reinforce the troops."

The Nazi Command drew up a detailed plan for the defence of the Berlin sector. It hoped that defensive battles on the Oder, the strategic forefront of Berlin, would be successful. The following measures were taken with this aim.

General Busse's 9th Army which defended the city was reinforced with personnel and military hardware. New divisions and brigades were formed in its rear. Units on the forward line were brought up almost to full strength. Particular attention was paid to deployment and use of tanks and assault guns in the defence.

An unbroken system of defensive works consisting of a

number of uninterrupted zones several trenches each was built from the Oder to Berlin. The main defensive line had up to five continuous trenches. The enemy took advantage of certain natural obstacles: lakes, rivers, canals and ravines. All towns and villages were adjusted to an all-round defence.

Army Group Steiner was being formed in an area northeast of Berlin with the aim of attacking the flank of the First Byelorussian Front. Picked marine units were also transferred to this area.

In addition, special measures were taken to defend Berlin. The city perimeter was divided into six defensive sections. Besides these there was a special, ninth section, including the centre of Berlin with the government buildings, Imperial Chancellery, Gestapo and Reichstag.

Three defence lines were built at the immediate approaches to the city: the outer protection zone, the outer defensive perimeter and the inner defensive perimeter. Heavy barricades, anti-tank obstacles, obstructions, and concrete structures were erected on the streets of the city. House windows were reinforced and turned into embrasures.

A newly formed headquarters for Berlin's defence warned the population that it should be prepared for disparate street and house fighting and that the struggle would be waged on the ground and underground. It was recommended to take advantage of the subway, underground sewage system and communications. A special order of the defence headquarters advised to turn residential areas into fortresses. Every street, square, lane, house, canal, and bridge became elements in the overall defence system of the city. Two hundred battalions of the Volkssturm created for street fighting underwent special training.

All the anti-aircraft artillery at the approaches to and in Berlin was used to reinforce artillery defence of the city. More than 600 anti-aircraft artillery pieces of large and medium calibre were mounted for anti-tank and anti-personnel action to defend the city. In addition, tanks undergoing repairs with operational guns were used as fire points. They were buried in the ground on street corners and at railway bridges. Anti-tank groups were manned by members of the Hitlerjugend, the Nazi youth organisation. They were armed with Faustpatronen.

More than 400,000 people toiled on the defences of Berlin. Picked units of police and SS were deployed in the city. Numerous SS regiments and separate battalions from the vicinity were brought in to defend the special section. These SS troops were headed by the chief of Hitler's bodyguard Monke.

The Nazi Command expected that it would force us to lose one line after another, delay the battle to the utmost, exhaust our troops and stop them at the nearest approaches. It was meant to do the same thing with our troops as had been done with the German troops by the Soviet Armed Forces at the approaches to Moscow. But these plans were not to be realized.

Events preceding the Berlin operation had developed in such a way that it was very difficult to conceal our intentions from the enemy. It was obvious to anyone, even a person with no idea of military affairs, that the key to Berlin lay on the Oder and the forcing of that river would be immediately followed by a direct attack on Berlin. The Germans expected this.

Subsequently, General Jodl said:

"It was clear for the General Staff that the battle of Berlin would be decided on the Oder, and for that reason the bulk of the 9th Army's troops defending Berlin was deployed on the forward line. The reserves that were being urgently formed were to be deployed north of Berlin for a subsequent counterattack against Marshal Zhukov's forces..."

Preparing the offensive we were fully aware that the Germans were expecting our thrust on Berlin. That was why the Front Command pondered over the way to organize the attack more unexpectedly for the enemy in all the details.

We decided to attack the enemy troops in the defensive with such force that they would at once be stunned and crushed by using masses of aircraft, tanks, artillery and other equipment. But to muster secretly all the arms and military hardware on the theatre of military operations in so short a period of time required titanic and I would say highly skilful work.

Numerous trains with artillery, mortar, and tank units moved through Poland. Outwardly they were not military trains at all: timber and hay were being transported on the flatcars. But as soon as the train arrived at its destination, the camouflage was quickly removed and tanks, artillery pieces and tractors came off the flatcars and were immediately sent off to shelters.

The empty trains returned to the east, and in their stead more and more new ones appeared with military equipment. The Front was reinforced with a large number of heavy guns, mortars, tractors and other supplies.

On March 29, when the last shots had been fired in Pomerania, artillery and tanks moved south under the strictest camouflage. All the woods and groves along the eastern bank of the Oder were filled with troops. Tens of thousands of guns and mortars of various calibres were deployed on the Berlin sector. It was necessary to equip firing positions for every gun, make a dugout for the crew, and an ammunition pit.

The positions usually looked deserted in the daytime, but they came alive at night. Thousands of men worked with spades, crow-bars and picks in complete silence. The work was made more difficult by subsoil spring waters and the beginning of spring mud. More than 1,800,000 cubic metres of earth were excavated during those nights. On the morning of every next day no traces of the tremendous night work could be seen. Everything was carefully camouflaged.

Endless lines of tanks, artillery, lorries with ammunition, fuel and food moved along numerous roads and without roads at night. Only in terms of ordinance it was necessary to have 7,147,000 shells available by the beginning of the operation. There could be no interruptions in supply if the success of our offensive operation were to be secured. The nature of the operation required ammunition to be forwarded from Front dumps to the troops in an unending stream without the usual army and divisional dumps.

The railway tracks were converted to the Soviet gauge, and ammunition was carried almost to the very Oder. To provide an idea of the scale of these transport operations suffice it to say that if the trains supplying this operation were placed along a straight line one after another, they would stretch for more than 1,200 kilometres.

We were absolutely sure that the troops would have no shortage of ammunition, fuel and food. Indeed, logistics were organized so well that when we began the assault of Berlin proper, we had as much ammunition as when we left the bridgehead on the Oder. The supplies were evenly replenished during the entire advance from the Oder to Berlin.

On the whole preparations for the Berlin operation were unprecedented in scale and intensity. A total of 77 rifle divisions, 3,155 tanks and self-propelled guns, 14,628 artillery pieces and mortars and 1,531 rocket launchers were deployed on a relatively narrow area of the First Byelorussian Front in a short period of time. We were certain that with these means and forces our troops would smash the enemy in the shortest possible time.

This entire mass of military equipment, manpower and supplies was carried across the Oder. It was necessary to build a large number of bridges and crossings not only for the troops to go over but also to supply them later on. The Oder was 380 metres wide in some places. The ice began to drift on the river. Engineer and construction work was done very close from the front lines under systematic enemy artillery and mortar fire and air raids. Nevertheless, by the moment the units began to occupy starting positions 25 bridges and 40 ferry crossings had been built across the Oder. The area of the crossings was protected by many lines of anti-aircraft artillery fire and patrols by many dozens of fighter planes.

Beginning with the first days of February the enemy was very active on the Oder. During March and the first half of April, the intense fighting for our bridgeheads in the Küstrin area did not cease for a single day. In addition to massive bombing raids, the enemy used the missiles and floating mines to destroy the bridges and ferry crossings, but the bridges continued to exist. The damage was being quickly repaired. Thousands of kilometres of telephone wires were ready to operate both underground and on poles.

On the sector of the Front's main attack there were up to 270 artillery pieces (76-mm and larger calibre) per one kilometre of the front line to be breached.

Simultaneously with operational, tactical and material preparations for the operation, the military councils, political bodies and Party organizations carried on extensive Party-political work to prepare the personnel for the final Berlin operation.

We celebrated the 75th anniversary of Lenin's birth on those days. Educational work among the troops was inspired by the name of the leader of the revolution. The Party consciousness among the officers and men was very high in that historic final period of the war. The number of people joining the Communist Party increased. I had occasion to be present in mid-April at a Party meeting in the 416th Rifle Division of the 5th Shock Army.

All those who spoke pointed out that every Communist was to lead the men forward by force of personal example in the coming operation, particularly during the assault of Berlin. Not only Communists but also non-Party soldiers spoke with great inspiration assuring the Party that they were ready to finish off fascism.

I must say a few kind words about member of the Front Military Council, Lieutenant-General Konstantin Telegin, who directed the entire Party-political work among the troops with great creative energy through the Front Political Administration. He managed to visit many units personally urging the men and commanders to perform feats of arms for our Motherland.

At the same time an extensive explanatory work was conducted among the troops on their loyal behaviour towards Germany's civilian population which had been cruelly deceived by the Nazis and was now experiencing all the vicissitudes of war. Due to timely instructions by the Party Central Committee and extensive explanatory work among the troops we managed to avoid undesirable actions by men whose families had suffered terrible atrocities and violence at the hands of the Nazis.

It has already been mentioned that the First Byelorussian Front was to smash the Berlin group and take Berlin with assistance from part of the forces of the First Ukrainian Front.

Constant operational and tactical cooperation was envisaged between the First Byelorussian and the First Ukrainian Fronts coordinated and corrected by the Stavka.

Thus, in the course of the operation the Stavka specified cooperation between the group on the right flank of the First Byelorussian Front and the 4th Tank Army of the First Ukrainian Front reaching the Potsdam, Rathenow and Brandenburg area so as to close the operational encirclement of the enitre Berlin enemy group.

It was decided, in planning the operation, to strike an auxiliary blow with the 69th and the 33rd armies from the Frankfurt-am-Oder area (south of the Frankfurt-Berlin railway) in the general direction of Bohnsdorf so as to prevent the enemy 9th Army from retreating to Berlin after the breakthrough by the First Byelorussian and the First Ukrainian Fronts on the Oder and the Neisse.

The Stavka ordered the Commander of the First Ukrainian Front to attack from the Kottbus area with part of its right wing towards Wendisch-Buchholtz so as to cut off the 9th Army from Berlin and rout it jointly with the left wing of the First Byelorussian Front.

By the strikes of the 69th, 33rd and 3rd armies of the First Byelorussian Front and the 3rd Guards, 13th, part of the 3rd Guards Tank and 28th armies of the First Ukrainian Front the entire 200,000-strong German south-eastern group of General Busse's 9th Army was cut off from Berlin and soon routed.

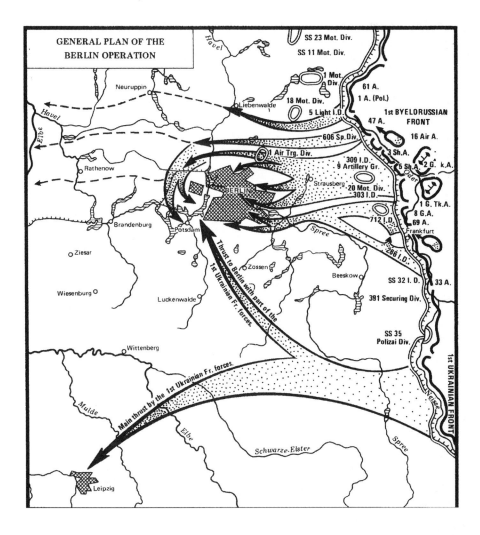

The important role played by the 1st Guards Tank Army (First Byelorussian Front) should be emphasized: it reached Berlin's south-eastern outskirts blocking the 9th Army's escape routes to Berlin. This made it easier for the 8th Guards Army to fight in the city.

At this point I would like to recall more or less consecutively how the historic Berlin operation unravelled.

Reconnaissance was carried out two days before the beginning of the offensive along the entire front line. For two days, on April 14 and 15, 32 recon groups consisting of up to one reinforced rifle battalion each, were reconnoitring in force to reveal the enemy fire defence system, his deployment and probed the strong and the weakest points in the defence zone.

This reconnaissance in force also pursued another aim. It was in our interests to force the Germans to deploy more men and equipment on the forward line so that they would be hit by all the Front's artillery and mortars during the artillery barrage before the offensive on April 16. The reconnaissance on April 14 and 15 was accompanied by strong artillery fire, including large-calibre guns.

The enemy mistook the reconnaissance for the beginning of our offensive. Suffice it to say that some German units were dislodged from their forward positions as a result of action by our recon groups, and almost the entire German artillery took part in repelling the recon group attacks.

The aim we had pursued had been attained. The enemy rushed his reserves to the second positions. However, our troops stopped their advance and dug in. This was perplexing for the enemy command. As it was learned later, some of the German commanders decided that our offensive had failed.

In the years of the war the enemy had become used to the fact that we usually began our artillery barrage before an attack in the morning, because infantry and tank attack was restricted to the daylight. We decided to take advantage of the enemy not expecting a night attack.

Late at night, a few hours before the artillery and air barrage, I set out for the observation post of 8th Guards Army Commander, General Chuikov.

Along the way I managed to meet many commanders of rifle and tank units and the 1st Guards Tank Army Commander,

General Katukov, and his Chief of Staff, General Shalin. All of them had not slept and were checking the combat readiness of the troops under their command once again in all the particularities.

I was pleased by the foresight shown by generals Katukov and Shalin. It turned out that yesterday morning they had sent their unit commanders assigned to the first echelon of the tank army to the observation posts of the corps commanders of the 8th Guards Army to coordinate the details of cooperation and conditions for their units to be committed into the breach.

From the 1st Guards Tank Army command post I called HQ of S. I. Bogdanov's 2nd Guards Tank Army. He was not at HQ but with Army Commander V. I. Kuznetsov. My call was answered by 2nd Guards Tank Army Chief of Staff, General A. I. Radziyevsky. When I asked Radziyevsky about the whereabouts of the formation commanders assigned to the forward echelons he answered:

"They're up in front, with Kuznetsov's people in connection with the coming job."

I could only marvel at our commander tank-men, how they had raised their operational and tactical skills during the war.

It was in such high spirits that I arrived together with Member of the Military Council K. F. Telegin and Front Artillery Commander V. I. Kazakov at the observation post of 8th Guards Army Commander Chuikov. The member of the Army Military Council, Army Chief of Staff, Artillery Commander and other army generals and senior officers were already there.

It was 3 a.m. Moscow time. Last-minute checks of combat readiness for the operation were being made in all the units. Everything was done efficiently, calmly, and at the same time without unwarranted self-assurance and underestimation of the enemy. It could be felt that the Army was preparing to fight in all earnest, as one has to fight against a strong and experienced enemy.

The checks were completed in an hour and a half. Artillery barrage was fixed for 5 a.m. Moscow time. The hands of the clock moved slowly as never before. In order to fill the

remaining minutes we decided to have some hot strong tea
which was made for us in the dugout by a girl. I remember that
she had a non-Russian name Margot. We sipped tea in
silence, each deep in his thoughts.

At exactly three minutes before the beginning of the
artillery preparation we all went out of the dugout and took
up positions at the observation post which had been built with
particular care by the 8th Army Chief of Engineers.

The entire vicinity beyond the Oder could be seen from
here in the daytime. Now there was a morning mist there. I
looked at my watch: it was five o'clock sharp.

And at this moment, the vicinity was lighted up by the
fire of many thousands of guns, mortars and the legendary
Katyusha rocket launchers followed by a tremendous din from
the discharges and explosions of shells and aircraft bombs. The
continuous roar of bombers was steadily growing louder.

A few bursts of machine-gun fire were heard from the
enemy side in the first seconds, and then everything quieted
down. It seemed as if there were not a single living creature
left on the enemy side. The enemy did not make a single shot
during the 30-minute powerful artillery barrage. This showed
that the enemy was completely suppressed and the defence
system disrupted. For this reason it was decided to shorten
the time of the artillery preparation and immediately begin
the general offensive.

Thousands of flares of different colour flew into the
air. This was the signal for 140 searchlights placed at intervals
of 200 metres to flash spot lights equalling more than 100,000
million candlepowers, lighting up the battlefield and blinding
the enemy and snatching objects for attack by our tanks and
infantry from the darkness. It was a striking picture, and I
remember having seen nothing like it during my whole life!

The artillery fire grew denser; the infantry and the tanks
drove forward in a single wave, their attack accompanied by a
double rolling barrage. By dawn our troops had taken the
first position and began to attack the second.

With a large number of planes in the Berlin area the
enemy was unable to use his air force effectively at night,
while in the morning our attacking forces were at such close
quarters with the enemy troops that their pilots could not

bomb our forward units without risking hitting their own troops.

The Nazi troops were virtually swamped in a sea of fire and metal. A thick wall of dust and smoke hung in the air, and in places even the powerful anti-aircraft searchlights were unable to penetrate it, but this troubled no one.

Our aircraft flew above the field of battle in waves. A few hundred bombers hit targets that were too far for the artillery in the night. Other bombers cooperated with the troops in the morning and day time. More than 6,550 sorties were made on the first day of the battle.

It was planned for the artillery to make 1,197,000 shots, actually 1,236,000 shells were fired: 2,450 railway cars of shells or nearly 98,000 tons of metal hit the enemy. Enemy defences were being destroyed and suppressed to a depth of 8 kilometres, and some resistance points even to 10-12 kilometres.

Here is a subsequent account of the events by the commander of the 56th Panzer Corps, Artillery General Weidling at an interrogation at Front HQ:

"On April 16, in the first hours of the offensive the Russians broke through on the right flank of the 101st Army Corps on the sector of Division Berlin, thereby threatening the left flank of the 56th Panzer Corps. In the second half of the day Russian tanks broke through on the sector of the 303rd Infantry Division, of part of the SS 11th Panzer Corps, and threatened to attack units of Division Müncheberg from the flank. At the same time the Russians exerted strong pressure on the front of the sector occupied by my corps. In the early hours on April 17 units of my corps, suffering heavy losses, were forced to retreat to the heights east of Seelow..."

In the morning on April 16 Soviet troops advanced successfully on all sectors of the front. However, having recovered from the initial shock the enemy began to resist by means of his artillery and mortars from the Seelow Heights, while groups of bombers appeared from the Berlin direction. The closer our troops approached the Seelow Heights, the stronger became enemy resistance.

This natural defence line dominated over the surrounding terrain, had steep slopes and was a serious obstacle on the way to Berlin in all respects. It stood like a wall before our troops blocking the plateau where the battle at the nearest approaches to Berlin was to take place.

It was here, at the foot of the Seelow Heights that the Germans expected to stop our troops. It was here that they concentrated the largest amount of manpower and equipment.

The Seelow Heights not only restricted the actions of our tanks but were also a serious obstacle for artillery. They blocked the depth of enemy defence making it impossible to observe it from the ground on our side. The artillerymen had to overcome this difficulty by more intense fire and occasionally fired at random.

It was also important for enemy morale to hold on to this major line. Berlin lay behind it. Nazi propaganda made a point of the decisive importance and invincible strength of the Seelow Heights calling them "Berlin's Castle" or an "invincible fortress".

By 13:00 I clearly realized that the fire system of the enemy defence was largely intact there, and we would be unable to take the Seelow Heights in the battle array in which the offensive had been started and continued.

After seeking the advice of the army commanders we decided to commit both tank armies of generals Katukov and Bogdanov to battle in order to reinforce the attacking troops and break through the defence by all means. At 14:30 I watched the advance of the forward units of the 1st Guards Tank Army from my observation post.

At 15:00 I called the Stavka and reported that the first and the second defensive positions of the enemy had been breached, the Front's troops had advanced up to 6 kilometres but had encountered serious resistance on the line of the Seelow Heights where enemy defences appeared to be largely intact. I committed both tank armies to the battle to reinforce the offensive of the infantry armies. I thought that tomorrow we would breach enemy defences by the end of the day.

Stalin listened attentively and then said calmly:

"The enemy defence on Konev's Front has proved to be weak. He has easily crossed the Neisse and is advancing hardly meeting any resistance. Support the attack of your tank armies with bombers. Report in the evening how things will be going."

In the evening I reported to the Supreme Commander again about difficulties at the approaches to the Seelow Heights and said that the line could not be taken earlier than tomorrow evening.

This time Stalin spoke with me not as calmly as he had in the daytime.

"You should not have committed the 1st Guards Tank Army to battle on the sector of the 8th Guards Army instead of where the Supreme Command had instructed." Then he added:

"Are you certain you'll take the Seelow line tomorrow?"

Trying to appear calm I answered:

"Tomorrow, April 17, by the end of the day the defence on the Seelow Heights will be breached. I believe that the more of his troops the enemy hurls at our forces here, the quicker we will later take Berlin, because it is easier to defeat the enemy in the open field than in a city."

"We intend to order Konev to move Rybalko's and Lelyushenko's tank armies towards Berlin from the south and Rokossovsky to hurry with the force-crossing and also make a thrust out-flanking Berlin from the north," Stalin said.

I answered:

"Konev's tank armies have every possibility to advance rapidly, and they should be directed to Berlin, but Rokossovsky won't be able to start the offensive before April 23, because he will be delayed in forcing the Oder."

"Goodbye," said Stalin rather wryly instead of continuing and put down the receiver.

Soon we received a directive of the Supreme Command for the First Ukrainian and Second Byelorussian Fronts. It prescribed Konev to move the 3rd Guards Tank Army via Zossen to Berlin from the south, and the 4th Guards Tank Army to reach the Potsdam area, and Rokossovsky to force the Oder faster and advance part of his forces outflanking Berlin from the north.

Fierce fighting flared up on all sectors of the front early in the morning on April 17. The enemy resisted desperately. However, in the evening the enemy began to retreat, unable to withstand attacks by the tank armies committed to battle on the previous day which had breached the defence in a number of places on the Seelow Heights cooperating with infantry armies. In the morning on April 18 the Seelow Heights were taken.

Having broken through the Seelow line we gained an opportunity to commit to battle all the tank formations on a broad front.

But on April 18, too, the enemy still attempted to stop the advance of our troops throwing all available reserves and even units withdrawn from Berlin defences against them. Only on April 19, having sustained heavy losses the Germans gave in to the mighty onslaught of our tank and infantry armies and began to retire to the outer perimeter of the Berlin defence area.

A few days later Malinin reported that instructions had been received from the Supreme Command annulling the directive to Rokossovsky prescribing the Second Byelorussian Front to attack Berlin outflanking it from the north.

It was obvious that the troops of the Second Byelorussian Front forcing a most complicated water system on the Oder and overcoming the German defence there would be unable to begin the offensive with all its forces before April 23.

As the actual course of events showed, the Second Byelorussian Front was able to mount an offensive with its main forces not earlier than April 24, when street fighting was already underway in Berlin and the right-wing group of the First Byelorussian Front had already outflanked the city from the north and north-west.

In the course of the fighting on April 16 and 17, and later, I repeatedly analyzed the way the operation had been carried out by the Front's forces to ascertain whether there were any mistakes in our decisions which could lead to the operation's failure.

There were no mistakes. It is to be admitted, however, that we made a slip which dragged out the fighting for one or two additional days in breaching the tactical zone.

In preparing for the operation we somewhat underestimated the complicated nature of the terrain in the Seelow Heights area where the enemy had an opportunity to organize a defence that was difficult to overcome. Situated 10 to 12 kilometres from our initial positions, having dug in deeply, particularly on the opposite slopes of the heights, the enemy managed to preserve his manpower and equipment from our artillery fire and air bombing. Of course we had a very limited time to prepare the Berlin operation but even that cannot serve as an excuse.

I must assume the blame for the slip above all.

I think that the responsibility for not being sufficiently prepared to take the Seelow Heights on the army scale will be taken by the relevant army commanders, if not publicly then in private. In planning the artillery attack, account should have been taken of all the difficulties involved in destroying enemy defences in this area.

Today, a long time after the events, in pondering over the plan of the Berlin operation I have reached the conclusion that the defeat of the Berlin enemy group and the taking of Berlin itself were done correctly, but it was also possible to carry out the operation in a somewhat different way.

There is no denying the fact that now, when everything is completely clear, it is much easier to draw up an offensive plan than at the time when we had to practically solve an equation with many unknowns. Nevertheless, I would like to share my thoughts on the subject.

The capture of Berlin should have immediately and by all means been assigned to two Fronts: the First Byelorussian and the First Ukrainian with the boundary line between them as follows: Frankfurt-am-Oder-Fürstenwalde-the centre of Berlin. In this variant the First Byelorussian Front's main force could have attacked on a narrower sector outflanking Berlin from the north-east, north and north-west. The First Ukrainian Front's main force would have attacked Berlin by the shortest possible route enveloping it from the south, south-west and west.

Of course, there was an alternative: to assign the First Byelorussian Front the mission of taking Berlin alone, reinforcing its left wing by not less than two infantry, two tank and one air armies and relevant artillery and engineer units.

This alternative would have made preparations for and control of the operation more complicated, but the overall cooperation between troops in routing the Berlin enemy group would have been much simpler, particularly in taking the city. There would have been less friction and vague points.

As to the offensive by the Second Byelorussian Front, it could have been organized more simply.

A small covering force may have been left on the Stettin-Swedt sector, the Front's main forces deployed south of Swedt adjacent to the First Byelorussian Front's right wing, or perhaps even the offensive launched from behind its flank (after it has forced the Oder) attacking in a north-western direction and cutting off the Stettin-Swedt enemy group.

When the Supreme Command considered and approved the plan these variants, for a number of reasons, were not mentioned. The Supreme Command implemented the idea of an attack on a broad front...

However, let us return to the events of those days.

In the first days of the fighting the First Byelorussian Front's tank armies had no opportunity to forge ahead. They were forced to fight in close cooperation with the field armies. General Bogdanov's 2nd Guards Tank Army acted somewhat more successfully with the 3rd and 5th Shock Armies. Moreover, enemy resistance was slightly weaker on its sector after April 18.

The First Ukrainian Front's advance developed more swiftly from the very first day. As expected, in the direction of its attack enemy defence was weak enabling both tank armies to be committed to battle in the morning on April 17. They advanced 20 to 25 kilometres on the first day, forced the Spree river and began moving towards Zossen and Luckenwalde in the morning on April 19.

However, as Konev's forces approached the Zossen area enemy resistance stiffened and progress by units of the First Ukrainian Front slowed. In addition, the nature of the terrain made it difficult for Rybalko's tank army to deploy in battle formation. In this connection Front Commander Konev sent General Rybalko the following radio message:

"Comrade Rybalko. Moving like a snake again. One brigade fighting, the whole army waiting. I order you to cross the Baruth-Luckenwalde line through the swamp along several routes in battle formation... Report the fulfilment. Konev. April 20, 1945."

On April 20, the fifth day of the operation, long-range artillery of the 79th Rifle Corps of the First Byelorussian Front's 3rd Shock Army commanded by Colonel-General Kuznetsov opened fire at Berlin. It was the beginning of the historic storming of Nazi Germany's capital. Simultaneously, the 30th Guards Gun Brigade's lst battallion of the 47th Army commanded by Major Zyukin also fired a volley at the Nazi capital.

On April 21, units of the 3rd Shock, 2nd Guards Tank, 47th and 5th Shock armies broke into the suburbs of Berlin and engaged the enemy there. The 61st Army, the lst Army of the Wojsko Polskie forces and other formations of the First Byelorussian Front moved swiftly bypassing Berlin towards the Elbe where the meeting with Allied forces was expected.

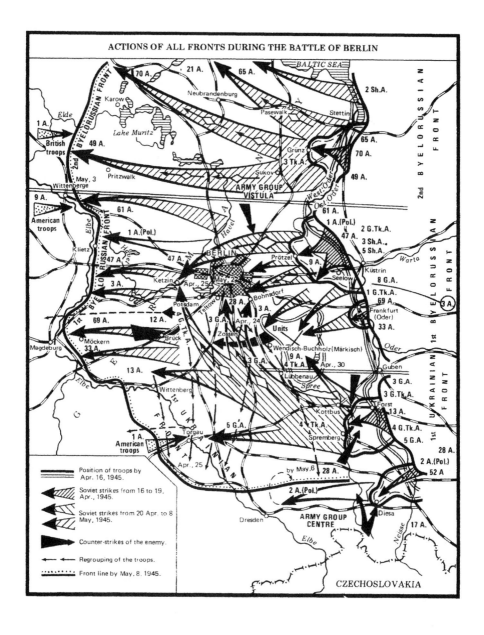

Extensive Party-political work aimed at securing high attacking spirit among the men was carried on by the political departments of the advancing troops: 47th Army (chief of the political department Colonel M. K. Kalashnik), 61st Army (chief of the political department, Major-General A. G. Kotikov), 2nd Guards Tank Army (chief of the political department, Colonel M. M. Litvyak), 3rd Shock Army (chief of the political department, Colonel F. Y. Lisitsyn), and 5th Shock Army (chief of the political department, Major--General Ye. Ye. Koshcheyev).

The Front's Military Council addressed the following appeal to the personnel:

"Privates, sergeants, officers and generals of the First Byelorussian Front!

"Dear comrades:

"The decisive hour of battle has come. In front of you lies Berlin, the capital of the Nazi state, and beyond Berlin — the meeting with the troops of our Allies and complete victory over the enemy. Doomed to perish the remnants of German units are still resisting. The Nazi Command is drawing on its last leftovers of Volkssturm reserves, sparing neither old men nor 15-year-olds to attempt to stem our offensive so as to delay the hour of its destruction.

"Comrade officers, sergeants and Red Army men! Your units have covered themselves with unfading glory. Nothing could stop you either at the walls of Stalingrad, or in the steppes of the Ukraine, or in the forests and swamps of Byelorussia. You were not stopped by the strong fortifications which you have overcome at the approaches to Berlin.

"You are faced by Berlin, Soviet warriors. You must take Berlin, and take it as swiftly as possible so the enemy has no time to come to his senses. Let us then bring all the power of our military equipment to bear on the enemy, let us rally all our will for victory and all our intelligence. Let us not disgrace our soldier's honour and the honour of our military colours.

"On to the assault on Berlin, to the complete and final victory, comrades-in-arms! By daring and courage, good teamwork between all arms of the service, good mutual support sweep aside all obstacles and forge ahead, only forward, to the centre of the city, to its southern and western outskirts — to meet the Allied forces moving from the west. Forward to victory!

"The Front Military Council is sure that the glorious soldiers of the First Byelorussian Front will fulfill the mission entrusted to them with honour, wipe off the face of the earth the last obstacles on the way to the new victory and raise their military colours over Berlin in glory.

"Forward to the assault on Berlin!

"Commander of the	Member of the Military
"First Byelorussian Front	Council of the First
"Marshal of the Soviet	Byelorussian Front
"Union	Lieutenant-General
"G. Zhukov	K. Telegin"

In order to crush the enemy defence in Berlin as swiftly as possible it was decided to commit the 1st and the 2nd Guards Tank armies together with the 8th Guards, 5th Shock, 3rd Shock, and 47th armies to the fighting in the city. They were to rapidly neutralize enemy defences in Berlin with powerful artillery fire, air attacks and a tank avalanche.

On April 23 and 24 troops of the First Byelorussian Front were mauling the Nazis at the approaches to the centre of Berlin. Units from the First Ukrainian Front's 3rd Guards Tank Army had engaged the enemy in the southern part of the city.

On April 25, the 47th Army's 328th Rifle Division and the 2nd Guards Tank Army's 65th Tank Brigade of the First Byelorussian Front which were advancing west of Berlin joined up with the 4th Guards Tank Army's 6th Guards Mechanized Corps of the First Ukrainian Front in the Ketzin area.

Thereby, the more than 400,000-strong Berlin enemy force was cut into two isolated groups: the Berlin and the Frankfurt-Huben group.

General A. V. Gorbatov's 3rd Army from the Front reserve committed to battle advanced further along the Oder-Spree Canal and exploiting the success of the 1st Guards Tank Army quickly reached the Königswusterhausen area.

From the latter area, turning abruptly south and south-east, it struck out towards Teupitz and joined up with the right-wing forces of the First Ukrainian Front advancing in a north-westerly direction. The ring had been firmly closed around the enemy group south-east of Berlin in the Wendisch-Buchholtz area.

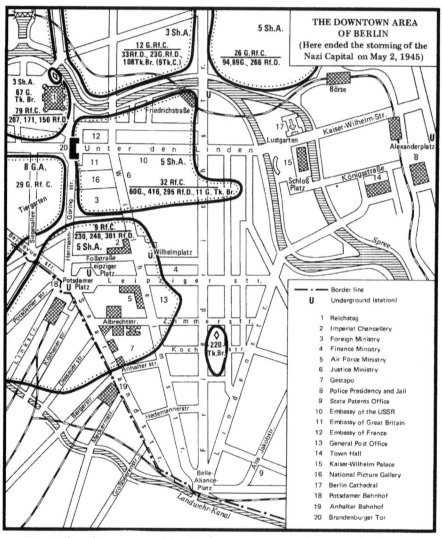

The fighting was developing successfully in Berlin, too. When the Front's troops broke into the capital of Berlin, the city's defence had been weakened already in some districts, because part of the Berlin garrison had been transferred by the Nazi Command to strengthen the defence on the Seelow Heights. Our units quickly found the weak points and outflanked the main resistance centres by manoeuvring.

However, as they approached the city's central part resistance stiffened sharply. The fighting became more fierce on both sides. Enemy defence was continuous. The Germans had used all the advantages offered to a side in the defensive within a city. An important part was played by multistorey buildings, thick walls, and particularly the bomb shelters and bunkers connected with each other through underground passages. The Germans could move from one block to another along these passages or even appear in the rear of our troops.

Cutting Berlin into two parts the Spree with its high concrete banks surrounded the ministerial buildings in the city's centre. Every house here was defended by a garrison, sometimes up to a battalion strong.

Our offensive did not abate either by day or by night. All efforts were aimed at preventing the enemy from organizing defence in new strongpoints. The armies' battle formations were well echeloned in depth. The first echelon attacked in the daytime, units of the second echelon at night.

Berlin's defence, prepared in advance with its sectors, districts and sections, was countered by a detailed plan of the offensive.

Every army storming Berlin was assigned an offensive zone in advance. Units received specific objectives to capture — districts, streets, and squares. A carefully drawn-up well-patterned system lay behind the seeming chaos of the fighting in the city. The main targets in the city were subjected to withering fire.

The most heavy fighting in the central part of Berlin fell to the lot of assault groups and assault detachments consisting of all the arms of the service.

The aim of the street fighting in Berlin was to deprive the enemy of the opportunity to deploy his forces in a shock group, split the garrison into individual parts, and rapidly destroy them.

The necessary conditions had been created to solve that problem at the beginning of the operation. First of all, our troops had badly mauled a considerable part of the enemy manpower and equipment at the approaches to the city. Second, having swiftly surrounded Berlin we deprived the Germans of the possibility to manoeuvre with their reserves. Third, the German reserves brought up to Berlin were rapidly defeated.

All this enabled us to reduce the street fighting to a minimum despite numerous obstacles and make it easier for the troops to destroy enemy defences within the city.

Every infantry and tank attack was accompanied by massive artillery and air strikes along all the sectors of the Front. At regular time intervals 11,000 guns of different calibre opened fire at the same time. Nearly 1,800,000 artillery shells were fired at Berlin from April 21 to May 2. On the whole, more than 36,000 tons of metal fell on enemy positions in the city.

On the third day of the fighting in Berlin fortress guns were transported to Silesia Railway Terminal along specially widened tracks and opened fire on the centre of the city. Every shell weighed half a ton.

Berlin's defence was blasted to smithereens.

Keitel later said at an interrogation:

"On April 22 it became clear that Berlin would fall if all the troops were not removed from the Elbe and thrown against the advancing Russians. After a joint conference of Hitler and Goebbels with Jodl and me it was decided: the 12th Army would leave weak rearguards against the Americans and attack the Russian forces surrounding Berlin."

Jodl continued:

"On April 22 Goebbels asked me if it was possible to avert the fall of Berlin by military means. I answered that it was possible only provided we withdrew all the forces on the Elbe and sent them to defend Berlin. On Goebbels' advice I reported my thoughts to the Führer, he agreed and instructed Keitel and me together with the Headquarters to be outside Berlin and personally command the counterattack."

The commander of the Berlin garrison, General Weidling said at an interrogation:

"On April 25 Hitler told me: 'The situation will improve(!). The 9th Army will approach Berlin and hit the enemy together with the 12th Army. This attack will be inflicted along the Russian southern front. Steiner's troops will advance from the north and hit the northern wing.'"

All these plans were the fantasies of Hitler and his entourage who had lost the capacity of thinking realistically. In the early hours on April 23 Keitel left Berlin for the Headquarters of the 12th Army with the mission of joining it up with the 9th Army. On the next day he was simply unable to return to the city. The Soviet troops were mauling both these armies.

Radio telegrams signed by Hitler were transmitted every day, such as the following: "Where is the 12th Army?", "Why doesn't Wenk attack?", "Where is Schörner?", "Attack, immediately!", "When will you begin the attack?"

Since actions by the 5th Shock Army commanded by Colonel-General N. E. Berzarin have been hardly described in our literature, I would like to tell about some of its feats of arms. Several of them I witnessed firsthand, I learned about others from army command and unit commanders.

In view of the particular importance of the mission this army was assigned — to capture the area of government blocks in the centre, including the Imperial Chancellery where Hitler's headquarters as well as Hitler and his henchmen were, we reinforced it with General I. I. Yushchuk's 11th Tank Corps in addition to elements attached to it earlier.

The most complicated task in the initial phase was the assault of the strongly fortified Silesian Railway Terminal and forcing of the Spree river with its high concrete banks.

The following forces were the first to burst into Berlin from the east (they belonged to the 26th Guards Corps commanded by General P. A. Firsov and 32nd Corps commanded by D. S. Zherebin):

the 94th Guards Division (commander General I. G. Gasporian, chief of the political department Colonel S. V. Kuzovkov);

the 89th Guards Division (commander General M. P. Seryugin, chief of the political department Colonel P. Kh. Gordiyenko);

the 266th Division (commander Colonel S. M. Fomichenko, chief of the political department Colonel V. I. Loginov);

the 60th Guards Division (commander General V. P. So-kolov, chief of the political department Colonel I. N. Artamonov);

the 416th Division (commander General D. M. Syzranov, chief of the political department Colonel R. A. Mejidov);

the 295th Division (commander General A. P. Dorofeyev, chief of the political department Colonel G. T. Lukonin).

Our heroic soldiers had awaited this historic moment for nearly four years. At last, the hour of the final reckoning with fascism had come.

It is difficult to describe the excitement which seized all the Soviet soldiers.

Here are the recollections of artillery piece commandeı in the 832nd Artillery Regiment's 6th battery of the 266th Rifle Division, Senior Sergeant Nikolai Vasilyev:

"Towards evening our battery reached the heights, and we saw an enormous city. We were overwhelmed by a feeling of joy and jubilation: it was the last enemy line and the hour of reckoning had come! We didn't even notice how a car drove up and our Commander-in-Chief, General Berzarin, climbed out. Hailing us he ordered our commander to open fire against the Nazis in Berlin! We had perhaps never shown such speed and efficiency in firing...

"The medical instructor Malanya Yurchenko wrote on the battery's shells: "For Stalingrad, for the Donbass, for the Ukraine, for the orphans and widows. For mothers' tears!'"

The 286th Guards Rifle Regiment of the 94th Guards Division (commander Lieutenant-Colonel A. N. Kravchenko) and the 283rd Guards Rifle Regiment of the same division commanded by Lieutenant-Colonel A. A. Ignatyev won particular distinction in the fighting during the storming of Berlin's eastern part.

The soldiers sought to advance and showed mass heroism. Seeing that it was difficult to capture the strongly fortified corner building that prevented the regiment from moving on by means of a frontal attack, company Party organizer of the 283rd Guards Regiment Alexei Kuznetsov with a group of soldiers sneaked round the building and attacked from the rear. The enemy strong point was captured.

Unparalleled valour was displayed by Senior Lieutenant

I. P. Ukraintsev of the 283rd Guards Regiment. During the attack of a house hand-to-hand fighting broke out, and he rushed at the enemy. The brave officer knifed nine Nazis to death. Following his example, Guards Sergeant Stepan Grobazai and his section killed several dozen Nazis.

The remarkable Komsomol leader of the 94th Guards Division Captain Nikolai Gorshelev, deputy chief of the division's political department, died the death of a hero in this fighting. He inspired the soldiers by his own example in combat, always being everywhere where the battle was decided. He was respected and loved by the division's men for valour and the concern he showed for the rank and file and officers.

The 9th Rifle Corps commanded by Hero of the Soviet Union Major-General I. P. Rosly achieved the greatest success in storming Berlin on April 23. The soldiers of the corps seized Karlshorst and part of Kopenick by a resolute storm and forced the Spree on the march.

As I was told later, the assault detachment headed by deputy division commander, Lieutenant-Colonel F. U. Galkin, won particular distinction in the fighting there. After taking Karlshorst, advancing on the Treptow Park the detachment captured on the march Berlin's largest electric plant, Rummelsburg, which the Nazis had intended to blow up. When Galkin's group burst into the plant it was still running at full capacity. The plant was immediately demined. Complete understanding was reached with the remaining workers. They pledged to continue the plant's technical maintenance.

Lieutenant-Colonel F. U. Galkin, Lieutenant-Colonel A. M. Ozhogin and Lieutenant-Colonel A. I. Levin were awarded the title of Hero of the Soviet Union for efficient organization, courage and heroism shown in capturing the Rummelsburg electric plant, forcing the Spree swiftly and capturing many objectives.

Brave actions were undertaken in forcing the Spree by the 1st River Boat Brigade of the Dnieper Flotilla, particularly by the brigade's motor-boat unit commanded by Lieutenant M. M. Kalinin. Despite strong enemy fire Petty Officer Georgi Dudnik ferried several rifle companies of the 301st Rifle Division to the enemy bank.

A fire broke out on board from a direct hit by an enemy shell. Dudnik was badly wounded. Despite the wound and burns, he drove the boat to the bank, landed the men, put out the fire and set out again for his bank. However, he failed to reach it being killed by mortar fire.

The helmsman of another boat, A. Ye. Samokhvalov, displayed exceptional bravery and ingenuity during the crossing by our units. Under enemy fire he repaired the boat and when his commander was killed by enemy fire he took over command and continued ferrying our troops.

Lieutenant Kalinin, Petty Officer Dudnik, G. P. Kazakov and A. P. Pashkov; sailors N. A. Baranov, A. Ye. Samokhvalov, M. T. Sotnikov, N. A. Filippov and V. V. Cherinov were bestowed the title of Hero of the Soviet Union by a decree of the USSR Supreme Soviet on May 31, 1945, for military valour and heroism displayed by the seamen of the 1st Bobruisk Brigade of the Dnieper Flotilla. The flotilla itself received the Order of Ushakov 1st Class.

Engaged in fierce fighting on April 24, the 5th Shock Army continued to advance successfully towards the centre of Berlin, to Alexanderplatz, Kaiser Wilhelm's Palace, the Berlin Town Hall and the Imperial Chancellery.

In view of the most successful advance by the 5th Shock Army, as well as the particularly outstanding qualities of its commander, Hero of the Soviet Union Colonel-General N. E. Berzarin, the command appointed him the first Soviet Commandant and Chief of the Soviet Garrison of Berlin on April 24.

Nikolai Berzarin was a loyal son of the Communist Party, a patriot, and an experienced, strong-willed and disciplined commander. As army commander in the Yassy-Kishinev, Vistula-Oder and Berlin operations Berzarin showed himself to be a talented military leader. He took a thoughtful approach to elaborating operations and controlling the troops and implemented the higher command's orders in a creative spirit. He always relied on the Communists in his work.

He was well assisted in army affairs by member of the Military Council, Lieutenant-General F. Ye. Bokov. Having worked formerly at the General Staff, Bokov gained considerable experience in operational questions and organisation of operations.

The fighting in the centre of Berlin proceeded with increasing intensity on April 25. Relying on strong defence points, the enemy resisted stubbornly.

Our troops sustained heavy losses, but surged forward, inspired by success, to the very centre of Berlin where the enemy High Command headed by Hitler still was. We knew this very well from German radio transmissions: Hitler hysterically called on his armies to save Berlin unaware that they had already been smashed by the forces of the First Byelorussian and First Ukrainian Fronts.

The fiercest fighting broke out in the city's centre on April 29.

The Town Hall was assaulted by the 1008th Rifle Regiment (commander Colonel V. N. Borisov) and the 1010th Regiment (commander Colonel M. F. Zagorodsky) of the 266th Rifle Division. The men of that division performed many exciting feats of arms which were described to me by firsthand participants in the assault.

Captain N. V. Bobylev's battalion was set the mission of breaking through to the Town Hall and capturing it jointly with Major M. A. Alexeyev's battalion supported by tanks and self-propelled artillery. Our men were met by such a strong avalanche of fire that further advance along the street was simply impossible.

It was decided then to break into the Town Hall through the walls by breaching them with explosives. Under the enemy fire the sappers put tolite and exploded the walls one by one. The smoke had not had time to disperse when assault groups rushed into the breaches and cleared the buildings adjacent to the Town Hall from the enemy after hand-to-hand fighting.

Tanks and self-propelled guns were committed to battle. Firing a few shots they smashed the heavy wrought-iron gates of the Town Hall, breached the walls while setting up a smokescreen. The whole building was engulfed in thick smoke.

Lieutenant K. Madenov's platoon was the first to break in. Privates N. P. Kondrashev, K. Ye. Kryutchenko, I. F. Kashpurovsky and others acted bravely together with the daring lieutenant. They used hand-grenades to clear the lobby and halls. Every room was fought for.

Komsomol organizer of the 1008th Rifle Regiment's 1st Battalion Junior Lieutenant K. G. Gromov climbed up on the roof of the Town Hall. Having thrown down the Nazi flag on the pavement Konstantin Gromov hoisted the Red Banner over the Town Hall. Gromov was granted the title of Hero of the Soviet Union for heroism and courage displayed in these battles.

Successfully advancing in the centre of Berlin the 5th Shock Army cooperated very well with the 3rd Shock and the 2nd Guards Tank armies, the 8th Guards Army, the 16th Air Army and other forces. The rapid success achieved in the fighting for the centre of the city was the result of skilful organization of cooperation between all the advancing armies.

At this point I must note the brilliant work done by the chief of staff of the 5th Shock Army, General V. K. Kushchev, his deputy General S. P. Petrov, Chief of the Intelligence Department A. D. Siniayev, HQ Party organizer V. K. Popov, Chief of Communications V. F. Falin and other staff officers.

Thus, the end was in sight.

What was the Nazi leadership counting on at this moment which was critical for Germany?

At interrogations Keitel said:

"Beginning with summer 1944 Germany was waging a war to win time hoping that in a war in which both sides were represented by different states, different military leaders, different armies and different navies, completely unexpected changes could occur in the situation as a result of the combination of various forces. Thus, we were waging a war waiting for events which were to happen but did not."

At the time of Berlin's fall Hitler could no longer count on these events and suggested the slogan: "It is better to surrender Berlin to the Americans and the British than to let the Russians into the city."

German pows in Berlin told us: "The officers maintained that all efforts would be made not to let the Russians capture

Berlin. If the city were to be surrendered, it would only be to the Americans."

The battle in Berlin had reached its peak. All of us wished to finish off the Berlin group by May 1. Although agonized, the enemy continued to fight for every house, for every cellar, for every storey and roof.

Despite this fierce but senseless resistance, the Soviet soldiers took block after block. The troops commanded by generals Kuznetsov, Berzarin, Bogdanov, Katukov and Chuikov advanced closer and closer to the centre of Berlin.

April 30, 1945, will always remain in the memory of the Soviet people and in the history of their struggle against Nazi Germany.

On that day, at 14:25 hours troops of the 3rd Shock Army (commander Colonel-General Kuznetsov, member of the Military Council General A. I. Litvinov) captured the main part of the Reichstag building.

The fighting for the Reichstag involved great bloodshed. The approaches to it were covered by strong buildings included in the system of the Berlin's ninth central sector of defence. The Reichstag district was defended by crack SS units almost 6,000-strong equipped with tanks, assault guns and strong artillery.

Here is how the events unravelled. The overall assault on the Reichstag was carried out by the reinforced 79th Rifle Corps of the 3rd Shock Army consisting of the 150th and 17lst Rifle Divisions and the 23rd Tank Brigade. The corps was led by a talented commander, Hero of the Soviet Union Semyon Perevertkin, an active participant in the Battle of Moscow in 1941.

The 150th Idritsa Rifle Division was commanded by an experienced general, Hero of the Soviet Union V. M. Shatilov.

Troops of the 79th Rifle Corps had burst into Berlin as early as April 22. Advancing they liberated block after block. Owing to their successful actions it became possible for the 3rd Shock Army to hit the centre of Berlin from the north.

The 79th Rifle Corps was turned south with the aim of capturing the city's northern part and exploiting the offensive towards Pletzensee and Moabit.

In the evening of April 26 the corps' units had forced the

Ferbindungs-Kanal and taken Boiselstrasse Station, and in the early hours on April 27, the north-western part of Moabit was cleared of the enemy. The vanguards of the 150th and the 171st Rifle Divisions reached the main Berlin electric plant, the Putlitzstrasse Station, and the Komische Oper theatre.

In the fighting the 150th Rifle Division took the Moabit Prison freeing thousands of pows and political prisoners. Red Army men found decapitating machines, guillotines, there, as they had at the Pletzensee Prison.

In the combat order No. 0025 of April 28, 1945, Major-General S. N. Perevertkin specified the missions for the units of the 79th Rifle Corps in taking the Reichstag:

"...3. The 150th Rifle Division: one rifle regiment to defend the line along the Spree river. Two rifle regiments to continue the offensive with the aim of forcing the Spree and **capturing the western part of the Reichstag...**

"4. The 171st Rifle Division to continue the offensive in its zone with the aim of forcing the Spree and **capturing the eastern part of the Reichstag...**

> "Commander of the 79th
> "Rifle Corps
> "Major General Perevertkin
> "Chief of Staff
> "Colonel Letunov"

Reinforced with Lieutenant-Colonel M. V. Morozov's 23rd Tank Brigade, the 150th and the 171st Rifle divisions' vanguard battalions commanded by Captain S. A. Neustroyev and Senior Lieutenant K. Y. Samsonov captured the Moltke Bridge in the zone of the corps' main attack in the early hours on April 29.

Fierce fighting took place from the morning of April 29 and all night before April 30 in the direct vicinity of the Reichstag. Units of the 150th and the 171st Rifle divisions were preparing to storm the Reichstag.

At 11 a.m. on Aprill 30, following an artillery and mortar attack, the assault battalions of these divisions' regiments and recon artillery groups commanded by Major M. M. Bondar and

Captain V. N. Makov went into attack attempting to capture the Reichstag building from three sides.

Following another 30-minute artillery barrage at 1 p.m. a new and rapid attack began. Small arms and hand-to-hand fighting flared up directly in front of the Reichstag building and for the main entrance.

At 2:25 p.m. Senior Lieutenant Samsonov's battalion of the 171st Rifle Division, Captain Neustroyev's battalion and Major Davydov's battalion of the 150th Rifle Division broke into the Reichstag.

However, even after the lower storeys of the Reichstag had been taken, the enemy garrison did not surrender. Fierce fighting took place inside the building.

At 6 p.m. the Reichstag was stormed once again. Units from the 150th and the 171st Rifle divisions cleared storey after storey of the enemy. At 9:50 p.m. on April 30 Sergeant M. A. Yegorov and Junior Sergeant M. V. Kantaria hoisted the Victory Flag received from the army Military Council on the main cupola of the Reichstag.

Witnessing the historic battle for the Reichstag personally the Commander of the 3rd Shock Army Kuznetsov immediately called me at the command post and reported rejoicing:

"The Red Flag is on the Reichstag! Hurrah, Comrade Marshal!"

"Dear Vasily, I congratulate you and all your men heartily with the wonderful victory. This historical feat by the troops will never be forgotten by the Soviet people!"

Order No. 06 of the First Byelorussian Front's Military Council on April 30 read:

"1. The Reichstag district in the city of Berlin was defended by crack SS units. In the early hours on April 28, 1945, the enemy parachuted in a battalion of marines to reinforce the defences of the district. In the Reichstag district the enemy resisted desperately our advancing troops having turned every building, stairway, room, cellar into strongpoints and defensive positions. The fighting within the main building of the Reichstag repeatedly took the form of hand-to-hand combat.

"2. Continuing the offensive the troops of Colonel-General

Kuznetsov's 3rd Shock Army overcame enemy resistance, took the main building of the Reichstag and today, on April 30, 1945, raised our Soviet Flag on it. Major-General Perevertkin's 79th Rifle Corps and his Colonel Negoda's 171st Rifle Division and Major-General Shatilov's 150th Rifle Division won particular distinction in the fighting for the district and the main building of the Reichstag.

"3. Congratulating with the victory won I commend all the men, sergeants, officers and generals of the 171st and the 150th Rifle divisions and the Commander of the 79th Rifle Corps, Major-General Perevertkin, who personally directed the fighting for the daring they displayed, and skilful and successful fulfilment of the combat mission. The privates, sergeants, officers, and generals who won particular distinction in the fighting for the Reichstag will be selected for government awards by the Military Council of the 3rd Shock Army.

"4. The hour of the final victory over the enemy is nearing. The Soviet Flag is already flapping over the main building of the Reichstag in the centre of Berlin.

"Comrade soldiers, sergeants, officers and generals of the First Byelorussian Front! Forward against the enemy — with our last swift blow let us finish off the Nazi beast in its lair and bring the hour nearer of final and complete victory over Nazi Germany.

"The order is to be read in all companies, squadrons and batteries of the front.

"Commander of the   Member of the Military
"First Byelorussian   Council
"Front   of the First Byelorussian
"Marshal of the Soviet   Front
"Union   Lieutenant-General
"G. Zhukov   K. Telegin

"Chief of Staff of the First Byelorussian Front
                                    Colonel-General M. Malinin"

At the end of the day on May 1 the Nazis in the Reichstag could no longer withstand the onslaught and surrendered. Only individual groups of Nazis in different sections of the

Reichstag cellar continued to resist until the morning on May 2.

Regiment commander Fyodor Zinchenko of the 150th Rifle Division was appointed Commandant of the Reichstag.

The fighting for Berlin was a life-and-death struggle. The men had come here from the depths of Russia from Hero Cities Stalingrad, Leningrad, from the Ukraine, Byelorussia, from the Baltic, Transcaucasian and other republics to complete the just war against those who had infringed upon the freedom of their Motherland. Many of them had wounds from previous fighting which had not healed yet. The wounded men did not leave the ranks. Everyone was intent on surging forward. It was as if there had not been the four gruelling years of war: morale had risen, the spirits were high, so it was easier to carry out the great undertaking, to hoist the Victory Flag in Berlin.

Our men showed great inspiration, heroism and valour in the fighting. The maturity of our armed forces and their progress in the years of the war were fully reflected in the Battle of Berlin. The privates, sergeants, officers and generals showed themselves to be creatively mature, resolute and extremely brave men in the Berlin operation. The Communist Party had made exceptionally experienced soldiers and true masters of warcraft out of them during the Great Patriotic War, and experience and knowledge are the most fertile soil for the comprehensive development of the art of warfare.

How many thoughts swept through our minds in those joyful minutes! We recalled the hardest Battle of Moscow where our troops stood firm to the death not letting the enemy reach the capital, Stalingrad in ruins but unvanquished, glorious Leningrad which withstood the fiercest blockade, Sebastopol which fought so valiantly against picked Nazi troops, the triumph on the Kursk Bulge, and thousands of destroyed towns and villages and the millions of lives the Soviet people lost, the people who endured and won...

And at last the most important moment for which our people suffered immensely had come: the complete defeat of Nazi Germany and the triumph of our just cause!

Only the Tiergarten and the government block remained in German hands on May 1. This was where the Imperial Chancellery was situated with the bunker of Hitler's General Headquarters in the courtyard.

On that day Martin Bormann wrote down in his diary: "Our Imperial Chancellery is turning into ruins."

CHAPTER 9

Unconditional Surrender of Nazi Germany

At 3:50 on the morning of May 1, General Krebs, Chief of the General Staff of the German Ground Forces was brought to the command post of the 8th Guards Army. He said he was authorized to enter into direct contact with the Supreme Command of the Red Army to negotiate an armistice.

At 4:00 General Chuikov telephoned to report me that General Krebs had told him about Hitler's suicide. According to Krebs it occurred at 15:50 on April 30. Chuikov read to me a letter from Goebbels addressed to the Soviet Supreme Command. This is what it said:

"In accordance with the Will of the late Führer, we authorize General Krebs to do the following. We inform the leader of the Soviet people that today, at 15:50 the Führer departed from this life of his own free will. By virtue of his legal right the Führer by his Will left all power to Dönitz, myself and Bormann. I authorized Bormann to establish contact with the leader of the Soviet people. This contact is essential for carrying out peace negotiations between the powers which have suffered the heaviest losses. Goebbels."

Enclosed with Goebbels's letter was Hitler's Will with the list of the new Imperial Cabinet. The Will was signed by Hitler, countersigned by witnesses, and dated April 30, 1945, 4 o'clock in the morning.

In view of the importance of the report I immediately sent my deputy, General of the Army Sokolovsky to Chuikov's command post for talks with the German general. Sokolovsky was to demand of Krebs the unconditional surrender of Nazi Germany.

I got on the line to Moscow straight away and called Stalin.

389

He was at his summer cottage. The call was answered by a duty general who said:

"Comrade Stalin has just gone to bed."

"Please, wake him up. The matter is urgent and can't wait till morning."

In a little while Stalin was on the line. I reported to him about Hitler's suicide and the letter from Goebbels proposing armistice.

Stalin answered:

"Now he's done it, the bastard. Too bad he could not have been taken alive. Where is Hitler's body?"

"According to General Krebs Hitler's body was burned."

"Tell Sokolovsky that there can be no talks — either with Krebs or any other Hitlerites — only unconditional surrender," said the Supreme Commander. "If nothing special happens, don't call me till morning. I want to have a little rest before tomorrow's May Day Parade."

The May Day Parade... the May Day demonstration... How much they mean to every Soviet man, especially if he is away from his homeland. I saw clearly in my mind's eye the troops of the Moscow garrison moving towards Red Square. In the morning, they would take their places and after the Commander who takes the salute finishes his speech they would march past the Lenin Mausoleum, past the Government and Party leaders. They would march past the walls of the ancient Kremlin, stepping firmly, proud to represent the victorious strength of the Soviet Armed Forces which had freed Europe from the menace of fascism.

About five in the morning General Sokolovsky phoned me to report on his first conversation with General Krebs.

"The Germans have something up their sleeve," he said. "Krebs says he is not authorized to decide on unconditional surrender. According to him, that can be done only by the new German government headed by Dönitz. Krebs claims that he seeks to arrange a cease-fire in order to assemble the members of the Dönitz government in Berlin. I think we should tell them to go to hell if they don't consent to unconditional surrender rightaway."

"Just so, Vasily Danilovich," I answered. "Tell Krebs that if Goebbels and Bormann don't agree to unconditional surrender before ten o'clock, the blow we shall strike will knock all ideas of resistance out of their heads. They had better think of the senseless sacrifices made by the German people and of their own personal responsibility for courting disaster."

No reply from Goebbels and Bormann was received at the appointed time.

At 10:40 our forces opened drum-fire on the remnants of the special defence sector in the centre of the city. At 18:00 Sokolovsky reported that the German leaders had sent their truce envoy. He said Goebbels and Bormann had rejected the demand for unconditional surrender.

In reply to that, at 18:30 the final assault of the central part of the city, where the Imperial Chancellery was situated and where the last of the Hitlerites dug in, began with incredible force.

I do not remember the exact time — as soon as it got dark — the commander of the 3rd Army, General Kuznetsov, rang me up. His voice sounded excited as he reported:

"At the position held by the 52nd Guards Rifle Division about 20 German tanks have just broken through, heading for the north-western suburbs of the city at a high speed."

Apparently someone was clearing out from Berlin.

This gave rise to most alarming conjectures. Somebody even said the tanks that had broken through were probably taking Hitler, Goebbels and Bormann out of Berlin.

The troops were at once alerted so as not to let a living soul leave the Berlin area. F. I. Perkhorovich, commander of the 47th Army, P. A. Belov, commander of the 61st Army, and Poplawski, commander of the 1st Army of the Wojsko Polskie, were immediately instructed to seal off all roads and passages to the west and north-west. Commander of the 2nd Guards Tank Army, General Bogdanov, and commander of the 3rd Shock Army, General Kuznetsov, were ordered immediately to organize pursuit in all directions, to spot and destroy the tanks that had broken through.

At dawn on May 2 the tanks were discovered 15 kilometres north-west of Berlin and quickly destroyed by our tankmen. Some of the tanks burned down; the others were blown to pieces. Among the dead crewmen there were no Nazi chiefs. The remains in the burned tanks could not be identified.

Late at night, at 1:50 on May 2 the Berlin Defence Head-quarters radio station broadcast several times in German and Russian:

"We are sending our truce envoys to the Bismarckstrasse Bridge. We are suspending hostilities."

At 6:30 on the morning of May 2, it was reported that General Weidling, commander of the 56th Tank Corps, sur-rendered at the sector held by the 47th Guards Rifle Di-vision. His staff officers surrendered too. At the preliminary interrogation General Weidling said that a few days before Hitler had personally appointed him commander of the Berlin defence.

General Weidling instantly agreed to order his troops to cease resistance. Here is what he signed and broadcast over the radio on the morning of May 2:

"On April 30 the Führer committed suicide, thus leaving us, who had sworn allegiance to him, alone. By the Führer's order we, the German troops, were to fight for Berlin despite the fact that we had run out of ammunition and that the general situation makes our further resistance senseless.

"I hereby order that all resistance be ceased immediately. Signed: Weidling (General of Artillery, former Commander of the Defence of the Berlin area)."

On the same day, at about 2 p. m. I was informed that the Deputy Minister of Propaganda, Dr. Fritsche, who had sur-rendered, offered to address the troops of the Berlin garrison over the radio telling them that all resistance should be stopped. We agreed to put him on the air so as to speed up the end of the hostilities.

After his radio broadcast, Fritsche was brought to me. During the interrogation he repeated what was on the whole known from the talks with Krebs. As is known, Fritsche was a close associate of Hitler, Goebbels and Bormann.

He said that on April 29 Hitler called together his cohort. The meeting was attended by Bormann, Goebbels, Axmann, Krebs and other high-ranking Nazi officials. Fritsche pro-fessed that he was not there, but that later Goebbels told him all about the meeting in detail.

According to Fritsche, during the last few days, especial-ly after April 20 when Soviet artillery opened fire on Berlin,

Hitler had been in a kind of stupor interrupted by hysterical outbursts. At times he would start gibbering about a close victory.

In reply to my question about Hitler's last plans Fritsche said that he did not know for sure but he had heard that when the Russians began their offensive on the Oder, some of the leaders went to Berchtesgaden and Southern Tyrol taking some freight with them. It was there that the High Command headed by Hitler were supposed to fly. At the very last moment, when the Soviet troops had reached Berlin, there was talk of evacuation to Schleswig-Holstein. Planes were kept ready near the Imperial Chancellery but they were soon destroyed by Soviet aircraft.

Fritsche did not have anything else to tell us.

The next morning he was sent to Moscow for a more detailed interrogation.

A few words about the final battle in Berlin.

On May 1 the 248th Rifle Division under General N. Z. Galai and 230th Rifle Division under Colonel D. K. Shishkov of the 5th Shock Army under General Berzarin stormed and seized the State Post Office and attacked the building of the Finance Ministry situated opposite the Imperial Chancellery. On May 1 the 301st Division (commander Colonel V. S. Antonov of Berzarin's Army) in cooperation with the 248th Rifle Division stormed and captured the Gestapo building and the Aviation Ministry. Under infantry cover a self-propelled artillery battalion rushed forward. A. L. Denisyuk, commander of a self-propelled gun, installed it in the aperture of the fence and saw the grey building of the Imperial Chancellery about a hundred metres away, showing through the foggy mist. A huge eagle with a swastika adorned its façade. Denisyuk gave the command, "Fire on the Nazi marauder!" The Nazi coat-of-arms was knocked off.

The final battle for the Imperial Chancellery, in which the 301st and 248th Rifle divisions were engaged, was strenuous. The fighting at the approaches to and inside the building was especially fierce. Striking was the courage of Major Anna Nikulina, instructor of the political department of the 9th Rifle Corps. Together with the assault group of F. K. Shapovalov's battalion, she made her way through the break in the roof, approached the metal spire and tied to it the Red flag she had carried under her jacket with a piece of telegraph wire. The Soviet Flag unfurled over the Imperial Chancellery.

After the capture of the Imperial Chancellery Colonel V. E. Shevtsov, deputy commander of the 301st Rifle Division, was appointed its commandant.

Since May 4, when the division was transferred to Treptow Park, this post was taken by Major F. G. Platonov, senior officer in charge of operations work of the 5th Shock Army.

By 15:00 on May 2, the enemy was crushed. The remnants of the Berlin garrison, over 134,000 men, surrendered. Many of those who had fought arms in hand apparently deserted in the last few days and went into hiding.

May 2, 1945, was a day of great jubilation for the Soviet people, the Soviet Armed Forces, our Allies, and the peoples of the whole world.

The Order of the Supreme Commander read:

"The troops of the First Byelorussian Front supported by the troops of the First Ukrainian Front after stubborn street fighting have completed the routing of the Berlin group of German forces and today on May 1, have gained full control of Berlin, the capital of Germany — the centre of German imperialism and the hotbed of German aggression."

After the seizure of the Imperial Chancellery I went there with Colonel-General Berzarin, Lieutenant-General Bokov, member of the Military Council of the Army, and some other officers who had taken part in the assault in order to make certain of the suicide of Hitler, Goebbels and other Nazi leaders.

On our arrival we found ourselves in an embarrassing situation. We were told that the bodies of the suicides had allegedly been buried by the Germans, but no one knew who exactly did it or where. Different hypotheses were put forth.

The pows, mostly wounded, knew nothing about Hitler and his entourage.

In the Imperial Chancellery only a few dozen people were found. Apparently, at the last moment the high-ranking officers and the SS men had left the building by secret tunnels and gone into hiding in the city.

We looked for the place where the bodies of Hitler and Goebbels were burned, but could not find it. Admittedly, we saw the ashes of some fires but they were obviously too small. Most likely German soldiers had used them to boil water.

When we had almost finished inspecting the Imperial Chancellery, it was reported to us that the bodies of Goebbels's six children had been found in an underground room. I must admit I had not the heart to go down and look at the children killed by their own mother and father. Shortly afterwards the bodies of Goebbels and his wife were found close to the bunker. Dr. Fritsche, who was brought to identify the bodies, testified that they were those of Goebbels and his wife.

At first circumstances made me doubt the truthfulness of the account of Hitler's suicide, all the more so because we could not find Bormann either. At the time I thought that Hitler might have escaped at the last moment when there was no hope of any help for Berlin from without.

I stated that surmise at a Berlin press conference for Soviet and foreign correspondents.

Some time later, after an inquiry and the questioning of Hitler's personal medical staff, etc. we started to receive additional, more concrete evidence confirming Hitler's suicide. I became convinced that there were no grounds for doubting Hitler's suicide.

Most of the Nazi ringleaders, among them Goering, Himmler, Keitel and Jodl, fled from Berlin in different directions in good time.

Like reckless gamblers, they, together with Hitler, hoped till the last moment to draw a "lucky card" which would save Nazi Germany and themselves. On April 30, and even on May 1, the Hitlerite ringleaders still tried to deter final defeat by starting negotiations on summoning to Berlin the newly-brought-to-light Dönitz government allegedly to make decision on Germany's surrender.

General Krebs, an experienced military diplomat, did his utmost to involve us in long-drawn-out negotiations, but his ruse failed. I have already mentioned that General Sokolovsky, who was empowered to carry on negotiations, told Krebs categorically that the cessation of hostilities was only possible after complete and unconditional surrender of the Nazi troops to the Allies. That was the end of their talk.

And since the Germans at that time refused to agree to unconditional surrender, our troops were ordered to finish the enemy off immediately.

In the morning of May 3, I inspected the Reichstag and the scenes of the fighting in that area together with the Berlin Commandant General Berzarin, F. Ye. Bokov, member of the Military Council of the 5th Army, K. F. Telegin, member of the Military Council of the Front, and others. We were guided by Wilhelm Pieck's son, Arthur, who fought in the Red Army during the war. He knew Berlin well, and this helped us to learn more about the conditions under which our troops had had to fight.

Each step, each inch of land, each stone, told us clearer than any words could do that at the approaches to the Imperial Chancellery and the Reichstag and inside these buildings a life-and-death battle had been fought.

The Reichstag is a huge building whose walls could not be breached by shells of medium calibre. Heavy guns were needed. The cupola of the Reichstag and the massive upper structure made it possible for the enemy to concentrate fire from several levels at all approaches to the building. Conditions for fighting inside the Reichstag were extremely difficult and complicated. They required of our soldiers not only courage but also instantaneous orientation, watchful care, quick movement from shelter to shelter and accurate fire on the enemy. Our soldiers coped with these tasks.

The columns at the entrance to the Reichstag and the walls were all covered with inscriptions written by our soldiers. In the laconic phrases or just signatures of soldiers, officers and generals one could feel their pride for the Soviet people, for the Soviet Armed Forces, for the Motherland and the Leninist Party.

We, too, put our signatures there. Having thus learned who we were, the soldiers surrounded us. We had to stay with them for an hour, talking heart to heart. The soldiers asked us many questions. They asked when it would be possible to go home, whether Soviet troops would remain in Germany to occupy it, whether we would wage war with Japan, etc.

On May 7 Stalin called me in Berlin and said:

"Today, in the town of Rheims, the Germans signed an act

of unconditional surrender. It was the Soviet people who bore the main brunt of the war, not the Allies," he went on. "Therefore the Germans should sign the surrender before the Supreme Command of all the countries of the anti-Hitler coalition, and not just before the Supreme Command of the Allied Forces.

· "I also did not agree to the unconditional surrender being signed not in Berlin, the centre of Nazi aggression," Stalin went on. "We reached an understanding with the Allies that the surrender act signed at Rheims should be considered a preliminary protocol of surrender. Tomorrow, representatives of the German High Command and representatives of the Supreme Command of the Allied Forces will arrive in Berlin. You are appointed representative of the Supreme Command of the Soviet Forces. Vyshinsky will join you tomorrow. After the act is signed he will remain in Berlin as your assistant in charge of political affairs."

Early in the morning on May 8, A. Ya. Vyshinsky, First Deputy People's Commissar of Foreign Affairs, arrived in Berlin. He brought with him all the necessary documents concerning the surrender of Germany and told me the names of the representatives of the Allied Supreme Command.

On the morning of May 8 journalists, correspondents and photographers of all the biggest newspapers and magazines of the world began to arrive to cover the historic moment when the defeat of Nazi Germany was put into legal form, when it acknowledged the irreversible fiasco of all the Nazi plans, of all its misanthropic ambitions.

The representatives of the Allied Supreme Command arrived at Tempelhof Airport in the middle of the day.

The Allied Command was represented by the British Air Marshal Arthur W. Tedder; the Commander of the US Strategic Air Forces, General Karl Spaatz; and the Commander-in-Chief of the French Army, General Jean de Lattre de Tassigny.

At the airport they were met by my deputy, General Sokolovsky; the first Berlin Commandant, Colonel-General Berzarin; member of the 5th Army Military Council, Lieutenant-General Bokov, and other representatives of the Red Army. From the airport the Allies went to Karlshorst where it had been decided to accept the unconditional surrender from the German Command.

General Field-Marshal Keitel, Admiral of the Fleet von Friedeburg and Colonel-General of the Luftwaffe Stumpff arrived from Flensburg, at the same airport. They had been authorized by Dönitz to sign the act of Germany's unconditional surrender.

There, in the eastern part of Berlin, at Karlshorst, in a two-storeyed building which used to house the canteen of the German military engineering school, a hall had been prepared for the ceremony of signing the document of unconditional surrender. After a short rest all the representatives of the Allied Command came to me to talk over the procedural aspects of the exciting event.

No sooner had we entered the room assigned for us than American and British journalists thronged in and plied me with questions. On behalf of the Allied forces they presented me with a flag of friendship on which greetings to the Red Army from the American troops were embroidered in gold letters.

When the journalists had left the conference hall, we began to discuss questions bearing on the surrender of the Hitlerites.

At that time General Field-Marshal Keitel and his companions were in a different building.

According to our officers, Keitel and the other members of the German delegation were very nervous. Turning to the people surrounding him, Keitel said:

"When we were driving through the streets of Berlin, I was terrified by the extent of destruction."

One of our officers replied:

"Mr. Field-Marshal, were you not terrified when on your orders, thousands of Soviet towns and villages were wiped off the face of the earth and millions of our people, including many thousands of children, were buried under their ruins?"

Keitel grew pale and shrugged his shoulders nervously but said nothing.

As had been agreed beforehand, at 23:45 the representatives of the Allied Command, Tedder, Spaatz and de Lattre de Tassigny, as well as Vyshinsky, Telegin, Sokolovsky and others, gathered in my office close to the hall where the Germans were to sign the act of unconditional surrender.

At 24:00 sharp we entered the hall.

The 9th of May, 1945, started...

Everybody sat down at the table. Behind it on the wall were the flags of the Soviet Union, the United States, Britain and France.

Sitting at the long tables covered with green cloth were the generals of the Red Army whose troops in the shortest possible time had crushed the defences of Berlin and forced the enemy to lay down his arms. Also present were numerous Soviet and foreign correspondents and photographers.

Opening the meeting I declared: "We, representatives of the Supreme Command of the Soviet Armed Forces and the Supreme Command of the Allied Forces, have been authorized by the governments of the anti-Hitler coalition to accept the unconditional surrender of Germany from the German Military Command. Bring in the representatives of the German High Command."

Everybody turned their heads towards the doorway in which were to appear those who had boasted that they could finish off France and Britain with lightning speed, crush the Soviet Union in one and a half or two months and conquer the whole world.

The first to enter, slowly and feigning composure was General Field-Marshal Keitel, Hitler's closest associate. He held up his Field-Marshal's baton in greeting to the representatives of the Supreme Command of the Soviet and Allied Forces.

Keitel was followed by Colonel-General Stumpff. He was a short man whose eyes were full of impotent rage. With him entered Admiral of the Fleet von Friedeburg who looked prematurely old.

The Germans were asked to take their seats at a separate table close to the door through which they entered.

The General Field-Marshal slowly sat down and pinned his eyes on us, sitting at the Presidium Table. Stumpff and Friedeburg sat down beside Keitel. The officers who accompanied them stood behind their chairs.

I addressed the German delegation:

"Do you have with you the instrument of unconditional surrender of Germany? Have you studied it and are you authorized to sign this document?"

My question was repeated in English by Chief Marshal of the RAF Tedder.

"Yes, we have studied it and are ready to sign," General Field-Marshal Keitel said in a muffled voice handing over to us a document signed by Admiral Dönitz. The document asserted that Keitel, von Friedeburg and Stumpff were empowered to sign the instrument of unconditional surrender.

Before us was another man, no longer that arrogant Keitel who accepted the surrender from defeated France. Although he tried to maintain some kind of pose, he now had a beaten look.

Rising I said:

"I ask the German delegation to come over to this table. Here you will sign the instrument of Germany's unconditional surrender."

Keitel quickly rose, shooting a malign glance at us. Then he lowered his gaze, slowly picked up his Field-Marshal's baton from the table and walked unsteadily to our table. His monocle dropped and dangled by its cord. His face was covered with red blotches. Colonel-General Stumpff, Admiral of the Fleet von Friedeburg and the German officers accompanying them followed Keitel to our table. Putting his monocle in place, Keitel sat down on the edge of a chair and signed five copies of the instrument of surrender. His hand was shaking slightly. Stumpff and Friedeburg affixed their signatures, too.

After signing the act, Keitel rose and put on his right glove, making another attempt to show his military bearing. But nothing came of it and he went over slowly to his table.

At zero hours 43 minutes, May 9, 1945, the signing of the instrument of unconditional surrender was finished. I asked the German delegation to leave the hall.

Keitel, Friedeburg and Stumpff rose, bowed and left the hall, their heads bent. Their staff officers followed them.

On behalf of the Soviet Supreme Command, I cordially congratulated everybody present on the long-awaited victory. Incredible commotion broke out in the hall. Everybody was congratulating one another and shaking hands. Many had tears of joy in their eyes. I was surrounded by my comrades-in-arms: V. D. Sokolovsky, M. S. Malinin, K. F. Telegin, N. A. Antipenko, V. Ya. Kolpakchi, V. I. Kuznetsov, S. I. Bogdanov, N. E. Berzarin, F. Ye. Bokov, P. A. Belov, A. V. Gorbatov and others.

"Dear friends," I said to my comrades-in-arms, "a great honour has been accorded us. In the final battle the people, the Party and Government entrusted us to lead the valiant Soviet troops in the storm of Berlin. The Soviet troops, and you, those who headed the troops in the battle of Berlin have justified this trust. It is sad that many of our comrades are no more among us. How happy they would have been to see this long-awaited victory for which they gave their lives without hesitation."

Remembering their friends and comrades-in-arms who were not to live to see this happy day, these people who were used to looking death in the eye without fear, could not keep back the tears.

At zero hours 50 minutes, May 9, 1945, the meeting at which the unconditional surrender of the German troops was signed came to a close.

After that a big reception was given. It passed off in an atmosphere of great enthusiasm. Opening the banquet I toasted the victory of the anti-Hitler coalition over Nazi Germany. The next toast was given by Marshal Arthur Tedder; he was followed by de Lattre de Tassigny and General Spaatz. It was then the turn of the Soviet generals. Each spoke of what was in his heart after all these hard years. I remember people speaking sincerely and in the most heartfelt manner. A great desire was expressed to consolidate for ever friendly relations between the countries of the anti-fascist coalition. This was stressed by the Soviet generals, by the Americans, the French and the British, and all of us then wanted to believe it would be that way.

The banquet ended in the morning with singing and dancing. The Soviet generals were unrivalled as far as dancing went. Even I could not restrain myself and, remembering my youth, did the *Russkaya* dance. We left the banquet hall to the accompaniment of a cannonade from all types of weapons on the occasion of the victory. The shooting went on in all parts of

Berlin and its suburbs. Although shots were fired into the air, fragments from mines and shells, and bullets fell on the ground and it was not quite so safe to walk in the open on the morning of May 9. But how different it was from the danger to which we had grown accustomed during the long years of the war!

On the morning of May 9, 1945, the Act of Unconditional Surrender was brought to the Supreme Command Headquarters.

The first clause of the Act read as follows:

"1. We, the undersigned, acting on behalf of the German High Command, agree to the unconditional surrender of all our armed forces on land, at sea and in the air and also all forces which are at present under the German Command, to the Supreme Command of the Red Army and simultaneously to the Supreme Command of the Allied Expeditionary Force."

In the afternoon I received a telephone call from Moscow and was told that all the documents on the surrender of the Germans had been received and handed over to the Supreme Commander.

So, that was the end of the sanguinary war. Nazi Germany and her allies were ultimately routed.

For the Soviet people, the road to victory was a difficult one. It cost the lives of millions. Today all honest people throughout the world looking back on the horrible days of the Second World War ought to remember with profound respect and sympathy those who fought against fascism and gave their lives to deliver mankind from fascist slavery.

The Communist Party of the Soviet Union and the Soviet Government proceeding from their internationalist duty and humane convictions, took all measures to make it clear to the Soviet soldiers as to who was actually guilty of the war and the atrocities perpetrated. There was never any thought of punishing the German working people for the crimes the Nazis committed in our land. The Soviet people took an unequivocal stand with regard to the common German people: they needed help in realizing their mistakes, uprooting the vestiges of nazism and joining the family of peaceloving nations whose supreme goal in the future was to be peace and democracy.

Fighting was still going on in Berlin and its environs when the Soviet Command, guided by the decisions of the Communist

Party Central Committee and the Soviet Government, set about organizing normal living conditions for the population of Berlin.

Order No. 5 of April 23, 1945, of the Military Council of the First Byelorussian Front provided the basis for the activities of military and civil administrative bodies.

It specified:

"All administrative power on the territory of Germany occupied by the Red Army is to be exercised by the military command acting through the military commandants of towns and districts.

"Military commandants are to be appointed in each city. Executive power is to be exercised by local citizens: burgomasters in the cities and aldermen in towns and villages. They are responsible to the military command for the observance by the population of all orders and ordinances..."

In keeping with this order, on April 28, 1945, the Soviet Military Commandant of Berlin, Colonel-General Berzarin, Hero of the Soviet Union, issued Order No. 1 on the transfer of all power in Berlin into the hands of the Soviet Military Commandant.

In this order he made it known to the city's population that the Nazi Party of Germany and all its organizations were thereby disbanded and all their activity banned.

The Order established norms of behaviour for the population and set forth basic conditions necessary for normalizing life in Berlin.

The Central Military Commandant's Office set up district military commandant's offices in all 22 districts of Berlin staffed with our officers, primarily administrative and engineering personnel. Military commandant's offices were also set up in some sub-districts. From the very beginning, the Soviet military commandants had to cope with numerous tasks under extremely complicated conditions.

In the course of fighting, almost 30,000 out of the city's 250,000 buildings were completely ruined, more than 20,000 were badly damaged, and over 150,000 buildings were damaged less seriously.

The city transport was not operating. Over one-third of the underground stations were flooded and 225 bridges had been blown up by the Nazi troops. The rolling stock and the power lines of the tram system had been put out of operation almost completely. The streets, especially in the city centre, were blocked with debris. All the public facilities — power plants, pumping stations, gas works and the sewerage system — had stopped functioning.

The population of Berlin had to be saved from starvation. The supply of foodstuffs, which had stopped before the Soviet troops entered Berlin had to be organized. It turned out that large groups of the population had received no food for several weeks. The Soviet troops stationed in Berlin began to extinguish the fires, organize the removal and burial of corpses, and demine whole areas.

The Soviet Command, however, could not solve all these problems without involving masses of the local population in active work.

The military councils, commandants and political department workers recruited for work at district councils German Communists released from concentration camps, anti-fascists and other German democrats with whom we at once established friendly mutual understanding.

That was how the German self-government bodies — organs of the anti-fascist democratic coalition — were set up. About one-third of their members were Communists who acted in comradely agreement with the Social-Democrats and loyal professionals.

Important work in Berlin was done by the political department of the Commandant's Office headed by Colonel A. I. Yelizarov.

In May 1945 the Military Council of the Front took a number of important decisions in order to normalize life in Berlin. Among them were the following:

May 11 — Ordinance No. 063 on supplying foodstuffs to the German population of Berlin. This document specified the order of and rations for issuing foodstuffs.

May 12 — Ordinance No. 064 on the restoration and maintenance of normal functioning of the public utilities in Berlin.

May 31 — Ordinance No. 080 on supplying the children in Berlin with milk.

There were also other decisions which improved living conditions and food supplies to the population, primarily the working people engaged in restoration work.

As first aid from the Soviet Government, 96,000 tons of grain, 60,000 tons of potatoes and some 50,000 head of cattle, as well as sugar, fats and other foodstuffs were sent to Berlin.

As a result of these measures the threat of famine among the German population was quickly eliminated.

An important role in normalizing the life of the German population was played by the Soviet commandant's offices and the political organs of the Front garrison and commandant's offices. They promoted the activity of the democratically-minded population which quickly rallied around them. Uncertainty and fear of reprisals with which the Nazis had frightened them melted gradually.

Once, while driving through the outskirts of Berlin I saw an unusually motley crowd in which there were some Soviet soldiers. There were many women and children in the crowd. We stopped the car and approached the crowd. We thought that they were Soviet people released from Nazi concentration camps. But they proved to be Berliners. As I stood there watching, I heard one of our soldiers, who held a fair-haired boy of about four in his arms, say:

"I lost my wife, my little daughter and son when my family was evacuated from Konotop. They were killed when the train was bombed. The war is ending. Why should I live alone? Give me this boy. The SS men shot his mother and father."

Somebody said:

"By the way, the boy looks like you."

A woman standing beside him said in German:

"No, I can't give him to you. He's my nephew and I shall bring him up myself."

Somebody translated what she said and the soldier's face fell.

I intervened:

"Listen, friend, when you return home you'll find yourself a son: we have so many orphans now. Still better if you take a child with its mother!"

The soldiers laughed and the German boy smiled. Our soldiers opened their kit bags and distributed bread, sugar, tinned meat and rusks among the women and children. The little boy whom our soldier held in his arms received sweets besides. The soldier kissed the boy and sighed sadly.

"What kind hearts Soviet soldiers have," I thought to myself as I went up to the soldier and shook his hand.

I was without my insignia and wearing only a leather jacket. Soon, however, I was recognized and had to stay for another half an hour answering many questions. I wish I had written down the names of those soldiers. All I remember is that those soldiers were from General Berzarin's 5th Shock Army.

On May 9 A. I. Mikoyan arrived in Berlin on a mission from the State Defence Committee. He wanted to see straight how the city's life was being normalized.

Leaving his car near one of the food stores where bread was being rationed out to the population, Mikoyan spoke to the women standing in the queue. They looked extremely emaciated.

"How are you feeling now that Berlin is occupied by Soviet troops? Speak your minds without fear," said Mikoyan. "This is Marshal Zhukov, he will take your needs into account and we will do all we can."

"And this is Anastas Ivanovich Mikoyan," I said, "Deputy Chairman of the Council of People's Commissars. He has come here on a mission from the Soviet Government to see how you live and what you need so as to give the Berliners all possible assistance."

The interpreter translated my words into German.

We were immediately surrounded by the German women. They began talking rapidly vying with one another.

"We could have never believed that such a big Russian official would talk to people in the queues and ask what the ordinary Germans need. They used to intimidate us with stories about the Russians..."

An elderly woman came up to Mikoyan and said, her voice trembling with emotion:

"Thank you very much on behalf of all us German women for not letting us starve."

She then turned to a boy standing by her side. "Bow to the Soviet Chiefs for the bread and good treatment." The boy bowed silently.

Mikoyan, A. V. Khrulev, N. A. Antipenko and I made a thorough study of the means at our disposal for assisting the population with food and medicine. Despite our own great difficulties, we were able to help the German people. One ought to have seen the faces of the Berliners when they were given bread, groats, coffee, sugar and sometimes a little fat and meat.

In keeping with the directives of the Party Central Committee and the Soviet Government we helped the German people in every way we could in order to normalize their productive life as quickly as possible. From the captured property we gave them lorries and seed, while the horses and agricultural implements taken on the estates of the German barons were handed over to the agricultural workers who organized cooperatives.

The leaders of German Communists arrived in Berlin. The German comrades noted that the workers, the ordinary people of Germany already regarded the Red Army as the liberator of the German people from nazism, not as a punitive force.

We recommended that German Communists should go to the units of the Red Army and talk with the soldiers. Our proposal was accepted. On coming back they spoke warmly about our soldiers, their broad political outlook and humaneness.

After the seizure of Berlin we often met Wilhelm Pieck, Walter Ulbricht and other German Communists. They worked hard to eliminate the heavy consequences of the war and Nazi domination.

I met Otto Grotewohl, who at that time was the recognized leader of the Left faction of the Social-Democratic Party of Germany which unmistakably gravitated towards the Communists. Soon Wilhelm Pieck, Walter Ulbricht and Otto Grotewohl started talks on the formation of a united socialist party made up of the Communists and Left-wing Social-Democrats. A year later, on April 21, 1946, these talks ended with the formation of the Socialist Unity Party of Germany. The leading Party bodies were elected and vigorous work began among workers, peasants and intellectuals.

In mid-May 1945 the Military Council of the Front convened a conference attended by the German public, industrial, transport, medical and public utilities workers, representatives of cultural institutions, and officers from the military commandant's offices. Mikoyan and German Party and public leaders participated in the work of this conference.

The conference discussed further normalization of life in the city, food supplies to the population and measures for the restoration of transport and public utilities and organization of cultural life in Berlin.

As early as May 14 Military Commandant of Berlin, Colonel-General Berzarin, together with the newly-established administration of the Berlin underground, opened traffic on the first line. By the end of May five lines with a total length of over 61 kilometres had been put into operation.

On May 19 the formal constituent meeting of the Berlin Magistracy (City Council) was held. The meeting was addressed by Berzarin who spoke on the policy of the Soviet authorities in Berlin. Oberburgomeister Dr. Werner introduced members of the Municipal Council to the public. The Magistracy was made up of the people known for their former anti-fascist democratic activities.

Large-scale restoration work was underway throughout the city. The huge piles of debris were cleared by German specialists and towndwellers with the assistance of Soviet engineer and special troops. By the end of May 1945 the city's main railway stations and river ports had been partially restored. They ensured the normal supply of Berlin with fuel and foodstuffs.

By that time 21 pumping stations of the city water supply system had also been put into operation. The seven restored gas works supplied the city with 340,000 cubic metres of gas daily. Industrial enterprises and the population in Berlin's main districts were almost fully provided with gas and water. In June the restored tram network was carrying passengers and freight on 51 lines with a total length of 498 kilometres.

On May 25, on the orders of Berzarin, the setting up of the city police, court and attorney's office was permitted. Paul Markgraf, an active member of the Free Germany movement was entrusted with heading the Berlin police.

The Berlin commandant's offices assisted by German Communists and democrats carried out considerable work in organizing and developing democratic order in the city.

Radio Berlin began to broadcast on May 13. The next day, the military commandants discussed preliminary measures for opening Berlin's theatres with their directors — Gustav Gründgens, Ernst Legal and Paul Wegener.

By the middle of June over 120 cinemas were operating in Berlin. They were showing Soviet feature and documentary films, viewed with interest by tens of thousands of Berliners.

Among the important political and cultural undertakings of the Soviet authorities in Berlin was the publication of the German version of the Soviet occupation forces' newspaper, *Tägliche Rundschau* (Daily Review), for the population of the city. The first issue was put out on May 15, 1945, and the paper quickly gained popularity.

The paper's objective was to explain to the German people the foreign and home policy of the CPSU and Soviet Government, tell the truth about the Soviet Union and the internationalist mission of the Red Army. The paper published detailed reports on measures to restore the public utilities, and cultural institutions in Berlin, and exposed the nature of nazism. It called on the Germans to make every effort towards the speedy restoration of normal life in Berlin.

A second newspaper, *Berliner Zeitung*, the organ of the Berlin Magistracy began to appear a few days later.

In June, all the democratic cultural forces of Berlin were united: the Kulturbund — the cultural union for the democratic renovation of Germany — was set up.

In the middle of May, in keeping with the Soviet Commandant's Office and the Magistracy directives, schools were reopened in most of the city districts. By the end of June normal lessons were on at 580 schools with a total enrolment of 233,000 pupils; 88 children's homes were founded.

Order No. 2 of the Commander-in-Chief of the Soviet Military Administration permitted the activities of anti-fascist parties on the territory of the Soviet occupation zone. Working people were guaranteed the right to associate in free trade unions and organizations with the object of safeguarding their own interests and rights. I shall speak about this measure of the Soviet Military Administration in more detail later on.

Meanwhile I shall cite the words of Otto Grotewohl who pointed out that this order "gave a powerful impetus to political life in the Soviet occupation zone".

"Where else in history," he wrote, "can one find an occupation army which five weeks after the end of war would give the population of an occupied state the opportunity to set up its own parties and publish newspapers, and grant freedom of assembly and speech?"

On June 16, 1945, the Soviet Commandant's Office and the 5th Shock Army suffered a great misfortune. Colonel-General Nikolai Erastovich Berzarin, Hero of the Soviet Union, Commander of the Army and the first Soviet Commandant of Berlin, who had done so much for the restoration of the city, died in a traffic accident while performing his official duties.

He was succeeded in the post of Military Commandant and Commander of the 5th Shock Army by Colonel-General A. V. Gorbatov, Hero of the Soviet Union. While in command of the 3rd Army during the Berlin operation he brilliantly coped with the task of routing the German forces surrounded southeast of Berlin. As Commandant of Berlin, Gorbatov demonstrated outstanding organizing ability and did his utmost to vigourously continue the work towards restoring the normal life of the German working people.

A word of praise should go to Lieutenant-General F. E. Bokov, member of the Military Council of the 5th Shock Army, and Colonel S. I. Tyulpanov, who rendered great assistance to the German comrades in organizing the Berlin Magistracy and the local self-government bodies, and the work of the Soviet Military Commandant's offices in Berlin.

The Prague operation was the final operation of the Soviet troops in the Great Patriotic War. The Soviet troops had to finish routing the remnants of the German forces in Czechoslovakia and liberate her from the German occupation.

On May 5 the Soviet Supreme Command learned that there was an insurrection in Prague and that the Czech insurgents were fighting the German troops. The First, Second and Fourth Ukrainian Fronts were ordered to speed up the advancement of our forces towards Prague so as to help the insurgents and prevent the Hitlerites from crushing the uprising.

In keeping with this order, the Fronts moved their mobile troops there. They reached the Prague area in the early hours of May 9 and in the morning marched into the city, enthusiastically greeted by the population.

After that the organized resistance of the German troops in Czechoslovakia, Austria and the south of Germany ceased. The German troops hastily retreated to the west in a bid to surrender to the Americans. Wherever the Soviet troops blocked their retreat, they tried to break through by force of arms, sustaining heavy losses. The American Command violating their Allied obligations, did not stop the retreat of the Nazi troops into their zone and even assisted them.

The same was observed in the areas occupied by the British forces. The Soviet Command lodged protests with the Allies, but to no avail.

The Vlasov Division made up of the traitors to their country also hastened to retreat towards the zone occupied by the Americans. However, its retreat was cut off by the resolute action of the 25th Tank Corps under the command of Major-General Ye. I. Fominykh. Vlasov himself was among the retreating troops. It was decided to capture him alive to make him pay in full for his treason. This task was entrusted to the commander of the 162nd Tank Brigade, Colonel I. P. Mishchenko, while the capture proper was assigned to a detachment under the command of Captain M. I. Yakushev.

Vlasov was captured while riding in a car in the retreating column. Hidden under a heap of bundles and covered with a blanket, he pretended to be a sick soldier. But he was given away by his own bodyguards. Later Vlasov and his associates were tried by the Military Tribunal and executed.

*   *   *

Thus, the monstrous fascist state had finally collapsed. The Soviet Armed Forces and the Allied troops, assisted by the people's liberation forces of France, Yugoslavia, Poland, Czechoslovakia and other countries had completed the rout of fascism in Europe. The best hopes of all progressive humanity were pinned on the victory over Nazi Germany.

It is difficult for me — and there is no need — to single out any of those who took part in the Berlin operation, that greatest final battle that signalled the end of the Second World War. Each Soviet soldier fought and did what he was charged with to the best of his ability.

In commanding the troops of the Front during this final operation I was greatly helped by the experienced staff officers of the First Byelorussian Front headed by General Malinin.

When summing up the results of the war, we should pay due tribute to the work of our staffs.

I would like to draw attention to the fact that the routing of the Berlin group of German forces and the seizure of the German capital — Berlin — took only 16 days. This is an unprecedentedly short time for such a complicated large-scale strategic operation.

Today some people in the West are trying to underrate the difficulties the Soviet troops faced in the final operations of 1945 and during the seizure of Berlin, in particular.

As a participant in the Berlin operation I must say that it was one of the most difficult battles of the Second World War. The enemy troops, totalling about a million, fought fierce defensive battles in the Berlin strategic direction. The fighting was especially strenuous on the Seelow Heights, on Berlin's outskirts and in the city proper. The Soviet forces sustained heavy losses in this final operation — about 300,000 killed and wounded.

From talks with Eisenhower and Montgomery, and other officers and generals of the Allied forces I knew at that time that after crossing the Rhine the Allied forces did not engage in heavy fighting with the Germans. The Nazi troops retreated quickly and surrendered to the American and British troops without much resistance. This information is corroborated by the insignificant losses of the Allied forces in the final operations.

Thus, for example, according to the data of F. C. Pogue cited in his book *The Supreme Command*, the 1st American Army of General Patton lost only three men on April 23, 1945, while on the same day it captured 9,000 German officers and men.

What were the losses suffered by the three-million-strong American army while moving from the Rhine in the eastern, south-eastern and north-eastern directions? Only 8,351 men, while the number of German prisoners of war ran to hundreds of thousands of officers and men.

Many Western military leaders, including the former Supreme Command of the Allied Expeditionary Forces in Europe, continue to allege that after the battle of the Ardennes and the emergence of the Allied forces on the Rhine, the German military establishment was crushed and there was no need for the spring campaign of 1945. Thus, US President Eisenhower in a

1965 interview granted in Chicago to Edward Foliance, a Washington correspondent, claimed that Germany had suffered a complete defeat after the battle in the Ardennes and that by January 16 everything was finished and every sensible person realized that it was the end... Any spring campaign should have been chucked. Then the war would have ended 60 or 90 days earlier, he said.

I cannot agree with this. As is known, by mid-January 1945, the Red Army had only started its offensive from the Tilsit-Warsaw-Sandomierz line with the object of routing the enemy in East Prussia and Poland. It was planned subsequently to launch an offensive on the centre of Germany in order to take Berlin and reach the Elbe, while on the southern wing preparations were under way for the final liberation of Czechoslovakia and Austria.

According to Eisenhower's speculations, the Soviet forces, too, should have also given up the idea of the spring campaign in January 1945. That would have meant ending the war without achieving either the main military-political goal, or even reaching the frontiers of Nazi Germany, to say nothing of seizing Berlin. In brief, that would have been tantamount to what Hitler and his associates dreamed about sitting in the bunkers of the Imperial Chancellery, that would have meant doing what is so much mourned about today by those who hate the great progressive changes of our days, who advocate policies in the spirit of the revival of fascism.

The defeat of fascism in Europe demanded of the countries of the anti-Hitler coalition the mobilization of enormous armed forces and material resources. The solution of this most important task revealed mutual understanding and the desire to bring the struggle against fascism to a victorious end.

No one can deny that the main brunt of the fight against the fascist armed forces was borne by the Soviet Union. It was the most bitter, bloody and difficult of all the wars that our people had ever fought. Suffice it to say that more than 20 million Soviet people died in that war.

No other country, no other people of the anti-Hitler coalition made such heavy sacrifices as the Soviet Union, and no country exerted such a tremendous effort to defeat the enemy which was threatening all mankind.

Not a single bomb was dropped on American territory, not a single shell hit an American city. In the war against Germany and Japan, the United States lost 405,000 men. Britain lost 375,000 men. While Poland, for example, lost 6,000,000 and Yugoslavia, 1,706,000 people.

The Soviet people give their due to the people of the United States and Britain, to their soldiers, sailors, officers and military leaders who did everything in their power to bring closer the victory over Nazi Germany. We sincerely honour the memory of the killed British and American seamen who despite the dangerous situation at sea, despite the fact that they faced death every mile of the way, delivered to us the cargoes under the Lend-Lease agreement. We highly appreciate the valiance of the participants in the Resistance movement in many European countries.

As for the valour of officers and men of all the arms of the Allied Expeditionary Forces in Europe, I must objectively note their excellent combat qualities and high morale which they displayed when fighting our common enemy.

It was no accident that when our troops and those of the Allies met on the Elbe and in other areas they sincerely congratulated one another on the victory over Nazi Germany, expressing their hope for postwar friendship.

The war unleashed by the Nazi rulers cost the German people dear too: Germany lost 7,000,000 killed in the battlefields. Among those who perished were also the Germans who selflessly fought against fascism. The Communist Party of Germany was always in the vanguard of the anti-fascist forces. More than 300,000 Communists died in Nazi torture-chambers. Many anti-fascists from among Left-wing Social-Democrats were also killed. The German people, along with other peoples of the world, had to experience great suffering and anguish.

Nazism turned young Germans, who had not yet reached maturity, into murderers. They ruthlessly shot, burned and trampled people to death, irrespective of the victims' age and sex.

How could this happen to the people who gave the world Karl Marx, Frederick Engels, Karl Liebknecht, Roza Luxemburg, Ernst Thaelmann and other fighters for the people's just cause and for communism?

How could this happen to the country which bestowed on mankind the greatest scientific discoveries, masterpieces of literature, music, painting and architecture, the country where men of genius — Bach, Beethoven, Goethe, Heine and Albert Einstein — lived and worked?

The historians have not yet got the full picture of the system and methods applied in Nazi Germany to instill in people a blind belief in fascism, in the arrogant — and unwarranted — greatness of the "German race" as a "super-race", in the all-conquering strength of the German state.

In order to re-educate people in the spirit of fascism, the Hitlerites set up a gigantic, ramified system of watching and spying. All the dissenters were thrown by the Nazis into Gestapo torture-chambers. The stick-and-carrot system was widely used. Awards, orders and ranks were lavished on the obidient ones, those who were lured by Germany's mythical greatness and world domination.

All this taken together produced the desired effect. Stupefied by the speeches of their Nazi ringleaders, including Hitler himself, and elated by the easy victories over European countries, the Nazis obidiently set out to conquer and annihilate until they were barred in their way by the Soviet Armed Forces inspired by the justest of all ideals in the world: the freedom of their Motherland, the equality and independence of all the peoples on Earth.

The war was a severe test of the Soviet social and state system which testified to its absolute superiority and viability. The course and outcome of the war revealed the decisive role of the masses. Every Soviet citizen, be it in the ranks, in a partisan detachment, at a factory, a designing bureau, a collective or state farm, spared no effort to contribute to the common cause of defeating the enemy.

Soviet workers, collective farmers and intellectuals worked under extremely hard conditions, without ever having enough food or sleep. Women and teenagers took the place of those who had gone to front lines. Based on a new economic foundation, the national economy proved its progressiveness. In the war years, under the most strenuous conditions of the armed struggle against the powerful enemy who caused us such an enormous material damage, our industry was able to manufacture nearly twice the amount of modern war materiel as Nazi Germany, which drew on the military potential of entire Europe.

Even at the most difficult moments, when it seemed that the enemy would gain the upper hand, the Soviet people did not lose heart, did not waver under the blows of the enemy but rallied round the Communist Party, surmounted all difficulties with honour and gained a historic victory.

Indeed, the Communist Party of the Soviet Union inspired and organized our efforts towards the victory. At a time of hard trials it led the fighting nation, and its best sons were in the front ranks of the armed struggle. By the end of the war over three million Communists — more than half of the Party membership — were fighting on the fronts (every fourth fighter was a Communist!). The greatest number of soldiers' and officers' applications for Party member-ship was recorded during the hardest months of 1941 and 1942. On the fronts and in the rear Communists and Komso-mols set examples of heroism in the struggle for their country. The people and their army saw in the Communists a model of lofty Soviet patriotism and allegiance to the internationalist cause.

I should like to make a special mention of the tremendously important role played by the Soviet press during the years of the Great Patriotic War in carrying on propaganda work and raising the patriotic spirit. Special correspondents, national and front newspaper reporters, fearless and ubiquitous press photo-graphers, radio reporters and cinematographers were always in the thick of things working heroically in the most difficult and dangerous combat conditions.

Sovinformburo, the Soviet news agency, merited the world-wide reputation of the most reliable source of information from the fronts of the Great Patriotic War.

German imperialism set itself the goal of eliminating the world's first socialist country and enslaving the peoples of many countries. Yellow with time are today the documents, directives and maps in which the Hitler hierarchy charted the destinies of Europe, Asia, Africa and America after the anti-cipated defeat of the USSR. But they should be recalled every time one comes to think of the significance of the Great Patriotic

War of the Soviet Union and of what claims to world domination may lead to.

Class irreconcilability and rejection of any compromise in the struggle against fascism and its armed forces had a decisive impact on the strategy, operational art and tactics of the Soviet Armed Forces guided by the Party Central Committee and the Supreme Command.

In the chapter on the Supreme Command Stavka I dealt with the matters of warcraft. I believe that at this point I ought to mention these matters again.

Soviet military leaders, having mastered warcraft, relying on the mass heroism and enjoying nationwide support succeeded in taking over the initiative and organizing a number of successful large-scale strategic offensive operations.

Improving the forms and methods of warfare, the Supreme Command, the General Staff, the commands of the Fronts and armies, and their staffs did tremendous work generalizing combat experience and promoting what was the most effective thus contributing to the overall success.

The most important factors in securing the success of the offensive operations of 1943-1945 were as follows: the new method of artillery and air force offensive; the massive use of tank and air force formations and their skilful cooperation with field armies in strategic operations; the radical improvement in preparations for such operations and in methods of troop control.

In the course of the war, our air force developed rapidly along with the land forces, and its tactics and operational art improved. This secured for us complete supremacy in the air in the final stage of the war. During the war our pilots displayed mass heroism. Acting in cooperation with the land forces, our air force dealt the enemy powerful, irresistible blows over the entire tactical, operational and strategic depth. By the end of the war our air force had excellent materiel.

In designing and building first-class military equipment, outstanding results were obtained by the teams directed by A. N. Tupolev, A. I. Mikoyan, A. A. Blagonravov, A. A. Arkhangelsky, N. N. Polikarpov, A. S. Yakovlev, S. V. Ilyushin, S. A. Lavochkin, V. M. Petlyakov, S. P. Korolyov, P. O. Sukhoi, Zh. Ya. Kotin, A. N. Krylov, V. Ya. Klimov, M. I. Koshkin,

V. G. Grabin,   P. M. Goryunov,   M. I. Gurevich,   V. A. Deg-
tyaryov,   A. A. Mikulin,   B. I. Shavyrin   and   G. S. Shpagin.

Along with the land and air forces our navy carried out successful operations. Scores of formations and hundreds of detachments of marines performed feats of courage earning the profound gratitude of the people.

Beginning with 1944 Soviet military strategy, relying on the
country's enormous military and economic potential and having
at its disposal superior forces and materiel started to carry out
offensive operations which involved simultaneously two, three,
four or more Fronts, tens of thousands of guns, thousands of
tanks, rocket launchers and combat aircraft. These powerful
forces and equipment enabled the Soviet Command to break
through any defences of the enemy, strike deep, surround large
groups of enemy forces, quickly divide and destroy them.

Whereas in the Stalingrad area it took the South-Western,
Don and Stalingrad Fronts almost two and a half months
completely to rout Paulus's army, in the final Berlin operation
the large group of the German forces was crushed and taken
prisoner in 16 days.

In the preparation of all the offensives of the Soviet forces,
great attention was paid to the surprise factor which was
achieved by thorough operational and tactical masking, by the
practice of elaborating operative documentation in secret and
providing strictly limited information of all levels from the
Supreme Command down to the troops. Special attention was
paid to the covert concentration of forces and materiel in the
directions of the main blows, and feigning regrouping of troops
in areas from which no offensive was intended.

During the war with Nazi Germany, the Soviet forces carried out a great number of major operations many of which are
unprecedented in the history of wars, either in scope or clas-
sical implementation. Among these operations were the Leningrad Battle, the Battle of Moscow, the Stalingrad Battle and
that of the Kursk Bulge, the Yassy-Kishinev Operation, the
defeat of the German forces in Byelorussia, the Vistula-Oder
Operation and the final Berlin Operation. Among the defensive
operations, unrivalled in mass heroism and staunchness
were the Battles of Smolensk, Leningrad, Sebastopol and
Odessa.

All the major offensive and counter-offensive operations of the Soviet troops, beginning with the autumn of 1942, were marked by their originality, determination, swiftness and thorough effectuation. Battles and operations continued almost without a break throughout the year. Neither severe frost and heavy snowfall in winter, nor pouring rain and impassable roads in spring and autumn, could stop the operations, although this required extreme physical and spiritual strain.

The most salient feature of Soviet strategy in 1944-1945 was its exceptional activity, the unfolding of strictly purposeful offensive operations along the entire Soviet-German front. Whereas during the first and partly the second period of the war the Soviet troops more often than not assumed the offensive (or rather counter-offensive) only after the German troops had exhausted their own offensive ability, the campaigns at the final stage of the war began straightaway with powerful offensive by our troops against well-prepared enemy defences.

This simultaneity and continuity of major offensives in several directions during 1944-1945 were possible due to the further shift of the balance of forces in favour of the Soviet troops and the shortening in the length of the Soviet-German front. That method of carrying on strategic offensive was extremely effective since it always deprived the enemy of the freedom of manoeuvre.

The strategic offensive operations greatly varied in form. The most characteristic of them were operations aimed at surrounding and destroying large groups of opposing enemy forces by dealing blows in converging directions or by pushing the enemy to the sea, and by striking smashing blows aimed at splitting the enemy forces and destroying them piecemeal. Operations aimed at surrounding the enemy proved the most effective form of strategic offensive operation. The most propitious conditions for initiating such an operation were provided by our troops taking an advantageous position, enveloping the enemy group.

Throughout the war the Soviet troops showed exceptional skill and boldness when operating at night. This type of military action, regarded as "operation in special conditions" before the war, became quite ordinary during the war. Night operations were carried out on an especially wide scale during 1943-1945, when our troops were engaged in the biggest offensive operations. As a rule the enemy forces avoided acting at night, and when forced to do so, they lacked initiative.

Since 1943 encounter battles gained special importance. The experience of the war showed that in encounter actions the victorious side is the one which had prepared for that type of action in good time. It is particularly important to remember that under any circumstances it is necessary to be ahead of the enemy even at the very first encounter — in the seizure of vantage lines, in deployment, in opening fire, outflanking and swiftly attacking the enemy. The nature of encounter operations demanded of the commanders an unfettered and bold initiative and constant readiness to assume responsibility for reasonable fighting activity.

The success of our offensive was bolstered by the heroic actions of the Soviet partisan forces who continually harassed the enemy for over three years, destroying enemy communications and terrorizing his rear. When the Soviet troops reached Poland, Czechoslovakia, Romania, Bulgaria, Yugoslavia and Hungary, they were greatly helped by the patriots of those countries who fought against Hitlerite invaders under the leadership of their Communist and Socialist parties.

According to incomplete figures 260,000 people's avengers fought in organized partisan detachments on the enemy-occupied territory of the Russian Federation, 220,000 in the Ukraine, and 374,000 in Byelorussia. The enemy command was in fact forced to set up a second front in his own rear to fight the partisans, thus engaging considerable forces. That factor seriously told on the general condition of the German front and, in the long run, on the outcome of the war.

I would like to recall the outstanding leaders of underground Party organizations and commanders of partisan detachments and formations, who did all in their power fighting the enemy in close cooperation with our regular troops: V. A. Begma, P. P. Vershigora, S. Ya. Vershinin, P. K. Ponomarenko, T. A. Strokach, A. F. Fyodorov, S. S. Belchenko, M. Gusein-Zade, F. A. Baranov, S. A. Kovpak, I. A. Kozlov, V. I. Kozlov, S. V. Rudnev, K. S. Zaslonov, A. N. Saburov, M. Šumauskas, D. N. Medvedev, M. I. Naumov, and P. Z. Kalinin.

Great service to our country was done by the frontier guards. They were the first to engage the German forces and did everything in their power to thwart Hitler's *blitzkrieg* plan, under which the frontier guards were to be crushed within one or two hours after the invasion.

The frontier guards fought staunchly along the borders, against the numerically superior enemy forces, and later together with the Red Army heroically defended every inch of Soviet territory.

In the Battle of Moscow a number of border regiments (former frontier guards detachments) fought to the end along with the Red Army forces on the Volokolamsk, Mozhaisk, Naro-Fominsk and Malo-Yaroslavets sectors. During the battle at the Kursk Bulge a brilliant performance was shown by the 70th Army, manned by frontier guards from the Soviet Far East, Central Asia and Trans-Baikal Area.

The frontier guards also performed important tasks in the enemy rear, eliminating its administration and disrupting communications. In the course of the war they guarded the Red Army rear and successfully warded off the penetration of every kind of Nazi agents and saboteurs. We could always be sure of success wherever border guards units and formations were fighting.

In modern warfare of great importance is efficient troop control at all levels. This embraces a wide range of military-political, moral, material and psychological factors, and constitutes the most important integral part of military science and art of warfare. In the prewar years Soviet military science failed to make a sufficiently profound study of this extremely important problem. In the course of the war, all of us had to master the science and practice of controlling troops. In this matter the Soviet Command was in a less favourable position than the Nazi Command which by the beginning of the aggression against the Soviet Union had already gained sufficient experience in warcraft.

As our armed forces gained general superiority over the Nazi troops, our skill in controlling troops and managing the materiel also improved.

* * *

In the middle of May 1945 the Supreme Commander ordered me to come to Moscow. I knew nothing about the reason for the summons and I didn't think it proper to inquire — nor is it the custom for the military men to do so.

I went to Antonov at the General Staff rightaway. I learned from him that the State Defence Committee was then considering problems relating to our new commitments to the United States and Britain—the Soviet Union's entry into the war against Japan.

At that time the General Staff was engaged in planning the forthcoming operations of our land, air and naval forces in the Far East.

From the General Staff I phoned Stalin to report my arrival. I was told to appear at the Kremlin at 8 p. m. Having enough time at my disposal, I went to see Mikhail Ivanovich Kalinin who had telephoned me in Berlin and asked me to call on him by all means when I was next in Moscow and tell him all about the Berlin operation.

I was sincerely fond of Kalinin, admiring his simplicity, his worldly wisdom and ability to elucidate even the most complicated things of life in plain words.

Kalinin gave me a hearty welcome. He had aged over the past few years and looked very tired. Despite his advanced years, he had several times visited the fighting troops, meeting officers and men, and always had a ready word of inspiration or comfort for all of them.

He asked me how Berlin had been captured, how the life in Germany was being normalized, how things were getting on in the German Communist Party, a great number of whose members was brutally killed by the Nazis.

After my talk with Kalinin I went to Stalin's office where, besides the members of the State Defence Committee, I saw the People's Commissar for the Navy N. G. Kuznetsov, A. I. Antonov, Chief of the Red Army Logistics A. V. Khrulev, and several generals who were in charge of organizational matters at the General Staff.

Antonov was reporting on the General Staff's blueprint for the transfer of troops and materiel to the Far East and their concentration on future fronts. According to the General Staff's draft plan the entire preparation for the campaign against Japan would require about three months.

Then Stalin asked:

"Don't you think we should celebrate the defeat of Nazi Germany with a Victory Parade in Moscow and invite the most distinguished heroes from among the soldiers, sergeants, petty officers, officers and generals?"

Everybody enthusiastically supported the idea and immediately started making practical suggestions.

At that time we did not discuss the question of who would take the salute at the parade and who would command it. However, each of us felt the Victory Parade should be reviewed by the Supreme Commander-in-Chief.

There and then Antonov was charged with drawing up the blueprint for the parade and preparing a draft directive. The next day all the papers were presented to Stalin and approved by him.

It was suggested that the Karelian, Leningrad, First Baltic, First, Second and Third Byelorussian, First, Second, Third and Fourth Ukrainian Fronts, the Navy and the Air Force should be invited to send to the parade one combined regiment each.

These regiments were to include Heroes of the Soviet Union, holders of the Orders of Glory, famed snipers and other outstanding award-holders from all ranks of the Armed Forces.

The combined regiments of the Fronts were to be headed by the Front commanders.

It was also decided to bring from Berlin the Red Flag which had been hoisted over the Reichstag as well as the military colours of Nazi units captured by the Soviet troops.

Intense preparations for the parade went on in late May and early June. Towards June 10 all the participants were issued new dress uniforms and got down to pre-parade drills.

On June 12 Kalinin conferred on me a third Gold Star of Hero of the Soviet Union.

I cannot recall the exact date but I think it was somewhere around June 18 or 19 that I was summoned by Stalin to his country house. He asked me whether I had not forgotten how to ride a horse.

"No, I haven't," I replied.

"Good," said Stalin. "You will have to take the salute at the Victory Parade. Rokossovsky will command it."

I replied:

"Thank you for the great honour, but wouldn't it be better for you to take the salute? You are the Supreme Commander-in-Chief and by right and duty you are to take the salute."

Stalin said:

"I am too old to review parades. You do it, you are younger."

The parade regiments were to be drawn up in the order of the Fronts, from right to left. On the right flank was the regiment of the Karelian, then the Leningrad, the First Baltic Fronts, and so on. On the left flank were the Fourth Ukrainian, the combined naval regiment, and units of the Moscow Military District.

Each regiment was to parade past to the strains of its favourite march. The next to last rehearsal for the parade took place at the Central Airport and the last dress rehearsal was held in Red Square. Over a short period of time all the combined regiments had been excellently trained and produced a formidable impression.

On June 22 the newspapers published the following order of the Supreme Commander-in-Chief:

"To celebrate the victory over Germany in the Great Patriotic War I hereby order a parade of troops of the active army, navy, and the Moscow garrison, a Victory Parade, to be held on June 24, 1945, in Red Square, Moscow...

"The salute at the Victory Parade shall be taken by my deputy, Marshal of the Soviet Union, G. K. Zhukov, the parade shall be commanded by Marshal of the Soviet Union K. K. Rokossovsky.

> "Supreme Commander-in-Chief
> Marshal of the Soviet Union
> J. Stalin

"Moscow, June 22, 1945"

Here at last was the long-awaited and unforgettable day. The Soviet people had firmly believed that it would come. The heroic Soviet soldiers, inspired by the Party of Lenin, led by their famed commanders, had traversed an arduous four-year road of battle, ending with a brilliant victory in Berlin.

On June 24, 1945, I got up earlier than usual. The first thing I did was to look out of the window to see if our weathermen had been correct in forecasting a cloudy sky and drizzling rain. How I wished that they should be wrong this time!

But unfortunately on that day their forecast came true. The sky above Moscow was cloudy and there was a fine drizzle. I rang up the Air Force Commander-in-Chief who informed me the weather conditions at most aerodromes were unfit for flying.

It looked like the Victory Parade was not going to be as festive as we had all wished. But no! In high spirits and with brass bands the Muscovites were streaming towards the Red Square area to take part in the demonstration on this historic day. Their happy faces, the great number of slogans and posters, and songs generated a feeling of universal jubilation.

Those who were not participating in the demonstration in Red Square were crowding the sidewalks. Their joy and cheers in honour of the victory over fascism made them one with the demonstrators and the troops. This unity conveyed the invincibility of the Soviet country's might.

At 3 minutes to 10 a.m. I was in the saddle at the Spassky Gate.

I heard the clear command: "Parade, shun!" A thunder of applause followed.

The clock began to strike 10 o'clock.

Honestly speaking, I felt my heart beating faster... I sent my horse forward and headed for Red Square. The powerful and solemn sounds of Glinka's *Glory* dear to the Russian heart rang out. Then abruptly absolute silence fell on the Square. I heard the clear report of the parade commander, Marshal of the Soviet Union Rokossovsky, who was, to be sure, as nervous as I. But his report riveted my attention and I became absolutely calm.

The military colours of the troops under which the rout of the enemy was completed, the war-scorched gallant faces of the soldiers, their sparkling eyes, the new uniforms, ablaze with orders and medals, created a stirring and unforgettable impression.

How sad that so many sons of our country had fallen in the battles against the bloodthirsty foe and had not lived to see this happy day, this day of our triumph!

As I reviewed and saluted the troops I could see little streams of rain trickling from the peaks of the men's caps, but the spiritual uplift was so great that no one noticed that.

A particular feeling of jubilation overwhelmed all those present when the regiments of heroes began their ceremonial march past the Lenin Mausoleum. At their head marched generals, marshals of all arms of the service and marshals of the Soviet Union who had covered themselves with glory in the battles against the fascist forces.

Nothing can compare with the moment when to the sound of drums 200 war veterans flung 200 Nazi banners to the foot of the Lenin Mausoleum.

Let this historic act be forever remembered by the revenge-seekers, inspirers of military adventures!

The Victory Parade was followed by a government reception in honour of its participants. The reception was attended by leaders of the Party and the Government, members of the Presidium of the USSR Supreme Soviet, members of the Party Central Committee, People's Commissars and prominent figures of the Red Army and Navy, science, industry and agriculture, arts and literature.

There were many speeches honouring the Party which had rallied the Soviet people in the struggle against the enemy and organized the armed forces to rout the enemy; honouring the Soviet Armed Forces which had accomplished the rout of Nazi Germany; honouring prominent men of science, technology, industry, agriculture and the arts who had ensured the material and spiritual strength of our armed forces in the struggle against a powerful, experienced and ferocious enemy; honouring the great Soviet people.

Long after returning to their regular duties, the participants in the Victory Parade remained under the impression of that memorable event.

On coming back to Berlin, we suggested to the Americans,

British and French that a military parade in honour of the victory over Nazi Germany be held in Berlin itself. Some time later we received their consent. It was decided to hold the parade of Soviet and Allied troops in September in the area of the Reichstag and the Brandenburg Gate, the scene of the final battles, when the Soviet troops stormed Berlin on May 1 and 2, 1945.

By common agreement the salute was to be taken by the Commanders-in-Chief of the Soviet, US, British and French Forces.

All arms of the land forces participated in the Berlin Parade. It was decided not to call in the air forces and navies as they were considerable distances away from Berlin.

The appointed date was approaching. The Soviet troops carried out a thorough preparation. We sought to invite to this parade primarily those soldiers, NCOs, officers and generals who had displayed particular gallantry in the storming of Berlin and particularly its main strongholds of resistance — the Reichstag and the Imperial Chancellery. Everything was going on according to our agreement with the Allies.

But on the very eve of the parade, we were suddenly informed that for a number of reasons the Commanders-in-Chief of the Allied Forces could not come to Berlin for the Victory Parade, and had authorized their generals to attend.

I immediately put a telephone call through to Stalin. He heard my report and said:

"They want to belittle the political importance of the parade of troops of the anti-Hitler coalition countries. Just wait, they'll be up to something else next. Ignore the refusal of the Allies and take the salute yourself, all the more so, as we have more rights to do it than they."

The parade of troops in Berlin was held on September 7, 1945, exactly at the appointed time. Participating were the Soviet troops which had stormed Berlin, and American, British and French troops which were stationed in Berlin in order to carry out occupation duties in the western sectors of Berlin set aside for them.

After reviewing the troops drawn up for the march-past, I made a speech noting the historic merits of the Soviet forces and the Allied Expeditionary Forces.

The Soviet infantry, tanks and artillery marched in impeccable order. A particularly memorable impression was made by our tanks and self-propelled artillery. Among the Allied troops the best-drilled were the British.

About 20,000 Berliners gathered to see the Parade. It was a ceremony symbolizing the victory of the anti-Hitler coalition over the bloodthirsty fascist aggression.

CHAPTER 10

The Potsdam Conference:
The Control Council for
Governing Germany

Around May 20, 1945, Poskrebyshev called me at my home late in the evening and told me to come to the Kremlin.

With Stalin in his office were Molotov and Voroshilov. After mutual greetings Stalin said:

"While we have disarmed all the officers and men of the German army and placed them in prisoner-of-war camps, the British are keeping the German troops in a state of combat readiness and establishing cooperation with them. To this day the staffs of the German forces headed by their former commanders are enjoying complete freedom and, on Montgomery's instructions, are collecting and putting in order the arms and materiel of the troops.

"I think," Stalin continued, "the British seek to retain the German troops so that they can be used later. But that is an outright violation of the agreement between the Heads of Government on the immediate disbandment of all German forces."

Turning to Molotov, Stalin added:

"We must speed up the departure of our delegation to the Control Commission and it must firmly demand of the Allies the arrest of all members of the Dönitz government, and German generals and officers."

"The Soviet delegation is leaving for Flensburg tomorrow," replied Molotov.

"Now that President Roosevelt is dead, Churchill will quickly come to terms with Truman," remarked Stalin.

"American forces are still in Thuringia, and so far they don't seem to have any intention of withdrawing to their own occupation zone," I said. "According to the information we have, the Americans are hunting for the latest patents, searching for and sending prominent German scientists over to America. They are pursuing the same policy in other European countries. I have already written to Eisenhower about this, asking him to speed up the withdrawal of American troops from Thuringia. He replied that he was going to come to Berlin one of these days to establish personal contact with me and discuss all problems.

"I feel we should demand that Eisenhower immediately implement the agreement on the stationing of troops within the assigned zones of occupation. Otherwise, we will have to refrain from letting Allied military personnel into the zones of Greater Berlin."

"Quite right," Stalin said. "Now listen to why I have summoned you. The military missions of the Allies have informed us that Eisenhower, Montgomery and de Lattre de Tassigny will be coming to Berlin at the beginning of June to sign the Declaration on the assumption by the Soviet Union, the United States, Britain and France of supreme authority to govern Germany during the occupation period. This is the text, read it," he said, handing over to me a folded sheet of paper.

This is what it said:

"The Governments of the Soviet Union, the United States of America, Britain and France hereby assume supreme authority with respect to Germany, including all the powers possessed by the German Government, the High Command, and any municipal or local government or authority."

The Declaration stipulated:

— the complete disarmament of all German armed forces, including land, air, anti-aircraft and naval forces, the SS, SA and Gestapo, and all other forces or auxiliary organizations equipped with weapons, with the transfer of their weapons to the Allies;

— the arrest of the main Nazi leaders and all persons suspected of war crimes;

— adoption by the Allies of such measures for the disarmament and demilitarization of Germany that they will deem requisite for future peace and security.

I returned the paper to Stalin.

"In this connection," Stalin continued, "a question arises of setting up a Control Council made up of representatives of all four countries to govern Germany. We have decided to

appoint you Commander-in-Chief to govern Germany on behalf
of the Soviet Union. A Soviet Military Administration must be
established besides the headquarters of the Commander-in-
Chief. You will need a deputy for the affairs of the military administration. Whom would you like to have as your deputy?"

I named General Sokolovsky. Stalin agreed.

Then he informed me of the basic questions bearing on the
organization of the Control Council.

"Besides yourself, General of the Army Eisenhower is to be
appointed to the Control Council from the United States, Field
Marshal Montgomery, from Britain, and General de Lattre de
Tassigny, from France. You will each have a political adviser.
Yours will be A. Ya. Vyshinsky, Eisenhower's will be Robert
Murphy, and Montgomery's will be Strong. We still don't know
the name of the French adviser.

"All the decisions of the Control Council will be valid on
condition of unanimity. In settling quite a few questions you
will probably have to act alone against the other three."

Lighting up his pipe and smiling, he added:

"But it won't be the first time we've had to fight alone...
The major objective óf the Control Council," Stalin went
on, "should be a speedy normalization of peaceful life of the
German people, a complete elimination of fascism, and the
organization of the work of local government bodies. The
members of the local government bodies in Germany should
be selected from among the working people who hate
fascism.

"The fascists have ravaged and plundered our country, therefore you and your assistants will have to do some hard work so
as to speedily implement our treaty with the Allies on the dismantling of certain military-industrial enterprises by way of
reparations."

With these instructions I soon left for Berlin. The day after my
arrival I was visited by General Eisenhower with his numerous
retinue, among whom was General Spaatz, Chief of the US
Strategic Air Command.

We received General Eisenhower at the Front Headquarters
in Wendenschloss. Present at the meeting was Vyshinsky.

We greeted each other like soldiers and, I may say, in a
friendly way.

Taking both my hands in his, Eisenhower looked me over for a long time, then said:

"So that's what you're like."

Shaking his hand heartily, I thanked in his person the Allied forces who had fought together with us against fascism and noted with satisfaction that during the years of the war against Nazi Germany fruitful cooperation developed between our armies and peoples.

At first we talked of past events. Eisenhower told me about the great difficulties encountered in conducting the landing operation in Normandy, the problems in arranging communications and troop control and particularly the difficulties experienced during the surprise counter-offensive of the German forces in the Ardennes.

Getting down to business, he said:

"We'll have to reach understanding on quite a few questions related to organizing the Control Council and providing land communications through the Soviet zone to Berlin for American, British and French personnel."

"We'll obviously have to agree not only on land communications," I replied to Eisenhower, "we'll also have to decide on the procedure for flights to Berlin by American and British aircraft over the Soviet zone."

Hearing this General Spaatz, leaning back in his chair, remarked in an offhand way:

"American aircraft have flown and are flying anywhere without any restrictions."

"Your aircraft are not going to fly over the Soviet zone without restrictions," I replied to Spaatz. "You will only fly in the air corridors, specially established for the purpose."

Eisenhower quickly broke in and told Spaatz:

"I haven't authorized you to raise the question of air flights in this manner."

Then turning to me, he remarked:

"Today I have come here to meet you personally, Mr. Marshal. As for our business problems, we'll settle them when we have organized the Control Council."

"I think that as old soldiers, you and I will find a common language and work as a team," I replied. "And now I'd like to make only one request and that is for a quick withdrawal of

American forces from Thuringia which, according to the agreement among the Heads of Allied Governments at the Yalta Conference, is to be occupied by the Soviet forces alone."

"I agree with you and I'll insist on it," replied Eisenhower.

I did not feel like asking him where he was going to insist. For me it was quite clear that this was a matter which directly concerned big policy or, rather, Churchill and Truman.

We asked Eisenhower and his companions to lunch with us right there, in my office, after which they flew off to their headquarters at Frankfurt-am-Main.

Eisenhower's outward appearance impressed me favourably.

On June 5 Eisenhower, Montgomery and de Lattre de Tassigny arrived in Berlin to sign the Declaration Regarding the Defeat of Germany and the Assumption of Supreme Authority in Germany by the Governments of the USSR, the USA, Britain and France.

Before the meeting, Eisenhower came to my headquarters to confer upon me a high American military award: I was made Chief Commander of the Legion of Merit.

I called Stalin and told him about it. Stalin said:

"We, too, should decorate Eisenhower and Montgomery with Orders of Victory and de Lattre de Tassigny with the Order of Suvorov, First Class."

"May I tell them about it?" I asked.

"By all means."

At the ceremony of signing the Declaration I met Field Marshal Montgomery for the first time.

During the war I had closely followed the actions of British troops under his command. In 1940 the British Expeditionary Force had suffered a disastrous setback at Dunkirk. Later, British troops under Montgomery's command had routed the German corps under General Rommel at El Alamein. Montgomery had skilfully commanded the Allied Forces during their crossing of the English Channel, landing in Normandy and their advance up to the Seine.

Montgomery was above medium height, very agile, smart in a soldierly way and produced an impression of a lively and intelligent person. He began talking about the operation at El Alamein and at Stalingrad. In his opinion, the two operations were of equal significance.

I did not want to belittle the deserts of the British troops, but still I was obliged to explain to him that the El Alamein operation was carried out on an army scale. While at Stalingrad the operation involved a group of Fronts and was of large-scale strategic importance. It resulted in the rout of a major grouping of German and their allies' forces in the area of the Volga and the Don and subsequently, in the North Caucasus. It is common knowledge that it was an operation that actually signalled a radical turning point in the war and triggered the driving of the German forces out of our country.

After the Declaration had been signed, Montgomery turned to me and said:

"Mr. Marshal, we have decided to occupy our zone in Berlin within the next few days and I suppose our friends, Americans and French, will also wish to occupy their zones at the same time. So, I'd like to reach an understanding with you right away on establishing communication routes for our occupation units in Berlin."

"Before settling the matter of the routes by which the British and American units will move to Berlin," I replied, "it will be necessary to move all Allied troops to the areas in Germany which have been assigned by the Yalta Conference. Therefore, only after American troops have left Thuringia and British Wittenberg, I could agree to the passage of the Allied troops to Berlin and the stationing of Allied personnel of the administrative bodies of the Control Council."

Montgomery was about to object when Eisenhower quickly interfered:

"Don't argue Monty, Marshal Zhukov is right. You'd better get out of Wittenberg as soon as possible and we from Thuringia."

"All right," Montgomery gave in, "we won't argue now. Instead, let's have our picture taken to remember our first meeting. I have a very good photographer with me..."

When the photographer had finally used all his film I announced to all three Allied commanders the Soviet Government's decision to confer on them the highest Soviet military decorations. In reply to my question where and when I could present the awards, Eisenhower and Montgomery invited me to come to Frankfurt-am-Main on June 10.

Having seen off my future colleagues at the Control Council, I telephoned Stalin and told him of Montgomery's claim and the stand taken by Eisenhower.

With a laugh Stalin said:

"We ought to invite Eisenhower to Moscow sometime. I want to meet him."

On June 10, by prior arrangement, we flew to Eisenhower's headquarters at Frankfurt-am-Main. We were welcomed by a big guard of honour of American troops who favourably impressed me by their excellent bearing.

In the ceremony of awarding that followed Eisenhower and Montgomery and a group of American and British officers were presented with Soviet decorations. This was followed by an air display by the American and British air forces which involved several hundred aircraft. After the fly-past we were all invited to lunch.

We left Frankfurt looking forward to the establishment of friendly relations and concerted action in the four-power administration of Germany.

Eisenhower's headquarters was located in the huge premises of I. G. Farbenindustrie chemical concern which remained intact during the heavy bombing by the Allies that had left the city of Frankfurt in ruins.

It should be noted that in other parts of Germany, too, property belonging to I. G. Farbenindustrie also remained intact although they presented excellent targets for air raids. It was obvious that Washington and London had given the Allied Command special instructions to this end.

Several other big munitions plants also remained undamaged. As it became clear later, the financial strings from these biggest munitions plants led to the American and British monopolies.

Soon the Americans and British pulled their troops out of the areas they had occupied in violation of the earlier agreement. After this US, British and French occupation troops arrived in Berlin together with the personnel of the administrative agencies of the Control Council.

In the second half of June Field Marshal Montgomery paid me a visit. After an exchange of greetings, he told me the British Government had decided to present me, Marshal Rokossovsky and Generals Sokolovsky and Malinin with British military decorations.

Montgomery asked me to appoint the day and place for the presentation ceremony. I suggested that he should name the day and place himself.

With great tact Field Marshal Montgomery said:

"The Soviet troops dealt the *coup de main* at the Brandenburg Gate where they hoisted the Red Flag over the Reichstag. I believe this is the right place to present you with the British decorations honouring the merits of Soviet troops you commanded."

At the appointed day and hour Rokossovsky, Sokolovsky, Malinin and I arrived at the Brandenburg Gate where we were ceremoniously welcomed by a guard of honour of British Guardsmen and a large group of generals and officers.

The actual ceremony took place outside the Reichstag. I was awarded the G. C. B., Rokossovsky the K. C. B., Sokolovsky and Malinin, the O. B. E.

That night Field Marshal Montgomery gave a reception at his residence which was attended by many of our generals and officers.

I have mentioned these decoration ceremonies because in the past some newspapers published rather inaccurate accounts of them.

At the beginning the Control Council and all its bodies functioned without any particular friction. The Council's meetings were called as problems accumulated but no oftener than once a week. Prior to the meetings the problems were usually discussed in the coordination committees and directorates of the Control Council.

I remember one interesting detail: the participants in the meetings of the Control Council were fed on a rotation basis: one month by the Americans, then the British, the French and the Soviet. Whenever it was our turn, the number of people attending the meetings would double. It was easily explained by generous Russian hospitality, the Russian cooking shown to advantage and of course the famous Russian caviar and vodka...

From the outset it became clear that in all the committees of the Control Council a thorough study was made of the Soviet representatives, the policies and tactics of the Soviet side, and of our strong and weak points. We, too, were sizing up our Western partners and their moves.

I must say that the American and British personnel had been well prepared for work in the Control Council. They had systematized all pertinent documentation referring to Germany and its economic and military potential and they were all well versed in matters of economic policy with regard to the future of Germany.

The situation in which the Control Council began its work may be characterized by the following.

The peoples of the Allied countries were profoundly grateful to the Soviet Armed Forces for routing Germany and eliminating the danger of Hitlerism that had loomed over all the peoples of the world. The attitude towards fascists was extremely hostile. In these circumstances the US ruling circles felt it was untimely and dangerous for them to reveal their true plans and intentions and, therefore, preferred to continue cooperating with the Soviet Union.

Moreover, just as the British ruling quarters, they were interested in the USSR participating in the war against Japan and they were looking forward eagerly to our entry into it. It was only natural that they did not wish to do anything that might cripple their relations with the USSR.

This is why in the early stage the Control Council functioned fairly smoothly.

Yet, as a matter of fact, the US, British and French representatives were far from sincere. In their zones of occupation the decisions of the Yalta Conference and of the Control Council were carried out lopsidedly, often as a mere formality, or at times were simply sabotaged. This applies to the decision on Germany's demilitarization as well. Neither in the economic, nor the political or directly military fields was this decision fully implemented.

At the very start of our work at the Control Council we came to an understanding with Eisenhower to send a group of Soviet officers from the intelligence division of the Front Headquarters to the American zone to interrogate the major war criminals. There were more of them in that zone than in any other.

They included Goering, Ribbentrop, Kaltenbrunner, Field

Marshal Keitel, Colonel-General Jodl and other no less important figures of the Third Reich. However, obviously acting
on special instructions, the Americans did not permit our officers to question all the war criminals. In fact, only a few were
interrogated, and those did their best to throw off the scent,
seeking to accuse Hitler alone of all the crimes perpetrated
against humanity, and thus shun confessing their own guilt.

The records of the interrogations confirmed that there had
been some backstage negotiations between the Nazis and the
US and British intelligence about the possibility of a separate
peace.

Further on in the course of the Control Council's work it
became more and more difficult for us to reach understanding with the Americans and the British. Our colleagues in the
Control Council opposed our proposals concerning the implementation of various clauses of the Declaration Regarding the
Defeat of Germany which had been agreed upon and signed at
the conference of Heads of Government.

Soon afterwards we received reliable information that during
the final campaign of the war against Nazi Germany, Churchill
telegraphed to Field Marshal Montgomery directing him "to be
careful in collecting German arms, to stack them so that they
could easily be issued again to the German soldiers whom we
should have to work with if the Soviet advance continued".

At the next Control Council meeting we had to make a sharp-
ly-worded statement on this subject, emphasizing that history
knew few examples of such perfidy and betrayal of Allied commitments and duty.

We pointed out that the Soviet Union, which was strictly
abiding by its Allied pledges, believed the British Command
and its Government deserved serious condemnation.

Montgomery made an attempt to reject the Soviet accusa-
tion. His American colleague, General Clay, kept silent. He
obviously knew about the British Premier's directive.

Subsequently, addressing his constituents at Woodford, Churchill acknowledged that when the Germans were giving themselves up by hundreds of thousands he did send that secret order
to Field Marshal Montgomery. Some time after Montgomery
himself confirmed he had received the telegram.

As is known, during the war the Nazis deported millions

of Soviet people to Germany to use for forced labour or throw them into concentration camps. In the eastern part of Germany we did our best to return all those released to their homes which throughout the grim years of imprisonment they had all been yearning for. But large numbers of Soviet people and war prisoners were in the zones occupied by our Allies.

Naturally, we began insisting on their transfer to our zone for their return to the Soviet Union. I brought this matter up with Eisenhower. He met our request with understanding and we did bring a considerable number of our people out of the American and, subsequently, British zones.

But then we received reliable information that the Americans and British were brainwashing the Soviet citizens and war prisoners persuading them to refuse to go home. Efforts were made to induce them to stay in the West, where they were promised well-paid jobs and all kinds of comforts. Slander of the Soviet Union, and intimidation were brought into play, as is usually done in such cases.

At our meetings with Eisenhower and his deputy, General Clay, we strongly protested against this anti-Soviet propaganda effort among Soviet people. Eisenhower and Clay at first tried to allege it pursued "humane objectives" but later they agreed to allow our officers to interview the detained Soviet people in American camps.

After frank talks and a clarification by our officers of certain matters these people were concerned about, many of them realized their mistake, saw the falsity of the American intelligence propaganda, voiced their decision to go back to the Soviet Union and went to the Soviet zone to be sent home.

Towards the end of May 1945 Stalin warned me that Harry Hopkins, a special confidant of the US President, wanted to meet me as he would pass through Berlin.

In Stalin's opinion, Hopkins was an outstanding personality. He had done a great deal to strengthen business ties between the United States and the Soviet Union.

Right from the airport Hopkins and his wife, a very beautiful woman of about thirty, drove to my place. A man of medium height and very thin, Hopkins looked exhausted and unwell.

Vyshinsky took part in the conversation.

Over lunch Hopkins said he had been received by Stalin.

They discussed some matters of the forthcoming Conference of the Heads of Government.

"Churchill insists on meeting in Berlin on June 15," said Hopkins, "but we won't be ready to participate in such an important conference by then. Our President suggests convening it in mid-July. We are very glad that Mr. Stalin has agreed with us. There will be some difficult debates on the future of Germany and other European countries and there seems to be a lot of 'inflammable material' around."

"Since our countries succeeded in finding a common language to organize the rout of Nazi Germany even in the grim wartime conditions," Vyshinsky replied, "today the Heads of Government can surely be expected to reach agreement on measures completely to eradicate fascism and settle life in Germany along democratic lines."

Hopkins remained silent. Taking a sip of his coffee, he said with a deep sigh:

"It's a pity President Roosevelt didn't live to see these days, it was easier with him."

Hopkins and his wife stayed about two hours. When he was leaving he told me that he was on his way to London for talks with Churchill.

"I respect Churchill," he said, "but he is difficult to deal with. The only man who found no difficulty in talking with him was President Roosevelt..."

Soon afterward a group of top-ranking officials from the Foreign Affairs Commissariat arrived to make preparations for the forthcoming conference.

I explained to them that there was no suitable accommodation in Berlin for the conference of the Heads of Government. I suggested they look over the area of Potsdam.

Potsdam was also badly damaged, and it was difficult to accommodate the delegations there. The only big building in Potsdam that remained intact was the Palace of the German Crown Prince. It had enough room for meetings and for the work of numerous experts and advisers.

The heads of delegations, foreign ministers and principal advisers and experts could be well quartered in Babelsberg (outside Potsdam) which had remained practically undamaged. Before the war it had been the residence of high-ranking gov-

ernment officials, generals and other prominent Nazi leaders.
The suburb was made up of a large number of two-storeyed
villas amidst thick greenery and flowers.

Moscow approved our proposal to start preparations for the
conference in the Potsdam area. Consent to hold the conference there was also given by the British and the Americans.

There was a rush to put the territories, the premises and
the driveways in order. Numerous squads and units of engineers had to be assigned for this job. Work continued almost
round the clock. By July 10 everything was ready and the
premises were almost fully equipped.

Merit should go to the efforts of the officers of the rear
services who accomplished a great deal of work in very little
time. A particularly hard task fell to the Chief of the Quartermaster's Division, Colonel G. D. Kosoglyad.

Inside the palace itself 36 rooms and a conference hall with
three separate entrances were given a major repair. The Americans requested that the premises set aside for the President
and his staff be finished in blue, the British, for Churchill,
in pink. The Soviet quarters were finished in white. In Neuen
Garten (Sans Souci Park) countless flower-beds were laid
and up to 10,000 flowers and hundreds of decorative trees were
planted.

On July 13 and 14 the group of advisers and experts of the
Soviet delegation arrived.

They included Chief of General Staff, General of the Army
A. I. Antonov, the People's Commissar of the Navy, Admiral
N. G. Kuznetsov, Chief of Main Naval Headquarters S. G. Ku-
cherov. The People's Commissariat for Foreign Affairs was
represented by A. Ya. Vyshinsky, A. A. Gromyko, S. I. Kavta-
radze, I. M. Maisky, F. T. Gusev, K. V. Novikov, S. K. Tsarap-
kin, S. P. Kozyrev and F. Ya. Falaleyev. Together with them
came a big group of diplomatic personnel.

On July 16 a special train was to bring Stalin, Molotov
and their escort.

The day before, Stalin telephoned me to say:

"Don't take it into your head to bring up any honour guards
with bands to meet us. Come to the station yourself and bring
along those you feel necessary."

We all arrived at the station about half an hour before the

train was due. In the group were Vyshinsky, Antonov, Kuznetsov, Telegin, Sokolovsky, Malinin and other officials.

I met Stalin outside his coach. He was in good mood, walked up to the welcoming party and greeted them with a curt wave of his hand. Having glanced over the station square he slowly got into the car, then, reopening the door, invited me in beside him. On the way Stalin asked me if everything was ready for the opening of the conference.

Stalin inspected the villa placed at his disposal and asked who it had belonged to before. He was told it had belonged to General Ludendorff. Stalin never liked any lavishness. After he had inspected the quarters he asked for some of the furniture to be removed.

Stalin then asked where I, Chief of General Staff Antonov, and the other military men who had come from Moscow would be.

"Right here, at Babelsberg," I answered.

After lunch I reported on the basic problems bearing on the group of Soviet occupation forces in Germany and described the last meeting of the Control Council where, just as before, we were having our biggest difficulties in reaching understanding with the British side.

The same day the government delegations of Britain headed by Prime Minister Winston Churchill and of the USA headed by President Harry Truman arrived. Rightaway there was a meeting of Foreign Ministers while Prime Minister Churchill and President Truman visited Stalin. The next morning, Stalin paid return visits on them.

The Potsdam Conference was not just another meeting of the leaders of the three Great Powers, it was also a triumph of the policy which culminated in the complete defeat and unconditional surrender of Nazi Germany.

The Soviet delegation arrived in Potsdam firmly resolved to achieve agreement on a policy to settle postwar problems in the interests of peace and security of the peoples and to establish conditions which would rule out any revival of German militarism.

In considering these top-priority problems, the participants in the conference were bound by the decisions previously adopted at the Yalta Conference of the Big Three. The Soviet delegation once again succeeded in frustrating the designs of the reactionary forces and imparting a more concrete character to the plans for the democratization and demilitarization of Germany as a major condition for peace. At the same time, at Potsdam the desire of the US and British governments to take advantage of Germany's defeat in order to strengthen their own positions in the struggle for world domination was brought into sharper focus than at previous conferences.

The Potsdam Conference opened in the afternoon of July 17, 1945. The meetings were held in the biggest room of the palace, in the middle of which stood a round, well-polished table. It is an interesting point that we were unable to find a round table of the size we needed in Berlin. It had to be made urgently in Moscow at the Lux furniture factory and brought to Potsdam.

Present at the first official meeting were the Heads of Government, all the Foreign Ministers, their first deputies, and military and civilian advisers and experts. In between the subsequent meetings the military and civilian experts and advisers met separately and conducted negotiations on the matters assigned to them.

During the Conference the main burden was borne by the Foreign Ministers and the diplomatic personnel. They had to study, analyze and assess all the documents advanced by each side, work out their own proposals and defend them at preliminary talks, only after that the final drafts were prepared for the Heads of Government.

The military advisers were to discuss the main proposals on the distribution of Nazi Germany's naval ships and big merchant vessels. On these questions preliminary talks were conducted with British and American seamen by our admirals, headed by Admiral of the Fleet Kuznetsov.

The American and British sides kept dragging out these talks. During the round-table discussions with Truman and Churchill, Stalin had to make several rather sharp observations on the different size of the losses borne by the Soviet Union and by its Allies in the war and on the right of our country to demand appropriate compensation.

The first stage of the Conference proceeded in a strained atmosphere. The Soviet delegation came up against a united front and a preconcerted stand taken by the US and Britain.

The principal matter discussed at the Conference was that of postwar settlement in European countries and, mainly, the re-arrangement of Germany along democratic lines. Prior to the Potsdam Conference the German question was considered by the European Consultative Commission, the International Reparation Commission and also discussed in great detail at the Yalta Conference.

As is known, debate on the German question began at the Teheran Conference. In keeping with the previously proclaimed Allied policy for the unconditional surrender of Nazi Germany, the Heads of Government were unanimous with respect to the demilitarization and denazification of Germany, the complete disarmament and dissolution of the Wehrmacht, the liquidation of the Nazi Party and all its branches, the arrest and trial of the major war criminals by the International Military Tribunal and the strict punishment of all war criminals. The decisions adopted by the Potsdam Conference provided for the banning of the production of any kind of weapons by Germany.

The Conference reached agreement on the political and economic principles of a coordinated Allied policy towards Germany during the period of Allied control. After the Conference we received an extract from the decisions which stated in part:

"German militarism and nazism will be extirpated and the Allies will take in agreement together, now and in the future, the other measures necessary to assure that Germany will never again threaten her neighbours or world peace."

The text of the agreement[1] by which the Soviet side was guided in the Control Council for Germany said the following:

"A. Political Principles:

"1. In accordance with the agreement on control machinery in Germany, supreme authority in Germany shall be exercised, on instructions from their respective Governments, by the Commander-in-Chief of the Armed Forces of the Union of Soviet Socialist Republics, the United States of America, the United

---

[1] Cited in abridged form.— *Ed.*

Kingdom, and the French Republic, each in his own zone of occupation, and also jointly, in matters affecting Germany as a whole, in their capacity as members of the Control Council.

"2. So far as is practicable there shall be uniformity of treatment of the German population throughout Germany.

"3. The purposes of the occupation of Germany by which the Control Council shall be guided are:

"The complete disarmament and demilitarization of Germany and the elimination of or control over all German industry that could be used for military production.

"To destroy the National Socialist Party and its affiliated and supervised organizations, to dissolve all Nazi institutions, to ensure that they are not revived in any form, and to prevent all Nazi and militarist activity or propaganda.

"To prepare for the eventual reconstruction of German political life on a democratic basis and for eventual peaceful cooperation in international life by Germany.

"War criminals and those who have participated in planning or carrying out Nazi actions involving or resulting in atrocities or war crimes shall be arrested and brought to judgment. Nazi leaders, influential Nazi supporters, and high officials of Nazi organizations and institutions, and any other persons dangerous to the occupation or its objectives, shall be arrested and interned.

"All members of the Nazi Party who have been more than nominal participants in its activities, and all other persons hostile to Allied purposes, shall be removed from public and semi-public office and from positions of responsibility in important private enterprises. Such persons shall be replaced by persons who by their political and moral qualities are deemed capable of assisting in developing genuine democratic institutions in Germany.

"German education shall be so controlled as completely to eliminate Nazi and militarist doctrines and to make possible the successful development of democratic ideas.

"B. Economic Principles:

"In order to eliminate Germany's war potential the production of arms, munitions, and implements of war, as well as all types of aircraft and sea-going ships, shall be prohibited and prevented. Production of metals, chemicals, machinery, and other items that are directly necessary to a war economy shall be rigidly controlled and restricted to Germany's approved postwar peaceful needs...

"At the earliest practicable date the German economy shall be decentralized for the purpose of eliminating the present excessive concentration of economic power as exemplified in particular by cartels, syndicates, trusts, and other monopolistic arrangements.

"During the period of occupation Germany shall be treated as a single economic unit. To this end common policies shall be established in regard to:

"(A) Mining and manufacturing production and allocations;

"(B) agriculture, forestry and fishing;

"(C) wages, prices, and rationing;

"(D) import and export programmes for Germany as a whole;

"(E) currency and banking, centralized taxation, and customs;

"(F) reparations and the removal of industrial war potential;

"(G) transportation and communications.

"In applying these policies account shall be taken, where appropriate, of varying local conditions."

One can only be amazed by how easily these cardinal decisions unanimously adopted by the Great Powers at Potsdam were soon discarded by US and British leaders. As a result, militarism revived. What followed is well known.

I shall never forget the remarkable words, pronounced by President Franklin D. Roosevelt in 1943:

"After the Armistice in 1918, we thought and hoped that the militaristic philosophy of Germany had been crushed; and being full of the milk of human kindness we spent the next twenty years disarming, while the Germans whined so pathetically that the other Nations permitted them — and even helped them — to rearm... The well-intentioned but ill-fated experiments of former years did not work. It is my hope that we will not try them again. No — that is putting it too weakly — it is my intention to do all that I humanly can as President and Commander-in-Chief to see to it that these tragic mistakes shall not be made again."

After Franklin Roosevelt's death, however, the US policy took quite a different course...

As I have already mentioned, not all the questions were easily resolved by the Potsdam Conference. The most aggressive-minded participant there was Winston Churchill. Yet, Stalin was usually able quickly to convince him, in rather calm tones, that he erred in his approach to the questions under discussion. Probably due to his then limited diplomatic experience, Truman seldom entered into sharp political discussion, giving priority to Churchill.

The question of the division of Germany into three states: Southern Germany, Northern Germany, Western Germany raised for the second time by the US and British delegations came in for serious debate. The first time they brought this matter up at the Yalta Conference it was rejected by the Soviet delegation. At Potsdam the Head of the Soviet Government again rejected it.

Stalin said:

"We reject this proposal, it is contrary to nature: Germany should not be dismembered, it should be made into a democratic, peace-loving state."

On the insistence of the Soviet delegation, the Potsdam decisions of the Allied powers included a provision on setting up central administrative departments in Germany. However, because of the opposition on the part of the representatives of the Western authorities this provision was never implemented. Such departments were never set up, and peaceful, democratic unification of Germany, envisaged at Potsdam, was never attained either.

As for the restoration of Germany's economy, it was decided that major attention should be focussed on the development of peaceful industry and agriculture. The Conference mapped out measures to destroy Germany's military potential.

The size of reparations and the procedure for obtaining them were established. Admittedly, Truman and particularly Churchill were reluctant to accept the dismantling of industrial enterprises in the western part of Germany in the form of reparations. Finally, however, they did agree, although with all kinds of reservations, to assign for this purpose part of the equipment of the war plants in the western zones. Regrettably, this decision was adopted merely on paper, for in reality, just as many other decisions of the Potsdam Conference, it never was implemented by the Allies.

The Conference also adopted a decision on giving Königsberg and the adjacent area over to the Soviet Union.

In order to conduct preparatory work for the peace settlements the Conference decided to establish a Council of Foreign Ministers. This Council was made up of the Foreign Ministers of the USSR, the United States, Britain, France and China. The Foreign Ministers Council was invited to draw up draft peace treaties for Italy, Romania, Bulgaria, Hungary and Finland; and to prepare a peace treaty for Germany.

Another matter that aroused controversy was the question of Poland and its western frontiers. Despite the fact that the solution of these problems had largely been predetermined by the Yalta Conference, Churchill attempted, under various apparently unsupported pretexts, to reject the Soviet proposal to establish Poland's western frontiers along the Rivers Oder and Western Neisse, including Swinemünde and Stettin. After a detailed and well-argued statement by the Polish delegation headed by Boleslaw Bierut, which had been specially invited to Potsdam for the discussion of the Polish question, the decision on Poland's western frontiers read as follows:

"Pending the final determination of the frontiers in a peace treaty, Poland shall be given territories east of a line running from the Baltic Sea immediately west of Swinemünde and thence along the Oder and the Western Neisse to the Czechoslovak frontier."

The British delegation kept insisting that the Polish People's Government should undertake the repayment of all loans provided by Britain to the Polish emigre government of Tomasz Arciszewski who had fled to London in 1939. The Soviet and Polish delegations resolutely rejected these British claims.

At the same time, agreement was reached on the cessation by the United States and Britain of diplomatic relations with the former Polish Government (in exile) in London.

Having examined and settled several other important issues, the Conference ended on August 2.

The Soviet Union's victory over Nazi Germany was so overwhelming, that the ruling quarters in the United States and

Britain were at that time compelled to adopt concerted agreements. This ensured the success of the Potsdam Conference.

On the whole, the decisions of this high forum show that the democratic principles of the postwar settlement in the world triumphed. A decisive role in this belonged to the Soviet Union, which during the war vigorously promoted the setting up of the anti-fascist coalition.

I do not recall the exact date, but after the end of one of the Conference meetings, Truman informed Stalin that the United States now possessed a bomb of exceptional power, without, however, naming it the atomic bomb.

As was later reported abroad, at that moment Churchill pinned his eyes on Stalin's face, eager to observe his reaction. However, Stalin did not betray his feelings and pretended he saw nothing special in what Truman had said. Both Churchill and many other British and American commentators subsequently surmized that Stalin had probably failed to fathom the significance of the information received.

In actual fact, on returning to his quarters after this meeting Stalin in my presence told Molotov about his conversation with Truman. Molotov reacted immediately: "They are trying to bid up."

Stalin laughed:

"Let them. I'll have to talk it over with Kurchatov today and get him to speed things up."

I understood they were talking about the development of the atomic bomb.

It was clear already then that the US Government was going to use the atomic bomb for reaching its imperialist goals from a position of strength. This was corroborated on August 6 and 9. Without any military need whatsoever, the Americans dropped two atomic bombs on the peaceful and densely-populated Japanese cities of Nagasaki and Hiroshima.

Just as the Commanders-in-Chief of the American and British Forces, I was not an official member of the delegation, but I attended several meetings of the Potsdam Conference.

I must say that Stalin was extremely scrupulous with regard to the slightest attempt by the US and British delegations to take decisions to the detriment of Poland, Czechoslovakia, Hungary and the German people. He had particularly sharp controversy with Churchill both at the Conference itself and during their private talks. It should be emphasized that Churchill obviously held Stalin in high esteem and, I felt, feared to enter into debate with him. In all his arguments with Churchill Stalin was always extremely specific and logical.

Shortly before his departure from Potsdam Churchill gave a reception at his villa. Those invited from the Soviet Union were Stalin, Molotov, Antonov and myself. Present from the United States were President Truman, Secretary of State James Byrnes, Chief of Staff of the US Army, General Marshall. From the British side there were Field Marshal Alexander, Chief of General Staff Field Marshal Sir Alan Brooke and others.

Before the Potsdam Conference I had met Churchill once in Moscow, but only fleetingly and never had a chance to talk with him. At the reception he gave me a good deal of his time, questioning me about various battles.

He was interested in my assessment of the High Command of the British Armed Forces and my opinion on the operations carried out by the Allied Expeditionary Force in West Germany. He was obviously pleased with my praise of the Normandy landing.

"But I have to disappoint you, Mr. Churchill," I added.

"In what way?" Churchill asked, on the alert at once.

"I believe several serious blunders were made after the Allied landing in Normandy. And if it were not for the mistake in appraising the situation made by the German Command, the Allied advance after the landing might have been held up considerably."

Churchill made no objections. It was obviously not in his interest to delve deeply into the matter.

The first to speak at dinner was President Truman.

Noting the outstanding contribution of the Soviet Union to the defeat of Nazi Germany, Truman offered the first toast to the Supreme Commander-in-Chief of the Armed Forces of the Soviet Union, Stalin.

Stalin, in turn, offered a toast to Winston Churchill who in the grim wartime years had shouldered the burden of leading Britain in the struggle against Hitler's Germany and had successfully coped with his great mission.

Quite unexpectedly, Churchill offered a toast to me. I had no option but to toast him in reply. In thanking Churchill for his kindness I automatically addressed him as "Comrade". I caught the look of amazement on Molotov's face and was confused for a moment. But I quickly recovered and offered a toast to the comrades-in-arms, our Allies — soldiers, officers and generals of the armies of the anti-fascist coalition who had so brilliantly completed the rout of Nazi Germany. And in this I made no mistake.

The following day when I was in Stalin's apartment, he and all others present kidded at my having so quickly acquired Winston Churchill as a "comrade".

On July 28 the leader of the British Labour Party, Clement Attlee, who had replaced Churchill as Prime Minister, became the head of the British delegation. In contrast to Churchill, the new British Prime Minister was rather more reserved. However, he continued Churchill's political line without any modifications in the policies of the former Conservative government.

In the course of the Conference Stalin reviewed and settled several important matters concerning Germany I submitted for his consideration. In particular, he approved the decision of the Military Council of the Front on the organization of fishing off the coast of the Baltic Sea. According to the decision, the troops of the former First Byelorussian Front were supposed to catch 21,000 tons of fish in the second half of 1945.

Incidentally, this was a very important decision, as the number of livestock in the eastern part of Germany by the time it was occupied by Soviet troops had considerably decreased. Therefore, the supply of fish was of great economic importance for the German population.

Just before his departure for Moscow Stalin familiarized himself with the plan for the return of Soviet troops to the Soviet Union and the progress of the repatriation of Soviet people from Germany. Stalin demanded that every measure be taken to enable the Soviet people to return home as soon as possible.

Stalin left for Moscow as soon as the Potsdam Conference was over, having given all the necessary instructions for the implementation of its decisions by the Control Council.

To carry out the decision on the distribution of Nazi Germa-

ny's navy a Tripartite Commission was set up. The Soviet side
was represented by Admiral G. I. Levchenko. The British
appointed J. Miles and Admiral Burrough and the Americans
named Admiral King.

Admiral Levchenko had to make a great effort to make the
Allies implement the decisions and recommendations of the
Potsdam Conference. He had to talk, repeatedly and persist-
ently to Field Marshal Montgomery, Admiral Burrough and
Eisenhower on this matter, and then demand a discussion at
the Control Council. In the long run the matter was resolved
and the Soviet Union received a total of 656 naval ships and
various transport vessels, most of which did not need repair.

Despite inevitable controversy and differences, the Potsdam
Conference on the whole showed a universal desire to lay
the stage for cooperation between the Great Powers on whose
policies so much depended in the postwar years.

This was also reflected in the relationships between the
members of the Control Council both during the Conference
and immediately after it. The Soviet representatives in the
Control Council did their utmost to carry out the decisions
adopted by the Conference. In the early period after the
Conference our American and British colleagues, too, abided
by the commitments set forth in the Conference's decisions.

Unfortunately, this political atmosphere soon changed. A
serious impetus to a change in policy was provided by the
differences that arose at the conference of the Foreign Ministers Council in London. And this was especially prompted
by Churchill's anti-Soviet Fulton speech. As if by command,
the American and British administrations in the Control Council
became less compliant in all matters and started unceremo-
niously frustrating the implementation of concerted Potsdam
decisions on all cardinal issues.

The good relationships established since the first days in
the Control Council between Eisenhower, Montgomery, Koenig
and myself, as well as between Clay, Robertson and my deputy
for the Soviet Administration, Sokolovsky, began to deteriorate.
It became increasingly difficult to find ways to settle disputes
particularly when we were dealing with the principal issues.
These included the elimination of the military and economic
potential of German militarism, the disarmament of military

units, the vigorous eradication of fascism and of all sorts of Nazi organizations in the British and American zones. One could feel that our Western colleagues had received new instructions stemming from the hostile policies of the imperialist quarters of the United States and Britain towards the Soviet Union.

Through repeated checking we established for sure that despite our protest the British were still retaining German troops in their zone. I was compelled to submit to the Control Council a memorandum on the presence of organized units of the former Nazi army in the British zone. It reads as follows:

"In accordance with the Declaration Regarding the Defeat of Germany, signed on June 5, 1945, as well as the decisions of the Potsdam Conference on Germany:

"'All German armed forces, or forces under German control, wherever situated, including land, air, anti-aircraft and naval forces, the SS, SA, and Gestapo, together with all other forces or auxiliary organizations equipped with weapons must be completely disarmed...

"'All German land, naval and air forces, the SS, SA, SD and Gestapo, with all their organizations, staffs, and institutions, including the General Staff, the officers' corps, reserve corps, military schools, war veterans' organizations, and all other military and para-military organizations, together with all clubs and associations which serve to keep alive the military traditions in Germany, shall be completely and finally abolished so as forever to prevent the revival or reorganization of German militarism and nazism...'

"In the meantime, according to data in the possession of the Soviet Command and reports carried by the foreign press, German armed forces and German land, naval and air forces still exist in the British zone of occupation in Germany. To this day there exists a German army group under Mueller, renamed Army Group Nord. This army group has a field administration and headquarters. The headquarters of the army group includes an operations division, a chief quartermaster's division, a logistics division, an officers' division, a motor transport division, and a sanitary service.

"The Army Group Nord incorporates land, air and anti-aircraft formations and units. It includes corps groups Stockhausen and Witthoff, numbering over a hundred thousands personnel each.

"In the British zone of occupation in Germany there have been set up five German military corps districts with respective administrations and services. The administrations of the German military corps districts are located in the towns of Hammer, Itzehoe, Neumünster-Rendsburg, Flensburg, Hamburg.

"In addition to the German military districts in the British zone of occupation in Germany there have been set up 25 district and local German military commandant's offices in the following towns and points: Pinneberg, Segeberg, Lübeck, Lauenburg, Itersen, Herkerkirchen, Beringstadt, Itzehoe, Schleswig, Eckernförde, Husum, Westerland, Wenzburg, Heibe, Marne, Wesselburen, Hanstadt, Meldorf, Albersdorf.

"German air forces are maintained in the British zone in the form of the Second Air District which includes anti-aircraft formations (units of the 18th Anti-Aircraft Division), bomber squadrons, fighter squadrons, ground attack squadrons and close reconnaissance groups. The Second Air District has headquarters, similar to the headquarters of a wartime air army.

"German armed forces in the British zone of occupation in Germany have over five signal regiments and tank units as well as a network of military hospitals. German naval forces are at present termed the German Trawler Service. This German trawler service has headquarters, coast-guard divisions and flotillas.

"Apart from the mentioned German formations, units and services there are in the province of Schleswig-Holstein about a million German soldiers and officers who have not been placed on a prisoner-of-war status and with whom training drills are being conducted.

"All the above-listed land, naval and air force units, formations and services receive all rations and other supplies according to army norms. The personnel of the above-listed formations, units and administrations wear insignia and military decorations. The entire personnel are given paid leave.

"As will be seen from the above, the presence of German military, naval, and air force authorities, as well as land, air, anti-aircraft and naval formations, units and services in the British zone of occupation in Germany can be explained by no special features attending the occupation of the British zone.

"The maintenance in the British zone of occupation of:

"German Army Group Nord,

"Corps Group Stockhausen,

"Corps Group Witthoff,

"the Second Air District,

"military district administrations at Hammer, Itzehoe, Neumünster-Rendsburg, Flensburg, Hamburg,

"25 military district and local German commandant's offices,

"signal troops,

"tank units,

is contrary to the decisions of the Potsdam Conference and the Declaration Regarding the Defeat of Germany.

"The Soviet Command deems it necessary to raise the matter of sending a commission of the Control Council to the British zone of occupation for an on-site inspection of the state of affairs as regards the disarming and liquidation of the German armed forces."

During the discussion of the memorandum in the Control Council Montgomery was compelled under the pressure of facts to admit the presence of organized German troops in the British zone allegedly "awaiting disbandment" or "working" under his command.

He tried to account for it all by "technical difficulties" involved in the disbandment of German troops.

It was at this meeting that we saw plainly that Eisenhower also knew all about it.

Later, in November 1945, addressing a meeting of the Control Council, Montgomery said:

"I would be surprised if I were told there was any difference between our line of behaviour in this matter and that of my American colleague, since the line we are following was from the outset laid down during the joint command under the leadership of General Eisenhower."

Everything became absolutely clear. While signing on behalf of his country commitments to uproot German militarism immediately and once and for all, and eliminate the German Wehrmacht, Winston Churchill was giving secret orders to the military command to preserve the arms and military units of the former Nazi army as a basis for a reconstituted West German Army pursuing far-reaching anti-Soviet goals. And all this turned out to have been known to the Supreme Command of the Allied Expeditionary Forces and to Eisenhower personally. Frankly, I was very much upset then and changed my initial opinion of Dwight Eisenhower. But perhaps this was a logical development...

During the Potsdam Conference Stalin talked to me again about inviting Eisenhower to visit the Soviet Union. I suggested inviting him to attend the sports festival scheduled for August 12.

This suggestion was accepted and Stalin ordered an official invitation to be sent to Washington. It was specified in the invitation that during his stay in Moscow Eisenhower would be the guest of Marshal Zhukov. This implied that Eisenhower was being invited to the Soviet Union not as a statesman or political figure but as a prominent military leader in the Second World War.

Since Eisenhower was to be my official guest, I was to travel to Moscow with him and then to accompany him on his visit to Leningrad and on the return flight to Berlin.

With Eisenhower on his Moscow visit were his deputy, General Clay, General Davis, Eisenhower's son Lieutenant John Eisenhower and Sergeant Dry. During his visit we had ample opportunity for long talks and I felt then that Eisenhower was quite frank in all he said to me.

What interested me most were the activities of the Supreme Command of the Allied Expeditionary Force in Europe.

"In the summer of 1941," Eisenhower said, "when the Nazi Germany attacked the Soviet Union and Japan was manifesting its aggressive intentions in the Pacific, US Armed Forces were brought up to one and a half million men.

"For most in the War Department and in the US Administration Japan's attack on Pearl Harbour in December 1941 came as a surprise.

"When following the Soviet Union's unfolding battle against Germany," Eisenhower went on, "we were at a loss to guess how long Russia could hold out and whether she could at all resist the onslaught of the German army. US business circles, together with the British, were at that time greatly concerned over India's raw material resources, the Middle East oil, the Persian Gulf and the Middle East in general."

From what Eisenhower said it was obvious that the principal concern of the United States in 1942 was securing its military and economic positions, rather than opening a second front in Europe. Theoretically, the United States and Britain began to give thought to plans for a second front in Europe from the end of 1941, but took no practical decisions until 1944.

"We," Eisenhower said, "rejected Britain's demand to launch an invasion of Germany across the Mediterranean for purely military reasons and no other."

The Allies were obviously highly apprehensive of German resistance along the coast of the Channel, and especially in France, and deeply worried about the widely advertised "Atlantic Wall".

The plan for an assault across the Channel was finally agreed upon with the British in April 1942, but even after that Churchill repeatedly attempted to persuade Roosevelt to undertake a landing across the Mediterranean. According to Eisenhower, they could not open a second front in 1942-1943 allegedly because they were not prepared for this major combined strategic operation. That was certainly far from the truth. They could open a second front in 1943, but they wittingly did not hurry to do so, waiting for our troops to inflict greater damage on Germany's armed forces and, consequently, to become more exhausted.

"The invasion of Normandy across the Channel in June, 1944 began in easy conditions and proceeded without any particular resistance by German forces on the coast — something that we certainly had not expected," Eisenhower said. "The Germans did not have the defences they had been boasting of."

"And what in fact was the 'Atlantic Wall' like?" I asked Eisenhower.

"There was actually no 'Wall' at all," Eisenhower replied. "There were usual trenches, and those did not run in a continuous line. There were no more than 3,000 guns of different calibre along the entire length of the 'Wall'. On the average this was a little over one gun per kilometre. There were only a few ferro-concrete fortifications equipped with artillery and they could not serve as an obstacle for our troops."

Incidentally, the weakness of the "Wall" was quite frankly admitted by the former Chief of General Staff of the German Ground Forces, Colonel-General Halder. In his memoirs published in 1949 he wrote: "Germany had no defences against the landing force of the Allies which attacked under cover of aviation which was fully and entirely dominant in the air."[1]

According to Eisenhower, the chief difficulties in the invasion of Normandy lay in landing the troops across the Channel and their material supply. As for the German resistance, it was insignificant there.

Frankly speaking, I was somewhat puzzled when in 1965 I saw the American film *The Longest Day*. This film, based on the historical fact — the invasion of Normandy by the Allied Forces across the Channel in June 1944 — shows the enemy to be far stronger than it actually was. The political lining of this film is easily understandable ... but after all there has got to be a limit somewhere.

The Normandy landing which was truly an operation on a grand scale requires no false gloss. To give it the objective credit it merits, it was prepared and conducted ably.

The Germans did not put up any major resistance to the Expeditionary Force until July 1944 when they transferred their forces from all over the coast of Northern France. But even then it was rebuffed by the greatly superior Allied land and air forces. There were — and there could be — no Allied offensive operations in the full sense of the word, no operations involving penetration of a deeply organized defence or fighting against operational reserves and counterattacks as was the case on the Soviet-German front simply because there were no major opposing enemy forces there.

With few exceptions, the offensive operations carried out by the American and British troops were reduced to overcoming mobile enemy defence. According to Eisenhower, establishing communication routes over unfavourable terrain presented the main difficulty to the advancing Allied forces.

I was very interested in the German counter-offensive in the Ardennes in late 1944 and in the Allied defensive action

---

[1] Franz Halder, *Hitler als Feldherr*, München, 1949, S. 59.

there. It is to be noted that Eisenhower and his companions
were always reluctant to talk about that. From what they did
say, however, it was obvious that the German counter-offensive
in the Ardennes came as a complete surprise for the Allied
Supreme Command HQ and for the Command of the 12th
Army Group of General Bradley, and the Americans failed
to resist the enemy's blows.

The Allied Supreme Command was greatly alarmed and
concerned about further action by the enemy in the Ardennes.
These apprehensions were completely shared by Churchill.
On January 6, 1945, he sent Stalin a personal message which
revealed his anxiety. He said that heavy battles were under
way in the West and that the Allied Forces, having sustained
heavy general losses and forfeited initiative, had come up
against a complex situation.

Churchill and Eisenhower sent Air Chief Marshal Arthur
Tedder to Moscow to deliver the letter, thus revealing their
anxiety to receive a quick response from the Soviet Union.
They hoped that if the Soviet Government orders a swift
offensive that would force Hitler to remove his shock units
from the Western front and move them to the East, to fight
against the Red Army.

It will be recalled that, true to its Allied commitments, in
exactly a week's time the Soviet Government launched a
large-scale offensive along the entire front which shook the
German forces to their very foundations in all strategic directions and forced them to retreat with immense losses to the
Oder-Neisse-Moravska Ostrava line, and in the spring compelled them to abandon Vienna and the south-eastern part
of Austria.

Recalling that offensive, Eisenhower said: "For us it was a
long-awaited minute. We all felt relief, particularly after we
had received news that the Soviet offensive was proceeding
with great success. We were sure the Germans would now be
unable to reinforce their Western front."

Unfortunately, after the war, when the surviving Hitlerite
generals and some prominent military figures from among
our former Allies began to flood the book market with their
reminiscences, such objective assessments of the events of
World War II have become increasingly scarce while the

distortion of facts and insinuation have come to be a frequent occurrence. The most overzealous ones even went so far as to allege that it was not the Red Army that had helped the Americans in their battles in the Ardennes but the Americans who had saved the Red Army.

We also touched upon the deliveries under the Lend-Lease programme. Everything seemed clear in that respect then. Nevertheless, for years after the war bourgeois historiography has asserted that it was the Allied deliveries of armaments, materials and foodstuffs that had played a decisive role for our victory over the enemy.

True, the Soviet Union did receive supplies the economy needed so badly: machinery, equipment, materials, fuel and foodstuffs. For example, over 400,000 vehicles, a great number of locomotives and communication facilities were brought from the United States and Britain. But could all that have had a decisive influence on the course of the war? I have already mentioned that the Soviet industry developed on such a scale during the war that it provided the front and rear with everything needed. I see no sense in going into all that once more.

As for the armaments, what I would like to say is that we received under Lend-Lease from the United States and Britain about 18,000 aircraft and over 11,000 tanks. That comprised a mere 4 per cent of the total amount of armaments that the Soviet people produced to equip its army during the war. Consequently, there is no ground for talk about the decisive role of the deliveries under Lend-Lease.

As for the tanks and aircraft supplied to us by the British and US governments, they, to be frank, did not display high fighting qualities; especially tanks which, running on petrol, would burn like torches.

Eisenhower displayed great interest in the operations to lift the blockade of Leningrad, the battles of Moscow, Stalingrad and Berlin. He asked how hard was the situation physically for me as the Front commander during the Battle of Moscow.

"The Battle of Moscow," I replied, "was equally hard for the soldiers and the commander. In the period of particularly bitter fighting from November 16 to December 6 I never had a chance to sleep for more than two hours a day and even then in cat-naps. To keep up my strength and ability to work I had to resort to brief but frequent physical exercises outside in the frost, to strong coffee and sometimes to a 20-minute ski run.

"But when finally the crisis of the Battle of Moscow was over I fell into such a dead sleep that no one could wake me up for a long time. Stalin called me on the phone twice but he was told: 'Zhukov is asleep and we are unable to wake him.' Stalin replied: 'Don't wake him until he wakes up himself.' During my sleep the troops of our Western Front advanced at least 10 to 15 kilometres. It was certainly a pleasant awakening..."

On Eisenhower's arrival in Moscow, Stalin ordered Chief of General Staff Antonov to familiarize him with all the plans of actions of our troops in the Far East.

Stalin talked much with Eisenhower about the actions of Soviet and Allied forces against Nazi Germany and Japan, pointing out that the Second World War was the outcome of the extreme short-sightedness of the political leaders of Western imperialist states who connived at the Hitlerites' unbridled military aggression.

"The war cost the peoples of all combatant nations dearly, particularly the Soviet people," Stalin said. "And it is our duty to do all we can to prevent war in future."

Eisenhower agreed with him heartily then.

I met Eisenhower once more at the Geneva Conference of the Heads of Government of the United States, Britain, France and the Soviet Union in 1955. At that time he was President of the United States. We met several times and talked not only about the days of war and our countries' cooperation in the Control Council but also about the topical problems of coexistence of our two nations and about the need to strengthen peace between all peoples. What he said now differed from what he used to say in 1945. Eisenhower was firm in expressing and defending the policies of US imperialist circles.

As a person and military leader General Eisenhower enjoyed great authority among the Allied troops he had successfully commanded in World War II. He could do a great deal to bring about an easing of international tension in the postwar period too, and above all, to prevent the aggression in Vietnam. Unfortunately, he did nothing to achieve this end, and moreover, he supported the aggression.

After the war, progressive-minded people hoped that the great powers of the world would learn the lessons of history, that Germany would develop on a democratic basis and German militarism and fascism would be uprooted. But matters took this course only in Eastern Germany — where the German Democratic Republic was later to emerge.

When the Soviet Armed Forces liberated the countries of Eastern Europe from fascist occupation, their peoples took firm hold of state power and shaped life in their countries along democratic lines. The East European democratic countries clearly saw in the Soviet Union their saviour from fascism and regarded it as a reliable guarantee for the future against any encroachment on their destiny on the part of aggressive forces.

The situation that had taken shape by the end of the war was a serious test for the political parties and leaders at the helm in the Western countries, a test of their political foresight. The question was whether they would be able to lead their countries along the path of friendship among nations or would pursue a policy of hostility to other nations.

Guided by Lenin's behests the Soviet Government, our Party adhered to a firm policy of peaceful coexistence with all countries and did everything possible to strengthen peace and cooperation.

Shortly after Eisenhower's visit to the Soviet Union, Molotov rang me up in Berlin.

"There is an invitation from the US Administration for you to visit the United States. Comrade Stalin is of the opinion that such a visit may be useful. What would you say to it?"

"I agree."

After the end of one of the Control Council's meetings, General Eisenhower came up to me.

"I am very glad, Mr. Marshal, that you will visit the States," he said. "I am sorry circumstances do not permit me to accompany you on your flight to Washington. If you do not mind you will be taken care of by my son John, General Clay, and other people from the Headquarters of the US Supreme Command."

I agreed.

"As your pilots are not familiar with the flight conditions across the Ocean and in the States," Eisenhower added, "I suggest you using my personal plane, the Fortress."

I thanked General Eisenhower and reported our talk to Stalin.

Stalin said, "Well, get ready."

Regrettably, just before the flight I was taken ill. I had to telephone Stalin again to say, "I can't go in such a state. Will you get in touch with US Ambassador Smith and tell him that the flight will have to be cancelled because of my poor health."

On returning to Berlin I plunged into the work at the Control Council again.

Vladimir Semyonovich Semyonov, then political adviser to the Commander-in-Chief of the Soviet Military Administration in Germany and now USSR Deputy Foreign Minister, helped me greatly in solving problems related to democratic reforms in the Soviet zone. We worked together in the Control Council on implementation of the Potsdam Agreements pertaining to the whole of Germany. We worked as a team and very fruitfully.

A good job in the Control Council was done by our officers, generals and other comrades whom the Government had assigned to the Soviet Military Administration headed by General Sokolovsky. Not only were they burdened with their work in the Control Council, but they also had to organize the entire social, production and government activities in the eastern part of Germany.

We began our effort to unite the progressive forces among the German people in the Soviet occupation zone and make them more active by issuing Order No. 2 of June 10, 1945, which I have already mentioned. In view of the importance of this order, I shall cite it here in somewhat abridged form:

"On May 2nd of this year Berlin was taken by Soviet forces. Nazi armies defending Berlin surrendered, and a few days later Germany signed the Act on Unconditional Military Surrender. The Governments of the Union of Soviet Socialist Republics, the United States of America, Great Britain and France published the Declaration Regarding the Defeat of

Germany and assumption by the Governments of the above--mentioned Powers of Supreme Authority in all the territory of Germany. From the moment the Soviet forces took Berlin strict order was established in the territory of the Soviet occupation zone in Germany, local bodies of self-government were set up and the necessary conditions were created for the free social and political activity of the German population.

"In view of the above, I give the following order:

"1. To allow the formation and activity of all anti--fascist parties on the territory of the Soviet occupation zone in Germany, whose purpose is the ultimate eradication of the vestiges of nazism and consolidating of the principles of democratism and civil freedoms in Germany and the promotion in this direction of the initiative and activity of the population at large.

"2. To grant the working population in the Soviet occupation zone of Germany the right of association into free trade unions and organizations for the purpose of protecting the interests and rights of the working people. To grant the professional organizations and associations the right to conclude collective agreements with entrepreneurs, and also to organize insurance offices and other institutions providing mutual aid, and cultural and educational and other establishments and organizations providing education...

"3. In accordance with the above said, to repeal all Nazi legislation and all the Nazi decrees, orders, directives, and instructions and the like, relating to the activity of anti-fascist political parties and free trade unions, directed against democratic freedoms, civil rights and the interests of the German people.

"Commander-in-Chief of the Soviet Military Administration in Germany
Marshal of the Soviet Union G. Zhukov
"Chief of Staff of the Soviet Military Administration in Germany Colonel-General V. Kurasov

"June 10, 1945

Berlin"

As I have mentioned earlier in this book an important part in organizing life in Germany along democratic lines was played by German Communist organizations that were soon able to rally workers and progressive-minded people of the eastern part of Germany.

Guided by humane objectives, the Soviet Government continued to show great concern for the population in that time of trials for the German people; in the first instance, care was taken of the Berliners, whose plight was particularly desperate.

When Berlin was taken by our troops, its population numbered no more than one million, but a week later there were already over two million and in the second half of May, around three million. The population continued to grow because many more kept coming in from other parts of Germany.

Extremely active in eliminating the aftermath of the war in Berlin were German workers and technical personnel. They stayed at their jobs days and nights on end conscientiously doing their work.

Considerable assistance was rendered to the Soviet commandant's offices by the aid groups made up of German anti--fascists. They took part in all activities, in keeping public order, distributing ration cards among the population, controlling food distribution, guarding factories, plants, the city's major utilities and services, and property.

On June 11, the Central Committee of the Communist Party of Germany came out with a programme appeal to the German people. This document of exceptional historic importance put forward a programme for the creation of an anti-fascist democratic Germany.

The German people was granted the right to build its own way of life on a democratic foundation.

In the very first few months after the end of the war the democratic bodies of self-government in Berlin, just as everywhere else in the Soviet occupation zone, effected a number of socio-economic transformations under the supervision of the Communist Party of Germany and assisted by the Soviet Command. A democratic land reform was carried out which gave land to almost a million German working people. The big capitalist monopolies were abolished, and the associations of entrepreneurs were disbanded. Former Nazis were removed from top posts in various spheres of the city's economic, social and cultural life. An eight-hour working day was introduced at the factories and a single system of leaves for the workers was established.

I well recall how the CPSU Central Committee kept up with these vital processes, very attentively and with a specific knowledge of the living conditions of the German working people. Many valuable pieces of advice regarding the key trends in this effort came from Stalin himself; he regarded these questions from the point of view of the international working-class movement and the efforts to strengthen peace and security in Europe.

By the time the troops and authorities of the USA, Great Britain and France arrived in Berlin, the life of the population in the city had in the main been normalized, and all the prerequisites had been created for its further development.

Order No. 17 of the Commander-in-Chief of the Soviet Military Administration of July 27, 1945, testifies to our measures to facilitate the economic development of the Soviet occupation zone. From this order it can be seen that even at that time, in the early postwar months, attention was paid to the work of the bodies managing the main branches of the national economy, culture and the health service.

It was ordered that "by August 10, 1945, the following German central departments should be formed on the territory of the Soviet occupation zone:

"— Transport — for the management and control of the boards of the railways and waterways;

"— Communications — to supervise the work of the post office, the telegraph and the telephone;

"— The fuel industry — to manage the operation of all the enterprises in the coal industry, the coal mines, open-cast pits, briquette factories, and plants producing liquid fuel and gas, as well as dealing with internal sales of the output of these enterprises;

"— Trade and supplies — to control and organize the operation of trading and procuring firms, institutions and enterprises, to ensure the procurement of farm produce, its processing and storage, registration of goods and provision of the population with them, and the promotion of trade;

"— Industrial — to manage the restoration, launching and exploitation of all the industrial enterprises;

"— Agricultural — to manage and control the agriculture and forestry, and also the enterprises of the farm industry;

"— Financial — to control the operation of all the finance and credit institutions;

"— Labour and social security — to regulate payment for labour, the utilization of manpower and engineering and technical personnel, and to supervise the trade unions and also the social security bodies;

"— Public health — to manage public health bodies, medical institutions and schools of medicine, and also enterprises of the pharmaceutical industry;

"— Public education — to supervise the schools, orphanages and nursery schools, educational establishments, arts, scientific and cultural and educational institutions;

"— Judicial — to control the operation of all the offices of the public prosecutor, the courts, and the organs of justice...

"Commander-in-Chief of the Soviet Military Administration Commander-in-Chief of the Group of Soviet Occupation Forces in Germany
Marshal of the Soviet Union G. Zhukov.

"Member of the Military Council of the Soviet Military Administration in Germany Lieutenant-General F. Bokov

Chief of Staff of the Soviet Military Administration in Germany Colonel-General V. Kurasov"

I must say that our measures to develop democratic tendencies, the economy, culture and keeping order in the Soviet occupation zone were enthusiastically welcomed by the German people.

Subsequently, we continued to put into effect measures to preserve all the national and state values for the German people. Thus, Order No. 124 was issued on October 30, 1945, which stated the following:

"...For the purpose of preventing misappropriation and abuse of property belonging formerly to Hitlerite state and military institutions, societies, clubs and associations, banned and dissolved by the Soviet Military Command, and also for the purpose of the more rational utilization of this property for the needs of the local population ... I hereby order that:

"1. Subject to sequestration is property within the territory occupied by the Red Army in Germany and belonging to:

"a) the German state and its central and local bodies;

"b) people who held posts in the National Socialist Party, its leading members and prominent supporters;

"c) German military institutions and organizations;

"d) societies, clubs, and associations banned and dissolved by the Soviet Military Command;

"e) the governments and subjects (physical and juridical persons) of the countries that fought in the war on the side of Germany;

"f) persons mentioned by the Soviet Military Command in special lists or otherwise designated.

"2. Property without an owner in the territory of Germany occupied by the Red Army should be placed in the temporary charge of the Soviet Military Administration.

"3. All German institutions, organizations, firms, enterprises and all private persons who do at the present time have in their possession property or possess information on such property are obliged to submit an account of this property in writing to the local bodies of self-government (Stadtverwaltung, Bezirksverwaltung, Kreisverwaltung) not later than 15 days from the date this order is issued.

"The statement should contain the following details: the nature of the property, its precise location, to whom it belongs and a description of the state of it on the day the statement is submitted...

"The local organs of self-government (on the basis of the statements and materials received on the property directly under consideration) will compile a general list of property subject to sequestration or temporary supervision, and this list is to be presented to the relevant military commandant not later than November 20, 1945...

"7. Not later than December 25, 1945, the Chief of the

Economic Board of the Soviet Military Administration in Germany, Major-General Shabalin, is to present to me proposals regarding the manner in which this property proclaimed confiscated or under temporary supervision, is to be used in the future.

"8. I hereby warn all institutions, organizations, firms and enterprises and all private persons which or who have in their possession the property, listed in points 1 and 2 of this order, that they bear full responsibility for its safety and its uninterrupted exploitation in accordance with its economic purpose. Any deals regarding this property carried out without the approval of the Soviet Military Administration, are declared invalid...

"Commander-in-Chief of the Soviet Military Administration Commander-in-Chief of the Group of Soviet Occupation Forces in Germany
"Marshal of the Soviet Union

G. Zhukov

"Member of the Military Council of the Soviet Military Administration in Germany Lieutenant-General F. Bokov

Deputy Chief of Staff of the Soviet Military Administration in Germany Lieutenant-General M. Dratvin"

The Soviet people never forgot the revolutionary merits of the German working class and German progressive intellectuals, or the great merits of the Communist Party of Germany and its leader Ernst Thaelmann who perished in the Nazi dungeons at the close of the war. Our Party and Government deemed it their duty to extend a hand of fraternal assistance to the German people.

In all towns and villages the German Command had left behind thousands of wounded soldiers and officers. In Berlin and its environs alone there turned out to be more than 200,000 wounded soldiers of the German army. Our medical personnel and the Soviet Command showed a truly humane attitude to these wounded ex-enemies of ours and organized their treatment on an equal footing with Soviet soldiers.

One day as I was walking down the Unter den Linden with a group of officers, an accompanying officer from the Berlin

Commandant's Office pointed out a building in fairly good condition which now housed a hospital for Germans. We decided to go in.

The first thing that struck me was the fact that most of the wounded were teenagers, almost children, between 15 and 17 years old. They turned out to be Volkssturm soldiers from various detachments formed in Berlin in early April. I asked what had made them join the Volkssturm detachments at a time when Germany was already in a hopeless state.

Eyes lowered, the boys were silent. Then one of them said:

"We had no way out but to take up arms and join in defence of Berlin. Those who didn't want to go were taken away to the Gestapo and no one ever returned from there..."

Then we learned that several of the wounded — the older ones — had been in the fighting at Moscow in November 1941. I told them I too fought at Moscow. One wounded soldier remarked:

"It is better not to recall the tragedy that befell the German troops there. In our regiment over there not more than 120 were left out of 1,500 men, and even those were brought to the rear area."

"And where did your regiment see action?" I asked.

"At Volokolamsk," the wounded man replied.

"So you and I are old acquaintances then," I said.

The same man asked:

"Would you tell us where and in what sector you fought, Herr General?"

I told them I had been in command of the troops of the Western Front at Moscow.

We inquired about their food and the way the Russian doctors were treating them. There was a chorus of praise of the food and care of the Soviet medical personnel. One of our doctors present remarked:

"The Germans used to kill off our wounded, and now we are losing sleep trying to nurse you back to health."

"It wasn't the ordinary Germans who did that," a wounded old man said, "it was the German Nazis."

"Are there any Nazis among you?" I asked.

There was silence... I repeated my question. Silence again. At last one soldier in his fifties rose and, walking up to the bed of another man, nudged him in the back and said:

"Turn around!"

The man turned over reluctantly.

"Get up and tell them you are a Nazi."

As we were leaving the hospital, the wounded Germans asked that they all be left in the care of Soviet doctors and nurses.

In the first postwar days and months we frequently met the German Communist leaders Wilhelm Pieck, Walter Ulbricht, and their closest associates. With great sorrow they spoke of the terrible losses sustained by the Communist Party, the best of the workers and progressive-minded intellectuals. They were deeply concerned about the plight of the German working people.

At the request of the German Communist Party, the Soviet Government fixed higher food rations for the Berliners.

Thus the Soviet people acted after routing fascism.

And what were Hitler's plans for the Soviet people?

In preparing for the capture of Moscow, Hitler issued a directive which I want to recall once again:

"The city must be encircled so that not a single Russian soldier, not a single inhabitant — man, woman or child — can escape. Every attempt to leave is to be suppressed by force. The necessary preparations must be carried out so that Moscow and its suburbs are flooded with water with the help of immense installations.

"The site of what is today Moscow must become a sea which will forever conceal the capital of the Russian people from the civilized world."

No better fate lay in store for Leningrad.

"In the case of all other towns," said Hitler, "the rule should hold that prior to their occupation they should be reduced to ruins by artillery fire and by air raids."

Such was the extent of barbarism which no normal man can fathom.

To be frank, when the war was still on I was fully determined to get even with the Germans for all their cruelty. But when our troops had routed the enemy and entered the German territory, we checked our wrath. Our ideological convictions and internationalist feelings did not allow us to give vent to blind vengeance.

At the end of March 1946, when I returned to Berlin after the session of the Supreme Soviet, I was asked to telephone Stalin.

"The Government of the USA has recalled Eisenhower from Germany, leaving General Clay in his place. The British Government has recalled Montgomery. Perhaps you should return to Moscow as well?"

"Agreed. As regards my successor, I suggest that General of the Army Sokolovsky should be appointed Commander-in-Chief of the Soviet occupation zone. He is better acquainted with the work of the Control Council than anyone else and knows the troops well."

"All right, we'll think about it here. Wait for instructions."

Two or three days later Stalin rang me up late in the evening. Inquiring whether his call had woken me up, he said:

"The Politbureau agrees to appoint Sokolovsky in your place. Leave for Moscow after the next meeting of the Control Council. The order regarding Sokolovsky's appointment will follow in a few days' time.

"Just one more question," Stalin continued. "We have decided to do away with the post of First Deputy of the People's Commissar for Defence and have a deputy to deal with general questions instead. Bulganin will be appointed to do this position. Vasilevsky is appointed Chief of General Staff. We are thinking of appointing Kuznetsov Commander-in-Chief of the Navy. What post would you like to have?"

"I shall work at any post the Central Committee of the Party considers most expedient for me."

"I think you should be in charge of the land forces. We think that a Commander-in-Chief should be at the head of them. Do you have any objections?"

"No," I replied.

"All right. Come back to Moscow and work out the operation duties and rights of the top-ranking officers of the People's Commissariat for Defence together with Bulganin and Vasilevsky."

I returned to the Soviet Union in April 1946.

The last time I was in the German Democratic Republic in 1957. When visiting many towns, institutions and enterprises of the new, democratic Germany, familiarizing myself with the remarkable achievements of the German people, I saw with my own eyes that all that had been done by the Soviet Government and Party in Germany was correct and had yielded beneficial results both for the German working people and for friendship between our peoples and the defence capability of the socialist countries.

Conclusion

I spent a long time thinking how to finish this book, what kind of ending it should have...

I must admit that for me, a military man, it was no easy matter to sit down at a desk and write a book. The ending of *Reminiscences and Reflections* sums up the whole of my life. My life, like that of any other person, was marked by joys, sorrows, and losses. When a person of my age looks back, he inevitably tends to see everything in its place, what was most important and what was not worthy of attention. For me the most important thing in my life was my service to my country, to my own people. And I can say with a clear conscience that I did everything I possibly could to do my duty. The writing of this book was perhaps one of the last things that I considered it my duty to do.

The days of my greatest joys coincided with joyful moments for my homeland. The anxiety of my Motherland, its losses and griefs always affected me more than my own. I have lived my life with the awareness that I am being of use to the people, and this is most important in anyone's life.

With every passing year we draw further and further away from those years of war. A new generation of people has grown up. For them war only means our reminiscences of it. And the numbers of us who took part in those historic events are dwindling fast. But I am convinced that time cannot cause the greatness of all that we experienced during the war to fade. Those were extraordinarily difficult, but also truly glorious years. Once a person has undergone great trials and come through victorious, then throughout his life he draws strength from this victory.

This is just as true of a whole people. Our victory in the war against fascism, to use lofty words, was the star-lit hour in the life of the Soviet people. In those years, we became even more tempered and amassed huge moral capital. When looking back, we shall always remember those who did not spare themselves to attain victory over the enemy of our Motherland.

The Great Patriotic War was an armed clash between socialism and fascism, the most reactionary and aggressive force of imperialism. It was a nationwide battle against a malicious class enemy who encroached upon what is dearest of all to all Soviet people — the gains of the Great October Socialist Revolution, the Soviet power.

The Communist Party raised our country and the multinational Soviet people to a resolute armed struggle against fascist invaders. From the very first and to the very last days of the war I served in the Stavka of the Supreme Command and I saw the tremendous organizing effort made by the Central Committee of the Party and the Soviet Government in mobilizing the people, the armed forces and the national economy to the rout of the Nazi hordes.

I wish to say outright that we could never have triumphed over the enemy had we not had such an experienced and trustworthy Party as Lenin's Party, the socialist state and social system, the mighty material and spiritual forces of which made it possible to rebuild the country's entire life within a short span of time and create prerequisites for the rout of the armed forces of German imperialism.

The enemy pinned his hopes on fomenting national strife, resulting in the collapse of the multinational socialist state. His hopes were in vain. The peoples of the Soviet Union heroically fought on the fronts and worked selflessly for the defence of their socialist homeland, in the name of the victory over the pernicious enemy, showing unprecedented staunchness and courage. The historic victory won by the entire Soviet people in the Patriotic War vividly demonstrated the advantages of the socialist social system, the great viability and invincibility of the USSR.

Under the impact of the Soviet way of life and the great educational work done by the Communist Party the new man has been moulded, ideologically convinced of the righteousness of his cause and deeply aware of his personal responsibility for the destiny of his country.

Wherever the Soviet man found himself — in the front lines or in the rear, behind the enemy lines or in fascist prison camps — he did his utmost to bring closer the hour of victory. No one shall succeed in belittling the significance of the military and labour feat that the Soviet people performed in the Great Patriotic War.

I have dedicated this book to the Soviet soldier. It is with his will, his valour and his blood that the victory over the powerful enemy was gained. The Soviet soldier knew how to face mortal danger, and displayed a great valour and heroism. There is no limit to the greatness of his exploit in the name of his Motherland. Neither is there a limit to the greatness of his labour feat in the postwar years. Hardly was the war over when millions of Soviet soldiers found themselves on the front again, a working front. They had to restore the war-ravaged economy, raise towns and villages from ruins.

The greatness of historic victory of the Soviet Union over Nazi Germany lies in the fact that the Soviet people did not only defend its own socialist state but that it selflessly fought to attain the working-class internationalist proletarian goal — deliver Europe and the rest of the world from fascism and bring long-awaited peace to the peoples exhausted by the war.

As a result of victory of the Soviet Armed Forces over German fascism and Japanese militarism progressive peoples of a number of European and Asian countries have rallied under the banners of Marxism-Leninism, smashed the reactionary forces in their countries and formed socialist states. Today, together with the Soviet Union, they form an indestructible fraternal union of the socialist community, whose strength is a reliable guarantee against any political and military ventures.

The Soviet people have not forgotten the contribution made to the victory over the common enemy by the other members of the anti-Hitler coalition. Our army and our people remember and think highly of the courage and valour displayed by the Resistance fighters.

The USSR was the recipient of the main blow dealt by the Nazi German invaders during the Second World War.

The Soviet Union withstood this blow, and then crushed the

Nazi war machine. This victory cost the Soviet people many millions of human lives and this is why the Soviet people remember well the sacrifices made during the last war and are well aware of the price of peace.

We speak out as convinced opponents of solving disputes among states by military means because we know all too well of the catastrophic consequences that a third world war would bring to our planet. We proceed from the fundamental interests of all the peoples on the planet and also from a profound awareness that it is precisely in peacetime that the advantages of that social system, of that way of life, of that policy, the foundations of which were laid by the Great October Socialist Revolution, can be realized to the fullest extent.

Soviet foreign policy, like its home policy, actively influences the social transformations in the world, for it is aimed at eradicating such social evils as war and imperialists' interference in the affairs of other peoples within the framework of international relations. "All our politics and propaganda, however," Lenin stressed, "are directed towards putting an end to war and in no way towards driving nations to war."[1]

The Soviet state was born with the word "peace" on its lips. At that time, there were people who tried to interpret our appeal for peace as a sign of weakness. Military intervention, the sparking off of the civil war, blockade and starvation, this is how the old world responded to the emergence of the first socialist state.

More than half a century has passed since that time. Radical changes have occurred in the world — the world system of socialism has taken shape and the foundations of colonialism have been undermined. Our country has matured and grown strong. Today even our out-and-out enemies do not dare to call the USSR a weak power. But just as in the very first days of Soviet Government's existence, the struggle for peace remains the core of our foreign policy.

The tremendous sacrifices made by our people during the Great Patriotic War were not in vain. As a result of the victory a new correlation of forces was created in the world whereby it is no longer as easy as it was for the reactionary imperialist circles to unleash a new worldwide conflict.

---

[1] V. I. Lenin, *Collected Works*, Vol. 31, 1974, p. 470.

At each stage in historical development the Communist Party solicitously works out a programme for its foreign policy activity in accordance with the changing international situation; this programme is called upon to ensure the peaceful construction of our state of the whole people, to assist in the successful promotion of the world revolutionary process, to strengthen the base of the struggle for peace and social progress for all peoples. The Peace Programme was worked out by combined effort at the 24th Congress of the Communist Party of the Soviet Union.

This Programme singles out decisive and at the same time pressing key international problems, which are of principal importance for the fate of the world. The Programme put forward by the Communist Party of the Soviet Union presupposes a precisely defined, well thought-out, logically coordinated system of actions. It is a well prepared frontal offensive in the main directions of world politics today for the benefit of peace and the security of nations.

The fundamental peculiarity of the Peace Programme consists in its being addressed not solely to governments but also directly to peoples. People at large find it appealing because it furnishes a businesslike answer to the most burning questions in international life, and this has ensured it the support of the peace-loving states and the multimillion-strong popular masses throughout the world.

Soviet people fully approve and support the tireless activity of the Central Committee of the Communist Party of the Soviet Union and the Soviet Government to implement the Peace Programme. It is precisely thanks to these efforts supported by all people of good will that a halt was put to US aggression in Vietnam. It is precisely thanks to these efforts that an important turning point came about in foreign affairs, the changeover from the cold war to detente, to the peaceful coexistence of states with different social systems.

Strictly speaking, it had always been possible to develop relations between the USSR and the Western countries, including the USA, based on principles of peaceful coexistence. The early postwar years had been an especially promising time for this. We had fought shoulder to shoulder against a common enemy. At that time, many people, myself included, thought that relations between the members of the anti-Hitler coalition after the war would be typified by trust and cooperation for the benefit of peace and the security of nations. Indeed, if our cooperation had played the decisive part in gaining victory over a common enemy why could not this cooperation be furthered and expanded when the war ended?

But there were anti-popular forces in the world to whom it was of greater advantage to wield international relations to exacerbate tension and wage the cold war. And it took almost a quarter of a century for the heads of a number of Western countries to realize that there is no future in the policy of strength.

The Soviet Union is a peaceful state. Our people's short- and long-term goals serve the cause of building communism in our country. We do not need war to attain this. But to protect and safeguard the Soviet people's peaceful labour we must study our military experience in defending the socialist Motherland, and make use of what will help us ensure the country's defences in the most effective way. We should never forget that as long as imperialism persists, the threat of another world war lingers on.

I would like young people to read this book through particularly carefully. We, the older generation, are well aware what helped us to withstand that onslaught of colossal force. But young people still have to understand it.

I should like to tell the young reader once more that we would have been simpletons if we had not backed up our efforts to champion peace with our readiness to defend our Motherland, our social system, and our ideals. The gun powder should, according to the saying, constantly be kept dry. But now it is not us, who have given all we could in past battles, but the new, younger generation who are the hope of the people. My message to you, young people, is — always be vigilant! A day's delay in the last war cost us very dearly. Now, if a crisis does occur, it may be seconds that count.

What would I wish to see you to be like, defenders of our Motherland? I would like to see you knowing what you are doing and with powers of endurance. Today the army is equipped with extremely sophisticated technology. It is much more difficult to master it than when I was young. At that time, things were much simpler. Every age sets soldiers various tasks of its own. The latest technology is for people with comprehensive training and a good education. So, get down to your studies!

I would also appeal to young people to have a solicitous attitude to all that is connected with the Great Patriotic War. It is a must to study military experience, collect documents, set up museums and erect monuments, and never forget memorable dates and glorious names. But it is particularly important to remember that there are still former soldiers living amongst you. Show concern for them.

I have seen soldiers going into the attack many times. It is no easy matter to stand upright when death-bearing metal is raining down upon you. But they did get up! Though many of them had hardly had time to taste of life, only 19 or 20 years old, in the very best age with their whole lives ahead of them. But all they had before them frequently was a German trench ejecting machine-gun fire.

Of course, they experienced the joy of victory in battle as well, the camaraderie, helping each other out on the battlefield, the feeling of satisfaction they gained from the awareness that they were performing the holy mission of defending their homeland.

At that time, the Soviet soldier went through ordeals. But today the old wound is making itself felt, and his health is playing up. But the old front-line soldier would not dream of complaining to you, for that is not his manner. You yourselves must be attentive to him. Do not hurt his pride, but have a sympathetic and respectful attitude towards him. That is very little to pay for all he did for you in 1941, 1942, 1943, 1944 and 1945.

Having written this, I wonder whether I am finishing this book with trifles. But now I have put that thought out of my mind. These are not trifles. During the war the order of things was severe: no matter how difficult it was, the wounded were removed by all means from the range of fire. This was not only a demonstration of the concern to save human life. Those going into battle placed their faith in this, for they knew that whatever happened, their comrades would not leave them.

The remembrance of those who perished and a considerate attitude towards war invalids help to keep up this high code of morals.

I see that my conclusion has turned into a talk with young people. Let it be so. It is young people who will have to further our cause. It is very important that they should learn from our mistakes and our successes. It is no simple science to learn to win. But he who learns, who strives for victory, who fights for a cause, in the rightness of which he believes, is always victorious. I have been convinced of that in the many lessons I have learned in my own life.

I began this book by telling you about my childhood. And now, when summing up my life, I recall my boyhood again. What would life have been like if the October Revolution had not happened?

The Revolution offered me the opportunity to live a completely different way of life, a vivid, interesting life full of exciting experience and important deeds. I have always felt that I am needed by the people, that I am continuously in their debt. And that, if one reflects on the sense of human living, is the main thing. My life is but a small example of the life of the Soviet people.

When I go through all the landmarks in my life, I consider most important that moment from which we all begin to take our readings, namely the Revolution. The Revolution furnished everyone with the opportunity to try his strength, to seek for his own self and acknowledge himself part of the creative might of the people. And when the hour came to defend this all-important achievement, we knew what we were fighting for.

"A nation in which the majority of the workers and peasants realize, feel and see that they are fighting for their own Soviet power, for the rule of the working people, for the cause, whose victory will ensure them and their children all the benefits of culture, of all that has been created by human labour — such a nation can never be vanquished."[1]

I could find no better words than these uttered by Lenin to finish this book.

---

[1] V. I. Lenin, *Collected Works*, Vol. 29, p. 319.

Briefly about Stalin

Before 1940 I had not met Stalin[1] personally. I judged him only on the basis of the press and the stories of those who had come into contact with him.

Disregarding the Marxist-Leninist precept that only the people make history, from the beginning of the 1930s Stalin began to ignore the party Central Committee (CC). He relied on the Politburo, on the obedient performers he had selected, and on the party Secretariat, becoming an absolute dictator. Unquestioningly they implemented Stalin's instructions, glorifying him as the great leader of the party and the people, very often skipping Lenin's name altogether.

Thus began the personality cult that took on gigantic proportions in the years that followed. Thus was an idol created and propagated by such idolaters as Beria, Voroshilov, Malenkov, Molotov, Kaganovich, Zhdanov, Bulganin and Shkiryatov,[2] not to mention the leaders of republican and regional organisations who praised Stalin's prowess in every way.

Anyone who was in any way opposed to the personality cult, or disagreeable to Stalin, was quickly removed. Times were especially hard for the party and the people in 1937–1939 when, because of the fear and neglect of the Politburo, Stalin was able to squander many thousands of party workers and military officers who were talented leaders and devoted patriots of the motherland.

Stalin cannot, of course, be forgiven for ruining the lives of many thousands of innocent people, whose families' and children's lives were also crippled. But it wouldn't be fair to blame just Stalin. Surely the other members of the then Politburo, as well as Stalin, were aware of the anti-party bacchanalia being perpetrated, especially by the NKVD, in every corner of our country. At the CC plenum in June 1957, when the activities of Molotov, Kaganovich, Malenkov and others were discussed, I publicized some of the lists that were given to Stalin by Yezhov[3] and other NKVD officials. All the listed people were shot without trial with the approval of Stalin, Molotov, Voroshilov and Kaganovich. Terrified by the idea of a big military-political plot, Stalin, as well as his Politburo entourage, didn't bother to talk or listen to any of those arrested, to understand by what means confessions of their "hostile" activities were obtained. Animal fear, acute suspiciousness, and Stalin's claim that during the construction of socialism the class struggle sharpened – they all did their dirty work. Particularly serious complications arose when foreign intelligence infiltrated the organs of state security. Its agents spread false stories about the alleged anti-Soviet activities of our people that incited irreparable damage to our motherland and to the defence of our country.

I got to know Stalin closely in 1941–1946 and I often met him when I was Chief of the General Staff, a commander of Fronts, Deputy Supreme Commander, and chief of the occupation forces in Germany. I tried to study Stalin thoroughly but it was very difficult to understand him. He spoke very little and formed his thoughts in short sentences. It seemed to me that Stalin was not organically connected to the people, to their work activities, their conditions of life, their thoughts and their worries. He learned about them from Politburo and Secretariat reports and since things were presented to Stalin in an embroidered manner, he didn't know the true state of affairs in the country or in the life of the people.

To be fair to Stalin, he never made rushed decisions. Usually the questions to be solved were handed to Gosplan [the state planning agency], or to a representative commission headed by a member of Politburo, for detailed examination.

Feeling his weakness in the organisation of operations, and also under the influence of major setbacks in the south of the country in 1942, Stalin offered me the post of Deputy Supreme Commander. Initially I refused this offer, referring to my character and the fact that it would be difficult for us to work together, but Stalin said: "the situation threatens mortal danger to the country, the motherland has to be saved from the enemy by any means, by any sacrifice. As to our characters – let's surrender them to the interests of our motherland." I said that I was always ready to serve my country.

From that moment, it should be noted, Stalin hardly ever made any decisions concerning the organisation of operations without consulting me. For most of the war I enjoyed his favour and trust, and this helped me to successfully organize and carry out operations.

Near the end of the war, more precisely after the Kursk battle, Stalin's understanding of military affairs wasn't bad. However, if major operations were successful, Stalin liked to put himself to the fore and to overshadow their organisers, achieving this by the following method: when the successful outcome of an operation became known, he would call the commanders and staff of the Fronts, army commanders, and sometimes corps commanders, and, using the latest data on the situation put together by the General Staff, ask them about the development of the operation, offer advice, express interest in their needs and make promises – creating the impression that their Supreme Commander was vigilantly at his post, with the reins of an operation firmly in his hands. He did this over our heads and Vasilevsky[4] and I only found out from Front commanders about these phone calls of the Supreme Commander.

When the enemy was driven out of our motherland and operations transferred to Poland, East Prussia and Czechoslovakia, Stalin abolished the institution of Stavka representatives, who until then had coordinated the actions of Fronts, and ordered the switch of the management of all fronts directly to Stavka. Vasilevsky and I were ordered to command Fronts – me to replace Rokossovsky[5] at the 1st Belorussian, and Vasilevsky to the 3rd Belorussian to replace General Chernyakhovsky,[6] who had been killed in action. The calculation was obvious. Stalin wanted to crown a glorious victory over the enemy with himself in direct command, i.e. to repeat what Alexander I had done in 1813 when he removed Kutuzov from supreme command and made himself the Supreme Commander so that he could parade on a white horse into Paris at the head of the valiant Russian forces that had destroyed Napoleon's army.

One day in the autumn of 1944 Stalin said to me privately, "The 1st Belorussian Front is on the Berlin direction; we are thinking of placing you in command of this important direction, with Rokossovsky being relocated to another front." I replied that I was ready to head any Front but felt that Rokossovsky would take offence if he was removed from the 1st Belorussian. Stalin said: "you are more experienced and you will stay as my deputy. Regarding offence – we are not pretty maidens. I will talk to Rokossovsky at once."

Poskrebyshev [Stalin's secretary] connected Stalin with Rokossovsky immediately. After telling Rokossovsky of his decision, Stalin asked him if he objected to being moved to the 2nd Belorussian. Rokossovsky asked to stay with the 1st Belorussian but Stalin said "it can't be done. We have decided to put Zhukov on the main direction, and you have to move to the 2nd Belorussian." Stalin had an ulterior motive. From this moment the warm, comradely friendship between me and Rokossovsky that had existed for many years was no more. The closer the end of the war came, the more Stalin played games with his Marshals – with Front commanders and deputies – often making them go head to head, sowing differences or creating jealousy, pushing people to seek glory on an unhealthy basis. Unfortunately, some commanders, disregarding comradely friendship, violated rudimentary decency and pursued their career goals, using Stalin's weakness, stoking his disloyalty to those he had relied on during the gravest years of the war. Such people whispered tales to Stalin, trying to show their persona in an appealing light. Marshal I.S. Konev[7] was especially engaged in these activities.

Starting from the Kursk battle, when the enemy could no longer resist the blows of our army, Konev, like no other commander, diligently fawned in front of Stalin, praising his own "heroic" actions during the conduct of operations, at the same time compromising the actions of neighbouring commanders. I remember the Korsun–Shevchenkovsk operation, which involved the 1st Ukrainian Front commanded by N.F. Vatutin[8] and 2nd Ukrainian Front under Konev. I was coordinating the two Fronts' actions and the operation was going well. Vatutin's army was performing better. But at the end of the operation, in a snowstorm, the remains of the surrounded enemy broke through the lines of Vatutin's army.

Stalin rang me immediately and asked in an agitated tone, "Are you aware the enemy has broken through Vatutin's front and escaped encirclement in the Korsun–Shevchenkovsk region?" I replied, "No, I am not. I think it doesn't correspond with the real situation." Stalin scolded me and said that Konev had rung him and told him about the breakthrough, then he said, "I am thinking of passing completion of the operation to Konev, and you and Vatutin had better concentrate your attention on the external front and preparation of the Proskurovsk–Chernovitsk operation." I replied to Stalin that to finish the operation required not more than three days and that the main role in the Korsun–Shevchenkovsk operation had been played by the 1st Ukrainian Front and Vatutin and his soldiers would be offended if their efforts were not acknowledged. Stalin put down the phone, terminating our talk, and in two hours there was a directive issued regarding the transfer of the finishing of the operation to liquidate the encircled enemy forces. Did the situation demand this? No, it did not. It was necessary in order for Stalin to deepen the wedge between Konev, Vatutin and myself. Konev played an unseemly part in this.

Knowing my conscientiousness, during subsequent operations Stalin tried more than once to set me, Konev, Rokossovsky and others against each other. He slandered me to Vasilevsky, and vice versa, but Vasilevsky, being quite a decent person, didn't respond to Stalin's provocation. Why did Stalin find this necessary? Now, I think that it was all done intentionally, the aim being to disunite the friendly collective of the higher command, whom he had begun to fear because of the unfounded defamatory slander of Beria and Abakumov.[9]

At the end of April 1945 the Berlin operation, which ended the war, was in progress. Successfully breaking through German defences on the Oder and destroying their first line of defence, troops of the 1st Belorussian Front met with the hard-fought resistance of the enemy at their second line of defence, which was situated at the Seelow Heights, which were awkward for our troops to attack. In order not to break off the operation and not give the enemy the possibility of beating off our attacks on the Berlin direction, I decided to involve in battle immediately the 1st and 2nd Tank Armies to ensure the defeat of the enemy on the Seelow Heights.

On the evening of 17 April Stalin rang me. At this time I was at Chuikov's[10] 8th Army command post. Stalin said, "It turns out that you underestimated the enemy's strength on the Berlin direction. I thought you would already be approaching Berlin's outskirts but you are still at the Seelow Heights. Konev's actions have begun more successfully. Shouldn't we change the boundaries between the Fronts and turn the main forces of Konev and Rokossovsky towards Berlin?" I replied, "It's not bad that the enemy sends all his reserves from Berlin to meet my troops. We will defeat them away from Berlin, and this will simplify and speed up the taking of Berlin. Regarding the more successful start to the actions of 1st Ukrainian Front – there are very few enemy troops there, but the enemy will have to send more troops to meet Konev and then the tempo of his advance will slow down. The Fronts' boundaries shouldn't be changed. Konev's main group should move quickly to the Elbe, to the capture of Thuringia and then prepare to be thrown at Prague. I think that no later than 22 April will my Front's troops enter Berlin. As to Rokossovsky, he will be able to conduct a forced crossing of the Oder with his main forces by 22 April, but he won't be able to move into the Berlin region with his group, and anyway it is not necessary."

After an hour I phoned General A.I. Antonov,[11] the Chief of the General Staff, and asked him why Stalin had become worried about the fate of the Berlin operation. Antonov said, "I am not in the picture. I just know that Konev rang him and reported about the successful development of his operation."

At the beginning of March 1946 Stalin rang me in Berlin and said, "Bulganin has presented me a draft proposal on the postwar restructuring of the management of the armed forces. You are not among the key leaders of the armed forces. I consider it wrong. What post would you like? Vasilevsky expressed his wish to be the Chief of the General Staff. Would you like the post of chief of our ground forces, they are the most numerous?" I replied that I hadn't thought about this question and that I was ready to do any work entrusted to me by the Central Committee. Stalin continued: "At the same time he [Bulganin] has presented a draft proposal on the position of the People's Commissariat of Defence. I would like you to come and work on it together with Bulganin and Vasilevsky."

A couple of days later I was in Moscow and I called on Bulganin. He was obviously troubled, knowing, it seems, about my conversation with Stalin. After looking at the draft on the People's Commissariat of Defence I had serious disagreements with Bulganin about the legal position of our armed forces' top commanders and that of the Commissariat's first deputy. According to his draft, commanders would for all practical purposes deal not directly with the People's Commissar for Defence [Stalin] but with his first deputy [Bulganin]. Defending his draft, Bulganin tried to substantiate it with the fact that Stalin, the People's Commissar for Defence, was overloaded with party and state work. "That is not a valid reason," I said to Bulganin, seeking to reject his arguments. "Today the People's Commissar is Stalin, tomorrow it might be somebody else. The laws are written not for one particular person but for the specific post."

Bulganin relayed this to Stalin in a distorted fashion, adding, "Zhukov is a Marshal of the Soviet Union, he doesn't want to deal with me, a mere general." Bulganin's move was calculated so that Stalin would give him the rank of Marshal of the Soviet Union. Indeed, within a day there was a decree published assigning the rank of Marshal of the Soviet Union to Bulganin, and Stalin told me that the position in regard to the Defence Commissariat should be worked on some more. It was clear to me that Bulganin had become Stalin's right hand man in relation to the People's Commissariat of Defence. Bulganin's knowledge of military affairs was very poor and he didn't have a clue about operational and strategic issues. But an intuitively developed person, also cunning, he managed to get near Stalin and gain his trust.

Of course, Stalin realised that he [Bulganin] was not a great find for the armed forces, but he needed him as a smart diplomat and an unquestioning idolater. Stalin knew that Bulganin would do anything for him.

Passing the post of chief of the occupation forces to my deputy V.D. Sokolovsky,[12] I arrived in Moscow and accepted the post of chief of the ground forces.

During this period the demobilization from the army and fleet of older soldiers was being completed. Military life was not yet back to normal. Military order and service were not at the proper level. To bring the army to the normal state we designed a set of educational measures for the ground forces and prepared a draft decree regarding combat training for 1946. The draft decree was sent to Stalin and copied to Bulganin. Stalin, heeding Bulganin's whispering, saw my actions as separatism and as if I was ignoring him [Stalin]. There was a major and unpleasant talk about the content of the draft decree, especially in relation to drawing the reserve troops and units of the High Command into the joint field and command-staff exercises of the ground forces.

Bulganin said that "Zhukov wants to take all the reserves of the High Command under his power, leaving us empty handed". I said that was child's talk. But my reply did not go down well with Stalin. It was suggested that I rework the draft decree. I reworked it, but again Stalin didn't authorise it. Vasilevsky told me in confidence that "Stalin wants to issue a Defence Commissariat decree, not a High Command decree". They then took my draft and reworked it into a Commissariat decree. It was signed by Stalin immediately. It worked out even better. It seems I wasn't right to insist on a command decree rather than a Commissariat decree.

The more time passed, the more combustible material was building up in my relations with Bulganin and Stalin. I felt that there was some unseemly work being done around me. Finally, major trouble for me broke out. Stalin convened the Main Military Council, to which were invited all the members of the Politburo, as well as marshals, and generals, including F.I. Golikov[13] and A.V. Khrulev.[14]

Stalin entered the meeting hall. He was as gloomy as a dark cloud. Not uttering a word, he took a paper out of his pocket, threw it to the Secretary of the Main Military Council, General S.M. Shtemenko,[15] and said, "Read". Shtemenko walked to the tribunal and started reading. It was a statement about Zhukov from my former adjutant Lieutenant-Colonel Semochkin and Chief Marshal of Aviation A.A. Novikov,[16] who were in prison, having been arrested by the state security organs.

The statement filled several sheets, its main content being that Marshal Zhukov was not loyal to Stalin, considered himself, not Stalin, the main leader in the war, and that he repeatedly conducted conversations directed against Stalin. It was alleged that during the war I had gathered around me a group of disgruntled generals and officers.

After the reading of this statement Stalin proposed there should be speeches. Molotov, Beria and Bulganin spoke, criticising me for not being grateful to Stalin for his good treatment, for putting on airs, and for disregarding the authority not only of the Politburo but of Stalin himself, saying that I needed to be put in my place. General Golikov spoke in the same vein, alleging that I had no reason to remove him from the post of Front Commander because of the failure of his Front's actions at Kharkov in 1943. However, the majority of the generals present supported me. Marshal of Armoured Forces P.S. Rybalko[17] especially spoke keenly in my favour, speaking about how Zhukov in the most complicated circumstances and dangerous moments had helped troops to find the right decisions and crush the enemy.

It ended with my removal from the post of the chief of the ground forces and being sent to command the troops of Odessa military region. At the next Central Committee plenum, I was removed from membership of the CC without formal explanation, although A.A. Zhdanov said that "Zhukov is too young and not mature enough for the CC".

In 1947 a big group of generals and officers were arrested, mainly those who had worked with me. Among those arrested were Generals Minuk,[18] Filatov,[19] Varennikov[20] and Krukov[21], ex-member of the Military Council of 1st Belorussian Front K.F. Telegin[22] and others. All of them were physically forced to admit to the preparation of a Zhukov-organised 'military plot' against Stalin's leadership. This affair was led by Abakumov and Beria. Their efforts concentrated around my arrest. However, Stalin didn't believe that I was trying to organise a military plot and he didn't agree to my arrest.

Khrushchev[23] told me later that Stalin allegedly said to Beria, "I don't believe that Zhukov would do such a thing. I know him well. He is a straightforward person, harsh and able to look you in the eye and tell you something unpleasant, but he wouldn't go against the Central Committee."

So Stalin did not allow my arrest and when Abakumov was arrested himself it came to light that he had deliberately fabricated this story against me, behaving in the same way he did in the dark years of 1937–1939. Abakumov was executed, while at the 19th Party Congress Stalin personally recommended me for membership of the Central Committee.

Throughout this unfavourable time Stalin never said a bad word about me. I was grateful for his objectivity.

G.K. Zhukov, 'Korotko o Staline', *Pravda*, 20 January 1989.

Translated by Svetlana Frolova and Geoffrey Roberts.

Notes

1. J.V. Stalin (1879–1953), General-Secretary of the Soviet Communist Party, 1922–1953, Supreme Commander, 1941–1945, Defence Commissar/Minister, 1941–1947.

2. L.P. Beria (1899–1953), Soviet security chief, 1938–1953; K.E. Voroshilov (1881–1969), Defence Commissar, 1925–1940, Chairman of the Supreme Soviet, 1953–1960; G.M. Malenkov (1902–1988), Soviet Prime Minister, 1953–1955; V.M. Molotov (1890–1986), Soviet Prime Minister, 1930–1940, Foreign Commissar/Minister, 1939–1949, 1953–1956; L.M. Kaganovich (1898–1972), Ukrainian party secretary in the 1920s and 1940s, transport and industry commissar/minister, 1930s–1950s; A.A. Zhdanov (1896–1948), Leningrad party secretary, 1934–1944, Soviet ideology chief, 1945–1948; N.A. Bulganin (1895–1975), political commissar on various Fronts, 1941–1943, Deputy Defence Commissar, 1944–1947, Minister for the Armed Forces, 1947–1947, 1953–1955, Prime Minister, 1955–1958; M.F. Shkiryatov (1893–1954), Secretary/Deputy/Chair of the party control commission, 1934–1954.

3. N.I. Yezhov, Soviet security chief, 1935–1938, arrested 1939, shot 1940.

4. A.M. Vasilevsky (1895–1977), Deputy and Chief of the General Staff, 1941–1945, 1946–1948, Deputy/Minister of the Armed Forces/Defence, 1949–1957.

5. K.K. Rokossovsky (1896–1968), commander of the 1st and 2nd Belorussian Fronts, 1944–1945, Minister of Defence, Poland, 1949–1956.

6. I.D. Chernyakhovsky (1906–1945), the youngest Soviet Front commander of the war and the only Jewish officer to reach that rank.

7. I.S. Konev (1897–1973), commander of various Fronts, 1941–1945, commander in chief of ground forces, 1946–1950, Deputy Minister of Defence, 1956–1961.

8. N.F. Vatutin (1901–1944), staff officer and Front commander, killed by Ukrainian nationalist partisans.

9. V.S. Abakumov (1908–1954), Minister for State Security, 1946–1951.
10. V.I. Chuikov (1900–1982), commander of the 62nd/8th Guards Army, 1942–1945, commander in chief of ground forces, 1960–1964.
11. A.I. Antonov (1896–1962), Deputy and Chief of the General Staff, 1943–1948.
12. V.D. Sokolovsky (1897–1968), served as Zhukov's Chief of Staff during the war and as his deputy in Germany after the war, Chief of the General Staff, 1952–1960.
13. F.I. Golikov (1900–1980), head of military intelligence, 1940–1941, chief of the military cadres department, 1943–1950.
14. A.V. Khrulev (1892–1962), chief of supplies for the armed forces, 1943–1951.
15. S.M. Shtemenko (1907–1976) Chief of Operations/Deputy Chief of Staff, 1941–1946.
16. A.A. Novikov, Chief of the Air Force, 1942–1946, arrested 1946, rehabilitated 1953.
17. P. Rybalko (1894–1948) deputy and chief of armoured forces, 1941–1948.
18. L.F. Minuk (1900–1977). Served with Zhukov before the Second World War. Dismissed from the armed forces in 1947 on grounds of ill-health.
19. A.A. Filatov (1895–1956). Served with the Soviet occupation forces in Germany, 1945–1947. Arrested in 1947 and sentenced to ten years' deprivation of freedom. Rehabilitated in 1953.
20. I.S. Varennikov (1901–1971). Served as chief of staff for various armies during the war and on the staff of the Frunze military academy from 1946 until 1948 when he was 'repressed'.
21. V.V. Krukov (1897–1959), divisional and deputy corps commander, 1941–1947. Arrested in 1948 together with his wife, the singer Lidiya Ruslanova, who had been awarded a medal by Zhukov in 1945. Sentenced to twenty-five years but rehabilitated after Stalin's death in 1953, as were most of Zhukov's associates who had been repressed in the late 1940s.
22. K.F. Telegin (1899–1981). Political commissar who served with Zhukov during and immediately after the war. Dismissed from the army in 1947, arrested 1948, rehabilitated 1953.
23. N.S. Khrushchev (1894–1971), leader of the Soviet communist party, 1953–1964.

After the Death of Stalin

It was March 1953. I had just returned to Sverdlovsk from tactical exercises with the district's troops. The chief of my secretariat reported that Minister of Defence Bulganin[1] had rung on the VCh [secure line] and ordered that I phone him back.

I phoned Bulganin immediately. He told me: "Tomorrow morning you have to be in Moscow." I tried to clarify the reason for the summons but Bulganin replied: "Fly in and you will find out." In recent years I had rarely been called to Moscow to receive something pleasant and I thought about this summons for a long time but didn't reach any definite conclusions.

We flew from Sverdlovsk to Moscow in four hours. The weather was clear and I looked at the winter landscape from above with great interest. We landed, as usual, at the central city aerodrome where I was met by officers from Bulganin's secretariat, who told me that I was to go straight to the Minister of Defence. I wondered why there was such a rush.

I found Bulganin in his office. He had his greatcoat on and was talking on the Kremlin line. I introduced myself in military fashion. Bulganin said: "A plenum of the Central Committee (CC) is going to take place today. You have to be present at it. I am in a hurry to get to Kremlin." He shook my hand and then briskly walked from the office to his car.

After having a bite to eat I went to see Vasilevsky[2] – the Chief of the General Staff. After talking about current work I asked Alexander Mikhailovich if he knew what would be discussed at the CC plenum today. He said: "I swear I don't know. The Minister of Defence just rang me and said that there will be a plenum today. The time of the meeting will be announced later."

Having gathered for the plenum in the lobby we learnt that Stalin[3] was seriously ill. At the appointed hour the plenum participants took

492

their seats in the Sverdlov Hall. In 15–20 minutes the Presidium[4] appeared. Opening the plenum, Khrushchev[5] said: "The present plenum has been called because of the serious illness of comrade Stalin. Due to the condition of his health he most likely won't be back soon to lead the party and the state. Having discussed the situation, the Presidium presents for your attention a set of pressing issues regarding the improvement of the structure of ministries, central state departments and personnel appointments."

Khrushchev was proposed as a First Secretary of the CC. Malenkov[6] was proposed as the Chairman of the Council of Ministers. The Ministry of Internal Affairs was to be merged with Ministry of State Security and Beria[7] was named Minister of Internal Affairs. Bulganin stayed on as Minister of Defence. My candidature for First Deputy Minister of Defence was considered and confirmed.

It has to be said that my assignment as First Deputy Minister of Defence came as a complete surprise because Bulganin was not a figure of authority for me, and he knew it. I was told later that Bulganin was against my appointment. He said that it would be difficult for him to work with Zhukov because he doesn't acknowledge me as a military man. He was told that state interests required Zhukov's assignment as First Deputy of Minister of Defence. As for personal mutual relations with me, these would have to be managed by Bulganin.

In any event since I hadn't returned to Sverdlovsk I took on my new responsibilities immediately but before starting my assignment as First Deputy Minister of Defence I had a major talk with Bulganin. He began saying that while "in the past not everything was smooth between us", he wasn't to blame. It was necessary to draw a line under the past and begin again on a healthy, friendly basis in the interests of state defence. It was as if he had been the first to propose my candidature.

I told Bulganin: "Nikolai Alexandrovich, you did a lot of unpleasant things to me, placing me in harm's way under Stalin, but in the interests of the state I would like to forget that and if you sincerely want to work together on a friendly basis, let's forget about past unpleasantness."

When Khrushchev reported to the plenum the Presidium's proposals to simplify state governance and on the candidates for leading state posts, it gave the impression that Stalin was not a living person any more, that he would never again rule the party and the state. At the end of the plenum a bulletin was issued on the state of Stalin's health, which made it clear that Stalin, still unconscious, was living out his last days.

Studying the faces of the Presidium members, I came to the following conclusions about their current attitudes toward Stalin.

Molotov[8] was seriously pensive and visibly anxious, worried about what was happening. Voroshilov[9] looked clearly at a loss. It was hard to judge by his appearance if he was anxious, sad or had any definite opinion at all. One could see him acting like this when he worked under Stalin, or maybe he still didn't believe that Stalin's death was inevitable and, just in case, had decided to wait it out. Malenkov, Khrushchev, Beria and Bulganin were in high spirits and evidently knew better than anyone that Stalin would die soon. Their judgements and critique of the state order that had existed under Stalin showed that they were certain that he would soon die and they were not afraid to voice their opinion, as they had been during Stalin's time.

Beria sat next to Bulganin and tried to put a friendly expression on his face. Even though his eyes were covered by glasses, if you watched him closely you could see his rapacity and cold cruelty. His whole demeanour said: "enough of the Stalinist order, we suffered a lot under Stalin, now everything will be different". I knew Beria quite well, had seen his cunning subservience to Stalin and his readiness to remove from Stalin's path anybody who was disagreeable to him, and now he was posing as a true Bolshevik-Leninist. It was disgusting to look at this masquerade.

Bulganin was, as usual, the height of subservience and timeserving. He approached one person and then another, smiling sweetly at one, giving a firm handshake to another. Every now and then he responded to what Khrushchev was saying: "That's right, Nikita Sergeevich, that's right. It should have been done long ago."

The rest of the Presidium members didn't show anything. They sat silently, just as they did during Stalin's time. Amongst a majority of CC members and candidate members a mournful mood was prevailing. Most were sincerely saddened by Stalin's near-death condition. It could not have been otherwise. Stalin was the universally acknowledged authority and leader. The party valued his achievements and trusted him. Nobody knew then about the scale of the evil inflicted on the Soviet people by Stalin in 1937–38.

Notwithstanding the fact that Stalin had been unfair to me after the Great Patriotic War, personally I was sincerely sorry and still valued him for the gigantic work he had carried out after Lenin and during the years of the Patriotic War.

During Stalin's funeral Bulganin told me about the night misfortune struck Stalin. In the evening he, Khrushchev, Beria and Malenkov (three inseparable friends, as Bulganin always boasted about them) had gathered at Stalin's dacha. After talking about business, everybody sat down at the table for dinner. Stalin was in a good mood and joked a lot. The dinner, as often happened at Stalin's place, continued till 2.00am.

Bulganin and Malenkov departed at 2.00am and it seems that Beria and Khrushchev left at about 3.00am. Fifteen to twenty minutes after Beria's and Khrushchev's departure, General Vlasik[10] entered Stalin's dining room to help him to bed, and saw Stalin lying on the floor in a semi-conscious state. Vlasik immediately called Beria and the doctors. Apparently Vlasik and his security team carried Stalin to bed. The doctors arrived and in the presence of Beria, Malenkov and Khrushchev tried to help Stalin but it was in vain. Stalin was unconscious and deemed paralysed. A bit later Bulganin and other members of the Presidium arrived. It was decided that a member of the Presidium and specialists from the Kremlin clinic would be on duty at all times.

A short time later Stalin died without regaining consciousness. After Stalin's funeral the Soviet people sincerely mourned his death and placed all their hopes in the party, which in previous years had led them confidently on the path toward communism.

Soon I was inducted into the CC Presidium and had a good opportunity to get to know the post-Stalin method and the style of the work of the party's highest organs. As a rule, under Stalin the Presidium had examined only really important issues. Discussions were very short. Essential proposals only were tabled. Less important issues were dealt with and decided by the CC Secretariat or by commissions formed by the Presidium.

After Stalin's death twenty-five to thirty matters were examined by each meeting of the Presidium, more than half of which were not particularly important and could easily have been decided by the ministries. Due to the extraordinary overload of the meetings' agendas, it was not possible to discuss in detail even those issues of significance to the state.

It was a paradoxical situation. The substance of an issue was not investigated deeply. Because they were unable to probe deeply all twenty-five to thirty questions, the members of the Presidium simply declined or accepted proposals, essentially rubber-stamping the recommendations of their apparatus, their aides and their consultants. After a while it was concluded that it was necessary to relieve the Presidium of many secondary issues, obliging the ministries and Gosplan [the state economic planning organisation] to resolve their own issues. However, fearing what might happen, ministries were unwilling to decide issues for themselves and continued to bombard the Presidium with questions. This was an effect of the habit inculcated during Stalin's time – never decide anything without the Central Committee's sanction.

Initially after Stalin's death there existed an especially firm friendship between Khrushchev, Beria and Malenkov. In the Presidium and in the life of the whole country these three men played the decisive role. Bulganin grovelled in front of them. He told me several times: "Before putting a Defence Ministry matter to the Presidium it was necessary to elicit the views and agreement of Malenkov, Khrushchev and Beria, and then the other members of the Presidium will vote in favour unreservedly."

In order to toady to Beria, Bulganin followed Beria's recommendation and disbanded the TsSKA [army] football team, sending the best players to Dynamo, i.e. to the team of the MVD [Ministry of Internal Affairs]. The Soviet Army was left with no football team for a long time.

Molotov remained aloof, while Voroshilov, it can be said, did not play any role. I can't recall any occasion when Voroshilov made an active proposal. Material sent to him remained unread and he almost never prepared for meetings.

The main and leading role was played by Khrushchev. He was supported in every possible way by Beria, and by Malenkov when he was still Chairman of the Council of Ministers, not to mention Bulganin.

Then some very important things happened. Beria was arrested. It happened like this:

Bulganin rang me and said: "Come quickly, please, to me for a minute, I'm in a rush to Kremlin." I speedily went down from the 4th floor to the 2nd and entered Bulganin's office. He told me: "Call Moskalenko, Nedelin, Batitsky[11] and a couple more whom you consider necessary and go with them to Malenkov's office immediately."

In 30 minutes I and a group of generals were in the reception to Malenkov's office. I was summoned into the office immediately, where besides Malenkov there were Molotov, Khrushchev and Bulganin.

Having greeted me, Malenkov said: "We called you to give you a very important assignment. Lately Beria has been carrying out suspicious activities amongst his people, directed against members of the Presidium. We think that Beria has become a dangerous person for the party and the state. We have decided to arrest him and to neutralise the NKVD. We have decided to entrust the arrest of Beria to you personally." Khrushchev added: "We have no doubt that you will be able to do this very well, particularly since Beria brought you personally a lot of unpleasant troubles. Do you have any doubts about this?"

I replied: "What doubts could there be? The assignment will be executed."

Khrushchev: "Keep in mind that Beria is crafty and is physically quite a strong man, the more so since it seems he is armed."

I said: "Of course, I am not a specialist in arrests and I haven't had to do that, but my hand won't shake. Just say where and when he should be arrested."

Malenkov: "We have called Beria to a meeting of the Council of Ministers. But instead of a council meeting there will be a Presidium meeting, at which Beria will be accused among other things of ignoring the CC, of displaying a disloyal attitude to Presidium members, and of appointing leaders of the NKVD without the CC's agreement. During the meeting you should be in the recreation room and wait for two rings. After the two rings you will enter the office and arrest Beria. Is everything clear?" I replied: "Completely."

Beria arrived and the meeting commenced. The meeting lasted for one hour and then another, but the bell did not ring as agreed. I began to worry that Beria had arrested those who wanted to arrest him. Then the bell rang.

Leaving two military officers at the door of Malenkov's office, we went in. As agreed, the generals took out their pistols and I quickly approached Beria and said to him loudly: "Beria, stand up, you are under arrest," simultaneously grabbing both his hands, lifting him off the chair and briskly feeling his pockets. There was no weapon. His briefcase was immediately thrown into the middle of the table.

Beria became horribly pale and started to mumble something. Two generals took him by the arms and led him to the back room of Malenkov's office, where a thorough search and removing of not-permitted objects were performed.

At 11.00pm Beria was secretly moved from the Kremlin to the military prison and 24 hours later he was transferred to the command post of the Moscow Military District, where he was entrusted to the security of the same group that had arrested him. Thereafter I did not participate in either the guarding or the prosecution process.

After his trial, Beria was shot by the same people who had guarded him. During the execution Beria behaved very badly, like the worst coward. He cried hysterically, dropped to his knees and then soiled himself. In a word – he lived an unsavoury life and died an even nastier death.

After Beria's execution the Presidium worked in a friendly fashion for some time, but then there started serious disagreements and arguments that descended into personal insults, especially between Khrushchev, Kaganovich[12] and Molotov. It has to be said that old scores were being settled between Kaganovich and Khrushchev. Making themselves felt were hostile relations originating from when they worked together in the Moscow committee of the party and from when Kaganovich was party leader in the Ukraine and Khrushchev served under him. Kaganovich considered himself the more educated Marxist-Leninist, but Khrushchev didn't recognise this quality in Kaganovich and considered him an incorrigible, dogmatic Stalinist.

When the 20th party congress was being prepared, Khrushchev raised the need to address the issue of Stalin's personality cult. Molotov, Voroshilov, Kaganovich and Malenkov spoke out against raising the question of Stalin's personality cult. The rest, above all the younger members of the Presidium, supported Khrushchev.

Molotov, Kaganovich and Voroshilov were particularly ardent and hardline in their opposition to raising the question of Stalin's personality cult. Together with Stalin they had indiscriminately annihilated party, Soviet and military cadres in the dark years of 1937–38. They were against it because they feared they would be exposed alongside Stalin, and the congress would demand that they be severely held to account.

After the 20th party congress, and after the removal of Malenkov as Chairman of the Council of Ministers, mutual relations within the Presidium became even more strained. Malenkov distanced himself from Khrushchev and became closer to Kaganovich and Molotov. Malenkov's personal resentment was to the fore, not some principled point of view.

Bulganin was appointed Chairman of the Council of Ministers in place of Malenkov, and I became Minister of Defence.

I can't recall one meeting of the Presidium where there wasn't a fight or an argument between Khrushchev and Kaganovich or between Khrushchev and Molotov. To us, the new members of the Presidium, such hostile relations between the old members, some of whom had worked together with Stalin and even Lenin, seemed strange. Such disloyal attitudes towards each other couldn't but have an impact.

There were unprincipled arguments and the issues they related to remained unresolved. We tried to advise them to stop their abuse but our voices lacked authority.

Personally I thought Khrushchev's direction was more correct than that of Kaganovich and Molotov, who clung tightly to old dogmas and were not willing to change in accordance with the spirit of the times. It seemed to me that Khrushchev was always thinking about and trying to find more progressive methods, means and ways to build socialism and to develop the economy and the general life of the country.

I got to know Khrushchev well in Ukraine in 1940, in the years of the Great Patriotic War, and in the post-war period. I considered him to be a good man, consistently genial and, undoubtedly, an optimist. Stalin had regard for Khrushchev, but I noticed that sometimes he was unfair to him, giving the plaudits to Molotov, Beria, Malenkov and Kaganovich. Taking everything into account, I firmly supported Khrushchev in the arguments between himself, Kaganovich and Molotov.

In 1957 Khrushchev was away. In the Presidium somebody, either Furtseva[13] or Kirichenko,[14] raised the question of conferring on Khrushchev a second Hero of Socialist Labour medal for major achievements in the agricultural sector. Serious arguments ignited and it finally dawned on me how deep and impassable was the chasm between Molotov, Kaganovich and Khrushchev. Molotov and Kaganovich thought that there hadn't been any special achievements in agriculture or any personal achievements by Khrushchev in this regard. Malenkov supported them. They thought Khrushchev was conducting an incorrect policy in agriculture, ignoring the Presidium, and at regional agricultural meetings was promoting without prior agreement the unrealizable slogan "to catch up and overtake America in 2–3 years". Molotov said this was a reckless venture and that Khrushchev should be called to order. However, the majority decided to award Khrushchev the second gold medal of Hero of Socialist Labour.

While in Gorky, Khrushchev made a statement regarding the desirability of handing over to the state the bonds of all loans – some 260 billion rubles (in old money). Khrushchev was blamed again for talking about an important issue without prior ratification by the Presidium. When Khrushchev returned to Moscow there was another unpleasant talk and the decision was made to defer honouring the bonds for 25 years rather than having them handed over to the state.

Considering necessary the decentralization of industrial administration and the delegation of more power to the Soviet Republics,

Khrushchev proposed to the Presidium the liquidation of many industrial ministries. Kaganovich rejected this proposal as premature and badly thought out. Molotov supported Kaganovich and said that there should be general direction from Moscow, possibly with the ministries being replaced by industrial committees. In the end the majority of Presidium members supported Khrushchev's idea.

At first Bulganin meekly supported all Khrushchev's initiatives but gradually leaned more and more towards Molotov and Kaganovich. Bulganin's knowledge of the country's economics, especially of agriculture, was poor and not once did he present to the Presidium any issues from the Council of Ministers. Bulganin realised that he was doing badly in his role as Chairman of the Council of Ministers, that everywhere and in everything Khrushchev was outperforming him. It seems that privately he was fully prepared to join the anti-Khrushchev group, and he did join as soon as he got wind that the majority of Presidium members were against Khrushchev.

In the spring of 1957 Khrushchev's son Sergey got married. To mark the occasion there was a celebration at Khrushchev's dacha. As is customary at weddings, everybody drank hard and there were speeches. Khrushchev made a speech. As usual he spoke very well. He spoke about his genealogy. He spoke very warmly about his mother, who, in his words, loved to talk a lot. Then he made a passing jab at Bulganin. On another occasion Bulganin would have kept quiet, but this time he uncharacteristically flew into a rage and asked Khrushchev to be careful what he said.

We knew that Bulganin was embittered against Khrushchev and this understanding was confirmed. As soon as the dinner was over, Molotov, Malenkov, Kaganovich and Bulganin pointedly left the wedding and went to Malenkov's dacha. Khrushchev now realised that Bulganin had switched camps and he was clearly worried about the strengthening of his opponents' group.

After Bulganin, Malenkov, Molotov and Kaganovich left, Kirichenko walked up to me and started a conversation: "Georgy Konstantinovich! You do understand where all this is going, don't you? That group left the wedding the way they did for a reason. I think that we have to keep our ears pricked and be ready for anything that might happen. We place our hopes in you. To the army you are a great authority. One word from you and the army will do what is necessary."

I saw that Kirichenko was drunk, but I was immediately on my guard. "What are you talking about, Aleksey Illarionovich? I do not understand you. Where are you going with your words? Why are you talking about my authority in the army and about me saying only one word and it would do everything that's required?"

Kirichenko: "Have you not seen how maliciously they were talking to Khrushchev? Bulganin, Molotov, Kaganovich and Malenkov are determined and bitter men. I think this business could get serious."

It seemed to me that Kirichenko had not started this talk by accident and was not speaking just for himself. This suspicion was confirmed immediately by his next words: "In any event, we won't allow Nikita Sergeevich to get hurt."

I had always had a bad opinion of Kirichenko. I considered him an "Odessarite" in the worst meaning of the word.[15] Here is one example of his character as an unprincipled communist. In 1946 I came to Odessa to head the military district, where Kirichenko was the first secretary of the regional committee of the party. After a couple of weeks, Kirichenko called me from the Odessa party HQ. "Listen, Georgy Konstantinovich, things are not great with my car and the military district has many good trophy cars. I ask you, please, give me one or two cars."

I replied that there was a car for him in the district but its transfer had to be done by the book through the Ministry of Defence. "You hand over the cars", said Kirichenko, "and don't worry about the documentation; in Odessa we can make any kind of document, not only for a car, but if necessary for a Hero of Soviet Union award." Kirichenko was the leader of the party in the region and, to be honest, I was taken aback by his mentality. Well, of course, I didn't give him a car, though he reminded me about it a few times.

From the cultural point of view Kirichenko was quite primitive. I was surprised and puzzled how he had earned such friendship from Khrushchev. After Khrushchev moved from the Ukraine to Moscow, he recommended him as the first secretary of the Ukrainian party. After Stalin's death Kirichenko was transferred to the CC secretariat and soon became a member of the Presidium, where he showed the worst side of himself.

On the morning of the day the Malenkov–Molotov group decided to place before the Presidium the question of removing Khrushchev from the post of First Secretary, Malenkov called me and asked me to come to him to discuss an urgent matter. Thinking that Malenkov was performing some job on the orders of the Presidium, I immediately started for his office.

Malenkov greeted me very amiably and said that for a long time he had wanted to have a heart to heart talk with me about Khrushchev. He briefly outlined his view of the supposedly wrong leadership of Khrushchev, pointing out that Khrushchev had stopped considering the Presidium and gave speeches without prior discussion of issues by the Presidium. Khrushchev was extremely rude to the older members of the Presidium – Molotov, Kaganovich, Voroshilov, Bulganin and others. In conclusion he asked how I evaluated the current situation in the Presidium.

I asked him: "Malenkov, are you talking to me in your own name or did somebody ask you to speak to me?" Malenkov said: "I am talking to you as an old member of the party, whom I value and respect. Your opinion is very valuable to me."

I understood that behind Malenkov there were more experienced and stronger personalities. Malenkov was obviously being false and hadn't revealed the true aim of his conversation with me.

I said to Malenkov: "Since you have issues with Khrushchev, I advise you to go and talk to him in a comradely fashion. I am sure he will understand." Malenkov: "You are mistaken. Khrushchev is not the kind of person to recognise that his actions are wrong and need altering." I replied that I thought the issue would resolve itself gradually. On that we said our goodbyes.

In a few hours I was called urgently to a meeting of the Presidium. In the Presidium corridor I met Mikoyan[16] and Furtseva. They were excited. Mikoyan said: "There is a group on the Presidium that is not happy with Khrushchev and they have demanded a review of the question of Khrushchev in the Presidium today. This group consists of Molotov, Kaganovich, Voroshilov, Bulganin, Malenkov and Pervukhin."[17] I told him about the talk I had with Malenkov two hours ago and Mikoyan said they had talked to him an hour ago.

Khrushchev had been busy since morning meeting with Hungarian comrades and was just free. But he knew already that a big group of Presidium members had demanded an immediate meeting of the Presidium.

When the meeting started, Khrushchev asked: "What are we going to talk about?" Malenkov spoke up: "I am speaking on behalf of a group of comrades on the Presidium. We would like to discuss the question of Khrushchev and since this will be about him personally I propose that Bulganin, not Khrushchev, chair the meeting." Molotov, Kaganovich, Bulganin, Voroshilov and Pervukhin shouted "that's right". As the group had a majority, Khrushchev silently vacated the chair and Bulganin took his place.

Bulganin said: "Malenkov has the floor." Malenkov detailed all the issues with Khrushchev and proposed that he be relieved of his duties as First Secretary of the party.

Kaganovich spoke after Malenkov. His speech was clearly malicious. He said: "How can he be the First Secretary? In the past he was a Trotskyist and he fought against Lenin. Politically he is badly educated. He meddled in agriculture and he doesn't understand the field of industry, bringing confusion to its organisation." Accusing him of vanity, Kaganovich proposed the acceptance of Malenkov's proposition to relieve Khrushchev of his duties as First Secretary and give him other work.

Molotov joined Malenkov and Kaganovich in proposing that in place of a First Secretary there should be a secretary for general matters so that the personality cult would not be revived. Bulganin, Voroshilov, Pervukhin and Shepilov[18] also associated themselves with these proposals.

The matter had taken a serious turn. The Molotov–Malenkov group had a majority and could that day remove Khrushchev as First Secretary. Against the decision to remove Khrushchev was a group consisting of Mikoyan, Suslov,[19] Zhukov, Furtseva and Shvernik[20] but they were in a minority. Comrades Aristov,[21] Kirichenko and Saburov[22] were not in Moscow. To gain time to call in absent members, and to take other measures, we proposed that in view of the importance of the issue there should be a break until tomorrow while an urgent call was made to all members of the Presidium. We hoped that with the arrival of the absentees the balance of power would be to our benefit. But Saburov went over to the other side and upon arriving in Moscow made a speech against Khrushchev.

Seeing that the matter had taken a serious turn Khrushchev proposed the urgent convening of a plenum of the Central Committee. The group rejected this suggestion, indicating that first Khrushchev had to go and then we could convene the plenum.

I saw that the only way out was decisive action. I announced: "I categorically insist on the urgent calling of a CC plenum. The issue is far bigger than that proposed by the group. At the plenum I want to raise the question of Molotov, Kaganovich, Voroshilov and Malenkov. I have in my hands materials about their bloody evil deeds, theirs and Stalin's, in 1937–38, and there is no place for them on the Presidium or even the Central Committee. If today the anti-party group decides to dismiss Khrushchev from the post of First Secretary, I will not submit to this decision and I will appeal immediately to the party through party organisations in the armed forces."

It was an unusual but necessary statement. To be frank, I wanted to deliver a firm psychological attack on the anti-party group and gain some time until the arrival of CC members, who were already being brought to Moscow by military aircraft.

After my statement it was decided to postpone the Presidium session meeting for three days and this meant the Malenkov–Molotov group had lost their undertaking against Khrushchev. But I must point out that even though I was thanked for making such a decisive speech against the anti-party group, four months later, in October 1957, I was very sorry about my decisive statement in favour of Khrushchev because it was turned against me personally, on which I will elaborate.

The reconvened Presidium meeting lasted for three days, from morning till night. During the breaks between sessions the two sides prepared themselves for the next day's clashes and this is worth describing briefly.

The Malenkov–Molotov group most often conducted their conversations in subgroups of two or three people and only once did the whole group gather in Bulganin's office. By the end of the second day it was noticeable that their members' determination was diminishing as the activism and energy of Khrushchev's side grew and its counter-accusations became more threatening.

In the middle of day two a group of ten CC members arrived and demanded the Presidium listen to them as they were very worried about the unity of the Presidium. This group had earlier been informed about the situation in the Presidium. Right till the end of the session the Malenkov–Molotov group was not willing to listen to this group of CC members, but then, under pressure from the supporters of Khrushchev, it was decided to send Voroshilov, Bulganin, Khrushchev and Shvernik to negotiate with them. The meeting was held in the Presidium's lobby and the CC members demanded the convening of a plenum.

The Presidium members who had sided with Khrushchev from the very first day acted energetically to keep the organisational and ideological initiative in their hands. To ensure unity of action, we met in the evenings in the CC building to discuss the next day. On the first day it was decided to gather the CC members urgently in Moscow in order to conduct a CC plenum. We thought that the plenum would condemn the action of the Malenkov–Molotov group and would support Khrushchev.

To gather the CC members quickly it was decided to bring them from the provinces to Moscow by Air Force planes. The organisation of this was delegated to the Ministry of Defence. Besides that I took upon myself the responsibility to talk personally to Voroshilov in order to separate him from the Malenkov–Molotov group. I undertook this negotiation because we were to some extent related though we had never met as relations (his grandson was married to my daughter at that time). Nothing came of the negotiations. Voroshilov was on the side of the Malenkov–Molotov group and against Khrushchev.

On the first and second days Khrushchev was somewhat demoralised and appeared perplexed. Seeing that I resolutely stood for his defence and that many members of the Presidium and the CC were immediately drawn to me as if I was the central figure in the situation, Khrushchev said with emotion: "Georgy, save the day, you can do it. I will never forget you."

I calmed him down and said: "Nikita, be firm and calm. We will be supported by the plenum, and if the Malenkov–Molotov group venture to employ violence – we will be ready for it." Khrushchev: "Do everything that you deem necessary in the interests of the party, the CC and the Presidium."

On the second day of the Presidium Saburov (having got wind of something) spoke sharply against Khrushchev and said: "What are you up to, Khrushchev? Have you decided to arrest us because we are speaking out against you personally?" Khrushchev asked: "Where are you getting this from?" Saburov: "From the fact that tanks have appeared around Moscow."

I said: "What tanks? What are you babbling about, comrade Saburov? Tanks cannot come to Moscow without the Minister's order, and there has been no such order on my part."

This counterattack of mine was appreciated very much by the Khrushchev group and Khrushchev very often quoted it at plenums and in other speeches. But after a while this counterattack was interpreted quite differently. A different political complexion was put on it and it was elevated to a Bonapartist policy.[23]

For Khrushchev and other members of the Presidium the formation of such a large group opposed to him was surprising. We knew, of course, that Kaganovich, Molotov and Voroshilov were his opponents, but for Saburov, Shepilov and Pervukhin to rise up against Khrushchev was completely unexpected.

On the second day of the Presidium meeting Brezhnev[24] became ill and only came to the CC plenum when the situation had been fully clarified and resolved.

Mikoyan, Suslov, Shvernik, Furtseva, Aristov, me and Kirichenko stood firmly at Khrushchev's side. During the third day of the Presidium we decided to miss the evening meeting and to go straight to the plenum, which had already gathered in the Sverdlov Hall. I don't know what the Malenkov–Molotov group were hoping, but they thought the plenum would support them. It seems they had supporters among the CC members, but they didn't reveal themselves at the plenum.

Khrushchev's supporters feared the Molotov–Malenkov group would venture to arrest us and there were some grounds to suspect this. For example, the number of security officers looking after Bulganin, Molotov, Malenkov and Kaganovich rose sharply on the first day. Raising the question: what was this for? Bulganin and Malenkov had many friends in the KGB and the MVD and among MVD troops, if necessary the group could resort to their help.

Having gained the firm support and reassurances of CC members arriving in Moscow that they wanted to seriously sort out the Malenkov–Molotov group, Khrushchev felt a surge of energy and returned to his old self the optimist. He was not mistaken. The plenum supported him unanimously.

The June plenum of the CC harshly accused the Malenkov–Molotov group of anti-party actions. I won't quote the plenum memorandum, which is common knowledge. But it has to be said that while the Presidium's subject matter was Khrushchev's activities and his removal from the post of First Secretary, at the plenum the issues were much broader and the Malenkov–Molotov group faced serious charges in relation to issues of principle, including the documented role of Molotov, Kaganovich and Voroshilov, together with Stalin, in the destruction of many honest party, military and Soviet figures.

How did those opposed to Khrushchev behave? From the first hours of the plenum confusion and disorder reigned in the anti-party group. Pervukhin, Saburov and Shepilov began to confess their errors and beg for their repentance to be taken into account. Bulganin was at a loss, running like a cowardly hare, coming up with all sorts of unintelligible excuses. He looked very unauthoritative. Molotov and Malenkov held firm and defended their beliefs to the end. As ever, Kaganovich was very talkative, but his verbosity was badly received by the members of the CC. At first Voroshilov sided with Molotov, but then lost it, and began to make excuses saying that he hadn't realised the true aims and intentions of the Molotov–Malenkov group. This said it all about Voroshilov, about how he had behaved under Stalin, too.

After the plenum a new Presidium was elected. I was elected a [full] member of the Presidium and the work gradually came to its normal flow.

In September 1957 Khrushchev, Mikoyan, Brezhnev, Kirichenko and I went for a holiday in the Crimea. The Black Sea weather was beneficial for a good rest. We often met at Khrushchev's place, spent the time leisurely and productively, often discussing general political issues and the practical affairs of our motherland.

I was preparing for my visit to Yugoslavia and Albania, where I had been invited by Josip Broz Tito[25] and Enver Hoxha.[26] My holiday in the Crimea was nearing its end when a very unpleasant circumstance arose for me. While walking with Brezhnev and Khrushchev around the grounds of Khrushchev's dacha, the following talk took place between us:

Brezhnev: "Nikita Sergeevich, Kadar[27] phoned me from Budapest and asked that General Kazakov, whom comrade Zhukov is planning to transfer to the Far East, remain as the Commander of the Soviet troops in Hungary. The Hungarian comrades have got used to Kazakov and I think we should take into account Kadar's opinion. Marshal Zhukov will find another commander for the Far East."

I said: "In the interests of the defence of the country General Kazakov should be sent to command the Far East district, and for Hungary we will find another good commander."

Brezhnev (anxiously): "One has to consider Kadar's opinion."

I replied: "One has to consider my opinion, too. Don't get worked up, I am as much a member of the Presidium as you are, comrade Brezhnev."

Khrushchev kept his silence but I understood that he was not happy with my sharp reply.

In a couple of minutes Brezhnev, taking Khrushchev by the arm, walked with him to the side and started to convince him ardently about something. I guessed that they were talking about me. After the talk with Khrushchev Brezhnev left for his dacha without even saying goodbye to me.

After this first tiff another, more significant one happened. A couple of days later we were all invited to Kirilenko's[28] dacha on the occasion of his wife's birthday. During the dinner there were speeches and toasts and more speeches. Prevalent in the speeches was all-round praise for Khrushchev. All this praise he took as his due and, being in high spirits, he was interrupting speakers and taking somebody else's turn to make more speeches. I didn't like it and, straight as I am, said: "Nikita Sergeevich, according to the agreed schedule the next speech is by Aristov." Khrushchev said aggrievedly: "Well, I can stop speaking altogether if you are not willing to listen to me."

After that Khrushchev's spirits dampened and he stayed silent. I tried to make light of it but in vain. It was immediately picked up for use by sycophants and whisperers and I and Khrushchev parted very coldly. I have to say that later I kicked myself for having opened my mouth, knowing that Khrushchev, being resentful, didn't forgive anybody who attacked him personally.

I didn't manage to meet with Khrushchev before going to Yugoslavia. Having talked to him on the phone, I left for Moscow and was getting ready to go to Belgrade in a couple of days. On the eve of my flight I rang the Crimea to report that I was departing for Yugoslavia the next day but was told that Khrushchev and a group of the Presidium members had flown to Kiev, where the commander in chief of our ground forces, Malinovsky,[29] was, on my instruction, conducting a meeting with the higher command of our ground forces. At this gathering the commander of the Kiev district, Chuikov,[30] demonstrated the crossing of a water obstacle by tanks.

I was informed that Brezhnev, Kirichenko, Kirilenko, Aristov and Mukhitdinov[31] had gone with Khrushchev to the meeting in Kiev.

I phoned Kiev on the 'VCh' and Chuikov answered the phone. Having reported on the progress of the meeting, he told me: "You need to be at this meeting yourself. There's some important business going on here." I told Chuikov: "In accordance with the leadership's decision I have to leave for Yugoslavia tomorrow morning, and I hope that everything will be well, Vasily Ivanovich." Chuikov continued: "It will be so, comrade Marshal, but it would be better if you were here yourself."

Intuitively I felt that Chuikov had said that for a reason. I asked for Khrushchev to come to the phone. With Khrushchev I had a good talk. I said to him: "Should I delay my trip to Yugoslavia for three days and come to Kiev for the meeting, as they say there a lot of interesting issues coming up?" Khrushchev: "It is not necessary to postpone your trip to Yugoslavia. I think we will handle it ourselves somehow, and when you return from Yugoslavia I will tell you all that was interesting here."

Calmed down by such a friendly talk, the next morning I flew to Sevastopol with a group of generals and officers, where we left on the cruiser "Kutuzov"[32] through Bosporus strait for Yugoslavia.

We arrived at the Bosporus strait the next morning. I hadn't been there before and I looked with great interest at what was from an operational point of view an important strait, one connecting the Black and Mediterranean seas.

Early in the morning a motor boat with American officers demonstratively came up to the cruiser and photographed the "Kutuzov" from every angle. Apart from the American military, on the strait's banks there was not one Turkish soul. It was the same all along the Bosporus strait. There were many Greek islands scattered in the Mediterranean and the coastline of the Greek territory looked bare, gloomy and poor.

After skirting the Greek and Albanian islands, we came into the waters of the Adriatic. Italy could be seen in the distance. Approaching port, the Yugoslavian comrades met us in their ships. At the port we were met ceremonially by a guard of honour and there were many Yugoslavians present.

In Belgrade we had a meeting with Marshal Tito, Rankovich, Kardelj, Popovich,[33] the state secretary of defence, and many others.

After a couple of days comrade Tito invited us to the mountains to hunt wild goats. I was very lucky at the hunt. I killed four goats. Tito killed only one and it seemed to me he was dissatisfied with his results, but he had shot at least six times.

After the hunt we were able to go to Croatia, Serbia, Dalmatia and other places. Everywhere and always we were met with wild delight and joy towards the Soviet people, who had done so much to liberate the Yugoslavian people from German fascist occupation.

We conducted many talks with military, party and state officials, with workers, and with the intelligentsia. I was touched by the love and sympathy which they expressed towards the Soviet Union.

Before the flight to Albania I sent Khrushchev a coded telegram, in which I said that the Yugoslavian people and government regarded the Soviet Union with great sympathy and that it seemed that when our people visited the country before they were biased in highlighting the unfriendliness of the Yugoslavian leadership. I proposed a rethinking of our mutual relations in favour of their improvement.

It appeared that in the Presidium my suggestion was read as though I was trying to dictate my own line, one that did not correspond to the Marxist-Leninist line of the CC on the Yugoslavian question. However, within a few years of Khrushchev's visit to Yugoslavia [in 1955], it was regarded as a socialist country and undoubtedly friendly to our people. But in 1957 when I returned to Moscow I was scolded for this opinion even though nothing has changed in Yugoslavia during these past years.

From Yugoslavia we took a TU-104 flight to Albania, where we were met very cordially by the Albanians, their army and the ruling party. In Albania I received information that the Presidium had called a meeting of party activists in the armed forces but that until I returned to Moscow I couldn't be told what questions were being discussed – at this meeting attended by the leaders of the Army and the Navy as well as all the members of the Presidium.

Naturally, I couldn't but be alerted and worried about the fact that for some reason these activists had been gathered in my absence. I asked to talk to my First Deputy Konev[34] but he replied through the secretariat along the same lines. The atmosphere had soured. Two days later we flew from Albania back to Moscow.

We landed in Vnukovo. Through the airplane window I saw that there to meet me were all the Marshals of the Soviet Union and the chief commanders of all sections of the armed forces, amongst them Chernukha, technical officer of the Presidium.

After we all greeted each other Chernukha came up to me and said that I was invited to go now to the Presidium. Everyone would be there, said Chernukha. I said that I would go home first, change and then arrive immediately.

Arriving at the Presidium, I saw every member and candidate member of the Presidium at the table, as well as the marshals who had met me at the airport. It was proposed that I give a short report about my visit to Yugoslavia and Albania and I reported on the main points.

Khrushchev proposed approval of the report, except for my opinion about Yugoslavia's leadership, who were allegedly following an uncommunist line in the construction of [socialism in] Yugoslavia and in relations with the Soviet Union. Then Khrushchev said: "During your absence the Presidium held a meeting of the Ministry of Defence party activists. On this Suslov will report."

Suslov started his report by saying that "at the meeting of party activists it was determined that Minister of Defence Marshal Zhukov was conducting a wrong political line, ignoring political officers, ignoring the GPU [Chief Political Administration), and considered political officers to be idlers. Marshal Zhukov is rude in relations with his subordinates and gives encouragement to those who praise him as an outstanding military commander."

Mikoyan spoke up: "I am still puzzled by and can't understand one phrase of Zhukov's at the Presidium during the struggle against the anti-party Malenkov–Molotov group. Zhukov said: 'If Malenkov's proposal was accepted, then he – Zhukov – wouldn't obey that decision and would appeal to the army.' How is this to be interpreted?"

I replied there and then: 'Yes, this was said, but I said that I would appeal through the party organisations within the army to the party, not to the army itself."

"So you said this consciously? I thought that you had had a slip of a tongue."

"Have you forgotten the situation back then?" I replied to Mikoyan.

Then Brezhnev spoke. He cast aspersions about things that had happened and about those that had not. He said that I have gotten above myself, that I was ignoring Khrushchev and the Presidium, that I was trying to make the CC take my direction, that I underestimated the role of the Military Councils, etc.

Then Khrushchev spoke. He said: "There is a view that comrade Zhukov should be freed of his duties as Minister of Defence and in his place appointed Marshal Malinovsky. There is also a proposal to hold a CC plenum tomorrow, where the activities of comrade Zhukov will be considered." The proposal was accepted unanimously of course.

This entire story, concocted against me in an underhand manner, came as a complete surprise. The circumstances were complicated by the fact that at the time I had the flu. I could not get my thoughts together quickly, though it wasn't the first time I had come across such dirty tricks. I felt that Khrushchev, Brezhnev, Mikoyan, Suslov and Kirichenko had decided to dismiss me from the Presidium because I was too intransigent and dangerous a rival, and in order to free themselves from the person to whom Khrushchev was indebted as a result of the struggle against the anti-party Malenkov–Molotov group. This thought was confirmed by Mikoyan's speech at the plenum when he said "to be honest, we are afraid of Zhukov". That was the crux of the matter. That's why they needed to send me to Yugoslavia, so that they could organize against me, which would have been difficult to do in my presence.

Upon my return home from the Presidium I decided to call Khrushchev so that I could clarify personally the real reasons for my hurried removal from post and the staging of a plenum about me. I asked: "Nikita Sergeevich! I do not understand what has happened in my absence that has led to my immediate removal from the post of Minister of Defence and the staging of special plenum about me." Khrushchev kept silent. I continued: "Before my leaving for Yugoslavia and Albania the Presidium didn't have any issues with me and all of a sudden there are plenty of them. What's the matter? I don't understand why it had been decided to deal with me in such a way."

Khrushchev replied coldly: "When you come to the plenum, you will find out." I said: "I think our previous friendly relations give me the right to ask you personally about the reasons for such an unfriendly attitude towards me." Khrushchev: "Don't get excited. We will still work with you." This was, essentially, the end of our talk.

I hadn't learnt anything from Khrushchev, but realised that my fate was in his hands and the prospects were hazy.

At the plenum the first to speak were Suslov, Brezhnev, Kirichenko, Furtseva and Mikoyan. Their speeches were a bit mealy-mouthed but I knew it was heading towards getting rid of me, towards removing me from the Central Committee.

Brezhnev and Mikoyan said that I was ignoring Khrushchev as the First Secretary of the CC. To show this they relied on two facts.

The first fact: in the summer of 1957 Khrushchev visited the German Democratic Republic at the invitation of the CC of the SED [Socialist Unity Party]. On the eve of Khrushchev's arrival in Berlin I was phoned by Rokossovsky,[35] who was inspecting the military preparedness of Soviet troops in the GDR. Rokossovsky said: "Tomorrow Khrushchev arrives in Berlin, but the troops are in the field and the exercise will not be over for a couple of days. What should we do with Grechko?"[36]

I said: "Tomorrow Khrushchev arrives in Berlin at the invitation of the CC of the SED. You have to go through with the exercise that has started. When it has finished you and Grechko will introduce yourself to comrade Khrushchev." When Khrushchev arrived in Berlin, there was no welcome from [Grechko], the commander of the Soviet forces in Germany, from Marshal Rokossovsky, or from a guard of honour of our troops.

The second fact: that summer Khrushchev visited Estonia and was going to go by car to Leningrad. From Leningrad the commander of the Leningrad region, General Zakharov,[37] called me and said that the

Leningrad authorities were going to meet Khrushchev at the Estonian border and asked if he should join them. I instructed Zakharov to meet Khrushchev in Leningrad. General Zakharov reported to Khrushchev that I had forbidden him to meet him at the Estonian border together with the regional leadership.

It seems that these two incidents seriously hurt the pride and ever-growing vanity of Khrushchev. He didn't say anything to me at the time, but apparently vented his resentment in front of Brezhnev and Mikoyan.

I thought, and still do, that I was acting correctly, because the regulations of the Soviet army do not provide for a special reception for the Secretary of the CC of the CPSU; everybody should be equal before the law. I thought that nobody had the right to revive the personality cult and, even more so, to cultivate idolatry.

Hardly any party or Soviet leaders spoke at the plenum, but to the fore was a united front of the majority of the marshals who were Minister of Defence deputies under me, including Zheltov,[38] the head of the Main Political Administration. It was evident that they had been primed in advance to belittle and decry my work, especially Malinovsky, Sokolovsky,[39] Yeremenko,[40] Biruzov,[41] Konev and Gorshkov.[42] After their speeches the deal that had been done was apparent.

The speeches came down to the allegation that I had ignored party political work in the army, that I was trying to break the army from the CC, etc. But that was just a smokescreen; the real aim was to get rid of me immediately so that I wouldn't be standing in the way of those seeking glory by any means and who weren't willing to share it with anybody else.

It was clear, too, that it had been resolved to strike me mainly with blows by the military, who had been prepped beforehand and outdid themselves discrediting my work, belittling in every way my service during the Great Patriotic War with utter absurdities and falsifications.

Even Khrushchev had to correct Marshal Yeremenko, who in the heat of his loud sycophantic speech said: "What about this Zhukov, they say he personally led the battle of Stalingrad, but he wasn't even there."

Khrushchev: "Well, Andrey Ivanovich, you shouldn't chatter so. We knew Zhukov very well as a commander. If some commanders were not successful at the front, Zhukov was always successful."

At the plenum was displayed a picture by the artist Yakovlev, who had been dead quite a while. I had learned about the existence of this picture only two months before the plenum. At some stage Zheltov came to me and said that he had this picture by Yakovlev, which nicely depicted me against the background of vanquished Berlin. I asked to be shown the picture. Personally I liked the painting, not because it depicted me on a rearing horse but because I felt the artist's love for the Soviet Army, which has defeated the blackest stronghold of imperialism – fascist Germany.

Zheltov asked me what to do with the painting. I replied: "Give it to the Soviet Army museum, maybe it will come in handy." It seemed to me that the matter of the painting was now closed. But when the case was fabricated against me, Zheltov reported to the CC about this painting in a warped way, saying that I instructed him to hang the painting in the Soviet Army Officers hall. In order to defame and ridicule me the painting was displayed at the plenum for everybody to see, and then it was driven around to party activists' meetings in Moscow. The demonstration of the painting was accompanied by derogatory comments such as "look how Zhukov portrays himself as George the Conqueror". Those who didn't cover themselves in glory during the Great Patriotic War were especially concerned to paint me this way.

Khrushchev was the last to speak at the plenum. He said: "When Bulganin and I were in the Far East, after visiting the troops we were invited to dinner by Marshal Malinovsky. At the dinner Malinovsky said: 'Beware of Zhukov, he is a budding Napoleon. If needed – he won't stop at anything.' I didn't pay much attention to Malinovsky's words then, but I was later reminded of those words and their meaning by Bulganin."

It just goes to show how long Malinovsky was engaged in provocation and intrigue against me, but I did not suspect it. It seemed strange to me that such a statement by Malinovsky, made to Khrushchev in 1955, was the same one used by Beria to frighten Stalin in 1945. The question arises – did this provocative statement come from the same source? It would not be surprising if Malinovsky, who made such a provocative statement in 1955, had done the same in 1945.

During the plenum I came to realise that the question about me had already been resolved at the Presidium, therefore I didn't deem it necessary to exonerate myself, knowing that nothing would come of this.

I reported to the plenum that the armed forces were in a state of full readiness. In cutting the personnel of the political officers I was trying, above all, to raise the role and activity of party organisations, to improve the role of unitary commanders[43] and to cut expenditure on paid political organs.

It was not clear why the question about me was raised so sharply. If I had made mistakes – I could correct them. Why were such harsh methods needed? What was talked about had to a degree taken place but the facts were given a tendentious political spin.

At the plenum I was removed from the Presidium and from membership of the CC. The plenum resolution about me was announced a week later, deliberately timed to coincide with the report of the first rocket to go into orbit round the Earth.

In my presence the CC plenum only took a decision on the organisational issue, i.e. my removal from membership of the Central Committee. It was contrary to the usual procedure that the political resolution wasn't discussed and decided in my presence and I was denied the possibility of defending myself from the stated accusations. I absolutely cannot agree with the resolution passed, as it did not correspond to reality and was patently tendentious, aiming to blacken me before the people and the party.

The worst thing was that, as during the period of the personality cult, I was, without proof, being stuck with all kinds of anti-party labels, blamed without any evidence for trying to tear the armed forces away from the party and from the people.

I think this resolution cannot withstand critique. The question arises: how is it possible to separate from the people and the party an army of millions consisting of more than 90 per cent communists and Komsomol members, an army with a yearly draft of a million young people into its ranks who are discharged when they finish their term, an army in daily contact with the multifaceted life of the party and the people? I am sure that neither the people nor the party believed such strange charges.

Simultaneous with the announcement of the plenum resolution there was an article about me in the press written by Marshal Konev, which was full of lazy lies and libellous attacks.

Konev amazed me with his lack of principles. As is well known, Konev was my first deputy. For at least three months each year he acted as Minister of Defence, very often carrying out the basic tasks of the ministry and communicating daily with the CC and the government. I do not know of any instance when on issues of principle his view differed from mine. He often boasted that during many years of joint work we had worked out a common point of view on all the basic issues concerning the building and training of the armed forces. As he was an old political officer, I valued and listened to his advice on issues of personnel education and on practical questions of party-political work. Konev often reassured me of his devoted friendship.

Imagine my surprise then when Konev announced at the plenum that he had never been my friend, that he had always thought that I underestimated his work, that I ignored him and that he didn't agree with me on a multitude of questions but was afraid to place these disagreements in front of the Presidium, thinking that Zhukov had the agreement of the Presidium.

Six months after the plenum I accidentally bumped into Konev in Granovsky Street.[44] I did not want to meet and talk to him, but he noticed me, stopped at his car and waited for me. Between us the conversation went:

Konev: "Good day! Why haven't you visited? You broke away completely from us, forgot your old friends.'

Returning the greeting, I said: "Ivan Stepanovich! What friends are you talking about? If you mean yourself, then it was you who announced at the plenum that you never had been Zhukov's friend.'

Konev: "Of course, you don't know everything that happened before the plenum, when the matter was very serious. Come in, we'll talk."

I replied to him: "Why, Ivan Stepanovich, did you get frightened and disown our friendship? I really don't understand you. You are a Marshal of the Soviet Union, a member of the Central Committee, you knew that everything said about me was false, fabricated with a definite aim in mind. How come you did not object to this undertaking? As for your invitation to come to the Ministry of Defence, I think I have no business there."

Since pedestrians, recognising us, had begun stopping, we said our goodbyes. Konev got into the car and I went by foot wanting to clear my head after such an unpleasant talk.

After the exclusion of the Molotov–Malenkov group from the Presidium, Kirichenko, Aristov, Ignatov,[45] Furtseva and Pospelov[46] were removed from membership. Among the old guard only Mikoyan stayed on the Presidium. Well, he is an old diplomat. Nobody can navigate a situation and adapt to it like Mikoyan.

The CC plenum motion spoke about giving me a different post, but this resolution wasn't executed and I, quite able-bodied, was dismissed [from the armed forces].

For a long time after my dismissal my activities were portrayed in a distorted light in the pages of the press, in speeches, in lectures, etc., attributing to me a series of negative events that never happened.

But I can say a big thank-you to the party and the people because of the regard for me of the majority of Soviet people and communists.

'Posle Smerti Stalina', Rossiiskii Gosudarstvennyi Voennyi Arkhiv, F.41107, Op.2, D.1.

Published in *Georgy Zhukov: Stenogramma Oktyabr'skogo (1957g) Plenuma TsK KPSS i Drugie Dokumenty*, Mezhdunarodnyi Fond 'Demokratiya': Moscow, 2001, pp. 620–39

Translated by Svetlana Frolova and Geoffrey Roberts.

Notes

1. N.A. Bulganin (1895–1975), political commissar on various Fronts, 1941–1943, Deputy Defence Commissar, 1944–1947, Minister for the Armed Forces, 1947–1947, 1953–1955, Prime Minister, 1955–1958.
2. A.M. Vasilevsky (1895–1977), Deputy and Chief of the General Staff, 1941–1945, 1946–1948, Deputy/Minister of the Armed Forces/Defence, 1949–1957.
3. J.V. Stalin (1879–1953), General-Secretary of the Soviet Communist Party, 1922–1953.
4. This was the 1950s name for the Politburo – the top committee in the Soviet communist party.
5. N.S. Khrushchev (1894–1971), leader of the Soviet communist party, 1953–1964.
6. G.M. Malenkov (1902–1988), Soviet Prime Minister, 1953–1955.
7. L.P. Beria (1899–1953), Soviet security chief, 1938–1953.
8. V.M. Molotov (1890–1986), Soviet Prime Minister, 1930–1940, Foreign Commissar/Minister, 1939–1949, 1953–1956.
9. K.E. Voroshilov (1881–1969), Defence Commissar, 1925–1940, Chairman of the Supreme Soviet, 1953–1960.
10. N.S. Vlasik (1896–1967), chief of the protection section of the Ministry of State Security, 1946–1952. Vlasik could not have played the role Zhukov ascribed to him since he was arrested in December 1952.
11. All Soviet generals.
12. L.M. Kaganovich (1898–1972), Ukrainian party secretary in the 1920s and 1940s, transport and industry commissar/minister, 1930s–1950s.
13. E.A. Furtseva (1910–1974), leader of the Moscow communist party, 1954–1957.
14. A.I. Kirichenko (1908–1975), leader of the Odessa communist party and then the Ukrainian communist party, 1945–1957.
15. In Imperial Russia and the Soviet Union Odessa had a reputation as a centre of criminality.
16. A.I. Mikoyan (1895–1978), Soviet trade commissar/minister, 1920s–1950s.
17. M.G. Pervukhin (1904–1978), Deputy Prime Minister, 1953–1957.
18. D.T. Shepilov (1905–1995), editor of *Pravda*, 1952–1956, Foreign Minister, 1956–1957.
19. M.A. Suslov (1902–1982), Soviet ideology chief, 1940s–1970s.

20. N.M. Shvernik (1888–1970), Soviet trade union chief, 1930s–1950s.
21. A.B. Aristov (1903–1973), Politburo (Presidium) member in the 1950s.
22. M.Z. Saburov (1900–1977), Gosplan chief in the 1940s and 1950s.
23. Since coming to power in Russia in 1917 the Bolsheviks – later renamed the communists – had been obsessed by the precedent of the French revolution and the seizure of power by General Napoleon Bonaparte.
24. L.I. Brezhnev (1906–1982), leader of the Soviet communist party, 1964–1982
25. J.B. Tito (1892–1980), leader of communist Yugoslavia, 1945–1980.
26. E. Hoxha (1908–1985), leader of communist Albania, 1945–1985.
27. J. Kadar (1901–1989), leader of communist Hungary 1956–1988.
28. A.P. Kirilenko (1906–1990), Ukrainian communist party leader, 1940s–1950s.
29. R.Ya. Malinovsky (1898–1967), army-level commander during the war, Minister of Defence, 1957–1967.
30. V.I. Chuikov (1900–1982), commander of the 62nd/8th Guards Army, 1942–1945, commander in chief of ground forces, 1960–1964.
31. N.A. Mukhitdinov (1917–2008), Uzbekistan communist party leader.
32. The ship was actually called the *Kuibyshev*.
33. Leaders of the Yugoslav communist party.
34. I.S. Konev (1897–1973), commander of various Fronts, 1941–1945, commander in chief of ground forces, 1946–1950, Deputy Minister of Defence, 1956–1961.
35. K.K. Rokossovsky (1896–1968), commander of the 1st and 2nd Belorussian Fronts, 1944–1945, Minister of Defence, Poland, 1949–1956, Soviet Deputy Defence Minister, 1956–1962.
36. A.A. Grechko (1903–1976), commander of Soviet forces in Germany, 1953–1957, Deputy Defence Minister, 1957–1960, commander-in-chief of the Warsaw Pact, 1960–1967, Defence Minister, 1967–1976.
37. M.V. Zakharov (1898–1972), chief of the Leningrad military district, 1953–1957.
38. A.S. Zheltov (1904–1991), Chief of the Main Political Administration of the Soviet armed forces, 1953–1958.
39. V.D. Sokolovsky (1897–1968), served as Zhukov's Chief of Staff during the war and as his deputy in Germany after the war, Chief of the General Staff, 1952–1960.
40. A.I. Yeremenko (1892–1970), Front commander at Stalingrad, 1942–1943, chief of the North Caucasus military district, 1953–1958.
41. S.S. Biruzov (1904–1964), Deputy Defence Minister, 1955–1962.
42. S.G. Gorshkov (1910–1988), Soviet naval chief, 1940s–1950s.
43. Officers responsible for political as well as military commands and decision-making.
44. Both men lived on this street, which was not far from the Kremlin and the Ministry of Defence building.
45. N.G. Ignatov (1901–1966). Ignatov was a supporter of Khrushchev's in 1957 but later turned against him.
46. P.N. Pospelov (1898–1979), an editor of *Pravda* in the 1940s and 1950s.

Bibliography of English-Language Writings on Georgy Zhukov

V. Anfilov, 'Zhukov', in H. Shukman (ed.), *Stalin's Generals*, Phoenix Press: London, 1997.

A. Axell, *Marshal Zhukov: The Man Who Beat Hitler*, Pearson: London, 2003.

S. Bialer, *Stalin and His Generals: Soviet Military Memoirs of World War II*, Souvenir Press: London, 1970.

O.P. Chaney, *Zhukov*, rev. ed., University of Oklahoma Press: Norman, OK, 1996.

P.M. Cocks, 'The Purge of Marshal Zhukov', *Slavic Review*, vol. 22, no. 3, 1963.

T.J. Colton, 'The Zhukov Affair Reconsidered', *Soviet Studies*, vol. XXIX, April 1977.

J. Colvin, *Zhukov: The Conqueror of Berlin*, Weidenfeld & Nicolson: London, 2004.

J. Erickson, 'Zhukov', in M. Carver (ed.), *The War Lords*, Pen & Sword Books: Barnsley, 2005.

R. Forczyk, *Georgy Zhukov*, Osprey Publishing: Oxford, 2012.

B. Fugate & L. Dvoretsky, *Thunder on the Dnepr: Zhukov-Stalin and the Defeat of Hitler's Blitzkrieg*, Presidio Press: Novato, CA, 2001.

D. Glantz, *Zhukov's Greatest Defeat: The Red Army's Epic Disaster in Operation Mars*, 1942, Ian Allan Publishing: Shepperton, 2000.

D. Glantz, introduction to *Marshal Zhukov's Greatest Battles*, Cooper Square Press: New York, 2002.

T. Le Tissier, *Zhukov at the Oder: The Decisive Battle for Berlin*, The History Press, 2008.

G. Roberts, *Stalin's General: The Life of Georgy Zhukov*, Icon Books: London, 2012.

H.E. Salisbury (ed.), *Marshal Zhukov's Greatest Battles*, Sphere Books: London, 1971.

A.L. Sethi, *Marshal Zhukov: The Master Strategist*, Natraj Publications, 2008.

W.J. Spahr, *Zhukov: The Rise and Fall of a Great Captain*, Presidio Press: Novato, CA, 1993.

Name Index